The New Suburbia

The New Suburbia

*How Diversity Remade Suburban Life in
Los Angeles after 1945*

BECKY M. NICOLAIDES

OXFORD
UNIVERSITY PRESS

OXFORD
UNIVERSITY PRESS

Oxford University Press is a department of the University of Oxford. It furthers
the University's objective of excellence in research, scholarship, and education
by publishing worldwide. Oxford is a registered trade mark of Oxford University
Press in the UK and certain other countries.

Published in the United States of America by Oxford University Press
198 Madison Avenue, New York, NY 10016, United States of America.

CIP data is on file at the Library of Congress

ISBN 978–0–19–757830–8

DOI: 10.1093/oso/9780197578308.001.0001

Printed by Sheridan Books, Inc., United States of America

The publication was co-financed by the Erasmus + programme under the project "Urbanism and
Suburbanization in the EU Countries and Abroad: Reflection in the Humanities, Social Sciences,
and the Arts" (2021-1-CZ01-KA220-HED-000023281). The European Commission's support for the
production of this publication does not constitute an endorsement of the contents, which reflect
the views only of the author, and the Commission cannot be held responsible for any use
which may be made of the information contained therein.

Portions of this work were adapted from Becky M. Nicolaides, "The Social Fallout of
Racial Politics: Civic Engagement in Suburban Pasadena, 1950-2000," in *Making Suburbia:
New Histories of Everyday America*, edited by John Archer, Paul J. P. Sandul and Katherine
Solomonson (Minneapolis: University of Minnesota Press, 2015), 3–20, copyright 2015 by
the Regents of the University of Minnesota.

For David, Desmond, and Marina,
and
my brothers, Louie and Alex

Contents

Acknowledgments

This book has been years in the making, and I am so grateful to the many people and institutions that helped me along the way. I became an independent scholar in 2006, when I transitioned from tenured professor to freelance historian. By 2009, I began germinating the idea for this book. The individuals and funders who supported my work as an independent scholar, recognizing the particular challenges of that status, hold a special place in my heart, and I am particularly thankful for their generosity and sustenance.

Three funders provided crucial support with year-long fellowships during which I wrote three of the case studies of this book: the John Randolph Haynes and Dora Haynes Foundation, the National Endowment for the Humanities, and the American Council of Learned Societies. I am grateful to the Huntington Library for several short-term fellowships, to the UCLA Center for the Study of Women for a steady succession of Tillie Olsen Grants, and to Bill Deverell and Wade Graham of the *LA County Almanac* project for allocating funds to me to collect 2010 data on LA. Additional thanks to the National Endowment for the Humanities for a grant to the USC Libraries to help make my LA County data accessible to the public, and I am grateful to Andy Rutkowski, Deborah Holmes-Wong, Bill Dotson, and Tim Stanton for their work on this project.

The UCLA Center for the Study of Women and the Huntington-USC Institute on California and the West granted me research affiliations, which have been lifelines to me as a scholar. To Bill Deverell, I owe a huge debt of gratitude. He has been a steadfast friend who went above and beyond by ensuring I had uninterrupted library access at USC. Thank you, Bill, for your unwavering support.

Numerous librarians, archivists, city employees, and individuals helped me find sources, gave me access to off-limits rooms, provided information, and otherwise facilitated my research, and I am grateful to all of them, especially Dan McLaughlin, Mary Carter, Young Phong, and Tiffany Dueñas of the Pasadena Public Library; Anuja Navare of the Pasadena Museum of History; Bill Trimble of the Pasadena City Planning Office; Lilia Novelo of the Pasadena City Clerk's Office; Anne Peterson and Keith Holeman of All Saints

Church Pasadena; Judith Carter of the San Marino Historical Society; Debbie McEvilly, Raquel Larios, and Sonia Guerrero of the South Gate City Clerk's Office; Bill Grady, Public Information Officer of Lakewood; Sarah Comfort of Iacaboni Library, Lakewood; and Laura Verlaque, Julie Yamashita, Mary Lou Langedyke, and Mike Lawler of the Lanterman Historical Museum, La Cañada.

Students played a pivotal role in this book. Many shared superb insights in my courses on suburban history and a few wrote research papers that enriched my own thinking. I thank students in my classes at UCLA, Claremont Graduate School, and Pitzer College, particularly Graham McNeill, Mercedes González-Ontañon, and Jada Higgins. Over the years, a team of student research assistants compiled the large US Census dataset on LA suburbia, which provided crucial empirical context for this book: Angela Hawk, Ryan Stoffers, Jennifer Vanore, Matthew Bunnett, Sera Gearhart, David Yun, and Desmond Weisenberg. A special thanks to Avi Gandhi for her immense help with the dataset during the late stages of this project. Other students assisted with research and various tasks, including Jean-Paul deGuzman, Allison Lauterbach, Jared Levine, Samantha Oliveri, Crystal Yanez, and Veronica Hernandez. As some have gone on to jobs with the federal government, nonprofits, and universities, I feel fortunate to have worked with them over the course of writing this book, and I am grateful for their invaluable assistance.

I've had the opportunity to present or workshop parts of my research on this book at various institutions, and I am indebted to those who made that possible: Margaret Crawford at the University of California, Berkeley; Michael Ebner and Ann Durkin Keating at the Chicago History Museum's Urban History Seminar; Jo Gill at the University of Exeter; Dan Amsterdam and Doug Flamming at Georgia Tech; Adam Arenson at Manhattan College; Ken Marcus, Donna Schuele, and Amy Essington at the Historical Society of Southern California; Jem Axelrod at the Occidental Institute for the Study of Los Angeles; and Andrew Sandoval-Strausz at Penn State University. A special thanks to the LA History & Metro Studies Group, where I workshopped chapters. And to my fellow coordinators of that group over the years— Kathy Feeley, Caitlin Parker, Andrea Thabet, David Levitus, Gena Carpio, Alyssa Ribeiro, Monica Jovanovich, Ian Baldwin, Lily Geismer, and Oscar Gutierrez—I am so grateful for your friendship, feedback, and camaraderie.

A number of friends and scholars shared sources, ideas, maps, photos, and/or read parts of the manuscript. I thank you for your generosity and invaluable insights: Jake Anbinder, Steve Aron, Eric Avila, Hal Barron, Brian Biery, Gena Carpio, Wendy Cheng, Peter Chesney, Jenny Cool, Jean-Paul deGuzman, Peter Dreier, Phil Ethington, Lily Geismer, Adam Goodman, Richard Harris, Andrew Highsmith, Greg Hise, Matthew Kautz, Kathy Kobayashi, Nancy Kwak, Matt Lassiter, Bill Leslie, David Levitus, Willow Lung-Amam, Jennifer Mapes (cartographer extraordinaire), Nancy Dorf Monarch, Michelle Nickerson, Mark Padoongpatt, James Rojas, Eva Saks, Kathy Seal, Tom Sitton, Raphe Sonenshein, Michael Tierney, Don Waldie, Jon Weiner, Michele Zack, and James Zarsadiaz. I am grateful to members of the LA Social History Group for reading early work, especially John Laslett, Steve Ross, Frank Stricker, Jennifer Luff, Craig Loftin, and the late Jan Reiff. Members of our short-lived but mighty writing group provided excellent feedback and warm friendship, and I'm grateful to all of you: Elaine Lewinnek, Lisa Orr, Hillary Jenks, and Denise Spooner.

The many individuals who shared their life stories with me through oral histories played a crucial role in the making of this book. Their personal reminiscences filled in the details of everyday life and the emotional experiences of living in changing suburbia. I am immensely grateful to each and every one of them.

My recent involvement with the Erasmus + grant team on "Urbanism and Suburbanization in the EU Countries and Abroad: Reflection in the Humanities, Social Sciences, and the Arts" has been a truly enriching experience. It has enabled me to share my work with an exceptional group of European scholars and has facilitated the fruitful exchange of insights about the structures and experiences of suburbia transnationally. Thanks to the Erasmus + Programme for funding this initiative, and especially to Pavlína Flajšarová, Jiri Flajsar, Florian Freitag, Vit Vozenilek, Jaroslav Burian, Eric Langlois, Mauricette Fournier, and Franck Chignier Riboulon. And Andy Wiese, thank you for repping the US with me and sharing this adventure in a way that only two suburban history nerds can fully appreciate.

Several friends and fellow scholars went above and beyond during my years engaged in this project, and to them I owe a special debt of gratitude. Denise Spooner, dear friend and companion on this journey, thank you for your love and support. Susan Phillips, I thank you for your extraordinary kindness, love, and social justice leadership. Carol McKibben, your friendship and unflagging encouragement helped me through. I especially thank Erin Alden, Jonathan Pacheco Bell, Barbara Gunnare, Max Felker-Kantor, Jorge Leal, Elline Lipkin, Caitlin Parker, Andrew Sandoval-Strausz, Jen Vanore, and

Jake Wegmann for your boundless encouragement and, in many cases, direct help with this book. Tim Gilfoyle and Jim Grossman, I am grateful for your enduring support and friendship. John Archer and Margaret Crawford, you both became my guardian angels when I bolted from academia and became an independent scholar, writing letters of support for funding and otherwise offering moral support over the years. I am truly grateful to you both. I am indebted to Ken Jackson, Betsy Blackmar, and Eric Foner for their intellectual inspiration that began in graduate school and has continued unabated. And a special thanks to Dolores Hayden, whose scholarship set the groundwork for this book.

I also am grateful to two scholars who have passed, Mike Davis and my dear friend Clark Davis, who both deeply influenced my thinking about Los Angeles. One of the last classes Clark taught was an oral history seminar that resulted in the book *Advocates for Change*, which gave voice to the individuals living through school desegregation. I drew often from that book, which renewed my appreciation for Clark and the legacy he left behind in his life and work.

Andy Wiese, you have been a treasured friend and intellectual partner since our days at Columbia. I am thankful for your support and friendship, and your willingness to drop everything and talk suburbs when I needed those conversations. Your insights always elevated my understanding and have shaped this book in countless ways. I'm so grateful to have such a kind and brilliant friend. Allison Baker, friend and fellow historian, enormous thanks for sharing your research and personal archive on Lakewood, which you lent me at the start of the COVID shutdown. Your dissertation deeply shaped my understanding of that community, and your tremendous generosity enabled me to finish this book. While I thank my friends and colleagues who have helped me along the way, all errors are my responsibility alone.

To Susan Ferber of Oxford University Press, I owe enormous thanks for everything, starting with the interest you expressed in this project years ago, and continuing with your tireless work in guiding this manuscript to completion. I'm truly grateful for your editorial eye, personal encouragement, and sheer stamina. I am so lucky to have worked with you. I am also grateful to the scholars who reviewed the manuscript for Oxford—Josh Sides, Jerry González, and an anonymous reader—for their excellent feedback and belief in this project.

My family has been my bedrock, sustaining me in every way. For your love and support, thank you Tina Nicolaides, Jean Ramos, Anya Nicolaides,

Vicki Lohser, Liz Tekus, George Papas, Sophia Khan, Brad Thornton, Tom Huang, Yvonne and Scott Carlson, and Ron Weisenberg. To my extraordinary brothers, Alex and Louie, your love and rock-solid support have kept alive the spirit of family that we grew up with, and I'm so glad that we still live within eight miles of each other. Thank you for always being there for me. My kids Desmond and Marina have lived with this book for the last dozen years. As they got older, they got more directly involved—Marina taking photos, Desmond compiling data tables and offering input on passages I was struggling with. More than that, they patiently put up with a mom consumed with this book. I'm so grateful to you both, you are my heart and soul. David, you have the patience and heart of a saint. Your love, humor, sustenance, feedback, ideas, and fortitude truly carried me through. And when I needed it most, you sang "Three Little Birds," which somehow completely worked. I am eternally grateful to you.

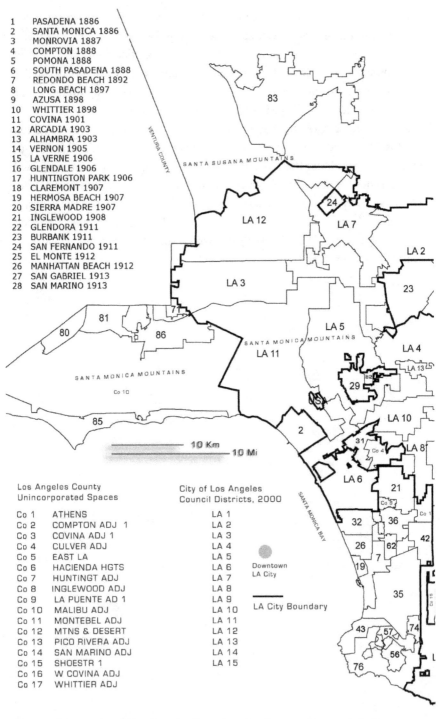

1   PASADENA 1886
2   SANTA MONICA 1886
3   MONROVIA 1887
4   COMPTON 1888
5   POMONA 1888
6   SOUTH PASADENA 1888
7   REDONDO BEACH 1892
8   LONG BEACH 1897
9   AZUSA 1898
10 WHITTIER 1898
11 COVINA 1901
12 ARCADIA 1903
13 ALHAMBRA 1903
14 VERNON 1905
15 LA VERNE 1906
16 GLENDALE 1906
17 HUNTINGTON PARK 1906
18 CLAREMONT 1907
19 HERMOSA BEACH 1907
20 SIERRA MADRE 1907
21 INGLEWOOD 1908
22 GLENDORA 1911
23 BURBANK 1911
24 SAN FERNANDO 1911
25 EL MONTE 1912
26 MANHATTAN BEACH 1912
27 SAN GABRIEL 1913
28 SAN MARINO 1913

Los Angeles County
Unincorporated Spaces

Co 1   ATHENS
Co 2   COMPTON ADJ 1
Co 3   COVINA ADJ 1
Co 4   CULVER ADJ
Co 5   EAST LA
Co 6   HACIENDA HGTS
Co 7   HUNTINGT ADJ
Co 8   INGLEWOOD ADJ
Co 9   LA PUENTE AD 1
Co 10   MALIBU ADJ
Co 11   MONTEBEL ADJ
Co 12   MTNS & DESERT
Co 13   PICO RIVERA ADJ
Co 14   SAN MARINO ADJ
Co 15   SHOESTR 1
Co 16   W COVINA ADJ
Co 17   WHITTIER ADJ

City of Los Angeles
Council Districts, 2000

LA 1
LA 2
LA 3
LA 4
LA 5
LA 6
LA 7
LA 8
LA 9
LA 10
LA 11
LA 12
LA 13
LA 14
LA 15

Downtown
LA City

LA City Boundary

Municipalities and neighborhoods of Los Angeles County. Cartography by
Philip J. Ethington ©2007.

Ethington base map edited and augmented by Becky Nicolaides.

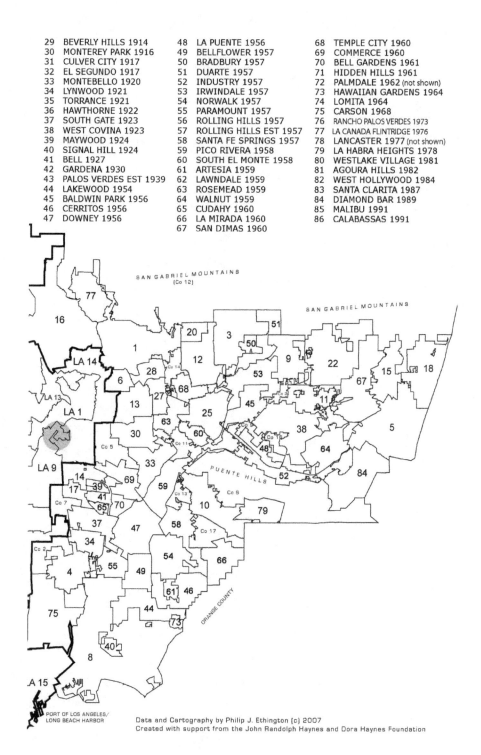

29 BEVERLY HILLS 1914
30 MONTEREY PARK 1916
31 CULVER CITY 1917
32 EL SEGUNDO 1917
33 MONTEBELLO 1920
34 LYNWOOD 1921
35 TORRANCE 1921
36 HAWTHORNE 1922
37 SOUTH GATE 1923
38 WEST COVINA 1923
39 MAYWOOD 1924
40 SIGNAL HILL 1924
41 BELL 1927
42 GARDENA 1930
43 PALOS VERDES EST 1939
44 LAKEWOOD 1954
45 BALDWIN PARK 1956
46 CERRITOS 1956
47 DOWNEY 1956

48 LA PUENTE 1956
49 BELLFLOWER 1957
50 BRADBURY 1957
51 DUARTE 1957
52 INDUSTRY 1957
53 IRWINDALE 1957
54 NORWALK 1957
55 PARAMOUNT 1957
56 ROLLING HILLS 1957
57 ROLLING HILLS EST 1957
58 SANTA FE SPRINGS 1957
59 PICO RIVERA 1958
60 SOUTH EL MONTE 1958
61 ARTESIA 1959
62 LAWNDALE 1959
63 ROSEMEAD 1959
64 WALNUT 1959
65 CUDAHY 1960
66 LA MIRADA 1960
67 SAN DIMAS 1960

68 TEMPLE CITY 1960
69 COMMERCE 1960
70 BELL GARDENS 1961
71 HIDDEN HILLS 1961
72 PALMDALE 1962 (not shown)
73 HAWAIIAN GARDENS 1964
74 LOMITA 1964
75 CARSON 1968
76 RANCHO PALOS VERDES 1973
77 LA CANADA FLINTRIDGE 1976
78 LANCASTER 1977 (not shown)
79 LA HABRA HEIGHTS 1978
80 WESTLAKE VILLAGE 1981
81 AGOURA HILLS 1982
82 WEST HOLLYWOOD 1984
83 SANTA CLARITA 1987
84 DIAMOND BAR 1989
85 MALIBU 1991
86 CALABASSAS 1991

Data and Cartography by Philip J. Ethington (c) 2007
Created with support from the John Randolph Haynes and Dora Haynes Foundation

The New Suburbia

Introduction

Certain images of the suburbs seem forever etched in our minds. The perfect green lawns. The cookouts. The lily-white suburbanites.

But the days of suburbia as a white monolith are over.

This book tells the story of how this came to be. It explores how the suburbs transitioned from bastions of segregation into spaces of multiracial living. The "new suburbia" refers to America's suburbs since the 1970s, which diversified at an accelerated pace.[1] It is the second generation of suburbs after 1945, which transformed from starkly segregated whiteness into a more varied, uneven social landscape. Diversity in the new suburbia refers not just to race, but also to class, household composition, and the built landscape itself. In the new suburbia, white advantage persisted, but it existed alongside rising inequality, ethnic and racial diversity, and new family configurations.

The racial transformation was a particularly dramatic turnaround. From 1970 to 2020, nonwhites living in America's suburbs rose from just under 10% to 45% of all suburbanites. From another vantage point, looking at the typical experience for Black Americans, Latinos, and Asian Americans, a majority of each group now lives in the suburbs. Something big has changed. Communities once imagined as "far whiter than most of the nation" have come to look like a cross-section of America itself.[2]

This matters because the suburb-city divide once defined deep inequalities that rested on racial difference. The suburbs were spaces of white advantage and privilege. For generations, they locked out nonwhites from access to those same privileges, bolstered by a thick web of biased policies. In the process, white suburbanites amassed generational wealth through homeownership, accrued political power from the local to federal level, and enjoyed the advantages of living in safe neighborhoods with good schools, green spaces, and community amenities. Through long-standing exclusionary practices, suburbia helped produce racial inequality in America.

The rise of diverse suburbia, then, signals an important transformation while also raising crucial questions. Did the Latinos, Asians, and Black Americans who moved to the suburbs enjoy the same privileges as generations of whites? Did they embrace older, white suburban political traditions, including the tendency to exclude? Or did they adopt wholly new suburban ideals, values, and ways of living? Are they remaking the suburbs? Or are the suburbs remaking them?

The New Suburbia explores these questions by tracing the process of suburban change over 70 years, from the 1940s to the early 2000s, traversing the era of postwar white suburbia to the era of diversity. It focuses on Los Angeles, at the cutting edge of this transformation, where trends have happened earlier and more widely. Governor Gavin Newsom likes to call California "America's coming attraction," and LA's suburban story is no exception.[3] The stories that are playing out in LA may very well be a bellwether for the nation.

At the heart of this book are stories of the people and their suburban communities undergoing these transitions. In the new suburbia, Asian Americans, Black Americans, and Latinos moved into white suburbs that once barred them. They bought homes, enrolled their children in schools, and began navigating suburban life. They included people like Tao Chia Chi, Sandra Martinez, and Derrick Williams, whose life pathways all brought them to the suburbs of LA.

Tao Chia Chi was born in 1949, in Shanghai, China, the year Mao's communist regime seized control of the country. Her father, a municipal employee in Shanghai, saw the writing on the wall—get the family out quickly or face certain persecution. Two months after Chia Chi's birth, her father paid off the right people, disguised himself as a farmer, and gathered his family—his wife, three young daughters, and a sister—to make their way to a rural village where they awaited a rowboat in the dark of night. When the fisherman arrived and saw Chia Chi, he asked, "Is this a new infant? If she cries, just choke her, otherwise we will all die." Because many people from the mainland were trying to get out by boat, the waters were heavily patrolled by communist soldiers. The girls managed to remain quiet, and the family made its way safely to a nearby island. From there, they hopped a cargo ship to Taiwan. The Taos started new lives and raised their children in Taiwan. At age 22, Chia Chi arrived as a student in the United States, where she eventually married a doctor and raised her own family.

Sandra Martinez was born in 1957, into a poor family in San Pedro Tlaquepaque, a town in Guadalajara, Mexico. Her father was a lawyer but didn't live with the family. Sandra had 11 siblings. Her mother raised them as a single parent, without financial help, making her living cleaning, cooking, and caring for other people's children. Without a home of their own, they lived with families willing to put them up, but they were cast out when the burden of housing 13 people became too much. When Sandra and each of her siblings reached the age of 10, they left school to work, cleaning homes or clerking in a shop. Their earnings went into the family pot, which eventually helped them move into their own rental house. When Sandra got older, she worked at a factory in Mexico making Brittania Jeans, a popular brand in the United States. In her early 20s, Sandra came to Los Angeles to join her sisters and marry her long-time boyfriend from Guadalajara.

Derrick Williams was born in 1965 and lived his early years in southwest Philadelphia. In 1972, his family purchased a home in West Oak Lane, an affluent community of Jewish and Italian families. They were one of the first Black families to move in. Derrick enjoyed a carefree childhood in a tight-knit neighborhood, with the freedom to roam and explore his surroundings. Within a 10-year span, however, rapid white flight flipped West Oak Lane from white to Black, and Derrick began experiencing intensive racial conflict at school, in the neighborhood, and in everyday life. As a teen, he was bussed to an all-white high school across town, where attacks on Black students by neighborhood youth became a daily routine. After graduating, Derrick served in the elite Army Rangers, then moved to Los Angeles after the death of his mother. He met his future wife Pamela while working in IT at Boeing.[4]

Chia Chi, Sandra, and Derrick all eventually ended up living in the suburbs of Los Angeles—San Marino, South Gate, and Lakewood, respectively. They brought with them rich and disparate life experiences, turning places once stereotyped as bland, predictable, and white into something quite different. They represent the faces of the new suburbia. This book tells their stories and the history of suburban places remade by individuals like them.

——

With every passing year, more and more Americans live in the suburbs. As of 2020, fully 54.6% of all Americans lived in suburban places, yet another milestone along suburbia's steady ascendance since World War II.[5]

As a paradigm of the suburban metropolis, Los Angeles represents an incredibly rich setting for probing suburbia's recent past. LA pioneered many facets of suburban development in the twentieth century. Its wide array of historic suburban landscapes allows for analysis across a range of built environments. LA stands at the forefront of suburban diversification nationally. From 1970 to 2010, the proportion of all suburbanites in LA who were Black American, Latino, and Asian American rose from 26% to 70%, much higher than national averages. Similarly, in 2010, 60% of LA's immigrants lived in the suburbs, compared to 51% nationally.[6] LA has been experiencing the reverberations of these changes for decades.

Los Angeles has a reputation as a diverse metropolis, but, in the immediate post-World War II years, whites overwhelmingly predominated LA County, especially in the suburbs. In LA, then, the contrast from 1950 to 2010 was dramatic. LA's suburbs flipped from being nearly all white to nearly all multiracial. By 2010, the suburbs had more nonwhite homeowners than white ones, and they housed more immigrants and poor people than urbanized areas. Suburbia looked less like an antiseptic haven of segregation and more like a space of multiracial America.

Suburban households also grew more diverse in other ways. In line with national trends, family structure in LA's suburbs evolved from young, straight nuclear families to more complex households after 1970, including more singles, divorced adults, LGBTQ individuals, cohabitating partners, extended families, and senior citizens. More suburban mothers worked outside the home, shattering earlier images of June Cleaver trapped at home mopping floors. By the end of the twentieth century, the older norm of breadwinner dad, stay-at-home mom, and kids had become entwined with class polarization. That suburban ideal found its fullest realization in the wealthiest suburbs. Despite these trends, the fact remained that married, homeowning families remained dominant in the suburbs; they often held a majority voice, and their vision continued to carry weight even as social realities shifted around them.

At the same time that suburbia's ethnic, racial, and household profiles were changing, middle-class suburbs were shrinking. As the middle class itself was squeezed by economic restructuring, a new hourglass economy emerged with rising numbers of high- and low-paying jobs and declining salaried jobs in between. These trends began showing up across suburban space as super-rich suburbs multiplied, as did suburbs of the poor. The gulfs dividing these communities—places like uber-wealthy Bradbury and, just two miles away, working-class Azusa—revealed an emerging suburban disequilibrium. Suburbia came to embody inequality itself. The notion of suburbia as a space of privilege was complicated by these patterns, which were appearing in LA and across the United States.[7]

Within a generation, the suburbs came to hold a much broader cross-section of people—rich, poor, Black, Latino, Asian, immigrant, the unhoused, the lavishly housed, and everyone in between. Through it all, the common denominators of suburbia remained—low-slung landscapes of single-family homes and yards, pervasive homeownership, and families seeking the good life. This familiar, recognizable landscape has encompassed a growing array of peoples, social processes, and lived experiences. An American dream endured even as the dreamers changed.

For more than a century, white suburbia has represented a bourgeois utopia, a "white noose" around the urban core, the generator of white generational wealth, the racialized American dream. Historically speaking, racial exclusivity was vital to the appeal of a significant grouping of suburbs. It drove homeowner politics and entitlement claims in the post-World War II years. Suburbia represented a crucial "wage of whiteness" that conferred numerous advantages through property ownership, superior schools, safe neighborhoods, and preferential tax breaks, passed down from one generation of white families to the next. All of this was bolstered by a web of policies—from the local to the federal—that protected those entitlements. These realities created a justified perception of suburbia as a space of white privilege, an idea that took hold in the 1950s and 1960s and retained its power ever since.[8]

The story that has been told of suburban political culture in the postwar era is one dominated by white, homeowning, taxpaying parents who consolidated their political power from the local to the national level. It was a bipartisan cohort—encompassing suburbanites left, right, and center—united around the shared goals of protecting suburban communities from such threats as racial and ethnic others, the poor, school integration, affordable housing, and challenges to zoning for single-family homes.[9] *The New Suburbia* continues that thread, but builds on stories of Asian, Latino, and Black American suburbanites who also took on suburban identities as homeowning, taxpaying parents. Diversifying suburbs indeed took a quantum leap forward by accepting nonwhites, but these residents had a range of responses once they found themselves on the inside.

As more and more nonwhites became homeowners, they began benefitting from the advantages of suburban life. Some adopted long-standing homeowner traditions, particularly the inclinations to protect property and community from various threats. In the new suburbia, those threats evolved to encompass the casualties of economic and global change—poor immigrants, the working poor, and the unhoused. At the same time, suburban political culture began to widen along a spectrum ranging from inclusive and progressive on one end, to defensive and exclusionary on the other. Racially diverse residents lived across that spectrum and participated in all of these political cultures.

In many diversifying suburbs, internal divisions surfaced. Homeowners mobilized against renters. Citizens against noncitizens. Long-term homeowners against the newly arrived. Whites against nonwhites. "Diverse" did not always mean integrated. These conflicts played out not just between ethnic and race groups, but also within them. So, in some suburbs, for example, Chinese American residents rebuffed Chinese businesses in an attempt to keep out the "riff raff," revealing Not in My Back Yard (NIMBY) proclivities toward other Chinese Americans. Suburban community dynamics began to reveal new power dynamics at play. In many places, the wealthiest clung tenaciously to power even as that group became more racially and ethnically diverse. In others, whiteness continued to confer power regardless of class. In other places, citizenship status delineated social divisions.

In some instances, then, new suburbanites of color continued long-lived habits of resisting the poor, the unhoused, the undocumented, renters, even ethnic landscapes—and that resistance became multiracial. They deployed well-developed exclusionary tools to serve their own needs.[10] Especially as nonwhite homeownership climbed, residents of color came to hold increasing sway in their towns and helped make decisions about who would be included or excluded. Suburban advantage began to take on new ethnic and racial hues. Their actions revealed divisions by class, citizenship, and race, in some ways redefining the protective boundaries around suburbia. The end result was persistent inequality across the metropolis, even as the suburbs themselves became much more diverse.

These exclusionary actions can be interpreted in a few ways. One is to see them as part of the politics of racial succession, a phenomenon in which minority groups struggle for their rights and then, after gaining a critical mass, work from the inside to protect the same system that originally marginalized them. As historian Scott Kurashige succinctly put it, "The more power you get within the system, the more you have a stake in upholding the status quo."[11] Working from the inside often included embracing the evolving racial hierarchies that privileged and subordinated different groups. This process played out in the nineteenth century for the Irish, Italians, Jews, and other Europeans once defined as racially inferior, who gained standing in part through differentiating themselves from other racial groups, such as Black Americans and Asians. Their own anti-Blackness, for example, elevated their status. In the post-World War II years, the suburbs themselves played a role in this racializing process. Suburban settlement was widely believed to promote the ethnic and racial assimilation of Italians, Poles, Greeks, Jews, and other European Americans who solidified their identity as "whites" in suburbia. These disparate groups found common ground around shared experiences, aspirations, interests, and racial solidarities in their segregated communities.[12]

After 1980, suburbia as a space of racial assimilation became murkier. As suburbia increasingly diversified, ethnic and racial identities could persist through the move to the suburbs. The impetus for this came from both without and within. Moving out of urban centers did not automatically erase white racializations of Blacks, Latinos, and Asians, somehow "whitening" them as suburbanization did to European ethnics in the postwar years. Blacks, Latinos, and Asians continued to be relegated to a racial terrain of nonwhiteness—Latinos pegged as illegal aliens, regardless of birthplace; Asians as inassimilable aliens; and Blacks as racially inferior.[13] No geographic move could fully erase those racial designations. At the same time, many Asians, Latinos, and Black Americans embraced their racial and ethnic identity even as they became suburbanites. The emergence of Asian "ethnoburbs" illustrates how this worked. In the ethnoburbs, ethnicity was reinforced through an embrace of ethnic aesthetic designs, businesses, and professional services catering to Asians, and ethnic community institutions. Ethnicity thus persisted in suburbia through proactive community-building and economic development aided by infusions of transnational wealth. These spaces not only complicated suburbia's relationship to assimilation, but also presented arenas where new divisions might emerge. Some Chinese American suburbanites, for example, rebuffed the touchstones of ethnoburbia—the Chinese language signs, the 99 Ranch Markets, and architectural flourishes on homes—and fought to keep them out of their own suburbs. They favored a more Euro-American appearance, which they believed signified a higher status and a badge of American cultural citizenship. In this way, suburbia became a site of emerging cleavages by class, national origins, citizenship, and race. NIMBYism in multiracial suburbia, then, could strike in many directions—not only between groups but within them.

In diversifying suburbs, as in any multiracial society, the tensions between conflict and solidarity constantly hovered, posing choices to residents. Would they find common cause with other people of color or even neighbors of similar ethnic heritage? Or would divisiveness prevail? With their long-lived cultures of exclusivity and homeownership, the suburbs presented a context that made solidarity something of an uphill battle. Diverse suburbanites often felt compelled to protect their assets, which could foster conflict within communities and a defensiveness against perceived threats by outsiders.

Another way of interpreting the exclusionary tendencies of diverse suburbanites takes into account the total context of suburbia and race. For generations, whites were given unfettered access to suburban life. Over those same generations, Black Americans, Asians, and Latinos were shut out. Once these groups finally made it in—after years of civil rights struggle— their grasp of the suburban dream represented a racial achievement not to be taken lightly. The right to hold property signified full citizenship. The fragility of this status in a society based on white supremacy, then, perhaps merited a defensive posture to protect their gains, even if it meant excluding others in the process.[14] Suburban defensiveness was a hedge against a system that perennially racialized them as subordinate. The attainment of homeownership and access to decent neighborhoods was a seed planted to begin the process of accruing the sort of generational wealth and advantages that whites had enjoyed for decades. For many, suburban advantage was a goal worth defending.

If tendencies toward suburban exclusion persisted, the new suburbia also witnessed the emergence of more progressive, inclusive values that contradicted long-standing suburban norms. These communities embraced what political scientists Tom Hogen-Esch and Martin Saiz termed the "multicultural suburban dream," which entailed a shared ethos of small-scale home and business ownership, a belief in the positive benefits of government, support for programs to help renters become homeowners, and encouragement of minority-owned small businesses.[15] *The New Suburbia*, then, probes the range of values embraced by suburbanites—inclusive and expansive in some cases, exclusive and protective in others, even coexisting within certain communities.

The new suburbia invariably stoked white anxiety. Whites, after all, were being challenged to change long-standing ways of doing things, and their hold on power was under threat. Racial segregation had been a long and persistent dimension of suburban life for at least a century, ensuring white residents a high degree of social comfort and insulation. When the racial wall cracked, many whites perceived a sense of loss—of community, of control, and of social predictability. Their response invariably involved efforts to reassert control, whether through maintaining local political power, protecting the look of their neighborhoods, intensifying calls for law and order, or even withdrawing from public life. This has been a recurrent dynamic as the suburbs become community spaces of difference.

Suburban inequality—not only across suburbs but within them—also defined the new suburbia and deeply shaped the texture of everyday life. Suburban fortunes came to vary radically. Some suburbs, such as South Gate and Van Nuys, were ravaged by plant closures and disinvestment. Others thrived from infusions of transnational capital and wealth, including Chinese ethnoburbs in the San Gabriel Valley. Some affluent suburbs, such as San Marino, drew on the social and fiscal capital of residents to ensure property protection and foster robust communities. Experiences varied widely depending on how larger structural forces—including economic restructuring, globalization, immigration, and rising neoliberalism—were affecting local life. These forces fueled the spread of wealth and poverty across suburban spaces, which in turn influenced how communities grappled with their newcomers.

Suburbia's transformation occurred at a moment of deep government retrenchment. During the 1980s Reagan era, the federal government passed on the responsibilities of social services, welfare, and even immigration enforcement to states and localities. In this colossal handoff, the suburbs emerged as a new, important locus of authority. They formed policies and asserted new forms of social control, often targeting those most marginalized—the poor, undocumented, and unhoused.[16] In California, the passage of Proposition 13 (1978) was another force of retrenchment. That property tax cutting measure was passed on the cusp of suburbia's massive demographic transformation. One direct impact was LA County's defunding of its human relations resources, civic initiatives to promote interracial cooperation and "the full acceptance of all citizens in all aspects of community life."[17] Prop 13 cuts left suburbs to fend for themselves when grappling with ethnoracial change. While well-resourced towns like San Marino and Pasadena managed to form their own human relations entities, many other suburbs, such as South Gate and Lakewood, were left to muddle through on their own.[18] This confluence of enhanced authority and fewer human relations resources created yet another dimension of uneven suburban fortunes and prospects for inclusive democracy.

These emerging community cultures tended to demarcate who belonged and who didn't, who had a social place and a civic voice and who did not. Those voices on the inside were the ones shaping local policy and community priorities. This affected not only the potential for democracy at the local level, but also for meaningful, fulfilling community life.

———

At the heart of this book are social histories that explore how social and civic life evolved in suburbs undergoing significant demographic transitions. How did community traditions evolve? What were people's everyday experiences like? How did diversity affect involvement in clubs, volunteer work, schools, and other local institutions?

These questions speak to broad assumptions that many observers have made about how suburban life has changed from 1950 to the 2000s. According to conventional wisdom, in the 1950s and 1960s, social life was marked by intensive community engagement, even excessive by the standards of some. Yet, by the 1980s, just one generation removed, suburbia had become a place of fear, social disconnection, privatism, and community decline.[19] What's fascinating about this pendulum swing is that suburban design was often implicated in these radically different social outcomes. The same built environment that was initially thought to foster community connectedness in the early years was blamed for deep social alienation by the 1980s.[20] Some observers blamed the decline on suburbia's social homogeneity and long commuting times, which sapped free time and dampened civic energy.[21] Still others blamed ethnoracial diversity for the disengagement.[22] Whatever the reasons, this led to the era of "bowling alone," as political scientist Robert Putnam memorably described this increasing social disconnection.

The New Suburbia questions the simple declension narrative, asking if it truly describes what was happening on the ground. Looking at specific suburbs suggests a mixed picture depending on factors like the class composition of a suburb or a suburb's position in the regional economy.[23] Some evidence suggests that community engagement persisted over the long haul, pivoting especially around suburban children and the schools. In suburbs rich to poor, children and the schools were crucial conduits of social integration, particularly for new immigrant suburbanites, belying the narrative of social breakdown in the post-1980 era.[24] While *The New Suburbia* does not presume to be the last word on the question, it does offer insights that point to arenas of persistent engagement, like the schools, as well as the disparate impacts of structural forces, like political economy, on the prospects for social and civic health in suburban places. It's unlikely that a design fix can solve the problem. Rather, suburbs that took proactive steps to integrate diverse newcomers seemed to offer the best chances for successful communities.[25]

Recently, histories of suburban life have emphasized two trends: suburban crisis and suburban regeneration, especially in the years after 1960. They are often told separately, in parallel lanes so to speak. The crisis narrative emphasizes the story of the white American middle class, which experienced a rising sense of victimization. Its crisis mentality arose around suburban issues including crime and drugs, child safety, encroachments on suburban land, and even dysfunctional social life. These concerns impelled white suburbanites to mobilize politically, advancing policies that perpetuated their advantage and interests while subordinating racial minorities, the poor, and disenfranchised, which in turn fueled such trends as mass incarceration and inequality.[26]

Diversifying suburbs convey a very different story about what was happening in America's suburbs in this era. Asians, Latinos, and Black Americans brought their own—sometimes transgressive—sensibilities to suburbia, reviving "dead malls," introducing new cultural traditions, and essentially regenerating the suburbs. Just as Latinos were revitalizing declining cities, the suburbs, too, were rejuvenated by the arrival of diverse residents.[27]

The *New Suburbia* builds on these perspectives and seeks to interweave them. In each of the book's case studies, specific places grappled with some sort of crisis. The nature of the problem varied as widely as the suburbs themselves and often depended on their position within the regional political economy and their relation to globalization. In one suburb, the crisis was school desegregation, in others it was factory closures or rising crime. In some places, the arrival of nonwhites was the perceived "crisis." But it all depended on who you asked. That arrival might be a crisis to some, but for others it was the realization of the American dream itself.

Many criteria have been used to define a suburb—political status (an independent municipality laying outside a central city), economic and social function (dependence on a central city, especially true for "bedroom suburbs" lacking an economic base), the built environment (single-family homes, set in yards), ideology and way of life (values of homeownership, nuclear families, privacy, local control, etc.), and process of development (the decentralization of homes, jobs, and other function from the urban core).[28] Initially class and race were tied to the suburban definition, with some claiming that a suburb was a suburb only if it was inhabited by upper- and middle-class whites. A generation of scholarship has challenged that assumption, and this book builds upon that inclusive approach. This book defines suburbs as places that stretch beyond the city core yet still lay within the orbit of the city. They are places with neighborhoods of single-family homes set in yards. Those homes might be big or small, rich or poor, but they are part of a low-slung landscape. A similarly capacious definition of suburb applies to its residents. Suburbs house rich, poor, nonwhites, whites, and everyone in between, even more so in recent times. Finally, suburbanization as a concept relates to the broader process of decentralization—of people and functions—that collectively make up metropolitan areas.[29]

Calling a place a "suburb" can trigger emotional reactions. Many Americans hate admitting that they live in the suburbs. They hold many negative stereotypes associated with suburbia—from mind-numbing mediocrity to environmental irresponsibility to racism and to just plain dullness. In the 1961 novel *Revolutionary Road*, Frank and April Wheeler shared that discomfort. They saw themselves as *in*, but not *of* the suburbs. They were above it. While that aversion lives on in many Americans, it misses not only new qualities in suburban places but also obstructs a full-bore encounter with these places—as spaces to investigate and understand.

In its analysis, *The New Suburbia* combines social and political history, spatial and social analysis, macro- and micro-level perspectives.[30] It focuses on Los Angeles County. While it makes references to the Southern California metropolitan region (which includes Orange, Riverside, San Bernardino, and Ventura Counties), the principal focal point is Los Angeles. It draws on suburban municipal records, local and regional newspapers, visual analysis, maps, memoirs, city directories, photographic evidence, local history archives and sources, voting and economic data, and oral histories and interviews, including more than 56 conducted for this project. A large US Census dataset on all 86 municipalities of LA County from 1950 to 2010, compiled for this book, provides an empirical basis for the analysis.[31] To accompany data provided in the book itself, supplemental tables appear on the book's companion website; they are designated in endnotes with an A preceding the table number (e.g., Table A2.1). *The New Suburbia* also draws upon the rich scholarship of Los Angeles history to flesh out county-wide portraits and patterns and is heavily indebted to this work. Both "race" and "ethnicity" are terms used throughout this book; sometimes one word best applies to the context of the discussion, at other times the terms overlap.[32]

Part I, "Suburban Metropolis," examines suburbia at the county-wide scale. It surveys the evolution of LA's historic suburban landscapes over 100 years, tracks changes in the demography and housing of LA's suburban municipalities from 1945 to 2010, and characterizes the spectrum of suburban political and civic cultures across LA County. Part II, "On the Ground in Suburbia," explores everyday life in four suburbs—Pasadena, San Marino, South Gate, and Lakewood. As they vary by age, class, demography, size, and historic suburban landscape, they are representative of a range of suburban types in LA. Pasadena evolved into an "edge city" that contained a range of historic suburban landscapes as well as long-standing racial diversity; San Marino was a small, elite, picturesque enclave that transitioned from all-white to white and Chinese American; South Gate was a working-class suburb that transformed from white to nearly all-Latino; and Lakewood was a post-World War II mass-produced suburb that started as all-white before becoming one of LA's most racially balanced towns (white, Black American, Latino, and Asian). Los Angeles abounds with many other suburban profiles—working-class Asian, middle-class Latino, white-majority exurbs, and more. These case studies offer only a few examples, yet their particularities allow for deeper exploration of the nuance and texture of everyday experience. Future research, alongside the many stories already told, will no doubt bring new insights to help fill in the mosaic that makes up the Los Angeles suburban story.

———

As suburbia is coming to look more like America itself—in all of its rich diversity—it's imperative to understand what is changing and what isn't. In the years after 1970, suburban history in Los Angeles revealed vivid variations. In some suburbs, an inclusive suburban ideal was taking shape, reflected in an acceptance of ethnic and racial newcomers. In others, long-lived traditions of homeowner politics and culture first honed by whites persisted

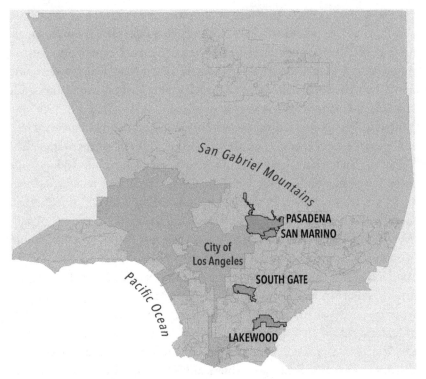

Figure I.1 Map of *The New Suburbia's* case study suburbs: Pasadena, San Marino, South Gate, and Lakewood.
Cartography by Jennifer Mapes, Kent State University.

even as these places diversified. When property values and a sense of community were threatened—whether by the opening of an Asian 99 Ranch Market, a jerry-rigged garage conversion, day laborers, or rising crime—homeowners of all races reacted to defend their neighborhoods. They were behaving just as white suburbanites had for generations. Property and the power it confers was becoming re-racialized. This new framework contributed to the reproduction of metropolitan inequality in the midst of profound demographic change.

The new suburbia matters because it has become home to a majority of Americans. These are the places where people struggle and prosper. In some cases, the suburbs became incubators of economic, social, and civic progress; in others they impeded it. The new suburbia has brought nuance and diversity to the American political landscape. Given the range of ideological proclivities across these communities, there is no such monolithic bloc as "the suburban vote." Wide-ranging loyalties help explain why the suburbs have become crucial swing districts in every major election: they house enormous numbers of voters with a variety of political outlooks.

Despite the assertions of some naysayers that the suburbs have reached their end, American suburbs in fact continue to grow and diversify at a steady pace.[33] Los Angeles stands at the leading edge of that change, pointing the way toward trends that may yet spread across the nation. The better we can understand the civic and social dynamics of these places, their histories, and the forces that shaped them, the better we can grasp where America itself is headed.

PART I
SUBURBAN METROPOLIS

1

The Historic Suburban Landscapes
of Los Angeles

For much of their history, the suburban landscapes of Los Angeles have been a varied milieu. Suburbs housed the artists, intellectuals, and domestic workers creating communities in early Pasadena, the doctors and businessmen settling with their families in the handsome homes of 1920s Westwood, and the African Americans living in the blocks surrounding Central Avenue. In early South Gate and Bell Gardens, working-class families built humble homes in rustic surroundings, while Mexican American families forged family neighborhoods in El Monte and the Eastside. After World War II, throngs of families filled the acres and acres of new mass-built homes in Lakewood, Carson, Westchester, and the vast reaches of the San Fernando Valley, while further east Chinese Americans families later settled the sprawling tracts of the San Gabriel Valley. In Los Angeles, suburbia had become a residential space for all.

The historic suburban landscapes of Los Angeles are a crucial starting point for making sense of suburban life in the region. They lay the foundation of place, establishing how communities would look, be built, serviced, and regulated; how insulated or connected they would be to the greater metropolis; and, ultimately, how open they would be to change. Over 130 years, suburban communities were built across the entire region. Early on, there was a palpable balance between city and country, between the clustering of life within suburban villages and the surrounding green acres of farmland, groves of oranges, rhythmic oil derricks, and rolling golden hills. Within a few decades, that would change.

In successive eras, particular suburban landscapes took shape, products of the historic contexts of their time—political, economic, aesthetic, technological, social. Each landscape type reflected these historical forces and constituted a foundational layer of place. Some suburbs had strong controls in place, limiting future transformations. They were residential spaces of buffered, protected wealth that remained remarkably stable. Others had only the loosest of regulations, opening the door to all manner of change. These historic landscapes bring into focus a legible geography of suburban places and help make sense of LA's expansive built landscape.

This geography matters, given LA's reputation for illegibility. Newcomers often feel an overwhelming sense of disorientation, complaining that the city lacks a sense of coherence, of familiar markers that help ground a person and signal where they are in relation to the whole. Usually, the suburbs are to blame. They do not radiate gradually from downtown, but rather spill carelessly from one to the next, seemingly oblivious to the city core. This sentiment was first articulated by visitors in the 1920s, who famously quipped that Los Angeles was "six suburbs in search of a city." Historian Jeremiah Axelrod dates the genesis of LA's "crisis of illegibility" to the late 1920s, when an explosion of unregulated suburban subdivisions raised alarm among civic leaders and city planners.[1] Even a century ago, people already experienced Los Angeles as a place of formless, bewildering sprawl.

Despite these long-standing complaints, it is possible to make sense of Los Angeles and its many suburbs. An exceptionally useful tool for identifying them is Dolores Hayden's concept of historic suburban landscapes, referring to the cutting-edge suburbs of their day.[2] While "suburb" can denote a particular political status—an incorporated municipality, with powers of local control over land use, infrastructure, and the like—"suburban landscape" is a more flexible concept that can encompass suburban areas that might exist in different political jurisdictions. What matters most is the nature and genesis of the built environment. In Los Angeles, a good example is the San Fernando Valley—dubbed "America's suburb" by its biographer—which lies within the borders of Los Angeles City and yet exhibits quintessential traits of mass-built suburbia.[3] Suburban landscapes can likewise exist in unincorporated territory (like Hacienda Heights or Altadena) or within suburban towns like La Cañada, Carson, or Compton. Some municipalities have a range of suburban landscapes within their borders, like Pasadena, with its streetcar suburb old town, its elite enclaves to the south and hilly western areas, its multiracial suburban neighborhoods in Northwest, and its postwar tract homes in Hastings Ranch to the east. In short, suburban landscapes can exist within and across political borders.

The physical look and feel of a place offer immediate clues about a suburb's age while conveying signals about neighborhood life and social possibilities. What is the scale of development? How do people get around? Are there people visible outside? How is the housing stock organized and changing?

Figure 1.1 Contrasting suburban landscapes in Santa Clarita and South Pasadena.
(top) Courtesy the City of Santa Clarita; (bottom) photograph by Marina Weisenberg, 2022.

Is it a navigable place? Driving around the pastel stucco, red tile-roof homes of Santa Clarita, with row after undulating row of similar looking houses, differs dramatically from walking around the quaint shops along Mission Street in South Pasadena, with its streetcar-era bungalows along the side streets, shaded by stately, mature trees. Crucial variations in how suburban landscapes look usually link back to a place's roots.[4]

This chapter surveys the historic suburban landscapes of LA, noted with their date of emergence or peak era: borderland (1880s), streetcar suburbs (1890s), picturesque enclaves and garden suburbs (1900), modest subdivisions (1910–1940), sitcom suburbs (1940–1960s), and edge cities and corporate suburbs (1970).[5] Even for a book that focuses on the years after 1945, the history of LA suburbia must necessarily begin earlier. By 1945, a vast array of suburban landscapes filled in myriad spaces and represented a mature starting point for a number of LA communities. By that time, 43 towns were already in place with significant geographic reach.

Even so, the pace of development was weighted heavily toward the postwar era in terms of population and housing, a period of immense growth in the region. In LA County, the population more than doubled between 1950 and 2000, rising from 4.15 million to 9.51 million, sparking a sharp rise in population density.[6] New people and new housing were overtaking and redefining the county. In the San Fernando Valley, a 212-square-mile suburban expanse, the population jumped from 112,000 in 1940 to 1.8 million in 1970.[7] In truth, development was happening all over LA, including in older towns whose vacant lots or outlying farmlands were converted into suburban homes for eager buyers. Another sign of postwar vigor was a spike in the number of municipal incorporations from 1950 to 1969—fully 32 towns incorporated, which outpaced other periods. This wave of incorporations was partly spurred by the "Lakewood Plan," a newly conceived system that gave suburbs the ability to secure their civic autonomy on the cheap by contracting with LA County for services like police and fire. It made the prospect of civic independence and local control a much more attractive, affordable option.[8]

Housing trends were even more dramatic. By 1970, newer postwar housing had come to outnumber older pre-1940 housing by a whopping margin— 75% to 25%. In 2000, the postwar "sitcom suburb" era remained dominant in terms of when housing was built.[9] By this time, pre-1940 housing represented a scant 13% of the total housing supply, underscoring the importance of postwar housing and validating the old axiom that LA is all about the future, with little appreciation for a preserved past. Between 1940 and

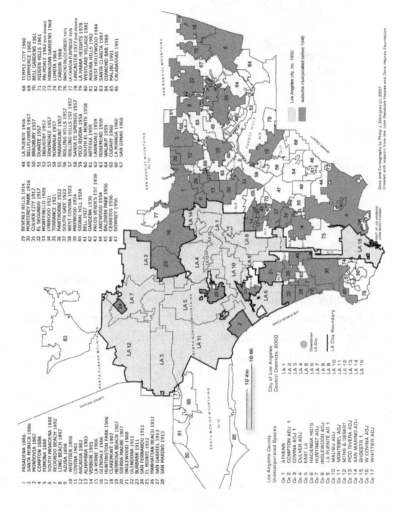

Figure 1.2 Suburbs of Los Angeles County, including LA City and all suburban municipalities. The dark-shaded towns were incorporated before 1945.

Cartography by Philip J. Ethington © 2007. Ethington base map edited and augmented by Becky Nicolaides.

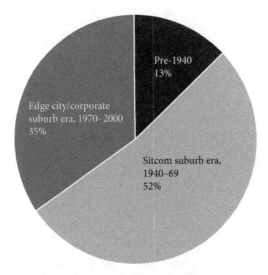

Figure 1.3 Year structures built in Los Angeles County, shown for all existing housing in 2000.
Source: US Census of Housing, 1970 and 2000.

2000, at least half a million older housing units (pre-1939) were demolished to make way for new ones.[10]

Despite this postwar dominance, the older suburban landscapes of LA established critical precedents in shaping the built landscape and social geography of the region. Certain areas were pegged as high class, others as modest, rendered so by the imposition—or absence—of certain land use regulations. The historic footprints of these places had remarkable staying power, etching deep imprints on the region's built environment.

Early Suburban Ideals and Land Development

LA's suburban identity had roots reaching back to the early twentieth century, when a powerful set of ideals and innovative land development practices were pioneered in the region. City boosters and leaders envisioned a unique path forward for LA, one that learned from the hard lessons of nineteenth-century industrial cities like New York, Chicago, and Pittsburgh. The pathway forward would veer outward. Los Angeles would revel in nature, open spaces, and light. It would use decentralization to create a calmer, healthier way to live and work, close to greenery and open air. As some Progressive reformers back east lauded early suburbs like Llewellyn Park, New York, and Riverside, Illinois as an antidote to big city problems of congestion, pollution, unrest, and poverty, Los Angeles leaders would take this suburban solution and apply it wholesale to the entire region. In 1890, LA represented a new urban canvas, a metropolis on the verge of growth with unique possibilities for experimentation. It was a hopeful, almost utopian vision of a healthful garden city, a place that could teach an America exhausted from the grind of industrial life how to rejuvenate and live better.[11]

LA reformer Dana Bartlett captured this vision in *The Better City* (1907), writing that Los Angeles would spread out to avoid the slums, congestion, and strife of eastern cities. He considered the low-density suburban pattern of development an advance that enhanced the quality of life. Many local leaders also believed suburban homeownership would diffuse labor radicalism.[12] In line with the national suburban movement, this vision had a racialized dimension, with Los Angeles as a final settling place for white Americans at the edge of the frontier. City leaders called it the "white spot," devoid of the diversity and its attendant corruption they believed were dragging down big cities. City leaders, planners, and real estate developers ultimately worked together to translate these ideas into practice, turning Los Angeles into a paradigm of the racialized suburban metropolis.

Along with these powerful ideological currents among the elite, other factors promoted suburban expansion. One was the cultural proclivities of LA's early, numerous Midwestern settlers who carried with them a community ideal that was thoroughly suburban: "spacious, affluent, clean, decent, permanent, predictable, and homogenous."[13] Another factor was the natural geography of oil fields in Los Angeles, which pulled development southward toward these productive sites.[14] Transportation played a more nuanced role. While it was once thought to have caused suburbanization in Los Angeles and the nation as a whole, transportation was in fact more of a facilitator than a cause. More important than transit technologies per se were the policies dictating how they would be used. During the streetcar era, for example, the United States was unique among nations in allowing transit owners to sell real estate along their lines. This policy sped the process of suburbanization, as did policies favoring the automobile after 1920.[15]

While new transportation forms may not have caused decentralization, they powerfully determined its shape. Since LA began its first phase of concerted urban growth at the very moment when electric streetcars came into widespread use, this coincidental timing meant that streetcars systems had an exaggerated impact on the shape of the city's growth, stimulating sprawl even before the arrival of the automobile. Subsequently, the automobile played a critical role in sustaining the suburban paradigm in Los Angeles. By the 1920s, LA's dispersed form had become entrenched.[16]

Just as important as ideology, culture, and transportation were the decisions made by the region's power brokers—political and business leaders, planners, and land developers—in determining the character of LA's built form. Numerous early planning efforts worked to promote a suburban ethos. They launched public improvements in line with the City Beautiful movement, which included limiting the building height to 150 feet and promoting civic centers, parks, and boulevards that radiated horizontally. The height limit had the effect of tempering the density of downtown. In 1908, the Los Angeles city council passed the nation's first zoning ordinance, which separated industrial and residential districts.[17] The original law mapped out three large areas of the city where most industry was prohibited and residential neighborhoods would be protected as tranquil, clean spaces.[18] As the original measure was somewhat imprecise and unevenly enforced, a second, stricter zoning law passed in 1921, which established clearer categories of land use, including one restricted solely to single-family detached homes; these became known as R-1 zones.[19] Despite these efforts, fairly haphazard private development predominated into the 1920s, which prompted some civic-minded citizens to push for more comprehensive planning. In the 1920s, planners began articulating a vision for Los Angeles as a dispersed network of "garden city" hubs—independent communities with industry, commerce, and homes—knit together by roadways. While only some aspects of this vision were realized, it further solidified LA's suburban future.[20]

The process of real estate development in Los Angeles also promoted and even revolutionized the suburban trend. From the 1880s to 1920s, profit-minded speculators and subdividers ran the gamut from highly capitalized large-scale operators to curbstone hucksters. In LA, the promotion of suburban real estate was elevated to a sophisticated art, complete with excursions to remote lands to hear lively sales pitches over barbecue roast beef.[21]

Three modes of suburban land development prevailed in the area in the early twentieth century. The first was led by moguls who owned both transit lines and suburban land. A leading example was Henry Huntington, whose ownership of LA's electric streetcars and subdividable land along the routes allowed him to reap spectacular profits from suburban land sales. To bring even larger pools of capital to their ventures, some developers formed land syndicates such as the Los Angeles Suburban Homes Company, which purchased 47,500 acres in the San Fernando Valley in 1910.[22] Second, Los Angeles pioneered a number of innovations in the areas of real estate, planning, and land use regulation, culminating in the emergence in the 1920s of a new type of developer: the community builder. These men moved beyond the method of simple subdivision and sale of individual lots to the professional planning of large residential neighborhoods. Typically operating at the upper end of the real estate market, they subdivided in newer areas or in established towns amenable to stringent land use restrictions. Community builders like William Leimert and Harry Culver planned entire developments with numerous rules and restrictions on land use, including the exclusion of racial and religious minorities. In later years, the community builders were succeeded by operative builders, merchant builders, and corporate builders, who took a similar approach but on larger scales and targeting a broader range of homebuyers.[23]

The third and arguably most common type of developer through the 1920s was the small-scale, bare-bones subdivider. These individuals would purchase acres of undeveloped land, divide it into allotments, and then sell them to prospective homeowners and speculators. The quality of their developments varied widely. On the low end were subdivisions with minimal improvements to the land—a few stakes in the ground, an ungraded road, an unrecorded plat, and defective title. More typical were subdivisions with some street grading, minimal services, and clear land titles.[24] These curbstone subdividers benefitted from the lack of coherent subdivision map laws, which allowed them to operate legally without clear oversight by city regulators. As a result, they often divided up land in a haphazard way without much concern for lot sizes, standard street widths, tree planting, or provisions for public parks, parking, and other public spaces. The dogged efforts by large developers and planners to clamp down on these smaller operators attested to their prevalence well into the late 1920s.[25]

Whether planned or unplanned, suburban real estate development expanded briskly from the 1890s through the 1920s. This was an era of unabashed pro-growth sentiment in Los Angeles, when the public and private sectors shared the goal of propelling LA into the ranks of the nation's leading metropolitan centers, an agenda that lasted well into the 1950s.[26]

Early Los Angeles, of course, was not all suburban. Distinct areas were given over to urban landscapes and functions. Downtown was the most obvious example, with its dense buildings and mixed land uses. Another example was multifamily housing—the apartments, lodging houses, flats, and bungalow courts that had become widespread within the LA city limits. From the 1920s to the 1940s, multifamily structures comprised nearly half of the city's housing units. Some of this housing accommodated an unusually large tourist population, many of whom stayed for long-term visits. But it also housed permanent residents—young couples, the elderly, workers, and the more cosmopolitan set, who lived in apartment clusters in Hollywood, the Wilshire district, and other LA city neighborhoods.[27] In the rural and suburban periphery, the single-family home remained dominant, representing three-quarters of all housing types in LA County by 1940. And despite the elites' platitudes about the virtues of suburban homeownership, many early Angelenos lived in suburban homes as renters.[28]

Race and the Suburban Ideal

By the early twentieth century, white racial purity had become a fundamental feature of the suburban ideal, a definitional element of what "suburbia" meant, not only in LA but across the globe. Underlying this ideal was a long-lived perception that racial purity ensured the social, economic, and civic health of neighborhoods. It also contained a class element. In suburban landscapes for the elite and middle classes, physical distance from the city's "undesirables" became a coveted value, conferring social status, economic benefits, and physical health on those who could afford the "country life" in these socially buffered neighborhoods. They were the most successful at achieving racial separation. In working-class suburbs, racial aspirations were equally powerful. Here, suburbanites staked their social and economic identity on their status as homeowners in stable, white neighborhoods. Often on the racial borderlines of metro areas, these suburbs were most vulnerable to racial change and, as such, became sites of the most volatile conflicts over integration. White suburbanites in their various landscapes shared the belief that, if racial and ethnic minorities moved in, community life and property values would suffer, a concept that scholars dubbed the "racial theory of property value." These beliefs reached beyond personal biases against people of color, reflecting an intrinsic consciousness of a "system" that asserted the same idea.[29]

Adding to these suburban racial assumptions, in Los Angeles certain ideological tides swept forward a powerful movement for white racial purity in the region. By 1900, after Americanization had largely marginalized the indigenous people, Californios, and Mexican settlers who had once dominated California, the Anglo elite who came to power imagined Southern California as a bastion of racial purity. It would be America's white racial frontier. Charles Lummis was a leading promoter of this idea. The editor of *Land of Sunshine/Out West* magazine and one of LA's biggest boosters, Lummis championed the idea that Los Angeles would be "the new Eden of the Saxon home seeker," an antidote to eastern cities filling up with "undesirable foreigners." These overtones found full-bore expression in a regional eugenics movement led by people like University of Southern California founder Joseph P. Widney and Robert Millikan of Caltech, who envisioned LA as an Aryan city of the sun. These ideas aligned easily with the ideology of suburban racial purity spreading nationally. In LA, it all came together—an emerging suburban metropolis guided by leaders embracing the tenets of white superiority and separatism.[30]

Somewhat predictably, by the 1910s and 1920s, LA pioneered and honed the tools of racial exclusion in suburbia. Real estate leaders and developers played a pivotal role in developing these mechanisms of segregation. By the 1930s, the federal government reinforced these efforts through its own biased housing policies. And in suburbs across LA, residents used intimidation and violence against people of color who tried moving in despite these barriers.[31]

The result was stark racial segregation. Most of LA's outlying suburbs were exclusively white. People of color were confined to multiracial sections east and south of downtown, which expanded gradually over the years, in neighborhoods like Boyle Heights and the Central Avenue district. They housed African Americans, Mexicans, Japanese, Jews, Italians, Anglos, and small numbers of Chinese and Korean residents.[32] While Black Americans were the most segregated group, they did gain footholds in a few far-flung suburbs such as Pasadena, Pacoima, and Watts due to early labor needs in those areas. Latinos and Asians likewise settled the periphery in the early twentieth century, especially near agricultural jobs.[33] While these small pockets represented important footholds for future suburban settlement, the overarching pattern from the 1880s to well into the 1960s was one of white dominance in suburbia.

The Historic Suburban Landscapes of Los Angeles

With this larger suburban vision in place to guide LA's future development, distinct suburban landscapes began to emerge. What follows is a survey of these places. While some municipalities contained a variety of suburban forms within their borders (such as Pasadena, Culver City, and Burbank), in other towns there was uniformity, especially in suburbs at the high and low ends of the class spectrum. This survey captures LA's historic suburban landscapes at their point of origin, clarifying the forces driving their formation. In some areas, ideological and aesthetic considerations were paramount, linking to broader national movements in suburban development and design. Other suburbs were the product of land development practices meant to maximize profit and minimize community investment. Still others reflected the aspirations of suburbanites themselves and the many ways they shaped suburban landscapes to fulfill needs based around class, race, and ethnic identity. The end result was a mosaic of distinct suburban landscapes spread across acres and acres of Los Angeles County.[34]

Borderland, 1880s

The elite suburban ideal that emerged in the eastern United States in the 1840s to 1860s signaled a profound redefinition of urban space. Residents, designers, and pattern book writers recast the urban periphery as a place once detested into one highly coveted, where lovely homes would nestle in a green country landscape. In this period, the ideal of a suburban cottage set in picturesque nature, linked to urban life by regular transport, was first defined and became a new, desired, permanent living space by the middle and upper classes. This borderland zone would lie between country and city. The rustic, unspoiled landscape of the borderland was inherently unstable, vulnerable to the advance of new development. Yet the borderland ideal endured, with residents seeking habitation in this natural space for generations.[35]

For Los Angeles, the borderland period began later than in the East, coinciding with LA's emergence as a young city in the late nineteenth century. Nature was a powerful draw for many pioneer white residents. In contrast to the lush, green woodlands surrounding cities they left behind back east, here nature was sunny and fragrant, and the mountains, ocean, and arid land seemed to evoke the Italian countryside. This warm, mild nature was healing, a salve to body and spirit, a draw for those suffering from tuberculosis and others simply seeking relief from harsh winters in the East and Midwest. The suburban borderland also reflected the region's agrarian qualities. Well into the 1940s, the rural life in Los Angeles was not an idealized abstraction but a living reality. In 1935, 23% of LA County land was devoted to farms and ranches.[36] Across the region, farmlands were plentiful, along with the open spaces of rolling hills, mountains, and chaparral.

The earliest borderland suburbs existed within this natural and agrarian environment. In the farming areas, these were not simply farming villages. They were a melding of agrarian and suburban cultures, so much so that historian Paul Sandul dubbed them "agriburbs." Residents could inhabit a small farm home close to the city and commute to work downtown. Expressions of this "ideal country life" proliferated in early Los Angeles—visions of homes set in lush, overgrown gardens, their owners upstanding, independent gentlemen farmer-businessmen. In the San Gabriel Valley, enthused the LA Chamber of Commerce, "may be found beautiful rural homes, whose owners are within touch of social life, and enjoy the best features of the city and country combined."[37] The ideal suggested that Southern California existed in a superior cultural state, where borderland life was marked by refinement, uplift, and sophistication, in contrast to regions like the rural South or urban East. Boosters promoted this idea from the 1880s well into the 1920s.[38]

In this LA borderland, suburban farming took on a distinct cast centered on the idea of "gentleman farming," a therapeutic version of farming that would invigorate minds, bodies, communities, and democracy. The actual farm work was a refined pursuit, worlds apart from the labor-intensive, exploitive toil of the South and much of California. It was recreational farming in a sense, enabling the professional or businessman returning home after a day in the office to get outside, get his hands dirty, and feel a visceral connection to the natural world. Since many suburban "farmers" had little or no agricultural experience, they relied on the copious advice of local government agencies, universities, chambers of commerce, and newspaper columns, which all promoted the virtues of this borderland life.[39]

Examples of this semirural suburban life abounded across Southern California, especially in the citrus orchards of the San Fernando and San Gabriel Valleys and among the dairy and produce farms of Southeast LA. Real estate sales agent Charles B. Hopper became one of the region's most effective promoters of these tracts, beginning in 1907 with the sale of semi-sustaining garden homes in Lawndale and Hawthorne. He peddled the same

Figure 1.4 Suburban borderlands imagined and realized in early Los Angeles, 1919 and 1891. In 1891, Charles Dudley Warner described the rich possibilities of a life in Southern California, a "new country" where "a roomy, pretty cottage overrun with vines and flowering plants, set in the midst of trees and lawns and gardens of tropical appearance and luxuriance" housed the fortunate newcomer. This life epitomized the "borderland" ethos.

(top) "A Little Land and a Living," postcard c. 1919, Little Farms Magazine, San Fernando Valley History collection, Special Collections and Archives, University Library, California State University, Northridge; (bottom) Courtesy of the Archives at Pasadena Museum of History (Photo C12b-11b; photo by Jarvis). Caption text: Charles Dudley Warner, "The Outlook in Southern California," *Harper's New Monthly Magazine* 82 (January 1891), 176.

type of suburban homesteads in South Gate in the 1920s, and Lakewood Village in the 1930s. Nearby Bellflower was pitched as the town "where farm and city meet," with deep narrow lots perfect for small farm homes, connected to the city by streetcar. In Hansen Heights in the northeast San Fernando Valley, the Meyer family raised persimmons, quinces, almonds, peaches, pears, and citrus fruits on their five-acre lot in the 1920s, while running a real estate business.[40] Even early Pasadena exemplified the borderland ethos. There, George Hoffman claimed a foothold in both urban and rural worlds. On his expansive 125-acre property in the picturesque Linda Vista section, he grew 1,800 avocado trees while serving as president of the American Radiator Company. He used his home and barn as a laboratory where he developed the Thermador heater, which made him a millionaire by 1926. The Hoffman family reveled in the country life but was firmly linked to urban capitalism.[41]

Despite the boosters' platitudes celebrating independence and self-sufficiency in this suburban borderland, these settlements were tightly linked to the city—for jobs, infrastructure, and even labor. Many of these areas excluded nonwhites from land ownership, even as many "gentleman farmers" relied on nonwhite and immigrant labor to help keep their small farms functioning. In the San Gabriel Valley's citrus belt, dependence on Asian, Mexican, and Native American workers was particularly acute, even as these towns touted the virtues of the "Ideal Country Life." The notion of "gentleman farming" was a racially exclusive concept applied to white landowners while eliding the labor performed by people of color who were segregated into separate neighborhoods. The citrus belt towns of Pasadena, Monrovia, Duarte, Glendora, Covina, Pomona, Claremont, Upland, and Ontario all had their origins in this semirural borderland culture, where orange "groves came right to the doorsteps of growers' homes."[42]

Many of these borderland areas gave way in later years to denser suburban development as their rural atmosphere dissolved into something more modern, paved over, and generic. In a few suburban areas, especially on the metropolitan fringes, residents clung to the rustic aesthetic and worked tenaciously to preserve a semblance of borderland living well into the twenty-first century. These were typically high-end semirural suburbs, whose "nature" was the product of vigorous activism and careful planning, placing them more under the rubric of "picturesque enclave." The true borderland had become obsolete, its intimacy with nature eroded as bulldozers cleared the way for one suburban wave after another.

Streetcar Suburbs, 1890s

Streetcars and roads would link the amorphous borderland into a more coherent built landscape. The emerging metropolis would be delineated by an
audaciously huge network of trains, trolleys, water mains, and roads that together made vast spaces remarkably accessible. The streetcar suburbs were
an early outcome of this infrastructure. Electric streetcar technology was a
revolutionary breakthrough, democratizing access to the suburban outskirts
with its clean, fast, and inexpensive service. Streetcar fares were generally affordable to a broad cross-section of riders, making the possibility of daily
commuting a new reality for many. The streetcar suburbs would reflect this
affordability.[43]

Streetcars caught on quickly in Los Angeles, stimulating a robust period
of suburbanization that greatly expanded the size of the metropolis.[44] The
coincident timing of LA's first major land boom in the 1880s and the national
introduction of electric streetcar technology positioned Los Angeles to adopt
this system of urban transit with exceptional fervor. In 1888, the city installed
its first electric streetcar line on Pico Boulevard, west of downtown. Over
the next few decades, the system expanded to become the world's largest
interurban network of its time.

The streetcars were the sinews of a regional body whose growth was driven
in these early years by agriculture, oil, nascent industry, and real estate. The
distinctive geographic character of these endeavors—spread far and wide—
were key vectors for regional development and the placement of streetcar
lines. For example, agricultural activity in the far reaches of the county drew
the lines deep into the San Fernando and San Gabriel Valleys. Oil fields in
southern LA likewise anchored transit systems, with heavy concentrations
around Dominguez, Torrance, Brea, Whittier, and El Segundo. The lines did
not always simply stretch into terra incognita, but rather connected a geography already buzzing with economic activity.

LA's world-renowned streetcar system took shape between 1888 and the
1920s. After early piecemeal development by separate competing traction
companies, a merger in 1911 consolidated the various electric railways into
two major systems. The first was the Los Angeles Railway (LARy), owned
by the Huntington family. Known as the "Yellow Cars," they operated over
397 miles of track by 1925, mostly within the city limits of Los Angeles. The
cars were small and nimble, traveled on narrow-gauge track, had the heaviest
usage of all the systems, and charged a flat five-cent fare. The second was the

Pacific Electric (PE), or "Red Cars," which was owned by the Southern Pacific Railroad after Henry Huntington relinquished his interests in 1910. The Red Cars were high-speed interurbans that traveled on standard gauge track and traversed 1,200 route miles across Southern California, from Owensmouth (now Canoga Park) in the west to Redlands in the east, from Mt. Lowe above Pasadena to Newport Beach to the south. By the 1920s, when the electric streetcars had been built out, the accessible metropolis had expanded immensely in all directions, reaching towns and suburbs up to 90 miles away.[45] Line expansions and ridership increased in the 1910s and 1920s, peaking in the mid-1920s. Thereafter, in a series of ballot measures, voters supported road building and rejected funding for the trolleys. By the late 1920s, the streetcar's impact on the built environment in Los Angeles had essentially ended.[46]

The electric streetcars shaped not only the broad patterns of development in Los Angeles, but also the built environment of suburbs and settlements along the lines. Two main patterns prevailed. First were lines that ran out to existing towns. They included Pasadena, South Pasadena, Monrovia, Santa Monica, Long Beach, Redondo Beach, Watts, and Hollywood, among others. All experienced fast population growth after the arrival of the streetcars. Watts, for example, was transformed from a sleepy outpost into a vibrant multiracial hub.[47] The second pattern was lines that ran into undeveloped areas that were quickly subdivided. From 1900 to 1920, fully 23 towns incorporated, most of them along the streetcar routes. Some sprang up after the arrival of the streetcars. By this measure, 27% of LA County's suburbs have some early identity as a streetcar suburb. By the 1920s, nearly every town was touched by the lines, although they barely grazed the outskirts of a few communities, such as South Gate, Monterey Park, Montebello, and West Covina. The streetcars likewise stimulated early suburban growth within Los Angeles City, notably in the San Fernando Valley where towns like Van Nuys, Lankershim, and Reseda grew after the Red Cars arrived. By contrast, several elite suburbs that were developed in the 1920s—such as Palos Verdes Estates, Pacific Palisades, and even Westwood—were deliberately designed away from the lines, largely to keep away the "riff-raff."[48]

Historian Robert Fishman views the streetcar era as the most successful period of suburbanization in LA history for striking the optimal balance between country and city. These suburbs were small, coherent villages of modest bungalows, surrounded by citrus groves and irrigated fields, linked

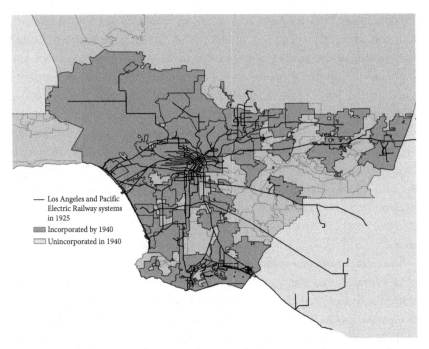

Figure 1.5 The location of streetcar lines in relation to towns incorporated before 1940.

Cartography by Jennifer Mapes, Kent State University.

to a vibrant downtown through an efficient, far-flung rail system.[49] They ran the gamut from wealthy to working class, reflecting the early class-inclusive nature of the streetcar system itself. From the higher-end suburbs of stately Victorians to the lower-end working-class suburbs of modest bungalows and self-built homes, streetcar suburbs reflected a range of class profiles well into the 1920s.[50]

The streetcar lines influenced commercial and residential neighborhood development in important ways. These were pedestrian-oriented suburbs, with few streets more than six blocks from a depot or rail line. A typical streetcar suburb was anchored around a small Main Street near the trolley stop, with groceries, barbers, pharmacies, and hardware stores serving the local populace. The nature of local land use restrictions varied across these suburbs. In South Pasadena's Oneonta Park, for example, the purchaser of a one-third acre plot had to build a home worth at least $3,500, with a minimum 40-foot setback. In Owensmouth (present day Canoga Park), aimed at lower middle-class residents, local guidelines allowed boarding and rooming houses, apartments, and hotels, with a minimum cost of homes set at $2,000.[51]

Suburbs linked by streetcar also varied by their urban–rural orientation. Some leaned toward the city's culture and economic base, others outward toward farming. For families living in towns like Highland Park, Eagle Rock, Glendale, Pasadena, South Pasadena, and Huntington Park, the commute downtown was routine and their ties to the city strong. Life in South Pasadena was touted by developers as a suburb where "beauty shall prevail—and hundreds of homeseekers will be eager to seize upon this opportunity of finding such a resting place from the turmoil and stress of business life." This enabled the perfect balance between city and country living.[52] Further toward the outskirts, farming was a powerful anchor. Towns like Pomona, Claremont, Gardena, Hawthorne, El Monte, Whittier, and Van Nuys were semirural streetcar suburbs, with productive farms and their own independent community institutions typically dominated by white middle-class residents. Mexican, Asian, and indigenous people also inhabited these suburbs in segregated neighborhoods, working as hired

Figure 1.6 Early streetcar suburbia in Highland Park, 1915. Shops and homes were typically within walking distance of the streetcar lines and depots.
USC Digital Library. California Historical Society Collection.

help or tenant farmers and commuting to jobs elsewhere when the harvest cycle dipped.[53]

Streetcar suburbanization left two important imprints on the built environment of Los Angeles. At the county level, it created a skeleton for the metropolis that was truly gargantuan in scale, geographically larger than any metropolis of its time. The county, then, was a bit like an overgrown child with huge, gangly limbs, not yet filled out with muscle and flesh but impressive for its massive reach. The skeleton was there. The region would gradually grow into it. The streetcars thus led to a geography of massive dispersal, linking up a series of small towns, villages, and suburbs. Some of these outlying towns gradually matured and spread, with places like Pomona, Claremont, Whittier, and Van Nuys becoming important nodes for future growth.[54]

A second imprint appears in the pedestrian-oriented core of these communities, usually a commercial Main Street near the old depot. These remain intact, particularly in smaller suburbs with a penchant for historic preservation, such as South Pasadena, Glendora, Monrovia, and Claremont.[55] Each has an "old town" section of mostly gentrified but well-preserved original commercial buildings, previously anchored by their streetcar stop. In South Pasadena, the historic Mission District has seen a rebirth of its link to transit as the Metro Gold Line stops near the old walkable shopping district. Restored buildings housing bakeries, coffee houses, and boutiques, and a New Urbanist development are clustered to take advantage of the pedestrian scale of this one-time streetcar suburb. Other towns have retained the streetcar suburb footprint in different ways. In northern Duarte, along the picturesque foothills of the San Gabriel Mountains, the Red Car line that ran through town was converted into a recreational trail for walkers and bikers, adjacent to modest homes. In Azusa, the town's civic center is located near the old streetcar stop. Lynwood is one of few suburbs that kept its actual Red Car depot, which it relocated to Lynwood Park.[56] Perhaps the most eccentric footprint is a series of public stairways carved into the hillsides of Echo Park, El Sereno, Highland Park, Hollywood, Mount Washington, Pasadena, Silver Lake and Santa Monica. These stairways were built to make the transit lines accessible to residents of hillside neighborhoods. Today, they represent a quirky piece of local history—about 400 stairways remain in greater Los Angeles—with historic ties to the once vibrant streetcar system.[57]

In most towns that once existed as streetcar suburbs, the old landscape has vanished. From Arcadia to El Monte, Inglewood to Van Nuys, no physical traces of this history remain.[58] Broad thoroughfares like Huntington Drive, Colorado, Pico, Sepulveda, and Hollywood Boulevards—where the streetcars once ran—appear simply as extra-wide streets with their own distinct spirits. The more profound impact of the streetcars was the way it stretched Los Angeles out to distances that virtually redefined the meaning of metropolitan space.

Picturesque Enclaves and Garden Suburbs, 1900

While picturesque enclaves in America originated in the mid-nineteenth century, the form found striking expression in Los Angeles in the early twentieth century. In some cases, LA's picturesque enclaves were designed by the direct descendants of the form's earliest practitioner, Frederick Law Olmsted, a principal designer of iconic Riverside, Illinois. In these highly planned suburbs aimed at affluent buyers, the principles of landscape architecture were applied to whole subdivisions. Curving roads followed the natural contours of the land, homes were sited in naturalistic settings, and ample green space was allotted for common use. The whole idea was to plant homes within an existing natural area, giving the appearance of minimal tampering with the environment.[59] By the time the picturesque enclave reached Los Angeles in the early twentieth century, it had evolved from its purest form— expressed in places like Llewellyn Park and Riverside—into what became known as the *American garden suburb*. In this rendition, there was a more visible manipulation of the natural landscape via landscaped parkways, community parks, country clubs, and the like, but careful attention to aesthetic design and natural surroundings remained.[60]

Community builders were key figures in the creation of picturesque enclaves. They used design and careful regulations to create whole communities as a way of stabilizing property values for prospective buyers. During the 1920s, they operated at the high end of the real estate market and were responsible for creating some of LA's most iconic and enduring suburban enclaves, though these were few in number.[61] From 1906 to 1925, fewer than 10 subdivisions in Los Angeles fell into the "planned community" category, all showing traits of the picturesque enclave.[62]

These high-end enclaves were sited in some of the most scenic locations in the region—rolling hills overlooking the vast Pacific, the peaceful foothills of the San Gabriel Mountains, the lush hillsides of the Santa Monica Mountains.

Elevation equaled wealth. These areas were beautiful then, and remain so, thanks to astute site selection, strict restrictions, prohibitive pricing, and community consensus to protect the status quo.[63] Important early examples include Palos Verdes, Pacific Palisades (including the Huntington Palisades section), Bel Air, Holmby Hills, San Marino, and portions of Beverly Hills, the Hollywood Hills, Pasadena, and Altadena, among others. The Olmsted Brothers Firm, run by the sons of Frederick Law Olmsted, was involved in several of these projects, including Bel Air, portions of Pacific Palisades, Palos Verdes, the Benmar Hills section of Burbank, and the San Rafael section of Pasadena. From 1891 to 1950, they designed 16 suburban developments in LA County, making them leading figures in bringing the picturesque aesthetic to Los Angeles suburbia.[64]

A few examples illustrate the character of these places. Huntington Palisades, a 250-acre section of what became Pacific Palisades, was initially subdivided in the late 1920s. Set along the western edge of the Santa Monica Mountain foothills, the land's striking natural features included tall trees, pastoral stretches, and breathtaking views of the Pacific. Curving roads followed the land's natural contours and left much of the native vegetation intact. Lot sizes ranged from one-quarter to over one acre. Restrictions included minimum construction costs ranging from $5,000 to $15,000 depending on lot size, residential-only uses of property, a two-story height maximum, a five-foot maximum on hedges, setback specifications, and the exclusion of non-Caucasians. A property owners association was established to enforce these guidelines.[65] Typical of elite developments, Huntington Palisades was sited away from the streetcar lines to insulate the community from the masses. As federal appraisers observed in 1939, this lack of public transit "was not a serious handicap in a district of this type." They used descriptors like "dignified," the "highest type," and architecture that was "the last word in the art," a clear testament to the persistence of the area's high status even through the Depression.[66]

Situated on a dramatic rise of hills overlooking the Pacific, Palos Verdes is perhaps the most well-known picturesque enclave in Los Angeles. Designed by Frederick Law Olmsted, Jr. and Charles Cheney, the elegantly planned community launched in the early 1920s, with Spanish colonial homes, a golf course, 800 acres of park land, winding parkways that followed the hilly terrain, a nursery school, and small shopping area. Stringent restrictions were applied to both the physical and social landscape. All house designs had to be approved by the community's Art Jury to ensure architectural harmony. Minimum house costs ranged from $6,000 to $25,000 depending on lot sizes,

Figure 1.7 Views of Pacific Palisades under development, ca. 1920s, and built up, 1933. With its dramatic vistas of the Pacific, careful planning, community design, restrictions, and high pricing, Pacific Palisades exemplified crucial traits of the picturesque enclave—a suburb for the wealthy, protected from future change.
Security Pacific National Bank Collection/Los Angeles Public Library.

supporting Olmsted's assertion that he designed the community "for fairly prosperous people."[67] The town was also restricted to the white race through deed restrictions "in perpetuity." When federal appraisers surveyed this area in March 1939, they described it as a town of "great charm" with "a magnificent view of the Pacific Ocean. . . . One authority ventures the opinion that 'Palos Verdes Estates' is one of the highest-class subdivisions in Southern California."[68]

As the picturesque enclave evolved into the garden suburb, developers continued to integrate natural elements into the design but in a more manipulated way. They used curving streets, though sometimes divorced from the natural contours of the land, and flora was often imported rather than conserved. Windsor Square (at Wilshire and 3rd Street) was designed in 1911 as an exclusive, privately owned neighborhood. In this 200-acre subdivision, residents owned the streets as well as their homes.[69] Deed restrictions required minimum home values of $12,550. Walls and fences were discouraged so that the garden from one home would ramble into the next to create a park-like feel. Power lines were installed below ground, and a dense grove of bamboo trees was destroyed to make way for new plantings. Though the area was located only five miles west of downtown, it was sufficiently cordoned off to retain its prestige and bucolic ambience.[70] Another example lay further north along the foothills of the San Gabriel Mountains. Altadena Country Club Park was laid out to follow the natural contours of the hilly terrain. It included 180 mansion-size lots sited along curving streets. In this case, the developers planted palm and camphor trees, introducing a striking—but artificial—natural element to the environment. A number of 9- and 10-room estates lined Midlothian Drive, while medium-sized bungalows filled out much of the rest of the neighborhood. Like the others, this neighborhood was blanketed with race restrictions.[71]

In later years, other picturesque enclaves were developed in scenic locales, such as Rolling Hills, Rolling Hills Estates, Rancho Palos Verdes, Malibu, Hidden Hills, La Cañada, La Habra Heights, and Bradbury. In a throwback to the borderland aesthetic, towns like Shadow Hills and Hidden Hills to the west and La Habra Heights embraced frontier pastoralism in their community design and land use regulations. Hidden Hills, a small village in the western San Fernando Valley, was incorporated in 1961. Its design style was nostalgic Old West, which it created through white three-rail fences, bridle trails, and the absence of sidewalks and streetlights. Developed by A. E. Hanson, who also developed Rolling Hills on the Palos Verdes Peninsula,

Hidden Hills preserved its original design through controls on growth. As late as 2000, only 1,875 people resided in Hidden Hills, 88% of whom were white. To the east, towns like Diamond Bar, Walnut, and La Habra Heights embraced a "country living" aesthetic, with equestrian properties and plenty of open spaces. These were mid- to late-twentieth century examples of a western-style picturesque enclave catering to the affluent.[72]

The picturesque enclave was the most protected of the suburban landscapes, buffered by high pricing, deed restrictions, and stringent land use controls. More than any other suburban landscape, these areas retain their original aesthetic feel, frozen in place by a protective force field of class and property restrictions.

Modest Subdivisions, 1910 to 1940

At the other end of the spectrum were the ordinary subdivisions, ranging from thoughtfully planned neighborhoods to bare-bones tracts. Many were nondescript places without much planning that otherwise might have brought green spaces or an appealing design to the community. During the boom decade of the 1920s, real estate peddling became a kind of recreational pursuit in the southland. Subdividers held barbeques out in the middle of nowhere, on a future subdivision, to attract possible buyers. A wider range of options for home building at the time—including precut mail order homes, owner building, and small-scale speculative building—meant land could be subdivided on the cheap. As such, many of these tracts lacked decent planning, adequate infrastructure, and public spaces. Many of LA's suburbs in the 1920s and 1930s fell into this category—minimally planned subdivisions whose shortcomings would stimulate major reform by the 1940s.[73]

These suburbs generally followed the pattern of the "speculative gridiron." Subdividers carved up lots along a grid pattern, a cost-effective way of selling street frontage while allowing for future expansion. As supply mostly outpaced demand, purchased lots were often surrounded by vacant lots, and it took years or even decades for neighborhoods to fill in. Because many of these neighborhoods had few land use restrictions, they were sometimes mixed-use towns; stores were located near homes, which were sometimes near factories. The simple, unregulated designs of these towns left open the possibility of future infill and change. In later years, some of these modest suburbs filled in so tightly they became the highest density tracts in the region.[74]

Just as the streetcars and scenery helped dictate the geography of some early suburban landscapes, the automobile and jobs influenced the location of these modest suburbs. Cars spurred infill development, allowing subdivisions to spread out away from the streetcar lines. Within these newly accessible spaces, industry helped anchor developments and shape their class profile. Choices about industrial locations not only dictated where factories and workers would cluster, but also the areas that the middle and upper classes would avoid. If the automobile allowed for unprecedented levels of spatial freedom in development, industry drew new critical boundary lines dictating who would live where, what land would be despoiled, and what areas would be protected. A new geography of real estate value—from high to low—was thus taking shape. Race was crucial to these valuations. Stringent controls over where nonwhites could live added another dimension of social sorting within these modest subdivisions. When it all came together, LA County took on a social and physical geography with remarkable staying power.

By the mid-1920s, the automobile eclipsed the streetcar as the primary mode of transportation in Los Angeles. At the forefront of car culture, the city by 1924 had the highest rate of auto ownership in the world, and local citizens supported policies that favored road building over public transit.[75] One major initiative, which passed by a wide margin, was the 1924 Major Traffic Street Plan for Los Angeles, drawn up by Frederick Law Olmsted, Jr., Harland Bartholomew, and Charles H. Cheney. More than a mere street map, their report articulated a unifying vision for the metropolis, ordered around the rationalization of traffic movement and a commitment to decentralization. Although only a small proportion of the Master Plan was implemented, from 1910 to 1930, a series of streets and thoroughfares were built covering the greater metropolitan area; the early highways generally followed the routes of existing streetcar lines.[76]

The automobile accelerated the sprawling nature of LA's built landscape while altering it in important ways. By the 1920s, the automobile eclipsed the streetcar in determining the location of real estate development as subdivisions were typically laid out away from the streetcar lines. Areas once inaccessible by streetcar, like the foothills, were opened up to broader development. Suburban landscapes began to incorporate car-oriented features like curbs, gutters, sidewalks, driveways, and garages.[77] As well, the auto and truck enabled manufacturers to build on cheap land away from rail lines, critical during the 1920s when the region saw a major influx of industry. Shopping likewise dispersed along these roadways.[78]

There was a class dimension to the development of auto-oriented suburbs. The price of autos put them within the reach of the middle class in the 1910s and the working class by the 1920s. Reflecting this trend, the earliest automobile suburbs were oriented toward the well-to-do, appearing as early as 1908, while working-class subdivisions were still oriented to the streetcar lines. By the 1920s, development aimed at all classes of buyers—including laborers—accelerated.

Jobs and industry also influenced patterns of development. Manufacturing had an early and important place in LA, though early leaders hoped to integrate industry in a manner superior to eastern cities. As they imagined it, clean, bright factories blowing "golden smoke" would dot the countryside, surrounded by villages of contented workers living in vine-covered cottages.[79] This utopian vision aside, developers, planners, boosters, and reformers shared two assumptions: industry should be zoned into specific

Figure 1.8 Suburban home in Glendale, 1926. By the 1920s, built landscapes in suburbia were designed to accommodate the automobile, with features such as sidewalks, curbs, driveways, and detached garages.
USC Digital Library. Dick Whittington Photography Collection.

districts and segregated by type, and these "production landscapes" should be surrounded by residences, services, and community institutions. Given that the early zoning laws prohibited factories from encroaching on neighborhoods of single-family homes, industry increasingly pushed out into the periphery, where it would anchor working-class suburbs.[80]

By the 1920s, an industrial geography began to emerge in Los Angeles, marked by both clustering at the core and dispersal to the hinterland. Close to the center, the East Side Industrial District was the city's old industrial hub, east of Alameda between Broadway and Ninth Streets. Here were locally owned, sweatshop operations, producing mainly for home markets. A second industrial zone lay southeast of downtown in the Central Manufacturing District and stretching into suburban areas east and south of downtown.[81] This was the zone of mass-production factories, including a significant contingent of branch plants producing for local and regional markets. It included parts of Boyle Heights, East Los Angeles, Vernon, Bell, and Commerce, and extended south into suburbs like Huntington Park and South Gate. A third industrial zone reached clear out into the farms and orange groves. Here, the oil, motion picture, and later aircraft industries best exemplified the imagined "machine in the garden."[82]

Landscapes of modest suburbs emerged around these job hubs. Some were launched by reputable developers, such as the Janss Investment Company (famous for developing tony Holmby Hills and Westwood), J. B. Ransom Corporation, and Walter H. Leimert. Janss developed parts of Belvedere in East Los Angeles, where residents could purchase a modest home or an empty lot and then self-build a house.[83] Further south, in the heart of oil country, the Olmsted Firm master-planned Torrance as a "model industrial suburb" in the 1910s. Real estate investment and cooperative building firms, such as the Los Angeles Investment Company, sold both empty lots and homes on lots aimed at middle- and working-class buyers.[84]

Arguably more common were the minimally planned suburbs for people of modest means, subdivided by small-scale, profit-hungry developers with little social vision. In working-class suburbs to the south, like Huntington Park, South Gate, Lynwood, Maywood, and Bell, factories cropped up in and near these towns, such as the large General Motors and Firestone plants just west of South Gate's borders. While comprehensive planning did not always drive this development, as factories sometimes followed residential development, there was some thought given to siting factories near suburbs of working families. Varied levels of planning were evident in far-flung towns producing oil, motion pictures, and aircraft, such as Hollywood, Long Beach, Santa Monica, Culver City, west Los Angeles, El Segundo, Lomita, and Whittier.[85] As a federal survey confirmed by 1941, small industrial districts spread throughout Los Angeles County, even in such "noteworthy residential suburbs as Hollywood, Beverly Hills, Santa Monica, Pasadena, and Long Beach."[86] This pattern, according to reformers, would help Los Angeles dodge the problems of industrial congestion plaguing eastern cities.

Other modest suburbs also developed around jobs, including domestic labor, streetcar labor camps, and farming colonias. Domestic service suburbs housed the maids, gardeners, and household workers who serviced the homes of upper-class suburbanites. They often took the form of modest enclaves near elite homes, as in Pasadena. Pacific Electric labor camps likewise became job-based anchors for working-class suburbs. Some of these temporary labor camps that sprouted up at key junctions or ends of the line transitioned into permanent towns in places like Watts and West Hollywood. Both domestic service and labor camp suburbs were open to all races and ethnicities, creating pockets of residential diversity that would later be surrounded by all-white suburbia.[87] *Colonias*, which formed adjacent to farms and orchards, were segregated enclaves that housed Mexican farmworkers and their families. The land was often owned by the growers, who rented out parcels to their employees, cutting off opportunities for homeownership otherwise common in many working-class suburbs.[88]

Modest subdivisions housed an array of middle- and working-class whites, African Americans, Mexicans, Asians, and other immigrant groups. Yet, even within this landscape, unbending color lines were drawn to separate whites from people of color. Because early mechanisms of segregation like race-restrictive covenants cost little to implement, even the poorest of white suburbs could maintain racial barriers.

Like their elite counterparts, these modest suburbs were predominated by single-family detached homes set in yards, inhabited by residents seeking the benefits of homeownership and "country living." But they also diverged in significant ways, particularly when working-class families used their residential property to help them meet their pressing economic needs. Many of these towns contained a mix of blue- and white-collar workers who experienced the realities of economic instability in pre-New Deal America, before the safety net of social security and unemployment insurance was in place. As a hedge against hard times, many residents drew on sweat equity to turn their suburban property into a source of economic security. Some constructed their own homes in subdivisions with lax building standards.[89] Others purchased their homes from mail order catalogues and hired builders to assemble the precut pieces or did the construction themselves or with the help of friends. It took just two days for a small team of carpenters to build the frame of a mail-order home and less than a month to complete it. Pacific Ready-Cut, which operated from 1908 to 1940, was the leading mail order home company in Los Angeles, selling 37,000 precut homes costing between a few hundred to a few thousand dollars. These homes were built in many neighborhoods around Los Angeles, including South Los Angeles, Highland Park, Hollywood, Larchmont Village, Studio City, Van Nuys, and Monrovia. Walt and Roy Disney purchased Pacific Ready-Cut homes in 1928 for lots they owned on Lyric Avenue, within walking distance of their Silver Lake studio.[90] The result was a built landscape of humble bungalows and cottages, sometimes of marginal quality.

Residents of modest prewar suburbs maximized the economic potential of their properties in other ways. Some grew fruits and vegetables and raised small livestock in backyards. Rather than a cultural pursuit like "gentleman farming," this was a strategy to help stretch the family dollar. Towns like South Gate, Cudahy, Bell, Bell Gardens, Lynwood, and parts of Huntington Park, Watts, Belvedere, East Los Angeles, Canoga Park, Reseda, and Van Nuys allowed these practices. In some cases, land was subdivided into ample lots to facilitate backyard provisioning. In Cudahy and Watts, for example, deep, narrow lots enabled residents to cultivate their backyards. This "sustenance farming" on suburban property was also practiced in far-flung towns like Glendora, Pomona, Azusa, El Monte, Pasadena, Bellflower, and Hynes/Clearwater (later Paramount), in some cases well into the late 1930s.[91]

Modest subdivisions contained the self-builders, backyard homesteaders, and working- and middle-class home dwellers. This was a landscape of nondescript suburbia, blocks of single-family stucco homes surrounded by a patch of grass and a backyard garden. These tracts overtook farmlands, they surrounded the Main Streets of streetcar suburbs, and they otherwise began filling in the spaces of LA County. Architectural critic Reyner Banham called this landscape the "Plains of Id," the endlessly sprawling central flatlands of LA with an unremarkable built landscape he dubbed "Anywheresville/Nowheresville."[92] Urban historian Dolores Hayden concurred, noting this generic landscape was partly a result of the standardized designs of pattern books and mail order catalogues produced by national corporations, which began to eclipse local architectural traditions.[93]

The landscape of modest subdivisions left important legacies in Los Angeles. It generated acres and acres of modest (even poor) housing which would be passed on to succeeding generations of middle- and working-class families. The tight link between workplace and residence—signified by factories tucked next to residential tracts—became a noxious liability in years to come. As these factories shuttered, they left behind a toxic footprint of industrial waste and contaminated land and groundwater. Subsequent generations of residents suffered related health risks despite never benefitting from the flush years of local industry.[94] Some of these towns evolved into what urbanists refer to as "at-risk" inner-ring suburbs, places with few resources and multiple challenges, including the costly consequences of earlier historical decisions. Compounding these risks were rising density levels, which reached astronomical levels in the modest suburbs of Southeast LA, rivaling even New York City, Chicago, and San Francisco.[95]

In the prewar years, the lack of extensive building and land use regulations in these modest suburbs, combined with the cheapness of property, left open the strong possibility of future change. While many of these neighborhoods were segregated early on, after racial restrictions were dropped, many became the destinations for aspiring Black, Latino, and Asian home seekers. The wall of "class"—so high and strong in the picturesque enclaves—was a more porous border around these modest suburbs. Once race barriers fell, it opened the way for all manner of social and physical change.

Sitcom Suburbs, 1940 to 1960s

The postwar era was the heyday of suburbanization in LA, as it was nationwide. No longer did most families—particularly white families—live on the brink. The stresses of the Great Depression and World War II began to fade, and new federal programs helped usher in greater economic stability and opportunity. Families gained the means to purchase homes, food, and the new staples of life, benefits directed especially to whites.

In LA, the Helms man symbolized this change. A familiar figure in the suburbs of postwar Los Angeles, he drove his yellow and blue truck up and down residential streets, sounding his two-note whistle to signal the arrival of fresh baked goods. If customers wanted something, they posted an "H" sign in their front window or hurried outside to flag him down. When the driver stepped out and opened the side door of his truck, a delicious smell of jelly donuts, cakes, and cookies drifted out. The trucks had wooden compartments for 150 kinds of bread, cookies, cakes, cream puffs, M&Ms, and other fare suited to the suburban palate. The Helms man delivered for the Helms Bakery, which opened in Culver City in 1931 and did booming business in the rapidly spreading sitcom suburbs. Suburban kids treasured memories of the Helms man, for his kindness, warmth, and delicious products. At its peak in the 1950s, the company turned out over a million loaves of bread a day, employed 1,850 people, and covered 950 sales routes between Fresno and San Diego. The Helms man embodied potent elements of sitcom suburbia—automobility, a "gee whiz" affect that echoed the suburban sitcoms on television, and a tangible sense of neighborhood.[96]

At the same time that the mobile Helms man lent a personal face to consumption, trends were also moving toward mass-produced food and chain groceries. In the 1950s to the 1970s, Los Angeles was at the vanguard of fast-food restaurants, suburban chain supermarkets, and the consumption

Figure 1.9 The Helms Man and his truck on a typical suburban route, 1931. The Helms Bakery reached its peak during the sitcom suburb era of the 1950s, distributing fresh baked goods to individual homes across Southern California—a potent symbol of postwar prosperity and the creature comforts of everyday life.
USC Digital Library. Dick Whittington Photography Collection.

of highly processed food. It was a leading producer of these foods and the birthplace of several iconic fast-food chains, including McDonalds (begun in San Bernardino, with a flagship franchise in Downey), Taco Bell, and Carl's Jr.[97] The Helms man and McDonalds symbolized two facets of life in postwar suburbia, an aura of neighborliness in an era of mass consumption.

The postwar period was the era of the sitcom suburb, named for the popular television shows set in these familiar surroundings. Defined especially by their rapid mass production, sitcom suburbs resulted from a confluence of forces—a huge pent-up demand for housing brewing since the early 1930s, federal housing policy that encouraged single-family homeownership and large-scale building, and the maturation of the construction industry. Home building had stagnated during the Great Depression and World War II, creating an intensive housing shortage during the war. As LA's population boomed with the influx of wartime workers and continued in-migration after the war, it put even greater pressure on a tight housing market. The stage was set for an explosion of home building.

The federal government played a crucial role here. It committed gargantuan subsidies to private builders to construct single-family homes on vast tracts of land while making a much smaller commitment to public housing. The outcome was sitcom suburbs, large-scale subdivisions exemplified in places like Lakewood, California; Levittown, New York; and Park Forest, Illinois, but they cropped up in all regions of the country. The Federal Housing Administration (FHA) and GI Bill, moreover, underwrote long-term, low-interest mortgages for individuals, making suburban homeownership affordable to a wide class of buyers. In Lakewood, a World War II veteran could secure a home loan with no down payment and a 30-year mortgage at 4% interest at a monthly cost of $44 to $56 including principal, interest, and insurance—cheaper than rent in many parts of LA. On the first day homes went on sale, 30,000 people lined up to tour the seven model homes; by the next month, 1,000 had purchased homes.[98] The prime beneficiaries of these housing programs were white, middle- and working-class, male-headed households; everyone else was mostly excluded. The lifestyles of these residents were reflected back at them in the hugely popular sitcoms of the era, such as "Father Knows Best" and "Leave it to Beaver."[99] Those shows presented innocent, idyllic portraits of postwar suburban life, masking discriminatory factors that underpinned these segregated communities and glossing over nagging economic insecurities felt by many white suburban families.

While sitcom suburbs in Los Angeles were adding onto a diversified suburban landscape already in place, they soon outnumbered everything that came before them. The biggest building frenzy took off in the San Fernando Valley. More than 900 square miles of farmland were bulldozed into suburban tracts. Builders like Leonard Chudacoff's Coronet Construction advertised three-bedroom, 1,270-square-foot homes for $11,130. By 1955, the Valley housed over a million residents, and, by 1970, its 1.8 million population would have made it America's sixth largest city had it been an independent municipality (it is mostly part of Los Angeles City). Lakewood was perhaps the most famous sitcom suburb in Los Angeles, gaining national recognition as the world's largest and fastest built postwar suburb and earning the nickname of "the instant city." Between 1950 and 1954, Lakewood's developers transformed 5,600 acres of farmlands into vast, parallel rows of tract homes. They constructed 17,500 homes during the first three years, and, by 1957, the population was approaching 70,000—double the size of New York's Levittown. Other lesser-known sitcom suburbs, such as Artesia, Carson, and Norwalk, were also built up nearby.[100] Postwar homes were also constructed within existing suburbs to fill in vacant land. The working-class suburb of South Gate, for example, was incorporated in 1923, was fairly well built up by 1940, and was the site of extensive new home construction in the undeveloped eastern end of town in the 1940s and 1950s. Homebuyers were offered a choice of several floor plans, exteriors, fixtures, and interior amenities. Even in South Gate, with its fair share of prewar housing, the number of single-family homes built after 1940 exceeded the earlier housing stock.[101] This pattern was repeated all over Los Angeles.

Certain features were common in these suburbs, partly as a result of new FHA standards that guided everything from site planning to the design of the house itself. The FHA's guidelines for site planning reflected principles of modern community planning, which evinced an optimism about the power of well-planned neighborhoods to foster healthy social interaction, if within highly segregated communities.[102] The building blocks of these designs were the "neighborhood unit," a self-contained area housing 1,000 to 1,500 families. Outlined by progressive planner Clarence Perry in 1929, the neighborhood unit was intended to be a single-family residential superblock with curvilinear streets, buffered along its edges by major arterials, small shopping districts, and apartments. A cluster of community institutions would sit at the heart of the unit, including an elementary school which served as a "mini-capitol" for local family life.[103] Perry placed high hopes in the neighborhood unit's capacity to promote a sense of neighborhood consciousness, unity, and stewardship. The concept assumed class and race homogeneity and insulated the suburb from the broader city; during the civil rights era, it came under fire as a justification for racial segregation.[104] The FHA encouraged the neighborhood unit plan in its technical bulletin series beginning in 1936, and the idea influenced postwar developments nationally, including many in Los Angeles.[105]

At the same time, LA community builders pioneered certain development practices that served as models for postwar suburbs nationwide. For one, they adopted synergistic planning for industry, homes, and commerce all at once. Cutting their teeth on developments for defense workers in the early 1940s, they designed places like Mar Vista and Panorama City to incorporate a tight workplace–residence link, as historian Greg Hise has shown.[106] LA community builders also pioneered mass-production building techniques that would be emulated elsewhere. For example, in 1939, Fritz Burns and Fred Marlow began work on Westside Village (Mar Vista), a development of 788 homes located two miles from a major Douglas Aircraft facility in Santa Monica. Here they first experimented with mass-building techniques, using precut and preassembled materials and employing specialized crews who worked through each step of the building process from foundation to finishing touches. The result was a sizeable community, built quickly and cheaply, that was affordable to blue-collar workers. A similar approach guided the development of Toluca Wood in 1941, built near the existing Vega and Lockheed Aircraft plants in Burbank/North Hollywood, and of Westchester in 1942, where 3,230 homes were built in just three years. In the San Fernando Valley, Kaiser Community Homes (KCH) perfected the community planning approach in places like Panorama City, North Hollywood, Westside Terrace, Monterey Park, and Westchester.[107] In Lakewood, postwar homes were built adjacent to existing industries, such as the newly built Douglas Aircraft plant and decades-old oil refineries around the Southeast.[108]

At the same time that some postwar community builders were promoting a workplace–residence link, LA's new freeway system encouraged the opposite pattern. Suburbanites could live where they wanted and commute to work along these high-speed, space-age corridors. The freeways essentially untethered them, with uneven consequences for Los Angelenos and their communities.[109]

The Los Angeles Regional Planning Commission (RPC) had a hand in reinforcing suburban and industrial momentum in different parts of the County. It imagined certain areas as "buffered suburbs," where communities

of single-family homes would be spared the nuisance of industrial production, while other sections would have a closer mingling of factories and
homes. This mattered especially in the sitcom suburb era, when heavy industry was peaking at the same time suburbs were multiplying.[110] For the
east San Gabriel Valley, for example, the RPC in 1957 envisioned an area
of new, spacious suburban developments surrounded by a ring of carefully
zoned-off industrial areas. Evincing a wide-eyed faith in the salubrious
effects of suburban sprawl, the RPC asserted that low-density development
would ease traffic congestion and preserve the natural beauties of moun-
tainous areas, the latter "most satisfactorily accomplished by maintaining
large lot area requirements." Industry would exist nearby, but it would in-
trude only upon working-class Latino suburbs like Azusa and La Puente.[111]
For the San Fernando Valley, the RPC drew up a master plan at the end of
World War II that most fully realized the synergistic approach of integrating
industry, homes, and commerce. The original plan envisioned 18 "self-
contained" communities, each surrounded by suburban truck farms, with
the whole conglomeration ringed by more intensive agriculture, in line with
the "Garden City" ideal. Designs for the self-contained communities of
Chatsworth, Northridge, and Reseda followed modern community planning
precepts, including the use of superblocks, long residential loop streets, and
local parks, schools, and civic centers, all sited near stores and factories.[112]

   In the Southeast area, the RPC in 1959 recognized the tight, historic link
between factories and suburban homes and appeared to sanction that design going forward. In contrast to the carefully separated zones of the San
Gabriel Valley, Southeast LA's homes would continue to abut factories. As
such, 8 of 11 towns in the area allowed residential development in industrial
zones. Despite the inclusion of Lakewood in this study area, the RPC had
pegged the southeast area overall as a fairly working-class, less protected suburban space.[113] Finally, in the Central Area, where older, working-class suburban districts dated back to the 1920s, the RPC's goal was to help manage a
humane balance between intensive industry and suburban neighborhoods.
The area already had a distinct working-class profile. At the same time, it
maintained a suburban aura—66% of local housing units were single-family
homes. Encompassing Latino East LA, Black South LA, and white blue-collar
suburbs, this planning district posed formidable challenges, but, in its 1963
report, the RPC offered only tentative recommendations for more studies
and common-sense advice such as balancing future high-density residential development with adequate public services. The RPC praised the area's

existing suburban landscapes and encouraged their protection even while acknowledging the area's massive industrial presence.[114]

Certain features were common in the sitcom suburbs. House designs were strongly influenced by the FHA, specifically its minimum house standards, which translated into a home modest in size and appearance. The typical Kaiser Home in Panorama City was 900 square feet, smaller than the typical prewar home. In Lakewood, homes averaged between 850 and 1,200 square feet set on a 5,000-square-foot lot (the minimum size allowed in LA County). Buyers could choose from 13 different floor plans, but each had a living room, kitchen, two or three bedrooms, and one bathroom. The houses looked alike, apart from some small exterior variations the builders used to break the monotony. Most of these developments anticipated that homeowners would embellish upon the original house through add-ons and cosmetic changes. By the late 1940s, house styles evolved to include ranch homes, split-levels, and other designs. In Los Angeles, ranch-style tracts began appearing in 1948 and spread through the 1950s, especially in the San Fernando Valley. These suburbs were designed with gridiron or curving street patterns that were artificially imposed upon flat terrain.[115]

Figure 1.10 The sitcom suburb of Carson, located just west of Lakewood, 2009. The modest housing in this town was built mostly in the 1950s and 1960s.
Photo by Michael Tierney.

Some sitcom suburbs deliberately housed blue- and white-collar workers side by side. Builders like Kaiser Community Homes programmed occupational diversity into its plans, believing that it helped prevent un-American social stratification. In other places, entire suburban neighborhoods were segmented by wealth, a pattern that intensified in later years.[116]

In terms of race, the sitcom suburbs were blindingly white. Though legal cases began to overturn some segregation tools, such as the *Shelley v. Kraemer* (1948) Supreme Court ruling that made race-restrictive covenants unenforceable, some white suburbanites engaged in hostile everyday actions meant to intimidate—if not physically prevent—people of color from buying into their communities. Developers and realtors further refused to sell property to nonwhite buyers. Despite this continued resistance, people of color during this era of civil rights sought to assert their right to live where they chose. It was, then, a time of intensive ethnoracial conflict, resistance, and courage playing out in everyday suburban environments. Most people of color remained excluded, a tremendous blow given that this was a moment of maximum housing affordability in America thanks to FHA and GI Bill underwriting.[117]

While drum-tight segregation and architectural monotony prevailed in the postwar sitcom suburbs, these communities held the potential for change.[118] Homes could be remodeled or expanded thanks to permissive building standards. In subsequent years, their affordability made these suburbs natural destinations for upwardly mobile Latinos, Asians, and Black Americans. As residential integration campaigns heated up and legal barriers to residential segregation continued to be overturned, a number of these suburbs became spaces of notable ethnoracial diversity, including Lakewood, Bellflower, Carson, and Artesia in Southeast LA and communities across the San Fernando Valley.[119]

The fate of the Helms man offers a poignant postscript to the sitcom suburb story in LA. The Helms Bakery became the victim of its own urban crisis. Though the company president blamed the firm's 1969 closure on "the irreversible reality" of modern supermarkets, other forces were at play. In 1966, the ranks of friendly Helms men voted to join the teamsters' union after a 35-year-long campaign to unionize. Up to that point, it had been the only non-union bakery in California. A rash of truck robberies on the modest suburban streets of South LA also influenced the decision. In July 1967, three Helms bakery trucks were held up at gunpoint, and one of the drivers was shot. More incidents followed, culminating in a record 400 robberies

Figure 1.11 A home redesign in the sitcom suburb of Carson, 2009. Loose local regulations allowed homeowners in sitcom suburbs to alter their property according to individual tastes. In Carson, one homeowner put an indelible stamp of individuality on his property.
Photo by Michael Tierney.

of commercial vehicles in South LA that year.[120] This upsurge signaled the discomfiting inequities in metropolitan life and punctured the shiny veneer of the sitcom suburb, whose reality was never as predictable as TV made it out to be.

Edge Cities and Corporate Suburbs, 1970s to 2000s

After 1970, a new wave of suburbanization was anchored by mature economic centers known as "edge cities," combinations of corporate offices, industrial parks, shopping centers, cineplexes, and chain hotels and restaurants. These developments included all elements—jobs, retail, and housing—on a larger scale than previous suburbs. New mass-produced subdivisions built by corporate builders surrounded the malls and office parks, always scaled to the car and offering few pedestrian accommodations or public spaces. In addition, some developments were sited in the "exurbs," fast-growing residential developments at the metropolitan edges where at least 20% of residents commuted to jobs in an urbanized area.[121]

Development during the edge city era marked the second largest building period in LA County, after the sitcom suburb era.[122] This pattern is even more striking given that it occurred during an era of slow-growth politics in LA. Beginning in the 1960s, suburban homeowners in places like the San Fernando and San Gabriel Valleys and Westside began concerted lobbying against growth, aimed at protecting their own suburban quality of life, open lands, and property values. Their success reversed years of breakneck development. While they slammed the brakes on growth especially within LA City borders, they pushed it into the suburban hinterland where big corporate developers often found more welcoming terrain.[123]

If jobs helped anchor suburban development in this period, urban analysts differ on exactly how that looked. Joel Garreau, who coined the phrase "edge city" and declared LA the birthplace and model of edge cities worldwide, identified 24 established and emerging edge cities in the LA metro area. The vast majority were within LA County: Warner Center/West Valley, Sherman Oaks/Van Nuys, Burbank/North Hollywood, Beverly Hills/Century City, LAX/El Segundo, South Bay, and Pasadena, among others.[124] Other analysts developed different lists of job subcenters, including Santa Monica, Hollywood, Glendale, Commerce, San Pedro, Inglewood, Hawthorne, Lawndale, and Downey.[125] Still others emphasized a more dispersed pattern of suburban employment, organized less as pinpoint centers and more as a diffuse scattering into "edgeless cities." This includes the meandering blocks of offices, apartments, and retail often sited near freeway corridors.[126] The exurb pattern points to suburban growth relatively untethered from job centers at all, with long commutes an everyday fact of life.[127] Los Angeles, then, contained multiple patterns—edge cities, diffuse office/commercial corridors, and more isolated exurbs—emblematic of the decentralization of economic activity that was tipping the balance of power from central cities to suburbs nationally.[128]

Proposition 13 (1978) also had dramatic impact on suburban development in this era. This California ballot measure limited property taxes and, in turn, reduced funding for public services. In response, developers shifted the cost of infrastructure on to new buyers, creating a "welcome stranger tax" and helping drive up housing prices. Fees, new infrastructure, and other required expenses doubled the price of a new home "before they begin digging the first hole in the ground," as one real estate lobbyist put it. Even despite those "growth taxes," many post-1980 developments got far fewer public amenities, like parks, playgrounds, and community centers. Not only were homebuyers paying more, they were getting less than earlier suburbanites.[129]

The origins of edge cities could vary widely. Several evolved in older towns like Pasadena, Burbank, Beverly Hills, and North Hollywood. In these places, the local economy diversified and matured as redevelopment introduced new offices and housing, in some cases gentrifying older neighborhoods. In other areas, the edge city and its surrounding suburbs were built on greenfields, massive-scale developments plunked down in the middle of nowhere. Good examples were Warner Center in the West Valley and Irvine in Orange County, with their generic landscapes of chain restaurants, bulk housing, and nondescript office towers and shopping malls. A third variety was the edge city that developed around a new regional shopping center or freeway interchange.[130]

Although some of LA's edge cities began in the 1960s, building accelerated in the 1970s and 1980s. A key catalyst was LA City's 1957 elimination of its height restriction on buildings (limited to 150 feet up to this point). This unleashed the construction of tall buildings in dispersed hubs around LA, such as gleaming Century City in west LA.[131] This high-density center of tall, modern office buildings, apartments, hotels, theaters, and shopping centers was a $500 million master-planned project, the most expensive privately financed development of its time. It was conceived as a "city within a city," a bigger, updated version of New York's Radio City. Sited on a shuttered 20th Century Fox backlot, its initial construction involved the literal dismantling of Old Hollywood, including the sets for the colonial mansion that appeared in both "Grapes of Wrath" and the Shirley Temple film "Littlest Colonel," the buildings of "Old Chicago," the town of "Tombstone," and an old railway station that appeared in numerous Fox wartime films. The main boulevard of Century City was dubbed "Avenue of the Stars," not to commemorate the place's cinematic history but rather to evoke a futuristic space-age vision. The first tall building went up in 1963, followed by others over the next decade.[132] By the 1970s, Century City was nationally recognized.

The nature of suburban residential areas around these nodes depended on how they originated. They differed depending on whether they were completely new growth centers developed on open land (like Irvine), new centers built in well-developed areas (like Century City), or older towns modernizing into edge cities (like Pasadena). In some cases, the conversion

of existing elite suburbs into new edge cities challenged the typical redevelopment debate, pitting affluent suburbanites against high-rise developers.
Century City was a case in point. When the project began, residents of adjacent suburban streets raised objections to the noise and hassle of intensified
traffic the development would generate. When they failed to stop the project
altogether, a group of property owners demanded the erection of an 8-foot
cement block wall to cordon off their neighborhood, in addition to a planned
15-foot buffer zone of trees and shrubberies. Similarly, in the early 1960s, a
group of Westwood homeowners opposed a rezoning measure that would
allow the construction of tall apartment buildings in the area. They feared
traffic congestion and other nuisances. While these groups initially lost out
to edge city development, Westwood homeowners ultimately secured zoning
restrictions that protected large affluent suburban properties.[133]

In areas of totally new development on open lands, a new type of suburb
emerged, the "corporate suburb." These were built by corporations, even
global conglomerates, entities far bigger than the postwar community
builders. Corporate America, in fact, was entering real estate in profoundly
new ways. The scale of home production was spurred on by a series of structural alterations in real estate finance that allowed developers access to much
greater stores of capital—via new real estate investment trusts (REITS),
pension funds, and a host of corporate and Wall Street investors—a trend
facilitated by government deregulation. In addition, government-sponsored
entities such as Fannie Mae funneled even more money into real estate
through the sale of mortgage-backed securities to investors worldwide. The
tethering of real estate finance to global financial markets allowed these new
corporate builders to operate at unprecedented scales while introducing new
levels of volatility to the housing market.[134]

Pumped up by this new steroidal capital, the scale of suburban
developments soared. Developments in Thousand Oaks and Simi Valley were
in the 11,000- to 12,500-acre range, making once record-breaking tracts like
Lakewood (6,000 acres) look small by comparison.[135] In Los Angeles, corporate builders such as KB Home, TransAmerica, William Lyon, and Pulte
Home were active at the far edges of the county, in the west San Fernando
Valley, east San Gabriel Valley, and north Antelope Valley. KB was especially
active in huge, fast-growing peripheral suburbs like Santa Clarita, Lancaster,
and Palmdale. Pulte Home, which by 1995 became the nation's largest home
builder, constructed new housing in West Hills in the west San Fernando
Valley, as well as in Mexico, Argentina, and Puerto Rico.[136]

KB Home typified the corporate builder. Founded in 1957 in Detroit by Don Kaufman and Eli Broad, the Kaufman and Broad Building Company started small, investing $25,000 to build two model homes in the suburb of Madison Heights. After selling 136 homes in its first year, the firm moved into new markets, selling entry-level priced homes in Arizona, then "suburban townhouses" in Southern California. Kaufman and Broad soon expanded and diversified.[137] In 1962, it became the first home builder to go public on the American Stock Exchange. It also acquired several smaller, regional builders, spurring the company's rapid growth. Over the next few years, it expanded into San Francisco, Chicago, New York, France, Canada, and West Germany. In the mid-1960s, it formed its own mortgage company to provide financing directly to homebuyers, started a cable television subsidiary, launched a manufactured housing company, and acquired Sun Life Insurance.

In the mid-1960s, the corporation established its headquarters in Los Angeles, seeing huge potential in the region. It weathered the booms and busts of the 1970s and 1980s, and, by the late 1980s, had become a billion-dollar global conglomerate. When markets in California went soft in the early 1990s, vigorous activity in Paris kept the corporation strong. More acquisitions of regional building companies in the Sunbelt continued in the 1990s, pushing revenues to $3.9 billion in 2000. It shortened its name to KB Home in 2001. By that time, it had become the largest home builder in America in terms of units built, focused on single-family homes for first-time

Figure 1.12 The uniform, repetitious built landscape of the corporate suburb of Santa Clarita. 2016.

Courtesy the City of Santa Clarita.

buyers in the western United States and Paris. KB's history exemplifies broader trends in American land development during this period, when large, publicly traded companies came to dominate.[138]

Even more than in sitcom suburbs, the landscape of corporate suburbia had a mass-produced feel, shaped by market research and production decisions made by corporate executives. To achieve profitable economies of scale, they standardized multiple aspects of home production while offering consumers a wide variety of choices on interior amenities. Reflecting a greater level of business sophistication than the Levitts, corporate builders relied heavily on market research to determine what people wanted. The emphasis was on more "domestic bling" inside the home—high ceilings, bigger walk-in closets, bigger kitchens with professional-style appliances—with much less concern for exteriors and overall community site design.[139] The end result was a terrain of even starker uniformity than sitcom suburbia in the shape, appearance, and siting of homes. Moreover, developers discouraged alterations to home exteriors through mind-numbing lists of Covenants, Conditions, and Restrictions (CC&Rs) enforced by homeowners' associations. In this way, the original mass-produced feel of these suburbs was frozen into place.

The sprawling and monotonous landscape of corporate suburbia typically separated housing, shopping, office parks, and civic institutions into clusters accessible only by car. Single-family homes were isolated into large residence-only areas, distant from stores. Community design was inward focused, exemplified by curving streets and cul-de-sacs that insulated homes from everything else. Carefully planned open lands reinforced the buffering effect. While this insular design was partly embraced to protect children playing on the street, children ironically played outside less and less in this era. The design intention backfired.[140]

Single-family homes were bigger and occupied larger lots compared to previous eras. In the 1950s, the typical home was 900 square feet on a 5,000-square-foot lot. From 1970 to 2000, the size of homes and their yards ballooned even as the number of people in each house shrank. By 1999, the average size of a new home was 2,250 square feet on a 12,910-square-foot lot.[141] Evolving population densities reflected these trends. Comparing two archetypes, Lakewood (sitcom) and Santa Clarita (corporate), Lakewood in 1990 was nearly three times denser than Santa Clarita (see Table 1.1). The relentless hunger for larger properties pushed development further and further into the periphery, straining natural resources, exacerbating climate change, and pushing ever deeper into the urban wilderness interface.[142]

Table 1.1 Density levels in a sample of historic suburban landscapes in Los Angeles and in the densest large US cities, 1990. Population density reflected significant class differences across LA's historic landscapes, as well as trends toward lower density in newer corporate suburbs.

	1990 population	Sq. miles	Pop. per sq. mile
Streetcar suburbia			
South Pasadena	23,936	3.4	6,975
Modest suburbia			
Azusa	41,333	9.0	4,592
Bell	34,365	2.6	13,433
Bell Gardens	42,355	2.5	16,856
Cudahy	22,817	1.1	20,728
Lynwood	61,945	4.9	12,757
Maywood	27,850	1.2	23,900
San Fernando	22,580	2.4	9,454
South Gate	86,284	7.4	11,738
Picturesque enclaves			
Beverly Hills	31,971	5.7	5,632
Bradbury	832	1.7	497
La Cañada Flintridge	19,378	8.7	2,236
Palos Verdes Estates	13,512	4.8	2,811
Rolling Hills	1,871	3.1	613
San Marino	12,959	3.8	3,441
Sitcom suburbia			
Lakewood	73,557	9.4	7,830
La Mirada	40,452	7.9	5,153
La Puente	36,955	3.5	10,586
Norwalk	94,279	9.8	9,661
Pico Rivera	59,177	8.0	7,419
Temple City	31,100	4.0	7,750
Corporate suburbia			
Agoura Hills	20,390	8.2	4,297

(*continued*)

Table 1.1 Continued

	1990 population	Sq. miles	Pop. per sq. mile
Diamond Bar	53,672	15.1	3,557
Lancaster	97,291	88.8	1,096
Irvine	110,330	42.3	2,607
Palmdale	68,842	77.6	887
Santa Clarita	110,642	40.5	2,733
Walnut	29,105	8.9	3,285
Westlake Village	7,455	5.2	1,432
Densest, large US cities			
New York City	7,323,000	309.0	23,700
San Francisco	723,959	46.7	15,502
Chicago	2,784,000	227.0	12,300
Boston	574,000	48.0	11,900
Philadelphia	1,586,000	135.0	11,700

US Census, "Land Area, Population and Density for Places in California: 1990," https://www2.census.gov/programs-surveys/decennial/tables/1990/1990-places-land-density/06ca.txt

Corporate suburbia also contained substantial multifamily housing—condos, townhomes, and apartments. The proliferation of these units after 1970 reflected the intertwined trends of rising home prices, land shortages, and a surging affordability crisis. Many condos and homes were built as part of common interest developments (CIDs), planned neighborhoods governed by homeowners' associations and bound by strict CC&Rs. Suburban municipalities, in turn, welcomed CIDs—despite higher densities and more affordable housing types—because private amenities such as pools, parks, and playgrounds reduced public expenditures, which mattered more in the wake of Prop 13. These trends also signaled a shift in the building industry, newly swayed in the 1980s by marketing consultants who identified a key demographic shift in suburbia toward households of affluent singles, retirees, empty-nesters, and single-parent families.[143] In many CIDs, an organic sense of civic life was "eclipsed by elaborately planned self-contained enclaves," ruled by homeowners associations and in some extreme cases by developer initiatives designed to teach neighbors how to be good neighbors.[144]

The repetitive landscape of corporate suburbia has been derided by contemporary critics, from New Urbanist planners to social commentators ruminating on the causes of suburban school shootings. They condemned the placeless and faceless feel, lack of accessible and authentic public spaces, total dependency on cars, and wastefulness.[145] Garreau captured this unease, writing that these developments give "people the creeps." "Irvine has been compared with the Stepford Wives—perfect, in a horrifying sort of way. The development's newest residential section, Westpark, is an unbroken field of identical Mediterranean red-clay roof tile, covering homes of indistinguishable earth-tone stucco.... Irvine has deed restrictions that forbid people from customizing their places with so much as a skylight. This is a place that is enforced, not just planned. Owners of expensive homes in Irvine commonly volunteer stories of not realizing that they had pulled into the driveway of the wrong house until their garage-door opener failed to work. Driving around, what one mainly sees is high blank walls."[146]

For many, the price of living at the edge was distance—not only the distance of homes from services, but also the distance of these suburbs from everything else. In the exurbs, the residents of corporate suburbia often inhabited the furthest fringes in "drive-til-you qualify" suburbs where affordability increased in tandem with commuting times. Vicky Ivanov's life embodied these challenges.[147] In the 1980s and early 1990s, she lived in Lancaster, a suburban municipality of 145,000 located in the Antelope Valley in the northern reaches of Los Angeles County, 70 miles from downtown LA. This area boomed after 1970, attracting those committed to owning a home set in a green yard and willing to commute punishing distances to make that happen. In a metro region where earning power slipped well behind surging housing prices, such a move forced tough life decisions. Ivanov described her home as "beautiful, incredible, big, nice. White. Lots of windows. I'd describe it as wonderful. That's how I do describe it. People say, how can you do that drive? How can you do this? I say, you should see the house I live in. The surroundings that I have here, more than I've ever had in my life." For the Ivanovs, this was an important step up, their house the physical reward of years of hard work.

But the factors that put the price of this suburban dream within reach were a brutal combination of population pressure, developer agendas, municipal competition, and poor regional planning.[148] The end result was a suburban landscape so far away that daily commutes of 90 minutes to 2 hours each way were commonplace. It was a fact of life in exurbs nationally, sprouting up in all regions but especially the South and Midwest. Urban reformers emphasize the environmental and fiscal costs of greenfield developments like Lancaster, whose location put a strain on resources to bring municipal services out to such distances. But for Vicky Ivanov, the price she was paying for her suburban lifestyle was steep, straining her marriage and her daughter's emotional health. Her husband was tiring of pressure from Vicky to do work around the house "so that things stay nice," and both were exhausted from their drives to and from work. Her teenage daughter came home every day at 3:00 to an empty house and did not see her mother until 6:30, when she returned from work after driving 90 minutes in heavy traffic. Ivanov felt guilty and sad about this. "Those are the worst things that have happened because it hurts relationships when you don't have time. . . . I think to own a house, that's a high price. Too high. So I wouldn't do it again. I wouldn't move out here again. I mean I love my house, but—not enough to repeat what I've got. It's hard."

The contradictions between a passionate desire for suburban homeownership and the constraints of metropolitan Los Angeles were captured in Vicky's answer to this question: What comes to mind when you hear the words Antelope Valley? "Home, now. Home. Kind of dread, in a way. Do I have to be here forever? I don't want to be here forever. This is kind a home for now, but not forever. It's not roots. But it's home."

History Embeds Itself in the Landscape

The suburban landscapes created in distinctive historical eras were shaped by different sets of practices and ideas about how to convert land into living spaces. These actions left a spatial legacy for subsequent generations—the housing stock itself, the way it was laid out in particular neighborhoods, and the way these neighborhoods fit into a broader mosaic, connected or isolated from the larger life of the metropolis.

Certain landscapes had more staying power than others. Some endured more or less intact, others showed flexible resilience. Still others vanished completely, overwhelmed by new design practices, tastes, redevelopment, gentrification, or the bulldozer. This was certainly the case with many borderland areas, which at one time existed along a physical edge that soon became interior. Streetcar suburbia endured most profoundly at the macro-scale of metropolitan life, as it laid the groundwork for massive dispersal, embedding the commuting habit into the very DNA of the region. Up close, streetcar suburbia was a landscape that faded quickly, engulfed by new building and community designs oriented to the car. Still, in a few towns, small traces of this landscape survived—in the compact siting of properties, in their rejuvenated old town Main Streets, and in their walkability and human scale.

Modest suburbia and picturesque enclaves left their own contrasting legacies, establishing distinctive social geographies in Los Angeles that would have remarkable staying power. On one end of the spectrum, modest suburbia left a problematic legacy for subsequent generations of working-class suburbanites—poor housing stock, lousy community design and planning, a dearth of greenery and public spaces, and proximity to industrial sites and their toxic residue. These towns are generally denser and more compact. Since the 1970s, they have become gateway settlements for immigrants who continue to comprise the region's working class. At the other end of the spectrum are the picturesque enclaves, the most desired and protected spaces of Los Angeles. These are the places of natural beauty, sealed in perpetuity through deft controls over land and people. These are arguably the most fixed spaces of Los Angeles. They achieved the residential gold standard from the beginning and stayed that way. Though they represent a small slice of the metropolis, their influence is enormous in the public and scholarly imagination.

Contemporary suburbia has been profoundly shaped by developments in the post-World War II years. The gargantuan footprint left by sitcom and corporate suburbia is hard to overstate, as these landscapes blanketed more of the metropolis than all the others combined. Sitcom suburbia created a vast panorama of average housing stock on modest lots, some anchored around employment and retail hubs, all thoroughly scaled to the automobile. The builders conceived of it as a democratic landscape, and it has remained so in ways they never imagined. Moderate regulations created an openness in both the physical and social landscape, securing a dynamic future for these places that upends every stereotype the TV sitcoms created. Corporate suburbia, the booming towns in the far reaches of the metropolis, represent the last and perhaps most recognizable suburban landscape. Distant and car-dependent as ever, these are townscapes of contemporary standardization, with a new fixedness of place enforced by mind-numbingly detailed CC&Rs. This is the far frontier of suburbia, the fringe destinations of urban flight for new generations who are chasing the American dream.

The variety in the tenor and built environment of these suburban landscapes, as they developed over time, set the stage for the tremendous social change that came to redefine the lives of their residents after 1970.

2

Change and Stability

Evolving Demography and Housing in the Suburbs

From 1945 to 2010, the suburbs of LA transformed from bastions of the white middle class to spaces of multiracial social diversity. This chapter traces the broad contours of that transformation, revealing patterns of both continuity and change. Some suburbs remained remarkably stable, while others were profoundly altered.[1]

After the postwar decades when the familiar suburban profile of white, middle-class nuclear families was set in place, the suburban context gradually began to shift. The movement of Latinos, Black Americans, and Asians into the city and its suburbs intensified, inspiring one research team to describe LA as an "ethnic quilt."[2] The suburbs also saw trends such as growing inequality and a rise in homeownership among people of color. The notion of "suburban advantage" shifted from white to something more multihued, while the expansion of suburban poverty upended a simplistic association of suburbia with advantage altogether. Other changes in family composition, homeownership, and the built environment together redefined the normative suburb and the typical suburbanite.[3]

Yet, at the same time, other trends persisted, such as suburban exclusion although increasingly it pivoted around class. Suburban mainstays like nuclear families with stay-at-home moms, children, and high rates of homeownership did not completely vanish; instead, their center of gravity drifted from middle-class to wealthier suburbs. And the suburban single-family home remained ubiquitous even as it was joined by other housing types.

All of these trends were shaped deeply by several larger forces—economic restructuring, globalization, immigration, and civil rights gains. LA's evolving economy crucially influenced suburban development, helping some areas, hurting others. The postwar period was the heyday of industry in Los Angeles—including high-tech aerospace and traditional unionized mass-production industries—which helped underwrite a middle-class standard of living for expanding numbers of Angelenos. In the 1970s, Los Angeles began experiencing the effects of economic restructuring driven by globalization and corporate cost-cutting that included outsourcing and shipping production to Latin America and Asia. The resulting labor market looked like a lopsided hourglass, fattest at the bottom. The restructured economy, indeed, was intensely polarized: high-paying, high-skill jobs on one end and low-skill, low-paid non-union jobs on the other. Middle-income jobs, meanwhile, began to dry up, such as the union jobs at shuttered factories like GM, Firestone, and US Steel. Large immigrant streams from Asia and Latin America after 1965 provided labor at both ends of the labor spectrum, from high-tech engineers and technical specialists to nannies and restaurant workers. In the process, the region's economy continued to grow rapidly by 31.2% during the 1980s (compared to 21.8% nationally), a pattern typical of Sunbelt metropolitan areas.[4]

Economic restructuring, in turn, shaped uneven suburban fortunes. Factories closed in south LA's industrial belt, new manufacturing opened in outlying areas, jobs themselves began to change, and economic inequality intensified. In the realm of industry, LA saw selective deindustrialization and reindustrialization all at once. Plant closures affected places like Van Nuys, Pomona and Fontana, but Southeast LA was hardest hit. In all areas, poverty followed. Following the closures of the Lockheed and GM plants in Van Nuys in 1992, for example, welfare caseloads in the eastern San Fernando Valley spiked by 80,000 over an 18-month period, reflecting a broader rise of poverty in the Valley. In Southeast LA, from 1978 to 1982 alone, more than 75,000 jobs were lost, leaving behind a hollowed-out landscape of scrap metal yards handling the refuse of a dying industrial economy. While these areas were suffering economic shock, other suburbs were thriving. Aerospace and electronics plants, for example, scattered south into Orange County and north into Ventura County, into places like Simi Valley and Thousand Oaks. By the 1980s, the residential patterns of engineers followed; they clustered in the South Bay, in some of LA's whitest, toniest coastal suburbs like Manhattan, Redondo, and Hermosa Beach, as well as the Palos Verdes peninsula. This sector was propelled by the steady rise in prime federal defense contracts to the region, which peaked in 1984.[5]

At the same time, LA saw a rise in low-paid, non-union industrial jobs, in apparel, furniture, printing, toys, and sporting goods. The garment industry employed the greatest number of workers, surpassing New York as the nation's leader in apparel production. Garment jobs were often occupied by low-wage, weakly organized, easily disciplined immigrant workers, especially undocumented immigrant women. By the 1990s, most of these factories were small, informal operations, employing fewer than 50 workers—typically Latino, Vietnamese, Korean, and Chinese immigrants. While most of these operations clustered in the downtown garment district, some were located in suburban areas like El Monte, Montebello, and City of Commerce. The garment industry had a reputation for labor exploitation and sweatshop conditions.[6]

The suburbs thus had come to contain the full range of economic opportunity and exploitation. They were the sites of the extremes of economic restructuring, within gleaming edge city buildings and decrepit suburban sweatshops. Vast variations in suburban density further illustrated these divides. In the protected green suburbs of wealth, homes were spread out in sparsely populated communities. In poorer suburbs, overcrowding reached astronomical levels, a result of the catastrophic confluence of low pay and exorbitant housing costs. LA County earned the dubious distinction of being the national leader in overcrowding from 1990 to 2020, due to its high levels of wealth inequality and home prices.[7] This crisis impacted urban and suburban areas alike, including places like South Gate, where informal housing crammed into suburban backyards. Elite suburbs, meanwhile, continued to be buffered from these problems.

In addition, the transformation of suburbia was driven by the civil rights movement, which gained particular force during the peak era of white suburbia. The two were closely intertwined. Racial justice activists challenged segregation and discrimination in all regions of the country, in heated battles that often erupted in the suburbs, from Pasadena to Canoga Park, Levittown to Cicero. These hard-fought civil rights campaigns helped trigger the transformation of suburbia, through the insistent claim that people had a right to live where they chose.

LA's suburbs experienced rising levels of ethnoracial diversity, as well as escalating inequality, uneven access to jobs, the emergence of new economic hot spots, and diverging economic fortunes. At the same time that people of color finally gained access to suburbia, the economic landscape was creating new, uneven stresses. The efforts of some suburbs to protect the status quo by excluding affordable housing and otherwise constricting the housing supply exacerbated these challenges. These tools of exclusion and segregation were originally honed in white suburbia, setting precedents that proved to be remarkably enduring.

Get Out: The Heyday of White Suburbia

In 1958, reporter Dick Degnon of the *Los Angeles Times* alighted in La Crescenta to profile a "bright new way of living" in the neighborly social world of suburbia. On the 3700 block of Anderson Avenue, neighbors did a lot together—dads helped each other with DIY home improvement projects, moms exchanged recipes, they took weekend outings together, and they shared everything from babysitting duties to cups of sugar. During daily kaffeeklatsches, they planned block parties and weekend activities for the group. In this tight-knit neighborhood, where people moved to "raise their children in a happy environment," the suburban good life seemed to be a lived reality.[8] Unmentioned in Degnon's piece was the suburb's racial profile. In La Crescenta, neighboring La Cañada, and nearly every suburb in postwar LA, the population was all white. This racial milieu fostered a sense of social comfort among neighbors and allowed for such a tight-knit community to blossom.

By the time Degnon wrote this profile, the notion of suburbia as a white space had become a normative reality. It was a part of everyday life that many whites took for granted, an image reflected back at them in popular culture from television sitcoms to dishwasher ads to Disneyland.[9] This perception was far from a natural outcome of settlement choices by different groups. Rather, systemic racial segregation across LA was the product of deliberate practices and policies refined over decades. It began at the local level through developers, realtors, municipal leaders, and homeowners; was fortified by the federal government in the 1930s; and persisted well into the 1950s and 1960s. Despite the movement toward fair housing in policies and court decisions, mid-century LA was racially split to a degree reminiscent of apartheid South Africa. Census data from the 1950s and 1960s confirms that more than half of all suburban towns had white percentages in the high 90s; the vast majority had white percentages of greater than 90%.[10] In a nutshell, segregation efforts effectively kept people of color out of most suburban towns.

An array of tools was developed over the twentieth century to create this social geography. One of the earliest and most effective tools was the racial restrictive covenant, used widely in Los Angeles and cities nationally from 1900 to 1948. This legal clause written into property deeds specified that the owner could only sell or rent the house to Caucasians, otherwise the owner could lose the property. Some covenants listed the excluded racial groups by name, such as "Negroes," Mexicans, Japanese, or Jews. Covenants predated zoning as a form of land use regulation. They were intended to be passed down with the land, despite future transfers in ownership, and typically lasted 20–30 years and sometimes in perpetuity. Two important court cases upheld their use. In *Los Angeles Investment Co. v. Gary* (1919), the California Supreme Court validated the restrictive occupancy clauses in such deeds, which essentially allowed a Black person to buy a home but not to live in it. In *Corrigan v. Buckley* (1926), the US Supreme Court allowed the enforcement of covenants. These rulings coincided with the 1920s building boom in Los Angeles, which unleashed their widespread use across the region, from Flintridge to South Gate to Leimert Park. By 1939, 22 areas within Los Angeles County deployed race restrictive covenants in perpetuity.[11] In 1917, one Black American resident described the impact of these covenants: they created "invisible walls of steel. The whites surrounded us and made it impossible for us to go beyond these walls."[12]

Despite the widespread use of such restrictions, they were only effective when all property owners in a neighborhood enforced them. To bring group pressure to bear, many suburban neighborhoods formed "protective associations" or "homeowner associations." Association members conducted covenant-writing campaigns, held meetings when the threat of "invasion" by people of color was imminent, and were often the party filing suit in cases where individual covenants were broken. Homeowner associations proliferated in LA after 1910, and, by 1920, their presence "heralded a more rigid and efficient era of residential segregation."[13] The developers of all-white Leimert Park required new residents to join a homeowner association to maintain "protective restrictions."[14] In the 1920s, the South Gate Property Owners' Protective Association handbook assured, "Practically all of the city's residential tracts have perpetual restrictions against occupancy by non-Caucasians," in contrast to some districts where the covenants were expiring.[15] In La Cañada, the Chamber of Commerce played the role of a protective association by launching a "race restriction campaign" in 1941, when local covenants were about to expire, taking cues from similar campaigns in nearby Flintridge, Pasadena, Glendale, Alhambra, and South Pasadena. Editorials in the *Crescenta Valley Ledger* called the campaign "necessary to insure a future of peace and happiness in La Canada Valley" because when "folk of one race force their way amongst other racial groups, there is often discontent and bitterness. La Canadans believe that they have a right to choose the neighbors in the community they have developed."[16]

Developers were also important catalysts for racial segregation. They attached race-restrictive covenants to properties in their developments, imposed their own restrictions, or simply refused to sell property to people of color, a practice that persisted well into the 1950s. These restrictions were often used as selling points for suburban subdivisions. For example, the developers of Windsor Hills stipulated "Caucasian race only" in its "Summary of Building Restrictions."[17] The Janss Investment Company used racial covenants widely in its new development of Westwood.[18] A 1920s ad for Eagle Rock real estate read, "As you journey about Eagle Rock . . . you will observe that the residents . . . are all of the white race."[19] As late as the 1950s, some of the largest developers of suburban tracts in Los Angeles refused to sell homes to Blacks, including Milton Brock Builders, Lakewood Village Builders, and Julian Weinstock Builders. This practice closed off huge segments of the booming housing market to people of color.[20]

To reinforce these efforts, white suburbanites used intimidation and violence to keep individual people of color from buying in their neighborhoods. In 1947, the Los Angeles Urban League identified 26 techniques that white homeowners used to turn back African American home seekers, including paying off neighbors to not sell to Blacks, vandalism, cross burnings, bombings, and death threats. Groups like the Ku Klux Klan fostered this climate of intimidation. From 1915 to 1944, the KKK counted about 18,000 members in the Los Angeles/Long Beach area. They held meetings in La Crescenta, South Gate, Watts, El Monte, and, in later years, Lakewood. White supremacists also operated in Glendale, Pasadena, and El Monte, through local branches of the Nazi Party and KKK, well into the 1970s.[21]

The real estate industry also played a pivotal role in codifying and enforcing racist norms. The Los Angeles Realty Board (LARB), founded in 1903, encouraged the use of racial covenants in property sales and urged members to steer people of color away from white neighborhoods.[22] A statewide survey conducted in 1927 by the all-white California Real Estate Association (CREA) revealed strong support of racial restrictions by realtors and described the association's efforts to prevent people of color from moving into white neighborhoods, in places like Compton, Pasadena, Santa Monica, and Bell. Respondents declared that, of all racial groups, African Americans posed the greatest threat to white neighborhoods. In 1924, the National Association of Real Estate Boards (NAREB) established a code of ethics that prohibited realtors from selling property to "members of any race or nationality" where they would threaten property values. NAREB reiterated this rule in its 1943 publication, *Fundamentals of Real Estate*: "The prospective buyer might be a bootlegger . . . a madam . . . a gangster . . ., a colored man of means who was giving his children a college education and thought they were entitled to live among whites. . . . No matter what the motive or character of the would-be purchaser, if the deal would instigate a form of blight, then certainly the well-meaning broker must work against its consummation."[23] If a real estate agent violated these rules, he could lose his license. The code of ethics stayed in effect until the late 1950s.[24]

Even after the CREA removed the racial rule from its code of ethics in 1951, local realty boards continued to punish or expel members who sold properties to nonwhites in white neighborhoods. This accelerated the process of realtors steering prospective buyers to specific areas well into the 1960s. For example, in Pico and Rivera (which were then separate towns), a Dow Realty listing for a house in the Pico Vista Park area in 1958 directed realtors, "Please show to Caucasians only." The LARB also refused to admit Black members up to 1960, despite numerous applications by Black real estate agents.[25]

As the real estate industry matured, codifying many of these racist practices in their own professional rules, they developed a reputation for respectability and knowledge of urban real estate markets. This positioned them to have enormous influence on federal policy when the government intervened in housing policy during the Great Depression. Two New Deal agencies, the Home Owners Loan Corporation (HOLC, 1933) and the Federal Housing Administration (FHA, 1934) played critical roles in perpetuating discrimination. The HOLC developed a system of rating neighborhoods as security risks for home loans that was laden with racial bias. This agency essentially defined neighborhoods as worthy or unworthy of federal assistance to homeowners. The worthy neighborhoods were white, suburban, stable, zoned, and homogenous. The unworthy neighborhoods were nonwhite, denser, closer to industry or other "odious" threats, and demographically and socioeconomically mixed. By blacklisting (or "red-lining," in real estate parlance) nonwhite or integrated neighborhoods, it entrenched the idea that these areas were financially untrustworthy and doomed to deteriorate, helping to make the "racial theory of property value" a self-fulfilling prophecy. In Los Angeles, neighborhoods with African Americans were nearly all assigned a red rating, including those with upper- and middle-class Black residents. For example, the upper-class West Adams district received a D-red rating purely on the basis of race.[26] African Americans had a more negative impact on HOLC ratings than other ethnoracial groups in LA.[27]

The HOLC's racially biased appraisal system ultimately influenced the FHA, which became the most important program for homeownership in the nation. The FHA, which insured mortgages granted by private lenders, was instrumental in spurring the postwar suburban boom and made homeownership possible for millions of Americans. People of color were largely cut off from these programs. Until 1948, the FHA supported the use of restrictive covenants and was reluctant to guarantee home construction loans in areas without them.[28] Entire subdivisions in the postwar period were financed by the FHA on the condition that they be exclusively white. Out of 125,000 FHA housing units built from 1950 to 1954 in Los Angeles County, only 3,000 (2.4%) were open to people of color. The FHA also refused to guarantee loans for home renovations in African American areas such as South Los Angeles.[29]

With this deeply inequitable policy in place as the nation stood on the cusp of its largest suburban expansion in history, these well-established techniques worked to fortify racial barriers around white suburbs. The "chocolate city–vanilla suburb" paradigm was firmly in place in Southern California, as it was across much of the nation. When LA's population surged during and after World War II, propelled in part by the in-migration of Blacks, Latinos, and Asian Americans, this diversifying of the overall population put unprecedented pressure on the region's racial framework.[30]

Even after civil rights activists won fair housing mandates, the segregation of white suburbs persisted, at times in reaction to these gains. Following the US Supreme Court decision in *Shelley v. Kraemer* (1948), which declared race-restrictive covenants unenforceable, it took two years for the FHA to agree to abide by the ruling. In practice, many local FHA officials condoned unwritten agreements and existing traditions of segregation until the Fair Housing Act of 1968.[31] Even after *Shelley*, nonwhite home seekers were rebuffed by racial steering, developers' refusal to sell, and incidents of violence and intimidation. Civil rights advocates continued to push back, only to be repeatedly resisted. To fortify fair housing in California, the state legislature passed the Rumford Fair Housing Act (1963), followed swiftly by a measure to undo it, Proposition 14 (1964), which would enshrine the right to practice housing discrimination in a state constitutional amendment. The proposition passed by a wide margin, boosted by a robust campaign led by the CREA.[32]

By the late 1960s, a number of fair housing breakthroughs occurred at the federal level. In 1967, the US Supreme Court overturned Prop 14, and, in 1968, Congress passed the Fair Housing Act. Despite numerous weaknesses in these and other housing laws—from enforcement problems to the spawning of new forms of housing discrimination—they gradually opened the suburbs to people of color and catalyzed new waves of racial resistance.[33]

One such reaction was a powerful homeowner movement that took shape in Los Angeles. A favored approach was to use colorblind land use tools as a means of excluding unwanted groups. Zoning, for example, became a way to bar multifamily housing, largely lived in by renters, poorer people, and people of color. The practice of blanketing suburbs with R-1 zoning—limiting building to single-family homes—was adopted in many communities and came to be dubbed "exclusionary zoning" for its power to defend white middle-class neighborhoods from "outsiders." Resistance to growth, a significant policy reversal in LA, also gained momentum among suburban homeowners. Putting a halt to growth helped existing property owners by locking in their existing advantages at a moment of white predominance. "No growth" pushed up property values by limiting the housing inventory, choked off possibilities for affordable housing, and thwarted ethnic settlement. This movement contributed to an overcrowding crisis in LA's poorest communities by limiting the overall housing supply. And in campaigns to protect open lands in the Santa Monica Mountains and the rolling hills of the east San Gabriel Valley, it turned access to nature into a suburban privilege. As urban theorist Mike Davis summed it up, anti-growth represented homeowner exclusivism, "whether the immediate issue is apartment construction, commercial encroachment, school busing, crime, taxes, or simply community designation," and it was based on only the flimsiest link to environmentalism.[34] This anti-growth position remained politically dominant in LA well through the 2010s.[35] In addition to zoning and no-growth policies, white homeowners asserted their interests through grassroots political campaigns against school and housing integration.[36]

Continued discrimination by developers and lenders also obstructed the efforts of people of color to buy suburban homes. In Los Angeles, Blacks reported experiencing housing discrimination three to five times more often than any other group. One Southern California study reported that Black and Latino applicants had a more difficult time securing conventional loans in suburban areas compared to inner-core areas.[37]

Discrimination in suburbia also targeted women, LGBTQ individuals, and single people. In the immediate postwar years, mortgage lenders tended to favor straight married white men when granting loans. FHA guidelines, for example, specified that a married man with a family was a more stable borrower since "he has responsibilities holding him to his obligations." Singles and those with "illegal connections"—at this time California law criminalized queer behavior and interracial marriage—would be disqualified from such loans. Women likewise faced bias in lending. Falling outside of the preferred borrower profile, they were essentially locked out of suburban homeownership.[38]

Decades of hostile acts, practices, and policies defined the suburbs as restricted spaces. Even as the legal barriers began falling, memories of antagonism could linger. In some communities, explicit hostilities persisted. The Crescenta Valley, where friendly neighbors enjoyed "a bright new way of living," was also home to California's head of the Ku Klux Klan and a publication arm of that group. This was the Janus-face of suburbia: the American Dream built upon a foundation of structural racism.[39]

Breaking Through: Social Change in Suburbia, 1945–2010

By the 1980s, the realities of suburban life had begun to shift. They were becoming home to a full cross-section of Angelenos: rich, poor, Latino, Asian, Black, white, straight, gay, singles, the elderly, single-parent families and working mothers. Poverty also found its way into many suburban communities, posing new challenges and controversies. After 1970, suburbs experienced growing ethnic and racial diversity, rising class disparities, changing household profiles, and evolving patterns of housing and homeownership.[40]

The most dramatic transformation from 1950 to 2010 was ethnic and racial change. There was a virtual reversal from a bulging majority of all-white towns in the 1950s and 1960s to ethnoracial diversity in all 86 suburban municipalities of LA County by 1990. The "vanilla suburb" had dissolved. This dynamic created a context of lively ethnic and racial transformation intermingled with intense white anxiety, tensions that underlay a great deal of the suburban zeitgeist in post-1970 Los Angeles. It also began redefining the racial meanings of suburbia itself.

Given the formidable efforts to maintain racial barriers for at least a half century, the process of crossing the suburban color line could be a tense,

Figure 2.1 The shifting social profile of suburbia, from the Cleavers to the Padoongpatts. The 1950s suburban profile—white, middle-class, nuclear family—was exemplified by the Cleavers of the TV sitcom "Leave It to Beaver," 1959. By the 1980s, the Padoongpatt family of the San Fernando Valley exemplified new demographic norms. In their Valley neighborhood of Arleta, about eight miles from where "Leave It to Beaver" was filmed, this Thai American family lived alongside Mexicans, Salvadorans, Filipinos, Vietnamese, Thais, and African Americans.

(top) ABC Television Network via Wikimedia Commons; (bottom) photo by Vitaya Chalermkij.

stressful, and sometimes ugly experience for new residents. One Japanese American woman recalled moving into Sierra Madre, where her family owned a nursery and wanted to build a home on the property: "It was property my grandfather owned from before the war. The neighbors circulated a petition trying to get us not to build a house there . . . we'd be their neighbor, right? This would be in the early sixties. It's kind of shocking if you think about it. It never got any place, and Dad built the house and we lived right there."[41] When Alfred Jackson, an African American veteran of the Korean War, moved into Compton with his wife Luquella and their children in 1953, they were greeted by a white mob spewing racist insults. They kept loaded pistols at hand while moving in, and a family friend stood guard with a rifle.[42] When Maria Avila and her husband tried to buy a home in Alhambra in 1958, they met immediate resistance: "I remember going to Alhambra one time and we walked into this real estate office. My husband is much lighter than I am and by looking at him . . . you would say he is not Mexican. And so he would go in and they would show him this possibility or that possibility. When I would get down from the car then the whole story would change. Then the down payment was higher or the criteria was another thing, but I didn't want to live there anyway. If they didn't want me, I didn't want to live there." They ended up moving to El Monte.[43]

Stories like these proliferated as people of color became "civil rights suburbanites." This process, at times fraught, was inflected with a sense of overcoming a racist system and perhaps an appreciation of the fragility of that accomplishment. Suburban living meant not just moving up the socio-economic ladder but also offered a training ground for living in a multiracial society for the children of these homeseekers. It was an achievement worth protecting.[44] These individuals helped drive the transformation of suburbia in LA, and their numbers were striking. From 1970 to 2010, the proportion of all suburbanites across LA who were Black American, Latino, and Asian American jumped from 26% to 70%. By another measure, by 1990, a majority of every ethnoracial group lived in suburban areas.[45] By 2010, the majority of all suburbanites across LA were people of color. This trend reflected LA County's changing demography as a whole. Whites had dominated in the 1950s and 1960s. In 2000, Latinos were the largest group, followed by whites, Asians, and Black Americans.

This profound demographic transformation was swept along by fair housing laws in the 1960s, the 1965 Hart-Celler Act (which spurred massive immigration from Latin America and Asia), and an expanding Black, Latino,

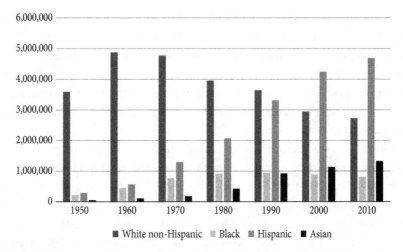

Figure 2.2 Ethnoracial groups in Los Angeles County, 1950–2010 (shown in raw numbers).
US Census dataset, 1950–2010.

and Asian middle class. By 1980, a majority of LA's immigrants also lived in the suburbs, and their numbers rose in subsequent years, a trend occurring nationally, with Los Angeles at the vanguard. Rates of immigration to LA, in fact, were among the nation's highest.[46]

In terms of pace of change, Asians and Latinos moved into suburbia faster than Black Americans. In part, this was due to the relative position of these groups within the American racial hierarchy. Both Asians and Latinos occupied what some scholars call the "racial middle," somewhere between white and Black. They didn't occupy the bottom, yet they didn't necessarily possess the advantages of whiteness.[47]

For Asians, after decades of exclusion, their entry into suburbia after World War II grew out of a distinct set of factors, including their growing wealth, the trend toward equal numbers of men and women (reversing historical imbalances) which conformed to suburban family norms, and the Cold War geopolitical climate. Asians went from being the most vilified racial group in California to an accepted, even admired minority group by the 1950s, a process that was clearly visible in housing patterns. World War II and the Cold War recast the place of ethnic Asians in American society. During the war, Japan's invasion of China began to erode the state's intense, long-standing anti-Chinese prejudice and fostered sympathy for ethnic Chinese, especially those fleeing Mao's communist regime. Acceptance came slightly later for Japanese people, prompted by their wartime mass incarceration and the sterling wartime record of Japanese American soldiers. By the 1950s–1960s, changing outlooks toward those of Asians descent translated into a greater Anglo willingness to accept them as neighbors in suburbia.[48] In addition, the post-internment federal policy of pressuring Japanese Americans to move out of ethnic enclaves and into dispersed neighborhoods implicitly encouraged suburban settlement.[49]

Great diversity came to characterize the Asian American population, and immigrants in particular. Asian immigration was driven, in part, by the normalization of relations with China in 1978 and Taiwan receiving its own quota in 1981. Quite quickly, the foreign-born came to predominate the Asian American population in the US. Among the post-1965 wave of Chinese immigrants were professionals and other highly skilled workers, pushed by political volatility in home countries and pulled by jobs, opportunity, and America's long-standing anti-communist stance. After 1980, Asian immigrants were more diverse by class, education, skillset, and profession. Immigrants from Hong Kong, Taiwan, the Philippines, and South Korea tended to be better skilled, joining the American middle-class upon arrival. Cambodian, Laotian, and Vietnamese refugees escaping genocide and war tended to bring fewer skills and capital, so often ended up in low-wage service jobs.[50] Across Los Angeles, suburban spaces began to reflect this growing diversity among Asian immigrants.

For Asian Americans, ethnic dispersal was by far the most common settlement pattern from 1950 to 2000. The first generation of postwar Asian suburbanites settled in white middle-class suburbs, such as Monterey Park, Gardena, and the Crenshaw district in southwest LA. In later years, they lived in a range of suburbs that spanned the class gamut, from wealthy enclaves like San Marino, Rancho Palos Verdes, and Bradbury, to the multiethnic suburbs of the San Gabriel Valley like Alhambra and Rosemead and master-planned corporate suburbs like Diamond Bar and Walnut. From 1990 to 2010, Asian clustering increased with significant concentrations in the San Gabriel Valley, which emerged as a national epicenter of Asian suburban settlement. By 2000, there were three majority Asian suburbs; by 2010, the number jumped to 10.[51] In overall terms, however, Asian residents settled widely across LA County, living in suburbs where they represented clear numerical minorities.[52]

Latinos also successfully breached the suburban color line. Access to FHA and GI Bill loans, combined with better paying jobs, allowed a small number of Latinos to move into previously all-white suburban neighborhoods in the 1950s and 1960s. Lighter-skinned Latinos more easily gained access to the suburbs, while darker-skinned Latinos continued to face harsher discrimination.[53] From 1970 to 1990, Latinos typically lived in ethnoracially diverse municipalities. Around 1990, resegregation began appearing. The most extreme examples were the southeast suburbs like South Gate, Huntington Park, Maywood, Bell, Bell Gardens, and Cudahy, which flipped from all-white to all-Latino. Even taking these areas into account, multiraciality was the most typical community experience for Latino suburbanites from 1945 to 2000.[54]

Latino suburban settlement followed two pathways from downtown—one to the east, the other to the south. Eastside suburbanization was shaped profoundly by the East LA barrio and the *colonias* that reached across LA county. Since the late nineteenth century, Latinos lived in working-class *colonias* that dotted the citrus belt of the San Gabriel Valley and Eastside areas adjacent to farms, brickyards, and oil fields in towns like Azusa and Pomona. Some of these Latino footholds lay directly in the pathway of future suburban expansion. Closer to downtown, East LA had been the region's most ethnically diverse hub until the 1940s. In the 1950s, as white ethnics left, more Mexicans moved in, many pushed by the displacement of freeway construction and urban renewal, turning the Eastside into LA's largest barrio and the center of Mexican American life and political activism. Those same push factors also drove middle-class Latinos to settle further east in suburbs like Pico Rivera, La Puente, Montebello, El Monte, and Santa Fe Springs, and Eastside-adjacent suburbs like Monterey Park, Alhambra, and San Gabriel. Middle-class Mexican Americans were drawn by industrial jobs, affordable homes, and good schools in these eastern suburbs. Working-class *colonias* became part of these communities when new suburban tracts enveloped them, setting the stage for mixed class profiles in these towns. If middle-class Latinos came to the suburbs, the suburbs also came to *colonias*.[55]

A different profile emerged in the gateway suburbs of Southeast LA. The largest numbers of Latinos arrived after 1970, and they were more heavily immigrant and poor. Some came from the Eastside, others from Watts and the Central American neighborhoods of Westlake and Pico Union, and still others directly from Mexico, Central America, or Cuba. They were drawn by inexpensive housing created by the huge exodus of whites in the wake of local plant shutdowns. Like most suburbanites, they were in search of decent neighborhoods and schools. By the 1990s, the southern suburbs represented the heart of Latino settlement in LA County; they had more Latinos than the Eastside.[56]

Black Americans faced the most difficulties in moving into white suburbia. After 1960, they made inroads into a very small number of suburbs, setting off frantic white flight in Compton and later Inglewood.[57] Exceptions were places like Pasadena, Monrovia, and Pacoima where African American communities had deep historic roots. After 1980, Black Americans moved into more and more suburbs. In some, they lived alongside Latinos in emerging majority minority suburbs like Compton, Inglewood, Hawthorne, Carson, and Gardena. In others, racial stability suggested growing acceptance and even some proactive efforts to welcome African Americans. In Altadena, a campaign of "managed integration" reflected the town's commitment to racial diversity, while in Brentwood an idealistic, modernist residential cooperative embraced racial integration as a core value.[58] Further south, the affluent Black haven of Baldwin Hills (part of LA City) offered handsome homes and hilltop views. These wide-ranging places mirrored Black suburban settlement nationwide after 1970, ranging from rich to middling to poor, some well-integrated, others less so. Some Black flight occurred into the exurbs or out of LA altogether. They were pushed out by plant closures, gangs, drugs, crime, underfunded schools, and racial profiling in historically Black areas, and they were pulled by affordable, newer housing on the outskirts. They settled in far-flung Lancaster, Palmdale, Upland (San Bernardino County), and Moreno Valley (Riverside County).[59]

Whites experienced the most jarring change, from total racial domination of the suburbs to multiracial coexistence. By 1990, most municipalities were multiracial and remained so for years.[60] The suburbs that stayed the whitest tended to be the wealthiest: Malibu, Manhattan Beach, and Hermosa Beach, along with picturesque enclaves like Hidden Hills, Westlake Village, Calabasas, and Agoura Hills. Even so, the days of 98% white suburbia were over. Even in Malibu, LA's whitest suburb in 2000, 11% of its residents were Latino, Black, and Asian. Geographically, the general direction of white suburban settlement was toward the edges. Equally notable was the white exodus out of Southern California altogether. Some whites relocated to Orange and Riverside Counties; more left for other parts of California, Arizona, Nevada, Oregon, and eastern and southern states. They were pushed out by plant closures, declines in aerospace, rising home prices and congestion, and unease over the immigrant influx, making this an outsized "white flight" that reached well beyond the metropolis.[61] This represented the most dramatic symbol of white unease in LA, a massive rejection of regional change altogether—packing up the U-Haul, saying goodbye, and wiping their hands of LA once and for all.

Immigrants were another driver of suburban diversification. Breaking with long historic traditions of settling in inner-city enclaves, immigrants began settling in the suburbs upon arrival, a trend that accelerated after 1970. They were extraordinarily varied in class, skill sets, and educational status, reflecting the socioeconomic polarization inherent in globalization itself. The greatest number of immigrants came from Latin America—Mexico, Guatemala, and El Salvador—many of them arriving with modest skills and education. This was followed by immigrants from Asia and the Middle East, who tended to be middle class and more highly skilled, though significant economic and skill polarization existed within these groups as well. As one research team put it, LA is a story of "diverging ethnic fates."[62]

Certain suburban areas became immigrant magnets. In the 1950s and 1960s, Santa Monica, Pasadena, Culver City, and Beverly Hills housed the most foreign-born residents.[63] The San Fernando Valley and Westside drew in European Jews, while Boyle Heights maintained its long tradition as an immigrant point of entry.[64] After 1970, new suburban immigrant hubs emerged, including Southeast LA, which housed high numbers of Latino newcomers, and the San Gabriel Valley, which drew upwardly mobile Mexican and Chinese immigrants.[65] Other suburban immigrant hot spots included Glendale, which was home to more immigrants than any other suburb in LA from 1970 to 2000, including Armenians, Koreans, Filipinos, and Mexicans; the east San Fernando Valley in areas like North Hollywood; the Gardena/Torrance area, where Japanese Americans had deep roots; Beverly Hills, which housed wealthy Iranian Jews; and Cerritos and Artesia, sitcom suburbs in Southeast LA that housed Latino, Korean, Japanese, Filipino, Chinese, and white residents.[66] The analogy of an ethnic quilt is an apt descriptor for the ethnic and racial landscape of LA suburbia after 1980.[67]

In terms of class, LA's suburbs evolved from a massive predominance of middle-class towns in the 1950s and 1960s, toward a more class-stratified landscape by 2000. The richer towns tended to stay rich, poorer suburbs stayed poor, and middling suburbs experienced the greatest volatility both up and down the class ladder. Suburbia, in essence, came to embody class inequality. These changes reflected a national rise in income inequality from 1950 to 2010. The suburban income gaps were largest in Sunbelt metros like LA, Houston, and Phoenix.[68] After 1970, suburbia no longer automatically signified a space of advantage and affluence. Instead, suburban residence meant something much more complex and more vexing all at once.

In the 1950s and 1960s, the vast majority of LA's suburbs fell into the middle-class range, reflecting the prosperity of even blue-collar families whose good wages in an era of strong unions and a flush economy enabled them to live middle-class lifestyles.[69] In these postwar decades, the swollen middle vastly outnumbered rich and poor suburbs. After 1970, the number of both wealthy and poor towns rose. Middle-class suburbs, meanwhile, dropped from 91% to 27% of all suburban towns between 1950 and 2010.[70]

A closer look at these communities is revealing. At the high end, an important cluster were LA's picturesque enclaves, including places like Beverly Hills, San Marino, Palos Verdes Estates, Bradbury, Rolling Hills, and Malibu. These towns maintained their position in the highest-class stratum of LA communities throughout their histories, enabling residents to maintain their social advantage over time.[71] Racially, they had disproportionate shares of whites and Asians.

The beach suburbs represented a unique subset of these rich towns. Their fortunes rose sharply from 1950 to 2000, thrusting them into the highest echelon of LA's suburbs. Beachfront affluence was not always a given in the

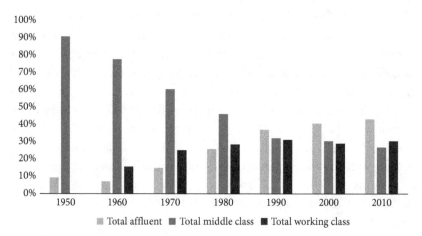

Figure 2.3 Affluent, middle-class, and working-class suburbs in Los Angeles County, 1950–2010.

Note: Shown as a percentage of all towns for each decennial year. Data are based on "median family income" for each town, classified in relation to the LA County "median family income" level for each decennial year.

US Census dataset, 1950–2010.

region. In the early twentieth century, southland beaches were a hodge-podge of oil derricks, seedy amusement parks, bodybuilder hangouts, ramshackle hot dog joints, and shoulder-to-shoulder crowding along the sand. Housing encompassed wealthy estates as well as low-rent apartments and oceanfront motels. African Americans frequented a beach called the Inkwell south of Santa Monica, while a string of gay bars flourished along Crystal Beach just south of that. This unregulated scene contributed to low property values in Redondo, Hermosa, and Manhattan Beach through the 1950s. During that decade, regional leaders launched vigorous campaigns to redevelop LA's beach communities, to make way for white middle-class residents. Modernization, demolition, and policing opened the way for a higher class of housing, marinas for yachts and pleasure boats, and a more sanitized and protected beach experience. This was LA's version of what historian Andrew Kahrl calls "coastal capitalism," the privatization and commodification of coastal areas.[72] As a result, the class status of Santa Monica, Redondo, Hermosa, and Manhattan Beach shot upward between 1950 and 2000. Malibu started near the top when it incorporated in 1991. These towns also were overwhelmingly white.

In addition to picturesque scenery and coastlines, jobs could also drive up suburban fortunes. This was true in edge cities like Pasadena, Burbank, Glendale, Culver City, Santa Monica, and El Segundo. They had substantial pockets of wealth and overall fiscal prosperity thanks to revenue generated by the aerospace, entertainment, and tech industries. While these areas did not rise to the top tier of suburban municipalities in terms of class due to their internal class diversity, they nonetheless represented fiscal winners in LA County.[73]

Poor suburbs stood in stark contrast. Poverty dispersed steadily across LA County from 1945 to 2017, touching the far corners of the metropolis from Pomona to the San Fernando Valley, Lancaster to Long Beach. Data since 1959 showed the presence of a suburban underclass even in the heyday of postwar affluence. After 1970, poverty climbed in certain suburbs, including older modest suburbs like Cudahy, Bell, Bell Gardens, Huntington Park, El Monte, and Maywood, and a few postwar suburbs like Hawaiian Gardens and Paramount. Some of these suburbs slid from "garden city to crabgrass slum," as Mike Davis put it, parallel to national trends in aging, inner-ring suburbs. Yet poverty showed up in newer suburbs as well, as a result of economic restructuring and downturns in defense spending. In the corporate exurb of Lancaster, poverty rates topped 19% in 2017. These trends revealed the fiscal strains shared by many suburbs, young and old, from the core to the farthest edges.[74]

Suburban poverty had deep roots. Suburbs historically had encompassed a wide range of class profiles, with varying degrees of restrictions and property requirements. Those restrictions were loosest in older modest suburbs, where poverty was "allowed in" to a degree, and in towns where people of color had gained early footholds. In 1959, more than half of LA's suburbs had poverty pockets within their borders. In some cases, these were neighborhoods of Latinos and African Americans, tucked within the borders of towns like Pasadena, Glendale, La Verne, Monrovia, Lomita, and Maywood. Some were domestic service suburbs inhabited by laborers servicing a wealthier class of residents.[75] In a few places, like Santa Monica and La Verne, towns began with poverty pockets early on but those shrank over time as wealthy and middle-class residents came to dominate.

After 1970, suburban poverty accelerated, driven by broad economic trends and new policy initiatives. It ushered in what some have called the "great inversion" of metro areas, the movement of wealth to the center and poverty to the periphery.[76] Economic restructuring was a crucial force as it expanded the low-wage workforce and pushed more and more families into poverty. Federal policy, in turn, pivoted in the late 1960s to support the dispersal of the poor into the suburbs, reversing its own decades-long role in promoting residential segregation. These policies included the Section 8 program (1974), a housing allowance to low-income tenants who could seek housing on the open market, including in the suburbs, and the US Department of Housing and Urban Development (HUD)'s Hope VI program (1992) which demolished high-density public housing and transitioned tenants to housing vouchers.[77] At the same time, localities, regions, and states— including California—instituted inclusionary housing programs to promote the building of low-income housing across metro areas. Despite limited results in the face of a lukewarm federal commitment and suburban resistance, these policies promoted the dispersal of the poor into suburbia.[78] By the 2000s, suburban poverty hit record levels across the nation. For the first time, more poor people lived in suburbs than in cities—by 2010, 55% of the metropolitan poor lived in the suburbs.[79] In Los Angeles, 57.7% of suburban tracts had poverty rates of 20% or higher that year.[80] A visible sign of suburban destitution was the gradually enlarging presence of unhoused people who camped under freeway overpasses, along the edges and corridors of suburban spaces, adjacent to big box stores and everyday homes.

Figure 2.4 The extreme end of suburban poverty shows up as homelessness in places like the San Fernando Valley, what one writer named "America's Suburb." Documentary filmmaker Eva Saks tracked this phenomenon in the heart of suburbia, along placid streets of single-family homes. The horizontal figure in the foreground is a person in a sleeping bag.
Photo by Eva Saks.

The most stunning difference between LA's richest and poorest suburbs related to crowding. In 2000, for example, population densities in the poorest suburbs were four times that of wealthy suburbs. Several poor suburbs in Southeast LA had among the highest population densities in California, rivaling the nation's biggest cities. These numbers were even more astounding because tiny suburbs like Cudahy and Maywood, with their one- and two-story dwellings, achieved astronomical levels of "horizontal density" by packing people into small rooms, add-ons, and even garages. Maywood was an extreme example: in 2000, it housed 28,083 people in a suburb of just over one square mile, creating a density rate of 23,799 persons per square mile (compared to Bradbury's 436 per square mile). These high rates of overcrowding continued into the 2020s.[81] (See Table 1.1.)

LA's middle-class suburbs experienced the most volatility, some moving up and others down the class pecking order, as measured by median family income and median home value. If a suburban home represented the American Dream, that dream rested on a foundation that grew flimsier by the decade. Local forces might affect a particular suburb. Mass layoffs in auto or aerospace, white flight, local corruption, or misguided redevelopment could bring neighborhoods down. Gentrification, transnational wealth infusions, or propitious economic development could raise a suburb's profile. As much as generations of developers tried to impose protections on property value, those defenses could not withstand the shocks of revamped home financing tools tied to volatile global markets or the decision of General Motors to shutter its factories.[82]

In terms of families and households, straight nuclear families overwhelmingly predominated in LA's suburbs during the 1950s and 1960s. A smaller number of established suburbs housed more varied family types, including Pasadena, Beverly Hills, Santa Monica, South Pasadena, and Glendale, where over one-third of adults were not married. These towns had high shares of widowers and seniors—the "little old lady from Pasadena"—who were aging in place. Claremont and La Verne had the most single adults, mostly college students attending nearby universities. From 1970 to 2000, the proportion of married suburbanites began a steady decline. By 2000, 50–59% of suburban adults were married. They still comprised a majority in nearly every suburb, signaling their continued demographic dominance, if by a narrower margin. One striking change was that the traditional nuclear family became a hallmark of affluent suburbs rather than middle-class ones.[83]

Another noticeable trend was the graying of the population in many suburban areas. In 1950, they clustered in larger towns that had greater housing variety, like Pasadena, Glendale, Santa Monica, and Long Beach, as well as smaller Beverly Hills, Claremont, South Pasadena, Monrovia, and Whittier. By 2000, a wider range of suburbs housed more and more seniors, including high-end towns on the Palos Verdes peninsula, where homeowning residents opted to age in place. Indeed, from 1980 to 2000, LA's richest suburbs also had the oldest residents—Rolling Hills, Palos Verdes Estates, Malibu, La Cañada, Westlake Village, and Bradbury had the highest median age. (By contrast, poor towns—such as the immigrant-heavy gateway suburbs—had the youngest residents on average, skewed by the younger age of parents and their children.) Suburban seniors in fact crossed the spectrum from rich to poor; in 1970, for example, 15.2% of them lived below the poverty line in LA.[84] Rising numbers of suburban seniors carried implications for political priorities, such as deciding between funding for schools versus adult programs or whether public parks should be used for quiet contemplation or rowdy basketball games.[85]

The mobility and clout of middle-class seniors were influenced over the years by Proposition 13 (1978). In the 1970s, one survey found that many seniors who were mobile and affluent relocated to the suburbs to live closer to their children. After Prop 13, more adults stayed put in their homes for the long haul. That measure was a powerful incentive for residents to age in place since it guaranteed them a low property tax bill (fixed near the 1978 rate) in perpetuity. This gave them a tremendous fiscal generational advantage. Their mortgage payments and tax bills remained affordable while housing costs skyrocketed around them. Thirty years later, these generational impacts reverberated as young millennials were moving in with their parents or grandparents due to unaffordable housing costs.[86]

A rising number of LGBTQ families also moved to suburbia beginning in the 1970s. One catalyst was a change in federal housing policy, specifically at HUD, which altered its definition of family away from heterosexual "marital or biological attachments" toward a more pluralist concept that would include "any stable family relationship," including LGBTQ households. While this definition initially applied to low-income families seeking housing assistance, it set the tone for a broader federal housing policy that "opened the door to queer recognition," according to historian Ian Baldwin. This may have created a more welcoming climate for gays in suburbia.[87] Silver Lake and Echo Park became a "gay mecca" in the 1970s, while West Hollywood's incorporation in 1984 as a city represented a milestone in gay activism in Los Angeles, where "'for the first time, an openly gay City Council' would control queer destinies."[88] As early as the 1960s, gay bars cropped up in suburban areas like Pasadena, Alhambra, Inglewood, and the San Fernando Valley, which continued to draw locals for decades. By the early 1980s, recalled one bar-goer, "All the crunchy Birkenstock lesbians were to the north" (North Hollywood, Sherman Oaks, Studio City, and Van Nuys), while West Hollywood drew in the more stylish crowd, sporting silk shirts, Jordache jeans, and Gucci shoes.[89] Cultural studies scholar Karen Tongson suggests that many queer suburban spaces were fleeting, pushed out by pressures like gentrification.[90] Still, suburbia had become familiar terrain for LA's LGBTQ population.

Another sign of changing families was the rise in working mothers, shattering earlier images of June Cleaver-type homemakers. These women were pushed and pulled into the workforce by several factors—the women's movement, which motivated many to seek out something beyond the grind of housework and childrearing; the economic slumps and soaring inflation of the 1970s, which meant that one paycheck was no longer enough to main-tain a middle-class standard of living; and the rising cost of housing in Los Angeles, one of the nation's most overheated housing markets.

Women's entry into the paid workforce did not automatically translate into autonomy when it came to real estate. Before 1974, women's income was routinely disregarded by mortgage lenders, reflecting a broader cul-ture of sex discrimination in the credit industry. Some lenders willing to consider a wife's income required what became known as a "pill letter" or "baby letter" from her doctor, ensuring that she was on the birth control pill or was infertile, thus negating any chance of a pregnancy that would inter-rupt the family's dual income. (They erroneously presumed that if a woman had a baby, she would stop working.)[91] Two measures passed by Congress in 1974, the Fair Housing Act and Equal Credit Opportunity Act, ended these practices by barring banks from discriminating in loan/credit decisions on the basis of sex. Banks were required to recognize a wife's income—pill or no pill—in qualifying applicants for a mortgage loan. Under these measures, more families and single women qualified for home loans, thus expanding the pool of buyers. Two-income families also qualified for larger mortgage loans, thus inducing them to buy higher-priced homes. Southern California lenders reported that one-third to one-half of loans in the 1970s were made to dual-income families, a significant jump from previous years. In a self-perpetuating loop, these factors helped drive up home prices and push more suburban wives into the workforce.[92]

Subjected to the greatest economic pressures, middle-class suburbs had the highest proportion of working wives after 1970, in towns like El Segundo, Carson, Cerritos, Walnut, Bellflower, Lakewood, La Verne, and South Pasadena. A tipping point was 1980, when over half of LA's suburban women worked outside the home; working women essentially traded places with homemakers as the new statistical norm in suburbia. By 2000, in suburbs like South Pasadena, La Verne, Sierra Madre, and Lakewood, more than 70% of women with children held paid jobs.[93] Among Black American families, mothers often went to work to bolster family income to pay for mortgages; their income was needed to offset racial wage discrimination. As one study noted, "black wives have to be more economically active in order to pursue the American dream."[94]

Trends among housewives split along class lines. In the 1950–1960s, more than three-quarters of mothers stayed at home with the children in nearly every suburban town—from rich, to middle- and working class. After 1970, while their numbers declined overall, the richest and poorest towns had the largest numbers of at-home wives. The implications of this broader decline were wide-ranging. For neighborhood life, it suggested a gradual disappearance of housewives' "eyes on the street," heightening parental anxiety about public safety and crime. It also had selective impact on neighborhood social unity. As working women had less time to spare, they withdrew from active engagement in community affairs, especially in the middle-class suburbs. It's no coincidence that some of the most vigorous voluntary activism happened in the poorest and wealthiest towns where stay-at-home mothers were fairly prevalent—from immigrant and environmental justice movements in South Gate, Maywood, and La Puente, to feverish philanthropic and educational work in Pasadena, San Marino, and Beverly Hills.[95]

Despite the trend toward household diversity, married couples held a statistical edge in the suburbs. They retained a majority voice, and their vision would continue to carry weight as social realities shifted around them.

Housing characteristics reflected another crucial dimension of suburban continuity and change. The single-family home persisted, but it was increasingly accompanied by other forms: condos, townhomes, apartments, backyard granny flats, even garage rentals. In most cases these traditional houses didn't disappear; they often remained in protected R-1 zones. They remained a fixture of the landscape across miles and miles of LA County, retaining numerical dominance over generations. The protections afforded to these R-1 neighborhoods made it difficult for higher-density alternatives to be built. As might be expected, the wealthy picturesque enclaves had the highest proportion of single-family homes, consistently, over time.

Even so, after 1970, a greater variety of housing types—especially multifamily housing—proliferated across many suburban areas, from wealthy to poor. By 2000, for example, in Covina, Downey, Malibu, and Lancaster, multifamily housing comprised between 20% and 50% of all housing.[96] Rentals were also common in edge cities and working-class suburbs, ranging from high-end condos to informal accessory dwelling units (ADUs). In LA, multifamily housing often blended into the suburban landscape, creating what historian Matthew Lasner described as "a new kind of hybrid built environment" of low-slung condos, townhomes, garden apartments, and, in poorer suburbs, stucco apartments.[97] In large metros like Los Angeles, New York, and Boston, by 2009, roughly one-third of homeowners lived in multifamily housing. This reflected, too, the changing social profile of suburban households, as seniors, singles, and

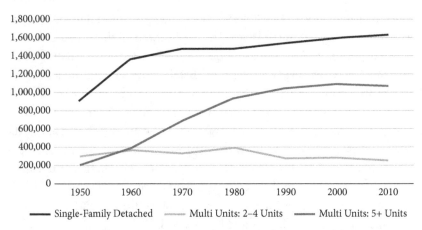

Figure 2.5 Type of housing in Los Angeles County, 1950–2010 (shown in raw numbers).

US Census dataset, 1950–2010.

single parents drove the demand for affordable homes that required less maintenance.[98]

A related trend was the rise of common interest developments (CIDs), a form of privatized communities. The three main types of CIDs were planned developments, condos, and coops, where individual property ownership and collective ownership of common areas (usually by a Homeowners' Association, or HOA) were divided in some way. They were usually self-governed entities that charged HOA fees, provided services for residents, and imposed rules and regulations on individual properties, called covenants, conditions, and restrictions (CC&Rs). CIDs emerged in the 1970s, with the greatest growth occurring after 1980. In California, by 2004, nearly one-quarter of the housing stock was part of a CID. Despite stereotypes about such communities being white, privatized havens, in the LA region CIDs were as ethnoracially diverse as other neighborhoods.[99] Gated communities were one subset of CIDs. In the LA metro area, by 2000, 11.7% of housing units were behind gates, while 18.2% were behind walls. This was much higher than the national average, though typical of Sunbelt Cities which led the way in walled-off communities. In LA, fear of rising crime in the 1980s and racial violence during the 1992 Rodney King uprising fueled some of this demand, which spread from elite Pacific Palisades to the Black middle-class neighborhood of Athens Heights in South LA, to the Mar Vista Gardens public housing project on the westside. One national study from 2000 found considerable diversity among residents living behind walls, including people of color, low-income families, and renters.[100]

Since 1970, the fastest rates of housing growth occurred in the newer corporate suburbs such as Palmdale, Walnut, San Dimas, and Lancaster. The slowest rates of growth occurred in some of LA's richest and poorest suburbs—including the gateway suburbs, which were fully built out by the 1970s, and elite enclaves like San Marino, Agoura Hills, and La Cañada, with their tight spatial restrictions.[101] Parallel pressures on the housing supply from rich and poor communities would help fuel LA's mounting housing affordability crisis.

Those pressures also helped create LA County's bifurcated housing landscape—overcrowded and undercrowded at the same time. On the one hand were the green suburban neighborhoods resistant to multifamily housing. On the other were "areas that are the Wild West," as real estate scholar Greg Morrow put it, where extreme overcrowding in tiny apartments, backyard garage units, and rental homes created a veritable human rights crisis. And despite LA's reputation for sprawl, in 1990 and 2000 Los Angeles-Long Beach-Santa Ana was the nation's densest urbanized area, ahead of New York-Newark; similar trends continued to the 2020s.[102] Both sprawl and severe overcrowding existed in the suburbs, exacerbating the extremes of wealth inequality itself. Los Angeles may have gotten denser over time, but this happened in highly uneven ways.[103]

From 1950 to 2020, a metric called "housing burden" rose steadily and painfully in LA County. Tracking the ratio of income to housing, it shows how housing costs rose much faster than income, thrusting Los Angeles into the ranks of the nation's most overheated housing markets. In 1950, a typical home cost three times the income of a typical family, which experts deemed a fiscally healthy ratio.[104] In 1990, it rose to nearly six times, and in 2010, it was seven times. Incomes for most families were falling far behind home prices, making homeownership an increasingly heavy burden on household budgets.[105] LA's rising housing prices reflected trends across coastal California, where home prices after 1970 raced far ahead of national averages. After the 2007–2009 Great Recession downturn, home prices in LA surged once again, while in LA's wealthiest suburbs, such as San Marino, even the Great Recession didn't stop the unrelenting upward trajectory of home prices.

Rising housing prices had myriad effects on life in Los Angeles, including spikes in homelessness, housing overcrowding, a population exodus of

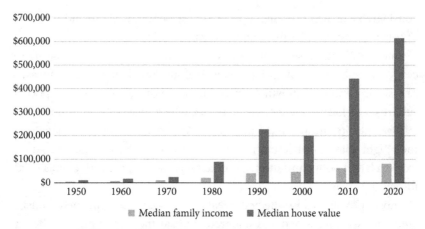

Figure 2.6 The "housing burden" in Los Angeles County, 1950–2020.
Note: Median house value is for owner-occupied housing units.
US Census dataset, 1950–2020; 2020 data from US Census American Community Survey.

whites and Blacks, rising commuting times to "drive-til-you-qualify" exurbs, and growing wealth inequality. Those who bought homes during opportune price dips benefitted from the long-term ballooning equity in their home. Some maximized their property by renting out spare rooms and backyard garages, parlaying homeownership into transfers of intergenerational wealth. To some degree, these advantages transcended ethnoracial lines. Those who missed these opportunities found that rising home prices became yet another stubborn barrier to entering the ranks of suburban homeownership.

If homeownership was a linchpin of the suburban experience, in Los Angeles it held on with an increasingly tenuous grasp. Homeownership gradually eroded in LA County from 1950 to 2010, part of California's overall lag behind the rest of the nation.[106] In the suburban municipalities, homeowners retained majority status from 1950 to 2010, if by a shrinking margin (57.7% to 51.2%). This suggested that, while suburban homeowners retained numerical power, they perhaps had a more tenuous hold on that power.

As with so many other metrics of "traditional" suburbia—such as the number of single-family homes, nuclear families with kids, and low density—the richest suburbs retained the highest levels of homeownership over time. In 1960, homeownership was common in an array of suburbs—from rich San Marino to blue-collar Duarte. By 1980, it was most prevalent in wealthy picturesque enclaves and a few sitcom and corporate suburbs. The suburbs with

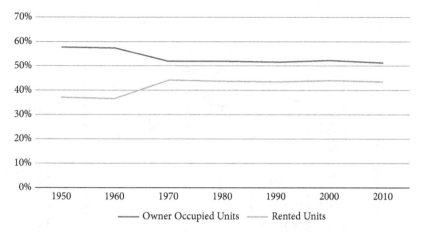

Figure 2.7 Housing tenure in Los Angeles suburbs, showing the percentage of homeowners and renters in occupied units of all suburban municipalities of the County, 1950–2010.

Note: This aggregates data from all municipalities in LA County, except LA City.

US Census dataset, 1950–2010.

the lowest homeownership rates—and thus highest tenancy rates—included edge cities like Glendale, Pasadena, and Santa Monica, with their abundant multifamily housing, as well as some of LA's poorest towns such as Cudahy, Huntington Park, and Bell Gardens, where tenants packed into apartments, single-family homes, and informal units in backyards.[107]

When it came to changes in suburban homeownership in Los Angeles from 1950 to 2010, the most profound transformation was racial. Over the years, the number of nonwhite homeowners rose steadily until they surpassed whites in 2010. In part, this can be explained by the simple demographic crossover from white to nonwhite in LA, yet it also signaled the overall economic advancement of Latinos, Asians, and Black Americans and their entry into suburbia. This trend began to recast the relationship between race and suburban property. While multiracial homeownership represented a breakthrough in some ways, giving nonwhites access to a crucial American pathway for opportunity and upward mobility, it operated unevenly across different ethnoracial groups.

By 1980, a small number of suburbs were havens of nonwhite homeownership. They were led by Compton, where Black homeowners tended to their tidy homes and gardens.[108] Then followed Carson, Cerritos, and Lynwood, and towns like Gardena, Monterey Park, Inglewood, Walnut, and Pico Rivera,

Table 2.1 Homeownership rates among white and nonwhites in Los Angeles, 1950–2010. Percentage figure shows the percent of all owner-occupied units.

	Los Angeles County				Los Angeles City				LA suburban municipalities			
	white owner occupied		non-white owner occupied		white owner occupied		non-white owner occupied		white owner occupied		non-white owner occupied	
	#	%	#	%	#	%	#	%	#	%	#	%
1950	705,516	96.0	29,199	4.0	284,052	93.0	21,341	7.0	421,464	98.2	7,858	1.8
1960	1,027,929	93.7	69,667	6.3	358,467	88.5	46,495	11.5	669,462	96.7	23,172	3.3
1970	1,056,148	89.5	123,795	10.5	349,820	83.3	69,981	16.7	706,328	92.9	53,814	7.1
1980	1,038,892	78.5	284,505	21.5	341,552	74.7	115,823	25.3	697,340	80.5	168,682	19.5
1990	897,462	62.7	543,368	37.3	304,354	63.4	175,514	36.6	593,108	61.7	367,854	38.3
2000	772,853	51.5	726,891	48.5	268,037	54.5	223,845	45.5	504,816	50.1	503,046	49.9
2010	714,542	46.3	830,207	53.7	261,431	51.9	242,432	48.1	453,111	43.5	587,775	56.5

which each had significant, varying shares of Asians, Blacks, and Latinos. By 2010, nonwhite homeowners represented majorities in nine suburbs, and they held substantial proportions in the more affordable exurbs of Palmdale, Lancaster, and Santa Clarita; the sitcom suburbs of Norwalk and Lakewood; the new corporate suburbs of Walnut and Diamond Bar, which were heavily Asian; and well-established diverse towns like Pomona, Inglewood, and Compton. By this point, Asian, Latino, and Black homeowners were well represented across LA's suburban landscapes. While predatory lending leading up to the Great Recession of 2007–2008 may have inflated these numbers, the overall trend of rising nonwhite homeownership marked a sea change in LA suburbia.[109]

Some ethnoracial differences persisted in Angelenos' ability to buy a home. For example, in the 1970s, the homeownership gap between Blacks and whites grew (despite consistency in income differences) due to persistent residential segregation and bias by lending institutions. In 1990, whites continued to have the highest rates of homeownership, followed by Asians, then substantially lower rates for Blacks and Latinos. Blacks and US-born Latinos were the most likely to own their homes free and clear, without a mortgage, ahead of whites and US-born Asians.[110]

For people of color, homeownership could present profoundly varied outcomes, both positive and negative. On the one hand, homeownership did not always confer the same advantages to people of color that whites enjoyed. Among Mexican Americans, for example, homeownership did not automatically generate upward economic mobility as it tended to for whites. In places like Pomona, Latinos homeownership and access to suburban amenities, such as good schools, were often diminished by white flight, fiscal abandonment, and exclusion from municipal resources. Persistent white racism underlay much of this inequity.[111] Among Black homeowners, some were the targets of what historian Keeanga-Yamahtta Taylor terms "predatory inclusion," the federally backed system that allowed the private real estate industry to extend mortgage financing on expensive, unequal terms. Especially in the late 1960s and 1970s, as part of HUD homeownership programs, Blacks were pulled into these nefarious real estate practices, paying higher prices for substandard dwellings, with costly origination fees. These programs zeroed in on poorer, segregated urban areas and older, segregated suburbs; in LA, this particularly meant South LA and Watts.[112] These practices seemed less prevalent in diversifying middle-class suburbs like Lakewood. In the 1960s and 1970s, one analyst found that a rising number of poor people lived in owner-occupied homes in both Black and white neighborhoods, often in substandard dwellings.[113] Even homeownership did not mitigate against poverty.

On the other hand, nonwhite homeownership could promote positive trends, such as wealth accumulation, community rootedness, community building, and political voice. Owning a home could confer economic advantages through property appreciation, tax breaks, and protection from market fluctuations through a fixed mortgage, together promoting generational wealth. For working-class people, such as the Latinos and Black Americans of South Los Angeles, homeownership could provide a means for "creating a sense of security, familiarity, autonomy, and future-making activities attached to place." South LA's rate of Latino homeownership rose from 25% to 32% from 1990 to 2000, and it remained stable even through the financial crisis.[114] For immigrants, homeownership was a powerful signifier of rootedness and a reinforcer of community and civic belonging.[115] Analysts often use immigrant homeownership as a proxy for gauging this attachment to place, and they have detected positive recent trends. In the last decades of the twentieth century, immigrant homeownership rose so significantly that it drove up homeownership rates overall. From 1990 to 2000, immigrants accounted for 73.9% of homeownership growth in California and 20.7% nationwide, making them a stabilizing force in the housing market. In Los Angeles in 1998, the 10 most common last names of homebuyers were, in descending order, Garcia, Lee, Rodriguez, Lopez, González, Martinez, Hernandez, Kim, Smith, and Perez. This was especially notable since immigrants spent more on housing than native-born residents of all ethnoracial groups. Though the price was high, the desire to own was strong enough to drive these trends.[116] Among Latinos, homeownership rates rose the longer they had been in the country. Other immigrant groups showed similar trends.[117] Even among undocumented immigrants, 31% of them owned a home in 2014; they were considered good mortgage risks by lenders.[118] These trends signified a crucial indicator of civic and economic commitment.[119]

More than race and ethnicity, an even stronger predictor of homeownership and home values was age. Older people had higher homeownership rates than younger people across all ethnoracial groups. In 2000, among whites in California, for example, the homeownership rate was 35.2% for 25- to 34-year-olds, 60.8% for 35- to 44-year-olds, and 81.1% for people aged 65–74. Older people also generally owned more expensive homes.[120]

While renters were a growing presence in LA County, they remained a numerical minority within suburban municipalities as a whole. While renters were vastly outnumbered in most suburbs in 1950, they became majorities in 26 suburban towns by 1980, and in 36 towns by 2010. With few exceptions, renters did not translate this numerical power into political power. This is evident, for example, in the difficulties that rent control has faced in Los Angeles since 1950.[121] In suburban communities, tenants' voices and interests were frequently overshadowed by homeowners, whose concerns have traditionally shaped local priorities and policy in America's suburbs.

———

By the turn of the new millennium, suburban fortunes spread unevenly across LA County. Wealth clustered in edge cities, in the beach towns, and in the picturesque enclaves. Poverty persisted in south LA and the suburbs surrounding downtown, but also alighted in suburban neighborhoods from the San Fernando to the San Gabriel Valleys. The extremes of inequality had sunk deeply into suburbia, creating both opportunities and strains. The suburbs also became a space of growing diversity by race, ethnicity, family composition, and homeownership. Perhaps most profoundly, suburban homeownership took on new racial meanings as people of color caught up to—then surpassed—whites. In places like Walnut, Carson, Cerritos, Pico Rivera, Diamond Bar, Baldwin Park, La Puente, and Compton, they were the majority of homeowners, making the decisions and determinations that would define community life. Would they adhere to well-established traditions enacted by generations of white suburbanites before them? Or would they embrace new values and possibilities? As these new suburbanites made choices about their neighborhoods, conflict and contestations emerged over definitions of belonging and who had a "right to the suburb." The variety of answers would expose both the promise and the limitations in this new suburban era.

3

Suburban Political and Civic Cultures, Across the Spectrum

In Los Angeles, diversity touched nearly all 86 suburban towns after 1980. This chapter takes a bird's eye view to explore how suburban political and civic cultures evolved across LA County in the wake of this shift. Did those places undergo changes in political and community values? And what happened when suburban whites were mostly out of the picture? Did the new suburbanites pivot away from time-worn suburban values toward something new, or did they stay the course?

Given the sheer variety of suburban places, drawing sweeping conclusions about their political cultures is difficult if not impossible. An alternative approach is to consider these cultures as existing along a spectrum.[1] At one end were communities that embraced well-established suburban ideals and defensive homeowner politics. The ideal looked something like this—single-family homes set in green yards, on tree-lined streets, in communities with schools, parks, and churches, locally controlled, and well-suited for raising children. Homeownership and low taxes were key, and for many years whiteness was part of the vision. To defend this ideal from social change, residents used the language of property rights, localism, neighborhood schools, and "quality of life."[2] At the other end were suburbs that embraced a more inclusive, multicultural suburban ideal. These towns accepted ethnic and racial newcomers, their spatial practices, and in some cases low-income residents by allowing multifamily housing. Moving beyond the first crucial step of accepting new population groups, the multicultural suburban ideal encompassed a fairly progressive approach to ethnoracial and even class integration and even embraced ideals of inclusive democracy.[3]

By offering snapshots of suburban political cultures at different points along this spectrum, this chapter reveals some of the variety of political cultures and civic ideals that began to find expression across suburban landscapes. As demographic diversity intensified, it spawned both defensive reactions as well as alternative suburban lifeways and ideals. This overview helps to situate the book's case studies within a larger schema of suburban political culture. For example, immigration profoundly impacted both San Marino and South Gate. Although one was affluent, the other working class, they responded similarly to immigrant newcomers in resisting the ethnic influences that new arrivals brought with them, be it an ethnic grocery store or a jerry-rigged garage conversion. Resistance in those suburbs was just one thread of a larger tapestry that made up suburban life in LA.

The chapter begins with the postwar period, when white residents articulated influential ideologies and honed tools to defend their communities and way of life. Some of these tools would be deployed by the next generations of suburbanites. It then moves into the era of diversity to explore various suburban reaction to social change. One thread explores the "warmth of welcome" ethnic newcomers received in suburbia. A second thread focuses on suburban responses to undocumented immigrants and day laborers who represented not only immigrant "outsiders" but also the working poor. Next, the chapter traces examples of progressive ideals and politics, showing that suburbia was far from a monolithic bastion of conservatism or self-serving liberalism. In scattered communities, suburbanites worked for social justice and pushed against deeply entrenched suburban norms. While their efforts did not always define the overarching political culture of their suburbs, they did bring alternative perspectives and agendas to their communities. Finally, the chapter briefly considers electoral politics concerning issues such as immigrant rights, law and order, and taxation.

Suburban political culture did not always align neatly with the major political parties, as scholarship on suburbs across the nation has demonstrated. Plenty of suburban causes—such as opposition to school busing, housing integration, taxation, or affordable housing—attracted support from conservatives and liberals alike, knitting together what historian Matthew Lassiter termed the "volatile middle," a bi-partisan consensus united around their interests as homeowners, taxpayers, and parents. In a similar way, non-partisan "Not In My Back Yard" (NIMBY) campaigns proliferated against projects like group homes, AIDS clinics, daycare centers, garbage dumps, and nuclear power plants.[4] The same tendencies were apparent across the LA metropolis, which grew increasingly blue and racially diverse. The cumulative effect of these actions reinforced metropolitan inequality while sustaining suburban privilege.

The larger context of California politics is an important framework for what happened in LA's suburbs. The 1990s were a decade of racialized politics and turmoil, when demographic and economic change and upheaval were reaching a boiling point in the state. Whites were slipping into the minority. LA's 1992 civil unrest laid bare festering racial anger. And recession woes were taking hold as the state suffered nearly one-half of the nation's net job losses in the early 1990s following factory closures and federal defense spending cuts. One result was a political backlash that embraced law and order, intensified policing, and punitive anti-immigrant measures. A series of racially oriented state ballot measures were proposed during this reactionary decade. These were joined by law-and-order measures that implicitly targeted people of color. All of these measures were taken up as models around the nation. After 2000, the state's contentious racialized political culture began to simmer down and it leaned leftward, propelling a blue wave. A confluence of factors spurred this shift, including economic and demographic change, structural political changes, and the rise of grassroots social justice activism that linked community organizing with voter mobilization. The result was a massive political realignment in California from red to blue.[5]

LA suburbs were part of this broader statewide shift toward liberalism. Voter registration in LA suburbs, in fact, revealed overwhelming Democratic dominance since 1962. From 1962 to 1980, around 70% of suburban towns had a predominance of registered Democrats, belying the image of Southern California as a bastion of right-wing suburban warriors.[6] In 1990, Republican registration surged in some suburbs, but those towns were still outnumbered by majority Democrat suburbs. In later years, suburban Democrats continued to dominate by ever-growing margins, reflecting the state's leftward turn. Another striking trend was the rise of "Decline to State" (DTS) as a party preference, reflecting a broader California pattern.[7] Similar to what other states would call "Independent," DTS began showing up in 1990 in Asian-heavy, middle-class Cerritos, Diamond Bar, Monterey Park, and Walnut and has accelerated since 2000. By 2010, in line with state-wide trends, the DTS category began to outnumber Republicans in a number of diverse suburbs. One analyst noted that younger voters, Asian Americans, and those leaving the Democratic Party but not yet ready to register Republican tended to select DTS; all of these groups leaned blue.[8] The trend contributed to an overall numerical decline in registered Democrats, suggestive of a possible moderation in liberal identity in these emergent suburbs and a move toward the middle.

The evolution of suburban political culture in LA, then, existed within a broader metropolitan context of liberalism punctuated by intensive moments of racial anger and anxiety, anti-immigrant panic, and economic angst. Along LA's spectrum of political culture, people of all political leanings, races, and ethnicities came down on all sides of the issues. Homeowners—of all colors—had a tendency to embrace long-standing white suburban ideals and defensive practices as a means of protecting communities and property values. But there were exceptions. These variations are a crucial part of the story.

White Baselines

White residents spearheaded the most powerful initiatives of suburban political culture during the 1950s and 1960s. Many derived their core political identity as white middle-class, taxpaying homeowners within the context of their own neighborhoods. They made a direct connection between their role as home-owning taxpayers and their right to a particular quality of life, defined especially as good schools, safe streets, and clean, well-maintained, racially segregated neighborhoods. They valued the privatism inherent in the single-family home. And they developed a sense of entitlement to these advantages, which they perceived as the just rewards for their own efforts. Although a broad web of state policies subsidized and privileged them, most white suburbanites didn't see it that way; they believed their achievement of the suburban dream was strictly the result of their own hard work. This suburban worldview transcended political party lines.[9]

Evoking the language of "white rights," color-blind meritocratic individualism, and homeowner entitlement, suburbanites across LA and the nation waged numerous political battles to protect their communities. These campaigns began locally but ultimately influenced federal policy and the national parties. The Republican Party first connected to this voting bloc at the national level starting in the late 1960s, but Democrats eventually came to support suburban political priorities as well. Although some white suburbanites supported a more racially inclusive, socially just vision for their communities, there were often limits to this racial liberalism. Whites continued to control the pace of racial integration, maintain class barriers around their communities, and hold on to local power. Their efforts etched deep patterns of race and class inequality across metropolitan areas as suburban agendas gained bipartisan backing.[10]

In LA, postwar suburban actions included outright resistance to people of color moving in, opposition to taxes, staunch resistance to affordable housing, and resistance to school busing via groups like BUSTOP, which gained widespread regional support. By the 1960s, a powerful slow-growth movement led by white homeowners waged successful campaigns to institute exclusive residential zoning, protect open lands, and block high-density zoning.[11] Homeowners in the San Fernando Valley, who were particularly militant on this issue, also pressed to protect large lot sizes and, in some areas, horse properties. In the San Gabriel Valley, the same anti-growth impulses manifested as opposition to apartment construction, intended to keep away poorer Asian and Latino immigrants. Together, these efforts represented "a reassertion of social privilege," as Mike Davis put it, to preserve and protect suburban landscapes of single-family homes and yards, homeownership, and racial purity.[12]

By the 1970s, after civil rights laws began abolishing older segregation tactics, suburbanites intensified their use of "color-blind" municipal tools—like ordinances on land use and behavior in public spaces—to exclude unwelcome groups. These groups included the working poor, the unhoused, undocumented immigrants, and even ethnic immigrants who sought to open ethnic businesses or put ethnic adornments on their property. The spatial policing of these "others" increasingly came to demarcate boundaries of inclusion and exclusion. Suburb after suburb began passing ordinances targeting newly conceived threats to the suburban ideal—from Asian-language characters and ethnic businesses, to yard sales, bright paint colors, day laborers, and multifamily housing—which together represented foreign threats to familiar landscapes. These efforts were first spearheaded by white suburbanites who were later joined by their Asian, Latino, and African American neighbors in many communities.

Zoning and housing policies in turn kept out working-class and poor people. After 1970, housing policies in California were in a tug-of-war between class inclusion, created by regional and state initiatives, and class exclusion, emerging from suburban localities. Until then, the California constitution had allowed suburbanites to block affordable housing by a local vote, which they repeatedly did. From 1950 to 1970, voters in local elections rejected about half of all public housing proposals in the state. In the 1970s and 1980s, suburbs like La Puente, Torrance, and South Gate used building moratoriums to block affordable housing, while Pomona passed a resolution to achieve the same end. As one middle-class Woodland Hills resident in

1971 put it, "low-income housing represents all the problems I moved here to the San Fernando Valley to get away from."[13] In a turn toward inclusivity in the 1970s, California enacted a series of Housing Element Laws, which required all municipalities and counties to include a plan for affordable housing in their master plans. Even small suburbs had to detail how they would provide housing for all income groups in order to meet their share of regional housing need. Yet there was virtually no enforcement of this law. It was up to individual suburbs to follow through. Without incentives or consequences, the law tended to promote "planning, not performance," as a 2002 state commission found.[14]

These tactics—from aggressive crackdowns to passive noncompliance—became powerful protective tools for the slow growthers and for suburbanites in general. By the time suburbia began diversifying in earnest after 1980, these tools for exclusion were firmly in place and available to the next generation of suburbanites—if they choose to use them.

From Warm to Cold: Ethnic Suburbs Along a Spectrum

In places with growing ethnic populations, a suburb's stance on built landscapes and public spaces became a telling marker of local political sensibilities. Groups that were free to fully use those spaces could claim cultural citizenship, including visible expressions of language, everyday customs, and artistic practices. This "right to the suburb" signaled membership in the community itself. Those denied that freedom lost something vital; in some cases, they acceded to that loss. Suburban spatial politics intensified in the 1980s, in reaction to the ethnic changes remaking many communities, a realm where political sensibilities were laid bare within the suburban world.[15]

It's no surprise, then, that suburban spatial practices became heated flashpoints. Across LA, some suburbs allowed ethnic practices to flourish fully while others sought to protect the "traditional" white American look of their suburb and suppress overt signs of ethnicity. This often became a vivid indicator of receptivity toward ethnic newcomers. If a suburb was warm toward them, they had a better chance for full integration. If it was cold, they were marginalized, and that process of integration could take longer.[16] That context of "warmth of welcome" is crucial for understanding the dynamics of everyday social and civic life in ethnically transforming suburbs. It exposes, too, new suburban cleavages along lines of class, national identity, and immigration status, dividing ethnic communities internally and complicating simplistic profiles of ethnic suburbia.

One of the most significant aspects of spatial politics in LA was the role played by pioneer ethnic suburbanites who gained the power to include and exclude newcomers who followed. Many in this generation saw value in assimilating to existing suburban norms. Within this milieu, the arrival of new or unacculturated immigrants tended to elicit the most hostile responses, at times revealing schisms between first- and subsequent-generation ethnics. While ethnic suburban residence represented a crucial breakthrough in some ways as a pathway toward opportunity and upward mobility, it could also work to reinforce inequality. But there were also cases where co-ethnics—across class, generations, and national identity—offered mutual support and understanding. These dynamics revealed variations around the struggle for inclusion in ethnic suburbs.

At the warm end of the spectrum were the "ethnoburbs," where ethnicity was allowed to fully flourish.[17] Ethnoburbs had heavy immigrant clustering, were often multi-ethnic, and contained ethnic businesses and institutions that reinforced a strong sense of ethnic identity in the place itself. They were continuously reinvigorated by the transnational inflow of people, investments, and goods, and they were often gateway communities—the first place that new immigrants settled. The economic development of the ethnoburbs revealed their growing power and clout over time as they evolved from ethnic service centers to global economic outposts.[18] Their vibrancy was bolstered by two interrelated patterns: the persistence of ethnic clustering (as opposed to gradual spatial dispersal) and the continued influx of new immigrants.[19] The ethnoburb concept upends the older theory that, when immigrants moved to the suburbs (especially European ethnics after World War II), they quickly assimilated and gained the advantages of whiteness. In the ethnoburbs, by contrast, ethnicity was reinforced and sustained.[20]

Ethnoburbs were especially recognizable by their built landscapes. They were replete with ethnic businesses and professional services, realty companies, immigration services, language schools, temples, and travel agencies, all displaying signs in native languages. Proto ethnoburbs in LA included Boyle Heights and Crenshaw. Boyle Heights was one of LA's earliest suburbs, first linked across the LA River to downtown by horsecar. It soon became one of LA's most racially open, multicultural communities, housing Eastern European Jews, ethnic Mexicans, Japanese Americans,

African Americans, Italians, Greeks, and Russians, among others. Many were immigrants, and their ethnic businesses, places of worship, and mutual aid groups found unabashed expression. In the Crenshaw district, Japanese Americans and African Americans broke the color line to settle the area in the postwar years. By the late 1950s, Japanese American developers planned a shopping center and suburban subdivisions. Crenshaw Square was designed with "Oriental" flourishes and hosted a Japanese summer festival to rival Little Tokyo's.[21]

After the 1980s, ethnoburbs flourished in the San Gabriel Valley, propelled by the process of globalization. They included San Gabriel, Alhambra, Rosemead, Hacienda Heights, Rowland Heights, and, above all, Monterey Park, which stood out as LA's quintessential ethnoburb. Monterey Park was LA's first suburb to become majority Asian American, and it experienced heated battles over ethnic claims to suburbia. The triumph of Chinese Americans and Latinos in these struggles resulted in the ascendance of Chinese American political power and a greater local acceptance of ethnic aesthetic influences.[22] In Rowland Heights, Hacienda Heights, and the City of Industry in the east San Gabriel Valley, Asian identity was also highly conspicuous in displays of Asian shops, offices, factories, and houses of worship. The Hsi Lai Buddhist Temple in Hacienda Heights was a vivid example. While initially whites resisted the planned temple, it was built and looms above a sea of mass-produced suburban homes. In retail areas, Chinese language signs, neon lights, dense design, crowds, and Asian wares lent distinctive aesthetics to ethnoburban spaces.[23]

Asian aesthetics were also visible in some ethnoburb residences, which might include bonsai-style landscaping, blue tile roofs, and gracefully curving roof lines. Some Chinese American suburbanites practiced *feng shui* in their homes, including the practice of cutting down trees that grew in front of the house (believed to block positive energy from entering the home). In Arcadia, liberal house demolition measures led to a wave of mansionization, some designed with *feng shui* elements and "wok-friendly kitchens aimed at wealthy transnational Chinese searching for American real estate investments."[24]

The emergence of the San Gabriel Valley ethnoburbs was propitious to say the least. They developed on the heels of Proposition 13 (1978), the tax-cutting measure that decimated local municipal revenues. With fresh, steady infusions of transnational wealth, ethnoburbs were replenished and

Figure 3.1 Ethnoburbia in the San Gabriel Valley, 2014. The Buddhist Hsi Lai Temple in Hacienda Heights was a vivid marker of an ethnic presence in suburbia, a hallmark of the ethnoburbs.

Photos by Becky Nicolaides.

Figure 3.2 The "enacted Latino landscapes" of suburban LA, 2013. These outdoor areas were dynamic and lively as residents turned front yards into spaces to express ethnic culture, sell wares, socialize, and replicate traditional Mexican house forms. This upended traditional suburban norms like privacy around single-family homes and conformity to a common architectural style.
Photos by James Rojas.

strengthened financially at a time when most municipalities were struggling to make ends meet.

Ethnoburbs also emerged in East and Southeast Los Angeles. There, Latinos used suburban spaces to support both their class and cultural needs, creating what James Rojas termed an "enacted Latino landscape." For example, in the suburban neighborhoods of East LA, an unincorporated area without strict land-use regulations, residents used their front yards, driveways, and adjacent streets as places to socialize, sell goods, and just hang out. They sold goods along sidewalks or propped items against front-yard fences, patterns of street vending that evoked the streetscapes of Latin America. Suburban homes incorporated touches like Mexican-style courtyards, and fences became places where people converged, a cultural landscape reminiscent of Mexico. Modest homes were thus transformed into spaces that served social, economic, and cultural purposes often in very public ways, challenging traditional suburban mores of privatism.[25] These spatial practices fostered the kind of interaction that could propel civic belonging and even unified activism.

In the southeast suburbs, Latino residents similarly used their property to meet their economic and cultural needs. During the 1970s and early 1980s, they sold goods from front yards, raised chickens and goats, and one man grew tall stalks of corn in his front yard, reminiscent of practices in Mexico. Street vending, sometimes without permits, was also common. This activity helped revitalize economically struggling suburbs and made the streets safer. One survey found that mothers in South LA often lacked transportation to stores with a decent selection of food; the street vendors partially met that need.[26]

At the other end of the spectrum were suburbs where ethnicity was suppressed, whether by coercion or cooperation. That suppression could occur in the realms of the built landscape, retail, public culture, housing, politics, or ethnic entrepreneurship.[27] San Gabriel Valley suburbs like San Marino, Diamond Bar, and Walnut retained an Anglo appearance even as they tipped to Asian American majorities. A suburb at the vanguard of this trend was affluent San Marino, which, after 1987, enacted some of the harshest measures in LA County to eradicate visible markers of the Asians living within its borders.[28]

One particularly effective tool against ethnic imprints in suburbia was the regulation of business signs. These measures dovetailed with the English Only movement that arose in the 1980s. While these measures (such as declaring English the official language) were largely symbolic at the state and national levels, at the local level their impacts were felt in everyday life, shaping the civic and physical atmosphere of a given community. This was particularly true of English signage laws, which began appearing in suburbs in the 1980s. These measures especially singled out Asian American and Pacific Islander (AAPI) groups, since their lettering was often indecipherable to English-speaking populations.[29] Signage ordinances laid bare local attitudes toward ethnic landscapes, often triggering emotional battles among residents.

One of LA County's earliest signage ordinances was passed in Gardena, a remarkably balanced suburb of whites, Blacks, Asians, and Latino residents. In 1982, the city council unanimously passed a measure requiring that foreign-language business signs include English and be easily readable from the nearest road. Gardena leaders cited public safety, to faciliate the work of police, firefighters, and the public in emergencies, an argument that would be repeated in other communities. Over the next seven years, other suburbs enacted similar measures that became even more specific in their restrictions. Most required a 50-50 balance of English and foreign letters. Temple City, Pomona, and Rosemead passed 50-50 laws, while Arcadia, San Gabriel, and San Marino passed stricter measures; San Marino demanded 80% English letters. Even two Latino suburbs—Bellflower and South Gate—tried to pass English-Only signage laws in the mid-1980s, setting off an immediate backlash from residents who found the measures both discriminatory and nonsensical given the region's deep history with Spanish-language place names. Measures in those two suburbs ultimately failed to pass.[30]

These laws essentially sought to codify the English language in the landscape and, in so doing, provoked debates around inclusion, exclusion, and the meaning of community. Proponents of the measures invariably cited public safety, the idea of English as a social unifier, and the concept of exclusion. Indecipherable signage, they argued, made long-time residents feel unwelcome, even segregated, in their own community. Opponents claimed the ordinances stoked racism, placed undue financial burdens on business owners, singled out the AAPI population, and interfered with their free speech right to advertise in their native language. They, too, invoked the argument of civic exclusion. As adult school teacher Luci Rios put it, "It would deny people the right to speak because it would make them ashamed to speak. I do not want to see any nationality humiliated in this way."[31]

The issue exploded most fiercely in Monterey Park, thanks in part to the efforts of Frank Arcuri, the self-styled leader of the English Only movement there. While trying to make English the official language of Monterey Park, then pushing for signage laws, Arcuri and his allies had inflamed racial tensions to a degree that the US Justice Department's Community Relations Service stepped in to mediate. After a protracted legal battle, the community finally reached a compromise measure in 1989 which required that the name and type of business appear in English without specifying a percentage of English letters. The signage controversy became a proxy for local race relations, triggering vigorous human relations work and ultimately sweeping in new Asian leadership, including Judy Chu, who was elected to the city council in 1988. The battle had laid bare strong racial resentments and coincided with intensifying white flight.[32]

Before long, Asian residents and business owners pushed back against signage laws, while civil rights groups like the American Civil Liberties Union (ACLU) and Asian Pacific American Legal Center (APALC) began monitoring developments around the issue. In 1989, Pomona, which had roughly a 5% Asian population, was the unlikely site of a legal turning point. The previous year, Pomona passed a 50-50 ordinance. As councilman Clay Bryant put it, the intention was to keep it from looking like another Monterey Park: "If [immigrants] are going to set up separate societies, I wish they'd just leave." Four months later, the Asian American Business Group of Pomona sued the city in federal court for violating their constitutional rights. They claimed the measure infringed upon their "personal, cultural, political and economic freedoms." In July 1989, a US district court struck down the Pomona signage law on the grounds that it violated the equal protection clause of the 14th Amendment by singling out a specific group—Asians—based on their national origin and obstructed their freedom of cultural expression.[33] Although not involved directly in the case, the ACLU vowed to sue other suburbs with similar laws, including San Gabriel, Arcadia, Rosemead, and Temple City. After this warning, communities scurried to enact alternative ordinances; Temple City revised its law merely to require nine-inch English letters, while Rosemead no longer specified a set percentage of English. The APALC said it didn't object to requiring an English description on signs, just not on every sign of a business, which would impose an undue financial burden on owners.[34]

Suburban battles over English-language signage flared up and then subsided by the 1990s, but they never went away. The issue had the effect of stoking racial animosity and, as historian Daniel HoSang observes, primed the public to support much harsher anti-immigrant measures, namely California's Proposition 187 (1994), which denied public benefits to undocuments immigrants, and Proposition 209 (1996), which nullified affirmative action in state hiring.[35] Even after the Pomona ruling, some suburbs retained their signage ordinances despite their legal precariousness. Others pursued the issue anew in later years. In 2006, for example, Hawthorne proposed an ordinance requiring English on most business signs. It had backing from Hawthorne's multicultural mix of business owners, including an Asian Indian, a Belize native, and an African American, illustrating how complex this issue was.[36]

English signage laws, design guidelines, and similar spatial policing measures together powerfully signaled to newcomers whose cultures were fully welcome. In some cases, anti-immigrant vandalism and social pressure reinforced local regulations. Quite quickly, many Asian American residents—especially those in the affluent suburbs where these regulations were strongest—came not only to accept but even champion the vision of an American design style. Among other benefits, this conferred a higher status on these Asian homeowners vis à vis those in the ethnoburbs. In these elite suburbs, property values were higher and schools were better. Clearly, there were payoffs for ethnic spatial suppression.[37]

In other suburbs with growing numbers of Latinos, similar efforts were made to protect Anglo suburban aesthetics while suppressing Latino landscapes and businesses. In a few cases, the suburbs led the way in devising these measures that became models for LA County as a whole. In some suburbs, these suppressive measures pitted middle-class homeowning Mexican Americans against recently arrived immigrants who engaged in practices like street vending and yard sales to make ends meet. After 1980, suburban leaders began backing measures that outlawed those practices as well as the use of vivid paint colors on homes and businesses and certain forms of outdoor socializing. Communities like Lakewood and South Gate passed measures banning piñatas in parks, while South Gate in 1993 outlawed sponaneous games of soccer in parks and began requiring permits.[38] While the stated goal was to restore a more traditional, residential suburban atmosphere, these measures effectively expanded policing authority over immigrants in the name of public health, order, safety, and aesthetics.[39]

Laws against push-cart vending—which targeted Latino immigrants selling products such as popsicles and fresh fruit—first appeared in the southeast suburbs: Norwalk, Cerritos, Lakewood, Hawaiian Gardens, Downey, Pico Rivera, Signal Hill, and Long Beach. Typical penalties were a $500 fine or six months in jail. Whittier required a $50 annual license, as well as a $30 fee for fingerprinting and photo, a burden on new cash-strapped immigrants. Similar measures spread into southeast suburbs like South Gate, Huntington Park, Montebello, Bellflower, and Hawthorne. In Huntington Park, vendors who couldn't show a drivers license or California ID card were subject to a citation and confiscation, which could mean the loss of a vendor's livelihood.[40] In June 1990, authorities there confiscated 32 coconuts, 85 watermelons, 120 mangoes, 743 bags of pork rinds, 53 churros, and 72 bags of spiced fruit. In African American-Latino Compton, a special enforcement team forced vendors out of the city and into unincorporated territory.[41]

Beginning in the 1980s, suburban yard sales also came under increasingly heavy regulation, which tended to penalize poor Latino residents. Historian Margaret Crawford notes that such measures reflected town leaders' views that a garage sale once or twice a year could be a "wholesome event" for eliminating residential waste, but the perennial vending of goods from front yards bordered on outright commerce, which contradicted suburban residential norms.[42] Yard sales were not only part of the enacted Latino landscape, but also a source of essential income for economically marginalized residents. During the 1980s, suburbs began passing ordinances that limited the number of days a resident could hold a yard sale (usually either once or twice a year), required a paid permit, and prohibited the posting of signs on public rights of way. Suburbs initially passing such restrictive measures included Azusa, Arcadia, El Monte, Pasadena, Pomona, and Sierra Madre; Glendale, Santa Monica, Inglewood, Artesia, Beverly Hills, Downey, South Gate, Maywood, Gardena, and Monterey Park imposed them by the 1990s. One early adopter was Azusa, which tipped toward a Latino majority in the 1980s. Suburban leaders there passed a measure in the early 1980s restricting yard sales to two per year. In response to push back, they exempted impoverished seniors who depended on yard sales for income and were subsequently allowed to hold them once a month.

The LA County Board of Supervisors took cues from these suburbs, passing its own measure in 1993 limiting yard sales to two per year and allowing only one posted sign. This rule applied to all unincorporated areas of the County. Repeat offenders could be charged with a misdemeanor and fined $1,000. By contrast, more lenient rules applied in LA City, which allowed five sales per year but also required a permit and the paying of taxes on all sales. Enforcement was an ongoing challenge, and in many areas—including East LA—yard sales persisted despite the measures. By 2015, Black and Latino residents in the West Athens and Florence-Firestone neighborhoods of South LA sparred over the issue. African American residents contended that daily yard sales were creating blight on the community as neighbors sold not just used goods, but also toilet paper, laundry detergent, and packaged foods, turning suburban front yards into "commercial enterprises." By this point, LA County had relaxed its rules to allow monthly sales, but enforcement remained difficult.[43]

Together, these suppressive spatial measures signified a desire for the recognizable touchstones of suburban Americana—English signs, tidy green yards, picket fences. In the late 1990s, majority Latino Huntington Park went so far as to help homeowners pay for that picket fence.[44] It was perhaps no coincidence that the proliferation of corporate-built suburbs in the 1970s and later—strictly controlled by covenants, conditions, and restrictions (CC&Rs)—occurred amid suburbia's rapid ethnoracial diversification. CC&Rs became a sweeping instrument for ensuring suburbia's bland, monotonous, generic built environment, devoid of any recognizable personal identity, ethnic or otherwise.

A suburb's receptivity to an ethnic presence was also revealed in policies toward immigrant entrepreneurs. On the one hand, in ethnoburbs ethnic businesses were supported and encouraged, reflecting a crucial interdependence between the ethnic economy and ethnic population. This synergy provided business opportunities, consumer necessities, immigrant jobs, and professional and managerial opportunities, all in one location. Fed by transnational flows of capital and people, this ethnic economic base was vital to both the formation and steady growth of ethnoburbs.[45] These patterns were strongest in the Asian ethnoburbs of the San Gabriel Valley, which became hubs of commercial activity. Asian malls were key centers of both commercial and social life. San Gabriel Square, dubbed locally as "The Great Mall of China" and the "Chinese Disneyland," housed an array of Chinese and Taiwanese shops and restaurants, anchored by a 99 Ranch Market.[46] By the 1990s, suburban businesses included the finance, insurance, and real estate sectors, with global ties. Realtors regularly worked with buyers from Asia who often paid cash for multimillion-dollar homes in upscale suburbs like San Marino, Arcadia, and Palos Verdes. Other global enterprises included import/export and logistics firms, making the ethnoburbs a focal point of international business, investment, and capital circulation.[47] In the process, these communities amassed ethnic wealth and built community resilience.

In less welcoming suburbs, immigrant entrepreneurs lacked such support. Asian suburbs like San Marino, Diamond Bar, and Walnut sought to avoid ethnic businesses altogether in order to preserve their carefully curated residential landscapes. Residents had easy access to the best, cheapest Chinese grocery stores, restaurants, and services in nearby ethnoburbs without having to alter the look of their own towns. Many expressed NIMBY attitudes toward ethnoburbia and prided themselves on the class advantage of their Anglo-looking suburbs.[48] This pattern was repeated in some southeast Latino suburbs as well. There, a different set of factors influenced local economic conditions, namely the deindustrialization of the area in the 1980s. Struggling to recover from that blow, these suburbs vigorously courted outside capital and investors, including corporate chains and Asian investors. Unlike the ethnoburbs, heavily infused by Asian investment capital which helped solidify Asian American claims upon these communities, in the southeast suburbs Latino capital played a much smaller role. In middle-class Downey, Mexican Americans and whites together resisted Latino businesses as a way of protecting the community's perceived class status.[49]

In some of these Latino suburbs, one consequence of this Anglo-centric development strategy was a civic disconnect: many business owners and workers did not live in these communities but instead commuted from surrounding towns. This trend contributed to a leadership void in these suburbs since fewer local business owners followed the traditional pathway to suburban political involvement, such as participation in the Chamber of Commerce.[50] In turn, South Gate, Maywood, Bell, and other southeast suburbs suffered a series of catastrophic political corruption scandals in the 1990s and early 2000s, a sign of these communities' fraying civic capacity. The warmth of welcome to immigrant entrepreneurs had clear civic and social consequences, influencing the process of integration or marginalization of the newest residents in these communities.

Suburban Responses to the Undocumented and Working Poor

If the spatial policing of ethnic landscapes was a form of soft power over ethnic and immigrant suburbanites, suburbs showed they could wield much harsher tools in their treatment of immigrants, especially the un-documented. While authority over immigration technically resided with the federal government alone—and was in fact denied to localities by the courts—federal retrenchment during the Reagan era began a process of passing authority to suburbs and other localities to do the work of immigration enforcement. As such, suburbs increasingly used their power over land use and behaviors in public spaces to essentially "do immigrant policing 'through the back door,'" as political scientist Monica Varsanyi put it.[51] At the same time, immigration control was increasingly framed as a law-and-order issue, creating a convergence of immigration control and crime control just as suburban authority was increasing. For example, some sub-urban city councils deployed local police powers to enforce immigration policy in partnership with Immigration and Naturalization Service (INS)/Immigration and Customs Enforcement (ICE) officials, or they imposed burdensome taxes and fees on the undocumented.[52] Through these tactics, suburbs cracked down on this increasingly vilified "other" in their communities and, in the process, suppressed their voice at city hall. This anti-immigrant activity and legislation notably hit Latino communities harder than Asian ones.[53]

Suburban reactions to undocumented immigrants consisted of a spectrum of policies. At one end were "sanctuary cities/suburbs," which extended protections to the undocumented, and, at the other, were suburbs that enacted harsh crackdowns. Both reflect varying levels of receptivity in the suburbs, some open and welcoming, others resistant and punitive. These actions could have deep consequences on the lives of the immigrants targeted, leading to possible loss of homes, jobs, and even deportation.

"Sanctuary city" status was an inclusive approach to immigrant rights that some suburbs adopted. While specific policies could vary, they generally forbade local officials—including the police—from notifying federal authorities about the immigration status of residents. They were based on the premise that all inhabitants should have the same basic rights regardless of their immigration status. One scholar estimated there were 45 sanctuary cities, suburbs, and states nationwide by 2008.[54] Los Angeles County was part of the trend. In the post-1980 era, a few municipalities declared themselves sanctuary cities, including Los Angeles City (in 1985),[55] Maywood (2006), Pomona (2006), and, in response to Trump administration anti-immigrant initiatives, Cudahy (2017), La Puente (2017), and Montebello (2017). By 2018, California declared itself a sanctuary state. Huntington Park telegraphed its pro-immigrant sentiments by appointing two undocumented immigrants to a municipal commission.[56]

At the same time, other suburbs took forceful stands in the opposite direction, such as majority white Santa Clarita and Lancaster, Asian/white Diamond Bar, and, in nearby Orange County, Costa Mesa, Los Alamitos, and Huntington Beach. Santa Clarita, which was 30% Latino in 2010, had its own Minutemen organization, a militia-based group seeking to stop undocumented immigration from Mexico. Lancaster, with a 37% Latino population, declared itself a "rule-of-law" city—meaning that undocumented immigrants were unwelcome—with support from Latino leaders and residents.[57] These were corporate suburbs along the county's edges, where home prices were cheaper and politics more conservative.

Day laborers, who came to represent the undocumented and working poor, were subjected to punitive policies in a growing number of suburbs. Their expanding presence after 1980 triggered harsh responses, including in areas with rising racial diversity. As an issue, day labor had a strong connection to suburbia, shaped by a confluence of shifting immigration policy and insatiable homeowner demand for help with various household projects, from home renovations to landscaping. After the postwar heyday of suburban DIY practices, suburban homeowners—increasingly two-income families strapped for time—outsourced labor for those projects. And Latino immigrants needed the work. This interdependence was a hallmark of the immigrant-based service economy that sustained many suburban areas.[58]

Day laborers, or *jornaleros*, were part of an informal economy that emerged from economic restructuring and government policy after 1980. A key facet of restructuring was the downgrading of workers into non-union jobs, with low pay, no benefits, few protections, and occupational hazards, which characterized day labor work. Some workers became day laborers after losing jobs when factories shuttered. Immigration policy, in turn, literally pushed workers into the streets. The Reagan-era Immigration Reform and Control Act (IRCA) of 1986 made it illegal to hire undocumented immigrants and penalized employers who did. When federal officials began enforcing IRCA in metro areas like Los Angeles, it forced many Latinos to seek work on a more informal basis. Day laborers typically clustered in groups outside of home improvement, lumber, and building supply stores to get ad hoc work from homeowners or contractors (Figure 3.3). One study conducted in Pasadena found that homeowners and contractors hired day

Figure 3.3 Day laborers speaking with a potential employer in Los
Angeles, 1986.

Photo by Jose Galvez, *Los Angeles Times*, Aug 17, 1986. Los Angeles Times Photographic Archive,
Library Special Collections, Charles E. Young Research Library, UCLA.

laborers about equally.[59] Most day laborers in LA were recently arrived male
immigrants from Mexico and Central America, many undocumented (one
national survey found three-quarters of day laborers were undocumented).
Their earnings were low while their job conditions were labor-intensive and
at times dangerous.[60]

The upsurge of day laborers spurred a punitive backlash in many suburbs.
The concerns of local residents and businesses hinged around two main issues: opposition to undocumented immigration per se and a desire to defend a suburban "quality of life." As day laborers were becoming synonymous
with "illegal immigrants," their visibility at the local level made them the
focal point of homeowner frustration with unauthorized immigration, and
residents began demanding that local officials do something about it.[61] They
also viewed working-class Latino men visibly clustered on street corners
or in parking lots as a scourge on the suburban landscape.[62] In truth, suburban homeowners drove both the demand for day laborers and the fight
against them. While this was in many ways a racialized issue, the racial factor
was denied in local battles, especially in communities where the NIMBY
homeowners were people of color. This underscored how class was coming

to shape social hierarchies in Los Angeles, where more affluent homeowners of all races positioned themselves above the working poor.[63]

Day laborers emerged in force across LA suburbs by the mid-1980s. One popular early site was affluent white Redondo Beach, where pay was higher. The laborers' presence raised a litany of local concerns about a few "bad apples" who were causing problems like urinating in public, showing up drunk, cat-calling women, and destroying property. The police arrested some of the offenders, and town leaders began considering ordinances to ban day laborers altogether. Local business owners claimed the proposed measures were not about race but about creating "an accommodating environment for good business." A day laborer named Pedro saw it differently: "A lot of us are Hispanic and I think people around here don't like us for that." The workers stressed their need to earn money to support their families.[64] Three years later, Glendale confronted the same issue and considered banning day laborers or creating a hiring center to contain the workers. The INS had been targeting day labor sites there for round-ups of undocumented immigrants, adding to the perils these workers experienced. At the same time, sheriffs in the corporate suburb of Santa Clarita stepped up arrests of day laborers in the heavily Latino Newhall section, signaling the cooperation of local authorities with the INS.[65]

By 1990, suburbs increasingly began using powers in their own legislative toolkits to control and, increasingly, criminalize day labor. Wealthy Redondo Beach and Agoura Hills led the way, passing anti–day labor measures that became models—and legal test cases—for California and beyond. In 1987, Redondo Beach passed an anti-solicitation ordinance prohibiting anyone on a street or sidewalk from seeking work, business, or contributions from passing drivers. In 1991, Agoura Hills in the west San Fernando Valley made it illegal to seek work on a city sidewalk, street, or parking lot, or to hire someone in such spaces, citing traffic and safety concerns.[66] In May 1992, La Mirada in Southeast LA followed suit, banning day laborers from using public streets, sidewalks, and medians to solicit work, subjecting them to fines of up to $1,000 and 6 months in jail. Three months later, Sierra Madre in the San Gabriel foothills approved a similar total ban, penalizing both workers and employers with a misdemeanor charge. There, open hostilities erupted between affluent white homeowners and Latino job seekers who tended to congregate near a local park. Homeowners complained that the men trampled the grass in the park, dirtied the public restrooms, ogled women, and urinated in public, making the park unusable in the morning hours when the men congregated there. For their part, day laborers saw the ban as depriving them of their right to work. Meliton Calderon, a 40-year-old worker who rode the bus every day from Pasadena to Sierra Madre, put it like this: "There's no drinking, no drugs, no nothing. We just come here for work." A construction contractor confirmed the complicity of area homeowners in the labor practice: "They [the men] want to work. Homeowners come and grab them all the time."[67]

A more high-profile conflict erupted in Ladera Heights, an upper middle-class, mostly African American suburb of rolling hills, tree-lined streets, and spacious homes just north of Inglewood. The controversy magnified race and class issues in uncomfortable ways for homeowners and leaders alike. Sitting in an unincorporated part of LA County, Ladera Heights fell under the political jurisdiction of the County Board of Supervisors. For years, homeowners and contractors there routinely hired Latino day laborers for short-term projects. The experience of 26-year-old Pedro Ortiz, a Salvadoran immigrant, was typical. He had a wife and three children to support and was unable to find regular employment after being laid off from a minimum-wage factory job in Carson two years earlier. "We come here because we have to," he said. "We have a right to be here. . . . I do not want welfare. I want work." For 51-year-old Matias Bonilla, who lost his regular job at a South Gate metal shop when it shuttered, seeking work was a matter of survival. "We come here to earn our daily bread. We do not do anything illegal—just look for work." Local homeowners, however, increasingly resented the presence of day laborers on their tranquil streets. In 1993, they organized the Ladera Heights Protective League to take back the neighborhood and began pressuring their representative, Supervisor Yvonne Brathwaite Burke, an African American, to pass an outright ban on day laborers. They believed curbside soliciting encouraged illegal immigration, and they called out the behavior of some day laborers who gambled, drank, urinated in the bushes, stole, and caused traffic tie-ups. While local sheriffs conceded there were a few thefts, they noted that most day laborers obeyed the law. Burke soon proposed a county-wide law, which would apply to unincorporated areas like Ladera Heights, banning soliciting for work within 500 feet of churches, schools, or residential areas, which encompassed much of the community. Responding to these complaints and pressures, the day laborers began to police their own behavior to cut down on littering, drinking, and other misconduct.

Charges of anti-Latino racism were quickly leveled. Many supporters of the ban were African American homeowners, a fact not lost on civil rights advocates who chastised them for showing the same intolerance they had faced 20 years earlier, when Blacks began moving into then-white Ladera Heights. As a trio of activists argued, "Some residents of the then-predominantly white neighborhood sought to prevent the formation of a basketball league by newly arrived African American residents, claiming that people would be 'frightened' by groups of Black men congregating in the park. Residents today point to this same pretextual 'fear' of groups of men, now Latino, as a justification for violating others' rights." A ban on curbside hiring, they believed, "criminalizes socially and economically beneficial activity . . . punishing workers and their families for the 'crime' of seeking work." Ladera Heights residents bristled at the charge of racism. "How the hell can you call me a racist?" asked Don Lopez, a Mexican American leader of a pro-ban group. Others denied any connection to race. "It's an issue of conduct," noted one. The issue of day laborers uncomfortably revealed homeowners' resentment of the Latino working poor in their middle-class suburb across the racial spectrum.[68]

Civil rights groups continued to push back, including the ACLU, the Coalition of Humane Immigrant Rights of LA (CHIRLA), Joe Hicks of the Southern Christian Leadership Conference of LA, and the Roman Catholic Archdiocese. In the most basic terms, they framed the issue as the day laborers' "right to the suburb." Workers had a right to occupy those public spaces and to seek work. Joe Hicks of the SCLC was one of few African American leaders to vocally defend the day laborers, seeing the situation in Ladera Heights as "determining who's here and who's part of society. . . . These men are participating in a time-honored American tradition: finding work. We should be celebrating that instead of attempting to criminalize it." Responding to these activist pressures, Burke and her fellow supervisors passed a lighter measure in March 1994, prohibiting the solicitation of work in some commercial parking lots (attached to home and building supply stores). Ladera Heights residents were furious. They renewed their campaign for a stricter ban and, two months later, they got it. Their cause was bolstered by a recent state appellate court ruling that upheld the Agoura Hills' ban on day laborers; this legal decision enabled other suburbs and cities to pass similar measures.[69] The LA County Board of Supervisors then quickly passed a law modeled on the harsher Agoura Hills ordinance that made curbside solicitation a misdemeanor, punishable by up to six months in jail and/or a

$1,000 fine. Burke voted for it. Ladera Heights homeowners were elated. The lone dissenter was Supervisor Gloria Molina, who called the ban "shameful." Suburban-led resistance to day laborers thus became a model for LA County, shaping policy for all unincorporated areas, which included Ladera Heights, East Los Angeles, Hacienda Heights, Rowland Heights, Altadena, and other portions of the Antelope, San Fernando, and San Gabriel Valleys. While the measure affected 10% of county residents, observers believed it had widespread symbolic impact, signifying suburban hostility to the Latino working class.[70]

In the immediate aftermath of the LA County ban, Burke faced heated criticism from civil rights activists, putting her in a deeply uncomfortable position given her track record as a liberal civil rights advocate. She emphatically denied that race factored into her decision to support the ban and claimed that the main issues were traffic, sanitation, and pressure from her Ladera Heights constituents. That interracial community, she asserted, was Democratic, liberal, and not racist. Ronnie Cooper, president of the Ladera Heights Civic Association, which supported the ban, asserted that local residents would call the sheriffs to help enforce the new law. She stated, "All we want to do is preserve and maintain our community and not have a bunch of outsiders who don't pay taxes come in and take advantage. We just wanted them not to be here."[71] Here was a clear statement of who had a "right to the suburb."

The practice, conflicts, and litigation around day labor continued throughout the 1990s and 2000s. More suburbs passed prohibitions, including Pasadena, Glendale, Alhambra, Monrovia, Duarte, Azusa, Santa Clarita, Malibu, and Lawndale; six of these nine towns had nonwhite majorities by this point.[72] The courts, meanwhile, sent mixed signals at first, then gradually began defending the rights of day laborers on First Amendment grounds. The 1994 state appellate court ruling upheld the Agoura Hills ban on day laborers on the grounds that it increased safety and served the public interest. In 2000, a federal district court struck down the LA County ban.[73] And yet law and policy seemed to matter less than what was happening on the ground. Suburbs continued to pass laws, and day laborers returned to communities daily to find work in the face of spotty enforcement.

Gradually, rights groups like the ACLU, the Mexican American Legal Defense and Educational Fund (MALDEF), CHIRLA, and especially the National Day Laborer Organizing Network (NDLON), which formed in 2001, organized and began achieving better results for both suburbs and the workers. Groups like CHIRLA advised workers to self-regulate, and many responded, prompting labor activist Pablo Alvarado to credit them with re-solving many of the problems themselves. At some pick-up sites, workers formed security details and cleaning committees and implored fellow laborers to follow the rules. These actions went a long way toward alleviating homeowner objections. The rights groups also advised suburban leaders to pursue alternative solutions, such as establishing hiring centers and phone job placement services to make conditions safer and more humane for workers. These centers—some funded by municipalities, others by private donations—offered food, bathrooms, skill training, English classes, and counseling for workers on how to avoid exploitation.[74]

Still, some workers were unhappy with the hiring centers, claiming they showed favoritism and didn't have enough jobs to go around, so they con-tinued soliciting in the streets. And harsh crackdowns continued. In Santa Clarita, for example, officials in 1997 vowed to bring in the INS to do monthly sweeps to bolster their day laborer ban. In Redondo Beach, po-lice arrested 63 workers and 7 potential employers in a two-month crack-down in 2004, actions later overturned by a federal judge. In Pasadena, conflicts persisted for more than a decade and were ultimately resolved by the near complete removal of day laborers from the streets. In increasingly gentrifying Pasadena, community appearance was an urgent priority for residents, and the visible erasure of the Latino working poor became part of that agenda. Through harsh measures such as police crackdowns and a $320 fine on drivers who stopped to pick up a worker, the activity of day laborers was fully criminalized. Raul Guardado Barrios, a 58-year-old laborer from Mexico, articulated what that felt like. When police came through to clear the pick-up sites, he felt like a "germ cluttering the landscape" in a town bent on beautifying its image. Latino workers were not a part of that picture.[75]

By 2011, the courts more firmly upheld the rights of day laborers. The Ninth Circuit Court of Appeals in 2011 threw out Redondo Beach's anti-solicitation ordinance, claiming it violated the day laborers' First Amendment rights. The US Supreme Court refusal to hear the Redondo Beach case on ap-peal signaled the high court's commitment to protecting immigrant rights in the face of local government hostility. Still, right-wing groups such as the Federation for Immigration Reform and the Minutemen would continue to agitate against day laborers and undocumented immigrants.[76] And in towns like Pasadena, local practices essentially erased day laborers from the landscape.

Across LA County's suburbs, residents and leaders made their attitudes toward undocumented immigrants known. While a few were welcoming, many more used their local authority to eradicate the immigrant working poor. The conflicts that erupted over day laborers from the mid-1980s to the early 2000s tended to pit suburban residents and business owners against day laborers and their advocates. Day laborers had few allies among suburbanites themselves, judging by local discussions around the issue.[77] In many ways, suburban resistance to day labor was emblematic of broader opposition to the poor in their midst, evinced by persistent campaigns against affordable housing, unhoused people, and Section 8 tenants. Such efforts were mainstays of local suburban politics.

These actions created community cultures that denoted who belonged and who did not, who had a voice and a place in the suburbs and who did not. In Los Angeles, where more and more immigrants were making up the social fabric of the region, local actions around issues like day labor had huge implications for the lives and fortunes of growing numbers of Angelenos. Suburban political culture dictated the extent to which ethnic and immigrant suburbanites might feel welcome, which in turn could shape their broader prospects for economic, social, and civic progress.[78] And those prospects were increasingly decided by suburbanites growing ever more diverse across LA.

Progressives in Suburbia

Over the decades, progressive suburbanites, though always a minority, offered genuine alternatives to widespread traditional suburban norms and values. While these individuals rarely made over their suburbs completely—through radical community design, for example—they did bring some measure of social justice to their communities while operating within existing landscapes and structures.

In LA, progressive activism was particularly robust at the metropolitan level, but it also surfaced in suburban areas of the Greater Eastside, the San Fernando Valley, and south LA.[79] In these communities, suburbanites pursued such goals as ethnoracial inclusivity, environmental justice, and affordable housing. Progressives seldom controlled entire suburbs. Rather, they lived alongside conservative and moderate liberal neighbors, exemplifying suburbia's motley mix of political and cultural agendas.[80]

The sprawling San Fernando Valley had a deep tradition of progressive activism, which existed alongside high-profile conservative movements like BUSTOP, Prop 13, and Valley secession. One example involved the small group of African Americans who gained a foothold in the Valley by 1955. They founded an NAACP chapter and later launched campaigns for fair housing, challenging the iron-clad race restrictions that blanketed the area. By the early 1960s, they had formed the Valley Fair Housing Council, waged the first successful housing anti-discrimination lawsuit in California, and campaigned against Proposition 14 (1964), which would make it legal to discriminate in housing. The Valley Japanese American Citizen League joined the latter effort, part of an ongoing collaboration between Black and Japanese American activists in the area. Black and Chicano activists subsequently fought for Ethnic Studies programs at Valley College, La Raza Unida Party ran candidates for city council in the small suburb of San Fernando, and residents battled against Valley secession on the grounds of racial justice.[81] The San Fernando Valley was also a site of ethnic cultural claims on suburban space. For example, Thai residents in the eastern Valley held lively festivals at the Wat Thai Buddhist temple and presented a vibrant public culture, in contrast to Anglo suburban traditions of privatism and homeowner rights.[82]

In other Los Angeles suburbs, progressive and even radical activism were spearheaded by suburban churches and synagogues, from Huntington Park to Pasadena. Although the region is better known as a bastion of conservative Christianity, some churches participated in a rising "politics of dignity" movement that pursued social justice activism in LA's religious realm. Churches in La Cañada, Glendale, Alhambra, and Pasadena, for example, began offering multilingual services to promote ethnic inclusion.[83] Pasadena's All Saints Episcopal Church moved leftward on a number of issues by the late 1960s, beginning with opposition to the Vietnam War and subsequent campaigns around civil and labor rights, affordable housing, healthcare, poverty, hunger, LGBTQ rights, the AIDS crisis, nuclear disarmament, homelessness, and environmental justice. In the 1980s, it offered itself as an immigrant sanctuary space.[84] Further south, St. Matthias Catholic Church in Huntington Park and Saint Rose of Lima in Maywood became key centers of immigrant rights activism.[85]

Pockets of activity also included South Gate, where a cell of the communist October League held regular meetings in the suburban living rooms of members during the 1980s as that community was coping with the devastation of plant closures. Responding to similar issues, including the toxic footprint left by shuttered factories and environmentally hazardous dumping, residents in Maywood, Huntington Park, and other gateway suburbs waged environmental justice campaigns.[86] And in Santa Monica in the late 1970s, progressives famously gained power at city hall. They passed one of the nation's strictest rent control measures; pushed policies requiring developers to fund day care centers, parks, and low-income housing; and debated social issues ranging from toxic waste to foreign policy.[87]

In other suburban areas, residents fostered multiracial social norms and values. In the Crenshaw area, Black and Japanese American residents together reshaped local life in the postwar years. Their activities found their purest expression at the Holiday Bowl. In 1958, four young Japanese Americans opened this bowling alley, which quickly became a popular hangout for this growing multiracial community. Bowling leagues there in the 1960s included Japanese Americans, African Americans, Chinese Americans, and whites. Rex Sullivan, a 40-year regular, described the Holiday Bowl as "our hub— the Black community and the Japanese community." Two life-long friends from Dorsey High—one African American, one Japanese American—met for breakfast at the Bowl daily for more than 50 years. In Crenshaw, residents literally bowled together for decades, countering the "bowling alone" stereotype of suburban community declension.[88]

In San Gabriel Valley suburbs like Alhambra, San Gabriel, and Monterey Park, Asian American and Latino residents similarly embraced inclusionary, multiracial values. They revealed a conscious desire to distance themselves from historically white suburban norms. The simple act of allowing and welcoming in nonwhite neighbors was the first step toward interracial inclusion. From there, friendships among neighbors, classmates, and residents created a wholly different social climate. A 21-year-old Vietnamese resident captured it well: "I like being around old men on their bicycles and Chinese people and Mexican people, and I like the fact that there's not a lot of white people out here because they would ruin a lot of things. Gentrification and everything, you know? They would ruin a lot of the things that have already [been] established." Residents in these suburbs revealed a deep-seated comfort with difference and a desire to raise their children in such an environment.[89] A similar dynamic prevailed in the working-class communities of South LA, where Blacks and Latinos lived as neighbors. While first-generation Latino immigrants "established a kind of next-door neighbor civility" with their Black neighbors, many next-generation Latinos developed a deep affinity for African Americans, embracing their culture, forming bonds of friendships, and creating a meaningful community. "We grew up together," recalled one young woman. "You know, they fed us collard greens; we fed them beans. You know, we grew up in each other's homes, and we grew up together. . . . They're our people. We struggle, we consider them our people." With shared loyalties to a common homeplace, these residents ultimately forged interracial coalitions that mobilized around social justice politics.[90]

To the east, El Monte and South El Monte stood as sites of convergence for "farmworkers, punks, white supremacists, suburbanites, Zumba dancers, and civil rights activists." These spaces blurred the lines between city and suburb, and melded conservatives and progressives in a common community space.[91] Even further east in the Pomona Valley, developers Ralph and Goldy Lewis broke ranks with their contemporaries to build suburban subdivisions open to buyers of all races. Staunch supporters of fair housing, their company, Lewis Homes, became "a model for multiracial exurban development."[92]

The Greater Eastside, in fact, represented a crucial site of emerging alternative political and civic cultures. Ethnic suburbanites in this area asserted their right to use public space, shaping policy and local culture in ways that diverged from Anglo norms. One vivid example was the local acceptance of *charrerías*, highly stylized, competitive rodeo-type events, with horse running, riding, and cattle handling, accompanied by mariachi music, dancing, and food. In the Eastside suburbs, *charrerías* were heartily supported by local leaders and most residents. As early as 1951, Mexican American members of the LA Sheriffs' mounted posse, many of them *charros*, paraded down Whittier Boulevard in East LA. By the 1970s, Pico Rivera leaders allocated municipal funds to build a Sports Arena, in part to host *charrerías* and other ethnic Mexican cultural events.[93] In a similar way, cruising culture showcased Latino influences on Eastside suburbia. At the heart of this scene was Whittier Boulevard, an 11-mile stretch that traversed East LA, Montebello, Pico Rivera, and Whittier. Chicano youth shaped this culture with their car clubs, souped-up cruisers with hydraulic lifts and chrome sides, and blasting music. Yet, unlike the welcome reception to the *charrerías* in Pico Rivera, cruising met with some resistance from homeowners, local businesses, and the sheriffs' departments during the 1960s and 1970s, even though Mexican Americans were 47% of the population in Montebello and 61% in Pico Rivera. For several months in 1979–1980, police and transit authorities shut down Whittier Boulevard, which only pushed the cruisers to other streets. They reached a compromise by July 1980: Whittler Boulevard was reopened but lined with barricades to protect the side streets that fed into residential neighborhoods. This placated homeowners while allowing car culture to own Whittier Boulevard.[94]

Ethnic assertiveness also emerged at the *colonia* called Flood Ranch in Santa Fe Springs. By the 1940s, Flood Ranch was a modest neighborhood of unpaved roads and jerry-built homes owned by working-class ethnic Mexicans. When Santa Fe Spring incorporated in 1957, its 16,000 residents were divided between whites and ethnic Mexicans. Almost immediately, local leaders launched a campaign to wipe out Flood Ranch through federally funded redevelopment. The cohort behind this campaign, which included middle-class Mexican Americans, labeled the area a "slum" and proceeded with a clearance program that would allow the land to be used for new tract homes and townhouses. The working-class homeowners of Flood Ranch countered by invoking the suburban language of taxpayer and homeowner rights. They were eventually joined by some middle-class Mexican American homeowners who came to recognize the rights and needs of their working-class co-ethnics. They pushed for a more equitable redevelopment program that would provide affordable housing, a neighborhood center, and a public park. As a sign of the plan's inclusionary spirit, many of the 150 displaced families from Flood Ranch moved back to the neighborhood in 1972, when the project was completed. This episode marked a Mexican American cross-class effort to shape local policy to meet the needs of the area's poorest residents.[95]

In La Puente, another Eastside suburb, a similar dynamic prevailed at the end of the century. La Puente in 1990 was 74% Latino, 15% white, and 7% Asian. Relations between Mexican Americans and Mexican immigrants there existed along a continuum from conflict to solidarity. At one extreme, older Mexican Americans who came of age during an era of discrimination and intense pressure to assimilate showed some impatience with Mexican immigrant neighbors who were slow to acculturate. Based on their own sometimes painful experiences, they believed that success came only to those willing to give up their traditions and language. They tended to resent immigrants who didn't do the same. Yet those relations and beliefs were never static. The two groups ultimately found common ground in the public schools, where they united against the white power structure in a fight for educational equity and bilingual education. This campaign unified neighbors around a shared sense of racial discrimination as they challenged long-standing suburban norms in La Puente.[96]

The fluidity and dynamism of local politics found in La Puente characterized Maywood as well. That southeast suburb flipped from being one of the most repressive spaces for immigrants in the 1990s to one of the most welcoming 10 years later due to the actions of a newly elected pro-immigrant city council. In other towns, a more gradual process of change unfolded as the children of immigrants—and their children—lived out suburban lives, their cultural identities and tastes evolving through their own process of adaptation.

From environmental justice activists in Southeast LA to bowling pals in Crenshaw, some new suburbanites embraced progressive values and elements of the multicultural suburban ideal. Their actions had the effect of widening the spectrum of suburban political cultures in LA and vividly illustrated how diversity was remaking everyday suburban life.

Electoral Politics: A Snapshot

While much political activity revolved around local, often nonpartisan, issues, it is worth exploring what, if any, links can be made between suburban political behavior in Los Angeles and national political party identification. Did more Democrats or Republicans tend to take certain stands on local issues? Did defensive suburban politics resonate more strongly with one party, or did it attract adherents of both? More significantly, did patterns change as more and more people of color moved into suburbia and became homeowners, slipping into that troika of homeowner-taxpayer-parent that so powerfully defined suburban political identity? Overlaying these questions was the relationship between partisanship and ethnoracial identity, adding further complexity to these dynamics.[97]

LA suburbs clearly expressed a range of political cultures, from progressive leanings in the Eastside, to racial inclusivity in certain part of the San Gabriel Valley, to NIMBYism against immigrants, ethnic landscapes, and the poor across LA County. How did these local actions correlate with partisan loyalties, if at all? The most progressive communities were the Latino suburbs of the greater Eastside, such as Pico Rivera, Santa Fe Springs, and La Puente, where the proportion of Democrats ranged from 68% to 73% in 1990, among the highest rates in LA County. Voter registration was relatively high in these communities, reflecting the long-term presence of Mexican Americans familiar with the American political system. In the mixed Latino-Asian suburbs of the San Gabriel Valley, such as Monterey Park, Alhambra, San Gabriel and Rosemead, Democrats were the largest group, though by smaller margins (from 48% to 59% of all voters, in 1990); they were accompanied both by more Republicans and DTS voters. Overall, Democrats dominated these communities by varying degrees.

In suburbs supporting bans on ethnic spatial practices and day laborers, party identification ranged from bipartisan to liberal Democrat.[98] Among suburbs that passed restrictive English-language signage ordinances, roughly half had a predominance of Democratic voters, the other half Republican, suggesting no clear-cut partisan pattern. Suburbs that supported bans on Latino spatial practices (such as yard sales, pushcart vending, and piñatas in public parks) were predominantly Democratic. Similarly, suburbs that passed laws restricting day laborers were mainly Democratic.[99] These examples suggest that multiracial suburban liberals supported restrictive politics meant to protect homeowner interests from variously defined "others," especially the Latino working poor.[100]

Suburbs with the highest numbers of nonwhite homeowners were selected to explore their political proclivities. Table 3.1 shows their ethnoracial racial breakdown.[101] This analysis revealed several patterns. Party registration in the vast majority of these towns leaned Democratic from 1980 to 2010, with heavily Latino suburbs the bluest (see Table 3.2). In towns with greater racial mixing (like Cerritos, West Covina, and Lakewood), party preferences were slightly more evenly divided. Some suburbs with heavy Asian American representation had moments of Republican dominance—such as Diamond Bar in 1990 and 2000, and Walnut in 1990—yet even they eventually leaned Democratic. The one exception in this subset was San Marino, heavily Asian and wealthy, which was consistently Republican for the duration. The other striking trend was the rise of DTS as a party preference, reflecting a broader California trend. DTS began showing up in 1990 in Asian-heavy Cerritos, Diamond Bar, Monterey Park, and Walnut—all middle-class—then accelerated after 2000. By 2010, in line with state-wide trends, the DTS category began to outnumber Republicans in a number of these communities and contributed to overall numerical declines in registered Democrats, defying easy categorization of party identity.

Also revealing are local voting patterns in these suburbs on three key state ballot measures: Proposition 187 (1994), the measure that would deny

Table 3.1 Racial/ethnic make-up of the suburbs with top percentage of nonwhite homeowners, 2000. Table shows both overall population of each ethnoracial group, and nonwhite homeownership rates.

	White non-Hispanic population (%)	Black population (%)	Hispanic population (%)	Asian population (%)	2000 Nonwhite owner-occupied housing units	Nonwhite owner-occupied as % of all housing units
Towns with highest percentage nonwhite homeowners						
Baldwin Park	7.3	1.6	78.7	11.6	8,860	50.8
Carson	12.0	25.4	34.9	22.3	15,354	60.6
Cerritos	21.4	6.7	10.4	58.4	9,068	58.1
Compton	1.0	40.3	56.8	0.3	12,438	52.3
Diamond Bar	31.0	4.8	18.5	42.8	8,777	48.9
La Puente	6.7	2.0	83.1	7.2	4,974	51.5
Lynwood	2.9	13.5	82.3	0.8	6,386	42.6
Monterey Park	7.3	0.4	28.9	61.8	8,973	44.4
Norwalk	18.9	4.6	62.9	11.5	12,036	43.7
Pico Rivera	7.7	0.7	88.3	2.7	9,944	59.2
San Fernando	7.9	1.0	89.3	1.1	2,472	41.7
Santa Fe Springs	19.2	3.9	71.4	3.9	2,126	43.1
South El Monte	4.8	0.4	86.0	8.4	1,923	40.7
Walnut	18.2	4.2	19.3	55.8	5,634	67.1
West Covina	23.0	6.4	45.7	22.7	13,214	41.2
Case studies						
Lakewood	52.4	7.3	22.8	13.5	6,140	22.5
Pasadena	39.1	14.4	33.4	10.0	9,519	17.6
San Marino	44.6	0.3	4.4	48.6	1,720	38.8
South Gate	6.0	1.0	92.0	0.8	8,947	36.9

US Census dataset, 2000.

Table 3.2 Voter registration in suburbs of LA County, with highest percentage of nonwhite homeowners as of 2000, and the book's case study suburbs, 1980–2010.

	1980 (%)			1990 (%)			2000 (%)			2010 (%)		
	Dem	Rep	DTS	Dem	Rep	DTS	Dem	Rep	DTS	Dem	Rep	DTS
LA County	58.2	32.3	7.2	54.6	35.4	8.0	53.3	27.6	14.2	51.4	23.6	20.6
LA City	63.0	27.0	7.6	61.3	28.6	8.0	58.8	21.7	14.3	56.7	17.6	21.1
Suburbs with highest percent nonwhite homeowners												
Baldwin Park	65.8	24.3	7.0	62.3	27.9	7.7	61.6	17.8	16.3	55.0	19.6	21.5
Carson	74.5	16.3	7.0	69.2	20.3	8.5	64.8	16.9	13.7	61.1	15.9	19.5
Cerritos	56.0	34.7	7.4	44.5	44.3	10.0	42.4	36.4	18.0	40.2	30.3	26.4
Compton	90.7	3.7	3.9	89.1	4.2	3.9	78.3	5.8	7.8	73.9	8.8	13.2
Diamond Bar				36.2	52.1	10.0	37.0	40.9	18.5	34.6	33.7	28.0
La Puente	73.0	18.5	5.5	68.0	23.2	6.3	65.9	15.6	14.0	59.5	17.9	18.9
Lynwood	77.6	15.3	4.8	78.6	13.7	5.3	72.9	9.2	11.9	68.1	10.9	17.2
Monterey Park	65.0	25.7	7.4	56.4	29.1	12.7	51.3	24.2	20.8	45.4	20.4	30.9
Norwalk	70.7	21.1	5.2	65.9	26.9	5.3	60.3	23.2	12.2	55.1	22.1	18.8
Pico Rivera	78.5	14.0	4.6	73.9	18.7	5.4	72.1	14.3	10.2	63.4	17.4	15.8
San Fernando	62.2	24.7	6.1	65.2	24.1	6.5	67.5	15.7	12.7	63.7	13.4	19.1
Santa Fe Springs	76.2	16.6	4.4	72.8	21.4	4.2	66.2	19.4	11.0	58.4	22.3	16.0
South El Monte	75.7	16.2	5.6	72.2	18.9	6.9	68.1	14.0	13.6	59.3	15.1	22.0
Walnut	49.0	40.1	8.7	41.3	46.1	10.8	37.2	36.1	22.8	33.5	29.8	33.1
West Covina	53.0	38.8	6.2	49.0	41.4	7.6	49.8	31.6	14.5	47.0	28.2	20.6
Case study suburbs												
Lakewood	60.7	31.4	5.8	50.1	41.4	6.6	48.7	35.2	12.1	44.7	32.9	17.8
Pasadena	50.3	40.1	7.8	50.1	39.8	8.1	52.4	30.1	13.4	50.0	25.2	20.4
San Marino	16.5	78.3	4.5	17.5	73.8	7.9	19.8	58.8	18.9	22.4	44.1	30.9
South Gate	64.3	28.9	4.9	60.5	30.3	7.0	66.5	15.8	13.0	63.5	14.2	18.3

DTS, Decline to State party affiliation.

California Secretary of State, *Report of Registration: State of California*, October 1980, October 9, 1990, September 8, 2000, October 18, 2010.

undocumented immigrants access to public services; Proposition 184 (1994), the "law-and-order," three-strikes initiative; and Proposition 30 (2012), which raised taxes on the rich and on retail sales. Table 3.3 compiles these voting results. Together, these propositions captured two phases of recent

Table 3.3 Voting returns on three statewide ballot measures from 1994 and 2012, in LA suburbs with highest rates of nonwhite homeownership as of 2000, and in the book's case study suburbs.

	Proposition 187 (1994): Undocumented immigrants (%)		Proposition 184 (1994): Three strikes (%)		Proposition 30 (2012): Raise taxes (%)	
	Yes	No	Yes	No	Yes	No
Suburbs with highest percent nonwhite homeowners						
Baldwin Park	43.3	56.7	79.3	20.7	68.6	31.4
Carson	55.5	44.5	70.3	29.7	66.8	33.2
Cerritos	60.9	39.1	80.2	19.8	51.9	48.1
Compton	58.9	41.1	52.5	47.5	77.5	22.5
Diamond Bar	61.6	38.4	80.9	19.1	47.1	52.9
La Puente	41.2	58.8	76.9	23.1	66.5	33.5
Lynwood	48.8	51.2	59.9	40.1	71.1	28.9
Monterey Park	47.0	53.0	74.5	25.5	62.0	38.0
Norwalk	57.4	42.6	80.5	19.5	61.7	38.3
Pico Rivera	36.9	63.1	76.6	23.4	66.8	33.2
San Fernando	40.4	59.6	76.9	23.1	66.7	33.3
Santa Fe Springs	46.9	53.1	78.2	21.8	59.6	40.4
South El Monte	37.1	62.9	76.8	23.2	69.3	30.7
Walnut	57.9	42.1	80.7	19.3	50.6	49.4
West Covina	59.3	40.7	79.6	20.4	55.9	44.1
Case study suburbs						
Lakewood	66.8	33.2	81.4	18.6	49.4	50.6
Pasadena	48.7	51.3	65.5	34.5	61.5	38.5
San Marino	63.7	36.3	74.8	25.2	34.1	65.9
South Gate	42.6	57.4	77.6	22.4	72.0	28.0

California Secretary of State, *Supplement to the Statement of Vote*, November 8, 1994, General Election (Sacramento, CA, 1994); California Secretary of State, *Supplement to the Statement of Vote*, November 6, 2012, General Election (Sacramento, CA, 2012).

California politics: the 1990s era of hostile racial politics and the 2010s, when racialized politics had diminished and a more progressive political climate prevailed in the state.[102] These measures addressed issues central to suburban concerns: immigration, law and order, and taxes.

One of the most contentious measures of the 1990s, Proposition 187, would apply to all ethnic groups but especially targeted Latinos. As a result, the election galvanized many Latinos in opposition. Prop 187 ultimately passed by a 59–41% margin, revealing strong opposition to undocumented immigrants in California although federal courts later declared it to be unconstitutional. Among the sample suburbs, the vote was split down the middle. Showing sympathy for immigrant rights by voting "no" were heavily Latino suburbs like Baldwin Park, La Puente, Pico Rivera, San Fernando, South Gate, and South El Monte. Lynwood's vote was fairly close, likely a sign of heavy African American support for the measure, combined with relatively low voter registration of Latinos there. Monterey Park and Pasadena were the only ethnoracially mixed communities in this subset that voted "no." Just as telling were the suburbs that voted "yes" to deny services for the undocumented They included three racially balanced suburbs—Carson, Norwalk, and West Covina—as well as Asian-heavy Cerritos, Diamond Bar, San Marino, and Walnut. This in part reflected the "No-on-187" grassroots focus on Latino immigrant communities rather than Asian American ones; Asian American groups, in turn, never contributbued substantially to the No-on-187 effort. While one statewide exit poll showed overall opposition to Prop 187 among Asian American, Latino, and Black American voters, in these particular LA suburbs, Asian Americans and African Americans voted in favor of the measure. These suburbanites of color revealed the limits of racial liberalism in diverse suburbia and a simmering intolerance toward undocumented immigrants.[103]

A more clear-cut suburban position emerged on Proposition 184, the "three-strikes" measure that mandated a 25-year to life sentence for a third felony conviction, raised the minimum sentence for a second felony, and didn't require the "third-strike" felony to be a violent crime. Support in these suburbs was overwhelming. With few exceptions, more than 70% of voters in this suburban subset supported Prop 184. Only Compton, Lynwood, and Pasadena showed narrower margins, although they, too, voted "yes" overall. These suburbs reflected statewide sentiments as the measure passed with 72% of the vote. Prop 184 reflected a surging concern with law and order in the wake of the 1992 civil uprising and rising crime rates in LA. Suburban homeowners of all races and ethnicities shared these concerns and supported pro–law enforcement politics in a number of suburbs, with Lakewood leading the way. Harsh criminal justice measures such as Prop 184 ultimately fueled the rise of racialized mass incarceration in California, and diversifying suburbs played a role in that process.[104]

Proposition 30 aimed to reverse the anti-tax reputation of California. This measure placed a higher tax on the wealthy while also increasing the state sales tax. For generations, suburbanites had reliably opposed taxes through measures such as the Lakewood Plan, Proposition 13 (1978), and numerous local campaigns around fiscal restraint. This bill, however, raised taxes for everyone and addressed income inequality by imposing a heavier burden on rich residents. In this subset of suburbs, Prop 30 won fairly decisive support. It predictably won in left-leaning Latino suburbs like Baldwin Park, La Puente, Lynwood, Pico Rivera, and South El Monte, but also won by a landslide in Latino-Black Compton. The towns opposing included Diamond Bar and San Marino, both upper middle class with large Asian American populations, and Lakewood by a slim margin, where whites remained a substantial portion of the electorate. The progressive outlook embodied in Prop 30 found warm support in most of these suburbs by 2012, suggesting shifting political inclinations. Yet a few towns remained tax averse, following generations of their suburban forebearers.

This brief survey of voting preferences reveals the limits of racial liberalism in diversifying suburbia with high rates of nonwhite homeownership. While half of these communities evinced support for immigrant rights— perhaps the clearest gauge of progressive leanings—those same towns also backed the punitive law-and-order measure. Even in Compton, where some families would feel the direct impact of a harsh three-strikes law, a majority of voters favored its passage. Perhaps the biggest break with suburban tradition was the vote to self-tax, although even that was becoming more common in individual towns contending with the fallout of Prop 13. These snapshots suggest that, in suburbs with rising numbers of liberal homeowning people of color, anti-immigrant and law-and-order politics could gain a foothold. While more research is needed to probe local politics in these places and its relation—if any—to partisan identification, this evidence suggests that certain conservative tendencies appear to have emerged in suburbs experiencing profound demographic change. The suburban identity of "homeowner" continued to shape politics and the desire to protect and defend neighborhoods. This, it appeared, was an unshakable constant.

LA's diversifying suburbs showed a range of political cultures across a wide spectrum. Some suburbs transformed into ethnoburbs that supported the values and needs of new immigrants, some spawned social justice movements, while others clung to deeply entrenched traditions and politics even in the midst of profound demographic change. While progressive politics and civic cultures gained a foothold in a number of LA suburbs, particularly in the Eastside, other suburbs created civic cultures of exclusion and even criminalized the working poor, with the support of residents of color. Suburban advantage, homeownership, and quality of life together comprised an enduring suburban ideal across generations and through the region's demographic transformations.

Like their white predecessors, suburbanites of color believed that they, too, had attained the American Dream through their own hard work. In addition, this hard-won achievement was reached without the structural advantages accorded to whites and, for some, in the face of racism and hostility. This experience did not automatically translate into a politics of inclusion and compassion. For Black, Latino, and Asian American suburbanites, buying a home and establishing themselves in their community entailed surmounting racial barriers. The fragility of their status and the challenges of becoming homeowners may have justified their desire to protect property. While on the surface these impulses may have resembled long-standing traditions of suburban defense, this distinctive path set them apart from earlier generations of white suburbanites.

These dimensions and nuances come into focus when specific localities are put under the lens. Part II of this book journeys into communities from north to south, starting in Pasadena, then moving into San Marino, South Gate, and finally Lakewood. These case studies reveal how diversity was remaking civic and social cultures, reshaping everyday life, and ultimately creating very distinct contexts for community participation. Those trajectories dictated the extent to which ethnic, immigrant, and African American suburbanites could find a sense of belonging and even stewardship of their communities. While some sporadic examples of expansive inclusivity appeared, in more cases fully inclusive democratic culture proved elusive. Suburbanites drew lines by class, citizenship, and race to define their communities. In some cases, the definition of suburban "other" changed over time, but the end result was stubbornly persistent inequality across suburban space even as suburbia became a much more diverse place.

PART II

ON THE GROUND IN SUBURBIA

4

White Flight Within

Pasadena

For over a century, generations of social observers characterized Pasadena as a deeply divided city. Willa Mae Robinson described 1920s Pasadena like this: "North Fair Oaks [Avenue], that was the dividing line between Blacks and whites. We lived over there on the Black side . . . and we couldn't even cross to this side, the white side." When Rector George Regas of All Saints Episcopal Church first arrived in Pasadena in 1967, his first impression was of a city profoundly divided by race. Historian Michael James conveyed a similar impression in a vivid vignette of 1990s Pasadena, juxtaposing wealthy, champagne drinking Pasadenans partying on the Arroyo Seco Bridge with the haunting image of three African American kids shot to death just a few miles up the road. Political scientist Peter Dreier, in 2007, dubbed Pasadena "Separate and Unequal."[1]

The lives of two famous early Pasadenans illustrate the gulf between its residents. Julia McWilliams was raised as a child of privilege. Born in 1912, into a family of blue-blood conservatives, she grew up in the southern part of town on a street with spacious suburban homes shaded by leafy trees. Julia attended two elite private schools, Westridge and Polytechnic. And yet she came to loathe it all. To her, it was a stuffy, right-wing, reactionary town that she couldn't leave fast enough. Her father, she wrote, "assumed I would marry a Republican banker and settle in Pasadena to live a conventional life. But if I'd done that I'd probably have turned into an alcoholic, as a number of my friends had. Instead, I had married Paul Child, a painter, photographer, poet, and mid-level diplomat who had taken me to live in dirty, dreaded France. I couldn't have been happier!"[2]

Jackie Robinson was born seven years after Julia Child. He grew up on Pepper Street, three miles north of Child's family home, in the northwest, working-class part of town. He lived a childhood of struggle and want, raised by a single mother with a fierce work ethic and rock-solid sense of family. Jackie's sense of racial injustice took root early. Though his neighborhood was the center of Pasadena's Black community, the racially mixed space was not always peaceful. Jackie recalled hostile white neighbors who did "unfriendly things" when he was a kid, like call the police when his brother skateboarded, sign petitions to "try to get rid of us," and, worst of all, call him "Nigger"—to which Jackie yelled back, "Cracker!" setting off stone-throwing fights. Jackie hung out with a mixed-race group of kids—Blacks, Japanese, and Mexicans—all from working-class families. They made trouble here and there, but "all the time we were aware of a growing resentment at being deprived of some of the advantages the white kids had." Jackie attended public schools, including John Muir Technical High School, where he began making his mark on the playing field.[3] Both Robinson and Child went on to great fame and achievement, yet each retained memories of Pasadena as a deeply flawed place.

The notion of Pasadena as a divided city contrasted sharply with the image it projected to the world through the Rose Parade, its annual flower-covered procession of floats down Colorado Boulevard. Pasadena prided itself on being a cultured, sophisticated place, with wealth, beauty, a cosmopolitan character, and an ability to grow in innovative ways. In contrast to postwar Southern cities such as Atlanta and Charlotte that confronted race in public discourse about growth and civic identity, Pasadena simply ignored race in its paeans to civic progress.[4]

Yet Pasadena's history was fundamentally shaped by race. Unlike many suburbs rooted in racial homogeneity, Pasadena was diverse from the start, a wealthy enclave serviced by a multiracial workforce of domestic laborers who lived in local neighborhoods.[5] Over time, it only became more diverse. White Pasadenans simultaneously embraced a vision of their neighborhoods as racially pure spaces, which they believed ensured the social, economic, and civic health of their community. Segregation would secure that ideal, and Pasadena enacted measures to fortify those racial borders.[6] For decades, its Black American community fought those restrictions on multiple fronts, culminating in two local court cases that influenced the national landmark Supreme Court cases *Shelley v. Kraemer* (1948) and *Brown v. Board of Education* (1954).[7]

In the 1960s and 1970s, years of steadfast civil rights activism began to pay off when the federal government made a genuine, if short-lived, commitment to eradicating the barriers of metropolitan segregation. With the passage of the Housing Act of 1968 and federal judges pressuring school districts to enforce *Brown v. Board of Education*, intense pressure built to stop practices of so-called de facto segregation in housing and the schools. While this moment of federal commitment proved fleeting and limited, it opened the door to profound changes in the racial composition and social experience of Pasadena. This change, in combination with key local initiatives such as redevelopment and freeway building, precipitated a resorting of the social landscape.[8]

One reaction to these transformations was massive white flight. Many white suburbanites left rather than face everyday life with diverse neighbors and schoolmates. This might mean moving to the next town, where municipal and school district boundaries insulated residents from these changes, at least for a time. It might mean moving to the far reaches of the metropolis into a newer exurb. It might mean moving to another county altogether, Orange County being the most common for Angelenos. In later years—when the Latino influx intensified—it might mean leaving California for another state, such as Arizona, Oregon, or Colorado.[9]

A second outcome was that whites stayed put, but a kind of "internal white flight" took hold. Partial to their hometowns, some whites elected to stay in place but withdrew from the public sphere, opting for private schools, private clubs, and sequestered neighborhoods.[10] Usually, the better-off could best afford this option. This resegregation, in turn, exacerbated inequality. Despite Pasadena's fame as a conservative hotspot, it had a strong liberal tradition for decades, and this story exposes the limits of racial liberalism.

This chapter considers the question: What were the social and civic consequences of racial upheaval in Pasadena? It begins by exploring how race and class shaped Pasadena, starting with the creation of the built landscape, then moving into the worlds of social and civic life. When that racial status quo was upset during the 1960s and 1970s, residents struggled to come to terms with a new civic commitment to racial equity, which shaped how they realigned their civic and social energies. The chapter looks closely at associational and group life as a lens into these social experiences. The focus here is on relations between whites and Black Americans, though other racial groups resided there.[11]

Pasadena represents something of an urban and suburban microcosm. By the postwar era, it possessed key elements of urban areas—rich, middling, and poor; center and suburbs; diverse people by race, ethnicity, political outlooks, and social experience. It was an important economic center, with a diverse jobs base, cultural institutions, Caltech, the Jet Propulsion Laboratory, and robust retail and service sectors, and was thus counted as a key edge city by the 1990s. The historical dynamics that shaped Pasadena also reflected major

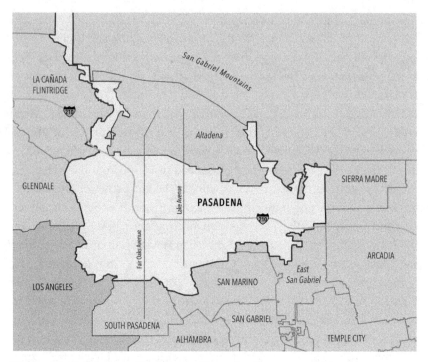

Figure 4.1 Pasadena and its surrounding suburban communities.
Cartography by Jennifer Mapes, Kent State University.

threads of metropolitan history, including redevelopment, freeway upheavals, segregated housing patterns, and an explosive busing crisis. Pasadena also contained nearly every type of historic suburban landscape within its orbit—wealthy picturesque enclaves, old automobile bungalow suburbs, multiethnic working-class suburbs, all-white sitcom suburbs of the postwar years, and post-1980 corporate suburbia. Beyond Pasadena's municipal borders lay unincorporated Altadena to the north and incorporated Sierra Madre to the northeast, both of which were part of the Pasadena Unified School District and were thus connected to Pasadena's racial and class politics.

Making the Divided Edge City

Founded in 1886, as the oldest incorporated town outside of LA, Pasadena has always had a dual identity—as a suburb of Los Angeles and an autonomous town. Developed upon land first inhabited by the Tongva people and later by Spanish and Mexican settlers, Pasadena grew gradually under American rule. When a group of migrants from Indiana settled the area in the 1870s, they brought with them a vision of communitarian life thoroughly steeped in an ideal of country living. These new residents, a number of whom were "dedicated professionals-turned-orchardists," immersed themselves in borderland living. Some of their dwellings were patterned on the cottage designs of Andrew Jackson Downing, the period's preeminent horticulturalist and suburban ideologue.[12]

The boom of the 1880s intensified both suburban and urban characteristics of the area. In 1886, a new interurban railway line first connected Pasadena to downtown Los Angeles, allowing for regular easy commuting. This set off a boom in residential subdivision and building as mature orange trees were chopped down to make way for homes. That same year, Pasadena incorporated as a municipality. Meanwhile, a number of opulent, high-end hotels were constructed to attract rich visitors from the East. Many liked what they saw and decided to stay, shifting the town's socioeconomic profile upward and downward at the same time, characterized by a wealthy white upper stratum and an ethnoracially diverse working class that serviced their needs.[13]

By the early twentieth century, waves of artists, health seekers, and affluent Easterners were drawn to this "village of orchards." Many built palatial mansions surrounded by elaborate gardens and lush groves of orange, peach, fig, and cherry trees. They fully absorbed the natural surroundings in the ways they built their homes and the town itself. This impulse found architectural expression in the Arts and Crafts Movement, which flourished in the area, its crowning achievement being the Greene brothers' Gamble House on Orange Grove Avenue.[14] Pasadena had evolved into a stylized West Coast picturesque enclave whose ethos found symbolic expression in the Tournament of Roses festival. First held on January 1, 1890, the day began with a leisurely parade of flower-draped carriages, followed by an afternoon of games played in open fields.[15] Pasadena's wealth, leisure, and scenic beauty had begun to define its identity.

A workforce of domestic laborers kept the Anglo residents' estates and mansions functioning. These laborers were initially African American, then Asian American by the 1920s. Latinos, meanwhile, labored in local orchards and railway yards. These historic roots gave people of color a foothold in the area, a pattern not always present in restricted white suburbs. Pasadena became a place where rich, poor, white, Black, and brown coexisted within common political borders.[16]

Figure 4.2 The picturesque life in wealthy Pasadena, ca. 1890. Pasadena emerged as an enclave for affluent easterners who wintered in this bucolic "village of orchards." This photo shows a Victorian mansion on Orange Grove Avenue, which came to be known as "Millionaire's Row." This leisured lifestyle was made possible by the domestic service workers who lived nearby.

Orange Grove Ave., Pasadena, approximately 1890, photPF 9550, W. H. Jackson Photo. Co., Denver Colo., The Huntington Library, San Marino, California.

Residential, social, and civic life was highly segregated before 1950. A core of modest suburban neighborhoods filled out the middle sections, surrounded by wealthy white enclaves on the scenic edges of town. The earliest African American settlers lived in homes adjacent to the mansions on Orange Grove. As more Blacks arrived, many settled in northwest Pasadena, where property was cheap and services sparse, and many seized the opportunity to buy land and become suburban property owners. This area evolved into a multiracial suburban neighborhood. In early Pasadena, ethnic Mexicans clustered in the south Raymond area, originally a labor camp for the Pacific Electric streetcar. In 1914, when the city passed its first zoning-type measure, this area was designated as Pasadena's primary industrial district. Here, Mexicans lived in old dilapidated rental homes adjacent to gas tanks, electric power plants, small factories, and laundries. They also settled farther out—in northwest Pasadena and the Titleyville area to the east—whose modest conditions were in line with working-class suburbia. The smaller population of Chinese and Japanese lived in the south Raymond Avenue neighborhood and in northwest Pasadena.[17]

Figure 4.3 Pasadena's early affluent residents were heavily dependent on a local labor force of domestic and agricultural workers who kept up the homes, gardens, and orange groves of property owners. Many of these workers were African Americans, who either migrated west with their employers or traveled independently to Pasadena, where they found work within the area's limited labor market.

Courtesy of the Archives at Pasadena Museum of History (BH-D-11-3, Ethel Houston photo album, Black History Collection).

Pasadena's white population inhabited the myriad suburban landscapes that radiated outward from the business core. Along Pasadena's edges, the picturesque hilly neighborhoods of Linda Vista, the lush San Rafael and Annandale area, and graceful slopes of Oak Knoll housed some of the area's wealthiest "old money" families on estate properties. One 18-room Mediterranean villa in Linda Vista, complete with a 1,200-foot long, rose-covered fence, acres of fruit trees, an artificial lake, and two lily ponds, was valued at $90,000 in 1925.[18] Along South Orange Grove, large mansions and stately Victorians lined the avenue dubbed "millionaire's row." In the vast middle of Pasadena, blocks of bungalows, cottages, and simple frame homes housed the white middle and working classes. The bungalow architecture style became closely associated with Pasadena; the Aladdin house pattern book even included a bungalow design named "The Pasadena."[19] To the east, sitcom suburban tracts were built up in the Hastings Ranch area starting in the late 1940s.[20] By the 1950s and 1960s, single-family homes and homeowners dominated Pasadena.

Figure 4.4 The contrasting suburban landscapes of Pasadena, 2010. Class and racial diversity were perennial features of Pasadena. Northwest Pasadena was a multiracial working-class neighborhood of tidy homes, such as this one on Pepper Street, the street where Jackie Robinson grew up. In the affluent white Oak Knoll section in southern Pasadena, homes conspicuously displayed their owners' wealth. Photos by Becky Nicolaides.

Various tactics ensured racial separation in Pasadena for decades. In 1885, Chinese residents were expelled from downtown Pasadena after a white mob attacked a Chinese laundry, lobbing stones and setting it on fire. City leaders and businessmen quickly signed a resolution barring Chinese people from the city center altogether, a blatant act of racial removal.[21] In subsequent years, as suburban home building picked up, race-restrictive covenants and homeowner associations operated in tandem to protect white residential areas. In 1939, the Pasadena Improvement Association formed, with the express purpose of perpetuating the use of covenants. This self-described group of "business and professional men" had the blessing of the Chamber of Commerce, the Pasadena Merchants' Association, the Civitan Club, and the Realty Board. "Negroes" were the chief concern of the Association, although their efforts targeted all nonwhites. Its prime goal was "purely materialistic," in the words of one officer—to maintain Pasadena property values by keeping Blacks out of white neighborhoods. Like door-to-door peddlers, Pasadena Improvement Association members sold this idea to white homeowners, charging those who signed a covenant $5 for the trouble of processing the paperwork. Though not all white homeowners supported this effort—as one Association member remarked, "There are too many nigger-lovers in Pasadena"—it nonetheless helped reinforce stark racial borders. By 1941, about 60% of all 7,500 parcels contained the restrictions.[22] Nearby La Cañada, Glendale, and South Pasadena waged similar campaigns of racial exclusion, limiting the residential choices of Pasadena Blacks.[23] In Altadena, hostile whites burned the gas meter of a home a Black couple was planning to buy. This and other scare tactics were used to intimidate Black homeseekers.[24]

Beginning in the 1910s, Black Americans were excluded from or sequestered in many of Pasadena's commercial venues, including theaters, restaurants, bowling alleys, golf courses, and roller-skating rinks. The Pasadena Playhouse, for example, always ensured that an empty seat separated Black and white patrons. By the late 1940s, the only racially open commercial establishments were movie theaters due to discrimination lawsuits brought against two local theaters. Many churches were also segregated. Pasadena's Episcopalians divided racially into two churches—All Saints, located across the street from City Hall in a stately gothic church, and St. Barnabas, a "mission" church housed in a modest chapel in Northwest, built in part because the white, upper-crust parishioners of All Saints did not allow Black worshippers. Many public spaces were likewise segregated. The public schools gradually began a process of racial sorting, certain parks were designated as white-only, and, most famously, the Brookside pool was racially segregated beginning in 1914 and remained so until the 1940s. In perhaps the most symbolic slight, African Americans were denied decent seating at the Rose Parade in the mid-1920s. Reinforcing these institutional segregation efforts were sporadic outbursts of violence and intimidation. Two Black churches were threatened with arson in the early 1900s, forcing parishioners to stand guard with rifles at night, while three Black-owned homes were burned to the ground. Such practices to ensure racial separatism—from formal to informal—were typical in towns whose "domestic service suburb" roots created a geography of racial proximity.[25]

As strong as the suburban ethos was in Pasadena, the town early on developed an urban identity, evident in its growing economic vitality. With the population climbing from 45,000 to 76,000 during the 1920s, it transformed into a predominantly middle- and working-class city. Colorado Boulevard, the main commercial thoroughfare, was lined with substantial two- and three-story brick buildings. Despite the early booster vision of Pasadena as a bucolic haven, the 1920s Chamber of Commerce vigorously campaigned to attract "clean" industry. By 1929, the growing local economy supported the tourist trade (with hotels and retail), over 150 industrial plants, a robust building trade, numerous cultural institutions, and a major university, Caltech. A City Beautiful initiative produced a stately civic center.[26] Pasadena seemed to strike the optimum balance between city and suburb. In *Your City*, a quantitative study ranking the quality of life in 310 American cities in 1930, Pasadena stood at the top, followed by Montclair, Cleveland Heights, Brookline, Evanston, and Oak Park—all iconic suburbs of the era.[27]

By the 1950s and 1960s, Pasadena emerged as a bona fide edge city. Driven by federal subsidies, local pro-growth initiatives, and unrelenting population growth, Pasadena transitioned from a tourist-dependent, old-money space into a more forward-looking, Space Age city. One catalyst was the 1940 completion of the Arroyo Seco Parkway, LA's first freeway, which linked Pasadena to downtown and drew business and shoppers to the area. In the 1950s and 1960s, the Chamber of Commerce and the city vigorously worked to attract more convention and tourism dollars, retail, offices, and clean industries. It paid off handsomely. A new business district opened along Lake Avenue, anchored by Bullocks, one of the suburban department stores proliferating in this era. Another shopping district opened in the new Hastings Ranch development in east Pasadena. By 1968, a group of economists named Pasadena's the largest "suburban" shopping district in Southern California. Office space likewise expanded. A surge of construction in the late 1960s

Figure 4.5 Pasadena as Edge City, 1988. The intersection of Lake and Colorado, shown here, became a key business node of Pasadena, with numerous offices and commercial enterprises.

Courtesy of the Archives at Pasadena Museum of History (PSN-Lake and Colorado; photo by Walt Mancini); used by permission of Southern California News Group.

turned the area at Lake and Colorado into the Pasadena Financial Center. Caltech and the Jet Propulsion Laboratory (opened in 1936), both expanding rapidly with infusions of Cold War defense spending, attracted high-tech and light industry in the 1940s and 1950s. Key local manufacturers included Hycon Manufacturing, United Geophysical, Aerojet Corporation, G.M. Giannini & Co., Consolidated Engineering Corporation, ElectroData, Stuart Pharmaceuticals, and Avon Products. Pasadena also had a reputation as an intellectual/cultural center: it was home to numerous scholarly oriented clubs, a symphony, an art museum, and the Ford Foundation. By the 1970s, the construction of a key freeway hub in Pasadena (the 210 and 134) cemented the area's preeminence in the LA region.[28]

As in many metropolitan areas, rapid growth posed critical challenges: housing shortages, influxes of low-income families, air pollution problems, and traffic. On a more existential level, it forced a fundamental reconsideration of Pasadena's identity: Would it be a city or suburb? In 1957, *Business Week* explored this dilemma in an article entitled "Pasadena Wants It Both Ways." Nailing the zeitgeist of many postwar city builders who were beginning to articulate a new aesthetic of urban "magic lands" and "cities of knowledge," the article explained, "Like many other bedroom suburbs Pasadena has been acquiring industry and thriving shopping districts. Now it is planning to keep the process up without loss of residential tone." It went on to describe a futuristic city plan—dubbed "Pasadena 1976"—meant to help manage the "bewildering changes" wrought by growth, like intense traffic and parking congestion. The plan, prepared for the Chamber of Commerce by four prominent local leaders, essentially proposed transforming the old suburb into a modern, high-tech office/retail/residential conurbation. It envisioned a high-tech office park adjacent to Caltech with "tall buildings in a

Figure 4.6 "Pasadena 1976," a futuristic city plan envisioned by four local leaders in 1957, reflected an ambitious urban vision for Pasadena. Likely because it tipped the balance too far to the urban side—in the urban–suburban balance—it was never adopted. Instead, the city continued to embrace a pro-growth agenda while softening that growth with ample protections for the local suburban environment.

"Pasadena Wants It Both Ways," *Business Week*, June 1, 1957, 37–38. Internet Archive.

campus-like setting"; an elongated shopping "park" along Colorado and Lake, complete with "trees, flowers, fountains, and moving sidewalks to transport customers from one store to another," as they were serenaded by piped-in music, "Bach at one time, Rodgers and Hammerstein at another"; and an elevated monorail system suspended above the freeways. Pasadena 1976 remained a fantastical vision that never materialized. Seeking a more sober strategy, the Chamber of Commerce commissioned a report two years later from the Stanford Research Institute. It made the same core recommendation: maintain Pasadena's ambience as an attractive suburb for downtown commuters while building a solid economic base, but without tipping the balance too far either way. The strategy worked. Pasadena maintained its dual identity, evident in its growing economic strength even as more than half of its residents commuted to jobs outside of Pasadena by 1980.[29]

Embedded in these postwar urbanizing forces were forward-looking mechanisms for segregation. The Stanford report, for example, singled out redevelopment as a key tool for stimulating economic growth. Over the coming decades, waves of redevelopment rebuilt Pasadena's physical landscape while wreaking havoc on certain older neighborhoods, poor and wealthy alike. In 1948, the city initiated the transformation of mansion-lined South Orange Grove into a corridor of garden apartments, symbolizing Pasadena's postwar modernization. Several Black and Latino neighborhoods were virtually wiped out to make way for freeways, industry, retail, and public housing. The Pasadena Redevelopment Agency, meanwhile, lured corporate giants Bank of America, the Ralph M. Parsons Corporation (an international engineering and construction firm), and Avery International (the label makers) to locate their headquarters in Pasadena. Colorado Boulevard was rejuvenated through gentrification, while Lake Avenue continued to thrive as a shopping destination for the San Gabriel Valley. Redevelopment was halted in the late 1970s, when Proposition 13 cut off funding.[30] But soon major projects were under way to recast central Pasadena as an upscale, post-industrial, gentrified neighborhood.

As an edge city, Pasadena represented a key urban node within the Los Angeles metropolis, an anchor for many suburban towns around it.[31] Even within its own borders, it represented a kind of metropolis in microcosm—"downtown" hubs surrounded by suburban neighborhoods. Colorado Boulevard and Lake Avenue were shopping and office districts; north Fair Oaks Avenue was the economic heart of Black Pasadena. Surrounding these downtown corridors were leafy residential neighborhoods of single-family homes, ranging from modest to opulent.

"We Came in Droves": Social and Civic Life
in Postwar Pasadena

Crystalline racial boundaries allowed for a vibrant public life to flourish in the 1950s and 1960s. Like their counterparts in postwar suburbs nationally, Pasadenans were joiners. They belonged to clubs, associations, churches, political groups, and PTAs. They embraced public education, sending their children to neighborhood schools buffered by segregation. Despite suburbia's aura of privatism—symbolized vividly in the single-family home—these suburbanites, especially the expanding white middle class, were active in local public life.

By contrast, Pasadena's elite straddled public and private worlds. They moved in rarified circles of private clubs and schools, creating for themselves a comfortable cushion of social distance. Although they may have lived in the most attractive, wealthiest suburban enclaves in the area, they had not completely retreated into their own insular worlds. As citizens of Pasadena, they also participated in public-minded clubs and service groups.

People made five- or ten-minute drives from their suburban homes to attend club meetings in central Pasadena and along its commercial corridors. Just as frequently, associational life happened in suburban neighborhoods, in members' homes, or in meeting rooms at the public schools. In the immediate postwar period, the suburban home was not simply a privatized domestic space but also a place of communal interaction and open doors, a site where public life entered in.

Pasadena's postwar demography set the backdrop for these activities. By 1950, its overall population surpassed 100,000, reflecting continued growth stimulated by World War II. It rose a bit more by 1960, then declined slightly by 1970, reflecting nascent white flight during the era of desegregation. Racially, whites dominated Pasadena through the 1970s. The vast majority were native-born and many celebrated those American roots. Immigrants comprised only a small portion of the population, hovering around 10%, with the largest groups hailing from Europe and Canada. Among nonwhites, African Americans were the largest group, followed by Latinos, then Asian Americans. The Black population nearly doubled every decade, from 1940 to 1960, and continued to climb until 1990.[32]

Socioeconomically, Pasadena was predominantly middle class, with a sizable share of modestly educated, blue-collar families. White-collar workers

Table 4.1 Demographic and social characteristics of Pasadena residents, 1950–2010

	1950		1970		1990		2010	
	number	%	number	%	number	%	number	%
Population total	104,577	100.0	112,951	100.0	131,591	100.0	137,122	100.0
Race/ Ethnicity								
White non-Hispanic	91,597	87.6	78,491	69.5	61,518	46.7	53,135	38.8
Black	7,820	7.5	18,256	16.2	23,436	17.8	13,912	10.2
Hispanic	3,202	3.1	12,991	11.5	35,400	26.9	46,174	33.7
Asian	1,594	1.5	3,308	2.9	10,340	7.9	19,293	14.1
Nativity								
Native born	94,752	90.6	99,487	88.1	95,364	72.5	95,860	69.9
Foreign born	9,825	9.4	13,816	12.2	36,227	27.5	40,589	29.6
Occupations								
White collar	22,641	53.5	29,422	61.5	45,313	69.0	48,841	71.8
Blue collar	12,098	28.6	11,501	24.1	10,543	16.1	8,745	12.9
Service	6,784	16.0	6,765	14.1	8,466	12.9	10,415	15.3
Females in labor force	16,979	34.4	21,148	43.5	31,502	57.3	33,594	58.2
Married females in labor force*			9,555	41.0	8,716	61.7	15,785	60.9

Note: Percentages calculated out of total population, except for occupations where it is calculated out of all adult workers, unless otherwise indicated.

* shown as a percentage of all married women over 16. For 1990, data is for mothers in labor force.

(which included sales clerks and office workers), only slightly outnumbered blue-collar and service workers. Despite the area's reputation as a center of high culture, high tech, and higher education, 84% of residents did not possess a college diploma, reflecting national rates during these years. Pasadena, in fact, compared only slightly higher in terms of white-collar work and education than the LA County average. Pasadena had its wealthy and well-educated—who dominated the social columns of the local press—but most residents were in the middle and working classes. In 1960, just 12.5% of Pasadena families fell in the "upper income" category.

Pasadena was a town with moderate levels of children, singles, and working women and a relatively large share of seniors. This was not simply a baby boom suburb, but also a community with a mix of ages and family types. The local proportion of children, in fact, fell below the LA County average for the entire postwar period. While married couples in Pasadena were the majority in the 1950s and 1960s, they co-existed with a substantial number of widowed residents who seemed to gravitate to the area.[33] Resident women gradually entered the workforce, reflecting the LA County average; by 1960, about one-third of married women worked outside the home, suggesting a healthy surfeit of housewives who stayed at home to raise children, tend to households, and volunteer.[34]

Associational Life in Postwar Pasadena

Like their counterparts nationally, Pasadena residents in the 1950s and 1960s were avid joiners. This impulse to participate flowed out of two streams: the older tradition of social, civic, and philanthropic activism that characterized early twentieth-century Pasadena and the wave of home-front activism that crested during World War II and carried forward. The postwar community had an immense array of civic and social groups, ranging from hobby groups and cultural organizations to service groups seeking to tackle local problems. During this apex of associational life, a remarkable 46 groups met on a weekly basis. Other groups typically met twice or once a month. Most were highly segregated, reinforcing racial separation in everyday life.[35]

Clubs and associations tended to reflect class differences.[36] Local fraternal groups, which peaked from the 1950s to early 1970s, attracted large numbers of middle- and working-class residents. With chapters dating back to the early twentieth century, these groups united philanthropy, ritual, socializing, patriotism, and belief in a "supreme being." Some were secretive. Pasadena had all of the usual male fraternal groups—the Eagles, Elks, Lions, Knights of Pythias, and Odd Fellows. But the Masons were by far the largest: 13 groups for men, 5 for women, and 5 for teenagers. These lodges met frequently; the men's groups convened weekly, while the others met either twice or once a month. Although membership numbers are elusive, one source suggests that local Masonic membership rose from 1,706 to 3,450 between 1945 and 1955. They held parades down Colorado Boulevard, hosted large picnics at Brookside Park, and honored local educators.[37]

Several fraternal groups had women's auxiliaries, but even more important were the many stand-alone women's clubs. Carrying forward the Progressive women's club movement, these groups gave women the chance to come together in communities of shared values and collective projects. Especially popular was the P.E.O., a women's group that melded philanthropy with socializing. Pasadena had 16 chapters in 1950, 20 in 1960. Meeting twice a month in members' homes helped reinforce the closeness of members. Sorority alumnae clubs were also very popular. The Woman's Civic League epitomized the spirit of civic engagement in Pasadena, embarking on its own projects while also honoring women for their contributions to local public life. In 1945, the award ceremony drew 700 people. The honorees were the intense "doers" of the community, involved in deep networks of social and civic associations. From 1945 to 1955, the League's choice of honorees reflected a broadminded spirit for its time. In addition to the predictable club women, it chose women involved in interracial progress, cultural diversity, and immigrant welfare.[38]

Ethnic and mutual aid organizations directed their energies inward toward their own members.[39] These groups remained strong in the postwar years, with many providing life insurance, welfare benefits, and sociability to their members as they had for decades. Several ethnic organizations reflected the Western European roots of residents—the Sons of St. George (English), the Dania Society (Danish), Sons of Hermann (German), and Order of Vasa (Swedish), among others. For all of the ethnic assimilation that suburbia purportedly caused, the vitality of these groups attested to the persistence of ethnic ties and identities carried over into postwar suburban life.[40]

Some groups were simply social spaces for fun and shared interests with like-minded residents. The Angelus Matchcover Club was a friendship group for people who collected matchbooks, several local bridge clubs met regularly, the Chess and Checkers Club met twice a week at a clubhouse, the Camera Club convened twice monthly in members' homes, several garden clubs met frequently in suburban homes, and groups oriented to arts and literature flourished.

African Americans were also joiners in the postwar years. Between 1950 and 1960, their population in Pasadena jumped from 7,800 to 14,500, suggesting an established community infused with new energies from recent migrants. Interestingly, there were more Black fraternal/philanthropic groups than civil rights organizations, reflecting the suburban zeitgeist of the times. In 1950, Blacks had nine Masonic groups (for men and women), two Elks Clubs, a Knights of Pythias chapter, the Harriet Tubman Club (a philanthropic group), the Scattergood Association (a temperance club that operated a settlement house for local youth), and likely two American Legion posts. To a striking degree, these mirrored white associations in Pasadena and thus underscored the segregated nature of associational life. Blacks also continued to sustain racial justice organizations, including the NAACP and National Council of Negro Women. Scattered sources suggest high levels of participation. In the 1950s, the NAACP had about 900 members (both Black

Figure 4.7 Four African American women share a convivial moment in a suburban yard in Pasadena, 1961.

Courtesy of the Archives at Pasadena Museum of History (BH-D-5-61, Black History Collection).

and white), while Blacks were also highly involved in PTA work. As well, Black churches continued to hold a vital place in local community life. In 1951, there were 14 Black churches in Pasadena, some catering to particular clusters of new migrants. Close neighborhoods facilitated these institutional connections.[41]

Beginning in the late 1940s, a handful of groups began conscious efforts to bridge the racial divide. The Pasadena Interracial Woman's Club was notable. Coalescing five years before a group of high-profile right-wing housewife activists burst on the scene, this group had its origins in a 1946 conference of church women representing 600 churches in Los Angeles, whose home study theme that year was "The Christian and Race."[42] In November 1946, 12 Pasadena women met over lunch to found the club. The group grew to 150 in the first year, rising to 300, and came to include whites, Blacks, "a few Mexicans, a few Japanese, an Indian princess and one Chinese." They spanned the occupational gamut, from college professors and businesswomen to domestic workers and housewives. Members connected at meetings and social gatherings at each other's homes, such as teas, luncheons, and "little Sunday evening suppers." Conscious of their transgressive stance, they recounted, "there was more than one quavering-hearted hostess at first who wondered what the neighbors would think when they saw a mixed group arriving." The misgivings soon dissipated. They formed subcommittees that included a Drama Section, a Music Section, a group of "victory gardeners," a Service Section devoted to philanthropic work, a Fun Section, and, most significantly, a Fellowship in Action Section, which once a month would venture out as an interracial group in public "at some important place or at some function." By enacting interracial friendship in a public way, they sought to pierce through the culture of racial separatism in Pasadena and model an interracial suburban ideal.[43]

Enacting Affluence: The Social Orbit of Elite Pasadena

The rich, too, engaged in civic life but could shut the door when they wanted to. Elite Pasadena straddled public and private worlds. Although elites comprised only 12–15% of the population during these years, their imprint on the city was visible and deep. Their social world was tightly controlled by scrupulous screening—whether to a charity group, a country club, or a private school—which acted as a means of social and racial filtering. As private as they made this world, wealthy Pasadenans relished their public role, put forth in adoring press coverage of their many fundraisers, parties, balls, and charitable endeavors. This was a private world to be gawked at, an "in-between space" between private and public that the privileged used to wield power and "craft and protect a class identity."[44]

Traditions of social exclusivity began early. Elite clubs, debutante balls, and private schools were well-established by 1950, comprising a potent network for facilitating the social reproduction of affluence and giving Pasadena a coterie of its own "old money" families. The most symbolic expression of this was the Tournament of Roses, the hugely popular annual parade organized by the Tournament of Roses Association, which had historic ties to the exclusive Valley Hunt Club. Dating back to the 1880s, that club was made up of affluent residents, who hunted jackrabbits, foxes, and coyotes in the nearby foothills, relishing the open-air rush of the chase.[45] The Valley Hunt Club soon became a social nexus of affluent Pasadena.[46] A few years after its founding, it shifted its emphasis from hunting to "a full social season"—festive balls held at the area's grand hotels, luncheons, teas, card parties, and, starting in 1891, the Tournament of Roses. Club members became leaders in the event, building a web of elite associational ties that intersected with various local institutions, including All Saints Episcopal Church whose Ladies Guild hatched the idea of the rose queen and court. For years, the Valley Hunt Club hosted the grand marshal, queen, and her court for a pre-parade breakfast at its clubhouse aptly sited along "millionaire's row" on Orange Grove.[47]

New members of the Club were admitted through nomination, and steep dues ensured their wealth. The Club's early rolls included scientist, inventor, and banker Thaddeus Lowe; banker Henry M. Robinson; Chicago businessman J. B. Durant; architect Myron Hunt; George S. Patton; and physicist Robert Millikan. The Club hosted dinners, dances, teas, themed balls, picnics, lectures, minstrels, cotillions, smokers, and billiards, supplemented over the years with golf, tennis, swimming, and bridge. By the 1940s, the regularity of these gatherings fostered strong bonds among members—"everyone knew everyone"—and "the Club was more or less your life," as Dorothy Macdonnell recalled.[48] Membership expanded rapidly in the 1950s, and the partying exploded.[49] The Club inaugurated its own debutante ball in 1949, which became a high point of the Pasadena social season, alongside other elite gatherings through the 1960s. In the late 1950s, the Club began highlighting tennis, sponsoring a number of tournaments and pro exhibitions, as well as matches with elite clubs in La Jolla, Palm Springs, and Montecito. The Valley

Hunt Club in this era was emphatically all-white, which Club members could innocently claim was not an intentional policy but rather a "natural" reflection of social/racial groupings in Pasadena. Other private clubs in Pasadena, including the University Club, the Overland Club, the Annandale Golf Club, and the Pasadena Athletic Club, were generally characterized by racial and religious exclusion—only white Protestants allowed.[50]

For their affluent white members, private clubs were a powerful means for shoring up elite privilege for themselves and their children, as were debutante soirees, women's clubs, and private schools. Debutante culture had a deep history in Pasadena, going back to 1908, and was invigorated in the 1950s and 1960s by balls at the Valley Hunt Club and the June Debutante Ball sponsored by the Pasadena Guild of Children's Hospital. These annual events drew full houses and regular "society page" press coverage, with at least a dozen young women coming out en masse. Often a generational tradition, families spent extravagantly on the debutante rituals—cotillion classes, formal dresses, pre-ball parties, and the coming out event itself. The balls

Figure 4.8 A debutante gathering at the Valley Hunt Club, ca. 1960s. Pasadena's affluent culture linked private schools, private clubs, and debutante soirees. The Valley Hunt Club's long history of hosting debutante events saw a resurgence in the 1950s and 1960s, which attracted regular media coverage. It was a prime way that Pasadena's elite families enacted their class privilege.

Courtesy of the Archives at Pasadena Museum of History (Photo C15-90h, Main Photo Collection; photo by Elton Sewell).

were lavish affairs, with girls in formal wedding-like dresses, copious flower adornments, cocktails, dinner, and live orchestras. While the road leading to a debutante presentation was often tied to charitable work, this was not the case for Valley Hunt Club debs.[51]

Another arena of elite community life was women's clubs, which encouraged civic responsibility in a context that reinforced white social privilege. Some, like the Shakespeare Club, had their roots in the early twentieth-century women's club movement in Los Angeles. By contrast, the Junior League was younger and more receptive to change. Their long histories offer powerful messages about the nature of civic and social engagement and their responses to transforming social contexts.

The Shakespeare Club, founded in 1888, was the oldest women's club in Southern California and was firmly rooted in the Progressive women's club movement with its ethos of self-betterment, sociability, and philanthropy. In the early years, the Shakespeare Club was engaged in an array of civic causes related to city building and philanthropy, interspersed with tea parties and literary discussions. It lobbied for the building of public restrooms for women, donated time and money to victims of the 1906 San Francisco earthquake, and, in 1920, founded Rosemary Cottage, a home for orphaned girls. Its membership reached 1,500 in 1927, then hovered at 800 by the early 1960s. Members were added by invitation only, which restricted it to Pasadena's white, well-to-do women. It met weekly on Tuesday mornings in the 1950s and 1960s, reflecting the stay-at-home status of its members, to hear presentations by "the very best artists in realms of music, drama, and current events." Its signature annual event was co-hosting the Rose Queen and her court at the annual "Queen's Breakfast" held just before Christmas. In the postwar years, the Club devoted its philanthropic efforts mostly to medical entities, such as the Red Cross and Woman's Hospital, raising money through bake sales, musical and fashion shows, and other charity events. Apart from aid to the Pasadena Council of Social Agencies and Community Chest, it kept a comfortable distance from the problems of poverty in Pasadena. Over the years it was a white organization because, as board members claimed, they had few requests from minorities to join. It also leaned rightward, hosting Republican Party meetings and events.[52]

The Junior League also began in the world of elite Pasadena but eventually evolved in tandem with the city's social transformations. The youthful age of members and their self-conscious commitment to serving a changing community helped ensure its flexibility and resilience. Founded in 1926, the Pasadena Junior League was a nomination-only group for women aged 18–35, while alumnae supported the group as "sustaining members." In the 1920s, it drew in the wealthiest daughters of Pasadena, who frequented country clubs and private schools and married Ivy League husbands. The Junior League held "frolics" and fashion show fundraisers at the Biltmore Hotel ballroom downtown, events covered by the society pages. Tempered by the Great Depression and World War II, the League gradually shifted away from extravagant social affairs to community voluntarism.[53] As League president Barbara Slattery put it in 1952, they emerged from the wartime "mole-like existence of black-out curtains, meat and gas rationing, and telegram fear. We blinked our eyes, breathed the fresh, free air of peace . . . [and] we came in droves like a plague of locusts." By the postwar years, the Junior League had a more socially modest, civic-minded aura. Partly because the age restrictions meant new blood was constantly flowing into the group, it reflected the diverse views of new members. Articulating of the postwar zeitgeist of participation, league members emphasized their civic purpose: "to foster an interest in its members in the social, economic, educational, cultural, civic, political and governmental conditions of the community, the state, the nation and the world."[54] The League stepped up its activities, many aimed at children, including theatrical performances in the local public schools, concerts, and the opening of the Junior Museum. To these events, they invited the wards of their charity ventures—the children from the Boys and Girls Aid Society, the Mexican Settlement, the Children's Training Society, and the Episcopal Home for Children. More than their predecessors, postwar Junior League members showed a greater comfort level in crossing well-established lines of class and race. By the early 1960s, they were helping to build an infrastructure of social services in Pasadena, including a Senior Center and the Court Relative Service, which gave guidance to relatives of mental health patients. The balance had tilted so far toward service that one League president worried over the "lack of social activity and personal relationships of our membership as it increased."[55] To remedy this, they planned two dances and continued a program of enrichment meetings on topics ranging from glamour tips to redevelopment in Pasadena. By the 1960s, the "society" element resurfaced, evident in the ritual announcement of new provisional members at luncheons at the Valley Hunt Club and an annual meeting downtown at the elegant Dorothy Chandler Pavilion. The number of active members topped 300 by the 1960s, and all were white.[56]

Perhaps more than any other institutions, private schools worked to ensure the social reproduction of affluent privilege. Pasadena always had a
higher than average share of its children in private schools.[57] In the 1960s,
even before school desegregation had fully set in, nearly 20% of elementary
children attended private school. Unsurprisingly, families in the wealthiest
neighborhoods had the highest rates of private school attendance ranging
from 18% to 25%, compared to 7% of children in multiracial northwest
Pasadena. Nearby Sierra Madre had fully 30% of its children in private school.
At four of Pasadena's most prominent private schools—La Salle High School,
Mayfield Senior, Polytechnic, and Westridge—the graduating classes were
all-white in the 1950s and early 1960s.[58] Private schools were a pathway to
top-tier colleges and universities, as well as strong links to private clubs and
debutante society. Graduation rites at private girls' schools were no less than
dress-rehearsals for "coming out" balls. At Mayfield School, graduates wore
"white French marquisette gowns fashioned over crinoline and will carry
bouquets of cerise roses and white sweet peas tied with cerise ribbons."[59]
While this formality also echoed the rituals of the Catholic sacraments such
as first communion—Mayfield was a Catholic girls' school—it also conveyed
the wealth of its families.[60]

From the picturesque enclaves where they lived, to their private clubs and
schools, Pasadena's elite forged strong social networks of mutual admiration
and favoritism. This was bonding social capital at its lucrative best. And it
was tightly segregated by race. The citadel the wealthy built would largely
buffer them from the threatening politics of race. At the same time, their
world would come to represent a model of refuge that middle-class whites
would later try to emulate.

While white socialite culture drew impenetrable racial lines in the 1950s
and 1960s, the Black community embraced aspects of this culture as well,
with its own cotillion classes, dances, and debutante events. In the early
1950s, annual festivities were spearheaded by the Pasadena chapter of the
Knights and Daughters of Tabor, an African American fraternal society with
historic roots in the abolition movement. In April 1953, six young women
were presented as debutantes in the Gold Room of the Pasadena Civic
Auditorium, adorned with a large rose-covered arch and floral displays.[61] By
1962, the Black women's sorority Delta Sigma Theta took the helm, hosting
its first annual debutante cotillion, a tradition that continued for decades. In
1969, at the swanky Biltmore Hotel downtown, 29 young women "bowed"
at a lavish ceremony, replete with sparkling indoor fountain and live music.

They wore long white ball gowns and formal gloves, clutching bouquets of American Beauty Roses. These occasions not only celebrated the "coming out" of debs, but also recognized their "excellence in scholarship, community leadership, talent and personality," reflecting the philanthropic culture of the Deltas. These events gave Black Pasadena's "leading families" an opportunity to celebrate themselves in a formal manner, with public recognition, in their own autonomous social spaces.[62] In these ways, polite society reinforced racial separation in Pasadena.

The Political World of Postwar Pasadena

Civic and political life was equally robust in the postwar years, animating partisans across the political spectrum. In the 1950s, Pasadena became known as a bastion of anti-Red conservatism, thanks to a local controversy that drew the national spotlight. Alongside this shrill conservative majority was a vigorous Democratic minority, which increasingly asserted itself by the 1960s. In the 1950s and 1960s, people believed that the local public sphere was the linchpin of democracy. Concern with community and its well-being—heightened by Cold War fears—stimulated robust civic and political engagement. The locality represented a compelling recipient of participatory energies, a space where residents felt they could make a difference.[63] This sensibility was expressed in the surging political club movement of both the Republican and Democratic Parties, in the proliferation of local political and patriotic groups, and in local high-profile battles over the future of public education—traditional versus progressive. In postwar Pasadena, public education was considered a community institution to be protected and fought for, not run away from.[64] Community-based groups energized residents to enact their political ideals in immediate, local ways and represented crucial sites of participatory democracy.[65]

Local conservatism was buttressed by a copious assortment of clubs devoted to the Republican Party, patriotism, Americanism, and the affirmation of WASP pedigrees. The Daughters of the American Revolution, for example, had four local chapters. In addition, Pasadena had at least eight chapters of white lineage groups, including the Daughters of American Colonists, Daughters of the British Empire in California, two chapters of the United Daughters of the Confederacy, and the Native Daughters of the Golden West. Intent on affirming their nativity and patriotism, these groups asserted white American identity and loyalty amidst the uneasy climate of Cold War and civil rights America. Similar men's groups proliferated, such as veterans' groups, which in the pre-Vietnam War era promoted patriotism while providing a supportive social community through twice-monthly meetings. Veterans' groups peaked in the 1950s and 1960s in Pasadena, with 10 American Legion posts and at least 14 similar groups.[66]

Republican women's clubs in fact exploded across Los Angeles in the postwar years, with a particularly robust showing in Pasadena. For women, the stay-at-home lifestyle of suburban mothers enabled them to imbue their political groups with neighborly hospitality. Much as a garden club might meet in members' homes, women's political groups met in homes to study issues, stuff envelopes, and organize activities. For example, the Tuesday Morning Study Club, a conservative women's group, held monthly meetings in the San Rafael home of its founder, Marjorie Jensen, where members gathered in the backyard to hear a guest speaker and then engage in discussion. They focused especially on education and threats coming from communists, UNESCO, and progressive educators. In the late 1950s, when the group's popularity peaked, about 50 women attended regularly.[67]

Pasadena's Republican women spearheaded a vigorous grassroots campaign centered around the public schools, which became nationally known as the "Pasadena Affair." What began as a scuffle around anti-Communism quickly veered into race, an opening salvo in a series of skirmishes around race that climaxed in the early 1970s. In 1948, the Pasadena Board of Education hired Willard Goslin as superintendent of public schools. A moderate liberal and an advocate of Progressive education, Goslin soon enacted Progressive education methods in Pasadena's schools, began working toward racial equity in education by changing racial school boundaries, and raised taxes to fund much-needed school construction. A small but astonishingly effective group of housewives mobilized in 1949 to oppose Goslin in a campaign that pegged him as a Red. Two local women, Louise Padelford and Frances Bartlett, were particularly influential. Padelford had moved to Pasadena in the 1930s with her husband into the tony San Rafael area. At their Spanish-style "mansion" with city views, she hosted numerous strategy meetings over luncheons. Bartlett lived with her physician husband in a spacious home right next to the Valley Hunt Club, where she launched a research campaign to expose Goslin's "suspicious" activity and associations. Their efforts worked. A tax bond pushed by Goslin to fund school construction was voted down, and ultimately Goslin resigned under the intense opposition building around him.[68]

In their diatribes during the controversy, Goslin's critics were particularly sensitive about charges of racism. Pasadena, they believed, had no race problems until Goslin came along. It wasn't until Goslin started labeling people as "minority, majority, white, Negro, rich, poor, and privileged or underprivileged" that tensions surfaced. Pasadena was handling race just fine, they argued, with its own Human Relations Committee that was making progress at an appropriately gradual pace. Bristling at charges of Jim Crowism, they portrayed Pasadena as a modern city with enlightened views, cultural richness, economic vitality, and the common sense to know how to handle its own racial situation.[69]

Democrats also established a presence, pushing back against their conservative neighbors and laying the groundwork for a political realignment in Pasadena. Under the rubric of the California Democratic Council (CDC), formed in 1953, a vibrant network of grassroots clubs spread across the state, devoted to participatory politics and left-leaning liberalism. By 1960, there were 100,000 members in 400 clubs statewide. These clubs supplied foot-soldiers in the highly participatory style of politics in this period. As Pasadena liberal activist Marvin Schachter recalled, "You ran your campaigns with volunteer help, with people ringing doorbells." The whole process was decentralized and deeply shaped by the input of the local clubs, a system that encouraged active participation by everyday citizens. In Pasadena, there were five Democratic clubs by the early 1960s, plus one in Altadena. Resident Joe Wyatt led the entire CDC in the late 1950s, and several other local figures were active as statewide CDC leaders.[70]

Like their Republican counterparts, the Democratic clubs slid easily into the suburban lifestyle. In Pasadena, three of the clubs met in members' homes, while the Pasadena Young Democrats met at Garfield Park in South Pasadena, a neighborhood gathering spot. The FDR Democratic Club had hundreds of members in this period and was somewhat interracial. Members of these groups gathered informally for dinner parties, get-togethers, and annual Fourth of July and Christmas parties, usually held in people's homes. Esther and Marvin Schacter hosted many of these dinners in their home just off Orange Grove. Though only blocks away from suburban homes where GOP rivals were gathering, it was ideologically a universe apart.[71]

Just as the Republicans were bolstered by a cabal of patriotic groups, the Democrats were buttressed by several local organizations committed to liberal principles and ideals. They included the Friends Committee on Legislation, a Quaker group committed to social justice; the Women's International League for Peace and Freedom; the Pasadena Interracial Woman's Club; the American Civil Liberties Union (ACLU); the NAACP; the Human Relations Committee of Pasadena/Altadena; the Interracial Committee of the Community Chest; and the League of Women Voters. Pasadena also claimed a heritage of pro-Union (Civil War) sentiment dating back to the nineteenth century. By the postwar years, Pasadena had five chapters of the Sons/Daughters of Union Veterans and two units of the Grand Army of the Republic. Their presence—alongside the local Daughters of the Confederacy chapters—suggests the Civil War was still playing itself out in Pasadena.[72]

Pasadena's Racial Turning Point

By the end of the Goslin affair, two intertwined trends were set in motion: a gradual approach to desegregating the local schools and the initial trickles of white flight. Moderate Republicans had gained control of the school board. And the civil rights movement began to gather steam. Under the impact of both local activism and federal mandates, civil rights emerged as the preeminent civic issue of the era. As the NAACP summed it up in the early 1970s, suburbia had become "the next frontier of the civil rights movement."[73]

As the legal barriers to segregation fell, Pasadena's deeply embedded racial geography began to alter, unleashing deep changes to the community's social and civic fabric. A series of three major developments accelerated that process: civil rights activism, sub/urban renewal, and busing aimed at school desegregation.

Civil rights activism gained momentum in Pasadena during the 1940s, spearheaded by the NAACP and local Black churches. Activists began with legal attacks on segregation and discriminatory practices, scoring several major victories; by the 1960s, the movement drew on tactics spreading nationally, including marches, public protests, and continued legal offensives. Its first major victory was the case to desegregate the public pool at Brookside Park. Under the leadership of Ruby McKnight Williams and Edna Griffin, the Pasadena NAACP sued the city and won in a 1942 decision handed down by the California Supreme Court. In response, the city closed down the pool for everyone. Only after another series of court battles was the pool reopened in 1947, and it soon began attracting mixed-race crowds. The NAACP, meanwhile, stepped up its fight against discriminatory hiring practices by the city. By 1963, the Fair Employment Practices Commission of California concluded that Pasadena was practicing discrimination and needed to re-dress it through a quota system. Though gradual and modest, victories were coming.[74]

Civil rights activists also targeted segregated housing, a long-standing pillar of the suburban ideal in Pasadena. The fight for open housing was a broad effort across LA, in places like Sugar Hill, Monterey Park, Torrance, and Pasadena. Different tactics were deployed, including the legal as-sault on race-restrictive covenants. NAACP attorney Loren Miller was the driving force behind this effort. One lawsuit centered in Pasadena, *Fairchild v. Raines* (1944), a California Supreme Court case involving an African American family trying to move into a racially transitioning neighborhood in east Linda Vista. They had purchased a home without a covenant but were sued by white neighbors on the grounds that the area was mostly covered by race restrictions. Miller won the case, building legal ammunition against the use of covenants which culminated four years later in *Shelley v. Kraemer* (1948).[75] White-instigated defensive violence ensued in Pasadena, including three cross-burnings in 1957 alone, one at Washington Elementary and two at Black-owned homes.[76]

In Pasadena, Black residential integration took place slowly and grad-ually in the face of white resistance, the persistence of racial steering practices by realtors, and continued discrimination by the Federal Housing Administration (FHA). Residential integration followed two common paths in this period—individual pioneering into all-white neighborhoods and spillover into adjacent white settlements. In the 1950s and 1960s, middle-class Black pioneers were numerically small but symbolically powerful figures. With the help of Black real estate brokers, crucial agents of deseg-regation, small numbers of Black families began moving into formerly all-white areas. Theodore Bartlett, a Black real estate broker in Pasadena, recalled that "selling to blacks into totally white neighborhoods was some-thing I had a lot to do with, and I've always been proud of it." Risking vio-lence and hostility, they often made the move as a conscious political act. The East Altadena and East Arroyo neighborhoods were both penetrated by Black pioneers and subsequently became the most racially mixed of the wealthier tracts.[77] More Blacks also spilled into areas adjacent to northwest Pasadena—north into Altadena and east toward Lake Avenue, which became a new racial borderline. Further east of Lake, most neighborhoods remained white, particularly Hastings Ranch at Pasadena's eastern edge. This area became a kind of racialized bunker for upwardly mobile white middle-class homeowners.[78] And white suburbs surrounding Pasadena—such as Sierra Madre, San Marino, Glendale, La Cañada, and South Pasadena—kept the door shut to Black residents.[79]

Meanwhile, local activists increasingly took to the streets in public protests and marches, following the tactics of the national civil rights movement. In September 1963, following the bombing of the Sixteenth Street Baptist Church in Birmingham that killed four Black girls, more than 200 Pasadena residents marched in silence from Central Park to City Hall in a show of solidarity. Three months later, activists set their sights on the Rose Parade to highlight racial disparities in their own backyard. The NAACP flirted with the idea of picketing the parade, to underscore its critique of the famously all-white Tournament of Roses Association, which had yet to admit nonwhite members or select young women of color as Rose Queen or Princess. The Tournament president denied any discrimination in selecting the court, claiming every parade welcomed Blacks as marchers and in the distinguished visitors' stand. Pasadena's Human Relations Committee stepped in to mediate and ultimately headed off a protest when it gained assurances from the Tournament that it would increase integration. Unconvinced, a group of Pasadena City College students staged a demonstration outside the Pasadena Civic Auditorium during the Roses Coronation Ball. Rejecting the Tournament's gesture of including a "Negro-sponsored float with a Negro queen," the student activists, as one put it, equated that float with "the separate but equal concept, and that's as bad as segregation as far as I'm concerned." In subsequent years, the Rose Parade—with its heady civic symbolism—represented a recurring site of the city's racial unease, even well after the first African Americans had served as Rose Princess and Queen in 1968 and 1985, respectively.[80]

Within this shifting milieu, local white supremacists surfaced but were quickly countered by a swelling interracial liberal movement. In 1964, about 300 people from across Southern California attended a meeting of the Citizens Council at Pasadena Civic Auditorium. At this self-professed "Caucasians only" conclave, several speakers from Mississippi assured listeners that "integration is not inevitable, it is impossible." Outside, more than 1,000 protestors encircled the building, mobilized with one day's notice by the Congress of Racial Equality (CORE), the NAACP, and the United Civil

Rights Council. A similar showdown happened a year later, when Southern white sheriff Jim Clark, notorious for his brutal assaults against civil rights workers in Selma, Alabama, spoke to the Citizens Council. Clark began his talk but was quickly squelched by boos and heckling from the 600 protestors who crowded the venue, watched by local police.[81]

In addition to the power of confrontational activism, these incidents revealed the growing muscle of liberal, racially integrated organizations, which were breaching color lines within their own groups while trying to bring that vision to the larger community. These groups symbolized an important change in Pasadena's long history with race. Groups like the Pasadena NAACP welcomed in more and more whites, the FDR Democratic Club had become well integrated, and the Interracial Women's Club of Pasadena continued its mission of promoting interracial understanding through social fellowship. Marge Wyatt exemplified this trend. She moved to Pasadena in 1956 with her family and remembered that the first group she joined was the NAACP. As a white mother of three, she was deeply concerned about the welfare of children, the community, and racial justice. As she put it, "I think racism in any form is so destructive and so anti-democratic that I don't see how we can do anything but fight it and try to bring equality and justice to this country." The Wyatts sent their kids to nearby Lincoln School, a nearly all-Black public school. And Marge became heavily involved in local progressive groups like the YWCA and the interracial FDR Democratic Club, for which she served as president.[82]

At the same time civil rights advocates were winning gradual victories—under both local pressure and federal mandates—race relations showed continued strain in Pasadena. Racialized policing was one persistent sore spot. The face of local opposition to police abuse against the Black community was Michael Zinzun. He grew up in northwest Pasadena, graduated from Blair in 1965, then had several skirmishes with the law. In 1970, he joined the Black Panthers, exploring his own sense of racial injustice born of his own experiences with the police and two years spent at a California Youth Authority facility for car theft. In 1976, he assumed leadership of the Coalition Against Police Abuse, formed in LA in 1974 to advocate for civilian control of the police, and was running a free breakfast program in Pasadena. He routinely showed up at police incidents to challenge abusive behavior by the police in Pasadena and Altadena. In 1986, a Pasadena police officer hit Zinzun in the eye with a flashlight when he intervened during a burglary arrest in his Northwest neighborhood. Zinzun lost his eye. The incident only accelerated his activism.[83]

The targeting of neighborhoods of color for redevelopment, slum clearance programs, and freeway building also produced racial inequities. The city of Pasadena began a series of redevelopment projects that decimated historic multiracial neighborhoods and resorted Pasadena's racial geography. Couched in the language of growth and progress, these projects were justifiably perceived by Blacks and Latinos as an assault upon their rights and the integrity of their communities. Redevelopment stimulated the dispersal of middle-class Blacks into formerly all-white neighborhoods at the same time that it concentrated the poorest people of color in a small area of northwest Pasadena. Pasadena, in effect, helped loosen the color line while simultaneously forging new geographies of class segregation.

The pro-growth agenda of local leaders that propelled Pasadena to regional prominence and gave the city a glossy veneer rested on policies that exacerbated racial and class schisms. As in many cities nationwide, the massive projects that orchestrated growth were often implemented at the expense of poor communities of color.[84] These initiatives were guided by federal policy, particularly the Housing Acts of 1949 and 1954, which encouraged city governments to work in concert with private developers to rejuvenate aging downtowns. These two laws ultimately privileged industrial, commercial, and institutional uses of redeveloped property over provisions for housing.[85] To leaders in Pasadena, the challenge was to eradicate so-called blighted areas, particularly those in the downtown area around Colorado and Fair Oaks. This included aging commercial establishments along Colorado as well as the old Black neighborhoods just to the south around Dayton, the Mexican neighborhood around South Raymond, and the mixed-race areas that had spread around that downtown nucleus. Portions of northwest Pasadena were likewise targeted. To local leaders, these "slum" spots of Pasadena had no place in the future of this forward-looking edge city.

In Pasadena, urban renewal began gradually. Early initiatives focused on suburban areas, part of a wave of suburban renewal happening in cities nationwide.[86] In the 1950s, Pasadena launched a program dubbed Operation Junkyard, which identified substandard housing in 197 blocks of the city's poorest multiracial areas. Officials nailed a red-lettered placard branding these structures as unsafe, then required the owner to fix the problems by a specified deadline. If owners faced financial hardship, they were referred to the city's Welfare Department or their church for assistance. About 4,300 properties were targeted; half of those property owners complied and got thank-you letters from the mayor.[87] Over the next decade, the city took a more heavy-handed approach that was less about rehabilitation and more about wholesale removal. Multiple initiatives were launched in the 1960s and 1970s: the Pepper Project, the building of the freeway, and the related expansion of the industrial district south of Colorado.

The first plan was the Pepper Project, an ambitious suburban renewal effort centered in northwest Pasadena.[88] It targeted a 102-acre area of modest, working-class suburbia including the street where Jackie Robinson grew up. It was mostly inhabited by long-time residents on limited incomes who lived in humble but well-kept homes. Tony Stewart had lived in the area since 1933, when her family arrived from Arkansas. Her recollections evoked the very essence of the Black suburban ideal: "We were a real community. Lots of different people, but most owned their houses, and that ownership meant so much to us. We had pride. Boys would be out mowing lawns, people liked their gardens and front porches. Although the neighborhood was racially segregated, it was not economically segregated—we had a couple of doctors, a lawyer, a pharmacist, a retired colonel down the street, along with regular folks, domestic workers, and such."[89] Despite the vibrancy and closeness of this community, Pasadena declared it blighted and condemned hundreds of properties between 1962 and 1964. Many Black residents voiced strong opposition, slapping the well-worn moniker "Negro Removal" on the project. Some families attempted to defy the bulldozers. The city ignored the pleas and moved forward. Modest suburban homes were torn down, replaced by public housing. As a result, the area transitioned from a vibrant middle- and working-class suburb to a neighborhood housing the "poorest of the poor," as Tony Stewart perceived it and census data confirms. By 1970, the tract encompassing the Pepper Redevelopment Area had the greatest concentration of both Blacks and poverty. Meanwhile, middle-class Blacks moved out of the area, accelerating a process of racial dispersal already under way following the early housing rights victories.[90] If slum removal was the ostensible goal, the Pepper Project had the opposite effect. It spatially concentrated Black poverty to an unprecedented degree while encouraging new patterns of class segregation within the Black community itself.

The next major urban renewal project involved the freeways and the related expansion of the industrial district south of Colorado. The construction of the 134 and 210 freeways in the 1960s had an acute impact on Pasadena. On the one hand, it sealed Pasadena's identity as a regional hub by weaving it into LA's rapidly expanding metropolitan highway system. Pasadena became a critical nexus between the San Fernando and San Gabriel Valleys via the freeways that cut horizontally through town. Boosters saw the project as nothing less than a colossal investment magnet, luring corporate headquarters, high-tech industry, retail, and tourism. Of all the San Gabriel Valley towns along the 210, Pasadena expressed the "rosiest predictions" about its impact. In tandem with the city's downtown redevelopment plan, the freeways sealed Pasadena's identity as an edge city. Its encircling suburban neighborhoods would still be there, but Pasadena's center would become more emphatically urban through gentrification, with upscale apartments for "well-heeled and free-spending single people," exclusive shopping centers, convention centers, hotels, and corporate offices.[91]

Public opinion about the freeways was far from unanimous. Some viewed this plan more as a battering ram than a growth opportunity. Affluent La Cañada to the northwest voiced strong opposition, fearing the environmental impact on this wooded picturesque enclave. LA County Supervisor Warren Dorn, who represented the still-unincorporated community, described the Foothill Freeway as "the best example I know of raping a magnificent community unnecessarily." Local citizens waged a two-and-a-half-year struggle to halt construction, but ultimately lost in 1966. The 210 freeway wiped out 500 La Cañada homes. While many were affected in Pasadena, the African American community was hardest hit, as was true of highway construction nationally. Many residents mobilized in opposition. In 1964, a multiracial group called the Freeway Action Committee for Thorough Study (FACTS) voiced its opposition to all of the proposed routes. FACTS, which included Pasadena resident Ruth Washington, the African American publisher of the *Los Angeles Sentinel*, gathered more than 20,000 "protest signatures" in Pasadena and surrounding suburbs. Pasadena leaders rejected these pleas. They ultimately selected a route that bisected northwest Pasadena instead of an alternative route along the Rose Bowl near wealthier white neighborhoods, which would have impacted fewer homes.[92] In March 1970, a group of 30 women and children from the National Welfare Rights Organization marched on City Hall, demanding that the city find housing for low-income residents displaced by the freeway. Many Blacks in Northwest perceived the project as a municipal ploy to cut them off from surrounding white communities. As local writer Don Wheeldin put it, "If some people had their way, we would be bulldozed right out of the city." In total, the freeways destroyed 5,600 housing units and displaced 13,000 Pasadenans.

A major interchange was sited directly atop the historic Black district at Vernon Avenue—the original nucleus of domestic service suburbia—while the northern spoke cut right through northwest Pasadena, particularly its poorest segment. The freeway became a massive barrier effectively buffering affluent Orange Grove while decimating a number of poor neighborhoods.[93]

In tandem with freeway construction came a push to remake downtown Pasadena and its adjacent blocks. Alarmed by a perceived exodus of "old line" Pasadena families to Orange County—the beginnings of white flight—city leaders fretted about the future of Pasadena's class identity.[94] The Pasadena Redevelopment Agency launched an aggressive gentrification campaign to replace old storefronts and mixed-race working-class neighborhoods with new corporate, industrial, and retail occupants. In the 1970s and early 1980s, a radical transformation of downtown Pasadena unfolded. South of Colorado, the old Latino Raymond Avenue section, the old Dayton Street hub of Black businesses, and surrounding mixed-race working-class neighborhoods would be cleared to make room for light industry, apartment complexes, and strip malls. In 1976, *Los Angeles Times* columnist Art Seidenbaum reported sympathetically on the plight of residents in the path of the bulldozers. He described homes "with neat screen porches and picket fences and big bougainvillea bushes." Residents described a community where people left their doors unlocked, neighbors were cooperative, and crime was nonexistent—a stable, quiet, safe working-class neighborhood. One survey found over 70% of residents wanted to stay put. Nevertheless, the redevelopment agency declared the area blighted and proceeded to transform it from residential to upscale commercial/industrial.[95] Along with the freeway, this redevelopment initiative worked to gentrify downtown Pasadena and push communities of color out of the highly visible center of town.

By far the most divisive arena of racial politics was public education. For about 15 years, the schools became the focal point of political activism from all points on the political, racial, and class spectrum. The federal mandate set in motion by *Brown v. Board of Education* challenged the web of long-standing practices and policies that had segregated Pasadena. With its daily impact on homes and families, school desegregation was the political issue that touched the greatest number of Pasadenans most directly and forced them to choose sides.

The Pasadena Unified School District (PUSD) was quite strong well into the 1960s, a jewel in the city's crown. Muir High was the district's shining beacon—80% of its graduates went on to college, while it boasted

7 National Merit scholars and 50 semi-finalists from 1957 to 1964. The city's public schools were among the most segregated in the country, even more so than in many southern states. Residents embraced the "neighborhood schools" concept—an outgrowth of the "neighborhood unit" idea— which meant that local schools reflected the demography of the immediate surroundings.

The district's claim that school segregation resulted from "natural" patterns of racial settlement disregarded not only the area's long history of residential segregation practices, but also school district policy itself. For example, the district gave transfers to white students to attend schools out of mixed-race areas while denying them to Blacks, and it allocated funds to build more classrooms in white schools instead of directing those white pupils into mixed-race schools where some classrooms stood empty. By the mid-1950s, the US Supreme Court's school desegregation cases pushed districts like PUSD to change by overturning the "separate but unequal" doctrine in public education and mandating that local districts desegregate "with all deliberate speed."[96] Pasadena thus began devising its own version of compliance to *Brown*. Its actions were remarkably salient on the national stage, representing a "classic model of Northern style school segregation" in the eyes of federal investigators and attracting periodic coverage by the *New York Times*. Over the next 15 years, Pasadena would attempt a variety of strategies to respond to the highly charged, emotional pressures of local residents, demographic and geographic changes, and, ultimately, federal and judicial mandates. Yet as Pasadena NAACP head George Jones saw it, things only got worse from 1955 to 1969, when control was more or less in the hands of the school board. Since *Brown*, Pasadena—and many northern towns like it— had showed steady slippage toward segregation, and Pasadena, the *New York Times* observed, "shows how the slippage occurs."[97]

After 1960, population shifts and new school construction complicated the situation. By this point, Pasadena showed a marked west–east racial divide—mixed-race neighborhoods to the west, all-white neighborhoods to the east, a racial configuration reflected in the schools. In Northwest was old Muir High School. This high-performing school had maintained a stable white majority for years, thanks to a predominance of whites feeding in from all parts of Pasadena and La Cañada. In 1961, wealthy La Cañada withdrew from the PUSD and proceeded to form its own school district (and later its own municipality). This removed about 900 white students from Muir, bumping up the proportion of Black pupils. Meanwhile, in the east, toward

Hastings Ranch, brand-new Pasadena High School (PHS) opened. Built to accommodate families moving into new all-white sitcom suburban tracts, the modern facility reflected the wealth of these neighborhoods. In 1964, a third high school, Blair, was built in the old south Raymond area. With this new configuration, the district began shuffling around pupils. Similar segregation patterns prevailed at the elementary school level, which led to a lawsuit brought by an African American family. In *Jackson v. Pasadena City School District* (1963), the California Supreme Court dismissed the de facto defense, a legal breakthrough for the national racial justice movement, though it offered little in the way of enforcement and implementation mechanisms.[98]

In a lukewarm effort to comply with *Brown*, in 1964, the district initiated the "open district" plan, which bused white and a few Black students from a designated "open district" in west Pasadena out of Muir and into the two new high schools. It was essentially a one-way busing formula: Blacks would be bused out east, but whites would not be bused west to racially mixed schools, putting the burden on Black children. As Black residents were gradually moving eastward and whites were leaving the district altogether, setting boundaries and devising equitable formulas were in constant flux.[99] By the late 1960s, the conflict escalated between Muir parents agitating for racial fairness and white parents in east Pasadena fervently resisting.[100]

Frustrated with the district's half-baked measures to redress school segregation, in 1967, three families filed a suit, *Spangler v. Pasadena Board of Education*. The plaintiffs were one Black and two white families, two from Altadena and one from east Pasadena.[101] Their initial lawsuit pressed for the district to enact a more equitable redistricting plan. To add weight to the lawsuit, a team of investigators from the Department of Health, Education, and Welfare's Office for Civil Rights came to Pasadena in 1968, to probe what they believed was "a classic model of Northern style school segregation." Along with 40 other cities, Pasadena was being investigated to determine if it should lose federal funds for violating the Civil Rights Act of 1964. After a three-week investigation, the team found nine violations, including the concentration of Black teachers in Black majority schools, refusals to send white pupils to schools with heavy Black enrollment, racial gerrymandering, the assignment of better teachers to predominantly white schools, and poor facilities at minority schools. The school board scrambled for a solution.[102]

In January 1970, the *Spangler* case went to federal court, where the Justice Department intervened on behalf of the plaintiffs, marking the first time the federal government interceded in a school desegregation case west of the Mississippi. One school board official in attendance resented the fact that Pasadena's good reputation was being exploited to build a high-profile landmark case. A Black community leader retorted, "The day of reckoning is here. Nobody's kidding anybody. The house has never been in order in Pasadena."[103] Pasadena's case attracted the national spotlight being shone on regional variations in compliance to *Brown*. In the eyes of Southerners, who were feeling the most intense heat from federal courts to desegregate school districts quickly (within two weeks in some cases), Pasadena came to symbolize the worst kind of regional double standard. They believed the Californians were not being held to the same standard as they were, despite its Jim Crow practices. In turn, the attorneys general of four Deep South states took the unprecedented step of intervening in the *Spangler* case on the side of the desegregation forces. They demanded that Pasadena—and all regions—be held to the same rules as the Southern states and called for a new national standard for the pacing and parameters of desegregation.[104]

After an eight-day trial, Judge Manuel Real ordered the PUSD to submit a desegregation plan within one month and to implement it by September.[105] In response, the district devised a comprehensive two-way busing plan that—for the first time—transported white students into Black areas and vice versa. White kids from the eastern suburbs went to Muir, Black kids from Northwest to PHS, and elementary school children in grades 4–6 to schools in opposite racial territory. The plan was cited positively in a US Senate hearing on equal education opportunity, and "education circles" favorably compared Pasadena's plan to similar ones in Berkeley, Princeton, Evanston, White Plains, and Seattle.[106]

It was a solution that some Pasadenans appreciated, but many disliked. White families in the eastern suburbs resented the "social engineering" of the plan and the perceived risk it brought to their children; a number of Black and Latinos resented having to leave their home school area in Northwest; and even the Spanglers thought the plan pushed things too far too fast. In particular, they believed the district stumbled in breaching both class as well as racial divides. As Jim Spangler saw it, the district "made big mistakes in how they integrated some of the westside schools. Lincoln Elementary, for one—I had a friend who lived in Chapman Woods. . . . Eastside, all white, upper income . . . and Lincoln Elementary was in mostly all black, lower

Figure 4.9 Outside the courtroom after the *Spangler v. Pasadena Board of Education* verdict was read, 1970. Judge Manuel Real ordered the district to implement its school desegregation plan by September 1970. The district's response was a comprehensive two-way busing plan that included both white and Black students.

Courtesy of the Archives at Pasadena Museum of History (PSN-Spangler decision); used by permission of Southern California News Group.

income. And they integrated those two communities. My friend was pro-integration, but when his grammar school was bused to Lincoln he said, 'They're not getting the education there.' The social bit was wrong. He wasn't afraid of blacks. He just wanted his kids to go to school with educated blacks."[107] That element of class fairness—though admirable in principle—drove white flight from the area, which accelerated swiftly after busing. The PUSD soon became majority minority, a turn of events beyond the jurisdiction of the courts by the late 1970s, as it became clear that both the federal government and liberals were retreating from a solid commitment to civil rights.[108] The PUSD quickly found itself on the road to white abandonment, with schools ultimately turning into a locus of resegregation in Pasadena.

"Magic Moment": Interracial Cooperation in the Busing Era

Busing set off a torrent of group formation and grassroots activity. For the many citizens committed to public education—for ideological, financial, or pragmatic reasons—school politics were virtually impossible to avoid. Civic engagement in turn reached a fevered pitch, and grassroots groups proliferated. While both sides mobilized, the pro-integration side had a broader, more organizationally powerful base of support, at times creating vibrant spaces of interracial unity. Though these efforts were ultimately fleeting, they had a broad impact on Pasadena. Racial politics helped tilt the balance of Pasadena's political culture from conservative to liberal and ushered in political leadership that was increasingly liberal and racially diverse.

Busing rallied a vocal, vigorous opposition—both Black and white. Several groups formed in the heat of the struggle, while some older groups redirected their energies to the school crisis. In public statements, they expressed the centrist discourse of racial innocence, meritocracy, and homeowner rights finding voice in suburban neighborhoods across the country. While most shied away from using blatant racist language, there were exceptions. One existing group that entered the fray was Taxaction Inc., an anti-tax home-owner group that shifted its focus to busing in 1970 and demanded the re-call of three pro-busing school board members.[109] Around the same time, the white supremacist Citizens Council circulated flyers claiming school desegregation was "maniacal" and meant "to force the white people of our community to associate with people of another race whether they wish to or not."[110] In 1970, several new groups formed, including the Pasadena Appeals Committee, which aimed to raise money to appeal Judge Real's decision. Within three weeks, they attracted 2,000 members and raised $30,000.[111] Other anti-busing groups included Pasadenans for a Better Way, which made its first order of business sending a telegram to President Richard Nixon to stop all busing in the nation until the buses passed a safety inspec-tion, and Citizens United for Proper Representation, based in Sierra Madre, some of whose members boycotted school on the first day.[112] A group of Black Pasadenans also questioned the concept of integration altogether, op-posing it on the grounds of Black cultural autonomy and self-determination. They formed a group called Parents in Support of Concerned Students of Pasadena, which had 300 members in 1970. Majority white schools, they believed, would overemphasize white perspectives and neglect Black culture and history. As the group's president Lawnie Taylor, an engineer, asserted, "Culture, pride, and identities of other racial and ethnic groups, especially that of the black student, cannot survive in such an atmosphere."[113]

As strong as grassroots anti-busing groups were, the pro-integration side had a broader organizational base of support. They favored racial moderation and legal compliance to busing, with motives ranging from Christian morality to economic self-interest. During the busing era, the pro-integrationists had robust support from liberal-oriented institutions in Pasadena, including leadership of 50 civic, educational, church, student, and city-connected organizations. That support began with the key civil rights groups, the NAACP and CORE. By the mid-1960s, a number of established groups stepped in to support desegregation and, ultimately, busing, including the League of Women Voters (LWV), the YWCA, the Pasadena Human Relations Committee, the ACLU, Council of Churches, the Ecumenical Council of Pasadena, and American Friends Service Committee. Several individual churches also backed the effort. Busing also had the vocal support of the Chamber of Commerce, Caltech, and the Pasadena Education Association (a teachers' group). The LWV was particularly active, viewing public education as an integral part of a healthy public sphere that comprised the foundation of good citizenship and individual opportunity.[114] New groups formed as well. One was called the Pasadena Action Committee for Equality and Excellence in Education (PACE), headed by Dr. Jerry Nims, a psychologist who lived in Altadena just east of Lake. PACE collected data showing that less-experienced teachers were concentrated in Black schools and proposed that new intermediate schools be formed to bring together a multiracial student body. Another group, Higher Opportunities in Pasadena's Education (HOPE), was a multiracial grassroots group focused on remedying deficiencies in the poorer schools. HOPE's initial goal was to muster resources to create a new reading program aimed at low-income kids; that program lasted 10 years.[115]

From the mid- to late-1960s, the tense period building up to Judge Real's busing order, a network of pro-integration advocates grew and strengthened. Members of PTAs, liberal civic groups, civil rights groups, and churches found in the issue of school desegregation a compelling common cause. By 1970, they came together in the Committee to Facilitate Integration (CRI), a coalition of 20 area organizations that met monthly. The LWV was the CRI's "watchdog," assigned to follow up on the progress of each group,

Figure 4.10 A coalition of progressive groups worked to ease the transition to busing in Pasadena, signifying a moment of interracial success during a period of racial change. This photo depicts early busing in Pasadena, when a multiracial group of parents offered cheerful assistance to Black and white schoolchildren. Courtesy of the Archives at Pasadena Museum of History (PCSN-6731F; photo by John Doran).

which included the Volunteer Bureau, the Ecumenical Council of Pasadena, Altadena Neighbors, YWCA, and Campfire Girls.[116]

Their efforts crested in 1970, as a groundswell of grassroots and organizational support coalesced to ensure a smooth, peaceful transition to busing following Judge Real's order. This moment marked the nominal end of suburban racial separatism and the beginning of a new racial convergence in the public life of Pasadena. To many, this was a hopeful moment signifying the ascendance of a new vision for the city, one where tolerance and moderation would supersede the forces of conservatism and separatism. It involved a loosely knit network of volunteers, including hundreds of parents, students, teachers, and community group members. Activities took place in homes, schools, libraries, and public gatherings. They included visits to classrooms by Black and white children who would soon be classmates, multiracial kaffeeklatsches for mothers, PTA-sponsored get-acquainted sessions for parents from 18 paired-up schools, and meetings on integration with speakers, film screenings, and literature hand-outs. Paired-up schools also took the initiative to build social connections, such as a picnic for Linda Vista, Cleveland, San Rafael, Lincoln, and Jackson elementary schools in June 1970 that drew 200. This was a remarkable union between affluent white suburbanites from the western picturesque enclaves and Black and Latino residents of Northwest. Students also held rap sessions on integration at the junior highs, and students from all three high schools formed a group called Students in Support of Integration. All of these events were designed to demystify difference, bring a human face to integration, and offer a nascent iteration of a new multiracial suburban ideal.[117]

School politics continued to dominate civic and political life in Pasadena throughout the 1970s. It remained highly contentious, marked by fiercely contested school board elections, recalls, lawsuits, injunctions, protests, and, as local businessman Joel Sheldon put it, "nasty, dirty, lies." "The two sides literally thought the other side was ruining the schools, the social structure, culture—Pasadena was going to hell in a hand basket."[118] At the extreme end, a local branch of the National Socialist White People's Party (formerly the American Nazi Party) weighed in against integration, the latest iteration of white supremacists surfacing around racial politics in Pasadena. They sprayed painted white power messages on the walls of PHS, showed up at integration demonstrations, and waged their own protests.[119] Tensions escalated from 1973 to 1977, when a reactionary "fundamentalist" school board took power with the promise of bringing order back to the schools and fighting busing altogether. This board embraced a fundamental curriculum and authoritarian style, stimulating more controversy and grassroots activism. In this revival of the old battle between progressive versus fundamental education, the fundamentalist position took on anti-busing overtones.[120]

One group that formed in direct response to this board was the Concerned Audubon Parents (CAP), a neighborhood group based out of Audubon Elementary School in Altadena. Led by resident Joel Sheldon, the group reflected the progressive spirit coming to pervade Altadena. Sheldon straddled many worlds: progressive politics, business (he managed his family business, Vromans Bookstore), and mainstream associational life (member of the Chamber of Commerce, Rotary Club, and the Red Cross). CAP waged a legal battle to prevent the board from turning Audubon into a fundamental school

Figure 4.11 The National Socialist White People's Party, headquartered for a time in El Monte, made periodic appearances in Pasadena when racial politics intensified. This photo captures one of their demonstrations in central Pasadena along Colorado Boulevard, ca. late 1970s to early 1980s.

Courtesy of the Archives at Pasadena Museum of History (PSN-Nazis, photo by Walt Mancini); used by permission of Southern California News Group.

and ran one of their members for the school board. In the process, Sheldon recalled, they were "activating a community." At one point they connected with the Black Panther Party, which also aimed to oust the fundamentalist board. CAP evolved into a close network that shared information, strategized politically, and formed social bonds. The core group of parents lived in a six-block area in Altadena. Though Sheldon was the self-described "front guy, conservative . . . my name was well known," most in the group were liberal progressives, "long hair, hippie types and yoga people." "Eventually," Sheldon recalled, "we had barbecues and parties. We all didn't sit around in a living room plotting strategy all the time."[121]

Community Together, which shared CAP's vibrancy and its opposition to the fundamentalist board, had a longer-term impact. It represented the future liberal power structure of Pasadena, bringing together Black activists with the NAACP, progressive student activists like Rick Cole, and moderate liberals like Bill Bogaard, Bill Thompson, Katie Nack, and Joel

Sheldon. As Sheldon saw it, "we lost all those [school] elections and yet those people effectively became the next generation of political leadership in the city of Pasadena." George Van Alstine, pastor of Altadena Baptist Church, remembers the peak year of that group in 1973 as a "magic moment" in the history of progressive activism in Pasadena.[122]

Race politics left a political realignment in its wake. Many of the hard-core conservatives who rose to prominence during the 1950s moved away, some of them carrying the spirit of conservatism to white suburbs at the region's edges, in places like Orange County and the west San Fernando Valley. What they left behind was a realignment in local political culture. At first a moderate Republican, then a multiracial liberal majority came to dominate Pasadena politics. During the 1970s, registered Democrats began to outnumber Republicans and would remain dominant for the rest of the century.[123] The public sphere—in local education, municipal politics, public-sector jobs, and public spaces—became racially diverse. By the mid-1980s, Blacks were serving on the city's board of directors and appointive commissions; the first Black mayor—Loretta Thompson-Glickman—served from 1982 to 1984; the first Black Rose Queen was selected in 1984; and, in 1991, a Black woman was elected president of the Pasadena Junior League.[124]

The Social and Civic Fallout of Racial Politics

If the early 1970s was a "magic moment" of interracial cooperation in Pasadena, over the next decades new kinds of separation set in. For a great many Pasadenans, withdrawal into separate spaces—whether defined by race, class, or zip code—became ever more common. The town thus turned more racially diverse and more liberal but also resegregated once again. Many of the whites who remained in Pasadena began moving quietly into Pasadena's well-established private worlds while also supporting discursively and politically the principles of postwar liberalism and racial justice. Progressive education—the bane of postwar conservatives—found a haven in local private schools, embraced by rising numbers of liberal families. Against a backdrop of racial and ethnic change, class increasingly reinforced lines of ethnoracial segregation, as it increasingly did in other privileged post-civil rights suburban spaces.[125] In the process, communities of engagement were likewise reshaped within these separate worlds, and participatory energy was increasingly divorced from the immediate context of suburban home neighborhoods.

These social shifts took place against the backdrop of profound change in Pasadena's demographic and housing landscape. After 1970, the white population declined (while still dominating numerically), the Latino population rose significantly, and the Black population rose and then fell. White flight and the influx of people of color drove these trends. Busing in itself did not instigate white flight but hastened a movement already under way. Significantly, the white population stabilized from 2000 to 2010, suggesting a pause in the exodus. Also notable was Black flight out of Pasadena after 1990, mirroring trends across LA County. At the same time, the number of Latinos and Asians rose. By 2000, Pasadena was a fairly stable, racially balanced city, with whites retaining numerical dominance (see Table 4.1). Geographically, Pasadena's elite enclaves and sitcom suburban tracts were white havens through 1980, then gradually incorporated Latinos and Asians. Blacks had a harder time moving into those neighborhoods, apart from upper-class east Altadena, where Blacks comprised 20% of residents in 2000. Pasadena's modest neighborhoods, including the Northwest area, transitioned from predominantly Black to multiracial. Asians, meanwhile, were the most evenly distributed group, signifying their class diversity.[126]

In terms of class, Pasadena experienced a gradual tilt upward, at the same time that schisms between rich and poor grew wider than ever after 1970. At the upper end, Pasadena had higher than average numbers of college-educated white-collar workers and professionals, rising substantially above county averages after 1970. There were notable socioeconomic disparities by race. From 1970 to 2000, Blacks continued to occupy a lower rung on the income ladder in Pasadena, even sliding downward by 2000, suggesting their continued struggle for economic parity. Latinos experienced a similar downward slide. In 1970, most of Pasadena's Latinos were middle class, with a median income level slightly above the city average; thereafter, they dropped well below the city average, reflecting the poorer and working-class status of Latino newcomers to Pasadena. By contrast, Asians showed steady upward mobility in income over these years. Meanwhile, the middle class fluctuated, peaking numerically in 1960, then ending at an all-time low by 2000. For many members of the middle class, the cost of living in Pasadena—with its private school surcharge and rising home prices—drove many away. Data on wealth from 2006 revealed that Pasadena was "the most unequal city in California."[127] In Pasadena, the income of households near the top

Table 4.2 Median household income by ethnoracial groups in Pasadena, 1970–2000

	1970		1980		2000	
	Median household income	% of Pasadena median income	Median household income	% of Pasadena median income	Median household income	% of Pasadena median income
Pasadena total	$7,276		$16,291		$46,012	
Non-Hispanic white			$18,175	111.6	$58,614	127.4
Black	$5,453	74.9	$12,205	74.9	$32,013	69.6
Hispanic	$7,781	106.9	$13,812	84.8	$34,842	75.7
Asian			$16,772	103.0	$49,010	106.5

Note: Blanks indicate data were not provided.
Source: US Census, 1970, 1980, 2000.

(in the 95th percentile) was 12 times greater than the income of those at the bottom (20th percentile)—$255,106 versus $21,277—the widest gap among California's 36 largest cities. The trend toward income inequality was driven by another wave of gentrification in the late 1990s, when the city accelerated initiatives to convert affordable apartments into expensive condos and slowed efforts to provide affordable housing. It reflected, too, a longer-term trend of wealthy whites staying in Pasadena, served both by city policies that privileged high-end development, retail, and services and by the maturation of their own privatized spaces.[128]

Housing and household composition revealed continued trends of diversification. The built landscape reflected the persistence of a "city–suburb" divide in Pasadena; suburban neighborhoods of single-family homes remained while mixed housing areas spread, particularly in the old areas of modest suburbia and near the business core. In essence, the trend toward mixed housing occurred against a stable, suburban backdrop.[129] Household composition also reflected some diversity, with rising numbers of young singles, declining numbers of seniors, and the persistence of two-parent households with children (they comprised about a third of all families in 1980). Working wives climbed from 41% to 62% of all married women from 1970 to 2000. Although they had less discretionary time to volunteer, join clubs, and engage civically, they did not all cease to participate. Rather, some adapted their routines and organizations to these new everyday realities. And affluent stay-at-home mothers continued their involvement in local group activity, as parent volunteers, coordinators of charity fundraisers, and club members.

Three realms of local life illustrate some of the ways racial change affected social and civic engagement in Pasadena: associations, the schools, and churches. This section spotlights associations and the schools while briefly exploring two churches. In the broadest terms, social patterns revealed a withdrawal of whites into separate social spaces. While some smaller, inter-racial spaces emerged, they were overshadowed by larger trends of racial and class separation.

Associational Life

Associations declined in number after 1970, reflecting a national trend.[130] In Pasadena, after a postwar peak, the per capita number of clubs and organi-zations experienced the largest drop between 1960 and 1970, then declined continuously thereafter. On the surface, the history of associational life in Pasadena comports with the idea that diversity strains the process of com-munity cohesion and engagement.[131] While the city's racial diversification did pose challenges to some groups, other factors also propelled the falloff. Conversely, some groups proved that an inclusive strategy could succeed with purposeful, persistent effort. Those entities, however, were generally in the minority. Within this broader context of numerical decline, Pasadena's groups tended to reinforce experiences of racial separatism.

Several factors affected the overall downward trend. First, the nature of some ethnicity- and race-based groups transformed, largely in response to local demographic change. White flight heralded an overall decline in the longstanding European ethnic and white lineage groups, which drove overall participatory numbers down. Latino groups remained proportionately small in number, despite this population group's increase. This goes a long way toward explaining the overall per capita decline in associations, as Latinos were likely also connecting outside the realm of formal organizations.[132] Second, some groups clung to old "member-by-invitation-only" policies, which constricted outreach to the limited social networks (often segregated) of members. The venerable Shakespeare Club, for example, maintained this "invitation policy" and remained lily-white in the postwar years. When membership numbers began sliding, the club instituted an application policy, but applicants still had to be sponsored by three members. From the 1960s to 1988, its membership dropped from 800 to 260, by which time most members were in their 60s and 70s. By 2001, 140 members remained. The club's 79-year-old president admitted that "new members come on very slowly today." To keep the group alive, the club abolished all barriers to admittance: "If you're breathing and you're a woman and you want to join us, that's fine. We want you," said one clubwoman. The group, then, had evolved from a highly civically engaged and influential women's organization to a philanthropic seniors' group.[133]

A third factor, completely external to Pasadena, was the waning of political party clubs by 1970. On the conservative side, anticommunists who had found outlets in grassroots political groups such as the Tuesday Morning Club and Pro America gradually faded as the Right shifted ideological focus. On the liberal side, the club movement was weakened by a move in the Democratic Party's campaign culture toward professionalization. As well, splintering within the party was reflected in the rejection of the clubs by Black militants and the radical youth movement, both alienated by the "white establishment" character of the clubs. Decline was swift. In California, membership in Democratic clubs fell from 100,000 to 10,000 between 1960 and 1970.[134] A final factor was the institutionalization of social services in Pasadena, which transferred the financing and delivery of services from charitable groups to non-profits, which proliferated after 1980. All Saints Church, a liberal congregation by that time, was alone responsible for establishing Union Station to serve the unhoused; the AIDS Service Center; the Foothill Free Clinic; the Pasadena Housing Alliance, a non-profit focused on developing low-income housing; and Young and Healthy, which provided free medical care to public school children.[135] While the creation of these agencies transferred the day-to-day delivery of services from volunteers to professionals, they did continue to use donations and fundraisers to finance their work.

Aside from the quantitative decline, the social experience of group life continued to be lively, meaningful, and marked by racial separation. For affluent white stay-at-home mothers, school fundraisers, charity balls, and society events continued to animate their social lives. Novelist Lian Dolan in *Helen of Pasadena* dubbed them the "neutron moms"—women who were overqualified and overcharged, the "once powerful business executives, now at-home mothers whose loss in status results in instability and possible implosion at any minute." With few productive outlets for their energy, they threw themselves into endless rounds of philanthropic work and charity galas. Dolan conceded her characterizations were based on reality; local media coverage attests to the continued vibrancy of this subculture.[136]

For elite Pasadenans, private clubs endured and retained their racial and class exclusivity. For example, after interest in the Valley Hunt Club waned during 1970s, a new coterie of younger members revitalized it in the 1980s. They ran two popular annual events, a Halloween costume party and The Big Splash, a "mixer" with other area clubs that drew 500 people in 1988. As the chronicler of the Club wrote during this peak moment of Pasadena's diversification, "As the rebellious times of the 1960s receded, a return to more traditional values has even stirred some nostalgia for the more settled past."[137] By the early 2000s, it had about 1,000 members, remained invitation only, and had a two- to three-year waitlist. Initiation fees were just under $20,000. And the Club's racial exclusivity persisted. That issue bubbled up in 1986, when the Club applied for a zoning change from a residential to a public designation. Local activists objected, claiming that—given the Club's racial exclusivity—the city would be endorsing segregation if it deemed this a public institution. The Club denied the allegations, claiming nothing in the bylaws "precludes any race or religion," although conceding that membership was contingent on "being well known to a number of members." Given the de facto segregation that permeated Pasadena social life, integration would be very slow in coming. In 2004, just one Black family belonged to the Club.[138] As a hub of influence and social networking, the Valley Hunt Club perpetuated generations-long patterns of racial exclusion from those networks.

Black groups also persisted as vibrant local organizations. Stalwart groups like the NAACP endured, joined by a local branch of the Urban League by the early 1970s; that branch closed in 2004, no doubt a casualty of "Black flight." Black women were particularly active, forming new groups like LINKS in 1963 and Women in Action in 1971, dedicated to bringing racial equity to municipal hiring. The Black women's sorority Delta Sigma Theta remained strong and hosted annual debutante balls through the early 2000s. Black churches likewise endured as important centers of community.[139] Civil rights and social justice continued to drive the efforts of these groups as postwar conditions posed new challenges.

Some groups embraced diversity, carrying forward nascent trends from the 1940s. They included the Interracial Women's Club, the League of Women

Voters, and the Interracial Committee of the Community Chest. One particularly successful group was the Junior League, which remained flexible and resilient thanks in part to its youthful composition. In one generation, it had evolved from a social beehive of white affluence to a multicultural women's service group. By the 1970s, by its own account, it traded in its "white gloves" for "work gloves" and stepped up its efforts to target local social need.[140] The service projects it took on in 1970 reflected the shift: it assisted the Foothill Free Clinic and provided volunteers to help PUSD teachers, staffers, and pupils during busing. In 1984, the League collaborated with Women in Action, the local NAACP, El Centro de Accion, and the Pasadena PTA to sponsor a conference on education to address the needs of youth and the local public schools. In 1986, the League articulated a key goal: to diversify its membership.[141] To that end, it eliminated sponsorship in its admission policy and held informational workshops for women of color. In perhaps its most dramatic move, in 1991, it selected as president an African American woman, Diane Scott, a 43-year-old mother of three and former pediatric nurse.[142] By 2010, whites made up half of the League's membership and people of color the other half. While the confluence of the group's membership surge and its embrace of diversity suggested a formula for organizational success after 1970, it was something of an outlier.[143] Many other groups that did not take this approach saw their memberships decline or disappear altogether.

Neighborhood associations multiplied after 1980, thanks in part to an initiative by the City of Pasadena. These groups had a long history locally dating back to 1912; new groups formed in Upper Hastings Ranch and West Pasadena in the early 1960s. By the 1980s, about 30 neighborhood associations existed. In 1987, Rick Cole, a member of the city's Board of Directors and former student activist, spearheaded the formation of the Neighborhood Connections (NC) office in city government. Its purpose was to help neighbors organize themselves into associations. By providing technical assistance and more importantly a mandate to ensure broad inclusivity, NC was a force for promoting neighborhood cohesion in diversifying Pasadena. With the stated goal of building caring communities, NC trained and assisted residents to organize associations in order to promote social cohesion, coordinate joyful activities, and advocate for neighborhood needs at city hall. Those needs could vary widely. NATHA (Neighbors Acting Together Helping All) in Northwest focused on physical revitalization, youth development programs, and community clean-ups. The Bungalow Heaven Neighborhood Association worked to prevent encroaching higher density development, to achieve landmark district status, and rid the local park of crime. The Garfield Heights Neighborhood Association also pursued land-mark district status and organized numerous social activities, such as block parties. Significantly, NC required that neighborhood associations include all residents – homeowners and tenants alike – to achieve city recognition, a break from the past when tenants had often been excluded. With the insti-tutional backing of NC, the number of associations expanded to 88 by 2007. While the vitality of these groups varied, in some areas they became sites of community integration across class, cultural, and generational lines, acting as social anchors within a city increasingly divided along those same lines.[144]

The Resegregation of Pasadena's Schools

School desegregation had an ironic—if familiar—denouement. After the in-itial politically self-conscious period of integration, during which the chil-dren of busing moved through their education and often celebrated lessons learned in the process, the public schools experienced a rapid process of resegregation. Pasadena's white middle- and upper-class suburban families largely abandoned them, along with the principle of education as a public good. Private schools became retreats for middle- and upper-class whites, and the public schools the province of people of color and the working class, mirroring national patterns of white flight away from multiple realms of public life.[145] It also paralleled the national retreat from busing and educa-tional civil rights, followed by severe resegregation of urban school districts, leaving America's public educational system in a perpetual state of crisis.[146] This resegregation had multiple effects—on the persistence of inequality by race and ethnicity, on the social reproduction of privilege and wealth, and on educational performance—stimulating years of hand-wringing and ed-ucational reform efforts among leaders at all levels of government. Beyond these well-known consequences, resegregation unmoored schools from their neighborhood settings and recast experiences of community along new lines of race and class segregation for adults and children alike. In Pasadena, the story unfolded in the parallel histories of public and private schooling.

In the 1970s, busing initially created an experience of new interra-cial understandings for public school children. Many students who daily interacted in this interracial setting expressed gratitude for the rare chance to get to know people of different backgrounds in meaningful ways. This spilled over into a raucous backyard party scene that brought together students of all races from Muir, Blair, and PHS to listen to bands like Mammoth, later renamed Van Halen. Members of that band were products of the Pasadena public schools during the busing era—David Lee Roth was bused to Muir where, one friend recalled, he "got very good at bridging the gaps." From that experience, public school students emerged "feeling wiser about racial difference than their parents or their peers from segregated schools." For many, this lesson stayed with them for years, helping them navigate life in an increasingly diverse, global society.[147]

Yet in Pasadena, this moment of interracial experience was largely fleeting. For one, mandatory busing halted in 1979, when a federal district court released the PUSD from its busing order. Thereafter, the district transitioned to a voluntary busing program which triggered a swift decline in the number of participating students.[148] More significantly, between 1970 and 2000, the PUSD transitioned into an institution that served a predominantly poorer and nonwwhite population and soon suffered the fiscal consequences of that demographic makeover. In the wake of the busing order of 1970, Pasadena's public schools continued to lose whites, to the distress of the activists who had fought hard for racial fairness in local education. Within the school district, whites tipped into a minority in the 1970s and by 2000 represented just 15% of public school pupils. At Muir High School, the number of whites dropped from 34% in the late 1970s to 9% by the 2000s. District-wide, white enrollment hit bottom in 2010.[149] White students either left Pasadena altogether or enrolled in private schools in Pasadena or other areas of LA. By 1980 over one-third of Pasadena's white children attended private school, and, by 2000, it was over half. The highest rates of private school attendance were in wealthy enclaves such as Linda Vista, Orange Grove, and San Rafael/Annandale. The abandonment of public education took on a momentum that was intensified by fading memories of earlier justice struggles and alarming performance drops within PUSD. Class segregation deepened in the process—only the well-to-do could afford private school tuition, while middle-class families found it increasingly difficult to afford this new privatized lifestyle.

The reputation of the once-touted public schools of Pasadena suffered as a result. Instead, they were perceived as sites of racial turmoil, declining achievement, and emaciated resources, further fueling the white exodus. There was no denying that school desegregation coincided with a fleeting uptick in violence in the schools, as it amplified emotions that occasionally exploded on school campuses. Around the beginning of busing, several racial skirmishes broke out at PHS, Marshall Junior High, and other schools. Animosities and accusations flew in both directions—Blacks blaming whites, and vice versa—yet Black students often bore a disproportionate share of punishment.[150] Many teachers and students resented the link made between racial diversity and school decline, blaming it on racism and negative media coverage. One African American teacher recalled that the front-page coverage of fights at Muir spread an exaggerated sense of danger at the school. A group of teachers, fed up with the negative reporting, met with the local paper asking them to stop the practice but were unsuccessful.[151]

Ultimately, the connection between racial diversity and school decline became a self-fulfilling prophesy. As whites withdrew their ample resources and energies, the PUSD's performance and resources plummeted. Just four years after busing started, notable drops in test scores were evident among all race/ethnic groups, a trend that continued for decades. White flight out of the schools also triggered a reduction in state funding for PUSD as enrollment numbers declined. The public schools became dominated by poorer minority students without the structural advantages to help them achieve academic success, so, by 2000, test scores in PUSD lagged far behind nearby affluent suburban school districts and were on par with declining cities.[152] Moreover, in school districts in neighboring affluent suburbs like South Pasadena, San Marino, and La Cañada, residents made up budget shortfalls with "soft money"—contributions from businesses, residents, and nonprofits. By contrast, in Pasadena by the 1990s, wealthy community members were not prioritizing public schools and providing such funds.[153]

The result was a striking disconnect between Pasadena's declining schools and its rising fortunes as a city. Bucking the trend of declining public education occurring in tandem with overall urban decline, Pasadena exemplified "white flight" from the public sector while whites physically stayed put.[154] Over the course of a generation, this became an accepted norm among newcomers to the area, a reality of inequality divorced from earlier racial politics, and the basis for profound community division.

Community engagement was shaken in two ways by school desegregation: first, by disconnecting education from local neighborhoods, and second, by depleting the participatory energies of middle-class families from public school communities.

For years, civil rights activists had justifiably lambasted the "neighborhood schools" movement as a euphemism for maintaining racial segregation. As accurate as this critique was, there had been a historic connection between neighborhood schools and community cohesion that was disrupted by the busing of Black and white pupils alike. Profound geographic dispersal diminished the role of the local suburban neighborhood in everyday life and placed new strains on families across the class/race spectrum. Harriet McGinley Webster grew up in the "bungalow heaven" area of central Pasadena in the 1960s, a community of modest suburban homes of mostly white and a few Black, Latino, Armenian, and Arabic families. Harriet, a white, attended Longfellow Elementary and recalled a strong feeling of neighborhood cohesion. She regularly walked to school "with complete safety. Most kids walked. And there were moms and grandmothers around during the day. . . . People were home." Neighborhood kids played together regularly at a nearby park. When she entered high school in 1969, she and one brother were sent to Pasadena High School, another sibling to Muir, and three others to Blair. After-school activities like Girl Scouts that had once been rooted in the neighborhood school were frequently moved to the new schools, but many parents wanted their kids in neighborhood-based groups. The result was attrition. For working-class parents, busing posed more substantial practical challenges. As one African American mother put it, "What does one do when the school calls and says your child is sick, come and get him. For poor people even if you have a car, sometimes there just isn't money for gas to drive the child to school or pick him up. I would like to see the return of neighborhood schools."[155]

While introducing logistical challenges into the everyday lives of families, busing also broadened the spatial horizons of the students on the buses. When groups of Black American children were asked to draw maps of Pasadena in the 1980s, their maps covered "virtually the entire metropolitan Pasadena." City planner Bill Trimble saw this as "in part related to school desegregation. They were all over the city in a way the adults were not."[156]

Besides the geographic disruptions, changes in the PUSD transformed the nature of community engagement through the PTAs, the long-standing conduit of parental involvement. The impending implementation of busing raised worries about the fate of the PTAs. The Pasadena Council of Parents and Teachers, the guiding body of individual PTAs in the district, officially supported busing, which broke with the National PTA's position. But they faced dissent within their ranks. As one mother asked, "Will the PTAs be bussed too?" Some parents were concerned about the dynamics of an integrated parent group given these mixed reactions. While the Eliot PTA backed integration, the Willard Elementary PTA registered strong opposition to busing. This schism hit the PTA at a time when participation nationally was already on a downward slide.[157] Between 1970 and 1976, membership in Pasadena's PTAs dropped from 14,000 to 8,248, a decline exacerbated by the Pasadena PTA Council's pro-busing stance. As one "disgusted mother" in Pasadena put it, she quit over this issue because "anyone against busing was not heard" within the organization. By 1997, membership in Pasadena's PTAs had dwindled to 3,370.[158]

The group struggled to attract working-class parents with little spare time or familiarity with the school system. Parents in San Rafael petitioned to have their school paired up with the school in East Arroyo, known as the "golden ghetto" for its affluence and racial diversity. "Those of us who were involved in PTA saw that it was class, not race, that was making the difference with parental involvement, and parental involvement made a difference in the school," recalled Ann Pursel, a school board member in the 1980s. "It's just really hard for poor parents, particularly if they don't speak English or they're not comfortable, to come around and tutor or help or do that kind of thing." The group Partners in Education, founded in 1995 by the Junior League, was formed in part to help address this problem by familiarizing families with the school system. Not only did declining parental engagement diminish the schools, but it also translated into a kind of political disenfranchisement of PUSD families within greater Pasadena. Without the presence of strong PTAs and a powerful parental voice, the PUSD grew increasingly isolated from the priorities of the city council. As well, since PTAs served increasingly as fundraising bodies in the post-Prop 13 years, the decline in the groups' vitality had fiscal effects that reverberated well beyond the school community experience.[159]

Black withdrawal from the PTA was also animated by the nuanced fallout of desegregation itself. In Pasadena, Black parents had participated within the PUSD's segregated system. Scattered evidence suggests that, during the 1950s, African American women headed up the PTAs at Lincoln Elementary, Washington Elementary, and Washington Junior High, all in the northwest section. Their efforts were bolstered by the Pasadena PTA Council which was quite progressive, welcoming an African American woman as treasurer in the mid-1950s, and, over the next 20 years, showing a dogged commitment to integration and busing.[160] Desegregation ultimately had mixed effects on the role of Blacks within the PTA. Nationally, when autonomous Black and white PTAs merged in 1970, Black parents lost power in the organization and PTA membership declined overall, a trend fed by the dissolution of Black-led

PTAs, the defection of some disgruntled whites, the women's movement, and changes in the workplace. PTA participation nationally fell from 50 members per 100 families in the early 1960s to less than 20 members per 100 families by the early 1980s.[161] Pasadena was caught up in these trends. As well, there was much local discussion about the need for outreach to Black and Latino families and the need to overcome language barriers. The local Black press called on Black parents to join to "take control of your child's life."[162] Wealthier suburban school districts, such as those in nearby Arcadia, La Cañada, San Marino, South Pasadena, and Temple City, were able to maintain higher levels of parental participation, while Pasadena had the lowest rate of PTA membership in the San Gabriel Valley. With their much greater class and racial diversity, Pasadena's PTAs could not stave off the malaise of parental withdrawal.[163]

Private schooling had always been strong in affluent Pasadena, but it surged in the wake of busing. Pasadena and Sierra Madre had among the highest proportion of children in private schools across LA County suburbs during these years. From 1970 to 2000, the number of area private schools jumped from 26 to nearly 50. Once the province of the "society" set, after 1970, private schools had become more diffuse, middle-class, politically diverse institutions. In 1990, about half of local private schools were parochial, three were progressive, and the remainder "traditional."[164]

With their pricey tuition, private schools created class-segregated school communities and also tended to reinforce separation by race. Although white children always outnumbered nonwhite in private schools, after 1970, this disparity grew wider. So while private schooling became a "typical" experience for the majority of Pasadena's white suburban pupils, it was increasingly unusual for Pasadena's children of color.[165]

Despite this trend, after 1970, a number of local private schools gradually diversified their student bodies. An analysis of the graduating classes of five schools found that, while most had less than 7% nonwwhite students in 1970, by 1990, the number rose to one-third, and to 40% to 55% by 2000 (this included Asian, Latino, and Black American students). Among this small sampling, Catholic schools, where tuition was cheaper, had the greatest diversity. Many public schooling advocates in the early 1970s chastised Pasadena's private schools for drawing the best and brightest minority kids and creating a PUSD brain drain. Blacks were still very under-represented, never exceeding 5% of any private school's graduating class from 1970 to 2000.[166] Moreover, since many of these schools drew students from beyond Pasadena, they were not necessarily serving Pasadena's nonwwhite families. In 1984, four private schools in Pasadena joined a regional effort by independent schools to recruit minority students by attracting corporate sponsors and offering scholarships. Polytechnic and Waverly used an organization called A Better Chance (ABC) to recruit Black and Latino applicants from across Los Angeles, all of whom lived outside of Pasadena.[167] With their careful screening processes, private schools ensured that the students admitted comported themselves with the values and cultural styles of the affluent white suburbanites who dominated these schools.

In this privatized sector of the education market, parents could shop for the educational style that most suited their tastes and avoid the debates over progressive versus fundamental education that perennially embattled the PUSD. For all the controversy progressive education elicited in the PUSD over the years, it ultimately found a comfortable haven in the private schools, attracting liberal/progressive parents. Traditional and parochial schools offered other alternatives. Pasadena parents could also seek out schools throughout the greater LA area.

Many private schools worked to foster communities of involvement among parents, which resonated among the post-1980 generation that embraced "hands-on" parenting. Several institutionalized this by setting a fixed number of required parent "volunteer" hours. Among six schools surveyed, four had such a requirement, ranging from 20 to 50 hours per year.[168] This policy not only ensured engagement, but also enabled schools to supplement their resources through volunteer labor. Other schools had active parent groups, often focused on fundraising. For example, Polytechnic, an elite traditional school located across the street from Caltech, had a parent organization that met regularly. The focus of its February 1991 meeting was the annual fund, with a "phonathon" carried out by parent volunteers. Many schools organized annual fundraisers, social activities, and community building events.[169]

At Waverly School, parental involvement became a central part of this progressive school's culture, because of its small size, the school's need for volunteer labor, and a parental motivation to be integrally involved in their children's lives. Parents created several annual events (fundraisers and social gatherings), did pro bono work on financial planning and site expansion, organized emergency preparedness, and served as classroom helpers. In a 2010 survey, one Waverly parent reported putting in 250 hours of volunteer work per year, during two years of running the Silent Auction fundraiser. Another described the parent community as providing "comfort and a source of meaningful and mutual support." One parent claimed Waverly "provides a foundation for our family as a whole, connecting with other families." This feeling was strengthened as many parents developed friendships among themselves. The head of school, Heidi Johnson, surmised this sense of school-based community replaced what once existed around neighborhood schools. Waverly families, moreover, clearly had the time and financial means to invest in this level of participation.[170]

The geographic disconnect between neighborhoods and schools that began with busing grew by an order of magnitude with the expansion of private schooling. Commuting became a daily fact of life for children attending schools well beyond their home neighborhoods. For example, the Sotomayors, both attorneys, had moved to the San Rafael area of Pasadena in 1987 and, for their family, public schools were never an option. Rande Sotomayor, herself a Catholic high school graduate, recounted that, when she first connected with the local elementary school, she determined there was "an insufficient local community commitment." The three Sotomayor children—the youngest and eldest five years apart in age—began by attending Clairbourn School, six miles away in East San Gabriel. When they got older, they attended Westridge School in Pasadena, Waverly School in central Pasadena, and Loyola High in central Los Angeles, the latter about 12 miles from Altadena, where the Sotomayors moved in 1998. So at different points in time, their children attended three separate schools significant distances apart. With extracurricular activities and parental involvement in the schools, life became a series of far-flung "commuter" activities. The main activity countering this trend was youth sports, like Little League and the American Youth Soccer Organization (AYSO), which connected the Sotomayors to multiracial families in the neighborhood.[171] Parental engagement around the schools, for the Sotomayors and most other families, did not cease in the world of private schooling: to the contrary, in many cases, it intensified even as it dispersed spatially. As with civic groups, schools continued to draw participatory energy, but often did so divorced from the immediate context of suburban home neighborhoods.

From 1970 to 1990, education was gradually depoliticized in the minds of many Pasadena residents. Whereas the choice between public versus private had once been a highly charged political decision—reflecting the tightly linked issues of race and education—by the 1990s the memories of that interconnection faded and a calcified system of educational separatism had become an accepted norm. In the process, the liberals who had come to dominate local political culture experienced a kind of existential shift, from visceral guilt over withdrawal to a new comfort level with educational apartheid. While this transition reflected the contingencies of local history, it also reflected broader, deeply intertwined trends—particularly the national retreat from civil rights, the widening gulf between rich and poor, and the rise of a centrist ideology of color-blind, meritocratic individualism as the basis for claims of suburban homeowner rights, used to explain social difference and persistent racial inequality. Thus, as the gaps between rich and poor, white and nonwwhite widened in income, housing, and schooling, there was less political willingness to address the structural forces exacerbating them.[172]

These ideological shifts around educational inequality happened both across the Pasadena population and within the psyches of individual residents. They manifested perhaps most dramatically among the children of busing. As one research team found, when these graduates—who uniformly valued their interracial experience during busing—became parents, about 50% of whites sent their children to all-white schools, and the remaining whites chose "somewhat diversified" schools. More Black and Latino graduates, by contrast, sought out diverse schools (both public and private) for their children, although about two-thirds of them noted that these schools were becoming less diverse as desegregation plans terminated and their communities were impacted by white flight.[173]

For many of these graduates, concern with quality education had come to overshadow their desire for integrated schools. Rebecca Fleming, who was bused as an elementary school pupil in PUSD, deeply valued that experience yet ultimately placed her own children in private school. "What saddens me the most," she recalled, "is that I did give PUSD a try with my daughter when she was younger. . . . As she entered the middle school years, I put her into Catholic school and she is now in high school and doing well. As for my son, I put him directly into Catholic school. It wasn't even an option for me to consider PUSD after these last five years with the declining test results, the administration that was in place and in general the negative press."[174]

The transition from integrated to segregated schooling was even more striking for one Black American graduate of Muir High School's class of 1980. The son of a truck driver and house cleaner, he grew up in a working-class section of Altadena. He was bused as a youngster from his west Altadena neighborhood to Field Elementary in the far east section of Pasadena, which he recalled as a rich experience academically and socially. By the time he attended Muir, he had continued making cross-racial friendships, particularly in his extracurricular activities, though his closest friends were Black kids from his neighborhood. Desegregation, he asserted, "can work, can produce good people, can produce good friends, can produce good experience, and . . . it's a necessity." He believed it was crucial to his own success. He went on to become a police lieutenant and, after marrying another Muir alum, moved into a large home in an affluent white suburb of Los Angeles. He bought the house because he and his wife wanted their daughters to grow up in a "better community where they would have a better chance of excelling . . . [where] they could concentrate on their academics and potentially also interact with people who . . . have a higher degree of education." They were one of two Black families in a community of 42 homes. He conceded that he experienced more racism in his upper-middle-class suburb than he ever did attending desegregated Muir, citing snubs at the local elementary school, racial steering in real estate, and even a cold shoulder from the wife of a white Muir alum who lived in the same neighborhood. Most of his closest friends were Black (not from the neighborhood), some of them from high school. For him, the tradeoff of living amid white suburban affluence was worth it. Despite his own positive memories of diversity during his youth, he chose a path to the American Dream that was affluent, suburban, and mostly white.[175]

A Tale of Two Churches

Houses of worship likewise grappled with the challenges posed by racial integration. Two examples briefly illustrate the challenges white churches had in adapting to racial change. All Saints Episcopal Church and Altadena Baptist Church were both committed to the principles of civil rights. Yet they had contrasting experiences in translating those ideals into congregational life. All Saints was a large, liberal congregation, deeply involved in social justice causes near and far, such as poverty, homelessness, nuclear disarmament, immigration, and LGBTQ rights. Thanks to its high-profile reputation, it drew thousands of parishioners from Pasadena and across LA. Altadena Baptist Church was a small neighborhood church, concentrating on ministering to the spiritual well-being of its members. While its pastor was highly active in local social justice causes, he did not incorporate them into his ministry. Altadena Baptist emerged as a racially diverse church, reflective of the changing suburban neighborhood around it.

By the 1960s, All Saints Church had established itself as a powerful force for social justice in Pasadena, supported by a parish of over 2,400 members. Its rector, George Regas, approached his ministry with a Bible in one hand and a newspaper in the other, as he put it, reflecting a strain of activist liberal Christian theology prevalent in LA and beyond.[176] For all of its passion, energy, and pragmatic understanding of inequity in Pasadena, the one issue Regas felt the church faltered on was race. From the perspective of All Saints' mostly white parishioners, this was an issue that hit perilously close to home. When Regas arrived in 1967, the school desegregation controversy had been building for years. With its long history of racial separatism, All Saints faced formidable challenges. The goal of integration—which parishioners embraced morally and spiritually—revealed profound schisms in the ways All Saints dealt with race and ultimately the ruptured ways that many white liberal suburbanites enacted their commitment to social justice.[177]

In the late 1960s, All Saints launched several initiatives—small and large— to promote interracial understanding. It began by forming a group called the Society To Act Rather'n Talk (START), which helped organize a weekend-long Black Arts Show in 1969, to highlight the work of local artists. The following spring, as the school situation was reaching fever pitch, All Saints presented a six-week series on minority self-determination, a program meant to familiarize parishioners with unfamiliar people.[178] The most substantial intervention was a program called Project Understanding, which ran at All Saints in 1970–1971. Its ambitious goal was to combat white racism in white suburban communities by placing seminary students in residence as interns at six suburban churches around Los Angeles, including All Saints. Program leaders perceived the situation in Pasadena as especially dire. The program was a kind of racial consciousness-raising for "white, middle-class, college educated parishioners." By the end of its run, Project Understanding's leaders declared it a moderate success but observed a tendency by parishioners to "talk less racist without behaving less racist." White liberal churches like All Saints tended to oppose "massive action in restitution for the disabilities inflicted by racism." In Pasadena, this was a coded reference to busing.[179]

These assessments captured the limitations of white liberalism at All Saints. Regas acknowledged the tremendous internal tensions that busing engendered among his parishioners. The church supported desegregation as a policy, and many of its members participated in the legal and political battles around the schools. As Regas put it, "the All Saints community, intellectually, agreed." But many also rejected busing as the proper mechanism for change, quietly sending their own children to private school. "It was hard, hard work, because the instrument to bring about racial justice was just a hard, harsh instrument. . . . The race issue, being so intimately tied to how your children are educated, was a dynamic explosive ingredient. And so it was harder to get people in a sustained involvement in the race issue in Pasadena that was so inextricably tied to the education issue. And so it's obvious that we failed in that, because of the enormous withdrawal of the white population." All Saints, as well, struggled to integrate its own parish, as whites were disproportionately represented, and it attracted a much smaller numbers of Black Americans, Latinos, and Asians.[180] In assessing his 28-year ministry at All Saints, Regas conceded with some regret, "I did better on the peace, ecology, hunger issues than I did on the race issue."[181]

Two and a half miles up the road, Altadena Baptist Church shared a common moral philosophy with All Saints, but it took a very different path in following those beliefs. It was a small, neighborhood church, more inwardly focused yet deeply aware of the demographic changes happening beyond its doors. In its successful adaptations to racial change, Altadena Baptist reflected a new multiracial suburban ideal in action.

When George Van Alstine arrived as the new minister in 1972, the church was all-white, drawing about 100 worshippers to services on Sunday mornings. Membership was around 330, but about 200 people were actively involved. By 1980, Blacks had surpassed whites in the immediate neighborhood, comprising 48% of residents, with whites at 39%, and Latinos at 11%. Van Alstine knew from the start that racially integrating his church was a "priority goal." At the same time, he fully embraced the idea that church life and political life were indisputably separate, which reflected his own religious upbringing as well as the culture of some Baptist churches. While in his spare time he engaged in busing politics, got elected to the school board, and joined the Interdenominational Ministerial Alliance, a group of Black ministers in the community—Van Alstine was the only white—he remained adamant about keeping politics out of the pulpit.[182]

Within Altadena Baptist, the goal of racial inclusion was gradually realized. After some early efforts to invite Blacks in failed, modest outreach began to pay off. Alice Blackwood, a newcomer to Altadena in the 1970s, visited the church one Sunday but because she didn't see any other people of color, she decided not to return. Within a few weeks, two deacons from the church came calling, saying "we didn't see you last Sunday." (It was church practice for the deacons to visit all newcomers.) Blackwood decided to give it another try. When she returned, she still did not see other Blacks, but was struck by the kindness of the congregation. "People were friendly and speaking to me, and me being born in the South, I wasn't used to white people speaking to you like that. It was a really friendly church."[183] On another Sunday, another African American family was there. Gradually, more and more Blacks found their way to Altadena Baptist, some through friendship networks but mostly independently. Eventually, Blacks came to comprise about one-third of the congregation, whites about 55%, and other nonwhites the remainder (including Filipinos, Koreans, and Lebanese)—and these proportions remained constant over the years.[184]

Altadena Baptist was particularly successful at building community within its diverse congregation. Like many churches in this period, it used small groups to do so. Dubbed TLC (tender loving care) groups, they began meeting in members' homes in the mid-1970s and continued for decades. The groups had autonomy in decisions about format, size, topics, and members. Alice Blackwood started the first group, partly as a way of pulling her husband into the church community because he didn't attend regular services. Her TLC group met weekly, sometimes over a meal, and generally spent their time together "sharing needs, being prayed for, [and] some bible study." Most of the groups were racially and ethnically diverse. Blackwood's group, for example, was comprised of four whites, nine Blacks, one Native American, and one Lebanese. It began meeting weekly in the mid-1970s and continued for the next 35 years, with some turnover in members over the years. "It's kind of like a family now," she said. This small church, linked in spirit and culture to its surrounding neighborhood, had found a workable formula for community engagement, offering interracial neighbors ways to connect and form lasting bonds of friendship.

In different ways, both churches made important contributions to the project of racial integration and social justice in Pasadena—All Saints at the level of programs and politics, Altadena Baptist at the level of community building. All Saints had a significant structural impact on Pasadena, helping establish a social justice infrastructure in the city. But it struggled with the challenges of building interracial community within its large congregation. Altadena Baptist left no political footprint. But it quietly found a formula for building community right in its own backyard. These two churches illustrate the ways that engagement—social and civic—manifested itself in diversifying Pasadena.[185]

Making and Remaking Inequality

Since 1950, race has had deep, complex effects on the history of social and civic engagement in Pasadena. This was not a simple story of declension. Rather, it involved shifting sites of involvement, changing cultures of class and race, the obstinate persistence of segregation, and the emergence of some interracial communities built within the challenging context of demographic change.

In the postwar years, social spaces in the city were highly segregated, clearly demarcated by race and social predictability. Within this segregated context, Pasadena suburbanites experienced a high point in local associational life, often centered around their homes. As political engagement reached its apex around the contentious politics of race and civil rights, there was a surge in grassroots activism from across the political spectrum. The progressive communities that emerged out of those battles paved the way for the ascendance of liberalism in Pasadena.

The liberal majority that emerged in Pasadena effected a kind of mental split—one that allowed for social justice activism in causes both local and distant while living in protected, affluent, suburban neighborhoods.[186] In the liberal, multiracial milieu of post-1970 Pasadena, the affluent set melded its progressive concerns with its own material resources of time and money through volunteer involvement in philanthropy and private schools.

It was within this multiracial liberal milieu, marked by rising income inequality, that lines of segregation were again drawn, separating rich from poor, whites from nonwhites. By supporting local policies like redevelopment and gentrification, which wiped out affordable housing, and by abandoning the public schools, white middle- and upper-class families exacerbated social divisions that long characterized Pasadena. Long-standing institutions like elite private clubs continued to close ranks and limit benefits to their own members. More than social hubs, these clubs were economic strongholds and political influencers; their racial and class exclusivity thus had public consequences. Low-income families of color, and eventually middle-class whites, found it harder to achieve upward mobility or even to afford to live in Pasadena. These actions helped create and sustain the city's resegregation.

Yet even within this bifurcated world, there were spaces where people breached the stubborn divides of class and race. In settings like the NAACP, the Interracial Woman's Club, Altadena Baptist Church, and the Junior League, diversity became a driver of engagement. Social justice activism also found a footing in progressive houses of worship such as All Saints and more recently in grassroots political groups. Moreover, the PUSD has seen a gradual return of white students since 2015, prompted by pocket-book pressures on families grappling with soaring housing costs.[187] These common sites of participation suggest nascent examples of multiracial suburban living.

Pasadena illustrates the possibilities and limits of multiracial coexistence in the new suburbia. White residents remained in Pasadena in their own separate spaces and as members of robust communities, all contained in a place that prided itself on being a world-class city of knowledge. Their pivot toward privatization in everyday life signaled an abandonment of Pasadena's public sphere, especially its schools, once a linchpin of local civic engagement and opportunity. This ultimately worked to disconnect the public schools from the city itself.[188] Trends of suburban inequality in turn accelerated. The city's fortunes rose as redevelopment brought high-end stores, restaurants, apartments, and condos to the refurbished Old Town. In nearby neighborhoods, poverty and homelessness, housing unaffordability, and racialized policing plagued the city's Black, brown, and poor residents. Within suburbia, the haves and have nots, poverty and progress, coexisted. As late as 2005, the rate of private school attendance in Pasadena was three times the state and national averages. Reflecting on those divides in 2013, PUSD president Renatta Cooper lamented Pasadena's persistent separate and unequal reality. She conceded, "The community is still . . . I think wounded is the right word."[189]

5

Learning Suburban Affluence

San Marino

What happens when a suburb that prides itself on stability and tradition becomes an immigrant receiving ground? And when that town is a landscape of privilege, savvy and dexterous with the tools of neighborhood defense, how does it handle the immigrant onrush? These challenges defined much of the recent history of San Marino. This stately, affluent suburb northwest of downtown Los Angeles is a community whose roots intertwined with the crème de la crème of the LA elite and became a favored destination of wealthy Asian immigrants after 1970. Like their Anglo counterparts, these newcomers were attracted to the town's fine schools and reputation as a dignified, old-money enclave. What they encountered was a suburb with strong traditions of community, aesthetics, and local identity bound together by a robust culture of voluntarism. In contrast to some affluent suburbs whose only social cohesion rests on a flimsy basis of shared allegiance to NIMBYism (not in my back yard), San Marino was a place where community had social meaning.[1] Full adjustment to local life meant participating and accepting these long-standing traditions.

San Marino, in effect, became a critical site where Asian suburbanites learned American democracy. Through quotidian activities around schools and neighborhood, participation emerged as an explicitly suburban value—sometimes the flashpoint of ethnic conflict, other times the incubator of assimilation and shared social experience.

Like most picturesque enclaves, San Marino's affluent status was predicated on a local culture of stasis. With a confident sense of the town's high value—social, aesthetic, and property—residents united around a shared belief that you don't change what works; you protect it and cement it in place as much as possible. This community philosophy applied to the built environment as well as social and political life itself. San Marino, then, was a town steeped in long-running local traditions. When immigrant newcomers confronted this firmly settled milieu, their only real path to local acceptance was assimilation. They had to learn the ways of suburban affluence—whether that meant embracing local design aesthetics, participating in critical hubs of social life, serving in political roles, or upholding the tools of class exclusion. In so doing, they reproduced the internal elements that ensured the remarkably consistent appreciation of local property values, even in periods of economic downturn. During the Great Recession of 2007–2009, for example, San Marino was the only wealthy suburb in Los Angeles where home prices did not fall.[2]

These habits did not come automatically to Asian newcomers. Many arrived without personal or family experience in community involvement. Yet this did not dampen their desire to integrate socially. A San Marino zip code may have been a vivid marker of what sociologist Lisa Sun-Hee Park terms "consumptive citizenship"—signifying status-laden economic and cultural capital that demonstrates social citizenship in the United States—but many Chinese newcomers also sought to fully experience an affluent suburban lifestyle that went beyond the prestigious address.[3] That meant learning the town's well-honed social and political traditions and showing a willingness to carry them forward.

Some scholars have argued that elite suburbs were retreats from the "psychologically unsettling processes of globalization," manifested in part as immigrant workers and the poor.[4] The history of San Marino, by contrast, demonstrates divergent ways that globalization has reshaped suburban geographies. Diverse groups of Asian immigrants—by nationality, class, education, and skill levels—settled in an array of suburban areas.[5] In the middle- to high-end suburbs, globalization meant the arrival of well-heeled immigrants and their wealth. While Anglo residents initially resisted this influx, eventually they reached a rapprochement and worked with Asian suburbanites in sustaining the privileges of affluent suburbia. In this way, globalization was not an oppositional force, but an integrative one in which class privilege—and in turn class inequality—was reproduced transnationally and across suburban space.[6]

As San Marino's multicultural populace converged around shared social and class interests, it ensured the continuity of the suburb's affluence, even as it drifted away from whiteness. Property values stayed high, schools strong, and landscapes elegant as Anglo and Chinese residents together protected these elements. The small size of the community with its own self-contained,

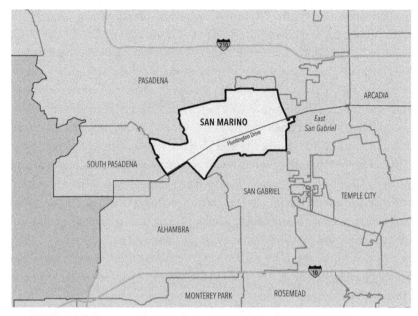

Figure 5.1 Map of San Marino and surrounding suburbs.
Cartography by Jennifer Mapes, Kent State University.

blue-ribbon school district assisted in that process. It helped neighbors learn
to build trust, find common cultural ground, and, ultimately, pass along
American traditions of suburban exclusivity. In San Marino, the social and
civic integration of Asian Americans served a broader purpose of protecting
one of LA's most venerated landscapes of privilege.

Moneyed Roots

San Marino sits approximately 8.5 miles northeast of downtown Los Angeles,
built along the escarpment of the Raymond fault. In the mid-nineteenth century, its rustic and picturesque landscape was covered with thick forests of oak
trees and wild grapevines. Originally settled by the Tongva people, the area
fell under the orbit of the San Gabriel Mission from the 1770s to 1830s. The
Mission's laborers built a dam and three mills, one of which still survives. With
secularization and Americanization came a series of land transfers that shifted
control into the hands of LA's emerging aristocracy. Two early landowners
were opposing Civil War leaders—Union General George Stoneman and

Confederate Colonel Edward Kewen—who each acquired vast tracts in the area, finding in this serene landscape a post-bellum Shangri La.[7] By the 1880s, the area had become a bountiful "fruit belt." Stoneman's ranch alone had almost 100,000 grapevines and an array of exotic fruit and nut trees—walnuts, almonds, figs, cherries, nectarines, tamarinds, berries, bananas, guavas, and oranges. The area's lush ecology and bluff-top vistas caught the attention of Henry E. Huntington, who chose the site for his own palatial estate and gardens in 1903. One of the area's biggest transit moguls and real estate developers, he amassed a fortune from subdividing farmlands into suburbs. An early neighbor was George S. Patton, land agent of Pacific Electric and general manager of the Huntington Land & Improvement Company.[8] Huntington and Patton developed a close friendship, playing poker, partnering on business ventures, and planning for the future of their land and community. Their estates were more sprawling, extravagant versions of the wealthy properties in neighboring Pasadena. This lush and picturesque part of Los Angeles was christened early and permanently as a landscape of wealth.[9]

By the 1910s, Huntington and Patton—the prime landholders at that point— guided San Marino's emergence as an affluent suburb. The first order of business was solidifying local control. In 1913, they spearheaded a movement for municipal incorporation in order to stave off annexation attempts by neighboring Pasadena, South Pasadena, and Alhambra. They had to muster signatures from 500 permanent residents, which proved a challenge given the area's lopsided social geography. It was essentially a sprawling expanse of ranch estates, sparsely populated by a few wealthy property owners, their families, and their laborers. The total 519 signatures they amassed represented less a democratic community than a plantation-like social structure of wildly unequal residents.[10] Like early Pasadena, whose estates depended on an army of laborers, early San Marino was characterized by cross-class interdependence. The difference was that San Marino's laborers did not form their own permanent working-class neighborhoods; they either became live-in staff or were squeezed out through exclusionary tools that made San Marino a sundown town.

By the 1920s, the Huntington estate had become an internationally renowned center of art and rare manuscripts, surrounded by expansive gardens. In 1904, Huntington hired German horticulturalist William Hertrich to develop his botanical gardens. Within a few years, Hertrich was raising more than 15,000 landscape trees in a nursery on the estate, which would eventually blanket the Huntington Gardens, as well as many elegant San Marino streets.[11]

Figure 5.2 The Huntington estate, shown in the top photo in 1913, was both the physical and aesthetic center of San Marino. Huntington took a special interest in imprinting his aesthetic vision on the homes and landscapes of San Marino to ensure a suitable buffer around his estate. Saplings raised in the Huntington Gardens were planted along many streets in the suburb in the 1910s and 1920s, still visible in the landscape today.

(top) PhotCL 402, Harold A. Parker Studio Collection of Negatives, The Huntington Library, San Marino, California; (bottom) photo by Becky Nicolaides.

With a bevy of savvy land developers and businessmen at the helm, San Marino entered its subdivision stage very carefully. Patton, the town's first mayor, conferred closely with Huntington on the town's early formation. Among Huntington's many developments in Southern California, this one was particularly important, representing a kind of residential buffer around his own personal estate. It was critical that it be fixed securely and permanently as a tasteful landscape of wealth. When he decided to begin selling off parts of his land, he enlisted agents to handle sales but remained actively involved in the process, detailing specific building and land use guidelines.[12]

One of the early and most important subdivisions was Oak Knoll Marino, developed in the early 1920s.[13] It occupied the western section of San Marino between Huntington's estate and the Huntington Hotel, just across the border in Pasadena. Huntington envisioned Oak Knoll Marino as a suburban sub-division imbued with the aristocratic air of his illustrious library. A sales brochure captured this well. Mimicking a rare manuscript, it opened with a translucent onionskin laid over a black-and-white copy of Gainsborough's "Blue Boy," Huntington's most famous art acquisition to date. Then, the hook: "Location Means Everything." Where we live "shapes our very destiny." In a dozen pages, the pamphlet described the makings of "the most beautiful residential park in California," with "large and satisfying" lots, up-to-date improvements, gracefully curving streets, and landscaping from the estate, including cocos plumosa, walnut, Australian and Canary Island palm, oak, and redwood trees. The Huntington connection was a clear and obvious selling point. Oak Knoll Marino also featured improvements and restrictions typical of growingly popular "country club districts"—modern sewers, curbs, sidewalks and ornamental streetlights, and race restrictions. The result was a lily-white neighborhood of extreme wealth, protected by restrictions that "guaranteed permanently desirable surroundings," as the sales brochure intoned.[14]

Subsequent 1920s subdivisions included "Huntington Hill" to the south, built on gentle wooded slopes.[15] Further east was "Gainsborough Heath," a 297-acre tract meant to conjure a direct connection to the English artist. Developers initially planned to build 1,000 homes ranging in price from $10,000 to several hundred thousand dollars.[16] In these high-end sections, residences were designed in classic, European influenced architectural styles—Spanish Revival, Tudor, French Revival—built by well-known architects, including Wallace Neff, Myron Hunt, and Roland E. Coate.[17]

Figure 5.3 Advertisement for the Gainsborough Heath development in eastern San Marino, 1928. Ads such as this made aesthetic connections between elite suburban real estate and the painter's masterworks housed at the nearby Huntington Library and Art Gallery.
Los Angeles Times, March 4, 1928.

While sales were healthy in the 1920s, the downturn precipitated by the Depression prompted the opening of new developments aimed at a broader range of buyers. From 1935 to 1937, San Marino experienced a mini-boom in home building. These included both high-end homes and moderately priced dwellings situated in more traditional middle-class subdivisions. In "San Marino Highlands," subdivided in 1939, 1,600-square-foot homes sat on 60-foot-wide lots laid along a denser constellation of gently curving roads.[18] These modest tracts were situated south of Huntington Drive, sufficiently distant from the wealthy estates, earning this area the derogatory nickname "Sub-Marino" in later years. The Depression, then, opened San Marino up to include a substantial share of middle-class residents. By 1940, the town was 52% built out; over the next two decades, it would be completely built out.[19]

From its suburban origins, San Marino had restrictions on its built and social landscape that were enforced by both private and public powers. In zoning measures passed in the 1920s and 1930s, the municipality designated the vast majority of local land as single-family residential (R-1), with minor commercial activity allowed along two commercial strips and in two small shopping clusters. Apartments and other multifamily housing were eventually banned, along with alcohol, firearms, and other odious enterprises. Private developers also worked to protect the town's high-end identity. In Oak Knoll Marino, minimum construction costs were set at $15,000, keeping out all but the well-to-do. Developers likewise enforced architectural integrity by offering "wise" guidance in areas like Gainsborough Heath. Unlike the planned community of Palos Verdes, San Marino did not exert municipal control over local design in its early years.[20] Reflecting this relatively lax approach, it formed a volunteer advisory "Board of Home Design" in 1952, to ensure that prospective homes conformed to size and design standards as well as "the general character and appearance of nearby residences."[21] The following year, this body was replaced by a new Planning Commission whose remit included enforcing residential restrictions.[22] For the most part, however, it took a light-handed approach to the regulation of local design up through the 1970s.

From the beginning, San Marino was a white man's town. While residents viewed Chinese, Mexican, and Black Americans as a valuable labor source, they vigilantly excluded them from permanent residence. The town's deeds of trust stated that local land should not be sold to Jewish, Black, or Chinese people. Race-restrictive covenants were also widespread. Early real estate promotions mentioned "race restrictions"; by 1939, federal HOLC appraisers noted that "deed restrictions are ample and rigidly enforced" in San Marino.[23] This persisted into the 1940s, when returning Japanese internees took jobs as domestics in many of the town's wealthy homes.[24] Along these lines, the Pacific Electric streetcar routes served two uniquely high-end purposes in

San Marino. One was a special spur track onto Huntington's estate to deliver precious cargo for his collection and to transport the family directly to their New York home.[25] A second was to give the hired help access to San Marino, a feature explicitly mentioned in sales pamphlets.[26] San Marino maintained racial exclusivity into the early 1970s through practices like racial steering by realtors, open opposition to fair housing laws, and outright refusal of owners to sell to nonwwhites.[27]

Among the Chinese people who later settled San Marino, some were keenly aware of these racist roots, calling San Marino a "sundown city" and otherwise noting the racial exclusivity that defined its origins.[28]

Life in Shangri-La: Creating Traditions of Voluntarism in Postwar San Marino

In 1956, in the throes of America's postwar fixation of domestic home life, San Marino parents started a tradition. Rather than let the high school seniors go off and party on their own, they would throw them an all-night bash to remember. This was the first graduating class of the newly opened public high school. Sensitized by media hype around juvenile delinquency and San Marino's own brush with tragedy the year before, when a drunk driver killed four students driving home from a prom, local parents took cues from high schools on LA's west side. Five years earlier University High in West LA started the first "Grad Night," a parent-supervised party to keep all the kids under one roof. In 1956, San Marino would begin its own version, one that would come to outdo every other town across LA County. San Marino's shindig would top them all in two ways—as an extravagant production and as an exemplar of community cohesion, voluntarism, and parental love. It also aptly symbolized the tenor of local social and civic life, rooted firmly and passionately around children and the schools.[29]

The first event was fairly modest. The 1956 Grad Night was themed "Carnival Français." It took place in the high school gym, decorated to resemble a French nightclub. The party went from 10 PM to the morning, with a firm "no exit" policy: "once they go out the door, they can't get back in." Students were served dinner by school parents, two bands played through the night, strolling singers serenaded the revelers, and swimming was encouraged in the adjoining Olympic-size pool. Local civic organizations sponsored games, a snack bar, a hamburger stand, a photo studio, a barber for the boys, and a hair salon for the girls. Finally, over a 5 AM breakfast, door prizes were handed out that included a TV, radios, and a "neatly framed" $50 bill.[30]

Over the years, Grad Night grew increasingly elaborate. Parents completely took over the planning and execution of the event, working with local social and civic groups. Although other suburban schools held their Grad Nights at country clubs, hotels, and even Disneyland, San Marino consistently held theirs on the high school campus but mounted bigger productions with every passing year. By the 1960s, parents spent six to eight months planning intricate set designs and entertainment that would "rival Disneyland for excitement, but beat it for supervision." For 1965's "Around the World in 80 Days" theme, parents of seniors converted the boys' gym into a "miniature Palace at Versailles—complete with Hall of Mirrors and famed outdoor gardens."[31] For the parents who devoted hundreds of volunteer hours, the event was a poignant moment, a coming together of families whose children had grown up together. For some, the social and emotional bonds formed were so strong they continued to volunteer for years after their own children graduated. Pat Connell put in "at least three months" of full-time volunteer labor for 15 years. Tom Santley recalled a group of fathers who stayed on as the lighting committee for 12 to 15 years after their children had graduated, enjoying the fun and camaraderie.[32]

Grad Night epitomized the San Marino community during the postwar years—child-centered, social, robust, and institutionally intertwined. Parents united with civic groups in shared projects of time, money, and energy. As a small community with a unified civic and educational structure, and the luxury of wealth—which afforded more time for volunteering—San Marino possessed key ingredients for robust community engagement. With children representing a critical source of social connection, it followed that the unified school district promoted a more seamless experience of social cohesion. Shielded from the divisions of more diverse school districts grappling with desegregation mandates, San Marino went through the busing era untouched. This civic insularity meant that residents could focus on the well-being of their own.

Postwar San Marino was well aware of emerging societal pressures gaining force around it. Grad Night, indeed, was a reaction to what many Americans—from neighborhoods nationwide to the White House—would perceive as a full blow suburban crisis by the 1970s. Fearing threats such as drugs, gangs, and integrated schools, suburbanites responded in both obvious and subtle ways.[33] Grad Night was one example of how suburban parents shielded their young from those looming threats. In the process, San Marino sealed its identity as a conservative, affluent, family-centered, and defensive suburban town.

Between the 1950s and early 1970s, San Marino completed its growth phase, settled comfortably into community stability, and reached an apex of affluent Anglo suburban life. The town hit its population saturation point in the 1960s, and, after a brief spike in 1970, settled in at 13,000 where it remained for the rest of the century. The town remained very white (98%) through 1970, dropping slightly in that decade with a minor influx of affluent Latinos, the first to break the racial color line. More than 93% of residents were native-born, the minuscule foreign-born element hailing from Europe or Canada. By the measures of median family income and median housing value, San Marino ranked among the wealthiest suburbs in LA during these decades.[34] As one resident put it in the early 1970s: "We are blissfully unaware of how the other half lives."[35] Even the neighborhoods of "sub-Marino" did not depress the town's overall affluence. A hefty proportion of breadwinners were white-collar workers, climbing from 80% to 87% over these years. It was a town filled with corporate vice presidents and their stay-at-home wives.[36] San Marino, in fact, had the highest proportion of housewives of all municipalities in LA County.[37] Two-parent families with children predominated. Demographically, this was a town well-positioned to be a hotbed of participation, given that husbands brought home hefty paychecks and wives were financially freed up to raise children and dive into volunteer work.

San Marino was a bedroom community of the first order—with single-family homes making up 99% of dwellings—served by four small clusters of shops and businesses. These "business areas" originated around the old Red Car stops. By the 1950s, each center had a grocery store, gas station, and pharmacy, providing a sense of neighborhood unity and pedestrian access, especially important to housewives without cars.[38]

Table 5.1 Demographic and social characteristics of San Marino residents, 1950–2010

	1950		1970		1990		2010	
	number	%	number	%	Number	%	number	%
Population total	11,230	100.0	14,177	100.0	12,959	100.0	13,147	100.0
Race/ethnicity								
White non-Hispanic	11,007	98.0	13,211	93.2	8,097	62.5	4,872	37.1
Black	110	1.0	24	0.2	36	0.3	53	0.4
Hispanic	70	0.6	868	6.1	635	4.9	855	6.5
Asian	36	0.3	71	0.5	4,166	32.1	7,010	53.3
Nativity								
Native-born	10,526	93.7	13,408	94.6	9,251	71.4	8,119	61.8
Foreign-born	704	6.3	796	5.6	3,708	28.6	4,995	38.0
Occupations								
White collar	3,370	80.6	4,432	87.3	5,150	90.3	5,174	91.7
Blue collar	242	5.8	294	5.8	228	4.0	162	2.9
Service	517	12.4	325	6.4	281	4.9	304	5.4
Females in labor force	1,067	21.8	1,452	25.9	2,389	44.6	2,730	48.2
Married females in labor force *			737	20.1	957	57.5	1,922	52.0

Note: Percentages calculated out of total population, except for occupations where it is calculated out of all adult workers, unless otherwise indicated.
* shown as a percentage of all married women over 16. For 1990, data is for mothers in labor force.

These small centers, along with nearby schools, helped create blocks of lively neighborly sociability. For example, in the 1950s along Las Flores—just off the Mission shopping district—neighbors gathered daily at 5 PM to sweep oak leaves off the sidewalks. On nearby La Mirada Avenue, there were 27 kids along a single block. The area lacked sidewalks, so children played in the streets, pulling their parents along into friendly social tribes. Perta and Tom Santley, who moved to this block in 1968 with their two small children, recalled: "all the families on this block were known to each other" and "they were all Caucasian." Youngsters attended the same elementary school a few blocks away, most walking or riding their bikes. Families socialized at frequent backyard parties, school fundraisers, and block parties. Similar scenes prevailed across the suburb. Local public schools reinforced children's social ties, which in turn pulled parents together.[39] For a small, homogeneous, independent suburb like San Marino, untouched by the pressures of school desegregation politics, the neighborhood unit concept was alive and well.

San Marino also had its "high society." Beginning in the 1930s, San Marino sons and daughters appeared regularly in the *New York Times* wedding pages, revealing the elite web of social connections that spanned from San Marino to the Ivy League to East Coast society. The local children of corporate presidents attended Stanford, Harvard, Princeton, and the University of Southern California (USC), and married partners with equally elite pedigrees.[40] In the 1950s and 1960s, the suburb produced a notable share of national-level tennis and golf players coming out of the local schools.[41] In the circles of debutantes and elite philanthropy, San Marino women were likewise well represented, garnering occasional coverage in the *New York Times*. In 1964, a local woman was named head of the Association of Junior Leagues of America.[42] To some upwardly mobile residents encountering this socialite culture for the first time, San Marino could seem "a little snobbish" or intimidating. Judith Carter, who grew up outside San Francisco, was the daughter of a carpenter-turned-independent building contractor. She met her future husband at Stanford, and, after marrying, they moved to San Marino in 1969. "I was not used to the wealth," she recalled. "We lived on this street, and houses were just kind of normal size. But as the kids went off to school, they would be invited to play in these houses that were just gigantic." In a town like San Marino, which mixed the middle and upper classes, the presence of extreme wealth could provoke some class anxiety. But, as Carter put it, "when you're busy raising kids, making sure they get their shots and all that, I'm not thinking too much about the downside."[43]

San Marino had a healthy share of civic and social groups. While the number of groups in San Marino appears fairly average, several had impressive longevity and social vitality. Nine groups had existed over 50 years, tracing their roots back to the 1920s and 1930s. The oldest, most important civic group was the City Club, formed in 1926. It began as a men's group combining monthly social gatherings with civic projects, oriented particularly around local youth. Membership was by nomination; in 1971, there were 550 members, with a substantial waiting list.[44]

In the 1930s, the Rotary Club, the Garden Club, the Woman's Club, and the Republican Women's Club were founded, all of which were quite robust in the postwar years. The Woman's Club, for example, was a hive of social and philanthropic activity. After an intense surge of civic voluntarism during World War II, the Club formed a "Philanthropy Guild" in 1947, to engage in civic and charity projects. From the 1950s to 1970s, the group had 300–450 members. The women met monthly at Huntington (Junior High) Auditorium, while the smaller Club guilds—such as art, music, drama, bridge, sports, and home craft—met monthly at members' homes. They also held garden parties, luncheons, fashion shows, and square dances while tirelessly fundraising to purchase a clubhouse, which they did in 1952. The Club established a Junior Guild in 1962, to bring in younger women; along the same lines, it formed a Debutante Guild in 1977. In 1983, the Club had 335 regular members, 54 juniors, and 78 debs. The Woman's Club catered to housewives who could attend daytime meetings that could last upward of four hours. In the 1970s, more than 100 women typically attended these lengthy gatherings, suggesting they fulfilled an important social function for the housewives of San Marino. In 1960, a San Marino chapter of the National Charity League (NCL) was established, giving the town its own socialite hub. With its recognized social cachet, the NCL became a stronger draw than the Woman's Club deb group, ultimately diminishing the latter's capacity to sustain itself in the long run. Like the Junior League, the NCL was structured to bring in younger members, with its focus on mothers and daughters together engaging in philanthropy. This built-in element of generational continuity helped ensure its longevity and strength over the decades.[45]

In addition to its garden variety civic groups such as the Rotary, Masons, Kiwanis, and Dancing Club, San Marino hosted one group that catapulted the otherwise low-key suburb into the national spotlight—the John Birch Society (JBS). Before the Birchers came to town, San Marino had a typical share of conservative organizations for a high-end suburb—the Daughters of the American Revolution, American Legion, and Republican Women's Club. In 1963, the JBS chose San Marino as the site for its new western headquarters. Its location in the quiet Mission shopping district gave the group a physical visibility meant to dispel its reputation for secrecy. The one-story rented office, which looked "as prosaic . . . as an insurance agency," housed a staff of six, headed by former Republican congressman John Rousselot, a native son of San Marino. The arrival of the Birchers magnified San Marino's conservative reputation and solidified the town's association with this ultra-right-wing, rabid anti-Communist group. Rousselot initially said he picked San Marino because "the rent was good," later noting its central location in LA and its favorable climate of conservative opinion. San Marino, in fact, had

Figure 5.4 Members of the San Marino Women's Club, 1952. As a hive of social and philanthropic activity during the postwar years, the Women's Club typified robust social engagement in the suburb and catered to housewives with the time and resources to participate.
USC Digital Library. Los Angeles Examiner Photographs Collection.

the highest rate of Republican voter registration of all LA suburbs in 1962 and 1970.[46]

San Marino hosted several local Birch Society chapters in the 1960s—five in all, proportionately more than neighboring suburbs with chapters, such as Pasadena, South Pasadena, Arcadia, La Cañada, and Monterey Park. Since

JBS chapters typically capped their membership at 30, it meant no more than 150 San Marino residents were directly involved. Despite its reputation as a fringe group of conspiracy-obsessed red baiters, the JBS played a key role in building a postwar conservative movement culture in LA, particularly in the close ties it forged with other grassroots Republican women's groups. In contrast to the red-baiting politics unleashed in nearby Pasadena, local Birchers didn't have many direct targets in San Marino given the town's small size, homogeneity, and conservative bent. So instead, they aimed their letter-writing campaigns at outside threats, such as the United Nations. Birchers tended to be somewhat marginalized socially, not necessarily cross-associating with groups like the Junior League or National Charity League in San Marino.[47]

More powerful and mainstream than the Birchers was a broader culture of open, good-natured voluntarism in San Marino. The values of participation and voluntarism were expressed in multiple ways. Setting the most vivid example was the city council, whose members contributed their time and labor without pay, a practice typical in LA's affluent suburbs.[48] Several leaders believed this beneficence created a political culture of honesty and courtesy, where council meetings remained civil and polite even when disputes arose. Voluntarism pervaded local social life as well. For many, it began with the Newcomers Club, an important vehicle for social integration in the postwar years. Established in 1950, the Newcomers Club was meant to "foster new friendships and to promote social activities for new residents," especially women. It held monthly luncheons, organized quarterly coffees and couples' parties, and hosted several special interest groups, some of which met weekly. After two years in town, members were gently prodded to join other local groups like the Hospital Guild, Women's Club, or Assistance League. Julie O'Reilly joined the group after arriving in San Marino, attending ladies' luncheons when she was off from work and progressive dinners with her husband. Then, she recalled, there was "a pressure" to join—"well you should join this, and you should join that." The Newcomers Club thus acted as a permanent institution to teach new San Marinians how to be good neighbors. As well, voluntarism as a social value was repeatedly articulated by community leaders.[49]

The focal point of volunteer energy was unquestionably the suburb's children. The driving triumvirate of suburban identity—parent, homeowner, and taxpayer—operated in multiple ways in San Marino. But on a purely social and voluntaristic level, it was the role of "parent" that thoroughly imbued local community dynamics.

Individuals often made their first neighborhood outreach by volunteering at schools, the Scouts, or youth sports, such as Little League, which began in the early 1960s. For a housewife like Mary Harrigian, who was not a natural joiner, it was easy for her to volunteer at her children's school. For Julie O'Reilly, a working woman with a Ukrainian-born husband who felt slightly alienated from the neighbors at first—"we were a little different, and me being a flight attendant, definitely a little different"—having a baby "kind of helped" them become part of the local "mainstream." She "brought cupcakes and was a room mother" at her son's elementary school. Soon she was inundated with invitations to join clubs and groups. Other women similarly recalled their first volunteer stints being tied to their children's lives.[50] The PTAs were active at every school and spun off other social groups. For example, the San Marino Women's Chorus was a group of PTA moms who convened in the 1950s and 1960s, while the San Marino PTA Fathers met regularly during the 1950s. In the 1980s, the San Marino Dad's Band was created to perform at various school gatherings.

Civic groups likewise often had a focus on youth. The City Club supported youth sports, a Boy Scout troop, Grad Night, and other school functions. The Rotary Club sponsored a high school club, career guidance for high school seniors, a Boy Scout troop, and various youth clubs, and participated in a student foreign exchange program. The Woman's Club also supported local school activities, lending their clubhouse for PTA functions. Grad Night, as the ritual capstone of San Marino childhood, drew everyone out to help. At Grad Night 1978, a dozen Exchange Club members manned the snack bar from midnight to 4:30 AM, serving Cokes, burgers, and popcorn. The Rotarians operated game booths all night, while the City Club purchased gifts for the graduates, including trips to San Francisco and "dinners in exclusive restaurants."[51] By the 1970s, strong traditions of parental involvement had been well established, contributing to a nurturing, convivial climate oriented around the well-being of local youth.

Within this milieu, a free-wheeling, affable social culture took root. San Marino parents liked to have fun. This was apparent on Grad Night, with the explosive outpouring of creative energy that drew on familiar popular culture tropes to create elaborate make-believe worlds—Never Never Land, the Roaring Twenties, the Land of Oz, Mardi Gras, the South Seas. It was on display at the "Fathers' Night Show" staged annually from 1928 to 1959 and sporadically thereafter. Originated by the PTA, these shows parodied life in San Marino through song, dance, comedies, and even a little cross-dressing. The tradition was revived in the late 1970s, when a group of local dads—including Merlin Olson, an actor and former LA Rams defensive lineman—staged an amateur melodrama called "Sneaky Fitch" in the Stoneman School auditorium as a school fundraiser. Several years later, the City Club put on annual Father's Night shows to raise money for the schools—"Founding Fathers" in 1976, then "Son of Founding Fathers," followed by "Son of Floundering Fathers"—all full of in-jokes about the community. Some likened the feel of these events and San Marino's social culture to a USC fraternity.[52]

The chummy community life of San Marino rested on a firm foundation of wealth and insularity. San Marinians could watch the travails of metropolitan life from afar, buffered by their suburban comforts. A *New York Times* reporter trying to figure out why the JBS was headquartered there immediately picked up on this in 1964. "San Marino is a sort of municipal Shangri-La, a monument to men's conviction that modern metropolitanism can be escaped—if you have the money."[53] Racial tensions and busing were a world away. San Marino came to represent an "escape hatch" suburb that received

Figure 5.5 From 1928 to 1959, the San Marino PTA sponsored an annual "Father's Night" show, like this one from March 1952 involving more than 180 male performers. Events like this illustrated the local culture of conviviality and hijinks among the suburb's residents.

USC Digital Library. Los Angeles Examiner Photographs Collection.

families leaving the hot zones. It was ironic that one San Marino resident in the 1960s was John McCone, who chaired the governor's commission on the 1965 Watts Riots. While placing most of the blame on the "spiral of failure" plaguing a fringe group of Blacks, the commission's report did acknowledge that whites fleeing to the suburbs "have developed an isolated existence with a feeling of separation from the community as a whole."[54] McCone's hometown was a textbook example.

Many African Americans saw San Marino in that light. *Los Angeles Sentinel* columnist Bill Lane wrote that McCone's appointment threw him "into abrupt contact with more Negroes than possibly he'd ever in his lifetime come to know even existed in the USA. (They generally come to San Marino only to do domestic work.)"[55] In nearby Pasadena, both white and Black leaders blamed San Marino and neighboring restricted suburbs for exacerbating the conditions of Blacks in Pasadena. Charges like this, along with the general fervor of civil rights activism, prompted a small group of San Marino residents in 1969 to form a Human Relations Committee, whose modest goal was to promote interracial contact "on a personal level." Given San Marino's racial profile, as a first step this meant inviting outside speakers "expressing the views of minorities." One was Samuel Sheats, former president of the Pasadena NAACP, who warned, "The world is shrinking and no community can remain an island." Though he refrained from attacking San Marino directly in front of the 25 attendees, his words touched a nerve, revealing a spark of racial liberalism in this overwhelmingly conservative town. One woman claimed they "were deprived in this white ghetto. There are more important things in life than wearing cashmere sweaters and being with whites." The small San Marino group joined a coalition of San Gabriel Valley human relations and housing rights committees, pledging their support for open housing.[56]

Although an awareness of racial discrimination, metropolitan inequity, and the inevitability of change found some purchase, San Marino largely retained its restrictions, hoping to ensure its continued insularity by maintaining the tony character of the suburb. As mayor Harry Hitchcock put it in 1965, "Those living here wish to preserve it as a homogeneous, high-grade residential neighborhood."[57] But as San Marino would soon discover, class barriers alone could not protect it. In San Marino, the barrier of whiteness wasn't breached by the people Samuel Sheats was talking about, but rather by a group of successful, wealthy newcomers with roots across the Pacific.

San Marino's Demographic Shock

By the late 1970s, this suburb that so highly valued stasis and stability faced two monumental challenges to its well-established order—one demographic, the other fiscal. San Marino's transition from white to multiethnic was a radical jolt, but one tempered by its static civic and spatial climate. Essentially, San Marino changed without changing—it transitioned ethnically without altering its fundamental identity as a conservative, affluent, family-centered, and defensive suburban town.

San Marino may have been an "island" within the LA metropolis, but there were larger forces it could not escape. Immigration was touching virtually every town in some way, even those that clung most tightly to their old ways. The twin pressures of the 1965 Hart Celler Immigration Act, which increased immigration from Asia and Latin America, and civil rights breakthroughs in open housing literally changed the face of suburbia.

Alongside those transformations, a succession of new fiscal measures revamped the ways that suburbs controlled local money. In essence, localities lost direct control over their property tax revenue, which had previously gone directly into funding local schools and services. The older system perpetuated great disparities of wealth, allowing rich towns like San Marino to hoard their wealth and fund their own world-class public schools and services while leaving poorer communities with a weaker tax base and diminished neighborhood services. This was the fiscal calculus of suburban local control.[58] Starting in the 1970s, this system began to unravel. It began with two court decisions (*Serrano v. Priest*, 1971 and 1976), in which the California Supreme Court ruled that a school finance system tied to property taxes was unconstitutional because it disadvantaged poor students, violating both their 14th Amendment rights and the California Constitution's guarantee of free education. The state was ordered to distribute funds more equitably across the spectrum of school districts. By unmooring local property taxes from local services, these rulings fed into growing anti-tax sentiments, culminating in the 1978 passage of Proposition 13. Further widening the chasm between localities and their property tax revenue, this measure not only depleted fiscal resources in general by freezing property taxes, but also shifted control over those resources to the state. Homeowners across California enthusiastically voted in the measure, which proved a boon for individual homeowners but a disaster for communities, at least in the short term. It placed suburban towns—from rich to poor—in dire financial straits and surrendered more fiscal powers than ever to the state. In response, towns began frenzied searches for new ways to raise revenue.[59] One result was a new set of practices that reinstated metropolitan inequity in novel ways. In wealthy San Marino, propelled by this emerging neoliberal climate, the implementation of those practices became a new basis of community invigoration.[60] Fiscal crisis spurred community engagement. But this worked best in wealthy towns where citizens had the time, resources, and money to give. Amidst this fiscal crisis, a new wave of Chinese immigrants arrived.

Chinese immigration to San Marino was one small stream of a larger wave of Asian immigration in the postwar era. San Marino's ethnic turn began gradually in the 1970s, then rapidly accelerated. In 1980, there were 822 foreign-born Asians in the community, split between Japanese and Chinese (mostly from Taiwan, but also Hong Kong). From 1990 to 2010, Asians rose from 32% to 53% of San Marino's total population, with Chinese coming to predominate. Early on, most came from Taiwan and Hong Kong, some of whom had escaped as children from Mainland China. These first Chinese arrivals settled permanently in America, in contrast to the immigrants who followed after 1990, many of them transnational sojourners cycling back and forth between the United States and East Asia (and increasingly Mainland China).

San Marino's ethnic transition was marked less by "civil rights suburbanization" than extraordinary buying power. Asian struggles over access were waged in more modest suburbs like nearby South Pasadena, where legal fights around race-restrictive covenants unfolded as early as 1947.[61] In San Marino, Chinese newcomers brought wealth, which resonated with the town's culture. By the time they began moving there in the late 1970s and 1980s, the strategy of overt white racial exclusion was no longer politically viable. The Chinese influx was facilitated by several factors: the willingness of cash-bearing immigrants to pay at or above the asking price for real estate at a time of spiraling inflation in home prices; the arrival of young Asian families seeking entrance, coinciding with aging Anglo residents looking to cash out; and the fiscal strain wrought by Prop 13, which created an openness to these affluent newcomers.[62] As well, San Marino's proximity to ethnoburbs like Monterey Park attracted newcomers who sought the best of both worlds—the superior status of living in an elite American suburb and convenient access to an array of Chinese grocery stores, restaurants, and services.[63]

The white belief that a minority influx would drive down property value—which historically underpinned much white resistance to racial integration—was thoroughly inverted with the arrival of Asians. Instead, whites saw Asians driving property values up. While this might have been a kind of fiscal expression of the "model minority" stereotype, the reality was that Chinese immigrants were bringing money into a suburb where wealth had always been a prerequisite for admission.[64] Any persistent concerns over the careful protection of those values were soon assuaged by the wealth and conservative inclinations of Chinese newcomers.

The Early Chinese Residents of San Marino

The earliest Chinese arrivals in San Marino were living examples of capitalist success and testaments to the felicitous outcomes of immigration in the Cold War world. They had escaped Communist China, seeking the freedom and opportunity to choose their own destinies. They arrived in the United States at a time when Chinese people were perceived less in racial than ethnic terms by the American mainstream. This shift from racialization to ethnicization created the potential for community integration, reflecting a higher level of Anglo acceptance of a group that decades earlier had been considered unassimilable.[65] In affluent San Marino, class and its attendant ideologies became a compelling common ground. Among the first wave of Chinese arrivals, many shared a strong belief in individual meritocracy and America's promise to enable its fulfillment. Chinese newcomers valued hard, diligent work and believed this—above all—determined a person's fate in life. As immigrants under the Hart Celler Act, they had family ties to citizens or permanent residents and/or expertise as skilled professionals, such as engineers, doctors, and pharmacists. A number of them arrived on student visas with aspirations to join these professions. With strong ambitions, these early arrivals embodied the Horatio Alger myth, inflected by Cold War imperatives to prove the superiority of the American capitalist system.

The life experiences of several Chinese pioneer residents illustrate these values and aspirations. Lily Wong was born in Shanghai and soon saw her well-to-do family separated when the Communists took control in 1949. Her parents fled to Hong Kong, and she did not reunite with them until 1958. She moved to Vancouver, and subsequently she and her husband began "hopscotching" across North America, moving to Columbus, Ohio; Portland, Oregon; and finally Monterey Park in 1967. At this point, she began investing in real estate. She and her husband borrowed $50,000 to buy an apartment complex in Glendale with several other investors. After that partnership failed, they purchased a six-unit apartment building in Monterey Park in 1971. From there, Wong followed a simple formula that worked in LA's steadily inflating real estate landscape: wait for the property to appreciate, then borrow against the increased value to buy another property. In the early days, she was a hands-on landlord, personally collecting rents and cleaning apartments when tenants moved out. Over the years, she bought 50 apartment buildings and "quietly" became "a major investor in the Los Angeles real estate market." Her husband ran a successful psychiatric practice on Wilshire Boulevard. In 1982, they moved to San Marino with their four children. They purchased a $1.4 million home on an acre-plus lot, with a tennis court and a hexagon-shaped swimming pool. In the late 1980s, a Rolls Royce sat in the garage. Musing about her wealth, Wong said, "People ask me how I got all this. I tell them, 'You didn't see the hard part.' " By the early 2000s, she was contributing generously to the Republican National Committee, embracing the credo of meritocratic individualism and the American dream.[66]

Tao (Rosa) Chia Chi was born in 1949, in Shanghai, just as the Communists were taking over. Her father, an administrative worker in the Shanghai municipal government under the Kuomintang regime, was eager to get his family out, knowing he would face persecution under Mao's regime. Two months after Rosa's birth, her parents and sisters made a harrowing escape by boat to Taiwan, where the family soon settled in. Her father, who harbored aspirations of owning a business, instead moved from one unstable administrative job to the next. Native-born Taiwanese resented the waves of refugees arriving from the mainland and suspected many of being Communist spies. "So my father felt, this is not a place for us, if your own flesh and blood people don't welcome you." He began "brainwashing" his daughters to leave, saying "go anyplace you want. This is not the place."

Rosa left in 1971, at age 22, to attend college in Eugene, Oregon, near her older sister who was studying in Corvallis. With few job prospects back in Taiwan, Rosa saw it as a permanent move. Through a friend, she met Zee Chi Shing, a medical student who grew up in Shanghai. They married in 1974, in New York, where Chi was an intern, and started a family, moving around for Chi's medical training. In 1978, they rented an apartment in Monterey Park before buying a house there. When their children started school in 1982, they purchased a home in the Gainsborough Heath section of San Marino. Rosa

Zee's rise to affluence was the reward of the couple's hard work and Rosa's energetic commitment to family and work. She valued their material comforts for allowing her to fully attend to her children's needs and participate robustly in local community life.[67]

Allan Yung was born in Hong Kong in 1940. He grew up in a rented apartment in a working-class neighborhood that was "shabby, somewhat dirty." He and his friends would play in the unpaved streets. As a child, he spent much of his free time in a little bookstore—no more than a "shed"—in a nearby alley, where the proprietors allowed him to read for a two-cent fee. Times were hard but, "the general feeling of the society in those days [was that] you make the best of it. If you don't make it, don't cry to anybody on their shoulders." There was little time for community or social life: "very individual, everybody's striving just to survive."

Hong Kong was a place of social extremes—both the wealth and poverty motivated Yung to strive for upward mobility. On a visit to a friend's house at age 13, he rode an elevator for the first time and it was a revelation. From their home, "we saw the sea, we saw the cars, and we looked far from the house. We looked at the harbor, then I realized there was a world out there. And at that time I was determined to get out of this rut." He also witnessed the city's crippling poverty, particularly among the refugees from mainland China, who lived on squalid sampan boats or as squatters, a few on the roof of his building. At age 15, he resolved to become a doctor and to get out of Hong Kong. Faced with the hypercompetitive educational system there, Yung decided to attend an American college, which was "very easy to come to . . . if you can afford it." He moved to Virginia in 1959, to attend Richmond College, went on to the Medical College of Virginia, and then began moving around the country for residencies and internships. In 1969, he joined the Navy to avoid getting drafted at the height of the Vietnam War. He and his wife started their family in the 1970s, while living on a naval base in Japan. In 1975, they moved to San Marino for the "good schools," then moved five times within San Marino as the family and their resources grew, eventually moving into an 8,000-square-foot home on elegant Lombardy Road. Based on his own life experience, Yung fervently embraced the idea that success comes to those who work hard, seeing this as a particularly strong Asian cultural value especially prized by an older generation. "Most Asians work their buns off, work at 6 in the morning 'til midnight. They will elevate their social and financial status." To Yung, his belief in meritocracy was personal, political, and cultural.[68]

For Wong, Zee, Yung, and other first-generation Chinese settlers who established the foundations of interethnic relations in San Marino, their experiences of self-made upward mobility predisposed them to the same conservative values as their Anglo neighbors. From different starting points—across oceans even—these Anglo and Chinese residents found common ideological ground, centered on the ideal of individual meritocracy that entitled them to enjoy the suburban good life. The Chinese arrived after the advantages of white suburban privilege had been deeply etched into metropolitan landscapes. Like most of their white neighbors, they were fairly oblivious to the structural advantages that accrued to elite enclaves like San Marino by decades of policy that protected these landscapes of privilege.[69]

This first wave of Chinese emigres saw themselves as permanent residents who acclimated to the ways of American life and culture. They established medical practices, businesses, and professions in the region, and they mostly made and spent their fortunes in the United States. While some maintained ties to their ancestral homelands, their lives were solidly rooted in San Marino. To them, the suburb was home.

The integration of Chinese immigrants into the community of San Marino was a varied process of assimilation, compromise, and, ultimately, some degree of cultural interpenetration. In contrast to the heated racial politics of nearby Monterey Park, the Chinese and Anglos of San Marino negotiated a more genteel, restrained racial peace. While Chinese residents acceded to long-standing customs in San Marino—the conservative spatial and political practices that shaped the suburb's elite identity—there was more interchange in the social realm.[70] Voluntarism and participation emerged as a firm basis of community integration, but getting to that place was not always a smooth process. It began when San Marino's Anglo residents realized that they had to grapple with the new reality of ethnic diversity in their midst.

Racial Strife Arrives in San Marino

By the late 1970s, San Marino's Asian population was still small, around 880 or about 6% of the total population. Jean Wang, who moved there in 1978, recalled an initial friendliness that soon gave way to hostility. A critical catalyst was Proposition 13, passed that June, which initially set off xenophobic resentment. As Wang remembered, this began with the publication of an article in the *Los Angeles Times* in November 1979 entitled "San Marino Schools,

City Struggle to Make Ends Meet." Although every town was hit by the fiscal retrenchment mandated by the measure, the article highlighted the strain that Asian newcomers were placing on the suburb's newly tightened coffers. Immigrant students in the San Marino school district—who comprised 10% of students and were mostly Taiwanese or Japanese—were expected to cost the district $30,000 per year for English as a Second Language (ESL) instruction. Because the district's ESL program was too small to qualify for state support, that money would have to come from the district's general funds. While the article described efforts to solicit donations "from foreign companies and governments" to help cover these costs, it stressed the pressures that immigrant students were placing on the district's shrinking resources. Superintendent Roger Lowney fed that sensibility: "The word spreads that this is a safe community with good school district so they just keep coming."[71]

While Lowney expressed faith in the intelligence of the "foreign parents," PTAs, and the community in general to address the problem, the article and his statements inflamed Anglo and Chinese residents alike. As Jean Wang later wrote, "To those Chinese-American residents of San Marino who had long been in the United States, the news was a heavy blow." Especially for those who had been in the country for years, built professional careers, and had American-born children who spoke flawless English, this conflating of ethnic difference and immigrant needs did not sit well.[72]

Perceiving the article as a hostile affront, a group of Chinese residents got together to formulate a collective response. Thus began a process of institutionalizing local ethnic relations, beginning with several mothers meeting in living rooms to address the "emergency" set off by the LA Times article. Recognizing the need to organize formally, they attracted more residents and, in 1979, formed the Chinese Club of San Marino with 80 founding families. Their mission was "to unite and solidify all Chinese Americans in San Marino, to heighten the good feeling of white Americans toward Chinese, and thus to build a better society."[73] Though it eventually would act as a social and cultural nexus for local Chinese families, the Club's founding purpose was less about insular Chinese unity and more about doing their share to serve the broader community. "It's not work inside. It's work outside, with outreach to the Caucasian [community]," recalled Jean Wang, who served as its first president.

The Chinese Club's immediate goals was to defuse the tensions over ESL and school resources. Wang's first task was to dispatch parent volunteers to the schools to assist with ESL instruction. In its first year, the Club also raised $5,000 for the public schools, purchased instructional material for ESL students, and sponsored booths selling fried eggrolls at school carnivals, with the proceeds going directly to the schools. While the Club hosted social events, such as picnics, fashion shows, and cooking classes, Wang emphasized that these were meant to attract new members who could then be sent into the schools to volunteer.[74]

In a suburb like San Marino, the Chinese Club's embrace of voluntarism around the public schools was an effective strategy for integrating newcomers into the town's participatory culture. The Club urged its members to "overcome the barriers of language and cultural mentality by encouraging them to become school volunteers and participat[e] in school activities."[75] For many of the Chinese parents, this was unfamiliar ground. Several Chinese residents recalled no personal experience with community voluntarism by their own parents back in Hong Kong or Taiwan.[76] Moreover, many harbored early memories of a culture that deferred completely to school authority and left no room for a parental presence. Rosa Zee recalled, "Where I grew up in Taiwan . . . parents were not welcome in the school setting. The parents felt like, if I send my kids to school, that's your job to educate my kids. I give 100% my rights to you. . . . They didn't feel like they have a place to tell the school, you have to do better, or it's part of my job to help you, to assist you, to make my children or the school environment better. That's not the Chinese culture."[77] Peter Chen noted that, for a typical Chinese parent, a visit to school happened only if a child was in trouble.[78] Jean Wang recalled that the strategy of voluntarism wasn't initially her idea but was recommended by the parents of high school students who had more experience with the American school system. They saw white parents volunteering, and, as Wang put it, "we want to bridge the [gap]." In teaching voluntarism, the Chinese Club gave members "a new concept of what American culture is."[79] Through their actions, these early Chinese residents moved directly into the heart of community life in San Marino.

Despite these early bridging efforts, subsequent years saw a rise in ethnic tension in San Marino, countered by earnest, sustained efforts to defuse them. Early conflicts occurred in the schools where Asians and whites were forced to interact.[80] By the early 1980s, a "small" group of white students, according to one report, aggressively harassed their Chinese classmates, yelling things like, "Why do you come to San Marino?" or "Why don't you go back to your country?", pelting them with apples and milk cartons in the cafeteria, and accusing them of cheating on exams and hogging all the scholarships. Some white hostility stemmed from the academic competitiveness of the Chinese students, a point made by the high school principal who claimed that the most overt white racists suffered from low self-esteem or bad school performance. In the winter of 1983–1884, two fights erupted between Chinese and white students at the high school. In both cases, school administrators showed some favoritism toward the whites when dispensing punishment. After one incident, the father of a Chinese student who had been harassed for months, confronted school authorities "but did not get full satisfaction." Many believed the prejudice was originating with the white parents and filtering down to the younger generation.[81]

By spring 1984, residents began meeting regularly to begin a dialogue about ethnic and racial relations in the suburb. Spearheaded by PTA parents and school superintendent David Brown, the group's goal was to facilitate a peaceful transition to multiethnicity. Four Asians and 12–15 Caucasians attended the first meeting. Unsurprisingly, the outnumbered Asians were assigned much of the blame and were the ones expected to change. Twelve Chinese attended the second meeting and challenged the earlier bias. Jean Wang recalled some tense moments at the outset when there was a frank airing of differences:

> We got together and the Caucasian people were accusing us what we did wrong. And we would accuse them, what they did wrong. And the point is—misunderstanding. . . . And then you don't speak English, and you go to the Chinese bank and the Chinese supermarket. . . . We just openly talked about it. Then my point . . . was [about] accusing. You parents in house, privately saying, "Chinese people this, Chinese people that." The children will hear it. They have the impression these Chinese are a bunch of gangsters or something. . . . I don't ask them to say, "Oh, Chinese are so good." I don't say that. But at least you don't—at the dinner table—you don't accuse.

At that second meeting, the Chinese parents successfully pressed the group to acknowledge the "joint responsibility" of Caucasians and Asians for local frictions. Attendance at the meetings swelled to 63 by late May and included members of the school board, the city council, the chamber of commerce, the board of realtors, the Chinese Club, Japanese groups, church groups, PTAs, students, the police department, the recreation department, and various civic groups.[82] This effort reflected this affluent suburb's capacity to do

human relations work in a grassroots way without relying on LA County resources reduced by Prop 13 cuts.[83]

Voluntarism emerged early on as a point of contention. Despite the early
work of the Chinese Club, some white residents perceived of Asian residents
as civic freeloaders. As one list of "Human Relations Issues" put it, "Parents
tired of giving dollars and time to Asians at expense of Anglo kids. Biggest
gripe is large number of Asian kids taking advantage of all facilities (Scouts,
Little League, Rec Dept., library, schools, etc.) with no parental volunteer
help."[84] In the social universe of San Marino, this shirking of responsibilities
was a breach of suburban culture.

By late spring, the multiethnic ad hoc group began to articulate some
proposed solutions, reflecting their broader social expectations. Given
the suburb's deeply ensconced traditions and regulations, the goal would
be to teach Asian newcomers the ways of the world in San Marino and expect them to adapt. By May, they began formulating specifics in a lengthy
list of recommendations: encourage English language instruction for both
children and parents through the schools and churches; the Chinese Club
and Japanese groups should "evaluate the significance of speaking English
as much as possible"; "Increase curriculum to emphasize cultural and social
traditions in America for all newcomers"; the Newcomers Club would "provide quarterly meetings to review the City of San Marino and its unique culture"; and increase Asian participation in the schools, both as volunteers and
paid staff. The list also recommended teaching Asians about local regulations,
specifically "R-1 zoning breakdowns, ordinance violations and property
care." The recommendations emphasized the importance of teaching voluntarism to Asian newcomers: "Volunteerism! Asians must be encouraged to
actively participate in San Marino community life. . . . Develop a servant's
heart, a helping hand and a greater cultural awareness." And it recommended
a campaign to make sure those volunteer opportunities were publicized in
both the English- and Chinese-language press.[85]

In June, the ad hoc group was formalized into a Human Relations
Committee (HRC), a resurrection of the late-1960s group, but this time intended to address real and immediate local issues. Composed of 9 Asians
and 10 Caucasians, the Human Relations Committee exuded "a sense
of accomplishment and optimism."[86] The group was recognized by both
San Marino City and the Board of Education, signifying an official sanction of its approach. The Human Relations Committee adopted the ad hoc
group's recommendations as its guiding principles, a move that signaled the

willingness of Chinese leaders in San Marino, those pioneer residents who had already spent some years in the United States, to embrace the assimilation agenda. Thus the tone of ethnic relations in San Marino was set around seeking acceptance and entering gracefully into the genteel lifestyle of this privileged social milieu.

Design Assimilation

After this consensus was reached, ethnic relations began to evolve more smoothly. When conflicts arose, which seemed less frequent and less aggressive, they were swiftly quelled by local community leaders—Anglo and Chinese alike—who united around the ideals of tolerance, civility, and assimilation. There was a remarkable politeness to it all. This contrasted with nearby Monterey Park, where conflicts among Anglos, Chinese, and Latinos were raging in highly divisive, racialized ways. In San Marino, wealth seemed to mute the discourse. Reinforcing this dynamic was a preemptive campaign by local Anglo leaders to enact policies to protect San Marino's built landscape. While extolling tolerance in one breath, in the next they supported measures to ensure that there would be few—if any—visible markers of the Asian influx.

By the 1980s, San Marino was taking cues from neighboring suburbs in the region, quietly observing the turmoil from a distance. San Marino began perceiving itself in distinct relation to other ethnic suburbs nearby—especially Monterey Park, just three miles away. It was discerning what not to do, what fights to avoid, and how to set their town apart from other suburbs being reshaped by Asian newcomers. Monterey Park emerged as San Marino's inverse touchstone. In Monterey Park, Chinese businesses were flourishing, reshaping the economic and built landscape into an "ethnoburb," a process that sparked intense political conflict as more liberal-leaning Chinese invoked the language of civil rights to assert their "right to the suburb."[87]

In San Marino, Anglo leaders launched a discreet campaign to avoid that fate. They enacted measures regulating the built landscape to protect the suburb's long-standing Euro-American identity, often with the consent of Chinese community leaders. Before Chinese immigrants arrived, a kind of community consensus existed around classic European and American architectural styles and decorative landscapes, so local design was lightly regulated. In the 1980s, some Chinese newcomers began introducing different styles onto their suburban property, threatening to bring a "foreign" look to the suburb. In 1987, a clamp-down ensued. The city council passed several measures—around homes, landscape, and signage—to protect Euro-American aesthetics, regulating what residents could or could not do on their private property. These measures were part of a push among some transitioning suburbs to demand "design assimilation" from ethnic newcomers.[88]

The first was an anti-mansionization ordinance, a somewhat ironic measure for this particular town. It limited homes to six bedrooms and to 30% of the lot size. Considered the most stringent law of its type in the area, the measure, declared city manager John Novak, was prompted by an unusually large number of permit applications.[89] "Mansionization" was a practice widely associated with Asians in places like nearby Arcadia, where liberal tear-down laws allowed it to spread unchecked. Some of these "monster homes" were designed with *feng shui* elements and marketed to wealthy transnational Chinese seeking American real estate.[90] Anti-mansionization was a tricky proposition for a suburb like San Marino, with its long history of opulent estates. Town leaders got around the contradiction by making distinctions between good and bad mansions, linked to proportionality. In 1991, the city council passed a measure designating the original Oak Knoll Marino area as an "estate zone," setting the minimum lot size at 60,000 square feet. This would be the protected space of the town's "crème de la crème." The anti-mansionization law, by contrast, targeted homes on smaller lots.[91]

A few years later, Anglo leaders realized that monitoring house size wasn't enough. Taste was also at stake. Paul Crowley, who grew up in San Marino and served on the city council from 1986 to 1999, was a key player. He instigated the formation of a Design Review Committee in 1992 to "give a subjective view on things."[92] One precipitating event was the construction of a home that became known locally as the "Taj Mahal," located two blocks east of the Huntington Estate among mostly one-story classically designed homes. This one-story residence had a vaulted dome at its center, with a silhouetted front wall echoing the shape of the dome, suggesting a vaguely Persian motif. Although it was owned by a Jewish family, the home became a cautionary tale for what could happen if Middle or Far Eastern tastes were allowed in. San Marino only needed to look nearby at what their suburb could become if left unregulated. Monterey Park's streets were lined with Chinese businesses and unchecked development, prompting a local newspaper publisher to remark in 1987, "I see a community that has become aesthetically and socially quite ugly." In Arcadia, a mansion built in 1985 by Sho Kosugi, the Japanese star of several "Ninja" movies, and his Chinese wife, was unapologetically Asian in design. It stood three stories high, embellished with a blue tile roof, Buddhist shrine, and a red bridge. The house was vandalized more than 20 times in two years. To San Marino's leaders, the protection of the town's architectural character wasn't just a matter of aesthetic frivolity, but a means of preserving both historical continuity and ethnic peace.[93]

During the 1990s, when Chinese in-migration was spiking, San Marino spelled out these standards in increasing detail. This was particularly evident in the Residence Guides passed out to newcomers. Guides from the 1950s and 1960s merely provided an overview of city services. By 1989, the guide—issued by the City Club that year—included five pages graphically depicting "Do's and Don'ts (Mostly Don'ts)" on how to properly use a suburban home.[94] The graphics and messaging strongly suggested its target audience was Chinese. For example, it warned against allowing extended family (such as grandparents) or auxiliary kitchens (such as "wok kitchens") that were common in some Asian households. By the late 1990s, the city

Figure 5.6 This suburban home, which came to be known locally as the "Taj Mahal," rankled many long-time residents and leaders of San Marino who criticized its nonconforming design. It ultimately precipitated the formation of the Design Review Committee, a body whose mission was to assess homeowners' plans and prevent structures like this from being built.
Photo by Becky Nicolaides.

DO'S & DON'TS
(MOSTLY DON'TS)

The unique residential character of San Marino has been preserved for seventy-five years by the enactment and enforcement of certain ordinances which are not always found in other cities and which are sometimes a surprise to prospective new residents and their realtors.

To stress the importance of some of the more important of these, we are setting them forth in illustrated graphic form. The titles are oversimplified but the details of each ordinance are available at City Hall. By avoiding bureaucratic language and lengthy prose, we hope to make the messages both interesting and clear.

ONLY ONE FAMILY PER HOME

ONLY ONE KITCHEN PER HOUSE

Figure 5.7   For the first time in its history, in 1989, San Marino published a detailed listing of "Do's and Don'ts (Mostly Don'ts)" regarding the usage of residential property. Warning against extended family, auxiliary kitchens, and privacy fencing, these guidelines were aimed implicitly at Chinese newcomers to San Marino.

"An Informational Guide for Residents of San Marino" (San Marino City Club, 1989), 14, San Marino Historical Society.

issued a 68-page document entitled "Residential Design Guidelines," which defined what good taste should look like in San Marino. Although not meant as "legally required development standards," it reflected the suburb's "desired design policies," intended to protect neighborhood character and property values. The guide tutored residents on acceptable architectural styles, including Spanish Colonial Revival, Mediterranean/Italian Renaissance, Tudor, Colonial Revival, and Cape Cod, and it warned that "common 'developer tract' styles are not authentic and are discouraged." Even "good taste" was spelled out. The guide defined "tasteful" in the glossary: "Having or showing good judgement [sic] in what is beautiful, appropriate, harmonious, compatible or excellent in art, architecture, decoration, etc." This definition essentially mandated continuity with San Marino's existing built landscape.[95] Paul Crowley, a driving force behind these measures, captured this ideal when he noted, "San Marino is a city that doesn't like to change much. Of course, I totally endorse that."[96]

The Design Review Committee ensured the protection of this style partly through the committee's racial composition—majority white from 1994 to 2006—but emerging Chinese leaders also shared the strong desire to protect the suburb's existing character. Hong Kong native Allan Yung served on the Design Review Committee in 2006–2008 and became an enthusiastic defender of San Marino's Euro-American aesthetics. Other Chinese leaders expressed a similar regard for existing regulations and the importance of teaching residents to learn and obey them. After 2000, Chinese residents served regularly on the Design Review Committee.[97]

While the city meticulously protected outward appearances, some Chinese residents found ways to subtly adapt properties to meet their own cultural needs. For years, San Marino had allowed second units in R-1 zones, originally as servants' quarters. Some Chinese residents found these units worked well as "granny flats" where they could house and care for their elders. Taiwan native Richard Sun, who had served on the city council since 2009 and as mayor in 2012, knew some Chinese families who used the second units in this way. In 2003, a local ordinance specified a minimum lot size of 12,000 square feet for these second-unit properties and mandated that the unit not be visible from the street.[98] The utilization of these units by Chinese families signified ways that they could maintain cultural autonomy by creatively using the restricted built spaces.

In addition to the style of homes, trees were another threatened aesthetic resource. In San Marino, old trees were a crucial facet of the picturesque landscape and a venerated link to the Huntington Estate. Old trees powerfully symbolized a connection to the past.[99] For Chinese newcomers who followed *feng shui* precepts, an ill-situated tree could block good energy from entering a household. What Anglos might perceive as stately, beautiful, and historic, some Chinese perceived as barriers to well-being. Others believed that trees were havens for insects. As a result, some Chinese residents began chopping down trees around their homes. City Manager John Nowak noted that an increasing number of large, healthy trees had been removed during the 1980s. Alarmed by the trend, the city council passed a moratorium on tree removal in October 1987, followed by a stringent ordinance regulating tree cutting. Taiwanese-born Jean Wang perceived early friction over tree cutting as a matter of cultural and language misunderstanding, but ultimately considered trees vitally important, making the community "very nice looking" and contributing to its "comfortable" feel and aesthetic value. Robert Lay, a Taiwan native who served as Chinese Club president in 1984, recalled that he and many Chinese residents felt that, when it came to trees, it was their private property so they could do what they wanted. But he soon realized the city's guidelines reflected a kind of expertise about trees and their value, a message he conveyed to fellow Club members. He also grew to appreciate the aesthetic beauty of trees.[100] At the Chinese Club's instigation, Mayor Suzanne Crowell declared March 12, 1992, Arbor Day in San Marino, which coincided with Taiwanese Arbor Day. The Club also donated trees to the city and participated in local Arbor Day celebrations in the late 1990s. With these very public gestures, the Chinese community symbolically defused a once-divisive issue and demonstrated their support for local aesthetic preferences.[101]

Finally, there was signage, which emerged as a hot-button issue in the San Gabriel Valley. San Marino's approach again revealed much about interethnic dynamics in the suburb. The contrasts between San Marino and Monterey Park were striking. In Monterey Park, signage became a fiercely contested, racialized fight for ethnic expression in the landscape that Chinese residents won. After 10 years of conflict, Monterey Park finally settled on a fairly liberal ordinance in 1989, requiring that the name and type of business appear in English but specifying no specific percentage of English words.[102] In conflict-averse San Marino, the town's sign ordinance passed quietly, but the nature of its passage revealed a somewhat cunning strategy. Local Anglo leaders essentially presented a tolerant public face in a high-profile controversy in early 1986, but then quietly passed one of the strictest signage measures in LA County the following year.

This turn of events began in early 1986, when Kevin Forbes, a 19-year-old recent graduate of San Marino High, proposed that English be made the official language of San Marino, tapping into the statewide "Official English" movement. Incensed by the brash, divisive nature of Forbes's campaign, the

San Marino city council voted down the proposal and denied his request to place the issue on the June ballot. Echoing moderate Republican opposition statewide—by Governor George Deukmejian, among others—local opinion in heavily Republican San Marino struck a tone of righteous indignation and colorblind inclusivity. Resident Chris Fastnow asserted, "a law proclaiming an official language is against everything our country stands for." Paul Crowley, who was running for city council, noted, "I think the resolution was insulting in the very least . . . [a] pointless matter that has no purpose because our Asian residents are totally in agreement with us."[103]

Crowley's comments proved more prophetic than he may have realized. The following year, well after the Forbes incident died down, the city council passed Ordinance No. 931, a measure that regulated all aspects of signage in San Marino. City council minutes registered no public discussion around the issue, while coverage in the *San Marino Tribune* was muted.[104] The ordinance required that 80% of the sign appear in English, much stricter than in other suburbs. The lack of public discussion, combined with the measure's stringency, suggested acquiescence by the Chinese community. As one Chinese businessman, comparing San Marino to nearby Alhambra with its visible Chinese presence, remarked, "Even the Chinese don't want Huntington [Drive] to look like Valley [Boulevard]. I don't want it to look like that."[105] As a result, San Marino's landscape would remain free of any outward traces of Chinese influence.

Chinese consent was not simply an amicable gesture but was also propelled by lingering ethnoracial tension. Anti-Chinese hostility bubbled up in late 1988, when a sign above the Golden Acres Realty office was repeatedly vandalized. The sign included just two Chinese characters—less than 10% of the sign's total area and thus legally compliant—yet prompted "a staggering" number of angry phone calls and letters to city hall. Crowley, serving as mayor at the time, defended the business for its compliance with San Marino's strict law and worried about the effects of this hostility on local interethnic relations. "Our history of harmonious and cooperative assimilation of Asians has been exemplary, and the possibility of major discord over such a small item is disturbing to me."[106] Although Crowley called out this racist hostility, his policies effectively stifled Asian visibility through more subtle, colorblind mechanisms.

The end result of these efforts—melding Anglo coercion and Chinese acquiescence—was a suburb where visible ethnicity was suppressed. The most striking example was the Chinese Club, which occupied a nondescript storefront along Huntington Drive, virtually indistinguishable from the insurance office next door. Even for this most ethnic of local organizations, the outward assertion of cultural identity was limited to a few small posters. In both its spatial presence and original mission, the Chinese Club signaled its recognition of the highly regulated nature of life in San Marino and an acceptance of both the payoffs and constraints of that regulation.[107] Even the Chinese-owned Colonial Kitchen—a long-time fixture in San Marino—prominently displayed American and British flags but hid any outward signs of Chinese identity.[108]

Ultimately, Chinese residents in San Marino accepted the prospect of living in a town that showed few physical traces of their presence. The multiple regulations put into place, as a backlash against the Asian influx, were meant to protect the original picturesque character of the community, a carefully tended space of physical beauty and American culture. This formula

Figure 5.8 The Chinese Club of San Marino, 2022. The lack of visible Chinese characters on the meeting place of the Chinese Club signified compliance to the suburb's strict regulations on English-language signage. The Chinese Club occupied two adjacent storefront spaces, shown here.
Photo by Becky Nicolaides.

had kept San Marino at the top of the metropolitan pecking order for many years, a lesson not lost on Chinese newcomers to town.[109]

A number of pioneer Chinese residents articulated their preference for the classical design styles and the ways it would ultimately benefit them through property appreciation. Allan Yung recalled his first impression of San Marino in the 1970s: "Big streets, clean, lots of trees, and it just seemed to be very comfortable." Taiwan native Robert Lay valued the open spaces and traditional "old fashioned" feel of the community. "It's like [the] country, beautiful." Though he was initially concerned about the upkeep costs of old local homes, he quickly came to recognize the high status and value these homes bestowed upon the suburb. His neighbor, an old friend from Taiwan, assured him that old heating and cooling systems could be easily upgraded. What San Marino homes delivered was value, which meant real estate appreciation, superior schools, and respectable neighbors, the bundled attributes of affluent suburban living.[110]

For some Chinese residents, San Marino embodied an imagined childhood ideal of America. Robert Lay recalled reading English-language primers as a boy in Taiwan about a fictional Taylor family living in American suburbia. From those books, he absorbed the vision of a single-family home where you can "have a backyard, have fun. . . . When we were in Taiwan, we saw those and, oh, that's my dream." When he arrived in San Marino, it reminded him of the world in the Taylor books.[111]

Some residents explicitly contrasted San Marino's identity with the ethnoburb of Monterey Park. One Taiwanese-born resident stressed the contrasting roots of both towns—Monterey Park, he claimed, started as chicken farms run by Mexicans, while Henry Huntington was concerned with creating a well-planned, nicely landscaped community in San Marino. Another Taiwanese native drew stark class distinctions, labeling San Marino as "level one" and Monterey Park as "level three." San Marino was also superior for its lush trees, good schools, upstanding kids, and the polite culture bred by high-level professionals and business people. The absence of major commercial areas or condos—which overran Monterey Park—allowed San Marino to maintain its bucolic character. Yet the proximity of Monterey Park gave these same residents the advantages of easy access to the best, cheapest Chinese grocery stores, restaurants, and services nearby without having to alter the look of their own town. As Taiwan-born Becky Ung put it, "You can do all that, just drive another two miles."[112] The Chinese of San Marino benefited from the cultural capital inherent in their town while maintaining a NIMBY attitude toward ethnoburbia itself.

Some locals linked Chinese preferences for Euro-American tastes to globalization itself. Janice Lee-McMahon, originally from Taiwan, moved to San Marino in 1985 and became a prominent realtor in the area. She perceived the Chinese appreciation for Euro-American aesthetics as a reflection of their cosmopolitanism and class position: "The second generation, or the really worldly Asians, have seen the masterpieces. . . . [I]f you have the same backgrounds, if you have the same education, most likely you'll have the same values. It doesn't matter if you're English, Jewish, Chinese. The *nouveau riche* is international."[113] Former City Manager of San Marino Matt Ballantyne echoed the idea that Chinese transnationalism and wealth contributed to their affinity for Euro-American landscape aesthetics: "the Taiwanese folks that are relocating here, they come from affluent families, and they may have been exposed to a lot more things. That means art, culture, just traveling in general. So maybe they've gone to Italy and then they see some of our design here, they understand it. I think money . . . provides this common bond here, and the reason why everybody gets along."[114] Affluence, then, helped create a common cosmopolitan outlook and design aesthetic, which acted as a cultural and political unifier in San Marino.

While some of these affinities can be explained as an outcome of governmental pressure, the evidence from San Marino suggests a more layered, complex formation of aesthetic sensibilities.[115] Chinese suburbanites melded personal homeland memories, expectations of American comforts and advantages, and an array of aesthetic predilections with hegemonic American suburban tastes, and out of it all they emerged as full-fledged members of affluent suburbia. At the same time, other Asians may have refrained from actively challenging these sensibilities due to unfamiliarity with local governance or insecurity about vocalizing their ideas to neighbors or local leaders.[116] A comparative perspective suggests another scenario. Many Asians were expressing themselves in nearby towns like Monterey Park, San Gabriel, and Hacienda Heights where spatial politics were open and contentious and ultimately created ethnoburbs. Landscapes of design assimilation existed in dialectic tension with ethnoburbs. Many Asian suburbanites wanted proximity to ethnic supermarkets, services, and restaurants close at hand, but just not in their backyards. Ethnoburban encroachment would puncture the bucolic suburban ideal and the suburban advantage that came from living alongside affluent whites. For them, too much visible ethnicity in their home neighborhoods was unwelcome. They perceived the American-ness of their communities as a marker of high status and their own social acceptance and integration.

By the 1990s, design aesthetics had come to pit pioneer Chinese residents against more recent arrivals from mainland China. Allan Yung, who served on the Design Review Committee and city council, articulated the impor-tance of protecting San Marino's Euro-American aesthetics against undisci-plined taste: "For people who come from China and look at this, [they say] wow. They pay $3 million for a flat that's 1,000 square feet [in China]. Now they have *two acres*, for $1 million . . . [and] they want to build 15,000 square feet. [laughs] We say no, you can only do 5,000, and only in a way that *we* like it. What you like doesn't matter. . . . We have to be compatible here. . . . You cannot mix the Italian, the French, and the German architecture—and put the house here. It's got to be pure in design."[117] Like other Chinese members of the Design Review Committee, Yung had become a fervent defender of San Marino's conservative design aesthetics. As more and more Chinese people moved in with every passing year, ethnic relations remained peaceful, and the landscape remained—as ever—unchanged.

Social Life in Multicultural Suburbia

If built aesthetics told a story of assimilation, San Marino's social life was a more nuanced tale of conflict and cross-cultural adaptation. In this realm, Chinese residents asserted their own lifeways and practices, at times critiquing Anglo culture, at other times melding with local traditions. Unlike their rejection of overt Asian design aesthetics, the Chinese of San Marino believed aspects of their ethnic culture had something to offer the community.

If they brought a distinct ethnic inflection to local social life, the suburb's Chinese residents also came to share core community values, especially around voluntarism and children. For many Chinese parents, the process of learning voluntarism was fraught with cultural missteps and cross-ethnic judgments. But with pioneer Chinese residents there to lead the way—the "bridge builders"—and second-generation residents to carry things forward, the process was remarkably efficient, accelerated by new fiscal pressures placed on the community by Proposition 13. Community members and leaders observed the growing strength of these shared values. In 1993, Mayor

Eugene Dryden—a San Marino resident since 1936—remarked that Chinese residents held "exactly the same long-term objectives as people who have lived here a long time. They want to preserve a residential town, with good schools and community participation. And that community participation is something that's growing in the Chinese community now."[118]

The "Bridge Builders"

Critical to this process was a group of Chinese residents who became ethnic "bridge builders." As active participants, they modeled the practices of voluntarism for their Chinese neighbors to smooth the way toward social acceptance and ethnic harmony. While their stories varied markedly—they came from different socioeconomic backgrounds and familial experiences of community participation—they did share certain traits. They were pioneer Chinese settlers in San Marino, and most had spent at least 10 years in the United States before moving to the suburb. They had lived mostly in majority-Anglo communities for years and had gained some familiarity with American community norms and customs. As parents, they had interacted with the American school system. Most were arriving from ethnically integrated communities, rather than insulated ethnic enclaves. They were, in short, familiar with American ways and experiences of ethnic diversity.

The bridge builders arrived with childhood memories of family and community experience from their home countries. Those who came from humble backgrounds recalled their parents had little time or inclination to get involved in local activities back in their home countries. Rosa Zee's father did not participate in the community or local government, partly out of suspicion; he believed that "China has never been government for people. It's always government for people in power."[119] In Hong Kong, Allan Yung recalled his parent's inability to participate because, in their modest working-class neighborhood, "Nobody joins anything, you don't have time. You can't afford time." He recalled no clubs or groups in his neighborhood.[120] Those from better-off backgrounds recalled parents active in their communities. From rural Taiwan, Jean Wang saw her father serve as president of the PTA of her elementary school and volunteer as a medical doctor for a local high school for 20 years. Richard Sun grew up in an affluent district of Taipei. His father owned garment factories, while his mother ran a private school and joined the Lions Club, Rotary Club, and Zonta International, philanthropic groups that raised money for the poor and disabled. In the 1960s, she was elected to the city council of Taipei. Richard followed her example at an early age, serving in school government in junior high and at his college in Taiwan.[121]

Though this group varied by class background, they shared similar patterns of life in the United States. Several were doctors or married to doctors, which required frequent moves for residencies and internships. By the time they arrived in San Marino, they had been exposed to an array of American towns, cities, and community experiences: Jean Wang lived in Chicago, Memphis, Buffalo, and Montebello, California; Allan Yung lived in Richmond, Virginia, and Orange County, Oakland, and San Diego, California; Rosa Zee lived in Eugene, Oregon; Berkeley; Flushing, New York; Danbury, Connecticut; Pittsburgh, Pennsylvania; and Monterey Park.[122] When they arrived in San Marino, they were familiar with American community norms, all had children, and they made their initial forays into community life through the local school system.

Because of their previous experiences, they recognized their potential to serve as ethnic bridge builders. They were somewhat self-conscious about this role, especially as the Asian population began to rise in San Marino. Looking back on the mid-1980s, Janice Lee-McMahon reflected: "I basically put it upon myself the task, not a job, but as a mission, of being the 'bridge.' Because my feeling was that most of the people who came from Taiwan at that time spoke very poor English and didn't know the new culture well at all. And most of the [Anglo] people in San Marino, even though they were wealthy, I hate to say this, but many were pretty narrow-minded, not very worldly." She believed they lacked empathy toward immigrants struggling to learn a new language because most had not experienced that struggle themselves. Lee-McMahon believed the best way to foster that empathy and build interethnic community was to emphasize the commonalities among white and Chinese families in San Marino—particularly the shared interests in children and the schools—and to get actively involved. Upon her own arrival in San Marino, she joined the PTA and began translating the district's educational codes into Chinese. "I encouraged the Chinese moms to be more involved and feel more connected with the school and their Americanized kids. . . . I came here when I was 12, so I went to junior high school, high school, and undergrad. So I know the importance of participation."[123]

Allan Yung arrived in San Marino in 1975, with his wife and two young sons, with a third born a year later. He described a pretty quick process of social integration. In Hong Kong, he recalled, neighbors were strangers. In

San Marino, his neighbors reached out quickly and warmly. To Yung, this was a singularly American custom. "You see neighbors, you see friends, you see kids. And we associate, we socialize. You take kids to school in the morning and you knew the families, you share rides, and you begin to go to school functions. . . . All of that was very foreign to me." Yung came to understand local traditions of voluntarism as a mechanism for social acceptance. Nonparticipation, he believed, exacerbated prejudice, and he worried that a tendency toward ethnic clustering would have a similar effect. The Chinese Club invited Yung to participate because he had lived in San Marino for a few years, and his decades in the United States made him comfortable and familiar with American ways. Many Club members, by contrast, were adjusting more slowly. Yung implored Chinese Club members to get involved in San Marino life. Although this was the Club's initial mission, he saw the need to reiterate the message as new immigrants continued to arrive. He told members, if you "plan to stay as a guest and never participate, you will never be accepted. You have to want to be a *part* of this, before they'll take you in as one of them." Yung himself was a member of established social and civic institutions, became one of the first Chinese Americans to serve in local government, and helped create new conduits for interethnic social connections.[124]

Rosa Zee forged a similar role for herself in the crucial arena of local public education. In the early 1980s, she enthusiastically threw herself into PTA work, driven by an intense desire to familiarize herself with her children's education. Previously, she had worked as a bilingual resource teacher in a Monterey Park school where the PTA was nearly defunct. Local parents wouldn't show up, so a tiny cohort of five teachers and teacher's aides—including Rosa—comprised the total PTA membership. After she moved to San Marino, she was constantly invited to "volunteer for this, volunteer for that." She started showing up at PTA board meetings, which were held on the one day she could take off from work. The difference between involvement in the two communities, as she saw it, related partly to ethnicity, partly to class. In Monterey Park, many parents—Asian and Latino alike—could not speak English, so they were reluctant to join. In San Marino, the PTA was bursting with Caucasian volunteers, many of them stay-at-home moms. For working mothers like Zee, participation was difficult because most meetings and volunteer activities happened during the day. Still, she increased her involvement, especially during the summers, and became president of the PTA at Carver Elementary School. Eventually she was the first Chinese

American elected to the San Marino School Board in 1992. All along, other Chinese parents relied on Zee as a conduit to the mostly Anglo-led school establishment.[125]

As early "bridge builders," these Chinese San Marinians modeled voluntarism for their Asian neighbors and brought them into the fold while setting the tone for local interethnic life. They shared a belief in assimilation and learning the ways of the mainstream, a philosophy that comported with the Human Relations Committee mandate. The role of "bridge builder" extended to the human relations liaisons placed in each school, typically a Chinese parent familiar with both cultures. Despite their enthusiasm, these residents often struggled to get Chinese newcomers to participate in the community and the schools. And they contended with lingering Anglo resentments toward the growing Chinese population. With every new immigration wave, the challenges escalated. Still, this nucleus of Chinese volunteers gradually pulled more and more of their co-ethnics into the heart of local social life. Ever so slowly, the well-entrenched social ways of San Marino began to adjust.

The Social Terrain of San Marino, 1970–2000

Through its ethnic transformation, San Marino's social and civic institutions remained fairly stable. Asian residents did not remake this landscape but joined existing groups and infused them with Chinese culture where they could. The health of social and civic life remained fairly robust, in spite of larger social forces like the rise of working mothers. Despite the surface appearance of statis, it was within this social life that cultural adaptations and interpenetration took place and Chinese suburbanites created their own sense of local belonging.

Between 1970 and 2000, San Marino demographically transitioned from predominantly white to multiethnic, reflecting a sizeable decline in its white population. By 2000, Asians outnumbered whites for the first time. While some Latinos moved in, their numbers remained low. During these years, a second Asian wave arrived, including transnational sojourners from mainland China, where the economy was booming. By purchasing homes in San Marino, these newcomers gained the dual benefits of a safe place to invest their money and top-flight schools for their children. In some cases, they settled their children in San Marino with a relative, then returned to

China. These "parachute kids" and their absentee parents posed particular challenges for the community and highlighted schisms between the
first and second waves of Asian settlers. The rising number of immigrants,
reaching 37% of the population by 2000, also reflected these divisions (see
Table A5.1). In terms of class, San Marino maintained its consistently high
standing, reinforced by the infusion of transnational wealth.[126] The proportion of white-collar professionals and college-educated adults also stayed
very high. In terms of family composition, San Marino remained remarkably
static throughout the ethnic transition. This was overwhelmingly a suburb of
working-age married couples with children. One big change was a steep rise
in the number of working mothers; they jumped from 20% to 60% of all married women, which aligned San Marino more closely with regional trends by
2000.[127]

Throughout this period, San Marino's elite aura endured. For incoming
Asian immigrants, a San Marino address represented an investment in an
American status symbol. The suburb continued to attract high-profile
residents, including Edmund Shea (founder of the mega developer Shea
Homes), LA County Sheriff Lee Baca and his Chinese wife, Reagan adviser
William French Smith, baseball player Jim Gott, football player and USC
athletic director Pat Haden, actors Jane Kaczmarek and Bradley Whitford,
Hall of Fame baseball broadcaster Jaime Jarrin, celebrity chef Joachim
Splichal, and even a Bolivian drug kingpin who lived there incognito with his
family.[128] The Los Angeles Times continued its regular coverage of residents
in its society pages during the 1980s and 1990s, detailing ritzy benefit galas,
weddings, debutante balls, and parties. San Marino high schoolers were perennially chosen for the Rose Court of Pasadena's Rose Parade.[129]

The public schools continued to play a vital role in interethnic community-
building. The Asian impact on the local schools was rapid and dramatic: from
1980 to 1989, the Asian school population jumped from 10% to 46%. In the
early 1980s—before any human relations work was launched—the PTAs
initiated cross-cultural programs with three-person committees at each
school (each with one Chinese, Japanese, and Anglo mother) that developed programs to help integrate new Asian families into the schools. Their
work included translating all school materials and policies into Chinese
and Japanese; holding informational meetings at the Chinese Club covering
school programs, medical forms, and general first-day information; and
rounding up ESL volunteers. Women devoted hundreds of volunteer hours to
facilitating the peaceful incorporation of Asian newcomers into the suburb,

paying particularly attention to the language barriers that intimidated many newcomer parents. Bridge-builders like Rosa Zee, Jean Wang, and Janice Lee-McMahon were crucial in these efforts.[130]

Rosa Zee recalled the infectious energy of the white stay-at-home mothers who volunteered in the PTA: "I realized these [San Marino] women do not work, they spend all their lives, pretty much 100% of their time, at their children's school. And they may not just be involved in one school—if they have two or three kids, they're at different schools. . . . They were very, very organized. All of those women treated the volunteer work like a full-time job." But she noticed few other Chinese mothers participating in the early 1980s, held back by their English-language deficiency or unfamiliarity with the community, and she wanted to involve these families. Local participation, she believed, was a crucial linchpin of American democracy: "We learn all of these wonderful things in democracy which we don't have much [in our background]. You learn here, you understand, you make your life better, you make the community life better."[131] When Zee ran successfully for school board in 1993, she vowed "to link the two cultures of San Marino."[132] Chinese families gradually responded by volunteering for school activities such as the country fair, pancake breakfasts, carnivals, and assisting with administrative tasks such as xeroxing.[133]

Proposition 13 was an unintended catalyst in this process. By 1986, the suburb's school district was characterized as *nouveau poor*, thanks to Prop 13 cuts, aging school buildings, and the suburb's conservative budget, which meant teacher salaries were among the lowest in LA County. As a bedroom suburb, San Marino had very few avenues for raising revenue. Rezoning to bring in large businesses would have destroyed its picturesque aura. The only real option was to lean heavily on the cash and sweat equity of residents. They soon delivered. Through vigorous fundraising and eventually the passage of parcel taxes, families donated millions of dollars to the local schools.[134] The parcel tax was a special levy tacked onto every resident's property tax bill. After failing to win the required 66.6% of votes in 1986, the parcel tax successfully passed in 1991, and enjoyed repeated success in subsequent years.[135] Another tactic was fundraising for the schools. San Marino institutionalized these efforts by forming a Schools Foundation in 1979. Helmed by 25 volunteer trustees, the foundation set out to raise enough money to close the gap between state funding and the funds needed to maintain San Marino's high-caliber school system. Between 1980 and 1986, the Schools Foundation raised $1.45 million. At one picnic fundraiser, the Chinese Club gave $9,000.

Families also donated computers, office supplies, and even a Volvo station wagon. In subsequent years, donations grew exponentially. By 2012, the Schools Foundation raised $3 million per year, supplemented by two parcel taxes ($5 million/year) and additional money from PTA fundraisers. Over its 38-year history, the San Marino Schools Foundation raised $45 million. This localized funding system illustrated how affluent suburbs worked to regain their own locally directed wealth, thus widening the gap between have and have-not suburbs.[136]

Just as significant was the social capital that Prop 13 generated. Parents stepped in to organize activities that the school district could no longer afford. Some parents volunteered to run music and other programs slashed by Prop 13. In 1984, 300 volunteers turned out to paint the high school, a project that quickly turned into a social occasion with donations of gourmet meals and a 1950s jukebox. A number of Chinese parents participated. In 1985, San Marino parents put in more than 75,000 volunteer hours, averaging over 27 hours per child per year, the majority logged by women. The fiscal crisis of Prop 13 thus invigorated San Marino's participatory culture. And, coming at the exact moment of the Asian influx, it created in the schools a bonding terrain for Anglo and Chinese parents. By the late 1980s, Anglos lauded Chinese parents as volunteers and especially as generous donors, signaling they had switched from being a fiscal drain to welcome community partners.[137]

San Marino's civic and social clubs, meanwhile, remained relatively strong from 1970 to 2000. On a purely quantitative level, the total number of groups declined somewhat following national trends, but the downturn was relatively slight.[138] Only two Asian groups formed during these decades: the Japanese Parents of San Marino in the 1980s and the Chinese Club, which became a permanent fixture. Despite their demographic ascendance, the Chinese of San Marino made only the lightest institutional imprint on the suburb. Existing Anglo groups retained their dominance as sites of social interaction, networking, and gateways to local political power.[139]

The turnover of groups suggested both broad and more subtle trends. Following national patterns, some fraternal groups such as the Masons and Kiwanis waned in San Marino, disappearing by the 1990s.[140] At the same time, others such as the Rotary and Lions Clubs thrived. Those diverging fates had much to do with globalization. The Rotary and Lions Clubs had a very strong presence in East Asia, compared to the Kiwanis, suggesting that robust fraternal group life in these feeder countries carried over to San Marino.[141] Taiwan had a significantly higher per capita rate of Lions Clubs than in the United States in 2013 (eight times higher), so the group was familiar to many immigrant arrivals in San Marino. In 1988, Robert Lay and a couple of dozen others formed a Chinese American Lions Club in San Marino. The Club was devoted to "the principles of good government and good citizenship . . . [and] the civic, cultural, social, and moral welfare of the community." It met monthly for socializing and service projects. Later, a few whites also joined.[142] The transnational character of certain fraternal groups, then, kept them relevant and vibrant in this ethnically transforming suburb.[143]

Among San Marino's older civic groups, those that retained vitality were the ones that welcomed diversity, such as the City Club. As one of San Marino's oldest civic groups, this club had a consistent history of robust membership and community influence. While membership was open to any male residing in the San Marino Unified School District, applicants had to be sponsored by a current member. By 1990, a small coterie of Chinese men had gotten in, including Allan Yung. In 1993, Yung sponsored others for membership—five Asians, one Caucasian—most of them fellow doctors. Gradually, a process of ethnic networking began to push the City Club toward ethnic diversity. Yung characterized the City Club as a "neighbor networking group." With its meetings held in a middle school cafeteria, it was free of the pretentiousness of other exclusive men's clubs and enjoyed a casual and convivial culture. The group attracted speakers from among business and political leaders, as well as movie directors, a newscaster, and high-profile athletes. It was a place where members formed social and business connections and supported community institutions like the schools. Yung, along with Mark Chen, Robin Chiu, and Matthew Lin, opened the door to other Chinese residents and used the club as a springboard into other civic roles, including human relations work and eventually municipal government. At the same time, their club participation made them familiar figures in the broader community.[144]

As a long-standing yet moderately flexible institution, the City Club retained its vitality and relevance in San Marino. Membership fell slightly from 500 to 400 between 1970 and 2010, and by the 2000s, Asian membership had grown to 25% of the total. Some of the overall decline occurred when women were admitted for the first time in 1995, driving some men away. While attendance at their monthly dinners dipped from between 140 and 180 to 100 by the 2000s, this was still a respectable turnout. As a sign of its adaptation to new demographic realities, it was fitting that a Chinese woman, Janice Lee-McMahon, served as its first female president in 2011.

The general culture and casual atmosphere of the club persisted, even as its social composition transformed. The group's flexibility allowed it to continue to serve as a kind of informal civic training ground and social resource for its members—Anglo and Chinese alike.[145]

By contrast, women's clubs had mixed fortunes. The most successful were ethnically inclusive, possessed some social cachet, and incorporated children in some way. For example, the local National Charity League (NCL) flourished over these years. A mother-daughter group focused on service projects and social functions culminating in debutante soirees, it was a powerful vehicle in San Marino where wealth and social status continued to matter. The centrality of youth propelled the club forward and ultimately fostered the process of ethnic integration. As children forged interethnic friendships, they drew their parents into social networks and ultimately began to open doors to even the most exclusive social groups like the NCL. Asian Americans first joined in the late 1990s, and, by 2013, they comprised nearly 50% of members. With their intensive commitment to philanthropy, members saw it as an opportunity to serve the community and train their daughters in continuing that service.[146]

By contrast, the long-lived Women's Club began a slow descent after 1980. By this point, the traditional activities of the club—fashion shows, plays put on by the club's drama guild members, lengthy daytime meetings—had become an outmoded form of women's sociability. The Club suffered from two problems, as long-time member Terry Golden saw it. First, there was drastic attrition as white members moved away and few new residents joined. Since the 1970s, she recalled only one Chinese woman joining the group. Second, women shifted how they spent their spare time and energy. Not only were they joining the paid workforce, but they were also embracing hands-on parenting and focused on their children's activities. The Women's Club failed to adapt to these changes, and, by 2000, membership declined to about 70 mostly aging long-time members.[147] A similar trend occurred within the Newcomers Club, a decades-long social fixture with its weekday luncheons, book club, and museum visits. These activities proved both logistically and culturally inaccessible to San Marino's new resident. By 2012, the group had dwindled to four members.[148]

The Chinese Club, San Marino's only ethnic group, walked a fine line in serving simultaneously as a site of ethnic identity, cultural interpenetration, and assimilation. While the group celebrated Chinese traditions and sought to pass along Chinese culture to the town's youth, it also sought to link

Chinese newcomers to the suburb at large. It went to great lengths to reach out to the Anglo community and demonstrate that it had San Marino's broad interests at heart. Perhaps because of this multidimensionality, the Club grew to become one of the largest, most robust organizations in San Marino, with 380 members by 1990 and growing.

The Chinese Club reached both inward and outward. For its members, the Club served the traditional functions of Chinese diasporic institutions. It ran a Chinese School and worked to teach and maintain Chinese traditions through activities, classes, and social functions. Over time, it also began to offer a wider variety of classes like line dancing (a trend among Asians in the San Gabriel Valley), Chinese painting, flower arranging, a book club, yoga, and yuen ji wu (a tai chi-like martial art). Chinese residents found a warm, welcoming environment, with familiar cultural touchstones, the comforting sounds of spoken Chinese, and plenty of co-ethnics eager to help newcomers navigate the social mores of San Marino. Its leaders emphasized this continuing role of social and civic integration. With this clear mandate, this institution—social-, civic-, and cultural-minded—was a critical presence that taught Chinese residents the ways of local life.[149]

The Chinese Club also gently brought Chinese culture to San Marino. In these efforts, its members showed some willingness to make their traditions palatable to Anglo residents in a show of neighborly goodwill and a recognition of the importance of cultural give and take. A key event was the Mid-Autumn Festival, an annual Chinese celebration of the autumnal harvest and full moon. In San Marino, the first festival was celebrated in 1984, as a Chinese-only affair held at a club member's home large enough to accommodate 200 guests. Families did all the cooking. Within a few years, it had turned into an upscale event held at swanky hotels like the Universal City Hilton or the nearby Ritz Carlton that took volunteers half a year to plan. By the late 1980s, leaders of the Chinese Club decided to open it up to whites as a way of building cultural bridges in San Marino.[150] The gesture was generous on two levels. Serving as gracious hosts, Chinese Club board members purchased expensive tickets or a table for their white guests, according to "the Chinese way," as Rosa Zee put it. And, in 1989, in a show of goodwill, the Club decided to donate all proceeds to the San Marino public schools.

Chinese Club members, however, lost a cherished gathering of cultural ease and comfort among co-ethnics when whites began attending. Chinese Club members were no longer fully able to relax there. As Rosa Zee described, "The people who were organizing it had to sit with people that they don't necessarily have a common interest. . . . They don't feel they are enjoying the night because they prepare so long but, deep down, they really don't understand American culture. They know they have to do it, but it's a painful experience to sit through the night."[151] Sensing this reluctance, when Zee became Chinese Club president in 1992, she cancelled the Mid-Autumn festival that year and instead hosted a paid trip to Taiwan for 10 San Marino school leaders—the superintendent, four school principals, and their spouses.[152] For Zee, who served on the San Marino School Board, this was a more powerful way to build intercultural understanding where it counted most—in the schools. The administrators learned many things, including how Taiwanese school transcripts worked, the scholastic challenges of many Taiwanese students who ended up in America, and the cultural richness of Taiwan itself. Bringing the white leaders closer to Taiwanese students in the district, she noted, meant "They have a lot more compassion . . . a lot more tolerance."[153] San Marino's wealth helped set a high standard for human relations work.

Other San Marino traditions were simply lost in translation. For example, the City Club's Father's Night variety show died off in the 1990s, because its sense of humor and hijinks "just didn't play" with Chinese members, according to Club president Tom Santley.[154] Moreover, the idea of donating time—instead of money—to community projects also met resistance from some Chinese families. Allan Yung believed the powerful work ethic of Chinese parents was one crucial barrier, especially in the early years. They would say,

> Why would I want to volunteer? I'm so busy, I have my life. Why you want me to go paint the schoolhouse? The Chinese say, okay, here's my contribution. You hire a painter and paint the schoolhouse. . . . Time is their own. They don't have much. Money they've got a lot. Caucasians [say] that's not enough. That's your kid so you go there, paint it, have fun with it, have time to mix with other people. Why do they do that? Habit. They get off work at 4. Work four days a week. Chinese work 7 days a week. . . . They ask the parents to come, help this, help that. . . . I can't help, I don't know how to help. Is this a conflict? Is this a misunderstanding? I don't know what you call this.

The white demand to participate, Yung contended, also overlooked the formidable challenge of the immigrant experience itself. As he put it, "The parents, mothers, they don't speak much English, so they're afraid to vocalize. They hide in the background. And the Caucasians say, why don't you say something? . . . So hey, you know, [she] can't speak English, why do you want [her] to say something?"[155]

To find common ground where neighbors could recognize and appreciate their common interests, social groups developed new modes of socialization. One example was "Dinner for Eight," a joint effort begun in 1993 by the city of San Marino and the Chinese Club. These were intimate gatherings that paired two Anglo and two Chinese couples.[156] Over a dinner cooked by the host couple, the group would get to know each other. They met once a month, with couples cycling through different groups, then the whole group converged at the Huntington Library for dessert and a multiethnic concert "mingling Anglo and Chinese musical traditions." About 150 people participated during its two- to three-year run. Yung recalled, "It was somewhat uncomfortable to begin with. But you realize that all the people who participated were the ones who want to meet new people. So, at first it was very odd, but after the drinks, it's easier, and after dinner it's much easier. And then, most of the time, people go home and say, let me do one."[157]

Grad Night remained the symbolic linchpin of San Marino social life, but it was not unaffected by the suburb's ethnic turn. While it remained strong from 1980 to 2000, Grad Night in the late 1980s was fraught with interethnic unease. The event continued to require hundreds of parent volunteer hours, and white parents continued to carry the heaviest load, even as Asians made up 38% of high school seniors and were leaders in student governance by 1990. The number of Asian parent volunteers, by contrast, was miniscule, partly because the event was imbued with formidable challenges for Chinese parents. First, Grad Night itself was designed around American cultural tropes, with themes such as "Mardi Gras," "Manhattan Magic," and "Pirates of the Caribbean."[158] Volunteers designed and executed elaborate sets and activities around these motifs, so familiarity with these cultural touchstones was important. Second, parents were expected to devote considerable physical labor. While Allan Yung was deeply impressed by all "that effort, that love, that emotion that went into it," he saw the call for such labor as unreasonable. "The work, the construction, the painting, the building, all that stuff . . . the Chinese never hold a hammer in their life [laughs]. How can you tell them, hammer this, hammer that?" Anglo parents also complained when Chinese parents didn't step up to help.[159] Third, the language barrier remained an insurmountable hurdle for many Chinese parents. Robert Lay, Chinese Club president in 1984, saw parents' shyness and insecurity about their English as the primary reason for not participating.[160] Despite these hurdles, by 1990, a noticeable uptick was evident in Asian participation and donations to Grad Night, and that involvement increased in subsequent years. More and more Asian parents helped stage the event, although they were still reticent to take on leadership positions. By 2000, Grad Night maintained its role as "a social sacred cow," drawing 95 parent volunteers on the planning committee alone. This local tradition stayed strong, invigorated by the slow, steady rise in Asian American participation.[161]

While the social terrain of San Marino showed some spaces of cultural amalgamation, such as folding the mid-Autumn Festival into the town's social calendar, for the most part Asian suburbanites were expected to learn the ways of the suburb's long-standing traditions. Again and again, community leaders in the 1980s and 1990s emphasized the importance of assimilation and participation, social strands braided tightly together. Asian Americans gradually made strides, a trend praised by community leaders both white and Asian. As Police Chief Jack Yeske put it in 1990, "Without a bunch of grandstanding or beating of the drums, [newcomers of Chinese ancestry] have become citizens of San Marino." Added Robin Chiu, president of the Chinese Club, "By and large, we're doing really well to assimilate."[162]

This suburban social ethos at its core was inclusive. Judgmental as white residents could be, their end game was to bring their Asian neighbors into the vibrant social life of affluent San Marino. The ability to participate and contribute to the community was a badge of privilege, a signal that residents had the spare time and resources to volunteer, to serve in office, and to bolster the social and civic capital of their town. Grad Night was a brilliant example. It took hundreds and hundreds of hours. It took generous donations of gifts and money. It was, in the end, a sign of community health. This tradition, in fact, spread to other communities in California, the nation, and beyond in the 1980s and 1990s, catching on especially in prosperous suburbs and cities. In Orange County, 70% of high schools held San Marino-style Grad Nights by 1990—indeed, they looked to San Marino as the tradition's originator. In many ways, this event was a luxury, a symbol of affluence. In poorer towns, where parents lacked the time and resources to stage these elaborate shindigs, this style of Grad Night was unattainable. As Michael

Figure 5.9 May Day celebration at Valentine Elementary School, San Marino, 1992. The adjustment of Chinese American residents to established suburban traditions helped smooth the way to local acceptance.

Courtesy of the Archives at Pasadena Museum of History (PSN-May Day San Marino, photo by Walt Mancini); used by permission of Southern California News Group.

Perez, assistant principal of Jordan High School in Watts, observed. "We're surrounded by junk yards. I honestly feel that economically, the majority of our parents could in no way participate in something like that." At schools like Jordan, parents participated in other, less lavish ways. In upscale San Marino, Newport Beach, Laguna Beach, and Palos Verdes, enthusiastic parental participation across ethnic lines worked to keep social capital rich and expansive, bolstering the advantages of living in suburban affluence and uniting multiethnic suburbanites around values like voluntarism, giving back, and parental love.[163]

The Gates of Heavenly Peace

In the heart of Beijing lies Tiananmen, the Gate of Heavenly Peace. This statuesque gateway sits at the entrance to the Forbidden City, directly across from Tiananmen Square. Through centuries of history in China, Tiananmen bore witness to foreign assault, internal dissention, and revolutionary change. The dramatic standoff of June 4, 1989, between protesting students and the Chinese military in Tiananmen Square drew the world's attention to China, ultimately triggering changes in Chinese policy that reverberated even in the suburbs of Los Angeles.[164]

In the aftermath of June 4, Deng Xiaoping set China on a new course, propelling it toward world power through a robust program of economic liberalization and fervent nationalism. Within a single generation, "Everyone got richer, much richer, as incomes rose exponentially. People shifted focus, devoting energies to buying apartments, setting up companies, and navigating the myriad of new opportunities."[165] After 1990, a new, somewhat unstable middle class emerged in China, defined by a lifestyle expressed in homeownership, consumerism, and economic liberalism. As anthropologist Li Zhang notes, this new middle class showed signs of *nouveau riche* insecurity; they were perceived as economically wealthy but lacking in higher education, manners, and taste. So they compensated through conspicuous consumption and homeownership. Their expectations as homeowners were remarkably similar to American suburban ideals, including a strong sense of homeowner entitlement to private property, a better neighborhood environment, quality services, privacy, and buffers from the poor. As a feeder country to the United States, China was closing the gap between homeland and American suburban culture, overlapping understandings about how to live in affluent suburbia. Standing as the ultimate personification of these connections were the transpacific sojourners who cycled back and forth between America and East Asian home countries, blurring everyday lifeways in suburban communities on either side of the Pacific.[166]

After 1990, San Marino felt the reverberation of these global forces as immigrants from mainland China became the second wave of Asian newcomers to the suburb. Seeking safe investments and good schools, they bought into the suburb, some paying cash for multimillion-dollar homes. These infusions of cash, along with enterprises like East-West Bank headquartered in San Marino, helped drive up real estate values.[167] While Chinese immigrants may have lacked familiarity with the suburb's social culture, they shared established residents' desire to protect property values and the suburb's affluent aura. The notion of gates and exclusion were familiar spatial practices from Taiwan to mainland China, particularly in the insecure context of post-independence Southeast Asia.[168] It was not such a stretch, then, for Chinese and Anglo residents to find consensus around suburban exclusivity and class privilege.

By the new millennium, San Marino's political culture was one of multicultural, moderate conservatism and a solid commitment to class exclusivity knit together by the suburb's enduring ethos of voluntarism. In terms of party preferences, San Marino leaned Republican like nearly all of LA's wealthiest suburbs with rising Asian populations.[169] The number of registered voters remained extraordinarily high throughout San Marino's ethnic turn, defying typical patterns among Asian Americans and suggesting that, as in other arenas of life, affluence fueled civic engagement.[170]

San Marino's embrace of a more moderate conservatism was signaled by the 1989 departure of the John Birch Society, which had grown sorely out of touch with new local realities. Although the JBS maintained its volunteer-staffed American Opinion Bookstore on Mission Street for a few more years, it had grown irrelevant in a suburb with a rising number of Chinese residents. The Birchers in fact had a deeply hostile relationship to mainland China, having been named for a man killed in 1945 by Chinese communists and valorized by the group as a martyr of the Cold War.[171] Moreover, the Birchers' simplistic anti-China position was out of touch with the complex, even contentious, nuances of ethnic Chinese politics.

By the late 1990s, mainland China had a kind of diffuse influence on San Marino political culture. On one level, it had bred a deeply rooted distrust of government and reluctance to participate among generations who had left the mainland. The process of overcoming those suspicions became part of their acculturation to San Marino, a formidable barrier that many successfully surmounted. The showdown in Tiananmen Square moreover pushed some to flee Hong Kong, fearing a similar fate when it transitioned to Chinese rule in 1997, and move to America. The Taiwan–China divide, too, had long fueled political enmity among Chinese Americans in Southern California. By the late 1990s, those divisions had begun to soften, reflecting a greater acceptance of Beijing as China's economy was opening up, transnational money was flowing, and more and more mainland Chinese were settling in Southern California—including in suburbs like San Marino. The San Marino Chinese Club—with 1,000 households claiming membership by

1997—consciously steered clear of the debates to maintain peaceful relations and to continue integrating into the community.[172]

At city hall, ethnic integration arrived gradually. In the 1990s, Chinese residents began serving on city commissions and the school board.[173] The city council was more difficult to penetrate. In contrast to Monterey Park, where two Chinese Americans sat on the city council by 1992, Asian Americans took longer to win those seats in San Marino. In 1992, Allan Yung was the first Chinese American to run for city council, part of a wave of Asian candidates running across the San Gabriel Valley. Typical of these campaigns, Yung downplayed his ethnic heritage while emphasizing issues like public safety and school funding. Yung lost this race. In 2000, Matthew Lin, an orthopedic surgeon, became the first Chinese American elected to the San Marino city council, followed by three more Chinese Americans in 2007 and 2009, including Yung.[174] These victories signaled the ascendance of multiethnic political leadership in the suburb.

By the turn of the twenty-first century, San Marino's multicultural consensus was firmly in place, committed to preserving the affluent status quo. Through well-established tactics like mandating design assimilation, copious fundraising for the schools, and shirking its responsibility to provide affordable housing by dubbing servants' quarters "low-income housing," San Marino's Anglo and Chinese residents together perpetuated a system that privileged and insulated their suburb.[175]

A vivid illustration of this multicultural effort to safeguard San Marino's affluence was the defense of Lacy Park, the suburb's treasured centerpiece. Designed in 1926, this verdant 30-acre park featured a large grassy center shaped like a teardrop, ringed by walkways, trees, shrubs and flowers, many donated by the Huntington Estate.[176] It was designed to be a "passive park," a space for quiet strolls and picnics.

In the early 1970s, Lacy Park had become the site of San Marino's own suburban crisis, a public space that had transformed from bucolic haven to unguarded portal to the outside world. In 1969, a widely advertised Fourth of July parade and picnic opened the floodgates, bringing in people from other communities who subsequently kept coming back. Attendance on a typical Sunday climbed from 150 to 2,000. It proved too much for many locals. At the 1972 Fourth of July parade, a van entry towed a huge sign that read "Lacy Park for San Marino Residents Only." Town leaders grew concerned over the perceived misuse of the park and incursions by outsiders who were disturbing the suburb's peace and quiet. Neighbors complained of parking congestion, motorcycle noise, people coming and going at all hours, and problems caused by "dogs, bicycle riders, and malicious mischief." The use of the park by certain people, moreover, scared away some residents who feared for the safety of themselves and their children.[177]

Following reports of "illegal or objectional behavior," the police launched foot patrols in 1972. And in 1974, the town's Planning Commission surveyed residents to gauge the scope of the problem and gather their ideas for solving it. The majority of respondents recommended fencing the park, erecting entrance gates, and imposing parking restrictions. Some advised a system of admission cards for residents. The idea, clearly, was to make this public space a little less public. The Commission ultimately recommended the initiation of police patrols on Sundays; the posting of rules signs throughout the park; and the prohibition of dogs, bikes, motorcycles, and "all forms of hardball play."[178] Yet the problems persisted, at least in the memory of some. Councilman Paul Crowley recalled, "it had gotten so bad it was attracting crime from all over Southern California." Police Chief James Moore, by contrast, recalled no such problems.[179]

A few years later, Proposition 13 handed town leaders a blunt instrument for controlling this public space—they would shut the park down altogether. They closed the park on weekends and holidays, using black iron gates to keep the public out. Town leaders claimed they no longer had sufficient funds to staff and maintain the grounds for full-time use. While the closures gave San Marinians a sense of relief, families from neighboring suburbs were frustrated. Claire Henze of Pasadena believed the move was meant to keep out "the riff raff" from other towns, while a mother from Alhambra expressed dismay that she could no longer bring her kids to "the one park for all the family." Town leaders were careful to blame Prop 13, which offered a neutral, colorblind excuse. City administrator Brice Stephenson retorted, "We could not discriminate against any element using the park, so we discriminated against everyone." Despite the subsequent passage of local parcel taxes to increase local revenue, the park remained shuttered.[180]

It took nearly 10 years before San Marino adopted a very gradual strategy for reopening the park on weekends. In 1987, the park was opened one Saturday per month, and visitors were required to get a park pass at city hall—free for residents, $3 for non-residents. Fewer than 600 people visited on those first trial Saturdays, a low turnout that reassured town leaders. The following year, they moved to every Saturday. These restrictive rules—requiring proof of residency and an admission fee for outsiders—were the

Figure 5.10 The entrance gates to Lacy Park, San Marino, 1984. Responding to community concerns about "outsiders" coming to this public park, local officials closed it down on weekends from 1978 to 1987. When they finally resolved to reopen it on weekends, the city charged non-residents a fee to enter.

Courtesy of the Archives at Pasadena Museum of History (PSN-Lacy Park, photo by Walt Mancini); used by permission of Southern California News Group.

strictest in the state, according to the president of the California Parks and Recreation Society.[181] Residents from neighboring towns continued to blast San Marino for elitism. As Bruce Holthaus of South Pasadena put it, "many of us felt that the park's closure was to prohibit entry to 'the wrong kind of people'. . . Americans generally pride themselves on being citizens of a country that is not bound by class restrictions . . . Except in San Marino. They have adopted India's caste system and are protecting themselves from the 'untouchables.'"[182] The strategy in fact was working; only 170 people used the park on those newly opened Saturdays, and fewer than one-quarter were nonresidents. Three years later, the park was opened on Sundays, with the same restrictions.[183]

By 2000, the restrictions remained in place and town leaders kept blaming Prop 13 and tight local budgets. Yet Lacy Park had received over $600,000 in state financing over the years, a fact revealed by *Los Angeles Times* columnist Steve Lopez. When he brought his four-year-old to Lacy Park to teach her to ride a bike and was charged a $4 admission fee, he questioned how a public park funded by state taxpayers could justify charging a fee to outsiders. He ended his article by sarcastically telling San Marino Mayor Matthew Lin and councilwoman Betty Brown that he planned to set up a booth at the entrance of Griffith Park—in the heart of Los Angeles—where he would charge anyone from San Marino $4 to enter. "I might charge $8 or $10 depending on how I feel at the time, or whether I think they really belong in my park." Lin and Brown replied that they love Griffith Park and would be happy to pay.[184]

Lopez's jab didn't ruffle the feathers of white and Chinese Americans living in suburban affluence. Lin and Brown's cheerful retort displayed a kind of class confidence, a unified, multicultural rejoinder to those who would question their right to live in a suburb of class privilege, bolstered through decades of careful town policies, a regenerated culture of voluntarism, and the ability to forge multicultural consensus around the protection of their landscape of privilege. Behind San Marino's gates, Chinese and Anglo Americans made their own peace, committed to the shared goal of protecting the everyday comforts they enjoyed in affluent suburbia.

6

The Death and Life of a
Working-Class Suburb

South Gate

In Los Angeles, the heart of working-class suburbia beats in the communities south of downtown, in places like South Gate. In these modest suburbs, middling and poor families have long lived side by side. There, the conditions of everyday life could be gritty, overcrowded, and even grim for the poorest of the poor, who experienced the living realities of suburban poverty.

These towns began as defensively lily-white before flipping to Latino. Paralleling the evolution of LA's working class since 1945, they shifted from predominantly white to nonwhite, unionized to non-unionized, well-paid to low-paid, homeowner to renter. As American-owned assembly lines gave way to sweatshops, national retail stores, and domestic work, these working-class suburbs tracked closely to the fate of workers themselves. Upward mobility accelerated in the immediate postwar years, skidded by the 1980s, then slowly rose. Throughout these decades, the suburbs remained havens for families making homes, raising children, and seeking a decent life. They were modest, but for many residents they meant something worth protecting.

The quality of life in these suburbs was always a subjective matter. A grizzled, white FBI agent investigating a drug-related kidnapping in 1995 saw South Gate as a "depressing little city." An immigrant arriving in 1989 from a poor neighborhood in Guadalajara, Mexico, considered South Gate "really beautiful."[1] These descriptions capture something elemental about South Gate's story: for newly arrived immigrants, it was a place of beauty and hope, the American dream materialized. For Anglo Americans, it was a failed place of decline and pathology, toxicity, and corruption. Reality lay somewhere in between.

South Gate sits among a constellation of towns dubbed the "gateway cities" for their role as portals for goods and people. These working-class suburbs sat along the spine of a massive regional logistics network. Imports shipped into the mammoth Port of Los Angeles traveled up the Alameda Corridor and the 710 Freeway, cutting through these towns on their way to downtown and then 40 miles east to the Inland Empire. They were also immigrant gateways, the first stop for new arrivals from Mexico, Central America, and Cuba. In contrast to working-class immigrant enclaves like New York's Lower East Side or Chicago's Back of the Yards a century earlier, these immigrant receiving grounds were suburban. And unlike the ethnoburbs of the San Gabriel Valley which welcomed an array of Asian and Latino immigrants, rich and poor, the gateway cities were entirely Latino and uniformly poorer. This class character had everything to do with the area's roots as working class, shoddily built, underserviced, and occasionally toxic. While their ethnic makeup transformed from white to Latino, their class makeup stayed fairly consistent.[2]

Clustered in Southeast LA, the gateway cities include Huntington Park, South Gate, Maywood, Lynwood, Bell Gardens, Bell, and Cudahy. With their detached homes, scattered parks, and low-slung profile, these towns are more accurately dubbed "gateway suburbs." They share a history as "inner ring" suburbs, originally built with modest homes and yards, minimal infrastructure, loose regulations, and factories in their midst. As the years passed, they endured the fate of many American inner-ring suburbs contending with job losses, aging infrastructure and housing, disinvestment, and middle-class flight.[3] On top of these challenges, LA's gateway suburbs shared a vulnerable position within the metropolitan political economy. Never bedroom suburbs, they were always highly dependent on a robust industrial jobs base. Collectively, they experienced the devastation of plant closures in the 1980s. While variations existed across these suburbs, particularly by class and attitudes toward immigrant newcomers, the common struggle for economic vitality, healthful surroundings, and responsible politics was strong enough to prompt several efforts to unify them into a regional entity.[4] South Gate contrasted in some ways with its neighbors—for example, it had the highest median family income among the gateway suburbs—yet it shared many of their challenges and experiences and conveys a broader story of suburban devastation and rebirth that reshaped all of these towns.

The vacillating fortunes of South Gate hewed closely to the fluctuating status of the American working class itself. After the insecure Depression

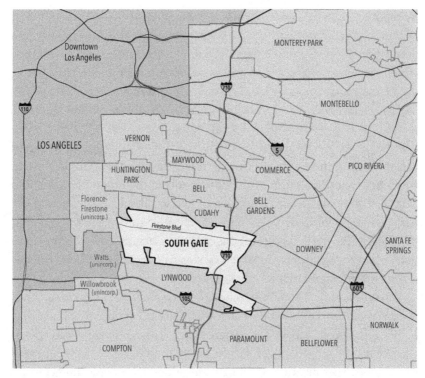

Figure 6.1   South Gate and the gateway suburbs of Southeast Los Angeles, shown with several Eastside suburbs. The gateway communities included South Gate, Huntington Park, Maywood, Bell, Bell Gardens, Cudahy, and Lynwood. By the 1990s, this heavily immigrant area housed more Latino residents than the greater Eastside.

Cartography by Jennifer Mapes, Kent State University.

years, workers emerged from the New Deal and World War II in an unprecedented position of strength. Emboldened by federal mandates that empowered unions and created the "security state," workers joined unions, waged strikes, and earned enough in Fordist industries to support a middle-class lifestyle. The prime beneficiaries were white male workers, reflected in the prosperity and profile of suburbs like South Gate.[5] When those payoffs disappeared with industrial flight in the 1980s, what remained was a fading echo of that vitality and stability. The industrial exodus nearly killed the suburb and created fresh problems for new residents to tackle, from community disinvestment to toxic waste. South Gate's transition from white to Latino further symbolized a shift in the profile of LA workers: from the older white, industrial working class to the new service-based working class of immigrants, minorities, and women.[6] This working-class suburb ultimately transformed through the infusion of new Latino arrivals, with their aspirations, energy, fears, and burdens—a pattern mirrored in cities across the country.[7]

This intertwined tale of industrial outflow and Latino inflow reflected, too, the evolving state of the political economy. By the 1980s, when those twin processes overlapped dramatically, they reflected the growing impact of globalization and neoliberalism. The same pressures that closed US plants and sent production south of the border stirred the economic turmoil in Mexico that ultimately led to neoliberal reforms, like privatization and free trade. As wages in Mexico plummeted and people suffered, many made the decision to head north despite a tightened border. South Gate sat at the crossroads of these capital and human flows, suffering the capital losses while receiving the migratory inflow.[8]

Amid these radical social and economic changes, South Gate clung tightly to crucial elements of the suburban ideal. A family community of suburban homes, schools, and jobs was a constant aspiration over the generations, even when that configuration wasn't always the best suited for its changing populace. Homeowner priorities dominated local politics, even as homeowners were gradually outnumbered by renters. Local leaders imposed stricter regulations, constricting opportunities for making the most of suburban property that early residents once used as a crucial stepping-stone to stability and upward mobility. South Gate changed from an unregulated to a regulated suburb. That transition made life harder for its most marginalized residents.

The South Gate story also reveals how rifts among the Mexican American generation and newer immigrants played out in suburbia. While some have seen the 1970s as a period of pan-Latino unity, in fact new divisions surfaced in the 1980s and 1990s within this ethnic suburb. Traditional suburban ideals were a compelling aspiration for homeowning Latinos who wanted to protect homes, built landscapes, families, and low taxes, but posed challenges for the poorer immigrant residents who lived alongside them.[9] This context shaped the degree of freedom and comfort immigrants felt voicing their opinions, joining clubs, helping at their children's schools, and taking their first steps toward involvement in their new country. That often happened at the neighborhood level, which was increasingly suburban.

Towns like South Gate thus faced formidable challenges as they adjusted to the economic, demographic, and spatial realities that defined the new suburbia. They not only had to sustain social and civic engagement, but they also had to rebuild from the ashes of economic catastrophe.

Working-Class Roots

Like many of the modest suburbs around it, South Gate began as a bare-bones subdivision of former farms and ranches, with minimal planning and infrastructure, intended for working- and lower-middle-class home seekers. When it was first subdivided in 1918, buyers could purchase a lot for a few hundred dollars and build a home themselves. Migrants from Nebraska, Missouri, Arkansas, and Oklahoma settled the area, pitching tents as temporary shelters before constructing permanent residences. In open-shop Los Angeles, where job instability always loomed darkly over a family's fortunes, the suburban home became a source of economic security, something to fall back on in hard times. To squeeze all they could out of the land, families grew fruits and vegetables and raised small livestock in their backyards. In the 1920s and 1930s, suburban homeownership became a crucial working-class strategy for surviving in a world where sickness, layoffs, or old age could sink a household. Sweat equity gave families access to property ownership. In a suburb like South Gate, it was an achievable goal.[10]

While the overwhelming majority of South Gate's early residents were white, ethnic Mexicans also found a place there despite race restrictions spreading across Los Angeles. During the interwar years, they owned homes in suburbs like South Gate, El Monte, La Puente, and Azusa.[11] South Gate's early Mexican households included immigrants, second-generation Mexican Americans, and a small colony of Mexican-born "white" Mormons who had been caught in a decades-long circular migration between the United States and Mexico.[12] By 1930, at least 175 local residents were part of Mexican immigrant families, many of whom fled during the 1910 Revolution. While they represented a miniscule portion of the suburb's population of 19,632, they had a relatively high rate of homeownership; among this group, homeowners outnumbered renters despite many being classified by federal authorities as "alien." Typical was Jesus Ramirez, a laborer for the Gas Company who lived on San Vicente with his wife Georgia and their two young children. The couple was in their 20s, Mexican-born, and undocumented as of 1930. They owned their home, valued at $3,000.[13] Yet, for most immigrants, the favorable, affordable local climate proved short-lived. By 1940, many Mexicans had left, possibly deported during LA's 1930s repatriation crackdown or voluntarily on the move in search of a better situation during the Depression. The security that whites achieved through homeownership eluded most of South Gate's earliest ethnic Mexican families, likely because of their insecure immigration status.[14]

In South Gate and other parts of southern LA, land was affordable and the town's loose regulatory climate allowed a family to live in a tent, jerry-build a house, and raise dozens of chickens behind the house. These practices flourished especially in Home Gardens, the southern part of town where lots were smaller and cheaper, but also in Watts, Bell Gardens, Cudahy, and nearby unincorporated pockets. In these towns, homeowners could take the initiative to develop their own kind of sustainable suburb. Their lifeways revealed a powerful ethic of self-reliance, frugality, hard work, and independence, which was reflected in their politics. The suburban home, in essence, became a crucial, attainable source of economic security—for whites and ethnic Mexicans alike.[15]

South Gate's working-class roots generated opportunities as well as formidable challenges. Early residents created a town of humble housing, minimal infrastructure, and loose regulations. Modest self-built homes, small detached garages, and cheap utilities characterized the young suburb. Early factories were also a local fixture, a crucial component of the community. Residents had an uneasy relationship with these plants: on the one hand, they welcomed the jobs they created; on the other, factories produced noise and waste virtually next door to homes, destroying the peace and purity promised by suburban living. But the payoffs outweighed the burdens. By 1940, South Gate emerged as an industrial hub with 900 factories within a two-mile radius, including enormous General Motors (GM) and Firestone plants that employed upward of 3,000 workers. By the late 1930s, it was dubbed the "Detroit of the Coast."[16]

Postwar South Gate's Community Profile

A home movie from South Gate circa 1944 provides a fleeting glimpse of life in a neighborhood of tidy, modest homes. A man in uniform, perhaps recently returned from the war, carries a baby toward an old jalopy parked in front of those houses. A group of smartly dressed adults horse around on the front lawn. These movies were likely taken by the Holloman family on Alexander Avenue, father a contractor, mother experimenting with her camera, and two blond elementary school-age boys. The movies suggest a life of some comfort, as the South Gate scenes are interspersed with footage from camping and road trips to Phoenix, Utah, and Mammoth Lake. This family enjoyed a nice home and a sense of belonging in a secure community and way of life.[17]

By the time South Gate emerged from the Depression and World War II, it resembled thousands of others suburbs nationwide that could be properly called middle class. While its modest homes persisted, they were joined by better housing constructed by professional builders, a sprawling regional park, and a respectable level of community voluntarism. This middle-class lifestyle all rested upon an unprecedented base of economic security, a product of both the federal "security state" and the flush state of the suburb's—and region's—economy. Through Social Security, the Federal Housing Administration (FHA), and the GI Bill, which created widespread access to affordable homeownership and education for white Americans, and laws protecting the power of labor unions, working families finally enjoyed some stability. Organized labor, which emerged powerfully even in open-shop Los Angeles, shifted its focus from workers' control to full employment, good wages, and benefits. Together, these elements created the material basis for family comfort and security, giving South Gate's white families access to the middle-class suburban dream.[18]

This prosperity was bolstered by California's flush economy, infused by millions of federal defense dollars pouring into West Coast cities. As part of the Sunbelt, postwar LA was a destination of plant relocations from the nation's Rustbelt. Gateway suburbs like South Gate were key hubs of this growth. The LA County Regional Planning Commission (RPC) recognized this when it dubbed this a "labor-importing" part of the county and "the leading center of industrial employment within the county, despite a county-wide trend toward decentralization of industry."[19] It was also becoming a center of the metropolitan logistics economy, capturing significant portions of the "distributive trades," and the RPC correctly predicted that its role would only expand. Between 1947 and 1973, the number of factories in South Gate spiked from 137 to 606, providing jobs to 25,000 by the 1970s. In 1959, its industrial sales volume far outpaced suburban neighbors like Huntington Park, Lakewood, and Lynwood.[20] The largest plants in South Gate were GM (employing 3,300 in 1970), Firestone Tire & Rubber (2,200), and Weiser Lock (1,400), and the vast majority of jobs were unionized. South Gate's one notable retail sector was automobiles: Firestone Boulevard was lined with car lots—new and used.[21]

Figure 6.2 The Philadelphia Quartz plant in South Gate, shown here in 1961, exemplified the ubiquitous presence of factories near homes. While industry underwrote financial prosperity in postwar South Gate, they also punctured the peace and quiet of the community and, in later years, often left toxic footprints.
Photo by Howard D. Kelly, Kelly-Holiday Mid-Century Aerial Collection/Los Angeles Public Library.

In everyday terms, this meant the suburb was a "production suburb" more than a "consumption suburb" like Lakewood, with its famous shopping mall, or a "bedroom suburb" like San Marino, intended as a residential retreat from production. Those were commuter suburbs. In South Gate, jobs lay right in the heart of the community. Industry supplied jobs and tax revenue. They helped finance upgrades of local facilities and infrastructure, including a new hall of justice; 125 miles of tree-lined streets, sewers, and water mains; and a 93-acre regional park complete with Olympic-size swim stadium, clubhouse, and municipal auditorium.[22]

Although the suburb was fairly evenly divided between blue- and white-collar workers, most lived a middle-class lifestyle with secure jobs, good pay, decent housing, and good schools. Residents' educational profile was working class; in the postwar years, 83–87% had a high school education or less. Yet, in 1950, it ranked in the top two-fifths of LA suburbs in terms of income.[23] It may have lacked certain trappings of middle-class culture, but financially it was holding its own. The suburb had a kind of dual personality—part middle-class, part-working class—where everyone was buoyed by the expanding local and regional economy.[24]

South Gate's population surged after 1940 and stayed overwhelmingly white. The population nearly doubled from 1940 to 1950, then stayed

Table 6.1 Demographic and social characteristics of South Gate residents, 1950–2010

	1950		1970		1990		2010	
	number	%	number	%	number	%	number	%
Population total	51,116	100.0	56,909	100.0	86,284	100.0	94,396	100.0
Race/ethnicity								
White non-Hispanic	50,131	98.1	46,451	81.6	11,957	13.9	3,233	3.4
Black	9	0.0	40	0.1	1,122	1.3	585	0.6
Hispanic	943	1.8	9,839	17.3	71,740	83.1	89,442	94.8
Asian	29	0.1	251	0.4	953	1.1	647	0.7
Nativity/ citizenship								
Native born	47,934	93.8	51,232	90.0	43,744	50.7	51,515	54.6
Foreign born	3,182	6.2	5,776	10.1	42,540	49.3	43,168	45.7
Not a citizen					34,139	39.6	27,505	29.1
Occupations								
White collar	9,349	44.8	10,972	45.1	13,021	37.6	17,041	44.5
Blue collar	9,983	47.8	11,191	46.0	17,222	49.8	14,421	37.7
Service	1,377	6.6	2117	8.7	4007	11.6	6795	17.8
Females in labor force	6,338	31.7	9817	42.4	15277	50.6	18,645	51.9
Married females in labor force*			5,235	37.1	6,534	54.6	8,599	48.9
Poverty								
Total families below poverty line**				7.4	2,763	15.2	20,196	23.1

Note: Percentages calculated out of total population, except for occupations where it is calculated out of all adult workers, unless otherwise indicated.
* shown as a percentage of all married women over 16. For 1990, data is for mothers in labor force.
** shown as a percentage of all local families.

steady to 1970. Less than 10% were immigrants, most hailing from England, Canada, and Germany. Latinos also settled in the suburb although their numbers are hard to pin down due to inconsistencies with census definitions. The census reported the number of "Hispanics" in South Gate rose from 2,205 to 9,839 from 1960 to 1970.[25] Latino's access to postwar white South Gate was facilitated by their early local foothold and their racial ambiguity.[26]

South Gate lay along the front lines of South LA's racial divide—which ran along Alameda Avenue, splitting white suburbs to the east from multiracial suburbs to the west—known locally as "the Wall" or "Cotton Curtain." It was situated in close proximity to diverse, often poorer communities, a configuration typical of working-class suburbs nationally. In the 1950s and 1960s, South Gate continued to exclude Black Americans, whose numbers were rising in nearby neighborhoods like Watts and South Los Angeles. When race-restrictive covenents were outlawed by the US Supreme Court in 1948, South Gate used other tactics to uphold the color line, like racial steering by realtors, activism against school integration, and violence and intimidation.[27]

As in the entire LA region, especially in areas near defense industries, South Gate experienced a massive housing shortage during World War II. Millions of defense workers poured into Los Angeles; South Gate's population spiked from 27,000 to 45,000 during the war. While federal housing programs helped, they fell far short of regional need.[28] By 1946, the crisis prompted 75 members of veterans groups in South Gate to petition the city council for immediate completion of city-sponsored emergency housing.[29]

Homeowners responded to the shortfall by converting spare bedrooms, garages, and add-ons into informal rentals. Officials framed the practice as a patriotic gesture to help alleviate the housing crisis for homeless servicemen, defense workers, and their families. "Rent your houses to a war worker with children, and be thankful those kiddies are speaking our American language instead of Japanese," implored the area's War Housing Council. In 1945, a 31-year-old veteran, his wife, and their two children spent nearly a year living in a garage in nearby Lynwood, without plumbing, heat, and flooring. They suffered no sickness, he claimed, because his wife "kept the place as clean as a pin." In 1946, a family of four was living in a single garage in South Gate after moving from Oak Ridge, Tennessee. Similar stories abounded. Even in the San Fernando Valley, hundreds of homes had conversions for rent.[30]

The popular discourse surrounding these units reflected the belief that informal housing was legitimate and patriotic. In the 1940s and early 1950s, the *Los Angeles Times* ran a series of features profiling garage conversions across the southland, from North Hollywood to Arcadia to Palm Springs. These stories offered "good housekeeping" style tips on how to design and decorate a garage, complete with floor plans, and they presented the profiled garages as "model dwellings." The message was clear: a wholehearted acceptance of garage rentals, with an appreciation for the resourcefulness of their

In the broad side of a carriage-size garage the front door was cut. The first floor is kitchen, garage and stairway, upstairs is living room and bath

By Janet McHendrie

OBVIOUSLY it was — and still is—a garage, but a very dignified and sophisticated one. No gay studio or arty atmosphere here, nor the apologetic "just camping until we can find something better". This garage is frankly elegant, with decorator touches that any city apartment might envy.

Its owner, Joseph A. Krone

tance from town, and hotels are no longer able to accommodate sudden late hour arrivals, Mr. Krone was often faced with the prospect of a long night drive at the end of his journeys. Finally he decided to reconvert a garage on some property he owned, conveniently located near the center of town.

At the time he began working on the garage, wartime restrictions limited materials which could be spent on a house

tained as a garage, with space for two cars. A double door at each end of the building permits the cars to be driven in from either end and stored facing each other. A large entrance hall, a kitchen and service porch, and a shower and small lavatory occupy the remaining space. The living room, · bedroom, dressing room and another small bathroom are on the second floor.

Figure 6.3 In mid 1940s to early 1950s, the *Los Angeles Times* ran a series of features profiling garage conversions across Los Angeles. In all of these features, the tone was admiration for the plucky, creative ingenuity of the people doing the conversions, which could serve as models for others.

"A Garage Goes Formal," *Los Angeles Times*, September 2, 1945; reproduced courtesy of Graig McHendrie.

white tenants who were making the best of a tough housing market. "The ga-rage apartment where Charles Hofflund and his British war bride are living is an excellent example of how ingenuity can triumph over necessity," declared a 1946 feature. The couple divided a double garage into a bedroom on one side and a living room and kitchen on the other. Through cozy decorating touches, they gave their garage "the air and informality of a cottage." Similar profiles appeared in subsequent years.[31]

The housing crisis ultimately triggered a building boom in South Gate. From 1940 to 1960, 13,500 new units were constructed, representing two-thirds of all local housing.[32] Many of these homes were built by professional builders and contractors, moving the town away from its jerry-built roots. The small-scale contractors operating in South Gate were typical of postwar builders nationally.[33] In South Gate, subdivisions like Meadow Park offered a choice of four floor plans, 12 exteriors, and GI and FHA financing. The homes featured two or three bedrooms, a paneled dining room, bay windows in the living room and breakfast nook, and "plenty of electrical outlets."[34] By the early 1950s, South Gate was virtually built out, with very little open space for new construction—the suburb had reached its housing saturation point. It remained a suburb of relatively small lots. From 1950 to 1980, this wasn't much of a problem as the population held fairly steady. The local density level was 7,724 people per square mile, comparable to postwar sitcom suburbs like Lakewood.[35]

While single-family homeownership had been a cornerstone of local culture since the 1920s, South Gate saw a rise in rentals and multifamily dwellings from 1950 to 1970. By 1970, about one-third of housing units were multifamily. The most typical buildings had three to nine units, some located on blocks of homes. Single-family homes were also rented out.[36] This trend signaled the growing presence of tenants in the suburb, which eventually reached a majority. The patriotic initiatives to offer rental housing during the war, it seemed, had shifted the balance away from the suburban norm of homeownership.[37]

Postwar South Gate was not a placid bedroom community of middle-class homes in a controlled spatial environment. It was a suburb of homes next to apartments next to factories. Its unplanned past continued to shape local life even as expectations were changing. Media images of clean-cut suburban streets, yards, neighborhoods, and people abounded in postwar America. In South Gate, it became a community aspiration, if city council meetings during the 1950s were any indicator. A litany of residential complaints about factory noise, workers parking and littering on residential streets, and other nuisances suggested two things: the reality permitted by local leaders and residents' aspirations for something better.[38] After 1960, this clash would usher in a new era of regulation, which took on altered meaning in the wake of South Gate's ethnic turn.

South Gate's Latino Suburban Pioneers

South Gate's Latino influx began in the 1960s and accelerated after 1970. In the 1960s, these Latinos were postwar suburban pioneers who breached long-standing color barriers. Those most likely to cross the color line were lighter-skinned, English-speaking, acculturated ethnic Mexicans. They were linked in outlook to the Mexican American generation, a cohort that came of age during the 1930s and 1940, some of whom rose into the middle class and embraced assimilation.[39] An important foundation of the postwar Latino community in South Gate, these residents were willing to integrate into existing social and civic structures.

Henry Gonzalez was one of these pioneers. Born at LA County General Hospital in 1935, Henry was the second child of Euloqio and Josephine Gonzalez. Euloqio was from Sinaloa, Mexico, and came to the United States in 1918; Josephine was the American-born daughter of Mexican immigrants. When Henry was three, the family moved to Watts, two blocks from his grandmother's home on Anzac Avenue. Euloqio—going by the name Joe—purchased a three-bedroom house at the back of a large grassy lot. Henry recalled the rustic feel of Watts in those days, the freedom of playing in the grassy expanse of their yard and eating "fresh eggs every day" and fruit off their trees. Henry's was a union family. His father was a mechanic at the Independent Paper Stack Company in Boyle Heights. His mother, aunts, and uncles also worked at the plant, with his uncle Socoro serving as president of the union local.[40]

Henry's early life was firmly rooted in Watts, about a mile west of South Gate. He attended public schools, including Jordan High where he excelled at football. He was courted by San Jose State to play at the collegiate level, but turned them down under some pressure from his girlfriend who said she "couldn't wait another two years for him to finish up." He earned his associate's degree at Harbor Junior College in Wilmington, taking courses in lathe and machine work, before landing a job at the GM plant in South Gate in 1955. He worked as a polisher and sprayer and quickly immersed himself in United Auto Workers (UAW) Local 216.

His girlfriend, Theresa Duarte, was also born at County General in 1935 and grew up in Watts, not far from Henry. Her father was born in Sonora, Mexico, her mother in Bisbee, Arizona. Theresa's father worked at a meat packing plant in Vernon, while her mother was a housewife raising eight children, Theresa the youngest. She described Watts as a close-knit neighborhood, with Latinos, Blacks, Jews, and Italians connected especially through their children. "We never knew discrimination," she recalled. "It was a very trusting neighborhood." From age 10 to 12, Theresa did housework for an African American family—the mother was a teacher, the father ran a grocery store. She did other odd jobs for the neighbors, where "everybody kind of watched out for each other." Her older siblings worked to help the family financially. Theresa left Jordan High School in the 11th grade to work full-time at JC Penney, completing her studies at night to earn her diploma.[41]

Sweethearts since age 14, Henry and Theresa married in 1956 while in their early 20s. Always living near extended family, they initially rented in south Los Angeles. They had two children, while Theresa worked at a faucet factory and Henry worked his way up the union leadership chain at GM. The GM plant had become quite racially diverse by that point—about 55% whites, the rest Latinos and Black Americans. In 1961, the Gonzalezes bought a two-bedroom home on Bowman Avenue in South Gate. Henry wanted to buy closer to the park, where there were "bigger, nicer homes," but realtors refused to show those homes. Theresa recalled an exchange with a white realtor they were working with. "He says to me–'When people ask if you're Mexican or Spanish, just tell them you're Spanish.' I said, 'I'm not Spanish, I'm Mexican.'" She immediately found another realtor, a white woman who never brought up such race talk. The realtor "suggested the little house on Bowman," which Theresa liked for its proximity to shopping, the elementary school, and Henry's job.[42]

In the early 1960s, Henry and Theresa encountered a suburb where many of their neighbors were white European ethnics. Theresa called it a "mixed" area—"they were white people but they were from another country." She recalled the neighbors being welcoming, kind, and "very friendly." Firm in their identity as Mexican Americans, Theresa and Henry didn't hesitate to confront any trace of racial judgment or innuendo. Theresa recalled, "The lady across the street always told me, you mean your kids don't speak Spanish? I said, no, that's my fault. I says, but you know what, do you speak

Italian? Of course not. I say, why not? Your mother speaks Italian. I put it to them that way—don't judge me because you're no better." Henry recalled similar exchanges. "My next-door neighbor north of me was German, the guy south of me was Dutch. Real funny because right away I started BS-ing them, because they all had accents. . . . I said, 'We're all one minority. I'm Mexican, you guys are German.' They took a liking to me [and]. . . became very good friends." Theresa surmised they received a warm reception because they both spoke English, which generally helped Latino newcomers "fall right in."[43]

The Gonzalezes joined a small stream of Latinos moving into suburbs like South Gate and Huntington Park, mostly English-speaking Mexican Americans who fit a middle-class profile.[44] They were moderately prosperous, about 72% owning their homes in 1950, though that dropped to 47% 10 years later.[45] While ethnic Mexicans were the largest Latino group in South Gate, a small number of Cubans fleeing the Castro regime also settled in South Gate, Maywood, and Huntington Park in the early 1960s. Mercedes González-Ontañon contended that her Cuban family was able to rent a duplex in South Gate in 1966 due to their "European appearance" and a letter of introduction from Catholic relief services.[46]

These Latinos wedged their way into a suburb that was overwhelmingly white and on the racial defensive. Many Americans internalized powerful ideas that linked property values to race and believed that people of color pushed property values down. In South Gate, newly prosperous blue-collar families worried for their economic security, which hinged partly on homeownership, fearing what an influx of racial "others" might do to their own status and wealth.[47]

Because Latinos occupied a relatively favorable position in the racial pecking order of Los Angeles, they experienced less resistance than their Black counterparts but were still subjected to some prejudice. In suburbs like South Gate, Lynwood, and Compton, described in the journal *Frontier* as "generally neat communities with well-kept lawns and painted homes," neighbors and realtors during the 1950s colluded to maintain racial segregation. The South Gate Realty Board, for example, fined and expelled realtors for selling to Mexican buyers. When realtor Harry Beddoe, a well-regarded member of the board in line for the chairmanship, sold a Lynwood home to the Portugals, an ethnic Mexican family, the board fined and then expelled him. A whisper campaign claimed Beddoe's real motive was "to open the gates to the Negroes."[48]

Beddoe, who had worked as a Seventh Day Adventist missionary in Africa and the Caribbean, saw a moral issue at stake. He refused to pay the fine and sued the South Gate Realty Board for damages totaling $42,000. The case drew the attention of the NAACP, Community Service Organization, and civil rights groups as far away as Hawaii that hoped a favorable decision would put an end to this insidious real estate practice. Though the Los Angeles Superior Court dismissed the case, claiming the Realty Board acted in good faith, the case nonetheless signaled the intention of some local white realtors to resist segregation practices. Meanwhile, the Portugals moved in and the neighbors—who earlier signed letters opposing the family—had a change of heart, describing the Portugals as "nice people."[49] This bumpy road into suburbia typified the pathway for South Gate's pioneer Latino settlers, who met both resistance and acceptance.[50]

These Latino suburban pioneers in postwar South Gate would adapt to local customs and traditions and be among the first to rise into local positions of social and civic leadership. They enjoyed a relatively favorable position compared to Black Americans, who made some progress in Lynwood and Compton but faced a more solid racial border in the other gateway suburbs.[51]

Not Quite Pleasantville: Community Life in Postwar South Gate

Against this backdrop of rapid growth, housing diversity, industrial expansion, and a nascent influx of Latinos, South Gate community life reflected an amalgam of middle-class and working-class experiences. Civic and social groups, churches, and schools were important hubs of local life. The postwar founding of many social and civic clubs signaled a greater sense of security and spare time among residents who had ascended from working-class struggle. Alongside these conventional groups were more radical groups and initiatives that operated largely unnoticed.

During this suburban era of "joining," the number and longevity of local associations in South Gate was fairly modest compared to San Marino and Pasadena but this was typical for community participation among working-class suburbanites.[52] Nonetheless, from 1940 to 1965, fully 71 new organizations formed in South Gate, including several groups launched by the newly energized Parks & Recreation Department, such as arts, theater, exercise, and hobby clubs. A good number of groups were short lived, replaced by new ones in the 1970s. These social spaces reflected a population that itself was in motion, moving in and out of the suburb.[53]

Some of the most enduring civic groups were the Chamber of Commerce, Eagles, Kiwanis, Optimist Club, Rotary Club, Sorpotimists, and the Women's Club, as well as the American Legion and Veterans of Foreign Wars, and youth-oriented groups like the Junior Athletic Association. Mostly predating the war, they outlasted a number of newer groups and persisted after South Gate's ethnic turn. The Kiwanis, Optimists, and Rotary Clubs—as well as the Democratic Club—were crucial civic hubs that served as springboards to local power. Members of these groups met weekly over lunch to network and socialize, learn how things worked in town, and "give back."[54] They devoted much of their energy to service projects, such as raising money for scholarships, sponsoring scout troops, and assisting with community projects. Along with the Chamber of Commerce, they also took the lead in coordinating public celebrations, such as July 4 galas and community fairs.[55]

The Soroptimist Club, formed in 1948, exemplified a particularly effective blend of social and service work in South Gate. With 90 chapters across Southern California in 1948, this professional women's service club engaged in an eclectic range of projects, from giving scholarships, to joining eye banks, to providing housing for college students or individuals facing a crisis. The South Gate-Lynwood Soroptimist club, in addition to holding scholarship fundraisers, helped launch an ambitious initiative in 1957 to build low-cost housing for seniors in the area. The chapter began with community surveys, then formed the Sorpotimist Village Foundation, a nonprofit corporation comprised of members of nine Soroptimist Clubs in Southeast LA.[56] The Foundation raised over $100,000 and secured a $297,000 loan from the federal Housing and Home Finance Agency to purchase land in Norwalk where they could build a 47-unit complex of patio apartments.[57] It took seven years of dogged volunteer work by 300 members of nine clubs to solicit individual donors and hold benefit sales and fundraisers. Drawing on their professional expertise, the women did much of the project work themselves, including drafting legal documents, designing the building, and overseeing its construction. Dedicated in 1963, the complex drew accolades from the US Department of Housing and Urban Development (HUD) as "an example of what can and should be done." Club members gave monthly parties for the residents and continued to raise funds to meet one-third of the project's operating expenses well into the 1980s. As a grassroots postwar housing initiative, it was remarkable for its suburban female-led character.[58]

If the Soroptimists drew a substantial number of professionals, some South Gate groups ignored occupational distinctions, enthusiastically welcoming white- and blue-collar members alike. This contrasted with civic groups in other towns that limited membership to businessmen and professionals. In South Gate, the Masons and Eagles had a good share of blue-collar members, while the Rotary Club welcomed Henry Gonzalez, an autoworker and union official. Perhaps the most inclusive groups were the PTAs, which drew in large numbers of parents and represented a true cross-section of the suburb. In 1949, 80% of parents at Tweedy School belonged to the PTA. Through fundraisers for the school—bake sales, spaghetti dinners, and paper drives—they strengthened ties among families, crossing bridges of occupation, class, and ethnicity.[59] This spirit of inclusion continued through the suburb's ethnic turn, providing a crucial hub of civic integration even as other groups declined.

PTA and youth work were often the gateway into community life that drew residents into a broader web of groups. Jane Blalock, the wife of South Gate High School's vice principal and mother of three sons, began her local involvement in the PTA in the 1950s. She remained an active PTA member for 35 years, volunteered 29 years for the Boy Scouts, and participated in the Ladies Missionary Society, South Gate Women's Club, Red Cross, Southeast Horticulture Society, Beautification Committee, and the Friends of the Library, among other groups. After moving from Kansas with her husband in 1940, Grace Shepherd quickly immersed herself in local volunteer work, earning a life membership in the Tweedy PTA by 1950. She gave hundreds of hours to the Boy Scouts, Girls Scouts, YMCA, and the Community Chest, and served 25 years on the South Gate Coordinating Council. Other South Gate women had similarly long community service records.[60] Youth-oriented volunteer work was also a civic entry point for Latina newcomers. Theresa Gonzalez gravitated first to the PTA "to keep an eye on my kids" but found only one other Latina in the group and felt that other PTA members "weren't too sure how to approach me because they hadn't heard me talk." She ended up getting very involved in the PTA and was eventually hired as a paid employee in the schools. By 1965, Mrs. Ralph Perez served as president of the Tweedy School PTA, having been one of the earliest Latina/os to show up in local organizational records.[61]

In contrast to the ladies and men holding club lunches and fundraisers, other residents of South Gate were pushing for ethnoracial equality on the factory floor and for socialist revolution, actions that broke with conventional expections of suburban life. A locus of those activities was UAW-Congress of Industrial Organizations (CIO) Local 216 at the massive GM plant on South Gate's westside. It had a fair share of Communists, Socialists, Trotskyites, and other radicals who aligned easily with the CIO's progressive stance on racial justice. Local 216 worked vigorously to integrate the plant after the war. By 1955 a notable number of Latinos and African Americans were hired, and their numbers grew substantially over the next two decades. Though this change was largely accepted by the rank and file, a schism grew between workplace and residential life in South Gate. The community wanted little to do with values expressed in the factory. In the late 1940s, for example, a union man lost in a campaign for city council, and the suburb did not celebrate Labor Day, despite the town being filled with factory workers. Moreover, when two local unions rented out their hall for "Mexican weddings," the city council and police cracked down on the "noise, trouble, and refuse" without much pushback.[62]

South Gate even had communist cells operating quietly in the suburb. Kathy Seal recounted her involvement in the October League (OL) when she, her husband Jim, and their young children lived there during the 1970s. Its members were ex-college students—well versed in Maoist doctrine—who were dispatched to work in factories across the country to support worker self-determination and combat racism, sexism, and capitalist oppression from within the workplace. Their goal was to build a new communist party by nurturing a revolutionary consciousness among workers. These cells convened discreet meetings in towns like South Gate and Huntington Park, while members took jobs in auto, rubber, and steel factories. Seal landed a job at GM South Gate, while Jim worked at the Ford plant in Pico Rivera. For this fairly introverted, intellectual young woman, the work of "integrating with the masses" could be painfully difficult, but it was not without its triumphs. She described the OL as "our little band of work boot–clad intellectuals, ex-Weatherpeople, veterans of the Chicano and Black liberation movements, lapsed Catholics, former high school cheerleaders, disillusioned academics, and a few actual factory workers." They held cell meetings in their darkened South Gate living room and attended countless other meetings for the cause. "I didn't mind devoting every minute of my weekends to meetings," she wrote, "since it provided a kind of intellectual although peculiar social life, and I felt that we were trying to accomplish idealistic ends." This radicalism contrasted with their everyday life in their two-bedroom house with a "beautiful orange tree, a great apricot tree, and spacious backyard." Although another GM worker and his family lived a few houses down, the Seals didn't socialize with them. "Making friendships was hard to do, and it was especially hard to do when you had an ulterior motive.... [P]robably the biggest factor was how very different I was from those folks." Devoting her spare time and energy to the OL, she felt disconnected from her immediate neighborhood and community.[63]

If political radicalism was muffled in South Gate, cultural transgression against middle-class suburban norms happened more openly in multiracial sports. South Gate hosted auto racing and professional wrestling at two local venues, Ascot Speedway and the South Gate Arena. The latter, which operated from 1946 to 1958, also held amateur boxing matches with an interethnic slate of fighters, including Ramon Tiscareno, Chu Chu Jiminez, Eddie Ramirez, and the "crowd-pleasing Mexican" Sammy Figueroa.[64] In a similar way, the Los Angeles Woman's Bowling Association presented a remarkable picture of interracial unity. Its 33,000 members included Black Americans, Japanese Americans, and whites who bowled in teams across LA's suburbs, including South Gate, Pico Rivera, Lynwood, Lakewood, Long Beach, the Manchester area, and Westchester. A few times a year they held awards banquets and meetings in places like the Westchester Elks Lodge in 1963 and the South Gate Optimist Clubhouse in 1967.[65] At a time when racial tensions were running high in Los Angeles, these women created a companionable multiracial leisure space that was suggestive of future suburban change.[66]

South Gate's Search for Order, 1945–1966

South Gate's civic leaders, meanwhile, had an uneasy feeling that their community was suffering from social and civic disunity and physical deterioration. With the spike in population, tenants, and factories; threats from civil rights activists; and a nascent Latino influx, they sensed disruptions to community life and a need for social and civic restoration. They launched postwar initiatives to unify the suburb and spark social and civic engagement. There was a cyclical rhythm to these efforts, which often recurred at moments of population growth, racial and ethnic change, and civic upheaval. They aimed to reinforce South Gate's identity as a suburb of law-abiding and community-loving homeowners, families, and taxpayers. Their efforts to foster community unity had mixed results.

The first initiative was the annual Christmas Parade, launched by local business owners in 1947, during the suburb's convulsive population boom. It began as a homespun affair, with Cub Scout marchers, 15 floats pulled on trailers depicting scenes like "Little Bo Peep," and Santa passing out candy to children lined up along Tweedy Boulevard. The event captured a feeling of small-town comfort, especially welcome after the stresses and tragedy of wartime. It was initially a small-scale affair that brought together residents, civic groups, and local shopkeepers who built and sponsored the floats and marching teams. By the 1950s, this event was featuring movie stars as grand marshals; drawing marching bands, floats, and equestrian units from neighboring suburbs; and attracting crowds topping 60,000. A crucial turning point was the outsourcing of the parade to a company called Pageantry Productions, owned by South Gate residents Bill and Ronnie Lomas and headquartered in Lynwood. The professionalization of the parade transformed it from a collective community endeavor into a commodified spectator event—complete with television coverage and crowds of 150,000 by the 1970s.[67]

In addition to launching events that they hoped would unify the suburb, South Gate leaders in the 1950s began searching for causes of the disunity. One immediate target was renters. Some leaders feared the lingering presence of tenants damaged the suburb's social cohesion. In 1955, the Community Coordinating Council (CCC)—an entity that brought together all social, school, and civic groups of South Gate—identified the expansion of the apartment population as "one of South Gate's greatest potential menaces" and called for a study of the challenges of "integrating newcomers into community life." Apartment dwellers, noted CCC president Rev. Norman Taylor of First Methodist Church, were a group without roots in the community and much harder to integrate socially than residents of single-family homes. Their presence resulted in a deterioration of community feeling, a diminished sense of responsibility, and "a greater drift toward delinquency." While South Gate leaders initially attempted to incorporate renters, they soon pivoted to focus on retaining community-minded homeowners who were leaving South Gate for better homes elsewhere. The best way to keep residents was by better controlling the suburb's housing stock.[68] Poor planning, they contended, had produced uncontrolled building, an uptick in tenancy, and the lack of a unifying town center and community cohesion. Instead of helping tenants, they resolved to shore up single-family homeownership.

Two planning studies conducted around this time conveyed a similar message. They recommended that South Gate shed its older working-class habits and embrace more conventional middle-class suburban standards. The first plan, commissioned by the city from Gordon Whitnall and Associates in 1959, observed that South Gate was overrun with small lots and was moving toward multifamily housing, which together portended an unappealing landscape of multifamily housing crammed onto tiny lots. Sound planning was needed to ensure a "desirable high-standard living environment" and to stave off decline caused by over-densification.[69] The city spent three years developing a new zoning plan for South Gate intended to codify the Whitnall report's recommendations. But zoning could go only so far in undoing past practices, such as the proliferation of small 5,000-square-foot lots. The 1960 Zoning Law did specify new frontage requirements (50 feet wide); eliminated trailer parks, junk yards, and used part storage yards; and defined "garages" as structures for the storage of vehicles only, not for human habitation. Subsequent ordinances reduced the number of chickens and rabbits allowed in backyards from 50 to 10.[70] These measures ensured the durability of tidy, modest homes on small lots and signaled a new regulatory culture in the suburb.

A second study was produced by a group of graduate planning students at the University of Southern California (USC) who took on South Gate as its studio project in 1964. They portended a bleak future for South Gate if it didn't change course. "The non-existence of any meaningful community identity, coupled with the lack of any identifiable planning goals and the continued out-migration of the young vigorous adults will create the environment that will encourage ethnic minorities and low-income groups to re-locate in South Gate," they wrote. If this continued, South Gate would become a "Negro ghetto." They perceived certain key problems in existing land use: too many tiny lots; not enough up-scale housing; rezoning of R-1 to R-3 areas, which encouraged multifamily housing on small lots; and an overdependence on car dealerships for revenue. The prime goal, the students perceived, was to bring back "new vigorous types (including higher income groups) of residents which South Gate needs." To attract them, they suggested retrofitting areas of small homes with "large residential developments" complete with recreational facilities, converting gridded streets to cul-de-sacs, bringing in better schools and shopping centers, and creating a discernable "city identity or image." Theirs was a vision of modern, postwar suburbia, branded clearly as white and middle class. The city council took all of these suggestions seriously when it hosted the students at a meeting in June 1965. Local leaders seemed to absorb both the message and the fears evoked by this student project. But with all of South Gate's land built out, undoing the effects of an unplanned working-class space would be difficult unless there was radical redevelopment.[71]

Around the same time, South Gate was embroiled in a battle over its racial future, compounding the sense of unease. In the early 1960s, the civil rights movement was stepping up its fight against segregation in south Los Angeles. South Gate found itself on the front lines of the battle, when the focus became two high schools that strikingly illustrated the "separate and unequal" problem within the LA Unified School District (LAUSD): South Gate High (97% white) and Jordan High (99% Black) in Watts, separated by just a mile and part of the same school district. Civil rights groups targeted this egregious example of educational inequality and, in 1963, filed a lawsuit. South Gate residents launched a vigorous counter-campaign to resist busing and school boundary changes, supported by the South Gate City Council, the Coordinating Council, the local press, and 17,500 signatories to anti-integration petitions. Their goal was to protect the "rights, privileges, and environment" of the suburb's children and the "community identity" of South Gate, which the City Council defined as a "close-knit family community"—despite the recent handwringing over South Gate's social fragmentation problem.[72] When the Watts uprising broke out in 1965, local police protected South Gate from the anger and fury of Black Americans fed up with discrimination and police brutality that erupted just a mile from its borders. The suburb turned inward, attempted to solidify a separate identity, and sought to brand itself in a new way.

Their solution was the Azalea Festival, which became South Gate's most enduring tradition. The festive community event at once reinforced the value of voluntarism; heralded the suburb's white, aging civic leaders; and catalyzed social cohesion by draping colorful natural beauty over a suburb a little coarse around the edges. It grew out of a revitalization campaign launched by the Chamber of Commerce in 1965. A Beautification Committee awarded prizes to the owners of attractive, spruced-up properties as a way to incentivize quality housing and civic pride. Leaders soon expanded the initiative by selecting a city flower and building a festival around it. Presiding over the fete was the Azalea Queen, "a woman who had worked for the home, school, church and community" and was at least 60 years old, along with her court of civic-minded volunteers. Given the suburb's racial roots, this ensured a white honoree. The Azalea Queen's "coronation" became a centerpiece of the festival, which began as a two-day affair, expanded into two weeks by 1976, and lasted a month by the 1990s. South Gate's civic groups were heavily involved in the Azalea Festival, hosting interclub lunches, a carnival, a golf tournament, a kite competition, hobby and club exhibitions, concerts, theater performances, a parade, and a fancy dinner-dance. An "outstanding male citizen" active in local civic work was chosen as grand marshal of the parade, and nearly all events were run by volunteers.[73] The Azalea Festival was an invented tradition meant to stimulate and celebrate volunteerism, invigorate local civic health, and encourage white residents to stay. This effort to create common ground for South Gate came late, at a time when rapid social change was already under way. Unknown to its founders, the Azalea Festival would act less as a lure to retain white residents and more as social anchor for a suburb about to be tossed violently by waves of social and economic change.

South Gate's Suburban Crisis, 1965–1982

In a tragic and symbolic twist, South Gate's one fatality during the Watts uprising was a Latino resident. Albert Flores, a 40-year-old auto upholsterer who lived on Dearborn Avenue, was fired at by 15 to 20 National Guardsmen as he tried to run a roadblock at 103rd St. and Compton Avenue. His brother Richard, a resident of Huntington Park, was shot in the chest by a National Guardsman while on his way to pick up his mother-in-law in Watts to take her to safety.[74] Both men were caught at the barricades, a racial border they had likely crossed many times to visit and care for family. This familiar ground turned deadly when law enforcement envisaged the barricades as the gates protecting white suburbia, where those Latino victims in fact lived.

Multiple vectors transforming south Los Angeles converged at this explosive moment in South Gate: ethnoracial change was under way, economic distress was spreading, and a sense of crisis loomed. Some, like the *South Gate Press*, tried to deny it; the newspaper ran no coverage of the civil unrest. For others, it served as a warning that it was time to leave. The Watts uprising was the beginning of the end of white South Gate. It was the first of multiple triggers that unleashed white flight out of the gateway suburbs. These communities were prime examples of what Lyndon B. Johnson's 1967 President's Task Force on Suburban Problems identified as suburbs in crisis.

Although different problems plagued different communities, South Gate belonged to a class of suburbs grappling with aging homes; industrial encroachment resulting in "pollution of air, water and landscape"; and, ultimately, poverty. These were not uncommon problems: 33% of suburbs nationally were industrial, while in 64 metro areas—including Los Angeles, Boston, San Francisco, and Pittsburgh—more poor families lived in suburbs than cities.[75]

From 1965 to 1982, South Gate experienced successive waves of crisis closely tied to the changing regional economy. These included a series of major plant closures, the buckling of infrastructure under the dual strain of population shifts and Proposition 13, and national economic woes and policy shifts that undercut working-class stability. National pressures included inflation, stagnant wages, new technologies, capital mobility to the US South, Asia, and Latin America, and Reagan administration policies such as deregulation and anti-unionism. As the security state that undergirded the postwar good life in South Gate crumbled, white residents moved away, leaving a void that would soon be filled by a Latino working class in search of its own suburban dream.

As a center of mass-production industry for Los Angeles, the southeast "production suburbs" had grown deeply dependent on factories for jobs, tax revenue, and ancillary business. In 1979, for example, Firestone Tire & Rubber pumped $34.6 million into South Gate's economy, providing 1,000 jobs and more than $1 million in tax revenue. Celebrated as "a major force for good in South Gate," the company donated money and volunteer hours to local Boy Scout troops, the Chamber of Commerce, career expos for high schoolers, Little League, and other programs. The GM auto assembly plant, which employed more than 4,000 in the 1960s and 1970s, invested $92 million into the community in 1980, making it the bedrock of South Gate's economic health.[76]

Periodic layoffs and shutdowns began in the 1970s. At GM, this became routine as the company struggled with mounting pressures from the oil crisis, foreign competition from Japanese automakers, and federal policies that together deeply undermined American manufacturers. In 1974, more than 1,900 workers at South Gate GM were laid off indefinitely. Among them was Peter Belsito, who worried for his "two kids and a house I have to make payments on."[77] Within the decade, full-scale plant closures hit. In 1979, Fibreboard and Weiser Lock shut down. A more devastating blow came in March 1980, when Firestone closed shop for good; the plant was considered

Figure 6.4 Firestone Tire & Rubber plant closes in South Gate, 1980. Firestone's demise was one of several plant closures to devastate South Gate's economy and community fabric during the early 1980s.
South Gate Press, March 22, 1980.

too old and obsolete to retool for the production of radial tires. About 990 people lost jobs, many with over 30 years of service to the company. They were "disturbed" to learn of their fate from television reports instead of their employer.[78]

At GM, the next two years were a roller coaster of temporary layoffs; plant retooling to produce smaller cars; union meetings, marches, and protests; and giddy media coverage of the company's enthusiasm about the future. Workers suffered the stresses of periodic layoffs as the corporation tried to figure out a plan. One African American worker said tensions and hostility ran so high that "fights broke out around the plant." A 36-year-old single mother from La Mirada described how the bosses handed out GM baseball caps the night before announcing a layoff. The next day, when she learned the news, she said, "I've thought about blowing my head off and ending it, but I won't. I just feel so down. I don't know what to do. I'm angry and hurt."[79] To fight back, in 1980, labor formed the Los Angeles Coalition to Stop Plant Closures, a South Gate–based group of labor unions, church groups, and citizens. UAW 216 was instrumental in its formation. The coalition held meetings, rallies, benefit concerts, and brainstorming sessions. Drawing about 40–50 people to its meetings, it explored innovative ways to replace

lost jobs, such as worker–community ownership of closed plants and producer cooperatives. Members envisioned their efforts lifting the entire south
LA region, including places like Watts and Compton. The *South Gate Press*,
meanwhile, ran optimistic stories about GM's plans to restart production
with new models and to produce electric cars by 1985. The GM comptroller
told his audience at the South Gate Rotary Club that the company was " 'a
sleeping giant' that intends to reawaken." At a Chamber of Commerce breakfast a month later, he claimed GM was "bubbling over with enthusiasm, confident and proud."[80] Exactly a year later, GM announced it would close its
South Gate plant permanently.

In late March 1982, rain drenched autoworkers who had hoped to hold a
rally at South Gate regional park to protest the plant closure the following
week. They moved over to the union hall where they "sang songs, carried
placards, and listened to speakers" calling for GM to reverse its decision.[81]
UAW 216 had been thrown into a frenzy over GM's offer for workers to
transfer to jobs in Oklahoma City or lose severance benefits. Workers with
highest seniority—men in their 40s, 50s, and 60s—got the first offers. If
senior workers refused to move, they lost their guaranteed half salary and
health insurance after their unemployment benefits ran out.[82] Yet these older
workers were also the least likely to relocate, given their deep roots in Los
Angeles and spouses who would lose their own pensions if they moved.
"Old lady won't never go to Oklahoma, leave her mother and sister here,"
said chassis inspector "Rod" Rodriguez. "What am I gonna do, live there
in a motel?" Moreover, these senior workers would slide down the seniority ladder in Oklahoma, ending up in "the dirtiest, hottest, and hardest
assembly line jobs," as Kathy Seal recalled. Younger workers would not get
these transfer offers or benefits. As Seal put it, this was a colossal "mind- and
body-fuck, courtesy of Generous Motors" that created an unimaginable rup-
ture in these workers' lives.[83]

By the mid-1980s, more than 40,000 jobs were lost to plant closings and
indefinite layoffs, many of these high-wage union jobs. South Gate alone lost
over 12,500 industrial jobs. The southern part of LA was on the losing end of
a metro-wide reshuffling of wealth and capital, marked by "a complex mix
of selective industrial decline and rapid industrial expansion" of high-tech,
high-end jobs in more peripheral suburbs, in the words of geographer Ed
Soja. This spatial reshuffling reflected national trends of economic restructuring triggered by the rapidly evolving global economy that created well-
paid, highly skilled jobs on one end and low-paid, unskilled non-union jobs

Figure 6.5 In February 1982, two inspectors at GM South Gate pondered their future as the impending closure of the factory loomed. It closed permanently a month later. The plant's demise upended the lives of GM workers, many of whom built middle-class lives in the surrounding suburbs. Older workers were faced with the choice of moving to GM jobs in Oklahoma or losing their severance benefits.

Photo by Paul Chinn, *Los Angeles Herald Examiner* Photo Collection/Los Angeles Public Library.

on the other. The hourglass economy left no place for middle-income blue-collar workers who had once been the beneficiaries of unionized, industrial growth.[84]

Restructuring also had a racial dimension. While whites could relocate for better jobs, like the ex-GM workers who moved to Santa Monica, Downey, and Orange County, this wasn't necessarily an easy option for Blacks and Latinos. Not only did they face continued resistance in many white suburbs, they often lacked access to affordable mortgages. Plant closures thus exacerbated income and racial inequality across suburbia.[85] If restructuring created a revamped hourglass economy, South Gate occupied the narrowing middle.

The factory exodus decimated the fiscal base of the southeast suburbs. Tens of millions of dollars were lost annually from declining tax revenue. Many merchants closed their shops, taking valuable tax revenue and their involvement in chambers of commerce and civic organizations with them. In South Gate, Chrysler closed three auto dealerships, reducing South Gate's sales tax revenue by 20%. In the midst of this crisis, Proposition 13 passed in 1978, which slashed property taxes and cut off another revenue stream for the community. The repercussions of lost industrial and property tax income would be felt as the community subsequently struggled to revive its economy.[86]

By 1982, town leaders were speaking of South Gate's "crisis condition." Local unemployment and poverty were on the rise, while church and club memberships were falling. The city council applied for a federal Urban Development Action Grant (under HUD) given to "economically distressed" communities. Little had improved a year later. A reporter visiting the UAW Local 216 union hall that Christmas found unemployed autoworkers wrapping frisbees which "came at a discount from a bankrupt store" as gifts for local children. About 1,500 GM workers were still out of work. Those without seniority were in dire straits: "Most of them can't buy food or pay their rent," said Bernice LaCour of Local 216. In nearby middle-class Downey, the PTA made Christmas baskets holding a week's worth of groceries for destitute families hit by the plant closures in South Gate, Bell Gardens, Bellflower, and Downey.[87]

This economic collapse also fueled South LA's expanding crisis during the 1980s and 1990s. The area was ground zero of the crack cocaine epidemic, crime and gang violence, and hyper-policing, as African Americans and Latinos continued to make their homes in these neighborhoods. These problems also spilled over into neighboring suburbs.[88]

The early 1980s represented the nadir of white South Gate, symbolized by the GM policy that frustrated so many of its workers. GM, in essence, closed South Gate's white migratory circle that started in Oklahoma in the 1920s and returned there in the 1980s. This was not the ending these workers imagined. Their hearts were in California, and few could envision a reverse "Grapes of Wrath" exodus. GM helped doom the future of white South Gate. And it was this suburban death that opened space for a Latino rebirth.

South Gate's Ethnic Turn

While South Gate always had Latino residents, their numbers boomed after 1970. Nationwide, Latinos moved into many cities and suburbs, especially those facing economic crisis. In the 1970s, the Mexican American population in the United States nearly doubled from 4.5 to 8.7 million, with immigrants driven by Mexico's slumping economy, painfully high joblessness (50%), and high birth rates. Among these were undocumented migrants, who comprised about two-thirds of Mexican immigrants by the early 1980s. Half of these immigrants ended up in California, concentrated in the Southern California region. After 1980, civil wars in Central America pushed north refugees from El Salvador, Nicaragua, Guatemala, and other hot spots.[89] South Gate and the other gateway suburbs were crucial receiving grounds.

The gateway suburbs had the highest levels of Latino clustering in LA as suburbs flipped from all-white to all-Latino. By 2010, these suburbs ended up as racially segregated as when they started.[90] Yet even accounting for this rising ethnoracial concentration, from 1945 to 2000, the vast majority of Latino suburbanites in LA lived in multiracial towns. Even the gateway suburbs were multiracial between 1960 and 1990, with a sizeable number of Black residents in Lynwood, Compton, and South LA during the 1980s and 1990s. While wholesale racial turnover was never a foregone conclusion, the demographic momentum underscored a high degree of white racial anxiety in these suburbs.

In contrast to the middle-class Latinos who settled in Eastside suburbs—like Pico Rivera, Montebello, and Whittier—the gateway suburbs were home to a more heavily immigrant, poor Latino populace. They came from towns like Watts, Westlake, and Pico Union or directly from Mexico, Central America, or Cuba. They were drawn by the affordability of homes, as well as the decent neighborhoods and schools. What they wouldn't find were well-paying industrial jobs. Even so, they embraced the opportunities that white flight created. They represented a wholly new suburban generation. By the 1990s, the gateway suburbs had more Latinos than LA's Greater Eastside.[91]

From 1970 to 2010, South Gate's overall population soared from 57,000 to 94,000, and racially flipped at the same time—whites plummeted from 82% to 3%, while Latinos rose from 17% to 95%. Most newcomers were ethnic Mexicans, with much smaller numbers from Central and South America and Cuba. By century's end, immigrants—many undocumented—comprised about half of South Gate's population (see Table 6.1). Residents' ages reflected the suburb's racial divide: a young Latino populace alongside aging whites.[92]

In terms of class, South Gate exhibited simultaneous trends of upward mobility and worsening poverty, suggesting a growing rift between the haves and have-nots. Median family income remained below the LA County average (about 70–75%) from 1970 to 2000. Still, South Gate residents showed signs of modest upward mobility. From 1980 to 2010, Latinos saw gains in managerial, professional, sales, and office jobs. At the same time, blue-collar jobs declined gradually while service jobs increased. Latinas drove some of these trends, occupying white-collar and service jobs. They increasingly held managerial, professional, sales, and administrative positions, helping propel some Latino families into the middle class.[93] At the same time that some were moving up, others were scraping by. From 1970 to 2010, South Gate's families living below the poverty line rose from 7.4% to 23.1%. By 2010 fully 20,196 families were in poverty, many living on the west side of town near abandoned factory sites.

Housing tenure reflected these divisions. Homeownership overall plummeted in the 1960s, reflecting the early exodus of white homeowners after the Watts uprising, then hovered between 44% and 49% through 2010. Among Latinos, homeownership fell in 1970—likely reflecting the influx of working-class Latinos—then climbed slowly over the next 40 years. Latinos drove a home buying surge in the 1990s across South LA, attracted by the affordability of its modest houses. As Guatemalan immigrant Jesus Sierra explained, "In your own house. . . you feel more secure. You are respected. You feel like a king." In some cases, extended families pooled resources to purchase a home, suggesting a more communal pathway to property ownership than traditional suburban nuclear families.[94] Overall, South Gate saw a persistent division between owners and renters from 1970 to 2010.

Situated between poorer communities in South LA and the middle-class Latino suburbs of the greater Eastside, South Gate became "a stepping-stone community" for upwardly mobile Latino families, as resident Hector de La Torre put it. Leticia Ortiz recalled, "When we moved here from Compton in the '70s, moved to South Gate, it was like, wow we had a front lawn and a backyard—it looked like a little suburbia compared to where we used to live."[95] Others shared similar perceptions. John Trujillo, who grew up in Watts, stated in 1984, "I moved (to South Gate) to better myself." Around 1982, Sandra Martinez immigrated from Guadalajara, Mexico, and moved into an apartment complex on California Avenue in South Gate. To her,

South Gate was "beautiful and better than Guadalajara," a town of "clean streets," calmness, and privacy, where "people lived comfortably." Latino residents appreciated South Gate's quiet, friendly, hardworking population; its responsive police force; and its clean, tranquil neighborhoods. For these newcomers, living there was the payoff for their hard work and sacrifice.[96]

South Gate's emerging Latino community also had its own internal divisions. At one end of the spectrum were middle-class Mexican Americans, including the pioneer Latino settlers, who were homeowners, taxpayers, and parents. Some were American-born, others were naturalized, some self-identified as white. They were small-business owners and union leaders, teachers and stay-at-home mothers, and local politicians. At the other end were recent immigrants from Mexico and Central America, many living below the poverty line and struggling to get by.

Whites and Latinos in South Gate made gradual, if bumpy, progress toward interracial acceptance. Many whites resisted the change—among them the 34,500 who left South Gate from 1970 to 1990. While it's difficult to pinpoint the motives of every white who left, some were clearly acting on racial anxieties triggered by the 1965 Watts uprising, the heated politics around school desegregation and busing, and the growing Latino influx. As in many suburbs undergoing integration, whites feared a decline in property values, wholesale racial turnover caused by blockbusting and panic selling, and the end of the community they had known. To staunch the white exodus, in 1972 the South Gate city council passed two ordinances meant to limit racial blockbusting, modeled on a 1971 ordinance passed in nearby Lynwood. "Blockbusting" was the realtor practice of persuading white homeowners to sell their homes at a low price by evoking fears of an impending racial turnover, then reselling the homes at higher prices to Latino and Black buyers. The following year, South Gate proposed the more radical measure of outlawing "for sale" signs altogether. Speaking in favor of the measure, Elizabeth Bradford, a 28-year resident of South Gate, implored, "Eight years ago I stood with . . . members of this council to stop the busing of our children out of South Gate. We were successful in that effort. Now, it seems to me, we are faced with an even bigger problem—the very survival of the city itself." While local opinion was divided on the proposal, it ultimately failed, partly due to opposition from realtors.[97]

White resentment against Latinos recurred in subsequent years. It especially focused on the strain on local services caused by Latino newcomers and the perceived decline in some residential areas. Virgil Collins, a liberal

Democrat who had been a committed union man at GM, admitted his resentment toward the "illegals coming in here" who put "a tremendous pressure on all our systems within the city." During his years on the South Gate
Planning Commission, he visited many properties and observed that "just
about every house was overloaded with people," which he believed diminished the standard of living. "So consequently, I've seen South Gate deteriorate to the point where we wanted to get out." He and his family decided to
move to Orange County.[98] At times, racial tensions were open and angry in
South Gate. Leticia Ortiz recalled "derogatory comments from these older
whites. They felt they had a right to say offensive things like, 'you stupid
Mexican' to me in the late '70s early '80s." Around the same years, Jose
Valenzuela, who arrived undocumented at age nine, was repeatedly called
"wetback" in elementary school.[99]

By 1980, the anger boiled over in a series of vitriolic letters to the editor published in the *South Gate Press*, most signed as "anonymous." They
complained of disheveled yards, litter, cars parked in front yards, crying children running rampant, loud gatherings, cruising, overcrowding in homes,
and threats of violence and theft. "You can't believe the mess in some people's
back yards: beer cans, plastic bags and trash stacked waist high, and weeds.
I have lived here 45 years, fell in love with it because it was such a quiet,
pretty city. . . . What a change has taken place! . . . I would like to be friends
with all the new nationalities that are moving into South Gate and to make
them feel welcome. But I do wish they would take an interest in helping an
older resident keep our city clean and beautiful." A "concerned resident on
Bowman" wrote that newcomers "ruined our streets and lawns. . . . I say
why give up . . . stay and show these newcomers that they don't belong in
this community, but go back to where they came from." Other letter writers
refered to Latinos as "invaders," "undesirable element" and "those people."
Speaking directly to these distraught white residents, the *South Gate Press*
ran regular ads for new housing developments in places like Bellflower,
Norwalk, Laguna Niguel, and Laguna Village, providing a virtual roadmap
for white flight.[100]

Other whites left when the factories were shuttered, including those with
more progressive views on race. Those who stayed—often with deep roots
in the community—tended toward acceptance of Latinos and more liberal
views in general, reflecting a broader shift to the left in local leadership.[101]
Their views paralleled a broader white acceptance of Latinos as neighbors
across the region.[102]

Figure 6.6 A suburban home in the gateway suburb of Maywood, 2017. In the early 1980s, white residents expressed alarm over the look of Latino residents' properties, including complaints about disheveled yards and cars parked in front yards. These uses of suburban property contradicted their sense of "normal" domestic practices.
Photo by Becky Nicolaides.

Although growing ethnoracial diversity and mutual racial tolerance had come to prevail, there were limits to this liberal vision. Suburban homeowners, taxpayers, and parents—Latino and white alike—would be the pillars of the community. Renters, undocumented immigrants, and the poor would occupy a more marginal position, not wholly excluded but targeted in multiple ways. It was one thing to diversify the suburb racially and ethnically, but quite another to embrace full inclusivity that bridged divides of race, ethnicity, class, and citizenship.

"Wall to Wall Rooftops": South Gate's Housing Revolution

Veronica Lopez thought she had seen it all. As a code enforcement manager for the South Gate Building Department, she had inspected all manner of jerry-rigged homes and rentals sheltering the poorest of the poor. Then, one day in early 2000, her staff found a property with a large backyard transformed into a stunning rent plantation: "This one was very innovative," she recounted. "You know those storage sheds you get at Home Depot? You know they're good sized. . . . This man had a big backyard so he bought six of them, set them up in the backyard, and rented each one to single people. Run electrical from the house. He bought the one that you could barely get a twin bed in, and you know, all they needed was a hot plate, and they could use the bathroom that was in the house. And that's how he was making his money. He was charging them, I believe, $400 per month. So he was making $2,400 a month for people living in those conditions."[103]

Lopez described an extreme example of how South Gate's built landscape transformed after 1970. Suburban homes and garages were converted into makeshift rental units, creating a system of informal housing—a shadow housing market—that granted minimal shelter and radically densified the community in the process. South Gate had a hand in creating this state of affairs since, like nearly all suburbs, it had rejected affordable housing when demand was mounting. Informal housing was a workaround by a working class desperate for shelter and willing to occupy overcrowded, substandard housing. Unlike historic urban tenements, these dwellings were in the hidden recesses of suburbia, out of sight in backyards and small detached garages.[104]

Local policy had contributed to the shortage of affordable housing. During the 1970s and 1980s, local leaders turned to redevelopment and federal block grants to attract new business and industry in an effort to salvage the town's collapsing economy. They quickly learned that the only way to gain voter approval for such projects was to guarantee they would include no low-income housing and that existing homes would remain unthreatened. They responded by focusing on creating jobs—not housing. This approach to redevelopment prioritized businesses and catered to homeowner fears that low-income housing would bring in more minorities and poor people.[105] In other gateway suburbs, redevelopment was deployed as a kind of "slow growth" tool to curb the influx of Latinos. The Huntington Park Redevelopment Agency, for example, replaced dense rental housing near city hall with single-family homes and condos, partly to decrease the local population.[106] These land-use policies uniformly backfired, leading to a swelling housing crisis.

Even federal funds earmarked for low-income housing fell into a similar pattern. In 1977, the Western Center on Law and Poverty sued both South Gate and Pomona for illegally spending HUD money allocated for affordable housing on building parking lots, curb repairs, and a water study. Both cities, the suit claimed, had identified the need for low-income housing but established housing goals that would help only an "infinitesimal percentile" of those in need.[107] In 1982, HUD rejected South Gate's "housing element" plan because it lacked provisions for affordable housing. Two years later, town leaders exacerbated the situation by passing a moratorium on building new apartments because they feared it would further increase population density. More significantly, over the next two decades, South Gate gradually downzoned residential land from multifamily to single-family districts. As a result, the construction of multifamily housing plummeted in South Gate and other gateway suburbs in the 1980s and never recovered, a pattern fueled further by Reagan administration cuts to federal housing programs.[108] While reflecting homeowner desires to maintain a suburban veneer of tidy single-family homes, such policies ended up pushing desperate shelter-seekers into the shadows and expanding what would become an intractable system of informal housing.

These suburbs, in turn, transformed into spaces of ultra-high-density living. While this took different forms, the shared trait was intensive crowding in horizontal suburban spaces, either apartments or spaces in and around single-family homes. Apartments in Cudahy, Bell, and Bell Gardens became what Mike Davis termed "rent plantations."[109] "Double bunking" was common—several families crowded into apartments or homes meant for one. Honduran immigrant Elsa Saravia lived with 11 family members in a two-bedroom apartment in Bell that had a leaky roof, rotting floorboards, a broken toilet, and rats. Long "dingbat" apartment buildings filled the deep, narrow lots in these towns that had once been backyard gardens.[110]

In South Gate, a system of informal housing developed around single-family homes. These units included conversions created from partitioning a single-family home into multiple separate living spaces, converting garages into living spaces, transforming a home into a bunkhouse for "hot-bedding," building onto a home in the back, and using a habitable vehicle or structure (like an RV or Home Depot tool shed). All were invisibile from the street and to code enforcement officers.[111] Although they shared the experience of jerry-rigging habitations with their white working-class predecessors in South Gate, these working-class tenants lost out on the ultimate goal of property ownership.

These informal units proliferated in Southeast Los Angeles during the 1980s. In 1981, in Huntington Park, three adjacent double garages along an alley housed 10 occupants. The living was rough—an extension cord ran from the front house to each unit, mattresses were spread wall to wall on

Figure 6.7 A backyard occupied garden shed in the Florence-Firestone section of South Los Angeles, 2013. These shelters exemplified the informal housing that spread across the gateway suburbs in the 1980s, as the search of affordable housing intensified.

Photo by Jonathan Pacheco Bell.

the dirt floor, and a hot plate and refrigerator served as a makeshift kitchen. Lacking plumbing, tenants used a five-gallon can or a laundry sink as a toilet. A Huntington Park building inspector estimated in 1980 that half of garage tenants were undocumented immigrants. A similar spike in conversions occurred around the same time in Bell Gardens. In Norwalk, in early 1981, a "small shed city" was erected behind two homes, consisting of 10 metal garden sheds sheltering 16 families. In nearby Bellflower, most of the conversions were built by professional contractors and were "quite attractive," according to a code enforcement officer. The situation was more dire in Maywood, where hazardous conditions were reported, from raw sewage running under floors to exposed light sockets. In Paramount, a mail carrier observed immigrants crowded into 75 of the 376 homes on his route, many asking him to post letters "stuffed with cash" to relatives in Mexico. Similar informal housing appeared in many poverty pockets across Southern

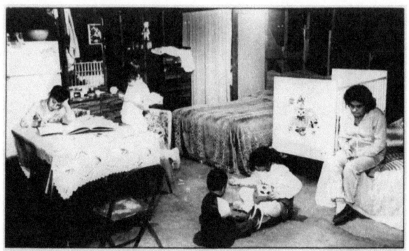

LAWRENCE K. HO / Los Angeles Times

Maria Torres with some of her children inside their garage home in the San Fernando Valley. Felix, 10, does his homework at the kitchen table in the photo above while Maria, 9, stands nearby. Guadalupe, 12, plays with Francisco, 2, as their mother watches.

Figure 6.8 In 1987, a *Los Angeles Times* exposé documented the widespread presence of garage conversions across Los Angeles County. In this image, Maria Torres was pictured with her children inside their garage home in the San Fernando Valley.

From "Garage Is Home to Mother, 5 Children," *Los Angeles Times*, May 24, 1987; photo by Lawrence K. Ho © 1987.

California, from San Fernando, Pacoima, and Arleta in the San Fernando Valley, to Santa Ana, Anaheim, and Long Beach to the south. But the practice was concentrated especially in the gateway suburbs.[112]

In South Gate, the practice had became so widespread that mayor Herb Cranton intoned in 1985, "If we don't do something, we're going to end up with wall-to-wall rooftops in the city."[113] From 1984 to 1987, approximately 24,500 people in South Gate—roughly one-quarter of the population—had inhabited a garage dwelling. In total, about 28,000 people participated in the system of informal housing in this period, including 4,000 landlords.[114] The practice persisted well into the 1990s, even after aggressive crackdowns. By 1996, at least 900 informal units existed in South Gate. On one block alone, six families huddled in converted garages.[115]

Informal housing had particular historical continuities in South Gate that lent itself to widespread use. As Veronica Lopez described, "The way that the garages are set up here in South Gate, they are detached from the home and they are in the rear third of the lot. So it was perfect for converting into a little granny flat. You're talking about 400 square feet of livable space. All you had to do was fix it up, and you were good to go." A conversion, which could cost anywhere from $5,000 to $8,000 in the 1980s, might involve installing dry wall, laying tiles on the floor, and dividing walls for a makeshift bathroom. The garage door was often covered over with dry wall, eliminating that exit and concealing the living quarters if the garage door was opened. Health hazards were rampant—cold drafts blowing through, inadequate and unhygenic kitchen facilities, and the absence of bathrooms. Other hazards were posed by lack of ventilation and gas pipes laid on the ground.[116] The tragic case of single mother Maria Castillo, a 31-year-old unemployed Salvadoran housekeeper, illustrated those risks. She lived with her three young girls in a small backyard rental, without smoke detectors. When a lace curtain caught on fire, it swept through the small dwelling, killing Castillo and two children. Yet despite the risks—health, legal, and otherwise—many South Gate residents living in poverty had no other choice of residence.[117] This was a built landscape that supported poor people in suburbia.

To tenants, informal housing was a survival strategy. They were often undocumented immigrants, many arriving cash strapped after spending hundreds of dollars to cross the border and ending up in low-wage jobs. For them, a garage rental enabled them to evade the costly, regulated procedures of a rental apartment. Because everything was handled under the table, there was no lease agreement, references, or credit check; instead of a hefty security deposit, a tenant could move in with just the first month's rent. In the 1980s, a typical rent was $200–300 per month, considerably lower than apartments. Details of available rentals spread through word of mouth or flyers posted at laundromats, churches, and other venues. For some, informal housing was a family-based strategy to provide shelter and pool resources. Lopez estimated that, in the 1980s, at least 60% of conversions were done for family. "Either the son that got married, or the daughter that got married, or the son that got divorced . . . or extended family that had come to live with them, they ended up in a converted garage." For the other 40%, tenants rented from strangers or acquaintances. Saving on rent could enable remittances or sending for relatives. In one case, a woman renting a home—who was receiving rental assistance payments from HUD—rented out her garage to seven or eight tenants.[118]

In the 1980s, many landlords were white homeowners—some moved out of South Gate but retained their homes as rentals, others inherited their house from their deceased parents, then rented it out. Jose Valenzuela's extended family of eight rented a two-story garage from a white "hippie" couple who occupied the main house. Before long, Latino homeowners also joined the system. (Lopez estimated that 75% of landlords of informal units lived in the main home.) Latino homeowners were motivated by a range of impulses to rent out units, ranging from exploitative to altruistic.[119] Some sought to help relatives recently arrived from Mexico, laid off from jobs, or otherwise facing misfortune. They charged only nominal rent as an act of kindness. In turn, landlords could trust family to avoid possible disputes, which might alert them to authorities. These cases represented a system of co-ethnic solidarity, a means of helping the recently arrived, poorest immigrants. As one Mexican-born property owner in Hawthorne saw it, he took pride in giving his fellow immigrants a "leg up" by charging low rents in his extralegal units.[120]

At the other end were landlords hoping to squeeze as much as they could out of their tenants. South Gate Councilman John Sheehy recalled an "illegal alien" who bought a small two-bedroom home and converted it into five apartments. He "crowded a Mexican family into each apartment," an act of exploitation resulting in a six-month jail term. For many homeowner landlords, the extra income from rents helped them cover their own mortgage and everyday expenses. As Veronica Lopez recalled, the 1980s were a tough time—"everything was so expensive, GM had closed . . . people had bought homes during the good times, they were trying to hang onto them, and this was one way to hang onto the home." Whether for altruism, survival, or profit, property relations in the informal housing market bound landlords and tenants together through shared participation in an illicit system. It was in both of their interests to protect and hide this system.[121]

By 1999, informal housing fueled an astronomical rise in density levels in the gateway suburbs. A study by the California Department of Finance found the Southeast contained four of the five densest cities in California, including Maywood, Cudahy, Huntington Park, and Bell Gardens—the first three ahead of San Francisco. Maywood had the highest density in the state with 25,083 residents per square mile. Only a handful of cities on the East Coast—including the boroughs of Manhattan, the Bronx, and Brooklyn—topped these levels. In South Gate, the population soared from 51,116 in 1950—when the suburb had reached its housing saturation point—to 96,418 in 2000. The gateway suburb numbers were remarkable because that density was achieved mostly in one- or two-story suburban homes or low-slung apartment buildings.[122]

If informal housing represented one important survival strategy for working-class Latinos—both tenants and their landlords—they also used suburban spaces in ways that supported both class needs and cultural tastes.[123] In South Gate and other gateway suburbs, Latino residents used their property most freely during the 1970s and early 1980s. Some built conversions themselves and grew food on their property. Others sold wares from front yards, grew tall stalks of corn, or raised chickens and goats, practices common in Mexico. Others painted their homes in lively colors— hues of turquoise, peach, or yellow—reflecting aesthetics from Mexico and Latin America. Together, these practices helped residents make ends meet and reminded them of home. Code enforcement officer Veronica Lopez recalled that one of the hardest parts of her job was "convincing people that they couldn't come to the United States, and buy a house, and do whatever they wanted with it. . . . They had the attitude that, 'well, it's my house, I should be able to do whatever I want with it.'"[124]

While homeowners had the means and latitude to reshape the public face of their properties, the tenants of informal housing were compelled to keep their presence as inconspicuous as possible. The housing on these properties often took up every last square foot of yard, leaving little room for personalized embellishments. These were hidden lives and landscapes. As geographer Jake Wegmann observed, residents living in these hidden spaces experienced the realities of dense urban living even as their streetscapes projected a suburban veneer. The crowded living quarters in the back expressed sheer poverty more than any ethnic aesthetic.[125]

This informal housing system created a novel scenario of interclass proximity in suburbia. Unlike traditional suburbs that excluded the poor, these communities housed the poor in the most integrated, intimate way—within the spaces of domestic homes and property. Not relegated to public housing complexes or old *colonias* on the fringe, the poor were interspersed in backyard garages, rental rooms, and ad-hoc dwellings. Despite all efforts to eradicate these units, the system persisted and adapted, housing a permanent resident underclass in South Gate. By 2011, South Gate had a comparatively low homeless population, suggesting that this system helped keep people off the streets even if dwellings were substandard.[126] Although both landlords and tenants were part of this system, tenants had the most to lose if

Figure 6.9 A section of southern South Gate, showing the dense footprint of housing and accessory units that fill up many backyards. The bustle of private activity that occurred behind homes was often invisible at street level, hidden behind the simple facade of single-family homes. The single-family home shown here masks the extensive building out in the property's backyard.
Google Maps.

discovered. This fraught context framed co-ethnic relations and limited the capacity of the most marginalized residents to participate in local life.

The Crackdown on Latinos and Their Landscapes

As the ethnic Mexican population expanded and the number of undocumented arrivals spiked in the 1980s, a neo-nativist backlash scapegoated immigrants for taking American jobs, draining public resources, and damaging the national economy. Strongest in large metropolitan areas like Los Angeles, Chicago, New York, and Boston, this backlash appeared as well in everyday suburban life.[127] If the segregated *barrio* represented a space of sustained interaction that might propel unified activism, suburban space could be a more fractured environment. It housed ethnic Mexicans with divergent interests: the pioneer suburbanites who owned homes and aspired toward middle-class status and *los recién llegados* (recent arrivals) who struggled for survival. This internal diversity characterized many Latino suburbs in Los Angeles but yielded a range of local responses—from co-ethnic solidarity to intraethnic hostility. In South Gate of the 1980s and 1990s, Latinos were pitted against each other within the delicate social context of a newly integrating suburb. These tensions surfaced most blatantly around land use, housing, and immigrant rights, as local leaders—both Anglo and Latino— took steps that marginalized the suburb's poorest residents, many of them undocumented. The ideal of suburban privatism, in the process, was turned upside down as these residents were subjected to aggressive intrusions into their home life with life-altering consequences.

Recently arrived and undocumented immigrants had the most precarious lives in South Gate. For much of the 1980s and 1990s, about one-third of local Latinos lacked citizenship. Some of these non-citizens may have chosen that status in hopes of returning to Mexico one day; others may have missed opportunities for amnesty, such as that granted by the 1986 Immigration Reform and Control Act (IRCA).[128] Either way, they found themselves in a marginalized, insecure position in suburbia. Federal immigration law posed inherent risks to undocumented immigrants, who faced persistent threats of deportation in this era.[129] Meanwhile, local leaders—including newly elected Latino officials—cracked down on immigrants in new ways to protect the suburban aura and reputation of their communities. Across the gateway suburbs, those responses took a variety of forms ranging from overt police brutality to more subtle prohibitions on cultural practices. In South Gate, these measures ushered in the most regulated era in the town's history. Even after many white residents left, Latinos were among those doing the regulating and policy-making to uphold suburban ideals and values. New ethnic suburbanites embraced old suburban values like protecting the quality of life, sanctity of the home, good schools, and the health and safety of children. Like generations before them, they felt a deep personal investment in their homes and pushed local policies to protect them. Undocumented immigrants, and their housing and spatial practices, bore the brunt of crackdowns during the 1980s and 1990s. These clampdowns represented a local layer of government power that criminalized undocumented Mexicans and rendered them "illegal" in the context of everyday suburban life.[130]

Deportations became a looming threat as the Immigration and Naturalization Service (INS) cast a wide net in workplace and neighborhood raids.[131] During 11 days of raids in June 1973, for example, the INS targeted factories, bus stops, and streets across Los Angeles, apprehending 7,100 Mexicans. A pre-dawn raid in Huntington Park yielded 400 detentions. One South Gate woman, five months pregnant, was apprehended at her factory job in Santa Fe Springs. She, her husband, and their five-year-old daughter lived in a home they owned in South Gate. In May 1979, INS raids in LA expanded into residential dwellings, such as two apartment complexes in Huntington Park where 80 people were loaded into INS vans and returned to Mexico the same day. Raids continued into the 1980s. Some Latinos from South Gate and Huntington Park were arrested in workplace sweeps during 1982, the year of GM's closure.[132] These practices left immigrant residents profoundly frightened. As one put it, "You feel humiliated because you realize you have no security in your own home."[133] Fear forced a 32-year-old single mother of two to socially isolate herself: "I can't afford to make many friends because I'm afraid they would turn me in if they got angry with me."[134] In Huntington Park, one mother was too afraid to leave home to buy milk at a store a block away. Mexican-born Jose Valenzuela, who arrived undocumented as a youngster in 1979 with his family, recalled being scared of the police and avoiding trouble "or they'll deport me." This visceral fear drove the undocumented to suppress their participation in community and civic life.[135]

Suburban municipal power was likewise deployed against vulnerable immigrants. Local police frequently aided the INS in its raids, even though such actions technically fell outside of their authority. Police forces in

Huntington Park, El Monte, Santa Ana, and Fullerton aided INS roundups, while the INS claimed that their stepped-up residential neighborhood raids were positively received by local law enforcement.[136] In South Gate, undocumented immigration became entwined with illicit housing as some residents believed rooting out one became a means for rooting out the other. Across the gateway suburbs, local police forces ranged from amiable to hostile during the Latino transition. Huntington Park and Bell/Cudahy, for example, led the gateway suburbs in police brutality claims in the mid-1980s, aimed particularly against Latinos. In Maywood, the police used DUI checkpoints to target unlicensed Latino drivers and subject them to excessive taxation and threats of deportation. South Gate had considerably fewer incidents of police abuse.[137]

Anti-immigrant sentiment and policy nevertheless surfaced by the 1980s in South Gate. Reeling from the mass exodus of factory jobs, locals fairly quickly scapegoated undocumented immigrants. In 1984, the *South Gate Press* ran a front-page story declaring, "Illegal aliens said to take most new jobs," citing a RAND study that found undocumented workers took 75% of new service and goods jobs in Southern California in 1983–1984.[138] Strains on local services and infrastructure were likewise blamed on undocumented residents who crowded into shadow housing and overtaxed water, sewers, and the schools. The issue of school crowding especially angered South Gate residents, who resented that it triggered the busing of local students to schools in Watts and the San Fernando Valley and forced the adoption of a year-round school schedule.[139]

With a pervasive sense that South Gate was facing its own suburban crisis, local leaders launched a spatial "law-and-order" campaign that built on city beautification efforts of the 1960s but took a more punitive, racialized approach. The campaign deployed local regulation and enforcement to codify the strictest land use measures in the town's history. These rules were meant to ensure a suburb of properly utilized single-family homes and public spaces, and they were implicitly aimed against Latinos who were perceived as the main violators. This spatial crackdown was a broad initiative across the gateway suburbs, as Bell, Bell Gardens, Cudahy, Maywood, Lynwood, and Huntington Park initiated similar campaigns against suburban "decay" and "eyesores." South Gate's measures were among the strictest.[140]

In South Gate, there were two waves of crackdowns—one in the 1980s, a second in the 1990s—aimed at pushing the community to become a more Anglo-looking, middle-class suburb. These efforts were launched and sustained by Mexican Americans newly elected to the city council and eager to prove their loyalty to the city. These campaigns exposed an important fissure within South Gate's Latino community—between middle class and working class, native-born and immigrant—and reflected how those divides were playing out in the suburban politics of place.

The first wave began in 1981, when city leaders launched a protracted campaign against informal housing. They began by beefing up the suburb's enforcement authority around building code violations. Local leaders added an amendment to the municipal building code, allowing the city to take violators "directly to a court judge" and re-designating violations from a misdemeanor to a fine-able "infraction" of the law. Henry Gonzalez, the first Latino elected to the South Gate city council in 1982, during his first mayoral term worked with Anglo city council members to initiate spatial policing. In a monthly "mayor's tour" of South Gate, he and other officials took a van around the suburb in a quest to "find the ugliest spots in town." They jotted down addresses in violation of city codes, including illegally converted garages. As city manager Bruce Spragg explained, "We want owners to take pride in their property." A 1983 ordinance sealed the effort by mandating the proper care of local properties. Residents were required to mow lawns, pull weeds, paint homes, keep yards clear of cars, clotheslines, and junk, and refrain from unauthorized conversions. Violators would face criminal misdemeanor charges, with a fine of $1,000 or six months in county jail.[141] The following year, Gonzalez's "fight against blight" campaign included volunteer anti-graffiti campaigns and ramped up enforcement. A new team of six building inspectors—equipped with new Ford Escorts—were empowered to patrol the suburb and issue citations on the spot. This system of spatial policing, adopted by Huntington Park in 1980 and South Gate in 1983, was fairly rare; one Huntington Park official estimated that 1 in 100 cities empowered inspectors to issue citations, much like a police officer. This new apparatus of enforcement represented a turn from a complaint-only, reactive system to a proactive, well-funded system of code enforcement. It gave inspectors legal authority to sniff out illegal garage conversions and indoctrinate Latino newcomers in the ways of American suburban living.[142]

By 1985, South Gate and neighboring gateway suburbs passed a series of measures to eradicate unpermitted housing altogether, South Gate's among the strictest. Previously the main tool was simply to enforce existing building codes and respond to neighbor complaints, but city officials enacted a more aggressive approach, including regular patroling of the suburb and stronger laws. In 1985, South Gate passed a pre-sale inspection ordinance, which required a city inspection of all homes for sale, a measure expressly designed to combat illegal conversions. It essentially inserted city authority into a private transaction.[143] The violations had to be fixed at some point in the home sale, and a later measure required the seller to pay for the inspection ($50). While it was up to the buyer and seller to work out what to fix or not fix, South Gate drew the line at unpermitted conversions. "The only thing that was not allowed to carry over from seller to buyer would be the garage conversion. We wanted that gone before they closed escrow," Veronica Lopez recalled. Seven gateway suburbs adopted similar measures by 2010.[144]

Public discussion following the law's passage reflected the widely shared view that unpermitted housing was a Latino problem. Only Anglos and American-born Mexicans felt empowered to speak up at city council meetings; no Latino tenants participated. Some white residents opposed the measure for penalizing white homeowners with conversions and advocated for garage conversions done before 1960 to be "grandfathered in." Others with a more progressive outlook claimed the measure seemed designed to target undocumented residents. Gregory Slaughter, for example, complained to the city council that inspectors "told him they wished to check his garage for illegal aliens," which he believed "to be a violation of people's rights particularly in regard to searches."[145] Larry Swisher claimed the city council's housing crackdown was meant "to get the illegals out of garages. They avoided saying it" for fear of offending Latino residents.[146] To these residents, housing inspection had become a local tool of immigration control despite city officials' claims to be "concerned about enforcing civil rights in this community."[147]

The system encouraged neighbors to turn in neighbors for housing violations. The city set up a hotline and dispatched code enforcement officers, the police department, and building inspectors to follow up on tips.[148] Housing law thus became a blunt instrument for regulating undocumented immigrants, one wielded by housing inspectors and neighbors. At this point, informal housing in South Gate—begun as a survival strategy in the 1920s and hailed as a patriotic duty in the 1940s—became fully criminalized in the 1980s, when the practice was racialized and linked to undocumented Mexican immigrants.

Building officials like Veronica Lopez in South Gate and Carlos Levario in Bell Gardens saw things differently. Their job was to protect the safety of vulnerable tenants in these illicit conversions and to ensure the quality of housing and services. Levario blamed absentee landlords: "It's greed. [They] are out to abuse people. They prey on them [immigrants] all the time."[149] Raised in a family of labor activists, Veronica Lopez had a deep and abiding sense of social justice and differentiated between her work and that of the INS. At the building department, she recalled, "I would get calls [from whites] like, 'There's a bunch of Mexicans living next door to us.' . . . Complaints. . . . We had to remind people that we were not INS, we were the building department." She recognized that garage conversions were often a survival strategy for homeowners struggling to make ends meet or an act of altruism to help those in need. Especially in later years, she recalled, "it was more the need, the family need for the money to stay afloat, than anything else." Still, she felt that eradication of these units was the best solution. She recalled the horrible conditions in some garage conversions: "There was a cockroach-infested garage that was so bad that I refused to go in and take pictures. I took them by sticking my arm in the door." Fire hazards were a major concern, along with poor insulation and temperature control. A more flexible approach to informal housing—as in some countries, where the practice was supported rather than criminalized—was not seen as an option by most of South Gate's leaders. Lopez felt that the safety issues, strain on services, and cluttering of property and streets were paramount, so she pressed city hall for even stricter laws, including the imposition of high fines to deter repeat offenders. By the 1990s, South Gate had empowered all city officials to act as spatial police, and fines had jumped from $75 to $1,000–5,000 for homeowners who illegally converted garages.[150]

The criminalization of informal housing added another layer of fear and insecurity to the lives of South Gate's most marginalized Latino residents as their dwellings came under siege. Rather than find suburban privacy, these residents were subjected to scrutiny in new ways, as local policy permitted official intrusion into their most intimate spaces. While the suburb's early loose regulatory climate had enabled Anglos to make the most of their property, many Latinos were prohibited from doing the same. For South Gate's poorest residents, the built environment became a formidable challenge to overcome rather than a resource to maximize to its fullest potential.

South Gate leaders spearheaded other attempts to regulate recreational and spatial practices, implicitly targeting Latino residents. In 1986, for example, local officials pressured the Latino representative of a local soccer league to deal with the "problems" their games were causing to residents living near the park or "the activity will be cancelled."[151] In the early 1990s, majority-Latino city councils passed another round of ordinances, including a ban on push-cart vending aimed at immigrants selling popsicles, fresh fruit, and snacks.[152] A 1993 measure outlawed spontaneous games of soccer in the park, requiring residents to obtain a city permit to play soccer, and confined their games to specific sections of the parks. Another measure prohibited loud boom-boxes and noisy parties or gatherings, designating a noise control officer to enforce it. A final measure clamped down on garage sales, a practice many Latino suburbanites used to supplement income and interact with neighbors. Sales were limited to twice a year by permit only and confined to the third weekend of the month to simplify enforcement. All of these measures passed without discussion at city hall.[153]

Other measures represented deliberate efforts to suppress Latino ethnic expression in the landscape. By the mid-1980s, the movement for English-only signage found its way to South Gate. Borrowing tactics from Monterey Park and San Marino, the South Gate planning commission proposed an English signage ordinance in 1985, making theirs the first southeast suburb to pursue such a measure. Local officials claimed English signage was needed to ensure public safety ("so police and paramedic units know where they're going") and clarity to customers. Residents blasted the proposal as discriminatory and ludicrous in a region long defined by Spanish-language place names. "Will the Pollo Loco and Wienerschnitzel now be called the Crazy Chicken and the Hot Dog?" asked South Gate resident John Trujillo. "Maybe in the future the Planning Commission will recommend that streets in South Gate such as San Juan and San Miguel be changed to Sir John and Sir Michael so the police and paramedic units will know where they are going." While most of the Anglo councilmen and the police chief saw no need for the law, Henry Gonzalez was the lone councilman to support it, stating, "I object to having a sign all in Spanish and no English whatesoever. It puts up a wall. . . . It tells Anglos and Blacks that they're not welcome in the store." Lacking council support, the measure was dropped. However, that same year, the council formed a new Design Review Committee charged with reviewing signage in the suburb.[154]

Twelve years later, Gonzalez led a push to regulate the paint color of local homes, a campaign that drew national media attention. Likening the effort to "color and design restrictions that are usually found only in affluent communities such as Laguna Beach and Westlake Village," the Los Angeles Times described the ensuing conflict as pitting Latino against Latino—between first and second generation, Chicanos and the assimilated, working-class and middle-class. On one side were homes and businesses painted in bright hues of turquoise, maroon, orange, and "banana yellow." As local artist Leo Limon explained, "It's part of our cultural identity. It's the colors of feathers and birds and trees, and the Latino population sees that and uses that." Felipe Gutierrez, an unemployed farmworker whose home was painted pumpkin, pink, and aqua, bristled at the criticisms, while Hilaria Contreras said of her bright lavender home, "It's for people who are happy. I would be depressed living in a house painted gray or beige." On the other side were councilmen Henry Gonzalez and Hector de la Torre, as well as other city officials and Latino residents who believed a more muted color palate would improve South Gate's image. "People are saying, 'It looks like hell,'" Gonzalez claimed. Citizen complaints, he noted, prompted the measure, and they were all from second- and third-generation Latinos, not Anglos. One such call came from Yolanda Arias, a native of Colombia and decade-long resident of South Gate, who described the "neon" paint as "ugly." She noted, "I sound racist. I'm not racist. But people coming from Mexico, people coming from other countries, they should know that this is America, that here it is different. . . . They put down this country with those colors." Lucy Bernal, a 39-year-old Mexican-born bank employee raising her family in a gray house, added, "I have a house around the corner from me, it's bright green with red trimming. It's an awful sight. When we moved here, it was a lot of retired white people in the area. They had such nice houses, and the yards were so well-kept. Now, I'm sorry to say, it's my own people that are causing the problem." The paint control measure was ultimately dropped by city officials.[155] Perhaps local officials gave in to the negative publicity, but the decision also signaled South Gate's immigrant community's greater assertiveness and effectiveness.[156]

South Gate also marginalized Latino entrepreneurs. Even as it embraced retail as a new economic development strategy in the face of factory closures, city leaders favored American- and Asian-owned enterprises over Latino ones.[157] For the most part, Latino entrepreneurs were not well supported, perhaps because they brought less capital and smaller operations, and they tended not to join the Chamber of Commerce. David Rodriguez, who opened Nana's Restaurant with a $75,000 nest egg, complained that South Gate authorities gave him a hard time "almost every time I try to advertise with flyers or banners. . . . You still need permission for this and permission for that." If he had to do it again, he mused, he would never start his business there. A 1996 RAND report confirmed Rodriguez's sense of the local climate for Latino entrepreneurs, noting that instead of bolstering small immigrant businesses South Gate tended to target them for regulatory violations.[158] Similar hostility was directed toward Latino entrepreuneurs in nearby Downey. In the gateway suburbs, Spanish-speaking merchants were generally not active in local chambers of commerce because meetings were conducted in English. While some formed their own ethnic chambers of commerce, they were separated from the seats of local power, oriented more toward hometown associations, and even worked with the Mexican government to invest back in Mexico.[159]

As a result, South Gate's retail was predominantly Anglo and corporate. El Paseo shopping center, sited on a former oil tank farm in the eastern part of town, opened in 2001 and was cited by one developer as a "turning point" because it represented corporate America's recognition of Latino buying power in mainstream retail. The center was filled with American chain stores and restaurants like Ross, Marshalls, Applebee's, Chili's, and, Starbucks.[160] A similar American-style shopping center—the Azalea Center—opened 10 years later on the former site of American Concrete & Steel Pipe Company, once a major local factory. In nearby Huntington Park, Lynwood, and Walnut Park, similar shopping centers were owned by Anglos, while shopkeepers were from Korea, Iran, Vietnam, Mexico, Cuba, and Nicaragua. While these shopping areas were designed for Latino customers and came to serve as vibrant community hubs, their ownership often lay in non-Latino hands, meaning they did not promote the accumulation of ethnic wealth in these suburbs. This contrasted sharply with Asian ethnoburbs, where immigrant entrepreneurs successfully leveraged investment and resources into a source of ethnic power and resilience. In the Latino gateway suburbs, that resource was mostly absent.[161]

South Gate's reception toward its immigrant residents—from enacting aggressive, racialized housing policy, to quelling ethnic expression in the landscape, to offering lukewarm support for immigrant entrepreneurs—revealed a desire among its leaders, including its newest Latino council members, to align South Gate's profile more closely with Anglo-style suburban values. These choices did not turn South Gate into an ethnoburb, but rather reflected Latino affinities for Anglo suburban aesthetics, landscapes, and capital. This approach, in turn, marginalized South Gate's more vulnerable residents and created a challenging context for fully democratic, inclusive social and civic life.

Social and Civic Engagement: First-Wave Assimilation

After 1980, the social and civic integration of Latinos in South Gate occurred in two phases. Pioneer Mexican Americans paved the way, joining mainstream clubs and organizations and carrying forward established traditions. Their embrace of certain facets of suburban social and political culture did not ensure a smooth road for the Latino newcomers who followed. They aligned with the dwindling population of aging whites who stayed in South Gate. For newer immigrants, participation could be a more daunting prospect. Class and citizenship divides thus played out in South Gate's social and civic life.[162]

In everyday neighborhood life, the sting of those fissures could be acute. While some Latinos recalled friendly, welcoming neighbors on their blocks where children played together and adults chatted in front yards, others remembered constant tensions around the issue of housing. Neighbors turned in neighbors for housing code violations, a practice encouraged by city officials. In nearby Huntington Park, every Monday and Tuesday morning blockwatchers reported to city officials about neighbors carting in sheet rock or lumber to convert garages. In South Gate in 1983–1984, city hall received 269 complaints about neighbors converting garages. For the vulnerable tenants of these dwellings, neighborhood surveillance fostered a reluctance to venture out, further reinforced by periodic INS raids and sporadic gang- and drug-related violence.[163] Pockets of neighborly goodwill coexisted alongside more hostile spaces.

In local group life, the suburb's well-established community institutions— such as the PTAs, the Azalea Festival, and major civic groups (Rotary, Optimists, Kiwanis, and Women's Club)—remained the most important nodes of civic life. At a time when the Latino population grew from 58% to 92%, South Gate lacked groups that consciously invited the mingling of whites and Latinos. No "human relations" committee existed to promote ethnic integration, as in San Marino and Pasadena. This void reflected a larger trend across LA County partly because of Prop 13 budget cuts to the LA County Human Relations Commission, charged with helping communities through these changes.[164] In South Gate, few proactive steps were taken to embrace Latinos, who were expected to join existing Anglo-American groups and traditions and adjust accordingly. Those most likely to join were English-speaking Mexican Americans already well acclimated to American life and open to assimilating.

GM employee Henry Gonzalez embodied that experience. As chairman of UAW Local 216, Henry built solid ties with other union men like Virgil Collins, financial secretary of Local 216 and a member of South Gate's planning commission, who lived one block away. "We'd go to Democratic meetings together. He was one of my mentors," Gonzalez recalled. Contacts Henry made in the Democratic Club, which he and his wife Theresa joined right after they moved to South Gate, helped him access more opportunities for civic involvement.[165]

Henry took much of the initiative himself, throwing himself into youth-oriented volunteer work. As a former football player, he helped organize a youth football program in South Gate and coached youth football, basketball, and baseball. He also volunteered for the Boy Scouts, founded the South Gate Booster Club, raised funds for his church, and served on the South Gate Bicentennial Committee in 1976. Gonzalez recognized the importance of building trust in a community undergoing ethnic change, and the only way to do that was "to get involved." That paid off especially when it came to coaching sports, a social space where parents entrusted their children to other adults: "People get colorblind when you get involved and you're involved with their kids. Kids come home and say, 'Oh, coach told me to do this, told me to do that.' They start talking about you." Theresa, meanwhile, was getting more involved in the PTA and Women's Club. Together, they were becoming a formidable couple in the community. They continued actively participating in the Democratic Club, where they met John Sheehy, South Gate's postmaster and a city councilman. The Gonzalezes' allegiances reflected South Gate's leftward shift after 1970, with a fair share of Democrats on the city council.[166]

Henry's local involvement took an important turn when he joined the South Gate Rotary Club in 1964, with sponsorship from John Sheehy. The club welcomed in Latinos only gradually and retained many of its white members well after white flight. In the 1960s and 1970s, there were about 60 members of this powerful group that served as a stepping-stone to local political power—and it served Gonzalez in this way. In 1982, Gonzalez became the first Latino elected to the South Gate city council, the same year that GM closed. He brought a liberal-labor mindset to the council yet would refrain from an overtly pro-union stance to avoid charges of favoritism. Gonzalez was part of the pragmatic progressive approach to Latino advancement, working within the system for reform, in contrast to leftist Chicanos seeking more radical change along nationalist, separatist lines.[167] His leadership trajectory was that of other South Gate first-wave Latinos—join existing groups, volunteer robustly, build trust, and pursue an agenda of moderate liberalism.

Following a familiar pattern, youth-oriented groups continued to serve as a first entry point for many early Latino joiners. To help out at school, on a sports field, or at the PTA was a relatively easy first step for a newcomer parent. Records of the Coordinating Council—a group that brought together reps from all local organizations—showed that the schools welcomed in Latina/o leadership more quickly than other organizations.[168] In the early 1960s, Theresa Gonzalez joined the "PTA right away." This led to deeper involvement in the community—she became a PTA leader, a school volunteer, a team manager for Pop Warner, and a member of the South Gate Women's Club, Azalea Festival planning committee, and, by 1990, president of the South Gate Coordinating Council.[169]

While the South Gate establishment expected assimilation to traditional ways, it began making modest overtures to Latinos after the population had tipped to majority Latino by the 1980s. The *South Gate Press*, for example, ran a small section of news in Spanish for a few years. It also ran the syndicated "Hispanic Link" column penned by conservative Latino writers, expounding on topics like eradicating the term "Chicano." A few local schools began celebrating Cinco de Mayo in 1980, and, three years later, South Gate celebrated the holiday with a Mexican lunch at the municipal auditorium. While South Gate feted Mexican Independence Day (September 16) with an annual carnival, it never adopted Cinco de Mayo as a regular holiday.[170] The Miss South Gate Beauty Pageant began receiving Latina entrants and crowned a Latina queen in 1979. The Christmas parade included several Latino entries, such as floats by Ernie's Mexican Restaurant and La Tapatia Restaurant of Huntington Park in 1980, which both lost out to Bob's Big Boy for top honors that year.[171]

The Azalea Festival, arguably South Gate's most important tradition, integrated Latino influences and individuals at a fairly glacial pace. It took some early steps in 1981 by including "low riders" in the festival's car show, a soccer skills contest headed by a Latina, and a "Mexican Fiesta" theme for the semi-formal dance. Over the years, the Azalea honor court, which included about 25–30 women from various civic groups, was slow to include Latinas. Theresa Gonzalez was among the first, serving on the court in 1971. Yet, over the next three decades, whites greatly outnumbered Latinas on the court and planning committee even though the white population had

WORKING-CLASS SUBURB   323

shrunk drastically. Six out of nine ladies on the court in 1995 were white, when South Gate was about 87% Latino. The festivities incorporated Latinos more as spectators than stewards.[172]

Some civic groups resisted Latino immigrant members for years, at the risk of self-destruction. The South Gate Women's Club was a case in point. Founded in 1919, this club was dedicated to "literary and philanthropic work" and promoted the "civic, social and economic" well-being of South Gate, including raising money for scholarships and assisting families in need. Its white, middle-class membership was controlled through careful vetting. In 1982, Theresa Gonzalez was the first Latina to break the color line. In subsequent years, the club was slow to admit Latinas: a few joined in the 1990s, and a handful more thereafter. By 2013, the club had 33 whites and 13 Latinas. It remained an English-only club. The Latinas who joined encountered hostility, according to Maria Davila, Mexican-born and raised in the United States. Davila recalled that, while some Women's Club members were "nice people," a few were openly prejudiced. "It came to the point that they started offending some of our—not me personally—some of our members and we just didn't take that." She was excluded from club board meetings, even though she was president of her own section of the club. Fed up, the Latinas broke away and formed their own group, the South Gate Women's Multicultural Club.[173]

If existing community traditions and groups were slow to integrate, some Latinos proactively worked to increase social and civic engagement by their co-ethnics. One of these initiatives flowed from the old UAW presence in South Gate. In 1984, Al Belmontez, former president of UAW Local 216 and unemployed for two years after the GM plant closure, worked on increasing Latino political participation in the area. The soft-spoken organizer lived in a converted four-car garage with his wife, Virginia Reade, regional director of the Mexican American Political Association (MAPA). Belmontez and Reade worked through MAPA to increase Latino voter participation, elect Latino candidates, and support local campaigns around issues like education, housing, immigration, and jobs.[174]

Another push came from Latino businessmen and professionals. They revealed a crucial reality in South Gate: since merchants were traditionally major community players in suburbia, the lack of support for Latino merchants erected a critical barrier to local participation. In 1983, a group of Latino lawyers, bankers, teachers, and corporate managers formed the Southeast Hispanic Business and Professional Association to support Latino entrepreneurs and educational advancement in the gateway suburbs. While the association supported Latino merchants by offering advice about everything from investments to regulatory rules, above all it preached the gospel of voluntarism as a means of ethnic group advancement. Members themselves served as leaders of local Chambers of Commerce, United Way chapters, Rotary, Elk, and Kiwanis Clubs, and Neighborhood Watch groups. Voluntarism, they contended, was a two-way street—participants helped the community, but they also gained in the process. As George Mirabal, owner of a Bell mortuary, put it, "The best way for newcomers to protect their interests in the area is to get involved in the area." People like realtor Raul Perez of Huntington Park emphasized the link between involvement and political power, especially crucial since "there's going to be a power struggle in the upcoming years." A native of Guadalajara, Mexico, Perez ran for the Huntington Park City Council five times before becoming the first Latino council member in 1990.[175] These Latinos all supported an assimilationist approach, seeking to teach immigrants the ways of suburban community life and how to make the most of it. In South Gate, Latinos were slow to join the Chamber of Commerce, reflecting the difficulty small business owners had in the community in general. In 1984, only 7.5% of the South Gate Chamber membership was Latino, although they were a majority of the overall population. The Chamber elected a Latina president that year, but very few Latinos served on the board of directors around this time. Only when the Chamber hired bilingual staff and published a bilingual newsletter in the 1990s did more Latinos begin to join.[176]

As it always had been, the ladder to local political power was through existing associations in these suburbs, and if Latinos aspired to city hall, they were expected to be part of these networks. After Henry Gonzalez's election to city council in 1982, Johnny Ramirez was elected in 1990, followed rapidly by other Latinos who came to comprise majorities on the council starting in 1992. Latino majorities in other gateway suburbs followed.[177] While racial politics dominated in Maywood and Bell Gardens, in South Gate and Huntington Park ethnicity was downplayed. As Bill Martinez, an insurance salesman elected in 1994, put it, "We were not running on a Latino or a *la raza* ticket. I don't think this is a victory for the Latino community . . . it's a victory for the people of South Gate." The assimilationist message prevailed. Despite this moderation, Henry Gonzalez experienced racist hostility from some residents unwilling to accept the prospect of Latino leadership in the suburb.[178]

Even with these Latino gains in local elected offices, whites continued to exert considerable power in city hall. As late as 2004, whites comprised 62% of city department heads, such as city manager, director of development, and chief of police. Long-time leaders like Bill DeWitt, owner of South Gate-based General Veneer Manufacturing, continued to serve on the city council—on and off—from 1980 to 2015.[179]

Up to the late 1990s, South Gate's enduring institutions were slow to adapt to new realities. As a result, civic and social groups began to disappear, and Latinos participated at low rates in general. Although spotty records on local civic groups do not allow for an accurate count over time, they suggest a general pattern of groups peaking in 1980, then dropping off. This downturn stemmed in part from the inflexibility of local associations, the lack of a "human relations" entity to encourage social integration, and policies hostile toward poor immigrant residents. Those Latinos most able to succeed in local groups were Mexican Americans who were fluent in English and willing to adapt. They emerged as leaders of a community whose identity was still deeply connected to those institutions. For others, particularly immigrants, they forged parallel, sometimes separate, spaces of community life in the suburb.

Social and Civic Engagement: Immigrants Claim a Place

After 1980, the suburb's immigrants began a gradual process of social and civic integration impeded by certain formidable barriers. In contrast to East Los Angeles where Mexicans Americans had a deep history of activism and political engagement, many immigrants arrived in the southeast suburbs with starkly different political sensibilities. Reporter Sam Quinones emphasized that those who came "straight from the ranchos—small villages on Mexico's frontiers," harbored a deep distrust of government, fostered by the Partido Revolucionario Institucional's (PRI) notorious political culture of paternalism, corruption, and electoral fraud. For some of South Gate's immigrant residents, their civic disengagement reflected a deep-seated ambivalence toward politics on both sides of the border.[180] It was a bitter brew that mixed historic suspicion of government corruption with a wariness toward local suburban officials who seemed to resent their presence. For others, fears of nearby crime, gangs, and drugs led immigrants to "shut in and shut out," as one research team put it.[181] Fears of deportation also loomed. For their own well-being, many immigrants withdrew from life in South Gate, to the detriment of local civic health.

Transnational loyalties also drew the civic energy of some immigrants who retained strong ties to native homelands. Some saw their sojourn as temporary, a way to earn money for a few years before returning to Mexico. Many sent remittances to family in home countries.[182] Others joined hometown associations, which fostered homeland identity, culture, sociability, and philanthropy among immigrants from the same state or region in Mexico and Central America. South Gate was the headquarters of the Jalisco hometown associations in Los Angeles, a federation established in 1989 by South Gate businessman Ruben Arenas that grew to involve 17 Jaliscan clubs with 3,500 members by 1992.[183] South Gate's Jalisco club especially helped those who arrived with little money or education by giving them a place to socialize and learn about local social services. They also raised funds for philanthropic projects back in Jalisco, such as purchasing hospital equipment, funding an orphanage, and mobilizing disaster relief. By 1998, Los Angeles had over 170 hometown associations from 18 Mexican states.[184] These transnational groups did not necessarily promote the accrual of wealth or social capital through suburban homeownership but instead revealed striking expressions of social and civic engagement across borders, toward family, friends, and co-ethnics in home countries. This complicated the prospects for immigrants' local participation.

Yet the situation began to shift in the 1990s, partially catalyzed by Proposition 187. This state measure, passed in 1994, denied undocumented immigrants public services like education and health care. Although the courts ultimately ruled against the measure, it propelled many immigrants to apply for citizenship.[185] In South Gate, voter registration jumped 40% over the next six years, thanks in part to the efforts of labor and civil rights groups.[186] By the late 1990s, South Gate's state assembly district was the only one in the state where Latinos made up a majority of registered voters.[187]

While gaining citizenship and the power to vote represented one pathway to civic engagement, immigrants pursued other avenues toward meaningful belonging in South Gate. Two important sites were the public schools and churches. A crucial turning point occurred in 1990, when the PTAs went bilingual. After the PTA decided to hold meetings at South Gate Junior High in Spanish and translate them into English (via headsets), membership rose from 466 to 1,455. This long overdue change was crucial in a school where

75% of parents spoke only Spanish and where only 95 of 3,700 students were non-Latino. PTA leaders realized that the organization would have to adjust or face collapse since attendance at meetings had plummeted. Latina/o parents rose into leadership positions, spearheaded membership drives, and volunteered in the classroom. Nora Gonzalez, mother of a sixth-grader and new joiner in 1990, captured the feeling of a PTA meeting: "They are my people."[188]

The inclusivity of the PTA aligned with its emerging role in integrating immigrants and the poor into the community. The group raised money for band uniforms and gym clothes for low-income students, delivered food to impoverished families, and, as part of a broader LAUSD PTA initiative, supported a dental and eye clinic for students lacking health insurance. A Newcomer Center at the junior high helped acclimate new immigrant families to American life, offering parents a two-week class on topics like shopping, health care, gang and drug problems, and community services. It even gave parents a tour of the suburb. The center was funded by a $200,000 federal grant. Project director Johanna Rivera believed her work was crucial for incorporating new immigrants: "They won't just be outsiders looking in. They'll be full-fledged members of the school community. They'll really have a chance to dig in and learn." Carmen Martinez, mother of an eighth-grader, was the first parent volunteer at the Newcomer Center. Through a Spanish translator, she recalled her own difficulties on arrival 15 years earlier: "When . . . I had to pay the light bill or go to a government agency, it was hard for me to relate. A lot of people go through this, and it motivated me to help."[189]

The schools, thus, became one of South Gate's most welcoming sites for immigrant residents, especially mothers. The stories of three women illustrate. Celene Leyva was born in Jalisco, Mexico, and immigrated to the United States at age 16. She moved to South Gate in 1979 with her future husband and had three children in the 1980s. Although her English was limited, she began attending PTA meetings when her children were in elementary school. When they entered junior high, PTA reps asked her, like other parents, to volunteer two hours a month at the school. Through this involvement, she began advocating more forcefully for her own kids, one of whom was wrongly placed in a special needs class. Leyva learned the ropes of the LAUSD administrative hierarchy and ultimately decided to become a district representative. She brought the concerns of immigrant parents to the attention of school administrators, sometimes to appeal charges like drug and weapons possession. For Leyva, this initial voluntarism spawned involvement in other groups.

Maria Davila was born in Michoacan, Mexico, and at age six immigrated to Los Angeles with her mother and siblings to reunite with her father, who was part of the Bracero program.[190] Maria grew up in Watts, where she attended elementary school, then was bused to South Gate for junior high and high school in the 1970s. After marrying, she and her husband moved to South Gate in 1985. When she was six months pregnant with her second child in 1990, her husband died suddenly from a severe asthma attack. Forced to find paid work, she took an office job at a garment factory, remarried two years later, and had two more children. She first got involved at her children's schools. "I volunteered in my child's classroom and just being there at the school—that is where all my time went during the day." She joined the PTA and went on to serve as president of the PTA and School Site Council. That work led to a job doing outreach to local families for MediCal, the state's Medicaid health care program. Davila went on to participate in many local clubs and ultimately politics.

Sandra Martinez was born in Guadalajara, Mexico, and immigrated in her mid-20s. She and her husband lived in an apartment complex where her seven siblings also rented. She had three children in the 1990s and soon got involved in the PTA. Speaking only Spanish, Martinez initially joined the PTA "to be there" with her kids and then stayed to keep informed. She ultimately served 13 years as a PTA community rep, attending LAUSD and city council meetings in that capacity. She valued the chance to share information with other parents. Along with her church, the school was the place where she met and made many friends.[191]

This parental desire to engage on behalf of their children manifested in volunteer work, participation in the PTA, and service club work. At South Gate Middle School, a cohort of Latina volunteers called Las Comadres formed in 1996, to act as surrogates for school administrators. They talked with parents of students having discipline problems and checked on truancies. They even washed piles of school uniforms for students who needed them.[192]

In a few cases, initial involvement in the schools spawned new groups formed by and for immigrants. For example, Padres Unidos, mostly Mexican immigrant mothers, began in 1998, specifically to address the problem of massive overcrowding in the South Gate schools. South Gate Junior High had more than 4,000 students in the 1990s, making it the nation's most crowded. As a short-term solution, the LAUSD transported students to schools in the

San Fernando Valley and Watts, but some parents feared for their children's exposure to gangs, drugs, and Black students. School buildings were also affected by the growing environmental problems caused by years of careless industrial practices and the toxic residue left by departing factories. In 1989, toxic waste from a chemical plant began seeping into the grounds of Tweedy Elementary, forcing its closure. Classes were instead taught in small bungalows at South Gate Park, a move that was supposed to be temporary but ended up lasting 15 years. Padres Unidos members demanded that LAUSD build more schools in South Gate. They attended LAUSD board meetings and enlisted the aid of city councilman Hector de la Torre, a well-connected politician who brought in state senators, members of the state assembly, and LA County supervisor Gloria Molina to help press their case. The mothers of Padres Unidos convinced fellow parents to attend crucial meetings and garnered media attention, finally winning a commitment by the district to increase the number of local schools from 12 to 21. Through this robust grassroots effort, South Gate's immigrant parents successfully battled the LAUSD behemoth.[193]

The South Gate Multicultural Women's Club grew out of Padres Unidos. A circle of 10 friends, all volunteer leaders at different schools in South Gate, met every Friday morning over breakfast and discussed their shared desire to raise scholarship funds for local students, something the Women's Club was already doing. After being rebuffed by that group, they decided to form their own. All meetings would be held in Spanish, but they opted for the name "Multicultural" because their group included whites and one Japanese woman, nearly all fluent in Spanish. (They translated for one white member.) During its early years the Club met monthly with around 25 members to organize a women's conference, a "day of the child" celebration, and an annual dinner dance to raise scholarship funds.[194] Around the same time, another parent group called Madres de South Gate also formed to raise scholarship money for local students. With few financial resources among its members, they were able to partner with city leaders.[195]

Even despite this growing multicultural involvement, the schools were not without problems, from fiscal to racial. As in Pasadena, San Marino, and Lakewood, schools were often the site of the most intensive racial conflict in this era of demographic change. South Gate was not immune. Anti-Black racism, for example, reared its head when Latino parents opposed busing local children to Watts. In 1997, a group of Black teachers and a student's family charged that racism had gotten so bad at South Gate Middle School

that they sued the LAUSD for redress. The teachers claimed they were harassed for speaking out against discriminatory policies and practices. The
student, 11-year-old Michael Collins, one of 16 Black pupils among 4,000
total, had been subjected to repeated harassment by Latino students, who he
alleged poured chocolate milk on him, put ink on his clothes and crazy glue
in his hair, and beat him with a stick with a rusty nail. His mother claimed
the sixth-grade counselor at the school said her son would "just have to get
used to being called a n***r." The teachers won the lawsuit in 1999, while
Collins settled out of court with the LAUSD.[196] Even as Latina/o parents were
finding a civic place within the orbit of the schools, racial hierarchies that
subordinated Blacks could persist and continue to suppress Black population
growth in South Gate (see Table 6.1).

Public safety was another focus of immigrant civic engagement. As in
other aging, working-class suburbs dealing with disinvestment and rising
poverty, crime and gang activity had been on the rise in South Gate for
years.[197] In 1997, residents formed a short-lived group called Comunidad
en Accion (CIA; Community in Action), a neighborhood watch, anti-gang
and anti-drug group. This grassroots law-and-order effort waged by immigrant suburbanites signaled their desire for safety in their neighborhoods
and a level of trust toward local law enforcement. The South Gate Police
Department partnered with them, attending neighborhood meetings and
working to help persuade local youth to stay away from gangs and drugs.
Turnout at monthly meetings was impressive, with each area group routinely
drawing 40–50 residents. For Celene Leyva, the shooting of police officer
Michael Hoenig right outside her home motivated her to become heavily involved in this group. In 1998, the CIA began holding marches "against violence and abuse; and to improve living conditions of the community and
the safety of our children," as a flyer announced. A typical march started
with 50–60, gathered others along the way, and sometimes ended up with
300–400 people. At their meetings, police officers also circulated flyers about
housing code enforcement and home security programs offered free to low-
income residents, to enlist members in the suburb's mission to help "beautify
the community." The CIA also held neighborhood clean-ups on Saturdays,
where residents and police together cleaned up alleys, painted over graffiti,
and repaired broken fences. In an unprecedented way, this group united
immigrant residents with the suburban establishment, making allies of
residents and the police and marking a high point in community–police relations in South Gate.[198]

Comunidad en Accion had allies in city hall who were part of a massive scandal, prompting the group to mobilize a vigorous grassroots campaign to oust them in 2002. This campaign became a crash course in US civics for many immigrant residents. In a rigorous series of kaffeeklatches held in suburban homes—five nights a week for four months—police officers like Frank Rivera explained how local government was supposed to work (such as open government, accountability, and budgetary oversight) and how a cabal of city leaders had circumvented that system for personal gain. As Rivera explained, "It was Government 101, right in their living room." One former member of CIA, Señorina Rendón, cooked pozole and tostadas to raise funds and held "neighborhood feeds" at her home where white seniors, Mexican immigrants, and local police officers gathered together to eat and strategize. This mobilization was an intensive moment of community engagement and unity to fight a common adversary.[199]

Figure 6.10 Comunidad en Accion (CIA), in South Gate, late 1990s. The CIA was a short-lived grassroots neighborhood group dedicated to public safety and cooperation with the local police. This group generated robust engagement among South Gate's Latino immigrant residents in monthly meetings and marches through the suburb's streets.

Photo courtesy of Celene Leyva.

Some churches served as community spaces that welcomed immigrant residents. Between 1977 and 1990, the number of churches focused on Latinos congregants rose from 1 to 15 in South Gate, comprising half of all churches by the latter date.[200] Over two-thirds of all churches held services in both Spanish and English by 1990. Parkview Foursquare Church, with a half Latino–half Anglo congregation, was committed to creating an inclusive interethnic community under the leadership of Pastor George Jameson. After his arrival in 1987, the church began offering an amnesty assistance program and English classes.[201] Jameson was vice president of the South Gate Ministerial Alliance, lending an inclusive voice to this community-wide leadership group. In nearby Huntington Park, St. Matthias Roman Catholic Church was a lively bastion of Latino life by the mid-1980s, drawing 8,000–9,000 worshippers to weekend masses, eight of them in Spanish. By 1990, St. Matthias had become a center of advocacy for immigrants and the poor, offering amnesty and English classes, supporting voter registration drives by the grassroots Latino group United Neighborhoods Organization, and organizing a food bank serving 2,000 people each month.[202]

Beyond the traditional suburban institutions of schools, groups, and churches, immigrant youth created vibrant communal spaces in the southeast suburbs. For example, Latina/o youth became "music activists" by staging concerts in repurposed spaces, such as restaurants, auto shops, veterans' halls, and warehouses—lasting a few days or weeks. They created social networks to share music, fashion, and fanzines both transnationally and within Southeast LA, flourishing especially around Rock Angelino. As historian Jorge Leal has shown, these connections, while often ephemeral, ultimately served as a springboard for regional political activism, particularly around immigrant rights and environmental justice.[203]

But it was the local attachments of parents sustained over generations that proved to be the most enduring in South Gate. The role of parent propelled Latino residents—including the most marginalized—to find a place and voice in the community, beginning with the schools and laying the groundwork for political activism. By the late 1990s, they began asserting claims to the right to a decent quality of life. They reacted to a series of local crises with new political muscle, ousting a cabal of corrupt politicians at South Gate City Hall and rebuffing the construction of a power plant in the suburb. Such impressive civic activism bubbled up during times of crisis and then often receded, but what proved more enduring was a suburban political culture of Latino parents, refreshed with every new generation. South Gate's Latinos weren't self-identifying as white, but they were embracing a deeply rooted suburban ideal that promised a safe, healthy place to raise children and a piece of the American dream.[204]

Up From the Ashes, Into the Dream

In early August 1990, three South Gate city councilmen—all Anglo—traveled to the White House, where President George H. W. Bush would bestow the All-America City Award on South Gate. The award was given by the National Civic League to 10 cities that year for excellence in community leadership, citizen participation, government performance, civic education, community volunteerism, and philanthropy. What clinched the honor for South Gate was its narrative of successful economic revitalization and cultural integration, a trajectory playing out in numerous towns across the country where Latinos had moved into depressed urban and suburban areas.[205] South Gate offered a story of rising up from the ashes of deindustrialization and creating a renewed community life of small business success, public safety, and cultural integration. As part of a 10-minute pitch, Reverend George Jameson, along with Guatemalan immigrant Al Cristales, who rose from janitor to janitorial service proprietor, gave passionate speeches about all of the ways South Gate had successfully progressed through a difficult transition. They were compelling, if somewhat skewed, examples of the South Gate story.[206]

Twelve years later, a corruption scandal involving local political leaders drew a different sort of attention to South Gate. It culminated in an explosive recall election that drew national attention. At the center of the storm was city councilmember Albert Robles. After being elected to municipal office, Robles embarked on a brazen series of actions, including 500% pay raises, rampant cronyism, the fleecing of city coffers, flyers falsely accusing opponents of child molestation, elaborate gift giveaways, the abolition of civil service requirements, and even an assassination attempt on Henry Gonzalez. Sam Quinones characterized this as Mexican PRI-style politics transplanted to American suburbia, with corrupt officials able to rise and carry on because few were keeping watch.[207]

On the surface, it may seem impossible to square these radically contrasting episodes in South Gate's recent history. If South Gate had achieved the National Civic League's criteria such as excellence in community leadership and citizen participation, how could its residents have allowed a man like

Robles to rise to power and wreak such havoc on the community? The answer lies in the fractured nature of the suburb and town leaders' overestimation of their bridging of those divides. Deep fissures still existed between the Latino suburban establishment—mostly homeowning, acclimated, invested—and poorer immigrant residents who continued to occupy a more marginal position. The establishment was committed to reasserting a prosperous, respectable, suburban identity. Through spatial policies that protected an Anglo-style suburban landscape of highly regulated single-family homes, fiscal policies to attract Anglo retailers, and a commitment to decent schools, healthy neighborhoods, and traditional civic groups, leaders worked to restore a suburban aura to South Gate. A 2004 study reaffirmed a strong desire to protect its built landscape from high-density development, even though South Gate suffered from an affordable housing crisis.[208] The study measured success by metrics including homeownership, length of residence in the community, and participation in traditional civic institutions. This suburban context, however, erected barriers to full participation for all residents, particularly the immigrants who comprised half of the population in the 1990s.

That half, thus, defined South Gate's other identity as an immigrant gateway. Urban sociologist Manuel Pastor, part of a South Gate advisory group in 2004, observed that South Gate, above all, needed to embrace its role as an "immigrant platform." "Neighborhoods that people churn through become entry points. People are going to be there, and then as they do better and their life changes they are going to go someplace else. There should be a rethinking of what the standards for success are, and what makes your city a good platform for people to succeed. Stability is important but understanding that people churn through your neighborhood is also important."[209] In South Gate, that "churning through" continued into the new century, much as it had for decades. The ephemerality of that experience showed up in different ways—in the "pop-up" music venues organized by immigrant youth, in the short lifespan of certain groups like Madres of South Gate, and in the fleeting nature of illicit housing.

At the same time, immigrants began claiming a more permanent place in the suburb in ways that gradually reshaped its civic terrain. Despite the hard crackdown on informal housing, residents continued to adapt single-family homes into illicit garage and backyard conversions well into the new millennium.[210] In the process, participants created an unconventional, permanent space of affordable housing in the suburb.[211] No political movement around housing rights arose, no doubt because many tenants were undocumented, yet their persistent occupation of suburban space represented an important claim to a "right to the suburb."[212]

Immigrant parents continued to join the PTA and activist causes on be-half of their children's welfare. Focal points of political activism after 1990 included movements against busing, for environmentally healthy school sites, and for equity within the LAUSD. Latino parents also remained consistent, active volunteers in youth sports, particularly the Junior Athletic Association, which, according to one local official, drew the strongest volunteer energy in South Gate. The suburb's Latino parents put in long hours at work, "but they'll get here to coach their kids' teams."[213] Maria Davila, elected to the city council in 2003, perceived of South Gate as "an educational city"—with more schools than businesses.[214] Issues involving children offered the most inclusive, democratic common ground and had the greatest potential to bring together all residents.

Perhaps nothing symbolized South Gate's shift more than the Azalea Festival. In 2007, the 42-year-old festival began a transition from past to future. It inaugurated the first Miss Azaleita, awarded to a girl aged four to seven living in South Gate. The Azalea Queen and Grand Marshall hung on for another 11 years, then phased out for good due to lack of community interest, while Miss Azaleita endured.[215] This adaptation was a sign that Latinos were finally shifting local culture, reflecting the priorities of its residents, and building on the crucial suburban identity of "parent." This was the space where immigrants could participate and begin connecting to suburban lifeways, the local establishment, and even the spatial politics of beautification and housing code enforcement. This was a space where they became most invested in the suburban ideal, even as it was gradually Latinized in South Gate.

7

From Neighborhood Trust
to Neighborhood Watch

Lakewood

Lakewood occupies a prominent place in the annals of American suburban history.[1] Along with Levittown, New York, and Park Forest, Illinois, Lakewood was part of a troika that exemplified the postwar suburb in American life. Built rapidly after World War II using mass production techniques that astonished observers at every turn, Lakewood had a spotlight trained on it from its very inception. Journalists and photographers documented its "instant" construction, while postwar writers documented its way of life. Historians considered Lakewood a textbook example of the "sitcom suburb." And native son D. J. Waldie penned a highly acclaimed memoir, *Holy Land* (1996), that revealed a deeper dimension to lived realities in mass-produced suburbia, powerfully conveying that simple ticky-tacky house exteriors do not tell the whole story.[2]

Waldie's book contested the cottage industry of cultural, urban, and social criticism of the 1950s and 1960s that took aim at mass-produced suburbs like Lakewood. Writers like Lewis Mumford, David Riesman, and William Whyte decried the conformity that these places encouraged and argued that they fostered mindless residents who were susceptible to authoritarianism, which in the post-Nazi era raised deep alarms. This new mass-produced type of suburb, Mumford wrote memorably in 1961, represented "a multitude of uniform, unidentifiable houses, lined up inflexibly, at uniform distances, on uniform roads, in a treeless communal waste, inhabited by people of the same class, the same income, the same age group . . . conforming in every outward and inward respect to a common mold."[3] William Garnett's series of aerial photographs, commissioned by Lakewood's developers, portrayed the "mass" in suburban construction in almost chilling fashion, depicting the denuding of the natural landscape into a vast sea of identical homes.[4] A series of staged photographs in *Life* magazine showed what happened next: thousands of people bought homes, then moved in and settled in at the same time, all choreographed to convey the magnitude and uniformity of that experience. Reinforced by popular culture, scholars, and the mass media, the image of suburbia as a space of oppressive homogeneity and social conformity was frozen into the American psyche. This monolithic portrait became a stereotypical backdrop for countless movies and stories about heroes struggling to break free of this suffocating uniformity and its mentally unhealthy atmosphere.[5] This portrayal of suburbia persists to the present day.

The history of Lakewood challenges this narrative in powerful ways, revealing varied social histories and lived experiences within the monotonous exteriors. Over the decades, it transformed from an all-white middle-class

Figure 7.1 William Garnett aerial photos of Lakewood, 1952. Although Garnett was hired by the builders of Lakewood to document the marvels of its construction, these photos came to represent something more sinister and troubling, according to cultural and social critics.

The J. Paul Getty Museum, Los Angeles. William A. Garnett, Plaster and Roofing, Lakewood, California, 1950, Gelatin silver print, 7 11/16 x 9 9/16 in. © Estate of William A. Garnett.

suburb to one of LA's most racially balanced and culturally diverse cities. The undercurrents of this change, where increasingly diverse families aspired to similar things—safety, security, opportunity, and joy—defined many sitcom suburbs.[6] This truth in and of itself upended the simple axiom that uniform built landscapes spit out uniform people. By the 1980s and 1990s, a Black Lakewood family was less concerned about keeping up with the Joneses than with keeping their children shielded from racism and other harms.

Over its 70-year history, Lakewood's social and civic culture changed from a place marked by neighborhood trust to one of neighborhood watch. Early on, close-knit neighbors nurtured an environment of social trust and childhood freedom. Gradually, public safety, law enforcement, and surveillance became core community values. Neighbors became more guarded, and children lost the freedom to roam, protected by parents who feared for their safety—against criminals, gangs, abductors, and even racist neighbors. Racially speaking, the fears cut in all directions. Black parents moving into a lily-white suburb feared for their children's safety within a milieu of white anxiety and racism. White parents feared the gangs and crime—often associated with the mere presence of people of color—that seemed to be closing in on them. By the 1970s and 1980s, Lakewood experienced its own "suburban crisis," as racial segregation crumbled, economic downturns and dislocation threatened family security, suburban housewives joined the workforce, and rising crime unsettled peace of mind. These local conditions reflected national trends, catalyzing reactions that included law-and-order politics, bipartisan pro-suburban politics, overpolicing of communities of color, and racialized mass incarceration.[7] In Lakewood, the law-and-order reaction reshaped community culture and the ways residents navigated the fragile process of racial integration. As a basis of social and civic engagement, law-and-order culture proved a tenuous foundation for community cohesion.

Policing in Lakewood ultimately emerged as a racial flashpoint, just as it did in LA's urban areas and nationally. Local law enforcement fell into patterns that often conflated blackness with criminality and treated whites as victims in need of protection.[8] As sociologist Andrea Boyles found, these policing biases were more intensely expressed in white suburban settings.[9] As law and order became more prevalent in Lakewood, unequal policing undermined community trust and inclusive democracy. These biases were shared by some city leaders and residents whose attitudes created formidable social barriers for people of color.

Located in Southeast Los Angeles, Lakewood is situated among a constellation of suburbs that spanned races and ethnicities. This area would become ground zero of multiracial suburbia in Los Angeles, containing the greatest number of "racially balanced" towns in LA County by 2010, meaning they had significant four-way mixes of whites, Blacks, Asians, and Latinos.[10] Nearby Bellflower, Carson, and Artesia shared Lakewood's history of rapid postwar building followed by intensive demographic change within a few decades, while Cerritos was described by one reporter as "little more than an expensive copy of Lakewood."[11] Just five to eight miles away lay Compton and the gateways suburbs, communities undergoing enormous racial and economic change. Lakewood and its surrounding suburbs shared political, criminal justice, infrastructure, and school districts. Lakewood became known as an aspirational destination for upwardly mobile people of color across south and Southeast LA. By 2004, the 13-square-mile area bordering Lakewood was deemed among the nation's most linguistically diverse territories, with 39 languages spoken, including Chinese, Japanese, Korean, Tagalog, Gujarati, Hindi, Urdu, and Spanish. In the ABC School District, covering parts of Lakewood, Hawaiian Gardens, Artesia, Cerritos, and Norwalk, at least 53 languages were spoken. These many cultures could both intertwine and collide. Food and personal care service might bring people together. Law enforcement and social relations could be more fraught. For example, when a Chinese Filipino man was pulled over and refused to look the police officer in the eye, the officer felt disrespected and became more aggressive until the man's Mexican American friend explained he was in fact showing respect.[12]

Just a few miles from Lakewood's borders, Black Americans began moving into suburbs like Compton and Lynwood, and the nearby gateway suburbs flipped from white to Latino after 1980. As this pattern of ethnoracial transformation encroached, white anxieties ran high. Lakewood ultimately emerged as a racially balanced city since its original white residents tended to stay put rather than follow other suburbs' wholesale white flight. It signaled community loyalty that endured through the generations, even despite the stresses of social transformation.[13]

Lakewood's history was shaped powerfully by the national and regional political economy. Writer Joan Didion summarized it well: in the early postwar years, Lakewood stood at the nexus of "two powerfully conceived national interests, that of keeping the economic engine running and that of creating an enlarged middle class." To meet these twin goals, the federal government

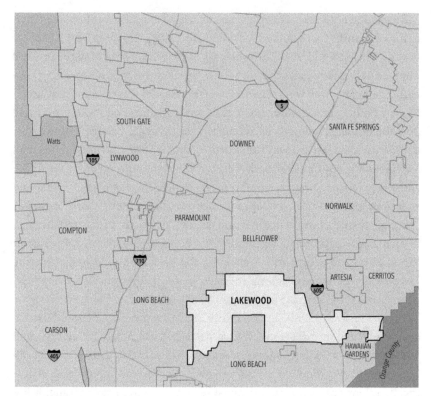

Figure 7.2 Map of Lakewood and surrounding suburban communities.
Cartography by Jennifer Mapes, Kent State University.

poured millions into defense spending in Southern California, which flowed into plants such as nearby Douglas, Hughes, and Rockwell and the Long Beach naval station and shipyard. Federal housing programs enabled white veterans and blue-collar families to purchase homes, thrusting them into the suburban middle class. This flush era shaped a conviction among these families that economic and social mobility "worked exclusively upward," as Didion put it. After 1980, when federal retrenchment ushered in a new "era of limits," Lakewood's once-solid basis of prosperity for local families began to falter.[14] This occurred, moreover, at the very moment Lakewood began racially diversifying.

More than most places, Lakewood has been highly conscious of narrating and controlling its story. It hired public relations experts to describe Lakewood's creation and in subsequent years maintained a first-rate public information office that wrote the town's history, curated its archive, and made material available to the public. Its booster narrative told a tale of progress that acknowledged some blemishes along the way but ultimately reached a positive, celebratory conclusion. Capturing mainly white voices, it elevated the "original" residents—of the 1950s—and their values.[15]

The ways that residents themselves remembered Lakewood offered numerous alternatives to this official account. Some original white residents adopted a narrative of declension—celebrating the golden era of the 1950s, then lamenting its perceived decline.[16] Other original residents embraced the change. For some new residents of color, the story was one of the American Dream achieved, marked by joy and love for Lakewood that seemed to echo the enthusiasm of Lakewood's first white residents. Others harbored memories of racism and discrimination. Despite the existence of multiple perceptions, the nostalgia-laden experience of the original settlers of Lakewood rose to dominate the official story. This reinforced the status quo and made it harder to change course when new conditions and needs arose.[17] For Lakewood, official local history served to perpetuate white power-holding in the community while masking simmering racism, unsettling residents who thought they had a safe and welcoming place in the suburb.

Demographer Dowell Myers claimed that post-1980 Los Angeles had "two competing stories. . . . One is that it's very segregated and there is a lot of hostility between groups. That's very wrong, but people want to hold onto it. The other story is that LA is diverse and people live close together with very little friction."[18] Reality lies somewhere between these extremes. Lakewood is a textbook example of that middle ground.

The Creation of Lakewood

The land that became Lakewood was part of the broad flat flood plain between the Los Angeles and San Gabriel Rivers. Natural aquifers lay underground and at times burst forth in earlier centuries, creating artesian wells. While this general area was originally home to the Tongva people, archeological evidence suggests indigenous people did not inhabit the immediate Lakewood area. These lands passed through the hands of colonial settlers after the 1770s—from Spanish, to Mexican, to American by the 1850s—and became Rancho Los Cerritos and Rancho Los Amigos by the 1850s, owned by Abel Stearns and Juan Temple. Ownership changed several times over the following decades, and, in the late nineteenth century, the land was used for sheep grazing. By 1904, new owners named the land the Montana Ranch and over the years grew sugar beets, alfalfa, barley, and beans on 3,500 acres, with another 3,000 acres devoted to truck farms, dairies, hog sheds, and pastures for thousands of cows and sheep. In the 1920s, it was still highly productive farm and pasture lands.[19]

As the conversion of farmland to suburban tracts intensified in LA during the 1920s, the lands around Lakewood were drawn into this process. New suburban tracts with modest dwellings in Wilmington, Signal Hill, and Long Beach housed oil well workers, longshoremen, and their families. Petroleum Gardens, developed in the 1920s, promised "Beautiful Homesites—All Oil Rights Included," although the lots were tiny.[20] Meanwhile, Montana Ranch's new owner, Clark J. Bonner, began contemplating what to do with his land as beet production declined and the sugar mill was shuttered in 1926. When the 1929 stock market crash nixed Bonner's idea of creating an industrial tract, he turned instead to suburban subdivision.[21]

Launching a real estate venture just as the Great Depression hit nearly doomed Bonner's plan. Still, he persisted and in so doing instigated Lakewood's suburban beginnings. Bonner's first idea was a development called the Lakewood Country Club Estates, envisioned as a high-end enclave of large, handsome homes adjacent to a planned golf course, an elite refuge for nearby Long Beach. Bonner chose the name Lakewood to connote money and exclusivity, after the posh New Jersey resort where his uncle owned an estate. The subdivision was announced in 1932, but the venture quickly fizzled during the Depression winter of 1932–1933 and the Long Beach earthquake of March 1933. Bonner proceeded to build the golf course and put the Estates idea on pause for more prosperous times. By earmarking a space for affluent residents, the stage was set for some class diversity within Lakewood.[22]

Responding to economic realities, Bonner pivoted to a modest proposal for a new Lakewood Village, a development of semi-sustaining suburban homesteads at affordable prices. He would sell two- and three-bedroom homes on half-acre lots for about $700 at low-interest monthly payments of $30–40, with gardens for growing fruits and vegetables. A few years in, only 50 lots had sold. By 1940, Lakewood Village had just over 2,000 residents, including naval officers, businessmen, professionals, and junior executives.[23]

As wartime housing demand skyrocketed, builders in Lakewood responded by constructing assorted small-scale subdivisions, such as County Club Estates, Mayfair, Lakewood City, and Lakewood Gardens. They were built by

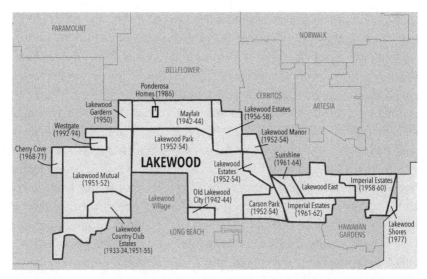

Figure 7.3 Map of the sections of Lakewood. From its inception, Lakewood had some class diversity within its borders, from the more affluent Country Club Estates neighborhood to the more modest sections in central Lakewood.

Cartography by Jennifer Mapes, Kent State University; based on City of Lakewood "General Plan" map, ca. 1994, Iacaboni Library, Lakewood.

different developers, on a relatively modest scale. The new housing helped alleviate the desperate needs of incoming defense workers who, in 1941, were being hired at the rate of 13,000 per month in Los Angeles.[24] Bonner also sold 200 acres to the Douglas Aircraft Company, which broke ground on a factory in November 1940. By war's end in 1945, 3,500 homes had been erected in Lakewood's three main tracts—Lakewood Village, Mayfair, and Lakewood City. Two years later, another 450 homes went up in the Lakewood Gardens tract. This patchwork of Lakewood developments, with hundreds of new structures, typified the relatively small scale of suburban building still prevalent in the mid-1940s. It exemplified, as well, the racial segregation of this era, as all developments were available only to whites, with race restrictions firmly and openly in place.[25]

Clark Bonner remained the driving force behind these developments. When he died unexpectedly of a cerebral hemorrhage in 1947, at the age of 57, Lakewood's history took a radical turn. Bonner's widow sold off the remaining 3,400 acres of the Montana Land Company two years later, and a new era began.[26]

The land buyer was the newly formed Lakewood Park Corporation (LPC), part of an emergent class of large-scale developer-builders that built entire communities. The LPC would launch one of the largest mass-produced suburban developments in the nation, using the same techniques as Levittown and Park Forest. The LPC's Louis Boyar, Mark Taper, and Ben Weingart secured over $100 million in federal construction loans and mortgage guarantees, while risking only $15,000 of their personal money. Ultimately, they made about $12 million from the development of Lakewood Park.[27]

After breaking ground in February 1950, the LPC began mass-producing homes at the rapid clip of 100 per day. The scene was like one huge, open-air house-building factory, where crews performed their discrete specialized task, moving from one house to the next. The result was a mind-spinning pace of productivity: by 1953, 17,500 homes were completed, and by 1957, Lakewood's population was approaching 70,000, double the size of Levittown, NY. *Time* magazine claimed Lakewood was the largest housing development in the world at the time. The result was a vast expanse of streets laid out on a grid, homes packed tightly on 50 × 100-foot lots on block after block, typically 46 homes to a block. Density in Lakewood Park was higher than in

Figure 7.4 Lakewood homes built on an assembly-line basis, 1950. Precut lumber was delivered in precise quantities to each home site to speed up construction. Crews of workers performed specialized tasks, like laying foundations, then moved onto the next home to do the same.
Photo courtesy of the City of Lakewood Historical Collection.

older suburbs, eight homes per acre versus five in prewar subdivisions.[28] The whole place had a feeling of newness and innovation, captured in Lakewood's town motto: "Tomorrow's City Today."

The homes of Lakewood Park were basic, with 13 simple floor plans to choose from. Two-bedroom homes were 800 square feet, three-bedrooms were 1,100 square feet. Buyers could purchase a refrigerator, gas range, and washing machine on a monthly installment plan added onto the mortgage. The terms for purchase made them cheaper than rent in many parts of LA. In 1951, a two-bedroom Lakewood home sold for $7,575, with a down-payment of $595 and monthly payments of $43. A three-bedroom sold for $8,525. Veterans on the G.I. Bill had no down payment requirement. For Verna and Barney Foley, it was an easy decision to trade their $75/month apartment in LA for a three-bedroom home in Lakewood with a monthly mortgage payment of $58.06.[29] They were members of the wage-earning middle class, or what *Architectural Forum* dubbed "the FHA class."[30]

Figure 7.5 A mass-produced home in Lakewood Park, 1950. The homes of Lakewood were modest and affordable, appealing to the tens of thousands of veterans and their families in the region desperate for housing after World War II.

Photo courtesy of the City of Lakewood Historical Collection.

In terms of community planning, the LPC's record was mixed. Lakewood was overwhelmingly residential, with only 6% of land zoned for business and other land earmarked for schools, parks, places of worship, and shopping. In contrast to master planned communities in LA like Westchester and Panorama City—which integrated homes, retail, and industry—in Lakewood, industry was more of an adjacent presence than a planned component.[31] Lakewood had the Douglas plant at its southern border, but other factories were not integrated in the LPC's original designs. It fared better in planning for retail. The most innovative elements were Lakewood Center Mall and 16 neighborhood shopping centers meant to be within walking distance (defined as a half-mile) of every home, enabling carless housewives to shop during the day. Located at intersections of major streets, these small centers would include a dry cleaner, barber, beauty salon, and either drugstore or five-and-dime; many had a grocery store. Lakewood Center Mall, the first regional mall built in Southern California, was conceived to draw in not just future Lakewood residents but shoppers from all over south LA. Anchored by the May Company, which helped design the mall, Lakewood Center included shops, restaurants, a movie theater, bowling alley, and grocery stores, as well as offices, a 250-bed hospital, library, post office, banks, county offices, and city hall. The mall became a cash cow for Lakewood, buoying municipal finances for decades and earning handsome profits for the LPC, which held 99-year leases on the mall.[32]

In terms of suburban infrastructure, the LPC provided basics like concrete sidewalks, street paving, and 5,000 concrete light posts, and it designed separator streets that ran parallel to major thoroughfares as a buffer for kids and families living on these blocks. The developers fell short when it came to parks despite their early promises to prioritize green space. In the early years, kids played in the streets, riverbeds, and drainage ditches, resulting in several accidental deaths. For Lakewood, park planning ultimately was in the hands of city leaders.[33] These elements illustrated the mixed record of the LPC, typical of postwar mass developers who built quickly and generally sought to maximize profits through the ownership of retail land and sale of homes while minimizing public space and public services.[34]

Beyond community planning and home designs, Lakewood's developers also shaped the suburb's racial profile. In the earliest tracts like the Country Club Estates and Lakewood Village, race restrictions were honored and advertised. By 1939, federal appraisers described "racial protection in perpetuity" in Lakewood Village.[35] Although race-restrictive covenants were outlawed by the Supreme Court in 1948, local developers found ways to circumvent the ruling. For one, the LPC simply refused to sell to Blacks, Mexicans, Jews, or Asians, including veterans. Lakewood Park sales manager Woody Smith described the process.

> [P]eople would cancel by the score if they knew there was a black person going to have a house on their block. . . . If there was a colored person in [the sales office], they'd start whispering. . . . The salesmen were scared of them. And when one would come and he was getting to the point where he wanted to buy, they used to turn them over to me and I used to have to do the p.r. I'd sit down and talk to them. I'd say, "Now, you're a reasonable person but these are the facts of life, and you know it as well as I do: if you move in there, you're not going to have any neighbors that are going to like you. It may not be in your best interest, so you better think about it carefully before you make this decision."[36]

While some Mexican American veterans were refused outright, others were told they would be considered if they self-identified as Spanish.[37] The NAACP chastised the LPC for these practices and also blasted LA County for purchasing land for a civic center in Lakewood Village, putting the County "in the position of assenting to racial discrimination."[38] Rising diversity surrounding Lakewood seemed to heighten local perceptions of racial threats. As the African American population in Long Beach grew and Japanese and Mexicans settled in the farm communities of nearby Norwalk, Artesia, and Bellflower, these families planted the roots of Southeast LA's diversity while also stoking anxiety in the new white "instant" suburbs like Lakewood.[39]

From the start, the creators of Lakewood self-consciously elevated the image of their project to something much greater than a real estate venture. They promoted Lakewood as a phenomenon.[40] The LPC hired Don Rochlen as Lakewood's first public relations director and Bobbe Frankenberg as assistant director to tell the story of "instant" construction in the most favorable way. While Foote, Cone & Belding devised the ads, Rochlen and Frankenberg wrote numerous feature stories and planted them at national publications like *Time*, *Look*, *Life*, *Women's Wear Daily*, and the *Christian Science Monitor*, resulting in a few cover stories. They used photography—often staged—to great effect. The PR team also hosted visitors from around the world to witness the miracle of Lakewood and bring home lessons in community building. Frankenberg hired buses with PA systems to take out groups of 20 visitors to traverse the streets of Lakewood and stop at homes where enthusiastic residents would welcome them with cake, tea, and coffee. "They were amazed that this was a workingman's home," complete with appliances and amenities, Frankenberg recalled.[41] Reversing the direction of messaging of the famous "Kitchen Debate" in Moscow which brought American suburbia to the world, in the early 1950s the PR team brought the world to Lakewood.[42]

Lakewood was incorporated in 1954, a process that reflected the twin goals of parsimony and local control. Residents wanted local control yet feared the higher taxes that would come with incorporation, a reasonable worry for families teetering on the edge of the middle class. Concerns over land use had already emerged in 1953, when residents protested the placement of an "honor farm"—a rehab facility for alcoholics—near the Lakewood tracts but failed to stop the facility from being built.[43] Exacerbating worries were efforts by Long Beach to annex Lakewood. When the newly formed Lakewood Committee for Incorporation hatched a plan in 1953 to contract for services on the cheap from LA County instead of the new city setting up its own expensive infrastructure, many cost-conscious residents were persuaded that incorporation might be a good idea.[44] Incorporation became the ultimate "have your cake and eat it too" solution. PR man Don Rochlen organized kaffeeklatches to promote the idea of incorporation and screen his recently produced film "The Lakewood Story." Local housewives knocked on doors to spread the word. Even before cityhood was declared, 39 nine city council hopefuls entered the race and joined in those kaffeeklatches. The collective "propaganda" campaign ultimately helped incorporation pass by a 3–2 margin, a decisive but not overwhelming victory, suggesting lingering doubts about independent cityhood for Lakewood driven mainly by economic anxieties.[45]

The practice of contracting for services from LA County became known as the Lakewood Plan. The suburb's early leaders saw it as a pathbreaking innovation and model for municipalities nationwide. The plan entailed contracting for a number of services at cut-rate prices, including law enforcement (through the LA County Sheriff's Department [LASD]), street maintenance, and building safety inspection, and securing fire protection, libraries, and waste-water treatment through County-based special districts. Trash collection, traffic signal and street light maintenance, tree trimming, and street sweeping were outsourced to private firms. Instead of forming its own unified school district, Lakewood piggy-backed onto neighboring school

Mass Moving Re-enacted for Benefit of Magazine Photographer

Figure 7.6 The staging and final version of the "moving vans" photo in Lakewood for *Life* Magazine, 1953. Bobbe Frankenberg and Don Rochlen of the LPC's public relations team were instrumental in staging publicity photos of Lakewood, like this one. The photographer wanted to capture blocks of new families moving in, so Frankenberg called moving van companies—about 40 were "anxious to get in the picture"—and they rigged up a fire truck with an extension ladder to help get the perfect angle. The result was "moving day," which ran in *Life* magazine in 1953.

(top) Photo courtesy of the City of Lakewood Historical Collection; (bottom) "A New Mayor, a New Councilwoman . . . and 400 New Angels Every Day," *Life* 35, 2 (July 13, 1953), 24. J. R. Eyerman/The LIFE Picture Collection/Shutterstock.

districts—the ultimate cost-saving measure.[46] While solving the suburb's immediate needs, the Lakewood Plan was highly controversial with critics who
charged that privileged white suburbanites took what they needed from the
County while shirking a broader responsibility for the County's overall fiscal
health. This critique grew stronger as more suburbs, many of them all white,
followed Lakewood's example.[47]

This municipal culture rooted in the Lakewood Plan persisted with mixed
consequences. On the one hand, thrifty city budgets and efficient service delivery continued to appeal to tax-conscious residents. Over the generations,
as more and more suburbs became racially balanced—and kept the contract
city system in place—they too benefitted from these fiscal advantages. On
the other hand, Lakewood residents lost something when they outsourced
services. Policing, for example, became a more transactional enterprise than
community-based presence. The LA Sheriff's Department serviced dozens
of communities across LA County, and the Lakewood Sheriff Station alone
policed several suburbs, pulling Lakewood into the broader Southeast
orbit whether it wanted that or not. As well, by relinquishing local control
over public education, Lakewood lost a crucial community hub. Low taxes
through the Lakewood Plan, then, unintentionally led to weakened local
control and even some degree of social disconnection.

By 1954, incorporation essentially unified a collection of housing
subdivisions into one municipality of over 60,000 residents, instantly making
it the 16th largest city in California. In 1960, 95% of dwellings were single-
family homes, and most households were middle class. The mass-produced
tracts built by the LPC occupied the broad center of town, surrounded by
smaller tracts like Mayfair, Carson Park, and Lakewood Gardens. The biggest
outlier was Country Club Estates, with its luxury custom-built homes
costing up to $150,000 in 1954. Along the edges, new tracts were added after
1960, including Cherry Cove, Lakewood East, and Imperial Estates. Eastern
Lakewood had older homes, some owner-built homes, substandard lot sizes,
and lower-income neighborhoods. Some tiny lots from the old Petroleum
Gardens subdivision survived in eastern Lakewood. To the west, Cherry
Cove was notable for its ethnoracial diversity by the 1970s. These tracts at
the edges of Lakewood eventually included apartments and people of color.[48]

Lakewood created an appealing formula for middle-class suburban
living: affordable homes, low taxes, and a semblance of local control, all
facilitated through the careful cultivation of community image. Never a
wealthy suburb, it represented a landing pad for families of modest means

seeking a safe and well-maintained community, a reputation that remained remarkably consistent over the generations and appealed to an increasingly diverse range of homebuyers.

Domestic Idyll: Everyday Life in Postwar Lakewood, 1950–1960s

For the white families who populated postwar Lakewood, everyday life offered a friendly, family-oriented, and socially comfortable environment. Newcomers poured in from other states, other parts of California, and nearby suburbs, growing the suburb from 15,000 to 67,000 between 1949 and 1960.[49] Postwar Lakewood exuded an energetic excitement, a feeling that residents were pioneering a new way of life in their tight-knit neighborhoods, reinforced by white exclusivity and a shared experience of family formation.[50]

Lakewood's original residents were 96% white, predominantly native-born members of nuclear families. About one-third came from the border South—Oklahoma, Arkansas, Texas, Missouri, some the children of Dust Bowl migrants.[51] Only seven African Americans lived in Lakewood in 1960, and they were all female, suggesting they may have been live-in help in the elite sections of town.[52] Latinos and Asians had a slightly easier time breaking the color line. Latino residents, who were mostly American born and middle class, gained some acceptance and remained the largest nonwhwhite group in subsequent decades. Among the early pioneers were the Baca family. Bill's second-generation Mexican American parents bought a home there in 1955 through the GI Bill. Typical of other early Latino families, they spoke English only, both worked outside the home, and they were relatively well-to-do.[53] By the end of the 1960s, people of color comprised 10% of Lakewood's population—including 107 African Americans—while immigrants were less than 5% of the population.[54]

Postwar Lakewood also skewed young. The average age of residents in 1960 was 25 for men and 26.7 for women, and the average household size was 3.8 persons, higher than the LA County average of 2.9. In 1960, children made up fully 45% of the population and seniors only 3%. Although the LPC targeted veterans in its initial marketing, by 1960 male veterans only slightly outnumbered non-veterans.[55]

Religion and politics also placed Lakewood in the moderate middle. The predominant religious denominations were Protestant and Catholic, with a smaller number of Jews (an estimated 3,000–5,000 in 1955). Voter registration rolls from 1962 to 1970 indicated that 65% to 60% of residents were registered Democrats.[56]

A decent-paying job—whether in a factory or office—was often enough to pull a family into the ranks of the suburban middle class. By income, Lakewood fell within the top half of all municipalities in LA County.[57] Managers and professionals (20.3%) and sales and clerical (27.4%) made up Lakewood's white-collar sector. Among men, blue-collar workers predominated in 1960. An estimated 3,800 worked in aircraft and aerospace, many of them at the nearby Douglas Aircraft plant or North American Aviation in Downey. The percentage of married women working outside the home rose from 32% to 41% from 1960 to 1970, reflecting national trends. They took jobs as factory workers (some at Douglas), secretaries, salespersons, waitresses, and teachers. They earned less than one-third as men, suggesting that families were not getting rich from women's paid labor.[58] But their income was essential to family budgets.

Despite these middle-class signs, life in Lakewood was not always flush.[59] Lakewood families often struggled to pay the bills, and some had experienced recent poverty. Economic insecurity underlay concerns about taxes and compelled families to cut corners by devising strategies for stretching family budgets, like DIY home maintenance or having mothers take up paid work.[60] Another sign of the marginal class position of residents was education: only 6% of residents were college graduates in 1960, while the largest cohort (42%) had not completed high school. Nonetheless, homeownership was high in Lakewood—85% in 1960. Together, these traits suggested a population earning middle-class paychecks and owning homes yet showing certain working-class traits.

Notwithstanding the trend toward female employment in the 1950s and 1960s, the majority of women were homemakers who played a critical role in fostering a safe, open environment of neighborly togetherness and childhood freedom.[61] They forged strong community ties through socializing, a culture of mutual aid, and local activism around family issues. For Lakewood housewives, everyday life was an endless round of housework, childcare, shopping, and economizing. Many stretched the family budget by sewing their family's clothes, cooking from scratch, borrowing from and lending to neighbors, and taking in work like ironing and babysitting. For the MacHale family, they opted to buy a two-bedroom instead of a three-bedroom home

Table 7.1 Demographic and social characteristics of Lakewood residents, 1960–2010

	1960		1970		1980		1990		2000		2010	
	number	%	number	%	number	%	number	%	number	%	number	%
Population total	67,126	100.0	83,025	100.0	74,654	100.0	73,557	100.0	79,345	100.0	80,048	100.0
Race/ethnicity												
White non-Hispanic	64,514	96.1	74,238	89.4	61,085	81.8	53,296	72.5	41,577	52.4	32,774	40.9
Black	7	0.0	107	0.1	1,494	2.0	2,606	3.5	5,825	7.3	6,663	8.3
Hispanic	2,477	3.7	7,787	9.4	8,630	11.6	10,526	14.3	18,071	22.8	24,101	30.1
Asian	77	0.1	673	0.8	2,209	3.0	6,529	8.9	10,716	13.5	12,811	16.0
Nativity												
Native born	64,270	95.7	78,792	94.9	68,659	92.0	64,038	87.1	64,287	81.0	62,857	78.5
Foreign born	2,856	4.3	3,955	4.8	5,995	8.0	9,519	12.9	15,125	19.1	17,002	21.2
Occupations												
White collar	11,387	47.7	16,743	49.9	20,478	55.0	24,093	64.5	23,908	64.0	26,665	66.9
Blue collar	10,058	42.2	13,046	38.9	12,572	33.8	9,325	25.0	8,611	23.1	7,371	18.5
Service	1,633	6.9	3,702	11.0	3,906	10.5	3,584	9.6	4,832	12.9	5,808	14.6
Females in labor force	7,392	33.5	12,797	44.9	16,784	56.7	17,354	59.0	18,802	59.8	20,824	63.6
Married females in labor force *	5,257	31.8	8,128	41.3	9,088	51.0	6,411	68.6	7,658	70.4	10,714	64.4

Note: Percentages calculated out of total population, except for occupations where it is calculated out of all adult workers, unless otherwise indicated.

*shown as a percentage of all married women over 16. For 1990 and 2000, data is for mothers in the labor force.

so they could afford to have Janet stay home with the kids; she didn't want to go out to work.[62]

Lois Smith was representative.[63] Born in rural Iowa in 1931, Lois grew up in a poor family and continued to struggle financially into adulthood. After marrying in 1950, she and her husband Jay moved to Omaha, Nebraska, and had two children. Jay worked with his father in the cattle business but didn't earn much. Lois recalled her mother sending them chicken broth so Lois could make noodle soup. She skipped trips to the pediatrician to save money. In February 1960, the Smiths decided to seek a better life in California. They loaded their furniture, beds, and household goods onto a truck and intended to avoid the cost of motels and restaurants by driving all night and packing their own food. The truck broke down six times along the snowy and icy journey, and money was running out. When they finally arrived, exhausted and bedraggled, Lois recalled, it felt as if they had come by covered wagon.

The family first rented a two-bedroom, one-bath home in Long Beach, which to Lois felt like "a castle." In 1964, they had saved enough to move into Lakewood, near Jay's brother. Lois had imagined California as a land of palm trees, sunshine, and white picket fences, and Lakewood did not disappoint. As the family's finances remained tight, she took in ironing and babysat the neighbor's kids. Trips to a local diner were rare. When her children were in sixth and eighth grade, Jay's pay was cut and Lois took a job outside the home, which would have been looked down upon for a married woman in Iowa. The job gave her independence and shifted Jay's attitudes in the process.

Lois especially appreciated Lakewood's neighborly culture, a stark contrast to her more isolated life in Iowa. "I wanted the people . . . I enjoyed having neighbors around me." Neighbors brought a feeling of security, in good times and bad. When Jay suffered a brain aneurysm soon after they moved in, the neighbors immediately stepped in to babysit their children and advise Lois on seeking medical care. Some of them became very good friends. While Lois participated in the PTA, her main focus was her family and job. For the first time in her adult life, she registered to vote, associating the Republican Party with her priorities of family and security. It was all about "a protective feeling . . . I just felt in my mind that this was the way to go to protect my family."

Lois Smith's life embodied the experience of many women in postwar Lakewood, a suburb that was family-focused, neighborly, resourceful, and a source of security and comfort for their children. As D. J. Waldie recalled his Lakewood childhood, "All was right in the world: dad went to work, mom stayed home, kids went to school, kids came home from school, mom looked after you, looked after all the kids who might drift in and out of your home, made dinner, and that's how the world went." By extending a bubble of warmth and safety in neighborhoods, Lakewood families created an open environment where children could roam and play, secure in the feeling that caring adults were always nearby. Its mothers were suburbia's "eyes on the street," belying the image of suburbia as a social wasteland painted by critics like Jane Jacobs.[64] "It was as if every mother in your neighborhood was your mother," recalled D. J. Waldie.[65] Anne Pechin Emigh, whose mother worked, remembered, "There were always moms home during the day. . . . The block was like a family, extended family." Sandra Jenkins Janich stated that neighbor parents not only looked after local children but reported on their bad behavior as well.[66] This collective social oversight grew out of the routines of everyday life.

Neighborhoods were also spaces of robust socializing and mutual aid. Margie Lehner Armstrong, whose family moved there in 1955, reflected on her tight-knit block of 16 homes with 33 children. One man across the street, who worked in construction, brought home used bricks, and at night the fathers would get together to clean the bricks and use them to build planters and even a fireplace. The fathers socialized frequently, visiting each other's homes for coffee after dinner to brainstorm business ideas and talk politics. Many of the mothers gathered to sew and socialize, and they helped each other, such as when Margie's mother drove a neighbor to the hospital when she went into labor. Other residents recalled frequent block parties, barbecues, card parties, and get-togethers. "There was a kind of small village feeling, in that everybody knew everybody else," Margie recalled. A strong sense of interdependence prevailed, and a "uniform pattern of casual but warm friendliness and co-operation" defined everyday life in this and other sitcom suburbs.[67] Resident Shirley Williams recognized the importance of Lakewood's insular environment to this communal culture: "Everybody kind of looked out for each other. But it was well-buffered from people who were not homeowners, who lived in apartments and maybe blighted areas and things like that. We were well-buffered from all of that in Lakewood, pretty much."[68]

Postwar women translated their family caretaking concerns into civic activism to maintain Lakewood's infrastructure as a "safe haven for families and young children," as historian Allison Baker has demonstrated.[69] They mobilized around issues like childcare, traffic safety, civil defense, school construction, parks, and recreation, community priorities valued in other mass-produced suburbs.[70] More than Lakewood's male political leaders, women were the driving force in creating a family-friendly suburb.[71]

Parks, sports, and recreation were a crucial pillar of this effort. When Lakewood took over park planning from the LPC, its survey of residents recommended creating a park or recreation facility within a quarter mile of every home that could be reached without crossing any busy streets. To fulfill this mandate, in 1957 Lakewood formed a Park and Recreation Commission—the one major exception to outsourcing under the Lakewood Plan—to oversee a robust program.[72] Mothers took turns supervising the "tot lots" where toddlers could be dropped off. They coached sports, formed booster clubs for park teams, and launched a three-year campaign to build a youth center for local teens. A few women also rose to positions of leadership, serving on the board of directors of the early Lakewood Park, Recreation and Parkway District.[73] The end result was 12 parks in Lakewood easily accessible to children, and Parks and Rec programs that were either free to residents or available at a nominal fee.[74]

Together, these efforts created a safe public sphere for Lakewood's youngsters, allowing them to roam, explore, and play, which they often did in groups. Lakewood's "original kids" have vivid memories of this freedom. At age six, Mike Rae went alone to the park across the street from his house—he would get there when it opened and come home when it closed—and his mother never worried about him. He played ping-pong, field hockey, ball tag, and chess, and "there was always somebody there supervising."[75] Keith Sharon recalled playing in the neighborhood on a daily basis, starting at age five. "School, my street, and the park were the cornerstones of my life. . . . The town was so set up for us." He rode his bike freely all over Lakewood. His parents, both of whom worked, didn't need to supervise him because there were always caring adults around.[76] Harry Henderson observed the same freedom in other sitcom suburbs, where children were "healthy, merry, energetic, out-of-door most of the time, and less dependent on adults . . . [they] respond to this environment as though given a new source of oxygen."[77]

Lakewood's parents were so easy-going and trusting that the city felt compelled to implore them to step up supervision of their children. To promote this, city leaders supported family togetherness through programmed activities for families, but parents weren't convinced. From 1958 to 1960, there was plenty of hand wringing about the lack of parental participation in Parks and Rec programs. At a 1960 city council meeting, city administrator

Figure 7.7 Lakewood children at Mayfair Park, under construction in 1957.
Photo courtesy of the City of Lakewood Historical Collection.

Henry Goerlick admonished the 110 adults in attendance: "You people must face up to your responsibilities. . . . Parents should know where their children are, but too often the teenagers don't even know where their parents are."[78] This rebuke was part of the broader conversation around juvenile delinquency, which blamed parents, especially mothers, for working and being absent, or for not working and being overly stultifying.[79] Actual cases of juvenile delinquency were miniscule in Lakewood, but a perception persisted that parents were giving their children too much freedom.[80] In truth, parents' trust in Lakewood underscored their trust in one another, a consequence of living in a racially and socially homogenous community.

Among Lakewood adults, organized groups also began creating social unity based on shared values, racial identity, and social class. Adding to older groups established in Lakewood Village like the Taxpayers Association, Lions Club, and Chamber of Commerce, new residents formed groups at the rate of one a week in 1953, including a Planning Council to organize the organizations. Some focused on the incorporation debate, including several taxpayer associations. Others had staying power, including civic groups like the Rotary Club, Optimists, Moose Club, Elks Club, American Legion, Veterans of Foreign Wars, the Jewish War Veterans, League of Women Voters, and various ladies' auxiliaries of the service clubs. Youth-oriented organizations included the Scouts, Lakewood Youth Council, Boys Club, and Junior League Baseball Club. Residents also formed the Lakewood Community Players and a book club. Sports and recreation also drew adult energy as parents volunteered as coaches, organized booster clubs, and participated in sports and activities themselves. John Rae recalled a men's club of volunteer coaches that met regularly at a park to socialize. Volunteer enthusiasm was so strong, he noted, that if he didn't get there early enough, he wouldn't get a team to coach. Women participated in housewives' leagues for softball, volleyball, and tennis. Lakewood's county-run golf course attracted a wide cross-section of players—laborers, aircraft workers, lawyers, business executives, and housewives—by the late 1950s. Social and civic life also reinforced the notion of a Greater Lakewood as tracts like Lakewood Village (technically part of Long Beach) remained a part of Lakewood life. Lakewood Village housed the Lakewood Chamber of Commerce offices, headquarters of Lakewood's major newspaper, two shopping areas, many of its churches, Lakewood's only

Figure 7.8 Lakewood square-dancers at Mayfair Park, 1956. In the postwar years, the social homogeneity of the suburb's residents—by race and class— eased the way for neighborly trust and social cohesion.

Photo courtesy of the City of Lakewood Historical Collection.

fire station, and its largest park (Pan Am Park). As was true of many suburbs, voluntarism was a pathway to local respect and influence, often a stepping-stone to local political power.[81]

Another hub of everyday life was the Lakewood Center Mall, where people walked, ate a meal, met friends, and shopped. On weekdays, it was a mostly female world. Malls eventually became central to Americans' leisure time. A 1973 study in *U.S. News & World Report* found people of all ages spent the most time in shopping centers, after work, school, and home.[82] With one of LA's largest regional shopping centers, Lakewood residents had especially easy access to this leisure activity.

The sense of comfort and openness that many felt in Lakewood rested on its racial segregation. Even as the civil rights movement gained momentum and generated liberal sympathy nationwide, residents might have admired its goals from afar but wanted little to do with it at home. Most Lakewood residents believed its all-white profile was an important community attribute and didn't hide it. When an African American moved into Lakewood Village in the 1950s, recalled LPC salesman Woody Smith, "we were ready to move them out on a rail . . . I mean, the community just rose up in arms."[83] Dr. Roy Gillespie of Lakewood, dubbed an "authority on racial problems," revealed open anti-Black sentiments when he delivered a talk to an anti-integration group in Whittier, where he called "integration a sin against God" and posited that the Christian solution was to send Blacks back to Africa.[84] A 1961 survey by the Lakewood Junior Chamber of Commerce confirmed broader community opinion against integration—60% of respondents believed a "mild influx of a minority group" would affect their residing in the community.[85] As a small but telling sign of the community's climate, the county-owned Lakewood golf club had only one Black member as of 1963.[86] It would remain to be seen whether the positive elements of Lakewood's social fabric could survive once Lakewood's racial insularity dissolved.

Many Roads to Lakewood: Diversity and Race Relations after 1970

After 1970, the Lakewood dream opened up as people of color broke the racial barrier and arrived in ever-growing numbers. In the wake of federal legislation—especially the 1968 Fair Housing Act—these new residents became the agents of civil rights suburbanization, spurring a trend that propelled Lakewood toward becoming one of LA County's most racially balanced cities by 2010 (see Table 7.1). Some of this growth reflected the movement of upwardly mobile Blacks and Latinos out of south LA, much to the consternation of those left behind who feared the economic and political drain on their communities.[87] Lakewood's share of immigrants also rose, from 5% to 21% between 1970 and 2010, with Asian outnumbering Latino immigrants two to one. While the white population in Lakewood experienced a steady decline, wholesale white flight did not happen. Instead, many original residents stayed, and their children returned to raise their own families. As in many suburbs in LA, Lakewood slid into diversity with little conscious effort to manage the change.[88]

Like its original residents, Lakewood's racially diverse newcomers sought a safe, attractive town where they could raise their children and own a home with pride. The experience of settling in Lakewood could vary widely, but the experiences of three families who arrived between 1970 and 2005 convey a general sense of social acceptance in the suburb. For these residents of color, feelings of accomplishment and joy at moving there were palpable.

Isidro and Rosario Pe were born in the 1940s and raised in the Philippines.[89] Isidro became an engineer and Rosario a nurse. After marrying, they immigrated to the US in 1967, when Firestone recruited Isidro for a job in LA. They settled first in Culver City, living with an aunt before getting their own apartment. When they had their first child, Ari, in 1971, they decided it was time for a move. Rosario had likely seen Lakewood on trips to visit her brother in Long Beach. In 1972, the couple purchased an affordable three-bedroom, two-bathroom house with a two-car garage in the small Cherry Cove section. Rosario got a job at Lakewood General, a community hospital, and eventually moved to a job at Kaiser. After their second child was born in 1974, both parents continued to work full time.

The family's neighbors in Cherry Cove included Black Americans, Mexicans, Filipinos, and whites. As a child, Ari's social life in Lakewood was "mixed right out of the gate. Growing up, I didn't see color lines at all"—an experience that contrasted sharply with Lakewood's "original kids." The elderly white couple who lived next door, whom Ari called "Grandma Gladys and Grandpa George," frequently watched Ari and his brother when their parents weren't home. When Isidro saw an African American neighbor enrolling their children in military school in nearby Signal Hill, he decided to send Ari there for kindergarten and first grade so the children could ride the bus together. Free and adventurous, Ari and his friends rode bikes and frequented the park across the street where park leaders ran activities and sports. Although they were busy with full-time jobs, Ari's parents launched the Lakewood Beautifies program, in which neighbors got together to celebrate their homes and hold a youth bike parade around the small neighborhood. Childhood for Ari was defined by his family's welcoming Filipino culture, as well as a community of caring neighbors and friends who watched out for him. Ari's parents were "notorious for throwing family parties.... We always had barbecues at the house . . . [for] the community and relatives, we always had people over."

In 1977, the Pe family moved from the edge to the center of Lakewood, just across from Mayfair Park. Their home was on a cul-de-sac of six homes, with neighbors who were all white except for one Japanese American family. Ari and his neighborhood friends—"all latchkey kids"—owned the streets. They biked, played outside until the streetlights went on, and played sports at the parks and at school. Ari attended private Catholic schools, and the church became a focal point of the Pes' lives. The family continued to share their Filipino culture with family and friends through volunteering at school and in their big social gatherings, cooking dishes like dinuguan (pork blood stew), oxtail, and egg rolls. With their warmth and openness, the Pe family infused central Lakewood with their culture and were appreciated and welcomed by their non-Filipino neighbors and friends.

Cassandra Chase was an "original kid" of the second generation.[90] Born and raised in Lakewood, she was the daughter of Caribbean immigrant parents. Her father, Louis Chase, was born in Barbados in 1943 and raised in humble circumstances by his grandmother. He had deep ties to the Methodist church from a young age. He recalled walking barefoot to school during the week and on Sundays donning his one pair of dressy shoes to attend church with his family. At 14, he quit school "because of poverty" and went to work. As a teenager, he moved to London, where he first worked in textiles and then transitioned into community organizing and social justice activism. He earned a degree at Oxford where he studied Pan-African movements, and met his future wife Marion, a nursing student at Coventry University who hailed from Jamaica.

In 1980, the couple immigrated to the United States and settled in Lakewood, where they purchased a home and started a family. For this young family, Lakewood was an ideal place to land. They were drawn to its safety, parks, sense of community, and peaceful and quiet atmosphere. Their home was in eastern Lakewood, directly across the street from an apartment complex, in a predominantly white area. They were the only Black family on their block in the early 1980s.

While enduring scattered incidents of racism and discrimination in Lakewood, Louis experienced a warm and life-changing welcome at Lakewood United Methodist Church, an all-white conservative congregation. The first day he attended service, which ran from 11 to 12, he returned home and at 12:30 a member of the church showed up on his doorstep inviting him to join the church. When Louis hesitated, explaining that he didn't have a car, the man offered to pick him up for Sunday services and meetings of the men's group. That church changed Louis's life. Louis had been struggling to land a job in human relations work in LA. The minister at Lakewood Methodist encouraged Louis to consider pursuing the ministry and put in a good word for him at the Claremont School of Theology, setting Louis on a new career path. He became a Methodist minister, serving a number of churches around Los Angeles, including Holman United Methodist Church, where he worked closely with James Lawson and other leading figures in the civil rights and anti-apartheid movements.

A year after the Chases moved in, their first child Cassandra was born, followed by Shaundra three years later. Louis recalled sitting on his front doorstep with his Claremont classmates, baby Cassandra on his lap, studying Latin and theology. As Louis pursued his calling, Marion took up full-time work as a behavioral health nurse at Long Beach Memorial Hospital. She worked the night shift so she could be home for her daughters after school.

Unlike a generation of children before her, Cassandra described leading a very sheltered childhood. "My early memories of Lakewood, our street specifically, was I remember us never seeing anyone that looked like me. . . . I was also very aware that my parents were immigrants, and so their story and experience were very different from that of our neighbors." Cassandra recalled being the sole Black among mostly white children—in the neighborhood, at school, at Girl Scouts, and at Parks and Rec activities. The Chase girls attended Catholic schools in Norwalk and Lakewood. Their mother instilled in them a sense of racial dignity from a young age. Cassandra remembered the day "I learned I was black," when at age six she donned a Halloween costume of cartoon heroine She-Ra, complete with plastic mask. When a friend told her she couldn't "be She-Ra . . . 'cause you're black," the comment confused and upset her. When her mother picked her up from school and heard this story, she told her daughter, "You know, Cass, don't let anyone ever tell you that you can't be anything because of the color of your skin . . . in fact, you can do anything and everything because of the color of your skin. Don't let that stop you." A defining moment for Cassandra, this incident perhaps reinforced Marion's inclination to protect her daughters.

Unlike Lakewood's postwar white generation, the Chase parents didn't allow their daughters to play on the streets because they did not put their full trust in the community and worried about heavy traffic on their block. The girls would look out the window and see other kids playing and want to go join them—"And my mom's like, you guys could study. You can read a book. There's other things you can do." Instead of letting the girls roam freely in Lakewood, her parents carefully monitored their friend groups and activities. Driven by the desire to shield their children from racism and to support their upward mobility, her parents carefully "curated" their social lives. So strong was this protective streak that they never carpooled or relied on other parents for rides. As middle-class immigrant parents with intense ambitions for their children, they showered them with opportunities—dance class, swimming, piano, classical guitar, Girls Scouts, and, through Lakewood Parks and Rec, gymnastics, karate, and Japanese class. The girls were immersed in a rich social and spiritual life at their father's church, where they connected with other Black families. "We were involved in so many things, sometimes it felt like home was just a place where we rested versus hung out." Her mother also insisted their daughters speak "the Queen's English," free of any Jamaican patois, outside of the home to fit seamlessly into American mainstream culture. To the parents, being Black and immigrant was "a double whammy in many ways, that you had to learn how to explore or to navigate the world through. I almost felt like . . . the guarding of our immigrant identity and culture was a way to protect us from having to deal with both of those things at the same time." Cassandra's aunt put it this way to her: the kids would have never known about any racial animosity because "we never left you guys alone in any setting where anyone can say anything to you." The Chases' parenting strategies were formulated around being Black and ethnic in white suburbia.

Pamela and Derrick Williams, an African American couple, grew up on opposite coasts but with common experiences of strong families and neighborhoods.[91] Pamela's parents were both born in Texas, married young, had six children, and then moved to Los Angeles in 1971, to escape racism and find stability. Her father worked as a bus driver, her mother as a nurse at Cedar Sinai. They purchased a home across from Van Ness Park in the Crenshaw district, a middle-class Black neighborhood of single-family homes. As youngsters, Pamela and her five siblings spent a lot of time at the park—swimming, playing sports, "just hanging out being kids." Their large extended family often gathered on the weekends for parties. As both parents worked, Pamela considered her adult neighbors an "extended family" in their close-knit, racially insulated community. "I was sheltered for many, many years because I lived around blacks," she recalled. Schools, stores, "it was just all black." Living in this Black "bubble," "I didn't have a clue about racial tension." Derrick grew up in Philadelphia, first in an apartment in southwest Philly and then in suburban West Oak Lane, where his parents purchased a home in 1972. This affluent area was nearly all-white—heavily Jewish and Italian—and his was one of the first Black families to move in. Like Pamela's parents, his stepfather was a bus driver, his mother a nurse. Derrick recalled tremendous freedom as a child within his tight-knit neighborhood where "everybody knew everybody." In the summertime, he and friends would leave home early and spend the entire day at the park, playing sports, riding go-carts, and biking to nearby Cheltenham Township, an all-white suburb where they rented boats and fished in the creek. Within a decade, West Oak Lane flipped from white to Black. Derrick's parents did their best to strike a balance "to not only give us freedom, but to still shelter us at the same time. . . . They did their best . . . keeping us informed, keeping us sheltered, keeping us covered—all at the same time." Pamela recalled similar parental protectiveness: "My parents were Southerners, so saw it all . . . [they] shielded us because of their own personal experiences."

Despite their parents' best efforts, Pamela and Derrick each experienced profound racial trauma in the early 1980s. For Derrick, it happened in high school when he was bussed to an all-white school across town, part of the tumultuous process of school integration.[92] Derrick earned good grades, was a member of the chess team, and was involved in swimming, diving, and track. Immediately after busing began, racial violence became a part of his daily routine: "We had race riots daily, weekly . . . we had an ongoing racial fight with . . . an all-boys Catholic school. . . . They would come and walk in mobs to our school. When we came out, they're throwing bricks at us, they're throwing chains, bottles. We would have to fight. . . . They turned one of our buses over one time . . . to try to stop us from getting on it so we would be in their neighborhood and be trapped. When we were out there, I mean fisti-cuffs, fighting, throwing bottles, hitting, beating each other. It was ridiculous. So that was my first experience of true racism and to a very high degree." Pamela's life changed when she was 12. In 1983, her 17-year-old brother

Anthony was hanging out with friends in the neighborhood when the LAPD showed up and everyone scattered. After Anthony ran into a friend's backyard to hide, the police shot him in the back, and he died that night. Though Anthony was unarmed, the officers claimed he had a weapon, although one was never found. The officer who pulled the trigger, Pamela recalled, had a record of excessive use of force and worked in a notoriously corrupt division.[93] The murder devastated the family. Both Pamela and Derrick proved resilient in the face of these experiences. Under threat of daily attack as a high school freshman and sophomore, Derrick resolved to claim his place at school. "I did not let fear rule my life where I could not enjoy those things that every other child out there was able to enjoy. If it meant I had to fight for it, then I'm going to fight for it." For Pamela, she followed her parents' advice, "Don't let that moment define you. Don't let that really define you because you can get burdened down with hatred, always looking over your back in that fear. And they never wanted us to fear anything." Both Derrick and Pamela resolved to move forward without fear and resentment. Pamela even came to hold "great respect for law enforcement" while still recognizing ongoing patterns of racialized police brutality.

Years later, after Pamela earned a college degree and established a career and Derrick did a stint in the elite Army Rangers and worked on the East Coast, the pair met in Los Angeles in 2003 and began dating. They both got jobs at Boeing, Derrick in IT and Pamela as an executive assistant. While living in Ladera Heights, they began attending Wednesday night Bible study at a friend's home in Lakewood and Derrick became "enamored by the neighborhood." They loved the hometown feel, the houses, the street layout, and the slower pace of life, perfect for raising a family. The parks especially resonated with them, since "we grew up in parks." To Pamela, a lifelong Angeleno who had never heard of Lakewood, it felt "like a little Mayberry." The couple married in 2005 and the following year bought a home in central Lakewood near Bolivar Park and welcomed their daughter. Their three-bedroom home had additions to the original model, and was located on a tree-lined street of single-family homes. On a block with many original owners, they were the second Black family to move in. The neighbors welcomed them warmly, bringing homemade fudge, cookies, and pies. For Pamela, settling in Lakewood raised a jumble of emotions. On the one hand, "the culture shock for me was not seeing so many black people." On the other hand, she and Derrick, as she put it, kept "falling in love with" Lakewood. The neighborly atmosphere reaffirmed their choice and allayed any apprehensions about not feeling welcome in white suburbia. "We don't know if you like fruitcake," as Derrick put it, "but here, we brought you a fruitcake. And just the gesture itself is enough to take whatever anxiety you might be feeling, and just drop it on down to the ground. Not only do you not have to worry about your surroundings or being welcome, but you *feel* welcome."

Like all newcomers to this community, the people of color moving in arrived with diverse life experiences and varied insights about race. Ari, Derrick, and Pamela all grew up in close-knit neighborhoods and carried those memories into adulthood in Lakewood. For Derrick and Pamela, their parents had actively tried to shield their children from racism and instill in them values of resilience and racial dignity. This shaped their own approach to social relations as they ventured into Lakewood community and civic life by the early 2000s.

While the Pe, Chase, and Williams families each had a fairly smooth transition into Lakewood, racial integration was marked by some moments of acceptance and others of deep resistance. Anecdotal evidence suggests that some people of color encountered warm neighborly welcomes like those of the Pe and Williams families. Mexican American Noel Baca and his older brother both bought homes for their families in Lakewood in the early 1950s. Passing as white, the Baca family embraced assimilation, which likely facilitated their acceptance by their neighbors. Both Noel and his wife worked full time—he as an inspector for the Department of Agriculture, she as a retail clerk at Sears and Roebuck—placing them in the solid middle class, which also aided their social acceptance. Joe and Patricia Esquivel found their neighbors "very friendly and helpful" from the time they arrived in Lakewood in 1963. Shortly after moving in, the Esquivels' second child Debbie was born, prompting the neighbors to step up to clean, wash, and cook while Patricia was in the hospital. The house "was just immaculate," Joe recalled. The Chase family moved into Lakewood in 1981 without incident and immediately befriended their neighbors, both Latino families. Vicki Stuckey grew up in a close-knit neighborhood in Compton, which she described as "kind of like Mayberry, but we weren't white, we were Black." An African American single woman with a demanding full-time job with the LA Sheriff's Department, Stuckey bought a home in Lakewood in 1992. Her cul-de-sac was near the Cerritos border and was mostly white with one "mixed" family (the grandmother was Asian, the grandfather African American). She recalled the neighbors being friendly when she moved in—they waved and said hello but brought no cookies or cakes. She eventually got to know them better after her sister and her two kids moved in with her, connecting with them through the children.[94]

By the 1980s and 1990s, a new Black or Latino family on the block became more routine and the process of buying into Lakewood easier. A 1996 housing study by Richard Sanders of UCLA found that realtors in nearby Bellflower were actually steering Black American home-seekers into Lakewood, suggesting that it was becoming known as a diverse community among the southeast suburbs.[95] Banks such as the Black-owned Broadway Federal Savings targeted people of color in their mortgage lending, opening up the possibility of suburban homeownership for this growing market. Samuel Martinez, a 29-year-old cargo operator, secured a loan to purchase a $78,000 home in Lakewood in 1998, noting the bank made him feel like a member of the family.[96] As early as the 1960s, Lakewood's racial geography began to shift. Latinos had the earliest breakthroughs, inhabiting all parts of Lakewood by 1960. In 1970, some Latino clusters appeared in west and east Lakewood, which would become centers of diverse settlement after 1980. In the west, people of color spilled over from similarly diverse neighborhoods in north Long Beach. Eastern Lakewood, with both homes and apartments, housed Blacks as well as Latinos, Vietnamese, and Japanese moving from Cerritos and Hawaiian Gardens.[97] In the Mayfair section, Blacks began moving in during the 1970s.[98] The concentrations of Black, Latinos, and Asians along the edges continued over the years, although all of these groups scattered throughout the suburb as well.[99]

At the same time, some Latinos, Black Americans, and Asian Americans encountered racial resistance in one form or another. Like most white suburbs in Los Angeles, Lakewood was largely unprepared for the human relations challenge that diversification posed and had few county resources to draw upon. Ironically, at the same time the county expanded services to individual suburbs for fire protection, policing, and infrastructure on a contract basis, it largely withdrew assistance in the arena of human relations— civic resources to promote peaceful racial integration—due to Prop 13 cuts, leaving many suburbs to contend with the changes on their own. In Lakewood, human relations work was delegated to the Lakewood Recreation and Community Services Commission in 1972; two former staff members had no recollection of Lakewood pursing the issue. The city did not form another human relations entity over the next several decades.[100]

As more people of color moved into Lakewood, evidence abounded of racial animosity ranging from individual acts of hostility to city actions on fair housing issues. Some examples illustrate how this played out. When Noel and Antonina Baca purchased their home in 1955, the realtor quickly backtracked, informing them they had to sell the house back since he didn't realize they were Mexican, and Mexicans weren't allowed to buy in Lakewood. When Noel responded, "we'll see you in court," the realtor backed down. While the family was ultimately welcomed by neighbors, this incident understandably left an impression on them.[101] For Sylvia Castillo's family, resistance came from the neighbors. When they moved into Lakewood in the postwar years, they immediately experienced prejudice. The neighbors circulated a petition against them, Sylvia heard the word "wetback" for the first time, and she and her sisters were ostracized. That reaction politicized her mother, who began attending fair housing meetings at night, taking her daughters along.[102] In 1964, Lakewood housewife and activist Betty McCune began campaigning for fair housing (in opposition to Proposition 14, meant to overturn the fair housing Rumford Act of 1963). She received death threats and was bombarded with about 100 anonymous phone calls, asking, "Why do you want to get housing for n—s?" and "Do you want to get a bomb in your home?"[103] In the 1970s, incidents in Lakewood and neighboring suburbs continued, some subtle, others more brazen. Even as the process of buying into Lakewood opened up for people of color, some were still rebuffed, such as a Latino couple unable to secure a mortgage loan for a Lakewood home despite the husband's well-paying job.[104]

In the 1970s and 1980s, a series of incidents in Lakewood and its neighboring suburbs signaled more troubling racial hostility. Busing was an early flashpoint. In the early 1970s, Black American students were bused as part of a voluntary program to Lakewood High School (part of the Long Beach Unified School District). Though they were only 100 Blacks amidst 1,400 whites, racial clashes quickly erupted.[105] On Halloween day in 1974, 50 sheriff deputies were summoned to break up a fight between Black and white students, leading to five arrests. In May 1978, a 25-minute melee broke out, resulting in several injuries, five arrests, and an early school closure. English teacher Wendell Milbrandt perceived a toxic climate of open racism at the high school—"cruel and constant on the campus." One of his students wrote in a weekly journal, "I hate all niggers," while another openly declared in class, "I wish all Blacks would die." Milbrandt believed that "Lakewood tends to be a red-necked, small-minded community" and requested a transfer. Science teacher Wellington Rogers, who had taught at the high school for 21 years, saw things differently. While he acknowledged racial tension, he blamed it on a small rebellious group of "rednecks" on campus. Most students "work to-gether beautifully," though they didn't socially integrate. He criticized the dis-trict for unleashing busing with "no warning and no orientation."[106] Mayor Paul Zeltner, who worked as "a police professional" in the area, responded by coordinating between the city and the Sheriff's Department, taking a law-enforcement approach to the problem.[107] Some parents launched unsuc-cessful bids to secede from the Long Beach district. Lingering resentments around busing lasted well into the 1990s.[108]

Rising white supremacist and skinhead movements in the south-east suburbs and nearby Orange County seemed to confirm Milbrandt's perceptions.[109] An early example was the Spook Hunters, a white teenage hate group that focused their attacks on Blacks who set foot in Compton, Downey, Lynwood, and South Gate. Their actions spurred the formation of Black clubs for protection that became the genesis of South LA gangs.[110] By the early 1970s, the LA Sentinel described neighboring Cerritos as a "racial tinderbox waiting for the explosion." A series of racial attacks there in 1972 and 1973 confirmed the prediction, when two African American sisters and their families became targets of racial violence, including physical beatings, death threats, racial epithets, hurling bags of gasoline and pop bottles at their house, picking fights with the children at school, and brandishing guns in front of their home. The harassment drove the sisters to move away.[111] In 1976, three Lakewood high schoolers burned a cross on the lawn of a Black American woman in the Mayfair section.[112] And in 1981, the Los Angeles Times reported on the existence of a Ku Klux Klan klavern in Lakewood, with 65 members drawn from the southeast suburbs. Donning white robes, members spoke at a city council meeting in nearby Paramount, charging that Black and Mexican youth were harassing white kids. They called for better law enforcement, expressed support for the police, and pledged to present plans for a neighborhood watch-type crime prevention program. As 26-year-old Mike Lyons, cyclops of the Lakewood Klavern put it, he watched these communities "go downhill" with the influx of Latinos and Blacks. Part of the Klan's motive in going public was to recruit new members. While they were shouted down by members of the National Chicano Moratorium Committee and La Raza Unida, they got their message across.[113] Ten years later, a swas-tika was painted on the front door of a Lakewood synagogue, along with initials "SWP," which likely stood for "supreme white power."[114] Skinhead culture, meanwhile, occupied a murkier racial space in Lakewood. Ari Pe recalled skinheads being part of the high school social scene in the 1990s, alongside Blacks, Asians, and Latinos within Lakewood's very active back-yard party scene.[115] While Pe described a youth culture in which radically different subcultures could at times peacefully coexist, in other instances, racial animosities erupted, creating a climate of intimidation toward Blacks, Latinos, Asians, and Jews in these suburbs.

Everyday slights were common, even for a family like the Chases who experienced warm receptions at church and from their immediate neighbors. Louis Chase was racially profiled by the Lakewood sheriffs who pulled him over without provocation, his two daughters were subjected to racial name-calling at school, and the family was often tailed by security guards on trips to the Lakewood Center Mall.[116]

By 1990, an incident in eastern Lakewood revealed the reluctance of city leaders to support residents of color victimized by racism. Eastern Lakewood, physically divided from the rest of Lakewood by the newly built San Gabriel Freeway (later called the 605), had a higher proportion of Latinos, Blacks, and low-income families and a higher share of apartment complexes. As early as the 1970s, residents there recognized that they were given short shrift when it came to public funding, infrastructure, and city responsiveness.[117]

An incident of housing bias reinforced this perception. In the early 1990s, the Park Apartments on Del Amo Boulevard began discriminating openly against its Black American tenants while leaving those of other ethnic-racial backgrounds alone. The middle-class Black families living in this complex included parents who held professional positions and their children who were good students involved in sports and other activities. Several families had lived in the complex for 14 years and never missed a rent payment. In the early 1990s, a new manager decided to crack down on security and began harassing Black American teenage males living in the complex. Management forbade them from gathering in groups of more than two, accused them of being in gangs, placed one teen under "house arrest," and threatened to evict one family if the kids hung out on the grounds at all. Fifteen-year-old Martin Crump, whose family had lived in the complex since 1983, was told he couldn't leave his apartment. He grew so afraid he asked friends to take out the garbage for him. The Walker family, whose son was being treated for lupus, had friends and family visiting him in around-the-clock shifts. Management perceived those coming and going from their apartment as drug traffickers and evicted the Walkers. When Reshrae Walker explained the situation to the managers, she said, "They didn't believe me. I was humiliated."[118] When several Black families were evicted, they banded together to file a class action lawsuit against the property management company in 1993.[119] The Long Beach Fair Housing Foundation (FHF), to which Lakewood outsourced its fair housing program, helped launch and support the lawsuit, in which the city of Lakewood and LA County were also named. In 1997, a federal judge approved a $1.7 million settlement in favor of the families in a consent decree that required the defendants to initiate sensitivity training for their employees, to learn anti-discrimination housing laws, and to maintain records of evictions and complaints.[120]

Just as significant as the discriminatory practices the case exposed was Lakewood's reaction to it. The response of city leaders revealed more concern about Lakewood's image than the plight of the evicted families. In July 1993, when the lawsuit was being launched, the FHF provided Lakewood a "case narrative" and a press release it was about to issue, which read "While many of these families have lived for years in this complex without a problem, it only took one ignorant and biased manager a few months to uproot and displace at least eight or nine such families and to send the message to yet another generation of young African-American that they are still not welcome in middle-class cities like Lakewood." City leaders claimed the statement accused Lakewood of racism. A few weeks later, Lakewood director of community development Charles Ebner accused the FHF of showing "poor judgement" which created "serious concerns for the future" of the FHF's contract with Lakewood. City officials began supervising the FHF more closely and asked it to "curtail the amount of exposure" it gave to discrimination complaints. Lakewood ultimately counter-sued the FHF and refused to renew its contract, which prevented it from carrying out its work in Lakewood. In an ensuing lawsuit alleging that Lakewood retaliated against the FHF simply for doing its fair housing work, the Ninth Circuit Court of Appeals ruled in favor of the FHF, citing protection under the federal Fair Housing Act and analogous California Fair Employment and Housing Act (FEHA), which bars interference with fair housing work.[121] This incident revealed the disinterest of Lakewood leaders in addressing housing discrimination within its borders while showing more concern for minimizing the bad publicity.

Other expressions of racial resentments in Lakewood emerged in the 1990s. Writer and "original kid" Alida Brill offered a pessimistic view of racial attitudes in her profile of the aging suburb. "Countless numbers of times," she wrote, "one hears the apprehension voiced in the question, 'Are we going to turn into Compton?'" One white Lakewood resident told her, "I've got three blacks [families] on my own block, right now. Three now, and well, you know the problem with blacks, they have friends, and they have visitors. That is the problem. We can't encourage our people to stay if this keeps up. Our housing stock has stayed pretty solid, but some people can't be encouraged much more to stay." One high school alumnus, looking back from the 1990s, blamed busing for the problems in Lakewood: "You will find Lakewood is a really racist town now; really racist now. Sometimes I guess I sound like a racist too. But it's because of what they did over there to Lakewood High." Another alumnus put it more bluntly, "The niggers and the Mexicans ruined everything we loved, everything."[122]

Race relations in Lakewood and other southeast suburbs was thus a twin story of progress and setbacks, of peaceful new arrivals and troubling racist incidents. Like many suburbs of LA County, Lakewood did not pursue human relations work as a bona fide civic issue. It also outsourced the matter of fair housing. This meant residents were mostly left to deal with incidents themselves or seek help from the local Sheriff's Department, without a robust civic entity dedicated to smoothing the waters for both old and new residents.

Social and Civic Life in the Era of Diversification, after 1970

In addition to racial diversification, other forms of social and demographic change set the backdrop for community life in Lakewood after 1970. The stereotypical postwar family structure was giving way to more varied households and higher rates of working mothers. At the same time, economic recessions and occupational shifts undercut local prosperity, introducing a greater level of economic insecurity into everyday life. These changes comprised a shifting context for social life in Lakewood.

Household changes were pronounced. A majority of married women worked outside the home by 1980, peaking at 70% in 2000. This suggested that two-income families increasingly became a prerequisite for Lakewood living, aligning with national trends.[123] Other trends included fewer children and more seniors. Seniors made up 12% of Lakewood's population by 1990, suggesting that many original residents were aging in place. Two-parent nuclear families also gradually declined. Lakewood had more widowed and divorced adults (they rose from 6% to 15% of adults from 1960 to 1990) and more singles, comprising a quarter of the adult population by 1990. Lakewood clearly housed a greater mix of household types, moving away from the nuclear family that so dominated the postwar years to a more complex profile.[124]

Housing evolved only gradually to match these changing demographics. Single-family homes continued to predominate, representing over 80% of all housing units through the 2000s.[125] Homeownership also remained relatively high in Lakewood, from 70–73% after 1980. Some of these single-family homes were used as rentals; in 1990, for example, roughly 12% of Lakewood homes were rented out. While whites consistently outnumbered people of color as homeowners, by 2010, 8,500 homes were owned by people of color, comprising 31% of all housing units. Throughout Lakewood's entire history, nonwwhite owners outnumbered nonwwhite renters, signaling their inclusion in the community by this important marker of suburban identity. Single-family homes were supplemented by several apartment complexes, which comprised about 15% of all housing units after 1980 and were concentrated in eastern Lakewood and along the periphery. In 1990, when Lakewood's first subsidized senior housing complex opened, with 201 units, its senior population topped 8,800, with most aging in place at home.[126]

The shift in Lakewood's occupational profile reflected broader trends in the regional economy away from blue-collar jobs and toward white-collar and service work. Most striking was the shrinking of the blue-collar workforce to just 18.5% of all workers by 2010. Some of this was fallout from the decline of the aerospace and aircraft industry. Occupational data also suggests a tilt by 1990 toward a more educated and specialized workforce, with more managers/professionals than blue-collar workers. Many women continued to work in lower-paying jobs, such as salesclerk, health care worker, and teacher. Living in a family household tended to buoy a family's economic fortunes; a relatively low 3.2% of families lived in poverty, compared to 14% of those living as "unrelated individuals." Among Lakewood's elderly, those 75 and older, living alone, 12% lived in poverty. While the differences were slight, Lakewood's Black and Asian households earned the highest median income in 1990, exceeding Latinos and whites.[127]

For white workers with generational roots in the aircraft industry, the years after 1980 revealed the precarity of their middle-class lives. In 1975, the national economic downturn led to layoffs at the McDonnell Douglas aircraft plant, adjacent to Lakewood. This was followed by a rebound in 1977, with a new US Air Force contract to produce aerial refueling and military transports, a program ultimately scrapped by the Carter administration. The 1980s saw expansion at the plant, followed by downturns in the 1990s spurred by the global recession, rising fuel costs, and reduced passenger loads on commercial flights.[128] Beyond these external factors, internal management at the plant exacerbated its problems. Since the late 1960s, the company had been only sporadically profitable and began consistently losing money by 1988. At that point, it was producing both civilian and military aircrafts, including C-17 transport planes on a $4.9 billion contract with the Air Force. To address these "deep-rooted problems," company leaders implemented a new team-based approach called Total Quality Management Systems (TQMS), which gave more voice and responsibility to workers. Some workers referred to TQMS as "Time to Quit and Move to Seattle"— the home of rival company Boeing. Analysts claimed the program created confusion and loss of morale. More painfully, management implemented a gut-wrenching series of layoffs as a way to raise profits. In July 1990, 8,000 workers were laid off at the local plant, and another 1,200 were let go three months later. Workers, who learned of the news by memo, were demoralized and depressed. Many had a hard time rebounding, remaining unemployed for long periods or taking lower-income service jobs. What had once been a bedrock of Lakewood had become shaky and unpredictable.[129]

While some white males were experiencing downward mobility, Black American families in Lakewood were faring pretty well. Blacks earned the highest incomes among married-couple families, indicating their solid economic standing and firm position within the middle class. This standing was also likely a result of dual incomes. National patterns showed more dual-income households among Blacks than whites, stemming partly from the wage discrimination people of color experienced and the added pressure for both parents to work in order to afford suburban living.[130]

Against this backdrop, social and civic groups had only marginal success as spaces of meaningful integration. Few appreciated the challenges that people of color might be feeling as they moved into a formerly all-white community. As a result, social integration was a gradual, at times uneven, process.

For new residents of color, integrating into local social and civic life unfolded in different ways. Scattered evidence suggests a few patterns: participating in racially defined groups that met in Lakewood, joining existing Lakewood groups, and connecting with neighbors. One social space open to Black women in the 1970s and 1980s was the Lakewood Center Mall and later the Centre at Sycamore Plaza. As early as 1972, the

May Co. department store hosted a sewing event that welcomed African Americans.[131] By 1976, Black women began holding annual luncheons and benefits at Bullock's department store at the mall. This high-end retailer supplied fashions for a host of Black women's groups, including Greek Letter societies, auxiliaries, and groups like the National Council of Negro Women, the United Negro College Fund, and the Compton YWCA. In 1977, for example, the National Council of Negro Women held its annual luncheon-fashion show at Bullocks Lakewood, to honor actress Beah Richards as Outstanding Woman of the Year. The Iota Phi Lambda sorority, an international organization of Black business and professional women, held its annual "Try It On For Size" fashion show-scholarship luncheons there, too.[132] Similar events followed in the mid-1980s to the 1990s, at the banquet room at the Centre at Sycamore Plaza.[133] These events exemplified the occupational success of these women and their dedication to Black-oriented philanthropy, which saw a resurgence in the 1980s.[134]

Recreation and sports were a conduit of participation for some Blacks and Latinos in Lakewood, in some cases continuing traditions established by nonwhite sports groups even before their members were allowed to move into the suburb. For example, as early as 1954, a Black woman's golf club, the Cosmopolitan Golf Club Auxiliary, was participating in golf tournaments at the Lakewood golf course. In the 1970s and 1980s, a robust Black women's bowling league played regularly in Lakewood and, by 1990, held its banquet at the Lakewood Country Club.[135]

Some nonwhite residents also began joining longstanding Lakewood social and civic groups. For families with two working parents, the process could play out gradually. This can be seen in two generations of the Mexican American Baca family. For Noel and Antonina (Toni) Baca, who purchased their home in 1955 and both held full-time jobs, their social lives revolved around family and bowling. They held frequent dinners and parties at the house with upwards of 40 members of their extended family. They were avid bowlers and participated in league games at least twice a week, often accompanied by neighbors. Noel also coached youth sports and played softball with a few other men in the neighborhood. When their son Bill moved to Lakewood to raise his own family in 1988, he began doing youth-oriented volunteer work, serving as a room parent at his children's school, coaching at Lakewood Parks and Rec for seven years, and leading a Scout troop. Lakewood Mayor Todd Rogers, impressed by Bill's energy, invited him to serve on the Public Safety Commission.[136] When Joe and Patricia Esquivel moved to Lakewood in 1963, Joe, a former high school football star, immediately volunteered to coach even before his children were old enough to play. He ended up coaching for a quarter century. He also joined the Jaycees, a community service group, serving as president in 1965 when the club had 100 members. His networking with local leaders led to an appointment to the Parks and Rec Commission. In 1990, Joe Esquivel became the first and only person of color to serve on the Lakewood City Council during these years. Around that time, he also became a Neighborhood Watch block captain and joined the local Democratic club. Joe conceded that he never felt compelled to connect with other Latinos in Lakewood.[137] For Cassandra Chase, the value of public service was instilled in her as a child. As a young adult, she joined the Lakewood Jaycees in 2007. She later ran for city council in campaigns that emphasized the importance of bringing more people into the civic decision-making process.[138]

Pamela and Derrick Williams, who moved to Lakewood in 2006, dove into local volunteer life with unbridled enthusiasm. Pamela, however, was concerned that the public schools, parks programs, and neighborhood streets they encountered were predominantly white. Having grown up in an all-Black community, Pamela worried about the lack of diversity for her daughter. "That was hard on me as a mother," she recalled. Within a month of moving in, they became Neighborhood Watch block captains as a way of connecting with their neighbors. They hosted a "meet and greet" for their neighbors and soon recreated the close-knit neighborhood experience they each grew up with. Pamela became actively involved in the PTA, and Derrick coached Little League, being one of only two Black coaches out of 30 or 40. Their children participated in numerous Park and Rec activities—team sports, tap dance, ballet, gymnastics, and cheerleading. Lakewood, as Pamela put it, had a "really good" impact on her family. And yet they saw few other people of color stepping up to volunteer, perhaps due to time constraints or racial discomfort. Derrick acknowledged, "It's not as if I didn't experience or go into it with not having any discomfort. But it wasn't that they pushed that discomfort on me. . . . I'm the only Black guy here, yeah that's uncomfortable. However, I got in and established myself regardless of what someone thinks. . . . I never felt any racial discord. None." To nurture Black identity and culture in their children, they attended a Black church, held frequent gatherings with extended family, and enrolled their daughter in Gems, the youth arm of the Black sorority Delta Sigma Theta. For the Williams family, participation was crucial to their investment in their future in Lakewood.[139]

Derrick Williams partially attributed the widespread hesitance of Black residents to get involved to Lakewood's white roots: "When the city was established in 1952, it was a white American working-class culture, and it has been maintained through today as such." A major factor was the persistence of whites "running the city, the city council, the structure of the government." Pamela noted, too, the lack of people of color working at city hall and as sheriffs, firefighters, and paramedics. The couple encouraged their African American friends in Lakewood to get involved, even run for office, but Derrick encountered naysayers who countered, "Lakewood is not gonna allow that to happen.'"[140] The reasons why whites held onto power in Lakewood even through the demographic transition were clear to residents of color. Combined with intermittent racial hostilities in the suburb, these forces could put a damper on community involvement.

For other families with two parents working jobs with long hours, participation in Lakewood could also be more muted. For the Chase and Pe families, church and parochial schools consumed most of their social energies. Louis and Marion Chase devoted their spare hours to church, family, and service projects, not to Lakewood community groups. As a minister's wife, Marion was deeply involved in the women's ministry, helped prepare meals, created floral arrangements, and sang in the choir on Sundays. Louis channeled his participatory energy into the wider LA church-based social activism scene, chairing the United Methodist Board of Church and Society and increasingly speaking out on issues such as abortion rights, gun violence, and police brutality. He was involved, too, in the religious community's response to the 1992 civil unrest following the Rodney King beating.[141] The family was also deeply committed to community service, whether ministering to the elderly at convalescent hospitals or at their church. Neither parent joined groups in Lakewood. The Pe family likewise focused its energies on family and church. Parents Isidro and Rosario volunteered at St. Pancratius Catholic Church and School, which their two sons attended. They helped out at the annual festival, where they started the first Filipino food booth. Isidro also joined the Knights of Columbus at church, which focused on community service.[142] These families were all involved in nurturing community, though not through Lakewood-centric groups.

If local civic groups had mixed success in integrating racially diverse newcomers, one unifier in Lakewood was pride in homeownership. As local columnist Bill Hillburg observed in 1994, pride of ownership was a constant from 1950 on. It showed up in "row upon row of well-kept homes, most of them expanded and improved because city policies allowed it. It shows up on the tree-lined parkways and in the 12 well-equipped parks that are focal points for life in Lakewood." Realtor Dave Emerson, who grew up in Lakewood, emphasized the continuity of aspirations: "Lakewood is still recognized as a safe place to live and raise a family. . . . There's more diversity among buyers, but they're coming here for the same reasons my parents did in 1951."[143]

These common throughlines were a tenuous basis of social cohesion at best. As social and civic groups fell short as meaningful spaces of racial integration, Lakewood moved toward diversity without a solid compass or vision for how integration should look in the suburb. It took few proactive steps to ensure racial peace and seemed unaware of challenges that people of color might face moving into this once-segregated community.

The Suburban Crisis Hits Lakewood

As early as the 1950s and intensifying after 1970, a "suburban crisis" struck the nation. Fueled by alarmist and sensationalist media coverage, suburban America was seemingly under siege from moral panics, even as it continued to draw in millions of home seekers nationwide. White middle-class suburbanites faced threats that ranged from rising crime, drug use among youth, and child predation, to mounting poverty, job losses, deteriorating housing, and toxic waste. While this crisis discourse painted white suburbanites as victims, the perpetrators were often portrayed as inner-city minorities, gang members, and random strangers.[144] "Marauders from Inner-City Prey on L.A.'s Suburbs," announced one expose by the LA Times in 1981 (which the newspaper has since apologized for).[145] Coming on the cusp of a full-blown war on gangs and drugs in the city, the alarmist rhetoric gave rise to a climate of fear and defensiveness in suburbia, touching Lakewood and many other communities. Coinciding as it did with Lakewood's racial diversification, the crisis would inevitably be linked to racial change in the minds of many despite a lack of evidence.[146] Although crime rates and racial change did not coincide in Lakewood, some white suburbanites would still scapegoat people of color for all of its problems.

Lakewood was caught up in these anxieties, from concerns about child safety to the economic dislocations fueled by inflation and defense cuts that threatened jobs, pressures that were upending the postwar social contract.

These apprehensions dovetailed with a broader malaise in America during this "age of fracture."[147] To some whites, Lakewood's changing demography and its unraveling model of middle-class success seemed intertwined. The cumulative result was a shift in public culture from convivial openness to a culture of fear and anxiety. Children especially felt it in the loss of freedom to roam and a move toward greater constriction and surveillance. Lakewood would place a new emphasis on law and order, which ultimately became a new—if tenuous—basis of community cohesion.

Crime existed in Lakewood from the beginning. Early news coverage was occasional but memorable, focused mainly on adult victims. The *LA Times* ran four crime stories on Lakewood residents from 1950 to 1961, including three attacks on white housewives, a marijuana bust involving a Lakewood Village resident, and a brutal assault on a Lakewood Village couple by youthful "wolf packs" terrorizing LA County. Such stories were outliers in a community known for its safety and openness.[148]

After 1970, the confluence of gangs, drugs, and imperiled children fueled a climate of alarm and fear in the suburbs of Southeast LA. Gang culture in fact was becoming widespread and diverse as Black and Latino gangs peaked in numbers and incidents of violence in the 1980s and 1990s, intensified by the crack cocaine epidemic.[149] Gangs emerged organically in the suburbs as well, from Asian gang activity in San Marino to Armenian gangs in Glendale and white gang imitators in affluent Agoura Hills.[150] Even Lakewood spawned its own homegrown white gang. Nonetheless, media coverage was often blatantly racialized, creating an association between crime, gangs, and people of color.[151]

In July 1972, 4-year-old Joyce Ann Huff was the victim of a gang-related shooting in nearby Hawaiian Gardens, a revenge killing following violence between rival gang members at a party in Lakewood. Huff's death made her "a martyr" in rising public alarm around youth gangs, whose activity "ranging from extortion, assault, burglary, inter-gang violence, to drug dealing" had become a "fact of police life" in towns like Norwalk, Hawaiian Gardens, Paramount, and Lakewood. While conceding that gangs transcended racial, ethnic, and religious lines, most gangs, a *Los Angeles Times* reporter asserted, were Black or Mexican American. The only way to stop this rising epidemic, he concluded, was to put more cops on the street.[152]

Beyond endangering children, gangs had come to threaten community safety in general. In 1976, the Lakewood Sheriff's Station launched an initiative targeting "hype-" (or heroin-) related crimes—burglary, petty theft, purse snatching, car theft—noting that women shopping alone at malls (like Lakewood Center) and empty homes during the day were common targets. The following year, the city voted to allocate $1,301 in matching funds for a sheriffs' anti-burglary program.[153] By 1988, Lakewood officials and sheriffs feared that "the gang activity gripping many Southeast cities is slowly working its way into the heart of this sleepy bedroom community." Gang members were reportedly hanging out at the Lakewood Mall, movie theaters, and local parks. "It's virgin territory here . . . [they] come here to get away from the troubles they find on their own streets," said Dale DuBois of the Lakewood Sheriff's Station. Even D. J. Waldie, public information officer for Lakewood, admitted that some gang members lived in Lakewood, although no gang was based there.[154]

Within a few years, a homegrown gang in Lakewood also inflicted serious damage on the suburb's climate of trust, openness, and childhood freedom. Composed mainly of white high school football players, the group called the Spur Posse had come to own Lakewood's public spaces—its playgrounds, streets, and parks—and committed a series of crimes and salacious acts, peaking in 1992. Resident Karin Polacheck described their activities.

> I'm talking about throughout the community. . . . At the baseball fields, at the parks, at the markets, on the corners of school grounds. They were organized enough that young children would say, "Watch out for that car when it comes around," "Watch out for these boys." I've heard stories of walking up and stealing baseball bats and telling kids, "If you tell anyone, I'll beat your head in." . . . I'm talking about young children, nine, ten years old. You know, it's a small community. . . . Younger kids knew that these older kids were out there.[155]

They harassed local kids with threats like, "You're dead," or "You're gonna get fucked up," or "You're gonna die." Their crimes soon escalated. At least two of the members committed burglaries, check forgeries, and thefts of credit cards, jewelry, bicycles, and guns, resulting in felony arrests. But their most egregious crimes were the sexual assaults of girls in Lakewood, ranging from age 10 to 16, who they treated as sexual conquests. When local authorities finally cracked down on the Spur Posse, the gang's exploits generated massive media attention and hand-wringing about what went wrong in Lakewood.[156] The public and media ultimately took a highly racialized view of gangs in the Southeast. When a gang was white like the Spur Posse, it was seen as an aberration, while Black and Latino gangs were deemed an endemic racial problem. The Spur Posse , nevertheless, deeply eroded trust and safety in the suburb's public spaces and escalated fears about child well-being.

Besides the gang threats, other crimes against children received graphic coverage in the newspapers. One 1976 story profiled the youngest "defenseless victims" of crimes—drug abuse, kidnapping, rape, assault, incest—torn from what one Sheriff's Department investigator called the "retch file."[157] As part of this rash of unsettling crimes against children, Lakewood and the Sheriff's Department were sued for enabling a "known juvenile sex offender" to get babysitting jobs through Lakewood's youth employment program. Even the schoolyard became a threatened space when a Lakewood man was arrested for threatening children with murder at Cleveland Elementary. Subsequent stories about local drug busts and drug pushers eroded the image of the community as a safe space for children.[158]

Sporadic stories about gangs and drugs with connections to Lakewood continued throughout the 1990s, including a local McDonalds that was reportedly part of a drug smuggling route of Mexican and Colombian cocaine traffickers, and a 1996 gang shoot-out in a Lakewood movie theater during a screening of "Set It Off."[159] In eastern Lakewood, some residents feared the encroachment of gangs on their neighborhood. As one remarked in 1992, "It seems we're right in between two gangs here. They're killing people right and left here."[160] A 1994 survey of Lakewood residents found that 62% felt their fear of crime had led them to change their daily activities or behavior.[161] A letter to the editor captured the feeling: "Recently my sister-in-law's purse was snatched while shopping near the Lakewood Center Mall; my friend's wife was harassed by gang members in the same area; and my boss' mother was held up at gunpoint in a store across from the mall. Now an innocent person has been murdered while parking his car at Lakewood Center Mall."[162] Lakewood, it seemed, had been swept into LA's treacherous crime wave.

As complex as the forces were that underlay Lakewood's own suburban crisis—which also impacted people of color—some whites made a simple racial calculus, blaming nonwwhites for the decline of safety and a sense of community in Lakewood. Social critic Alida Brill's disquieting portrait of Lakewood in the mid-1990s vividly captured white residents lamenting the "loss" of the parks, the high school, and mall to people of color. Reverend Robert Bunnett, who headed a large Protestant church in Lakewood, concurred: "We have a feeling of being encroached upon. I hear it all the time in the interfaith meetings we ministers have together, as well as from my congregation members and my neighbors. . . . [T]here are many people in Lakewood, not just in this church, who feel that we may be overwhelmed, and we are afraid." Larry Van Nostran, mayor and councilman since 1975, told Brill in 1993 about a visit he made to Mayfair Park, while he was mayor: "There was one white family, one white family—that was it. . . . Everyone else was black, or they were Spanish, Latino, Mexicans, whatever. . . . After 19 years as an elected councilman in this city, those people did not even know who I was. I told my wife . . . what am I doing here? Why am I working so hard for this town, what is it all for now? Maybe it is just time to go." Van Nostran continued to serve on the council and as mayor during Lakewood's ethnoracial transition through 2012, when he died while in office. Although Brill conceded that not everyone in Lakewood held these opinions, many did.[163] Longtime resident June Tweedy echoed this racial unease: "You sure don't feel safe when you're out. . . . Like today, I went over to the [ATM] and this is awful to say, but when I came out there was a couple of colored kids standing there, and I had my money and I had my keys and I thought I was ready to scream. Because they come up to you in those parking lots—you know, they're so bold."[164] White racial fear and mental associations of people of color with crime fostered an unsettled community dynamic.

For some parents, fears of crime and kidnapping curbed their willingness to allow their children to roam freely in the public spaces of Lakewood. Interviewed in 1996, Shirley Williams reflected, "One of the things I noticed with the change, neighbors were a little more apprehensive and frightened in letting their kids out to play. They played in their backyards. They just didn't feel it was safe. They had the feeling somebody was going to kidnap their kid out in front." Other residents echoed this change in long-standing suburban culture.[165]

Although the suburban crisis has been presented as one of white victimhood, Black and Latino suburbanites in towns like Compton and Whittier were experiencing their own suburban crisis, also fueled by rising crime in Los Angeles in the 1970s and 1980s. At times, these forces prompted their move to suburbs like Lakewood, perceived as safer spaces. Yet there was clearly no simple correlation between their arrival in Lakewood and spikes in crime. Lakewood's per capita crime rates peaked around 1990, when whites were 72% of residents—a period of heightened white anxiety—then declined steadily thereafter as Lakewood's diversity increased. Incoming residents of color were just as concerned about safety for their children as their white

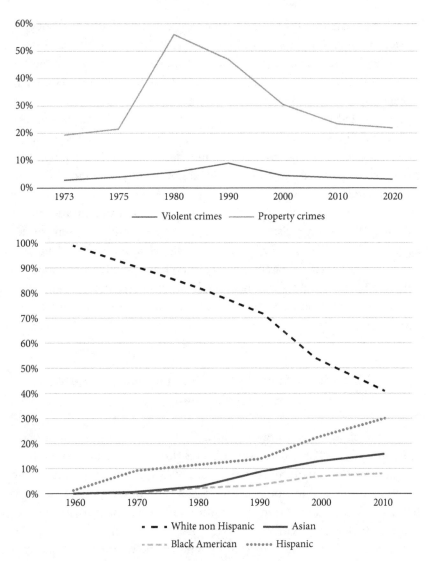

Figure 7.9 A comparison of crime rates and demographic change in Lakewood, 1960–2020. Crime in Lakewood peaked before the major demographic transition from white to multiracial.

(top) Crimes reported in Lakewood, per 1,000 persons, 1973–2020. For data sources, see note 166. (bottom) Ethnoracial composition of the Lakewood population, 1960–2010. US Census dataset, 1960–2010.

neighbors. If anything, they were a stabilizing force in Lakewood, judging by steadily declining crime rates from 1990 to 2020.[166] Overall, Lakewood's crime rates were average by LA County standards, and it was among the safest communities in the southeast suburbs.[167] Indeed, among newcomers to Lakewood, safety was often cited as a draw.

Because Lakewood's suburban crisis coincided with the beginnings of its racial transformation, many white residents fell into the easy trap of associating racial change with community declension. What that perspective missed were the aspirations and dreams of the Black, Latino, and Asian families gradually moving into Lakewood. They shared much with their white neighbors. For these families, safety for their children also meant shielding them from racism and harm. The Chase family, for example, accomplished this by creating a protective shield around their daughters through hyper-attentive parenting. Race fears clearly could cut both ways. As Lakewood increasingly placed new emphasis on public safety and security, it would remain to be seen whether these shared concerns might unite this diversifying suburb.

Surveillance Suburb: The Rise of Policing Culture in Lakewood

While the suburb had always prioritized the well-being of families and children, after 1970, safety would come through policing rather than neighbors. More institutionalized modes of law enforcement and public safety came to define not just how Lakewood would protect its own, but also an emergent community culture. Initiatives began with the city working in lockstep with the Sheriff's Department, moved into spatial policing, then percolated down to the grassroots, where neighbors were enlisted as agents of community surveillance. Together, these measures turned Lakewood into what one scholar called a virtual "police state," with at least 21 programs to fight crime, including the largest Neighborhood Watch programs in LA County by the 1990s.[168] The emerging culture of "see something, say something" could foster feelings of community stewardship, caretaking, and unity but, at the same time, invite suspicion, accusations, and punitive tactics into community dynamics. In the context of Lakewood's emerging public safety culture, race could be both a powerful unifier and powerful divider.

The relationship between Lakewood's public safety culture and its evolving racial profile was a nuanced one. While there were areas where policing was racialized, many of Lakewood's newest residents of color supported robust policing in their suburb and participated in neighborhood public safety initiatives.[169] This was not completely surprising given that a majority of nonwwhite residents were homeowners, just as concerned about property and family protection as their white counterparts (and, for that matter, suburban tenants). Yet the nexus of policing and race inevitably invited trouble, given the problematic track record of law enforcement in Los Angeles.[170] As the LASD's role and power grew, so did its mistakes. For Lakewood's second and third generations, it remained to be seen whether the cost savings of outsourcing policing was worth the tradeoff in loss of community control.

The rise of Lakewood's law-and-order culture began with Sky Knight, the city's highly visible and symbolic police helicopter program, a physical emblem of a new kind of surveillance. Neighborhood monitors were no longer attentive stay-at-home moms but LA sheriffs' deputies on the lookout for trouble from the air. Anti-crime initiatives undertaken over the following decades included city-sponsored programs, new policing technologies, and neighborhood volunteer efforts. Together, they turned public safety into a "core Lakewood value" and reoriented community culture in the process.[171]

A crucial catalyst was the 1965 Watts uprising. Fueled in part by frustrations over police brutality against Black and brown communities, the unrest ultimately provoked a law-and-order backlash in LA. The region responded by building up a martial infrastructure, drawing on federal funds from President Johnson's War on Crime and applying technologies developed in the Vietnam War to local law enforcement. While much of this mobilization was directed against communities of color, it also included a defense of white suburban spaces.[172]

In June 1966, Lakewood became a pioneer in applying military technology to policing, with the launch of Sky Knight. Initiated by the LASD, this helicopter patrol program was funded with a $159,000 federal grant. It was to be an 18-month experimental program with the Lakewood Sheriff's Station serving as the test site—a joint venture between Lakewood City, the Sheriff's Department, and the Hughes Tool Company. Sky Knight—which shared the nickname of the Douglas F3D-2 aircraft produced at the nearby plant—was an innovative form of crime control that linked helicopter patrols with ground units via radio.[173] The police helicopters were equipped with specialized radio equipment, camera, loudspeaker, and high-intensity floodlights. Three patrolled the area in single shifts, for about 20 hours per day. Owners of commercial buildings in Lakewood helped the pilots by installing rooftop markers and warning lights triggered by burglar alarms, sending a bright signal visible five miles away. In its first year of operation, Sky Knight helicopters were involved in tracking thefts and illegal dumping on vacant property, directing kids away from flood areas, breaking up a "teenage problem at a drive-in," and assisting in the capture of suspects.[174] One pilot made the military connection explicit in flight over Lakewood, asking his partner: "Remember when those squares were rice paddies in Korea instead of homes?"[175]

After some Lakewood residents initially feared the noise, the "snooping," and the "big brotherism," most ultimately embraced Sky Knight, especially after Hughes engineers modified the helicopters to reduce their noise. Many residents welcomed the aerial patrols for the perceived safety they brought to Lakewood. The Sky Knight made vivid impressions on area children. Linda Kay Gahan, whose father was a Lakewood sheriff, said they called it the "voice in the sky."[176] Nine-year-old Bill Baca remembered playing in the

Figure 7.10 Lakewood's Sky Knight program pioneered the use of aerial surveillance in law enforcement.

Photo used with permission of the Los Angeles County Sheriff's Department.

street at dusk with a dozen other kids and first "seeing this helicopter flying over knowing it was a sheriff. It was like, wow, we're in the safest city in the world. . . . It was like pulling the blanket over me. I felt like nobody can get away with anything."[177] Through the years, Lakewood celebrated Sky Knight in public events, produced videos about it, and touted the fact that other cities followed their lead—including Los Angeles. By the mid-1990s, Sky Knight was responding to calls about kids who didn't show up for dinner. As chief pilot Wes Pearson explained, "We'll fly over to the neighborhood and broadcast the child's description and name," and soon the child in question could be "seen scurrying home."[178]

Other public safety initiatives soon followed. In 1972, two months after the murder of Joyce Ann Huff, Lakewood formed a new anti-crime division called the Community Safety Department (CSD), a unit within city government to direct all operations involving law enforcement and administer the Sheriff's Department contract. Director Terry Mangan quickly launched a youth education program that deployed officers to "every school class in town, kindergarten through high school seniors" to discuss stranger danger, crime and drug prevention (and avoidance), and tips for reporting suspicious cars or persons. Home safety checks and inventories of personal property were also covered.[179] Some residents balked at these efforts, launching a recall campaign in 1975 against four city council members for, among other things, creating the CSD as a "second police department" without voter consent. While the recall failed, these dissenters gained seats on the council and helped abolish the CSD in 1976, moving those functions to the Sheriff's Department in the name of cost savings and efficiency.[180]

The city council learned its lesson and, rather than form duplicate departments, bolstered its support for law enforcement through direct subsidies and the formation of new programs. From 1977 to 1990, it approved, for example, city funds for the Southern Regional Burglary Team ($1,310), the LASD Crime Task Force ($59,277) and Street Criminal Apprehension Team ($4,910), a tip-line for reporting graffiti ($5,000), and a sheriffs' anti-drug program in the Long Beach Unified School District ($54,000). At a time when Lakewood felt a fiscal crunch from Prop 13, inflation, and defense cuts, these commitments signaled broad community support for law enforcement funding, a trend that accelerated in subsequent years.[181] Around the same time, Lakewood implemented a child fingerprinting program, part of a national trend in the wake of stranger-danger panics, as well as a car decal program to stave off a rise in car thefts.[182] And, in 1992, Lakewood instituted the Special Assignment Officer (SAO) program, hiring private security officers to focus on Lakewood's "hot spots"—the mall and eastern Lakewood where gang conflict was heating up. Sometimes plainclothes, sometimes uniformed, the SAOs would "saturate an area and they'll sit and they'll monitor what goes on in that area," Lakewood sheriff Barry Wulwick explained.[183]

The Sheriff's Department continually incorporated new technologies in surveillance and law enforcement, including night vision scopes similar to those used in Vietnam and heat-seeking "flirscopes," particularly useful for Sky Knight, which Wulwick noted produced "a nice red spot depending on how warm the body is." The Lakewood Sheriffs set up a facial recognition program, a Graffiti Watch program to immediately remove graffiti, and K9 units on 24-hour call.[184]

Like other suburbs around this time, Lakewood also launched new spatial policing efforts meant to better control the appearance and use of both public and private spaces. Some of these measures targeted people of color. In 1998, the suburb formed a Crime and Nuisance Property Abatement Team to enforce property upkeep, especially targeting rental properties (including houses) and businesses.[185] Lakewood's parks became a particularly fraught space. Long beloved for their robust programs and inviting green spaces, the parks by the 1980s had become a flashpoint of white racial resentment as they were used with increasing frequency by people of color, residents and nonresidents alike. Bolivar Park became especially popular among Blacks and Latinos. One "original" resident described being "in jail" on the weekend, trapped in their homes because, "They are everywhere. We cannot leave our houses, they park in front of our houses."[186] In response, the city began a more assertive program of park policing in the 1990s. The sheriffs introduced bike patrols in 1992, then stepped up Park Watch a few years later by stationing more sheriffs in the park to provide a visible law enforcement presence. The city banned piñatas, which one official said got one "particular group . . . very upset with me because it was a cultural thing."[187] (By 1990, Lakewood had over 10,000 Latino residents.) Councilmember Jackie Rynerson admitted that it was hard for some white residents to accept the fact that Lakewood residents were among these nonwwhite park users. Alida Brill put it this way: "There is no mentality present that suggests than any good could come from trying to integrate with people using the parks. Instead, the options are to retreat to one's own back yard, literally and metaphorically."[188]

The public schools were another site of intensified policing. Racial tensions continued at Lakewood High. In 1986, the Long Beach district held a weekend camping retreat near Big Bear for 130 high school students to promote interracial harmony. Students participated in bonding exercises like the "trust fall," team exercises in the woods that focused on problem-solving, small-group discussions of personal problems, and imaginary gift exchanges. Although the students reveled in their new friendships and perspective, some doubted how long these would last once they returned home. By the early 1990s, at campuses in Lakewood, Paramount, Compton and Long Beach, conflict between Black and Latino students had escalated. For example, a lunchtime altercation in 1994 at Lakewood High involving about 60 students resulted in 10 injuries and one arrest. (The racial breakdown at the school by then was 38% Latino, 34% white, 14% Black, and 9% Asian.) In response, the school installed metal detectors, beefed up police patrols, and instituted a "zero tolerance" policy for weapons, drugs, or fights on campus, resulting in swift disciplinary action that included suspension and expulsion. While principal Jon Meyer also hoped to form an "interracial committee" at school, the police crackdown was the more decisive response and followed the pattern that largely guided human relations in Lakewood.[189]

Finally, Lakewood enlisted residents as agents of community surveillance and public safety. While in the early years neighborly supervision was done informally, by the 1980s, the city directed these roles and relationships with a distinct emphasis on crime prevention. It made residents on-the-ground junior partners to law enforcement in their neighborhoods. Although these were institutionally directed initiatives, residents took these programs in different directions—some embracing the law enforcement mandate, others nurturing a more benevolent sense of community stewardship. Not surprisingly, whites and people of color at times diverged in their approach to community, law enforcement, and their role in neighborhood "watch." Meanwhile, crime rates fell in Lakewood as both these programs and Lakewood's multiraciality multiplied.

The culture of "see something, say something" was at the heart of these programs, which grew from an arsenal of protective measures spawned in response to the suburban crisis regionally and nationally.[190] They can also be seen as suburban versions of community policing, in their emphasis on the deputizing of private citizens to make them extensions of law enforcement.[191] In Lakewood, city leaders in 1972 created community education programs for adults and youth on how to recognize and report suspicious situations. In early 1978, the WeTIP (We Turn in Pushers) program spread to Lakewood. This was an anonymous phone hotline for tips about drug trafficking, which then expanded to other crimes like murder, robbery, burglary, arson, rape, and child abuse. Callers received $500 for information that led to an arrest and conviction, while their anonymity buffered them from the criminal justice system. Community organizations in Lakewood contributed financially to WeTIP. Ten years later, in March 1988, the new group Mothers Against Gangs in the Community (MAGIC) attracted over 850 members in just three months. Founded by Lakewood resident Patricia Patrick, whose close friend was shot in a gang-related drive-by in Long Beach, the group sponsored a series of public meetings on gang violence in the southeast suburbs. Lakewood also began hosting annual Crime Fighting Expos in the park. In 1995, it included displays by Lakewood Neighborhood Watch, the Sky Knight, Lakewood Auto Watch, Lakewood Sheriff's Station patrol cars, SWAT teams, K-9 units, and Kidprint (child fingerprinting).[192]

The heart of Lakewood's community-based crime prevention was Neighborhood Watch, a national program launched in 1974, originally sponsored by the National Sheriff's Association. The program had two goals: to protect homes against burglary and to foster the cooperation of residents with law enforcement as a way to deter crime. Activities might include citizen patrols, keeping an eye on neighbors' homes when they were out of town, and reporting suspicious activity in the neighborhood. In Los Angeles, LAPD Chief William Parker saw the value in community-driven policing in the sprawling suburbs of LA, and he launched a series of neighborhood meetings in the 1960s to urge residents "to become arms of the law."[193] This was a strategy for building consensus and trust between suburban residents and law enforcement.

As early as 1977, a Lakewood group convened a meeting on Neighborhood Watch with speakers from the Sheriff's Department. In 1981, their program officially launched and would become one of the largest in Southern California.[194] The *Los Angeles Times* soon began running a weekly feature of Neighborhood Watch tips targeting Lakewood and other southeastern suburbs, covering topics like safety tips for seniors, how to handle a rape threat, and how to protect children from abuse.[195] As one column put it, Neighborhood Watch "is designed to increase cooperation, respect, and understanding between the citizen and the police."[196] In 1987, the city began holding annual barbecue picnics for Neighborhood Watch block captains, who numbered 250 in 1990. By the late 1990s, Lakewood had nearly 35,000 active members in Neighborhood Watch groups—about 63% of the adult

Figure 7.11 Lakewood Neighborhood Watch, 1987. Lakewood's Neighborhood Watch program launched in the early 1980s and grew to become one of the largest in California. This program connected neighbors while also maintaining a tight link to law enforcement, eliciting mixed reactions from the suburb's diverse residents.
Photo courtesy of the City of Lakewood Historical Collection.

population—with 400 block captains. Many volunteers were white retirees or members of second- and third-generation Lakewood families.[197]

By the 1980s and 1990s, Neighborhood Watch had evolved to serve three functions in Lakewood: to report crime, to forge consensus between residents and the Sheriff's Department, and to foster neighborly connections. The crime aspect was crucial, from the perspective of both the Sheriff's Department and some long-time white residents. To the sheriffs, Neighborhood Watch's prime role was to report suspicious activities, "to be the eyes and ears for the sheriff's department and help us get that job done." This mindset was reflected in a one-page monthly newsletter that reported on crime statistics and trends, safety tips, and Sheriff's Department updates.[198] At times, volunteers could be overzealous. As Sheriff Barry Wulwick noted: "the biggest problem we have is that there are a lot of these people that are so excited and want to help so much, sometimes they put themselves in a precarious position," such as a resident who ran into the street to wave down a speeder rather than take down the license plate and call it in. In Lakewood, Wulwick noted, "sometimes you have to put them under your thumb and kind of simmer them down a little bit."[199] Especially in the context of a diversifying community, this sort of overreach was potentially dangerous for residents who were targeted.

Neighborhood Watch came to represent a neighborly connection that could bridge racial divides. Lakewood had experienced a sea change in social life by the second generation, and Neighborhood Watch was restoring some lost connections. As one resident stated, "Most people who buy a home want a neighborhood. And that's what Neighborhood Watch is about. It helps you have a neighborhood instead of just owning a home some place."[200] Perhaps the most vivid evidence of the program's social function was its "welcome wagon" role. As block captains Derrick and Pamela Williams explained, the city notified them when a new neighbor was moving in, it sent them a packet for the neighbors (which included useful phone numbers and information about Lakewood), and then the Williams hand-delivered this, along with a plate of cookies if they felt so inclined. The first official social outreach to new residents, then, came from Neighborhood Watch. Many groups also held social activities on the block, like barbeques, Fourth of July get-togethers, Christmas and New Year parties, and happy hours. Some Neighborhood Watch groups met four times a year, to connect socially and share information on local crime and safety. For Mrs. P, a white block captain, making friends was an unexpected benefit of participation.[201]

While Lakewood collected no data on this, interviews and anecdotal evidence through 2020 suggest that the racial breakdown of Lakewood Neighborhood Watch reflected an overrepresentation of whites as block captains, while group members included some nonwhite residents. Many white retirees served as block captains. Members tended to be mostly white, with smaller numbers of Latinos, followed by Blacks and Asians. This profile suggests some buy-in to Lakewood's self-policing culture by people of color. Interviews suggest they joined for a variety of reasons, including a desire to protect the safety of their streets, to foster connections with neighbors, and, ultimately, to help determine whom to trust.[202]

A few Black Americans who became leaders in Neighborhood Watch put their own imprimatur on the group, emphasizing mutual caregiving and trust while at the same time remaining deeply skeptical about the Lakewood Sheriff's

Department. They inflected the group with their own values, including stewardship and social justice. This defined the experience of Pamela and Derrick
Williams, who jumped at the chance to serve immediately after moving in.
Derrick recalled, "I love meeting people. And I love to help. . . . I welcome everything that it stood for, just going out and getting involved in the community,
watching over each other, having each other's backs, helping in any way." Derrick
chatted frequently with neighbors on a Saturday while mowing the lawn, turning
a two-hour chore "into a six- to seven-hour day." Pamela made flyers, passed out
Safety Expo tickets to neighbors, and helped welcome newcomers. Together, they
attended monthly block captain meetings to be briefed by sheriffs on local crime
trends and safety tips. Pamela became certified as a first responder as part of the
Community Emergency Response Team, an option offered to block captains.
The Williams were a visible and trusted presence on their block who neighbors
turned to in times of need. They cared much less about the law enforcement
aspect. Derrick described the tenor of their role: "We watch each other. When
there's a blackout, I'm outside and walking up the street, flashlights on my head
and everything else. And everyone's coming out. I'm checking on everybody,
they're checking on us." The Williams held more trust in their neighbors than the
sheriffs, who they believed were sorely disconnected from the community; the
sheriffs made no effort to introduce themselves, "to walk around and say hi and
interact with the neighborhood," as Derrick put it.[203]

Another nonwhite block captain also saw Neighborhood Watch as a promoter of neighborly trust, without necessarily leaning on the sheriffs. "It really has to be us policing our own communities," she noted. It wasn't enough
to rely on the sheriffs, who didn't have the resources to police all streets and
who at times showed racial bias, she believed. Their group, united by a crime
surge on their street, had the effect of fostering trust and sociability among
neighbors. "I have never been a really neighborly person, and not because
I didn't want to. I just didn't know who to trust."[204] In a diverse suburb where
racial suspicions might run high in multiple directions, the group played an
important unifying role.

While Neighborhood Watch could play a nuanced role in Lakewood
shaped by residents themselves, another resident-centered program put
crime front and center: Volunteers on Patrol (VOP). Begun in 1994, this program was run jointly by the city and Sheriff's Department. They recruited
and trained resident volunteers to patrol areas and keep an eye out for
criminal activity. Volunteers underwent a six-week training course at a
Sheriffs' facility in basic criminal law, first aid, patrol procedures, and, in

later years, homelessness, animal abuse, and cultural sensitivity. Within its first year, 90 volunteers had been trained.[205] Bill Baca, who joined VOP in 2011, emphasized that they were "representatives of the LA County Sheriff's Department." Some elderly volunteers assisted at the Sheriff's Department itself, giving tours of the station, doing office work, answering phones, and taking fingerprints.[206] Younger volunteers patrolled the neighborhoods in white patrol cars equipped with amber lights and marked "Volunteers on Patrol" on the back bumper. Baca and a partner worked a four- to eight-hour shift each week. "We pretty much do everything that deputies don't want to do"—such as direct traffic around accidents and downed trees, home vacation checks, and assist at alcohol checkpoints. In VOP, residents were essentially junior deputies. In 2020, Lakewood VOP had four vehicles and 62 volunteers, making it the second largest group in LA County. Baca estimated that about 40% were white, about 25–30% Latino, the remainder a mix of Blacks and "Middle Easterners," including several volunteer clergy members in the Sheriff's Department who were "predominantly Black."[207] In this program, a powerful consensus existed between a racially diverse group of Lakewood residents and the Sheriff's Department.

The final anti-crime initiative in Lakewood that enlisted residents was a series of city-produced cable TV shows in the early 1990s, including *Crime Stoppers*, *This Is Neighborhood Watch*, and *Behind the Badge*, which instructed residents on handgun use. Produced by Lakewood's City TV and the LASD, these shows encouraged residents to report suspicious activity and people, setting a precedent for subsequent social media anti-crime initiatives. In a 1998 community survey, *Crime Stoppers* was the most-watched show among Lakewood's cable television programming—73.4% of respondents said they watched it.[208]

The rise of a law enforcement culture in a community in the throes of racial diversification was, on one level, not surprising. Social life had become unpredictable, neighbors sometimes unknown and unfamiliar, creating challenges that were simply absent in the early years when everyone seemed to get along because they were so alike. On another level, the Black, Latino, and Asian families moving into Lakewood perceived both benefits and drawbacks in this public safety culture. Some enthusiastically participated in sheriff-driven efforts like VOP, while others reframed programs like Neighborhood Watch to support their own values. For people of color, neighborly protection could mean shielding one another from all kinds of harm—from racism to crime to the Sheriff's Department itself. Either way, the collision of race and policing in Lakewood inevitably led to conflict and concerns. With a rise in policing in Lakewood came a rise in police-related problems.

As a contracted service, the LASD lacked local mechanisms for ensuring police accountability and efficiency. A study conducted in 1980 by the office of Captain John Hammargren, commander of the Lakewood Sheriff's Station, acknowledged the difficulty of knowing the communities under their watch, adding that "increased community knowledge is desirable but beyond a certain point does not necessarily result in significantly better enforcement." Not surprisingly, they offered few remedies.[209] While Lakewood may have been an exception to this, given the station's location within Lakewood and the rise of a law enforcement culture locally, some residents still noticed the lack of on-the-ground interface between the sheriffs and residents. Louis Chase described it as "a certain militarization and apartness by the Sheriff's departments. . . . It's not like someone who would stop the car to get out to have a conversation with you. It is someone who when you're stopped, it's like you're almost under arrest." This applied particularly to Black people.[210]

In the 1980s and 1990s, several corruption and racialized police brutality incidents tarnished the Lakewood Sheriff's Station. One narcotics sheriff was convicted for peddling cocaine, another for planting drugs on suspects.[211] In February 1989, in perhaps its most egregious abuse of power, the Lakewood sheriffs stormed a Samoan bridal shower in Cerritos. The clash occurred at the home of the Dole family, a Samoan family well known to their neighbors for their friendliness. On the night of the party, a neighbor called the Lakewood Sheriff's Station asking if they could ask the family to turn down their music, which they did. Two hours later, the sheriffs returned clad in riot gear, with dozens of police cars and a police helicopter. Neighbor witnesses and deputies disagreed on what happened next. While the sheriffs claimed the partygoers hurled rocks and bottles at them, a video taken by neighbor Doug Botts, a 57-year-old Douglas Aircraft worker, showed no evidence of bottles or rocks at the scene. But it did show the sheriffs storming the home, pulling dozens of people outside, forcing them to lay face down on the ground, then beating them with clubs.[212] The sheriffs arrested 34 people, all Samoan, and seven were later charged with various felony and misdemeanor counts of rioting, assaulting officers, and refusing to disperse. The Samoan community and the Doles's neighbors believed the raid was a civil rights violation and a disturbing example of police brutality against a minority family, charges that prompted an FBI investigation. Neighbors who testified at the trial claimed the sheriffs had committed an unwarranted and unnecessarily brutal raid against the Dole family. One neighbor, who watched events unfold from her front lawn, stated, "If you would have seen what they did, you couldn't believe it. You saw them beating [the party goers] and no resistance from them at all, just taking them out and beating them." The arrested Samoans were acquitted. No sheriffs were disciplined.[213] This raid, not coincidentally, occurred around the same time as the LAPD's Operation Hammer, a broad crackdown on people who fit the "drug gang" profile—representing a heightened moment of law enforcement aggressiveness against communities of color in LA.[214]

The Lakewood Sheriff's Department faced further accusations of racialized abuse of power. Louis Chase was stopped several times while driving through his own town, which he perceived as racial profiling.[215] In 1992, an African American in his 20s relayed to an investigative panel his experiences at the hands of the Lakewood Sheriffs: "I've been living right across the street from this park for the last 15 years.... [A]s I got older in age the police force out here would pull me over, call me 'nigger' ... 'What are you doing out here? Where are you from, Compton?' This and that. Sit me on the curb, dirty my clothes. Tear out everything in my car.... To me, it's a crime to be Black and to be on the streets of the Lakewood sheriff's department after 11 o'clock."[216] Another resident described how her friend's Black sons were stopped regularly by deputies "for no reason" while walking to the Lakewood Mall.[217] Derrick Williams recalled how Black friends were pulled over by the sheriffs and recounted the confrontation like this: "they made me get out of the car and it was just, I'm going, 'what did I do?' Simply because you say, 'what did you do?' it turns into a whole—now you're being uncooperative, you're being threatening in your gestures." The Williams believed such encounters were commonplace in Lakewood.[218]

These incidents were part of a spike in police abuse, often racially driven, by the LASD around this time. In 1989, 151 excessive-force lawsuits were filed against the Sheriff's Department, nearly double the figure in 1985. Over a three-year period in the late 1980s, the department paid out $8.5 million in major settlements. In many cases, the deputies—some of them repeat offenders—were not disciplined and in a few cases were promoted. Leaders in the Black, Latino, Korean, Samoan, and gay communities were especially critical of the sheriffs, accusing them of unjustified violence, including five fatal shootings in 1989–1990.[219] For the Samoan bridal party assault, the LASD eventually paid out $23 million in damages to the victims, the largest assessed against an American law enforcement agency—and six times what Los Angeles paid Rodney King.[220] At the Lakewood Sheriff's Station, part of the problem was the lack of racial representation on the force. In 1992, 78% of officers were white, and they patrolled an area that was 49% white. Ironically, the Lakewood Plan, intended as an economizing measure, likely passed on the costs for these payouts to residents in the suburbs contracting with the Sheriff's Department.

The 1992 Kolts Report, based on a seven-month internal investigation of the LA Sheriff's Department, found "deeply disturbing evidence of excessive force and lax discipline." While the southeast Norwalk and Lynwood Stations were especially singled out, the latter harboring a neo-Nazi, white suprem-acist gang of deputies known as the Vikings, the excessive-force cases in-cluded actions by the Lakewood Sheriffs. While the Kolts report praised the Lakewood Station for implementing an excessive-force tracking system in 1989, it also acknowledged that the LASD was not reforming "with adequate thoroughness and speed."[221] In 1993, the Lakewood Sheriff's Station, seeking to seize control of the situation, set up a six-member advisory committee that could bring problems to the sheriffs' attention and work with Neighborhood Watch groups in a fully coordinated effort. As one sheriff put it, "We're trying to break down the us-versus-them mentality between the community and the Sheriff's Department."[222] This clear statement of consensus-seeking by the Sheriff's Department was yet another effort to forge a law enforcement culture in Lakewood.

And yet problems persisted, particularly as Lakewood continued to diver-sify. In 1997, an ACLU report showed that citizen complaints against the LASD actually rose from 2,048 in 1994 to 2,787 in 1996, while the department also stopped recording the race and age of people filing complaints. The Lakewood Sheriffs lodged the highest number of citizen complaints in LA County and had the worst record on neglect of duty and discourtesy and second worst on false imprisonment and excessive use of force. While the sheriffs spun these figures as a sign that their complaint system was working, the ACLU saw "a se-rious community relations problem."[223] For Lakewood in particular, this was a troubling signal that, for a community committing itself so thoroughly to law enforcement, the bedrock of that system was not treating everyone equally.[224]

"Tomorrow's City"

At the dawn of the new millennium, Lakewood was a suburb of social com-plexity. Residents of divergent backgrounds and identities inhabited blocks of similar homes, mass-produced 50 years earlier in a manner that once worried social critics for their supposed power to homogenize individuals. That worry was grounded in the unspoken expectation that suburban segregation would hold indefinitely, a supposition that enabled these critics to imagine whites as the victims of such societal forces as "mass production" or "mass culture." Lakewood's original white residents were of course the beneficiaries of numerous advantages conferred by postwar suburban living, including superior schools, safe and healthy neighborhoods, and asset accumulation through homeownership which fostered generational wealth. The social experience of a close and trusting community made a deep, positive impression on Lakewood's first generation, adults and children alike. They reaped those benefits fully—launching children into the world, forging lifelong friendships, and claiming ownership of Lakewood's story.

The civil rights movement disrupted this segregated idyll. Through their determined effort to claim a place in suburbia and benefit from its advantages, Blacks, Latinos, Asians, and other people of color broke the racial barriers and purchased homes in Lakewood and many suburbs like it. Their very presence challenged the assumption that suburbia was, by definition, white. As Lakewood's once easy, trusting social milieu became more tenuous and guarded, the suburb's culture pivoted to one of public safety and law and order. People of color settling in Lakewood at times found a more challenging, unsettling, and emotionally taxing environment than their white predecessors.

Residents of color often described how they loved Lakewood and were so happy to be living there. It was their attainment of the American Dream, a life in quiet, peaceful suburbia—and yet, one that could also bring experiences of overzealous police, prejudiced neighbors, and white overrepresentation at city hall. For decades, no public forums allowed for frank discussions about race. For whites, newcomers and long-time residents alike, the hope for Lakewood was to maintain itself as a safe place where neighbors took pride in their property and their community. Yet demographic change revealed their own discomfort and wariness around the "other" in Lakewood. Many didn't hesitate to express those misgivings. This created a formidable barrier to social and civic engagement. Lakewood's new law-and-order culture also created a problematic context for the social and civic integration of Lakewood's residents of color. Given the poor record of local police on race relations, the undercurrents of suspicion promoted by this culture were inopportune for building social trust and warmth.

Up to 2020, Lakewood took few proactive steps to promote peaceable human relations as it underwent demographic change, to understand the experience of living as an "other" in a well-established community and to proactively promote inclusive social and civic engagement. This context makes the actions of individuals like Pamela and Derrick Williams, Ari Pe, Joe Esquivel, Bill Baca, and Cassandra Chase even more significant. They stepped forward to become engaged members of the community and in so doing brought a multiracial sensibility to suburbia.

Diversity created a multiplicity of experiences that suggested something much deeper, richer, and more complex than Lakewood cared to admit. It was a suburb of conflict and consensus, inequity and contentment, American dreams and simmering racism, which together made up "Tomorrow's City." More than its founders could have imagined in choosing that moniker, Lakewood indeed was a harbinger of the future, reflecting continuity, change, and contradictions in the new suburbia.

Conclusion

The New Suburbia reveals how certain continuities in suburban culture persisted in communities undergoing rapid demographic change. Long-lived suburban ideals first defined by whites survived, at times to the detriment of equity and inclusivity across the LA metropolis. The desire endured to protect and defend suburban communities from internal and external threats in places like San Marino and South Gate, where Asians and Latinos became majorities and reinforced those goals. This book captures especially those fraught moments of transition, when defensive reactions led to clampdowns on newcomers and their unfamiliar ways. Both of those suburbs sought to protect Euro-American aesthetics and traditional suburban values, replicating some of the more exclusionary tendencies that long defined white suburbs. One might argue that a hegemonic white suburban ideal seemed to be alive and well in the new suburbia—and not just at the hands of whites, but among a multiracial cross-section of new suburbanites.[1]

Those white influences were more direct in Pasadena and Lakewood, two suburbs that saw some—but not total—white flight. The white residents who remained were committed to their communities, whether out of nostalgic loyalty or attraction to a certain way of life. In both places, white anxieties ran high during the transition, when fears of established whites losing power animated community dynamics. In these particular suburbs, ethnoracial change triggered shifts in local social life toward privatization among Pasadenans who could afford it and toward a law-and-order culture in middle-class Lakewood. Residents of color, who finally got the opportunity to achieve the American dream, had to navigate this fraught landscape as part of the suburbanization experience itself.

Social and civic engagement in suburbia did not die off between 1945 and 2010. Experiences varied in different suburbs, but these case studies showed that community involvement persisted over decades and pivoted especially around suburban children and the schools. This comports with the notion that homeowner, taxpayer, and parent defined suburban identity. "Parent" loomed especially large in the realm of suburban social and civic life. In

suburbs rich and poor, children and the schools were crucial conduits of social integration, particularly for new immigrant suburbanites. The context
of local education thus had an outsized impact on the nature of that engagement. Where local school systems were unified, drawing in the vast majority
of residents, they acted as a cohesive force. Where education was splintered
into public, private, and parochial schools, so, too, was social life. Schools
represented an important hub of participation over the years, belying the narrative of social breakdown in the post-1980 era. Yet there were also nuances to
this story. In class-divided Pasadena, for example, school communities split
starkly along class and race lines as white families retreated from integrated
public schools into private schools, where robust voluntarism remained alive
and well, if insulated within this privileged realm. In working-class South
Gate, the schools represented a particularly important stepping-stone for
immigrant Latino parents making their first tentative forays into American
civic life. Schools were an accessible gateway for acclimating immigrant
families to suburban lifeways. In wealthy San Marino, a small unified school
district represented a crucial site where new Chinese residents first got involved, learned the importance of voluntarism in suburban culture, and
from there entered local political life. In all instances, the schools represented
more than places for children to learn; they were essential sites for engagement, immigrant integration, and local political power.

In addition to the schools, community safety represented a hub of
civic and social engagement, if a tenuous one, within diverse suburbia. In
Lakewood, a shared concern around public safety united residents of different backgrounds. As that concern came into conflict with the problematic apparatus of law enforcement, the fragility of this consensus revealed
itself. These dynamics played out most clearly in Lakewood. It had pioneered
the "Lakewood Plan," which created a system of outsourcing law enforcement and in turn hindered police accountability, a system replicated in other
suburbs. Lakewood became a community fixated on public safety while
emerging as one of LA's most racially balanced suburbs. Its history illustrates
the important role that the LA Sheriff's Department played in policing LA's
suburban spaces, with its problematic record of racially biased policing and
the challenges this created in growing numbers of diversifying suburbs.
Lakewood also highlighted how residents could appropriate a public safety
culture to serve various ends—whether to police racially diverse newcomers
or to foster inclusive community cultures where residents genuinely looked
out for one another, even against racially biased law enforcement. This

bottom-up community building could steer public safety in a more racially sensitive, inclusive direction.

Suburbanites of different backgrounds, races, and ethnicities at times came together to build bonds of friendship and trust. These were simple, sometimes fleeting moments, but they represented proactive efforts to unite diverse neighbors in communities of engagement. It happened in "Dinners for 8" in San Marino and in bowling leagues in Crenshaw and the southeast suburbs, in TLC small groups at Altadena Baptist Church and certain Neighborhood Watch groups in Lakewood. These were hopeful moments and models for human relations in the new suburbia.

At the same time, suburbia could be a fractured environment marked by internal tensions. The people in power locally—namely homeowners—tended to hold on to that power and hew to traditional suburban ideals even as socioeconomic realities were changing around them. Those normative ideals represented continuity with an Anglo suburban past, staying relatively fixed and resistant to adapting to the differing needs of new suburbanites, including those seeking affordable housing. Significantly, these ideals were embraced by new ethnic leaders in the suburbs. By working to protect single-family home neighborhoods, such suburbs exacerbated metropolitan inequality by class, immigrant status, language, and race. These multiple vectors of difference drove community dynamics in the new suburbia, with class especially salient. As late as 2022, three-quarters of residential land in California was zoned R-1, a mechanism that has impeded the construction of housing across suburban areas. This slow-growth tool has tightened the housing supply, pushed up prices, and, ultimately, obstructed the building of mixed types of housing that might be more affordable.

In the southeast suburbs, neighborhood life in the 1980s and 1990s revealed a fractured Latino community, pitting co-ethnics against each other within the fragile social context of newly integrating communities. Residents divided around local issues such as land use, housing, and immigrant rights, at times marginalizing the poorest residents, many of them undocumented. Just as suburbia had conferred and fortified certain crucial advantages of whiteness for a generation of European ethnics, it did so for privileged Latinos, though many of them retained a strong sense of Latino identity through that process. The persistence of a Latino suburban working class with its own everyday norms—from informal housing to "enacted" Latino landscapes—suggested that, despite the crackdowns against these practices, these individuals could still find pragmatic ways to make meaningful lives in Southern California. In wealthy Chinese/white San Marino, spatial politics carefully protected long-entrenched Anglo aesthetics while suppressing visible traces of ethnicity in the landscape. Chinese residents embraced a NIMBY attitude toward ethnoburbia as a means of solidifying their inclusion in the suburb and protecting property values. The local interethnic consensus among Chinese and white residents worked to protect this "landscape of privilege" with iron-clad efficiency.

The suburbs of Los Angeles experienced the repercussions of the macro forces of globalization, economic restructuring, and immigration in intensely local ways. They displayed the abounding diversity of the suburban experience itself, from rich to poor, immigrant ethnoburbs that celebrated ethnic identity to immigrant suburbs that suppressed it, from suburbs that racially flipped to those that remained stably diverse. Some suburbs retained their insulated wealth. Others were ravaged by deindustrialization and poverty. Suburbia came to represent the dynamism of American life, a space where everything happened.

On October 10, 2022, a political scandal shook LA City Hall. A leaked audio tape exposed a litany of racist remarks uttered by LA City councilmember Nury Martinez, conversing with three other Latino leaders—councilmembers Gil Cedillo and Kevin de León and LA County Federation of Labor president Ron Herrera. The conversation was about redistricting, and, in expressing her frustration with the perceived unfairness toward Latinos within that process, Martinez disparaged Blacks, whites, Oaxacans, and gays using crude language. She resigned quickly under immense pressure that came from as high up as the White House. The incident set off weeks of public discourse in Los Angeles around the excruciating challenges of living in a multiracial society—the racism that can exist among all race groups, the hate that can spew across groups, in all directions.[2]

The Nury Martinez incident exposed the numerous layers of division that had been operating for decades in LA, including in its suburbs undergoing racial change. These were communities of diverse residents trying to figure out how to live together. Not everyone welcomed the changes or aspired to what Martin Luther King, Jr. described as "the beloved community," where people would live in mutual respect, where justice was not for any one oppressed group, but for all people. These histories challenge us to think about the complexities of justice in an era of re-racialized spatial privilege. Even more broadly, as social theorist Nicholas De Genova puts it, they force us to look at how racially oppressed people make claims on "American-ness." "Do they disrupt, repudiate, subvert, recapitulate, or endorse [it]? . . . Do their very efforts to challenge their subjugation by white supremacy become captive to its grinding machinations and even enlisted in the service of sustaining the efficacy and reenergizing the resilience of their own and others' oppression?"[3] These are urgent and important questions as demographic changes continue to remake suburbia and the nation itself.

Stories from the new suburbia offer both cautionary tales and hopeful signs. Even as racism and exclusion prevailed in many communities, some recent signs are pointing toward greater inclusion and equity. One indicator is attitudes among suburbanites toward diversity itself. In a 2020 Monmouth University poll conducted nationally, 74% of voters and 84% of suburban women stated that it was important to them to have more racially integrated neighborhoods and that trend was unlikely to affect property values or safety. They also supported the construction of new apartments nearby. Another 2020 poll conducted in Minnesota and Wisconsin found that a majority of suburbanites would not be concerned if new apartments, subsidized housing, or Section 8 tenants moved into their communities. By a two-to-one margin, they supported government vouchers for low-income residents to live in more affluent communities.[4]

Two developments in California signaled efforts to undo key mechanisms of suburban exclusion. In October 2022, the California Association of Realtors issued a formal apology for its past discriminatory efforts, including its proactive role behind Proposition 14 (1964), its endorsement of redlining and race-restrictive covenants, and its support of state measures to obstruct affordable housing.[5] More significant was a cluster of laws passed by the state legislature designed to dislodge the power of R-1 zoning. In 2016, California lawmakers began passing a series of laws that made it easier to densify R-1 areas. These bills allowed for the building of accessory dwelling units (ADUs) and for the subdivision of single-family lots to accommodate up to four units. The potential power of these measures was signaled by the pushback from opponents (homeowners and politicians) who feared the laws would destroy the single-family home neighborhood. Proponents see the measures as a way for the suburbs to help alleviate the state's housing crisis.[6]

In the area of race relations, social justice activism erupted in the summer of 2020, catalyzed by the murder of George Floyd. Across LA, many suburban communities joined #BLM protests—from sidewalk demonstrations in elite La Cañada-Flintridge, to miles-long car caravans snaking through the streets of Pasadena and Claremont. Indeed, in all of the suburbs profiled in this book—Pasadena, San Marino, South Gate, and Lakewood—residents took to the streets, on foot and in cars, to protest Floyd's killing, demonstrate solidarity with Black Americans, and, in some cases, press town leaders to reconsider funding priorities. For suburbs like Lakewood and San Marino, such demonstrations were a first.[7] Advocates in Pasadena followed up with a robust campaign at City Hall to establish a Community Police Oversight Commission with a full-time independent Police Auditor as a means of ensuring community justice and police accountability. In South Gate, youth activists Veronica Hernandez and Amanda Tapia mobilized residents behind a campaign for a "People's Budget," which would redirect municipal funding away from the police and toward basics like affordable housing and community development. In neighboring working-class suburbs, similar groups emerged, including SELA Chisme, Lynwood Youth 4 Radical Change, Downey Resistance, and Compton Rising. These collectives attracted mostly Latino youth in their early 20s, but also Black Americans and some whites.[8]

A number of suburbs also undertook their own racial reckonings. Several communities investigated and made public apologies for their racist pasts. In 2020, the Glendale city council issued a resolution apologizing for its history of racial exclusion, making it the first city in California to do so and third in the nation. South Pasadena's city council followed in 2022, with a similar resolution condemning its history as a sundown town and its practices of institutional racism. In June 2022, in Manhattan Beach, Bruce's Beach was returned to the original Black American family that was dispossessed of that land nearly a century earlier. And in 2022, elite La Cañada engaged in a series of community conversations about racial housing discrimination, past and present.[9]

Lakewood also finally confronted the issue of race head on. In June 2020, a #BLM protest march of 500 people culminated in a confrontation between protestors and law enforcement in front of the Lakewood Sheriff's Station. The sheriffs fired pepper balls and smoke cannisters at the marchers, which "eventually succeeded in dispersing the crowd," Mayor Todd Rogers reported.[10] At least 18 residents voiced concerns at the next city council meeting, including Black Americans, Latinos, and whites, calling on Lakewood to address racial inequality and prejudice in the community, bring greater accountability to law enforcement, and increase diverse representation at city hall.

This prompted Lakewood leaders to attend to race relations for the first time in its history. They convened two town hall meetings on race. Of the 80 or so residents who participated via Zoom, many expressed their love for Lakewood and their desire to see race relations improve. Then, stories of racism and discrimination poured out. Residents recounted numerous incidents at the hands of hostile neighbors and the Lakewood Sheriffs. Of particular concern was the Lakewood Regional Crime Awareness, Prevention, and Safety Group on Facebook, which took the spirit of Neighborhood Watch onto social media. With 21,000 members in 2021, the page had become a space where overt racism surfaced in response to BLM activism. One resident stated, "I was shocked at the level of hate on that page."[11]

In the wake of the Town Hall meetings, the city responded by forming an ad hoc task force and issuing a "Community Dialogue Action Plan" in January 2021. The following year, it formalized these efforts by establishing a city council committee on race, equity, diversity, and inclusion, which hosted regular meetings with residents. It also inaugurated a multicultural food and music festival. Lakewood proved to be one of the more proactive suburbs in the region in developing a civic infrastructure for local human relations, earning it recognition from the League of California Cities.[12] The racial composition of the city council also gradually shifted around this time. In its nearly 70-year history, Lakewood had elected only one nonwhite to the city council, Joe Esquivel, who served from 1990 to 2012. Esquivel conceded that race matters were never at the top of his agenda.[13] While a few people of color had run for office after 1990, they never won. That changed in 2020. In the city council election that year, five people of color ran for office—including Ari Pe, Cassandra Chase, and Pamela Williams. Ari Pe won the seat. That same year, Vicki Stuckey was appointed to fill a vacancy, becoming the first Black American to hold a council seat. A retired LA Sheriff's Department captain, Stuckey aligned well with the suburb's law-and-order culture.[14] A more decisive change occurred when Cassandra Chase was elected to the city council in 2022, under a new district voting system. With her more progressive political views, she brought a truly new perspective to Lakewood leadership.[15]

The stories don't begin and end with Pasadena, San Marino, South Gate, and Lakewood. Each of LA's approximately 84 suburbs have their own unique histories, with their own distinctive patterns and themes. Looking closely at individual communities and the dynamics that made them can point the way toward a more nuanced understanding of American suburbs in our own time.

Martin Luther King Jr. spoke often of the "beloved community," a vision of society based on inclusion and social and economic justice. For him, the ultimate goal was to end the scourge of segregation, which meant forging integrated communities based on genuine intergroup and interpersonal living. Given their racist histories, suburbs seemed highly unlikely places for realizing King's vision. And yet they were places where experiments in integration were unfolding, where communities moved from intentional segregation to diversity, where the potential for creating "beloved communities" was ripe. The process of change could be delicate, precarious, and treacherous. Not everyone wanted the same ends. And yet the suburbs became an unexpected incubator, a social petri dish, for observing how integration in America was actually playing out. The new suburbia emerged as a crucial site where people of different backgrounds, races, classes, and identities coexisted as neighbors, where people were trying to figure out how to live together in difference.

For Derrick and Pamela Williams of Lakewood, the summer of 2020 revealed the totality of this challenge.[16] Throughout a time of rabid, open racism, they remained loyal to Lakewood. As Derrick reflected, "Has it changed for me, or my outlook on Lakewood? No, because I've always understood where I was moving to. . . . [Early on], those small instances that we've heard about or may have experienced somewhat, were never a factor to change our outlook on the city because overall, we love our city. We will state it. That's why we're involved in it. That's why we moved here. I've lived in suburban America before. I've lived in inner-city America before. So, this wasn't anything new for me." In his view, the events of 2020 have "not changed our outlook on Lakewood. Not at all." Pamela added, "But I got a reality check." Derrick continued, "And it let her know that this stuff does exist. And it's not just in George Floyd's area, or anywhere else, it's right here where you are, too. It doesn't come up to Lakewood and jump over and go around. No, it comes and goes right on through here, too. And it's going to remain. It's not going anywhere. It is not going anywhere. But guess what? Neither are we."

Notes

Abbreviations

Newspapers

HPDS	*Huntington Park Daily Signal*
LAS	*Los Angeles Sentinel*
LAT	*Los Angeles Times*
LBIPT	*Long Beach Independent Press Telegram*
LBPT	*Long Beach Press Telegram*
LBP	*Long Beach Press*
LO	*La Opinión*
NYT	*New York Times*
PSN	*Pasadena Star News*
PW	*Pasadena Weekly*
SMT	*San Marino Tribune*
SGP	*South Gate Press*

Archives

CRPPL	Centennial Room, Pasadena Public Library
LHCIL	Local History Collection, Iacoboni Library, Lakewood
PMH	Pasadena Museum of History Research Library and Archives
SGCH	South Gate City Hall
SGHWL	South Gate History collection, Weaver Library, South Gate
SMCH	San Marino City Hall
SMHS	San Marino Historical Society

Introduction

1. Suburban diversity has a long history, but the pace of diversification after 1970 accelerated. Excellent overviews include Matthew D. Lassiter and Christopher Niedt, "Suburban Diversity in Postwar America," *Journal of Urban History* 39, 1 (January 2013), 3–14; Ruth McManus and Philip J. Ethington, "Suburbs in Transition: New

Approaches to Suburban History," *Urban History* 34, 2 (2007), 317–337; Michael B. Katz, Mathew J. Creighton, Daniel Amsterdam, and Merlin Chowkwanyun, "Immigration and the New Metropolitan Geography," *Journal of Urban Affairs* 32, 5 (2010), 523–547. Also see Becky Nicolaides and Andrew Wiese, eds., *The Suburb Reader*, 2nd edition (New York: Routledge, 2016); John Archer, Paul Sandul, and Katherine Solomonson, eds., *Making Suburbia: New Histories of Everyday America* (Minneapolis: University of Minnesota Press, 2015).

2. William H. Frey, "Today's Suburbs Are Symbolic of America's Rising Diversity: A 2020 Census Portrait" (Brookings Institution, June 15, 2020), quote on p. 1; William H. Frey, "Melting Pot Cities and Suburbs: Racial and Ethnic Change in Metro America in the 2000s," State of Metropolitan America series, no. 30 (Brookings Institution, May 4, 2011); William H. Frey, *Diversity Explosion: How New Racial Demographics are Remaking America* (Washington DC: Brookings Institution Press, 2018).

3. Newsom quote from "'Heavy Weight' on Newsom to Deliver in Second Term," *LAT*, November 14, 2022. On California as political bellwether for the nation, see Manuel Pastor, *State of Resistance: What California's Dizzying Descent and Remarkable Resurgence Mean for America's Future* (New York: The New Press, 2018).

4. Rosa Zee oral history conducted by Becky Nicolaides, June 4, 2012, San Marino, CA; Sandra Martinez oral history conducted by Becky Nicolaides, April 1, 2017, South Gate, CA; Pamela and Derrick Williams oral history conducted by Becky Nicolaides, November 20, 2020, via Zoom.

5. The proportion of Americans living in the suburbs rose from 13.4% in 1940, to 37.1% in 1970, to 54.6% in 2020. For 1970–2010, see Nicolaides and Wiese, eds., *The Suburb Reader*, 2; for 2020, figure gleaned from 2021 Population Survey, table 16, Metropolitan Mobility of Persons 16 Years and Over, by Labor Force Status, Sex, Age, and Race and Hispanic Origin, accessed at https://www.census.gov/data/tables/2021/demo/geographic-mobility/cps-2021.html. Thanks to William Frey and Erin Raftery for leading me to this table.

6. Audrey Singer and Jill H. Wilson, "Immigrants in 2010 Metropolitan America: A Decade of Change," State of Metropolitan America Series, no. 41, Brookings Institution (October 13, 2011), 5–9; Audrey Singer, Susan W. Hardwick, Caroline B. Brettell, eds., *Twentieth First Century Gateways: Immigrant Incorporation in Suburban America* (Washington, DC: Brookings Institution Press, 2008); for an overview of these changes, see Nicolaides and Wiese, eds., *The Suburb Reader*, chapter 14.

Works in sociology, geography, and urban studies and planning have been documenting these changes for several decades. Key recent works include Paul Maginn and Katrin B. Anacker, eds., *Suburbia in the 21st Century: From Dreamscape to Nightmare?* (New York: Routledge, 2023); Bernadette Hanlon and Thomas Vicino, eds., *Routledge Companion to the Suburbs* (New York: Routledge, 2019); Katrin Anacker, ed., *The New American Suburb: Poverty, Race and the Economic Crisis* (New York: Routledge, 2016); Bernadette Hanlon, John Rennie Short, and Thomas J. Vicino, *Cities and Suburbs: New Metropolitan Realities* (New York: Routledge, 2010).

7. Myron Orfield, *American Metropolitics: The New Suburban Reality* (Washington, DC: Brookings Institution Press, 2002); Willow Lung-Amam, Katrin B. Anacker, and

Nick Finio, "Worlds Away in Suburbia: The Changing Geography of High-Poverty Neighborhoods in the Washington, DC Metro," in *Suburbia in the 21st Century: From Dreamscape to Nightmare?* edited by Paul Maginn and Katrin B. Anacker (New York: Routledge, 2023); Todd Swanstrom, Colleen Casey, Robert Flack, and Peter Dreier, "Pulling Apart: Economic Segregation among Suburbs and Central Cities in Major Metropolitan Areas" (Living Cities Census Series, Brookings Institution, October 2004); Richard Fry and Paul Taylor, "The Rise of Residential Segregation by Income" (Social and Demographic Trends, Pew Research Center, 2012); Elizabeth Kneebone and Alan Berube, *Confronting Suburban Poverty in America* (Washington, DC: Brookings Institution Press, 2013); Becky M. Nicolaides and Andrew Wiese, "Suburban Disequilibrium," *NYT*, April 6, 2013.

8. A large, rich literature has documented this history. Key works include Kenneth T. Jackson, *Crabgrass Frontier: The Suburbanization of the United States* (New York: Oxford University Press, 1985); Arnold Hirsch, *Making the Second Ghetto: Race and Housing in Chicago, 1940–1960* (Cambridge: Cambridge University Press, 1983); Thomas Sugrue, *Origins of the Urban Crisis: Race and Inequality in Postwar Detroit* (Princeton: Princeton University Press, 1996); Thomas Sugrue, *Sweet Land of Liberty: The Forgotten Struggle for Civil Rights in the North* (New York: Random House, 2009); Matthew Lassiter, *The Silent Majority: Suburban Politics in the Sunbelt South* (Princeton: Princeton University Press, 2006); Kevin Kruse, *White Flight: Atlanta and the Making of Modern Conservatism* (Princeton: Princeton University Press, 2005); David M. P. Freund, *Colored Property: State Policy and White Racial Politics in Suburban America* (Chicago: University of Chicago Press, 2007); Robert Self, *American Babylon: Race and the Struggle for Postwar Oakland* (Princeton: Princeton University Press, 2003); Lily Geismer, *Don't Blame Us: Suburban Liberals and the Transformation of the Democratic Party* (Princeton: Princeton University Press, 2014); Becky Nicolaides, *My Blue Heaven: Life and Politics in the Working-Class Suburbs of Los Angeles, 1920–1965* (Chicago: University of Chicago Press, 2002); Katherine Levine Einstein, David M. Glick, and Maxwell Palmer, *Neighborhood Defenders: Participatory Politics and America's Housing Crisis* (Cambridge: Cambridge University Press, 2019); Richard Rothstein, *The Color of Law: A Forgotten History of How Our Government Segregated America* (New York: Liveright Publishing, 2017); Paige Glotzer, *How the Suburbs Were Segregated: Developers and the Business of Exclusionary Housing, 1890–1960* (New York: Columbia University Press, 2020). On racial segregation in Los Angeles, see Andrea Gibbons, *City of Segregation: One Hundred Years of Struggle for Housing in Los Angeles* (New York: Verso Books, 2018).

9. In addition to the works cited in Note 8, see Kenneth D. Durr, *Behind the Backlash: White Working-Class Politics in Baltimore, 1940–1980* (Chapel Hill: University of North Carolina Press, 2007); Kyle Riismandel, *Neighborhood of Fear: The Suburban Crisis in American Culture, 1975–2001* (Baltimore: Johns Hopkins University Press, 2020).

10. On similar internal dynamics among Black Americans in urban and suburban spaces, for example, see N. D. B. Connolly, *A World More Concrete: Real Estate and the Remaking of Jim Crow South Florida* (Chicago: University of Chicago Press, 2014); Andrew Wiese, *Places of Their Own: African American Suburbanization in*

the Twentieth Century (Chicago: University of Chicago Press, 2004); Mary Pattillo, *Black on the Block* (Chicago: University of Chicago Press, 2007); Bruce B. Haynes, *Red Lines, Black Spaces: The Politics of Race and Space in a Black Middle-Class Suburb* (New Haven: Yale University Press, 2001).

11. Kurashige quote in Frank Shyong, "Racial Coalitions Define Life in Los Angeles," *LAT*, October 18, 2022; also see Scott Kurashige, *The Shifting Grounds of Race: Black and Japanese Americans in the Making of Multiethnic Los Angeles* (Princeton: Princeton University Press, 2008); Scott Kurashige, "The Many Facets of Brown: Integration in a Multiracial Society," *Journal of American History* 91, 1 (June 2004), 56–68; Mark Brilliant, *The Color of America Has Changed: How Racial Diversity Shaped Civil Rights Reform in California, 1941–1978* (New York: Oxford University Press, 2010).

12. Karen Brodkin, *How Jews Became White Folks and What That Says About Race in America* (New Brunswick, NJ: Rutgers University Press, 1998); David Roediger, *Working Toward Whiteness: How America's Immigrants Became White: The Strange Journey from Ellis Island to the Suburbs* (New York: Basic Books, 2006); George Lipsitz, *The Possessive Investment in Whiteness: How White People Profit from Identity Politics* (Philadelphia: Temple University Press, 1998). Studies that challenge the straight-line white assimilation narrative include Deborah Dash Moore, *To the Golden Cities: Pursuing the American Jewish Dream in Miami and L.A.* (Cambridge: Harvard University Press, 1994); Lila Corwin Berman, *Metropolitan Jews: Politics, Race, and Religion in Postwar Detroit* (Chicago: University of Chicago Press, 2015).

13. Nicholas De Genova, ed., *Racial Transformations: Latinos and Asians Remaking the United States* (Durham: Duke University Press, 2006), 4.

14. Connolly, *A World More Concrete*, 10–14; thanks also to Jada Higgins for articulating this point.

15. Tom Hogen-Esch and Martin Saiz, "An Anatomy of Defeat: Why San Fernando Valley Failed to Secede from Los Angeles," *California Policy Issues* (November 2001), 56–58. On progressivism in suburbia, also see Sylvie Murray, *The Progressive Housewife: Community Activism in Suburban Queens, 1945–1965* (Philadelphia: University of Pennsylvania Press, 2003); Amanda Kolson Hurley, *Radical Suburbs: Experimental Living on the Fringes of the American City* (Cleveland: Belt Publishing, 2019); Christopher Niedt, ed., *Social Justice in Diverse Suburbs: History, Politics, and Prospects* (Philadelphia: Temple University Press, 2013).

16. An excellent discussion of the shifting of authority to suburbs is in Bernadette Hanlon and Thomas J. Vicino, "Local Immigration Legislation in Two Suburbs," in *The New American Suburb: Poverty, Race and the Economic Crisis*, edited by Katrin Anacker (New York: Routledge, 2016), 113–130; also see Genevieve Carpio, Clara Irazábal, and Laura Pulido, "Right to the Suburb? Rethinking Lefebvre and Immigrant Activism," *Journal of Urban Affairs* 33, 2 (2011), 185–208; James S. Duncan and Nancy G. Duncan, *Landscapes of Privilege: The Politics of the Aesthetic in an American Suburb* (New York: Routledge, 2004); David Harvey, *A Brief History of Neoliberalism* (New York: Oxford University Press, 2007); Lily Geismer, *Left Behind: How the Democrats Failed to Solve Inequality* (New York: Public Affairs, 2022).

17. "Human Relations Agency Enlists Help of Community Groups to Ease Tensions," *LAT*, July 6, 1980. See Shana Bernstein, *Bridges of Reform: Interracial Civil Rights Activism in Twentieth-Century Los Angeles* (New York: Oxford University Press, 2011), 78.

18. At the same time, the privatization of public services could act as a spur to participation in the suburbs, depending on factors like class and length of residency. See Scott Vandehey, "Suburban Citizenship" (PhD dissertation, UC San Diego, 2009), chapter 8.

19. Examples of works on robust suburban social life in the 1950s and 1960s include William H. Whyte, Jr., *The Organization Man* (New York: Simon and Schuster, 1956); John R. Seeley, R. Alexander Sim, and Elizabeth W. Loosley, *Crestwood Heights* (New York: Basic Books, 1956); Sylvia Fleis Fava, "Contrasts in Neighboring," in *The Suburban Community*, edited by William M. Dobriner (New York: G. P. Putnam's Sons, 1958), 122-131; S. F. Fava, "Suburbanism as a Way of Life," *American Sociological Review* 21 (February 1956), 34–37; Robert C. Wood, *Suburbia: Its People and Their Politics* (Boston: Houghton Mifflin, 1959); Claude S. Fischer and Robert Max Jackson, "Suburbanism and Localism," in *Networks and Places*, edited by Fischer et al. (New York: Free Press, 1977), 117-138; Murray, *The Progressive Housewife*, chapter 4; Rosalyn Baxandall and Elizabeth Ewen, *Picture Windows: How the Suburbs Happened* (New York: Basic Books, 2000), 146–156; Chad M. Kimmel, "Revealing the History of Levittown, One Voice at a Time," in *Second Suburb: Levittown, Pennsylvania*, edited by Dianne Harris (Pittsburgh: University of Pittsburgh Press, 2010), 30–36. Even sociologist Herbert Gans, whose participant-observer study of Levittown, Pennsylvania, was meant to challenge an emerging suburban critique of hyperactive socializing and conformity, conceded that suburbanites engaged in high levels of community engagement. See Herbert Gans, *The Levittowners: Ways of Life and Politics in the New Suburban Community* (New York: Columbia University Press, 1982 ed.).

    The literature that emphasizes social disconnection, fear, and privacy in suburbia after 1970 is large. Some important examples include Jackson, *Crabgrass Frontier*, chapter 15; Setha Low, *Behind the Gates* (New York: Routledge, 2003); Evan McKenzie, *Privatopia* (New Haven: Yale University Press, 1994); Mike Davis, *City of Quartz: Excavating the Future in Los Angeles* (London: Verso, 1990); James Howard Kunstler, *Geography of Nowhere* (New York: Simon & Schuster, 1993); Christopher Caldwell, "Levittown to Littleton," *National Review* (May 31, 1999); Andres Duany, Elizabeth Plater-Zyberk, and Jeff Speck, *Suburban Nation* (New York: North Point Press, 2000), especially chapter 7; and M. P. Baumgartner, *The Moral Order of a Suburb* (New York: Oxford University Press, 1988). A crucial work is Robert D. Putnam, *Bowling Alone: The Collapse and Revival of American Community* (New York: Simon & Schuster, 2000). Works critiquing Putnam's approach include Robyn Muncy, "Disconnecting: Social and Civic Life in America Since 1965," *Reviews in American History* 29, 1 (2001), 141–149; James Jennings, ed., *Race, Neighborhoods, and the Misuse of Social Capital* (New York: Palgrave Macmillan, 2007); Barbara Arneil, *Diverse Communities: The Problem with Social Capital* (New York: Cambridge University Press, 2006); Iris Marion Young, *Justice and the Politics of Difference* (Princeton: Princeton University

Press, 2011). On perennial narratives of community declension throughout American history, see Thomas Bender, *Community and Social Change in America* (Baltimore: Johns Hopkins University Press, 2000).

20. Suburban critics who focus on design as the cause of suburbia's social problems tend to offer design solutions; this includes proponents of the New Urbanism. By building mixed-use, walkable, and economically mixed spaces, community and civic spirit, they believe, can be revived. See especially Duany et al., *Suburban Nation*. For a critique of New Urbanism, see Bernadette Hanlon, "Beyond Sprawl: Social Sustainability and Reinvestment in the Baltimore Suburbs," in *The New American Suburb: Poverty, Race and the Economic Crisis*, edited by Katrin Anacker (New York: Routledge, 2016), 133–152.

21. Putnam, *Bowling Alone.*

22. J. Eric Oliver, *The Paradoxes of Integration: Race, Neighborhood, and Civic Life in Multiethnic America* (Chicago: University of Chicago Press, 2010); Robert D. Putnam and Lewis M. Feldstein, *Better Together: Restoring the American Community* (New York: Simon and Schuster, 2003); Zachary P. Neal and Jennifer Watling Neal, "The (In)compatibility of Diversity and Sense of Community," *American Journal of Community Psychology* 53 (2014), 1–12; Richard Florida, "The Missing Link Between Diversity and Community," *Bloomberg CityLab*, November 4, 2015.

23. This harkens back to Herbert Gans's observation about class and participation in his landmark book, *The Levittowners.*

24. This finding comports with observations on Dublin's suburbs in Mary P. Corcoran, Jane Gray, and Michel Peillon, *Suburban Affiliations: Social Relations in the Greater Dublin Area* (Syracuse: Syracuse University Press, 2010).

25. Two noteworthy studies address questions of participation in suburbia, from sociological and public policy perspectives: Patricia Farrell Donahue, *Participation, Community, and Public Policy in A Virginia Suburb: Of Our Own Making* (Lexington Books, 2017); and Corcoran et al., *Suburban Affiliations.* The study by Corcoran, Gray, and Peillon was especially instructive. In their sociological analysis of four suburbs in Dublin, Ireland, they argued for using the concept of suburban" affiliations"—rather than "community"—as a means of exploring the nuanced social texture of suburban places. This is a useful concept that I've tried to heed throughout this book, although I do use the term "community," more as a shorthand quotidian concept than a technical sociological one.

26. Matthew Lassiter, *The Suburban Crisis: Crime, Drugs, and White Middle-Class America* (Princeton: Princeton University Press, 2023); Matthew D. Lassiter, "Pushers, Victims, and the Lost Innocence of White Suburbia: California's War on Narcotics during the 1950s," *Journal of Urban History* 41, 5 (2015), 787–807; Matthew Lassiter, "Impossible Criminals: The Suburban Imperatives of America's War on Drugs," *Journal of American History* 102, 1 (June 2015), 126–140; Riismandel, *Neighborhood of Fear*; Paul Renfro, *Stranger Danger: Family Values, Childhood, and the American Carceral State* (New York: Oxford University Press, 2020); Charles M. Haar, ed., *The End of Innocence: A Suburban Reader* (Glenview, IL: Scott, Foresman & Co., 1972); Charles M. Haar, ed., *The President's Task Force on Suburban Problems: Final Report*

(Cambridge, MA: Ballinger Publishing Co, 1974). Also see Becky Nicolaides, "How Hell Moved from the City to the Suburbs: Urban Scholars and Changing Perceptions of Authentic Community," in *The New Suburban History*, edited by Kevin M. Kruse and Thomas J. Sugrue (Chicago: University of Chicago Press, 2006), 80-98.

The literature of geographers, planners, and sociologists sometimes conflates the crisis and diversification narratives. For example, see Maginn and Anacker, eds., *Suburbia in the 21st Century: From Dreamscape to Nightmare?*; Anacker, ed., *The New American Suburb: Poverty, Race and the Economic Crisis*; William H. Lucy and David L. Philips, *Tomorrow's Cities, Tomorrow's Suburbs* (Chicago: Planners Press, 2006).

27. A. K. Sandoval-Strausz, *Barrio America: How Latino Immigrants Saved the American City* (New York: Basic Books, 2019). Key recent works in this expansive literature include James Rojas, "The Enacted Environment of East Los Angeles," *Places* 8, 3 (Spring 1993), 42–53; Wendy Cheng, *The Changs Next Door to the Díazes: Remapping Race in Suburban California* (Minneapolis: University of Minnesota Press, 2013); Wei Li, *Ethnoburb: The New Ethnic Community in Urban America* (Honolulu: University of Hawai'i Press, 2009); Min Zhou, Yen-Fen Tseng, and Rebecca Y. Kim, "Rethinking Residential Assimilation: The Case of a Chinese Ethnoburb in the San Gabriel Valley, California," *Amerasia Journal* 34, 3 (2008): 55–83; Willow A. Lung-Amam, *Trespassers? Asian American and the Battle for Suburbia* (Oakland: University of California Press, 2017); Willow Lung-Amam, "Malls of Meaning: Building Asian America in Silicon Valley Suburbia," *Journal of American Ethnic History* 34, 2 (Winter 2015), 18–53; Niedt, ed., *Social Justice in Diverse Suburbs*; Jerry González, *In Search of the Mexican Beverly Hills: Latino Suburbanization in Postwar Los Angeles* (New Brunswick: Rutgers University Press, 2018); Romeo Guzmán, Carribean Fragoza, Alex Sayf Cummings, Ryan Reft, eds., *East of East: The Making of Greater El Monte* (Rutgers: Rutgers University Press, 2020); Josh Sides, *L.A. City Limits: African American Los Angeles from the Great Depression to the Present* (Berkeley: University of California Press, 2003); Wiese, *Places of Their Own*; Todd Michney, *Surrogate Suburbs: Black Upward Mobility and Neighborhood Change in Cleveland, 1900–1980* (Chapel Hill: University of North Carolina Press, 2017); Kurashige, *Shifting Grounds of Race*.

28. Nicolaides and Wiese, eds., *The Suburb Reader*, 7–9. There have been articles and at least one book written on how to define "suburb" and consensus remains elusive. See Ann Forsyth, "Defining Suburbs," *Journal of Planning Literature* 27, 3 (2012), 270–281; Richard Harris and Robert Lewis, "The Geography of North American Cities and Suburbs 1900-1950," *Journal of Urban History* 27, 3 (March 2001), 262–292; William Sharpe and Leonard Wallock, "Bold New City or Built-Up 'Burb? Redefining Contemporary Suburbia," *American Quarterly* 46, 1 (March 1994), 1–30; Richard Harris and Charlotte Vorms, eds., *What's in a Name? Talking About Urban Peripheries* (Toronto: University of Toronto Press, 2017).

29. Nicolaides and Wiese, eds., *The Suburb Reader*, 7–9.

30. Dolores Hayden also makes a convincing case for thinking about suburbs in terms of their historic landscapes, the recognizable emblems of place that were built over time. Her typology of historic suburban landscapes has deeply guided this book. Dolores

Hayden, *Building Suburbia: Green Fields and Urban Growth* (New York: Pantheon Books, 2003).

31. Over the past several years, a team of student assistants helped compile a dataset on all municipalities of LA County, 1950–2010, covering 53 variables, such as race, nativity, occupational category, age, educational attainment, private school attendance, median home value, median family income, housing tenure, and homeownership by race. These data provide an empirical basis for analysis throughout the book. Readers interested in drilling deeper into these data should consult the companion website to the book, which has a number of supplemental tables drawn from this dataset. Throughout the book, it will be referred to as the "US Census dataset."

    The full dataset and extensive methodology and source notes are available at the USC Libraries website, "Los Angeles County Demographic Data Project, 1950–2010," https://doi.org/10.25549/lademo-ouc1sto1757543. This project was funded by the National Endowment for the Humanities.

32. The US Census defines "race" as a person's self-identification as white, Black or African American, Asian or AAPI, and "ethnicity" as Hispanic or Latino or non-Hispanic. I do not adhere to this categorical difference per se, mainly because both the (white) power structure and ethnoracial groups themselves used both terms in different contexts. Latinos, for example, have been racialized by the white power structure for centuries. Ethnicity, in turn, can refer to AAPI culture and identity and might describe certain aesthetics in the built landscape (I use "ethnicity" in reference to the built landscapes of "ethnoburbs" for example). In other contexts, conflicts between white-Latinos, or white-Asians were articulated in "race" terms, so I used "race" in those discussions. I tried to use the term that best reflected the context in which it was being used. In general, when discussing whites and Blacks, I use "race." When discussing Asians and Latinos, I use both "race" and "ethnicity," depending on what the context dictates. I use the term "Latino" throughout this book to refer to people of Latin American descent. And as much as possible, I tried to refer to groups by their specific national origin, such as "Mexican," "Chinese," or "Cuban."

    Works that especially guided my thinking are Tomás Almaguer, *Racial Fault Lines: The Historical Origins of White Supremacy in California* (Berkeley: University of California Press, 1994); Eileen O'Brien, *The Racial Middle: Latinos and Asian Americans Living Beyond the Racial Divide* (New York: New York University Press, 2008); Michael Omi and Howard Winant, *Racial Formation in the United States* (New York: Routledge, 1994); Laura Pulido and Manuel Pastor, "Where in the World is Juan—and What Color Is He? The Geography of Latina/o Racial Identity in Southern California," *American Quarterly* 65, 2 (June 2013), 309–341.

33. See sources in Note 5. For contrasting views about the state of suburbia in America, see Leigh Gallagher, *The End of the Suburbs* (New York: Penguin, 2014); Thomas J. Sugrue, "The New American Dream: Renting," *Wall Street Journal* August 14, 2009; Jed Kolko, "2015 U.S. Population Winners: The Suburbs and the Sunbelt," *Bloomburg CityLab* March 24, 2016; William H. Frey, "Big City Growth Stalls Further, as the

Suburbs Make a Comeback," Brookings Institution, May 24, 2019, https://www.brookings.edu/blog/the-avenue/2019/05/24/big-city-growth-stalls-further-as-the-suburbs-make-a-comeback/; Samuel J. Abrams, "Millennials, Like Their Parents, Now Long for the Suburbs," *LAT*, May 29, 2021.

Chapter 1

1. "Six suburbs" from W. W. Robinson, *Los Angeles: A Profile* (Norman: University of Oklahoma Press, 1968), 27; quoted in Jeremiah B. Axelrod, *Inventing Autopia: Dreams and Visions of the Modern Metropolis in Jazz Age Los Angeles* (Berkeley: University of California Press, 2009), 238. This "six suburbs" line was later attributed to Dorothy Parker.

2. Dolores Hayden, *Building Suburbia: Green Fields and Urban Growth* (New York: Pantheon Books, 2003). Another useful survey is Linda Flint McClelland, David L. Ames, and Sarah Dillard Pope, "Historic Residential Suburbs in the United States, 1830–1960" (Washington, DC: Department of the Interior, National Park Service, 2002).

3. Kevin Roderick, *The San Fernando Valley: America's Suburb* (Los Angeles: Los Angeles Times Books, 2001).

4. I am indebted to the seminal article, Ruth McManus and Philip J. Ethington, "Suburbs in Transition: New Approaches to Suburban History," *Urban History* 34, 2 (2007), 317–337.

5. In addition to drawing on Hayden's typology, I drew insights from Michael Southworth and Peter M. Owens, "The Evolving Metropolis: Studies of Community, Neighborhood, and Street Form at the Urban Edge," *Journal of the American Planning Association* 59, 3 (Summer 1993), 271–287.

6. Roger W. Lotchin, "Population Concentration in Los Angeles, 1940–2000," *Pacific Historical Review* 77, 1 (2008), 87–101. Lotchin shows that, after 1980, LA's density levels were significantly higher than many other metro areas and notes that much of this high density was concentrated in the Latino suburbs south of downtown. See Figure A1.1 (Population density).

7. Greg Hise, *Magnetic Los Angeles: Planning the Twentieth Century Metropolis* (Baltimore: Johns Hopkins University Press, 1997), 191; Leonard Pitt and Dale Pitt, *Los Angeles A–Z* (Berkeley: University of California Press, 1997), 448.

8. Phillip J. Ethington, "The Spatial and Demographic Growth of Los Angeles," in *The Development of Los Angeles City Government: An Institutional History, 1850–2000*, edited by Hynda Rudd et al. (Los Angeles: City of Los Angeles Historical Society, 2007), 664; Michan Connor, "'Public Benefits from Public Choice': Producing Decentralization in Metropolitan Los Angeles, 1954–1973," *Journal of Urban History* 39, 1 (2013), 79–100; Gary Miller, *Cities by Contract* (Cambridge: MIT Press, 1981). See Figure A1.2 (Suburb incorporations).

9. For Los Angeles County, the *number* of dwellings classified by "year structure built" (as of 2000) breaks down as follows:

Pre 1940	421,785
Sitcom Suburb era 1940–69	1,712,185
Edge city/corporate suburb era 1970–2000	1,136,939

10. This number was calculated by taking the number of housing units counted in the 1940 census (961,531) and subtracting the number of pre-1939 housing units counted in the 2000 census (421,785). All figures are for LA County.

11. Robert Fogelson, *Bourgeois Nightmares: Suburbia 1870–1930* (New Haven: Yale University Press, 2007); Robert Fishman, *Bourgeois Utopias* (New York: Basic Books, 1987); Becky Nicolaides and Andrew Wiese, eds., *The Suburb Reader*, 2nd edition (New York: Routledge, 2016). Charles Lummis was a vocal champion of this vision, of LA's unique capacity to teach an overworked America the virtues of leisure, recreation, and healthful outdoor pursuits. See, e.g., *Land of Sunshine* 3 (Feb 1895), 134–135; also, Lawrence Culver, *The Frontier of Leisure: Southern California and the Shaping of Modern America* (New York: Oxford University Press, 2010). The notion of a "new urban canvas" refers to LA's urban development alone, and does not suggest the absence of the indigenous, Spanish, and Mexican people who inhabited the region.

12. Fishman, *Bourgeois Utopias*, 158; Robert Fogelson, *Fragmented Metropolis: Los Angeles, 1850–1930* (Berkeley: University of California Press, 1993), 192; Martin Wachs, "Autos, Transit, and the Sprawl of Los Angles: The 1920s," *Journal of the American Planning Association* 50, 3 (Summer 1984), 298; Mike Davis, "Sunshine and the Open Shop: Ford and Darwin in 1920s Los Angeles," in *Metropolis in the Making: Los Angeles in the 1920s*, edited by Tom Sitton and William Deverell (Berkeley: University of California Press, 2001), 96-122; Marc A. Weiss, *The Rise of the Community Builders: The American Real Estate Industry and Urban Land Planning* (New York: Columbia University Press, 1987); Culver, *Frontier of Leisure*.

13. Fogelson, *Fragmented Metropolis*, 144–145.

14. Fred Viehe, "Black Gold Suburbs: The Influence of the Extractive Industry on the Suburbanization of Los Angeles, 1890–1930," *Journal of Urban History* 8, 1 (November 1981), 3–26.

15. The classic refutation of transportation determinism is in Kenneth T. Jackson, *Crabgrass Frontier: The Suburbanization of the United States* (New York: Oxford University Press, 1985), 42–44, 111–112, 121–122, 124; also see Greg Hise, "Home Building and Industrial Decentralization in Los Angeles: The Roots of the Postwar Urban Region," *Journal of Urban History* 19, 2 (1993), 97, 120n9.

16. McClelland et al., "Historic Residential Suburbs in the United States," E4–E5; David Brodsly, *L.A. Freeway: An Appreciative Essay* (Berkeley: University of California Press), 82; Wachs, "Autos, Transit," 297; Scott L. Bottles, *Los Angeles and the Automobile: The Making of the Modern City* (Berkeley University of California Press, 1987), 180.

17. Weiss, *Rise of the Community Builders*, 13. This zoning law was upheld by the California Supreme Court in 1913 and the US Supreme Court in 1915, establishing the validity of land use planning as an exercise of municipal power.

18. George J. Sánchez, "The History of Segregation in Los Angeles: A Report on Racial Discrimination and Its Legacy" (Scheff & Washington, PC, for *American Civil Rights Foundation v. LAUSD*, 2007), 4.

19. Weiss, *Rise of the Community Builders*, 87–96.

20. Axelrod, *Inventing Autopia*; Hise, *Magnetic Los Angeles*; Hise, "Home Building and Industrial Decentralization," 95–125.

21. William Fulton, "Those Were Her Best Days: The Streetcar and the Development of Hollywood Before 1910," *Southern California Quarterly* 66 (Fall 1984), 237; Hayden, *Building Suburbia*, 98–100.

22. Jackson, *Crabgrass Frontier*, 121; Fogelson, *Fragmented Metropolis*, 144.

23. There are two mutually exclusive literatures that treat suburban land development in this era: one focuses on transit and real estate moguls in the early twentieth century, treating figures like Henry Huntington, Harry Chandler, Moses Sherman, and Eli Clark, among others; a second focuses on the rise of community, operative, and merchant builders. The latter literature generally does not discuss figures like Huntington and Chandler.

    On the early transit and real estate moguls (such as Henry Huntington, Harry Chandler, Moses Sherman, and Eli Clark), see Fogelson, *Fragmented Metropolis*; Jackson, *Crabgrass Frontier*; Fulton, "Those Were Her Best Days"; William B. Friedricks, *Henry E. Huntington and the Creation of Southern California* (Columbus: Ohio State University Press, 1992); William Friedricks, "Henry Huntington and Real Estate Development in Southern California, 1898–1917," *Southern California Quarterly* 74, 4 (Winter 1989). On "community builders," see Weiss, *Rise of the Community Builders*, chapters 1–2, pp 6–7, 46–47; Hise, *Magnetic Los Angeles*.

24. Weiss, *Rise of the Community Builders*, 40–41; Hise, *Magnetic Los Angeles*, 29. Though Weiss is describing subdividers nationally, his footnote includes an interview with community builder Fred Marlow, describing common subdivision practices in Los Angeles into the 1920s.

    On the predominance of small-scale builders during the streetcar era in Boston, see Sam Bass Warner, *Streetcar Suburbs: The Process of Growth in Boston, 1870–1900* (Cambridge, MA: Harvard University Press, 1978).

25. Weiss, *Rise of the Community Builders*, chapter 5; also see Fogelson, *Fragmented Metropolis*, 103.

26. Andrew Whittemore, "Zoning Los Angeles: A Brief History of Four Regimes," *Planning Perspectives* 27, 3 (July 2012), 393–408; on urban pro-growth regimes, see John R. Logan and Harvey L. Molotch, *Urban Fortunes: The Political Economy of Place* (Berkeley: University of California Press, 1987).

27. Todd Gish, "Building Los Angeles: Urban Housing in the Suburban Metropolis, 1900–1936" (PhD Dissertation, University of Southern California, 2007), especially chapter 1, and on tourists, see 51–53; Frederick Bode, "At Home in the Film Capital: The Economy and Culture of Hollywood's Working-Class Lodgers During the 1930s" (paper presented at the LA History & Metro Studies Group, Huntington Library, 2021).

28. Harold Brackman, "Making Room for Millions: Housing in Los Angeles," in *The Development of Los Angeles City Government: An Institutional History 1850–2000*,

vol. 1, edited by Hynda Rudd et al. (Los Angeles: Los Angeles City Historical Society, 2007), 384; US Housing Census, 1940. Census figures reveal the numerical significance of the single-family home in LA County by 1940: they comprised 62.2% of all housing units in the county; if LA City is excluded, they comprised 74.1% of all housing units in the county.

29. The literature on race and suburbia is vast. On the earliest manifestations of suburban racial and class separatism, see Carl H. Nightingale, *Segregation: A Global History of Divided Cities* (Chicago: University of Chicago Press, 2012); John Archer, "Colonial Suburbs in South Asia, 1700–1850, and the Spaces of Modernity," in *Visions of Suburbia*, edited by Roger Silverstone (London: Routledge, 1997), 26–54; Fishman, *Bourgeois Utopias*; Jackson, *Crabgrass Frontier*; on racial preoccupations of post-WWII suburbanites, see Arnold Hirsch, *Making the Second Ghetto: Race and Housing in Chicago, 1940–1960* (Cambridge: Cambridge University Press, 1983); Matthew D. Lassiter, *Silent Majority: Suburban Politics in the Sunbelt South* (Princeton: Princeton University Press, 2006); Kevin Kruse, *White Flight: Atlanta and the Making of Modern Conservatism* (Princeton: Princeton University Press, 2005); Robert Self, *American Babylon: Race and the Struggle for Postwar Oakland* (Princeton: Princeton University Press, 2005); Becky Nicolaides, *My Blue Heaven: Life and Politics in the Working-Class Suburbs of Los Angeles, 1920–1965* (Chicago: University of Chicago Press, 2002). An excellent overview of race and suburbia is in Andrew Wiese, *Places of Their Own: African American Suburbanization in the Twentieth Century* (Chicago: University of Chicago Press, 2004). For a broader overview of race in the history of suburbia, see Nicolaides and Wiese, eds., *The Suburb Reader*, chapters 8 and 11.

30. Mike Davis, *City of Quartz: Excavating the Future in Los Angeles* (London: Verso Books, 1990), 8, 56; Eric Avila, *Popular Culture in the Age of White Flight* (Berkeley: University of California Press, 2004), 21–24; William Deverell, *Whitewashed Adobe* (Berkeley: University of California Press, 2004); Laura Barraclough, *Making the San Fernando Valley: Rural Landscapes, Urban Development, and White Privilege* (Athens, GA: University of Georgia Press, 2011), 27.

31. Douglas Flamming, *Bound for Freedom: Black Los Angeles in Jim Crow America* (Berkeley: University of California Press, 2005), 69; Laura Redford, "The Intertwined History of Class and Race Segregation in Los Angeles," *Journal of Planning History* 16, 4 (2017), 308; Sánchez, "The History of Segregation in Los Angeles"; Gene Slater, "How Los Angeles Pioneered the Residential Segregation That Helped Divide America," *LAT*, September 10, 2021; Gene Slater, *Freedom to Discriminate: How Realtors Conspired to Segregate Housing and Divide America* (Berkeley: Heyday, 2021). On the "racial theory of property value," see Charles Abrams, *Forbidden Neighbors: A Study of Prejudice in Housing* (Port Washington, NY: Kennikat Press, 1971), 158; Nightingale, *Segregation*, 305–318, 344–348; Richard Rothstein, *The Color of Law: A Forgotten History of How Our Government Segregated America* (New York: Liveright, 2017), chapter 6.

32. Profiles of these multiracial communities include Mark Wild, *Street Meetings: Multiethnic Neighborhoods in Early Twentieth-Century Los Angeles* (Berkeley: University of California Press, 2008); Allison Varzally, *Making a Non-White America:*

Californians Coloring Outside Ethnic Lines, 1925-1955 (Berkeley: University of California Press, 2008); George Sánchez, *Boyle Heights: How a Los Angeles Neighborhood Became the Future of American Democracy* (Oakland: University of California Press, 2021); Flamming, *Bound for Freedom*.

33. Lawrence B. de Graaf, "The City of Black Angels: Emergence of the Los Angeles Ghetto, 1890-1930," *Pacific Historical Review* 39 (1970), 327, 346–347; Max Bond, "The Negro in Los Angeles" (PhD dissertation, University of Southern California, 1936), 69; Flamming, *Bound for Freedom*, 66, 68, 97–98, 290, 350; Josh Sides, *L.A. City Limits* (Berkeley: University of California Press, 2006), 98–99; Wiese, *Places of Their Own*; Matt Garcia, *A World of Its Own: Race, Labor and the Making of Greater Los Angeles, 1900-1970* (Chapel Hill: University of North Carolina Press, 2001); Jerry González, *In Search of the Mexican Beverly Hills: Latino Suburbanization in Postwar Los Angeles* (New Brunswick: Rutgers University Press, 2018), chapters 1–2.

34. See Table A1.1, for an alphabetical list of all incorporated municipalities in Los Angeles County with "year structure built" data classified by the era of the three main suburban landscape periods: the pre 1940 era, the sitcom suburbia era (1940-1969), and the corporate suburbia era (1970–2000). See Table A1.2 (Picturesque enclaves), Table A1.3 (Sitcom suburbs), Table A1.4 (Corporate suburbs), Table A1.5 (Older suburbs).

   The data on "year structure built" offer a rough gauge of when most of the housing was built in a particular municipality, so it helps situate these suburbs chronologically (and thus into their historic suburban landscapes). The picturesque enclave is one landscape that was built up throughout the years.

35. Hayden, *Building Suburbia*, chapter 3.

36. Kevin Starr, *Americans and the California Dream, 1850-1915* (New York: Oxford University Press, 1973), 204; Howard J. Nelson, "The Spread of an Artificial Landscape over Southern California," *Annals of the Association of American Geographers* 49 (1959), 189; Howard J. Nelson and William A. V. Clark, *Los Angeles: The Metropolitan Experience* (Cambridge, MA: Ballinger Publishing Co., 1976), 22; Douglas Monroy, *Rebirth: Mexican Los Angeles From the Great Migration to the Great Depression* (Berkeley: University of California Press, 1999), 118. Matt Garcia notes that land under citrus cultivation in Southern California increased from 83,600 to 329,700 acres from 1903 to 1944 (*A World of Its Own*, 23–24). As well, from the 1910s to 1949, Los Angeles County ranked first nationally in value of agricultural product sold.

37. Garcia, *A World of Its Own*, chapter 1, quote at 25. Garcia's chapter contains an excellent discussion of this "ideal country life" and its derivations from rural ideological traditions in America.

38. Paul Sandul, *California Dreaming: Boosterism, Memory and Rural Suburbs in the Golden State* (Morgantown: West Virginia University Press, 2014); Barraclough, *Making the San Fernando Valley*, chapter 1, especially 33–35; Garcia, *A World of Its Own*, 25; Becky Nicolaides, "'Where the Working Man Is Welcomed': Working-Class Suburbs in Los Angeles, 1900-1940," *Pacific Historical Review* 68, 4 (Nov. 1999), 548–552.

39. Barraclough, *Making the San Fernando Valley*, 31–35; Kevin Starr, *Inventing the Dream: California Through the Progressive Era* (New York: Oxford University Press, 1985), 45–47.

40. "Famous Rancho's Land Scheduled for Market," *LAT*, September 23, 1934; Nicolaides, *My Blue Heaven*, chapter 1, 340n15; Nicolaides, "Where the Working Man Is Welcomed," 551–552; Barraclough, *Making the San Fernando Valley*, 34; "A Diversified Farm," *LAT*, April 27, 1930.

41. Beverly Wayte, *At the Arroyo's Edge: A History of Linda Vista* (Los Angeles: Historical Society of Southern California and Linda Vista/Annandale Association, 1993), 50.

42. Garcia, *A World of Its Own*, 27–46, quote at 27; Barraclough, *Making the San Fernando Valley*, 33–35, 41; González, *In Search of the Mexican Beverly Hills*, chapter 1.

43. Warner, *Streetcar Suburbs*; Hayden, *Building Suburbia*, 71–73; McClelland et al., "Historic Residential Suburbs," E3–E7.

44. In Los Angeles, a small system of horse cars and cable cars preceded the streetcars, huddled around the downtown core. LA's first true suburb, Angeleno Heights, was linked by cable car to downtown, as were neighborhoods in Pico-Union, University Park, and West Adams. Boyle Heights was another early suburb, connected by horse car to downtown. Robert C. Post, *Street Railways and the Growth of Los Angeles* (San Marino, CA: Golden West Books, 1989), 36, 39.

45. Wachs, "Autos, Transit," 300; Spencer Crump, *Ride the Big Red Cars* (Corona del Mar, CA: Trans-Anglo Books, 1983), 91–94; Post, *Street Railways*, 147–148; Fogelson, *Fragmented Metropolis*, 137; Friedricks, *Henry E. Huntington*, 7; Bottles, *Los Angeles*, 35–37.

46. Crump, *Ride the Big Red Cars*, 94, 17; Fishman, *Bourgeois Utopias*, 166; John Heller, "Commercial Development Related to Street Railway Transportation," March 13, 2008, Historic Context Statement for Survey L.A. The Red Cars were dubbed "interurbans" because they were faster and larger than those running strictly within city limits (Jackson, *Crabgrass Frontier*, 122).

47. Crump, *Ride the Big Red Cars*, 97–100, 173–174; Brodsly, *L.A. Freeway*, 2–4, 68; Jim Walker, *The Los Angeles Railway Yellow Cars* (Charleston, SC: Arcadia Publishing, 2007), 27; Fogelson, *Fragmented Metropolis*, 164–165, 173; Fulton, "Those Were Her Best Days," 238.

48. Crump, *Ride the Big Red Cars*, 110.

49. Fishman, *Bourgeois Utopias*, 160–161.

50. This resembled the pattern in Boston, described in Warner, *Streetcar Suburbs*.

51. Brodsly, *L.A. Freeway*, 71 caption, 82; Merry Ovnick, *Los Angeles: The End of the Rainbow* (Los Angeles: Balcony Press, 1994), 142; Fogelson, *Fragmented Metropolis*, 154–155.

52. Jane Apostol, *South Pasadena: A Centennial History, 1888–1988*, 2nd edition (South Pasadena: Friends of the South Pasadena Library, 2008), 49.

53. Garcia, *A World of Its Own*, 24–28, 36–37; Bellflower Heritage Society, *Bellflower: People and Places* (Bellflower, CA: Bellflower Heritage Society, 1987), 38–42, 48, 104; Barraclough, *Making the San Fernando Valley*, 41, 44–45, 52–58.

54. Garcia, *A World of Its Own*, 23–25; Richard E. Preston, "The Changing Form and Structure of the Southern California Metropolis," *California Geographer* 12 (1971), 13 (1972); Viehe, "Black Gold Suburbs."

55. Also see Hayden, *Building Suburbia*, chapter 3. In some cases, the old commercial centers predated the arrival of the streetcars, but the streetcars clearly stimulated the growth and longevity of these areas.

56. Fletcher H. Swan, "The Big Red Cars: The Trolley Connected Los Angeles to Pasadena," *The Quarterly Magazine* (Winter 2009); on "Rails to Trails" see https://www.railstotrails.org/; "Celebration of 100 Years," *Lynwood 'n Perspective* 15, 7 (July 2021), 3; and visual surveys by author. See Figure A1.3 (Rails to trails).

57. "Taking a stairway to health," *LAT*, April 14, 2010; Charles Fleming, *Secret Stairs: A Walking Guide to the Historic Staircases of Los Angeles* (Santa Monica, CA: Santa Monica Press, 2010).

58. I base this claim on visual surveys I made and phone interviews I conducted with city officials, librarians, or local history experts in Pasadena, Altadena, Arcadia, Azusa, Glendora, San Marino, Alhambra, El Monte, South Gate, Whittier, Glendale, Gardena, and Hawthorne, in April 2010. I also consulted Michele Zack, *Altadena: Between Wilderness and City* (Altadena: Altadena Historical Society, 2004); Walt Dixon and Jerry Roberts, *Hawthorne* (Charleston, SC: Arcadia Publishing, 2005), 47; Apostol, *South Pasadena*, 47–59.

59. McClelland et al., "Historic Residential Suburbs," E16.

60. Hayden, *Building Suburbia*, chapter 4; McClelland et al., "Historic Residential Suburbs," E18.

61. Weiss, *Rise of the Community Builders*, 1–5.

62. Barry Neil Zarakov, "California Planned Communities of the 1920s" (MA Thesis, UC Santa Barbara, 1977), 131.

63. On these protective practices, see Duncan and Duncan, *Landscapes of Privilege*; Mary Corbin Sies, "Paradise Retained: An Analysis of Persistence in Planned, Exclusive Suburbs, 1880–1980," *Planning Perspectives* 12 (1997), 165–191.

64. *The Master List of Design Projects of the Olmsted Firm, 1857–1950*, compiled by Charles E. Beveridge and Carolyn F. Hoffman (New York: National Association for Olmsted Parks, 1987), 37. This list did not clarify which projects were brought to full fruition.

65. Fogelson, *Fragmented Metropolis*, 105, 155.

66. Home Owners' Loan Corporation, "Security Map and Area Descriptions, Metropolitan Los Angeles, California," and City Survey Files, Record Group 195, National Archives, Washington, DC, worksheet A-25 (hereafter HOLC City Survey Files). This source mentions the presence of race restrictions.

67. Fogelson, *Fragmented Metropolis*, 159; Margaret Marsh, *Suburban Lives* (New Brunswick: Rutgers University Press, 1990), chapter 6, quote at 170.

68. HOLC City Survey File, A-59; Fishman, *Bourgeois Utopias*, 169; Fogelson, *Bourgeois Nightmares*, 5–19. The Olmsted Firm, ironically, later chastised some of these hillside developments for despoiling nature. See Greg Hise and William Deverell, *Eden By*

Design: The 1930 Olmsted-Bartholomew Plan for the Los Angeles Region (Berkeley: University of California Press, 2000), 56n6, 92.

69. This was a precursor to a common feature of Common Interest Developments that proliferated after 1960.

70. "The History of Windsor Square and the Windsor Square Association," accessed at https://windsorsquare.org/neighborhood/a-brief-history-of-windsor-square/.

71. Zack, *Altadena: Between Wilderness and City*, 128; HOLC City Survey File, A-10.

72. Barraclough, *Making the San Fernando Valley*; http://www.hiddenhillscity.org; US Census dataset, Population 2000; James Zarsadiaz, *Resisting Change in Suburbia: Asian Immigrants and Frontier Nostalgia in L.A.* (Oakland: University of California Press, 2022); also see James S. Duncan and Nancy G. Duncan, *Landscapes of Privilege: The Politics of the Aesthetic in an American Suburb* (New York: Routledge, 2004).

73. Hayden, *Building Suburbia*, 97–100; Weiss, *Rise of the Community Builders*, 40–41; Hise, *Magnetic Los Angeles*, 15–29. Hise describes the problem of excessive unplanned subdivisions in 1920s LA (pp. 28–29).

74. Southworth and Owens, "The Evolving Metropolis," 273–274; Nicolaides, *My Blue Heaven*; Lotchin, "Population Concentration," 94.

75. Fogelson, *Fragmented Metropolis*, 92; Richard Longstreth, "The Perils of a Parkless Town," in *The Car and the City*, edited by Martin Wachs and Margaret Crawford (Ann Arbor: University of Michigan Press, 1992), 142; Wachs, "Autos, Transit," 304; Bottles, *Los Angeles and the Automobile*, 93, 170.

76. Wachs, "Autos, Transit," 306–308; Brodsly, *L.A. Freeway*, 85–91; Fogelson, *Fragmented Metropolis*, 92–95.

77. McClelland et al., "Historic Residential Suburbs," F55. See Ovnick, *End of the Rainbow*, for an excellent discussion of automobile-oriented suburbs.

78. Mark Foster, "The Model T, the Hard Sell, and Los Angeles' Urban Growth: The Decentralization of Los Angeles during the 1920s," *Pacific Historical Review* (1975), 477–78; Brodsly, *L.A. Freeway*, 92; Richard Longstreth, *City Center to Regional Mall: Architecture, the Automobile, and Retailing in Los Angeles, 1920–1950* (Cambridge, MA: MIT Press, 1998); Bottles, *Los Angeles*, 198–199, 207–208.

79. Greg Hise, "Industry and Imaginative Geographies," in *Metropolis in the Making: Los Angeles in the 1920s*, edited by Tom Sitton and William Deverell (Berkeley: University of California Press, 2001), 15–17. Early industrial dispersal was not unique to LA; see Nicolaides and Wiese, eds., *The Suburb Reader*, 2nd ed., chapters 4, 7.

80. Hise, "Industry and Imaginative Geographies."

81. Hise, "Industry and Imaginative Geographies," 28.

82. Davis, "Sunshine and the Open Shop," 96–122; Hise, "Industry and Imaginative Geographies"; on the geography of the film industry, see Stephanie Frank, "Claiming Hollywood: Boosters, the Film Industry, and Metropolitan Los Angeles," *Journal of Urban History* 38, 1 (2012), 71–88, and Barraclough, *Making the San Fernando Valley*, chapter 3.

83. Hise, "Industry and Imaginative Geographies," 28–29.

84. Robert Phelps, "The Search for a Modern Industrial City: Urban Planning, the Open Shop, and the Founding of Torrance, California," *Pacific Historical Review* 64 (November 1995), 503-535; Kim Hernandez, "The 'Bungalow Boom': The

Working-Class Housing Industry and the Development and Promotion of Early Twentieth-Century Los Angeles," *Southern California Quarterly* 92, 4 (2010), 352.

85. Hise, "Industry and Imaginative Geographies"; Viehe, "Black Gold Suburbs"; Hise, *Magnetic Los Angeles*; Nicolaides, "Where the Working Man Is Welcomed"; Nicolaides, *My Blue Heaven*; Nancy Quam-Wickham, "'Another World': Work, Home, and Autonomy in Blue-Collar Suburbs," in *Metropolis in the Making*, edited by Sitton and Deverell, 123–141.

86. Hise, *Magnetic Los Angeles*, 42.

87. Nicolaides, "Where the Working Man Is Welcomed," 543–548; Wiese, *Places of Their Own*, 25–27, 54–66.

88. González, *In Search of the Mexican Beverly Hills*, chapter 1.

89. Nicolaides, *My Blue Heaven*; González, *In Search of the Mexican Beverly Hills*.

90. Carolyn Patricia Flynn, "Pacific Ready Cut Homes: Mass Produced Bungalows in Los Angeles, 1908-1942 (MA Thesis, University of California Los Angeles, 1986), 38; "12,000 Easy Pieces: Was Your '20s House Built from a Kit?" *LAT*, July 16, 2006; Hayden, *Building Suburbia*, 115–116; Rosemary Thornton and Dale Patrick Wolicki, *California's Kit Homes: A Reprint of the 1925 Pacific Ready-Cut Homes Catalogue* (Alton, Illinois: Gentle Beam Publications, 2004).

91. Nicolaides, "Where the Working Man Is Welcomed"; Eileen V. Wallis, "'A Worth-While Living from the Soil': The Farmlet in Southern California from the Late Nineteenth Century to World War II," *Western Historical Quarterly* 49, 2 (Summer 2018), 185–208; Ryan Reft, "From Small Farming to Urban Agriculture: El Monte and Subsistence Homesteading," in *East of East: The Making of Greater El Monte*, edited by Romeo Guzmán, Carribean Fragoza, Alex Sayf Cummings, and Ryan Reft (New Brunswick: Rutgers University Press, 2020), 163–173. In Cudahy today, these deep narrow lots are filled out by "dingbat apartments."

92. Reyner Banham, *Los Angeles: The Architecture of Four Ecologies* (New York: Penguin, 1971), 172–177.

93. Hayden, *Building Suburbia*, 100.

94. Laura Pulido, "Rethinking Environmental Racism: White Privilege and Urban Development in Southern California," *Annals of the Association of American Geographers* 90, 1 (2000), 12–40; Karen Brodkin, *Power Politics: Environmental Activism in Southern California* (New Brunswick: Rutgers University Press, 2009).

95. Myron Orfield, *American Metropolitics: The New Suburban Reality* (Washington, DC: Brookings Institution Press, 2002); Lotchin, "Population Concentration," 93, 98; also see Chapter 6.

96. "Helms Man Always Delivered the Goods," *LAT*, October 17, 1994; "This Is His Town," *LAT*, November 13, 1969; Photo with caption "Hardy Gets Trophy," *LAT*, January 21, 1945. In the racially diverse Eastside, which the Helms company did not service, an independent operator, Herman Langley, delivered Helms baked goods, bringing the same congenial spirit to his route. See "A Baker's Dozen of Sad Goodbyes," *LAT*, November 11, 2006.

97. Robert Gottlieb, *Reinventing Los Angeles: Nature and Community in the Global City* (Cambridge, MA: MIT Press, 2007), 80; Lizabeth Cohen, *A Consumers' Republic: The Politics of Mass Consumption in Postwar America* (New York: Vintage, 2003).

98. City of Lakewood, "The Lakewood Story," chapter 3, https://www.lakewoodcity.org/About/Our-History/The-Lakewood-Story/03-Suburban-Pioneers.

99. Hayden, *Building Suburbia*, 128.

100. On the San Fernando Valley, see Deborah Dash Moore, *To the Golden Cities* (Cambridge, MA: Harvard University Press, 1994), 42–43; Pitt and Pitt, *Los Angeles A–Z*, 448; Kevin Roderick, *America's Suburb* (Los Angeles: Los Angeles Times Books, 2001); Barraclough, *Making the San Fernando Valley*; Hise, *Magnetic Los Angeles*; Hise, "Home Building and Industrial Decentralization, 95–125. On Lakewood, see Chapter 7.

101. Nicolaides, *My Blue Heaven*, 206.

102. On the segregation aspect, see Rothstein, *Color of Law*, chapter 4.

103. Benjamin Looker, *A Nation of Neighborhoods: Imagining Cities, Communities, and Democracy in Postwar America* (Chicago: University of Chicago Press, 2015), 56.

104. Ansley Erickson, *Making the Unequal Metropolis: School Desegregation and Its Limits* (Chicago: University of Chicago Press, 2016); 30–34, 63; Tridib Banerjee and William C. Baer, *Beyond the Neighborhood Unit: Residential Environments and Public Policy* (New York: Plenum Press, 1984).

105. Looker, *Nation of Neighborhoods*, 52–59; Hise, *Magnetic Los Angeles*, 31–35; Southworth and Owens, "The Evolving Metropolis," 274.

106. Hise, *Magnetic Los Angeles*, chapters 4 and 5.

107. Hise, *Magnetic Los Angeles*, 136–152, 165–166, 187–188, 195–208; Hise, "Home Building," 103–110; Brackman, "Making Room for Millions," 391.

108. See Chapter 7. In Lakewood, early land developer Clark Bonner sold 200 acres of land to Douglas Aircraft in 1940, which built its plant quickly to meet the wartime emergency. This plant was in place before Lakewood's postwar building boom.

109. Brodsly, *L.A. Freeway*; Avila, *Popular Culture in the Age of White Flight*, 195–223; also see Eric Avila, *The Folklore of the Freeway: Race and Revolt in the Modernist City* (Minneapolis: University of Minnesota Press, 2014).

110. See Figure A1.4 (RPC study areas).

111. Regional Planning Commission, County of Los Angeles, "The East San Gabriel Valley: An Area Land Use Plan," County of Los Angeles Regional Planning Commission (January 15, 1957), 4, 16–19, quote at 16 inset; Victor Valle, *City of Industry: Genealogies of Power in Southern California* (New Brunswick: Rutgers University Press, 2009), 119–120.

112. Hise, *Magnetic Los Angeles*, 190–195.

113. Regional Planning Commission, County of Los Angeles, "The Southeast Area: An Area Land Use Plan," Regional Planning Commission of Los Angeles County (June 1, 1959), 16–17, 20–21.

114. Regional Planning Commission, County of Los Angeles, "The East Central Area: An Area Plan," Regional Planning Commission of Los Angeles County (July 1, 1963), 32.

115. Hise, *Magnetic Los Angeles*, 201, 211; on Lakewood, see Chapter 7; Ovnick, *Los Angeles: The End of the Rainbow*, 283, 287–295. On the architecture of the postwar house nationally, see James A. Jacobs, *Detached America: Building Houses in Postwar*

Suburbia (Charlottesville: University of Virginia Press, 2015); Miller, *Houses for a New World*, 7–27. Also see Patricia Farrell Donahue, *Participation, Community, and Public Policy in a Virginia Suburb: Of Our Own Making* (Lanham, MD: Lexington Books, 2017).

116. On class democratizing, see Hise, *Magnetic Los Angeles*, 203–205; Waldie, *Holy Land*; Nicolaides, *My Blue Heaven*; on class stratification in postwar suburbia, see Cohen, *Consumer's Republic*. For broader class patterns, see Chapter 2.

117. Rothstein, *Color of Law*, chapter 11.

118. Some contemporary commentators believed the sitcom suburbs—with their cheaply built housing—would become the slums of the future. See Barbara Kelly, *Expanding the American Dream* (Albany: State University of New York Press, 1993).

119. "Local Suburbs More Diverse: Integration Along Class Lines Has Become a Norm," *LAT*, December 9, 2008; Myers and Park, "Racially Balanced Cities," Exhibit 3; and see Chapter 7.

120. Quote from "Helms Man Always Delivered the Goods"; "Helms Truck Drivers Will Join Teamsters," *LAT*, February 10, 1966; "3 Trucks Held Up on City Streets; One Driver Shot," *LAT*, July 9, 1967; "Fear Plagues Drivers in South-Central L.A.," *LAT*, November 26, 1967; "Parolee Admits 38 Holdups," *LAT*, December 29, 1967.

121. Hayden, *Building Suburbia*, chapter 8; Joel Garreau, *Edge City: Life on the New Frontier* (New York: Doubleday, 1991); Alan Berube, Audrey Singer, Jill H. Wilson, and William H. Frey, "Finding Exurbia: America's Fast-Growing Communities at the Metropolitan Fringe," Living Cities Census Series (Washington, DC: The Brookings Institution, October 2006), accessed at https://www.brookings.edu/research/finding-exurbia-americas-fast-growing-communities-at-the-metropolitan-fringe/. Joel Garreau's definition of "edge city" was a place with at least 5 million square feet of leasable office of space, 600,000 square feet of leasable retail space, and more jobs than bedrooms. The "Exurban" study team found that the South and Midwest had higher concentrations of exurbanites than the West and Northeast. They also noted that although New York and Los Angeles anchor dense mega-regions and each has a considerable number of exurbanites, those populations "are quite small viewed against the backdrop of total metropolitan population" (p. 11).

122. In the four outlying counties of the region, growth in this period was even faster than in LA, especially in Irvine, Orange County, a prototype of the edge city.

123. Davis, *City of Quartz*, chapter 3; William Fulton, *The Reluctant Metropolis: The Politics of Urban Growth in Los Angeles* (Point Arena, CA: Solano Press Books, 1997), 1–20, 43–66, 177–199; Whittemore, "Zoning Los Angeles."

124. Garreau, *Edge City*, 262–263, 269, 283.

125. Genevieve Giuliano and Kenneth A. Small, "Subcenters in the Los Angeles Region," *Regional Science and Urban Economics* 21 (1991), 163–182.

126. Peter Gordon and Harry Richardson, "Beyond Polycentricity," *Journal of the American Planning Association* 62, 3 (Summer 1996), 289–295. Also see Anne Vernez Moudon and Paulo Mitchell Hess, "Suburban Clusters: The Nucleation of Multifamily Housing in Suburban Areas of the Central Puget Sound," *Journal of the*

American Planning Association 66, 3 (Summer 2000), 243. While this team studied Puget Sound, their observations apply generally to Los Angeles.

127. Gary Pivo, "The Net of Mixed Beads: Suburban Office Development in Six Metropolitan Regions," *Journal of the American Planning Association* 56, 4 (Autumn 1990), 457–469; Robert E. Lang and Jennifer LeFurgy, "Edgeless Cities: Examining the Noncentered Metropolis," *Housing Policy Debate* 14, 3 (2003), 427–462. Lang and LeFurgy found that office space in Los Angeles was distributed as follows: 37% edgeless cities, 29.8% downtown, 25.4% edge cities (p. 443). For this, they dubbed LA's office sprawl "balanced" (p. 450).

128. Nicolaides and Wiese, eds., *Suburb Reader*, chapter 12; Self, *American Babylon*.

129. Peter Schrag, *Paradise Lost: California's Experience, America's Future* (New York: New Press, 1998), 171–172.

130. Also see Hayden, *Building Suburbia*, chapters 8 and 9; Garreau, *Edge Cities*.

131. Nelson and Clark, *Los Angeles*, 21.

132. "Huge Century City Project Will Begin This Spring," *LAT*, January 29, 1961; "Century City Set to Be Born Today," *LAT*, April 17, 1961; "Bulldozers to Topple Make-Believe World," *LAT*, July 16, 1961; "'Avenue of Stars,' Not Named for Movies," *LAT*, July 16, 1961; Stephanie Frank, "Why a Studio Without a Backlot Isn't Like a Ten-Story Building Without an Elevator: Land Planning in the Postfordist Film Industry," *Journal of Planning History* 15, 2 (2016), 129–148; Stephanie Frank, "Building Century City: Twentieth Century Fox and Urban Development in Los Angeles, 1920–1975" (paper presented at the Urban History Association meeting, Las Vegas, October 2010).

133. "Wall off Century City, Neighboring Area Asks," *LAT*, February 12, 1961; "Westside Committee to Hit at 'High Rise,'" *LAT*, April 23, 1961; Peter Sebastian Chesney, "The Playboy Mansion Must Be Destroyed," *Critical Planning* 26, 1 (2023), 63.

134. Andrew Wiese, "'The Giddy Rise of the Environmentalists': Corporate Real Estate Development and Environmental Politics in San Diego, California, 1968–73," *Environmental History* 19 (January 2014), 32–34; Davis, *City of Quartz*, 120–159; Elizabeth Blackmar, "Of REITS and Rights: Absentee Ownership in the Periphery" in *City, Country, Empire: Landscapes in Environmental History*, edited by Jeffry Diefendorf and Kurk Dorsey (Pittsburgh: University of Pittsburgh Press, 2005); Kevin Fox Gotham, "The Secondary Circuit of Capital Reconsidered: Globalization and the U.S. Real Estate Sector," *American Journal of Sociology* 112, 1 (July 2006); also see Becky Nicolaides and Andrew Wiese, "Suburbanization Since 1945," Oxford Online Encyclopedia of American History, published online 2016.

135. Wiese, "Giddy Rise"; "Ship Firm Subsidiaries Purchase Triunfo Ranch," *LAT*, October 3, 1963; "Union Oil Buys Simi Ranch for $20 mil, Plans City," *LAT*, March 17, 1968.

136. On KB's activity in LA County, see "For Antelope Valley, It's Hammer Time Again," *LAT*, August 8, 2000; "KB Home Cuts Holdings as Market Cools," *LAT*, August 30, 2006; on Pulte, https://www.pultegroupinc.com/about-us/pultegr oup-history/default.aspx; Garreau, *Edge City*; Becky M. Nicolaides and James Zarsadiaz, "Design Assimilation in Suburbia: Asian Americans, Built Landscapes,

and Suburban Advantage in Los Angeles' San Gabriel Valley since 1970," *Journal of Urban History* 43, 2 (2017), 352. KB Homes had 14 subdivisions in the Antelope Valley alone.

Some called these places "boomburbs," others "exurbs." See Robert E. Lang and Jennifer LeFurgy, *Boomburbs: The Rise of America's Accidental Cities* (Washington, DC: Brookings Institution Press, 2007). Lang and LeFurgy define a "boomburb" as an incorporated city with at least 100,000 in population, not the core city of their region, and with double-digit population growth in each census since 1970. Other "boomburbs" in the LA metro area included Irvine, Moreno Valley, Rancho Cucamonga, Simi Valley, and Thousand Oaks. On exurbs, see Berube et al., "Finding Exurbia."

137. http://www.fundinguniverse.com/company-histories/KB-Home-Company-History.html; Ned Eichler, *The Merchant Builders* (Cambridge, MA: MIT Press, 1982), 139–140.

138. Paul L. Knox, *Metroburbia, USA* (New Brunswick: Rutgers University Press, 2008), 67.

139. Seth Lubove, "Learning from Victoria's Secret," *Forbes*, December 19, 1994, 60+; "Domestic bling" from Knox, *Metroburbia*, 76–78.

140. Hayden, *Building Suburbia*, chapter 9; Southworth and Owens, "The Evolving Metropolis," 275–277.

141. Hayden, *Building Suburbia*, 190. More recently, the trend has been larger homes on shrinking lot sizes. See Knox, *Metroburbia*, 80; US Bureau of the Census, *Census of Housing, Characteristics of New Housing, 2014*, accessed at: https://www.census.gov/construction/chars/historical_data/.

142. Peter Calthorpe, *Urbanism in the Age of Climate Change* (Washington DC: Island Press, 2013); also see Char Miller, *Not So Golden State: Sustainability vs. the California Dream* (San Antonio, TX: Trinity University Press, 2016).

143. Nicolaides and Wiese, "Suburbanization Since 1945"; Evan McKenzie, *Privatopia: Homeowner Associations and the Rise of Residential Private Government* (New Haven: Yale University Press, 1994); Knox, *Metroburbia*, 74; Matthew Lasner, *High Life: Condo Living in the Suburban Century* (New Haven: Yale University Press, 2012).

144. Southworth and Owens, "The Evolving Metropolis," quote at 276; Sarah Elizabeth Richards, "Backlash in the Burbs," *Psychology Today Magazine* (September/October 2005), 66–72.

145. Examples of this criticism include Andres Duany, Elizabeth Plater-Zyberk and Jeff Speck, *Suburban Nation: The Rise of Sprawl and the Decline of the American Dream* (New York: North Point Press, 2000); Christopher Caldwell, "Levittown to Littleton: How the Suburbs Have Changed," *National Review* (May 31, 1999); Southworth and Owens, "The Evolving Metropolis," 285.

146. Garreau, *Edge City*, 271.

147. Ivanov's story from "Home Economics: A Documentary of Suburbia," produced and directed by Jenny Cool, distributed by New Day Films, 1994, 46 min.; and Jennifer C. Cool, "The Experts of Everyday Life: Cultural Reproduction and Cultural Critique in the Antelope Valley" (MA Thesis, University of Southern California, 1993).

148. While LA had its fair share of exurbs, the South and Midwest had even higher concentrations of exurban populations who had to contend with similar conditions of living. As one study found, "South Carolina, Oklahoma, Tennessee, and Maryland have the largest proportions of their residents living in exurbs, while Texas, California, and Ohio have the largest absolute numbers of exurbanites." Berube et al., "Finding Exurbia."

Chapter 2

1. At the center of this analysis is an extensive dataset drawn mainly from the US Census, which I compiled with the help of a team of graduate and undergraduate students. For each of LA County's 86 municipalities, we collected data on 53 variables for each decennial year from 1950 to 2010. These variables covered race/ethnicity, class, gendered labor patterns, education, lifecycle characteristics, family status, and housing. Despite the many flaws of the Census involving inconsistencies in method and definitions over time, these data present an invaluable empirical base for tracing various demographic, social, housing, and economic trends across the county's suburban areas over a 60-year period. All tables and demographic data for this chapter are drawn from this dataset. The full dataset and extensive methodology notes are available at the USC Libraries website: https://doi.org/10.25549/lad emo-ouc1sto1757543.

   I chose the municipal level as the main unit of analysis. If we had collected census tract data—which would have given a more granular view of neighborhoods—a somewhat different picture would surely emerge. Yet a compelling case can be made for the municipal scale, given that the municipality is the primary social and civic universe for most suburban residents: it holds the power of protecting and policing civil rights and freedoms, land use, public services, and infrastructure. Moreover, municipalities are often the jurisdiction where immigrant policies play out, helping elucidate the local context of everyday life in emerging ethnic suburbs. As one team of analysts put it, the municipal scale is important to consider since "a majority of people reside in incorporated cities, obtain government services from these entities, and cast votes for city council members to represent them at the local level" (Linda Lou, Hyojung Lee, Anthony Guardado, and Dowell Myers, "Racially Balanced Cities in Southern California, 1990–2010," Population Dynamics Research Group, USC Price School of Public Policy, February 2012, 4). And while the municipal scale waters down variations within suburban towns—and there were many—it still gives us a means of observing county-wide patterns of change in a manageable way, over a relatively long period of time.

   On the question of scale, see Philip Ethington, Julie Park, William Frey, and Dowell Myers, "Placing Segregation: Intersections of Isolation and Diversity in a Multiracial Metropolis, 1940–2000," (unpublished manuscript), 7; John Mollenkopf and Manuel Pastor, eds., *Unsettled Americans: Metropolitan Context and Civic Leadership for Immigrant Integration* (Ithaca: Cornell University Press, 2016), 2.

2. James P. Allen and Eugene Turner, *The Ethnic Quilt: Population Diversity in Southern California* (Northridge: Cal State Northridge Center for Geographical Studies, 1997).

3. On similar trends nationally since the 1980s, see Myron Orfield, *American Metropolitics: The New Suburban Reality* (Washington DC: Brookings Institution Press, 2002); Paul Maginn and Katrin Anacker, eds., *Suburbia in the 21st Century: From Dreamscape to Nightmare?* (New York: Routledge, 2023); Bernadette Hanlon and Thomas Vicino, eds., *Routledge Companion to the Suburbs* (New York: Routledge, 2019); Katrin Anacker, ed., *The New American Suburb: Poverty, Race and the Economic Crisis* (New York: Routledge, 2016); Bernadette Hanlon, John Rennie Short, and Thomas J. Vicino, *Cities and Suburbs: New Metropolitan Realities* (New York: Routledge, 2010); "Suburban Inequality, Parts I and II," *The Russell Sage Foundation Journal of the Social Sciences* 9, issues 1 and 2 (February 1, 2023); Tim Keogh, *In Levittown's Shadow: Poverty in America's Wealthiest Postwar Suburb* (Chicago: University of Chicago Press, 2023).

4. Edward W. Soja, *Postmodern Geographies: The Reassertion of Space in Critical Social Theory* (London: Verso, 1989), 191–196, 201–215; Edward W. Soja, *My Los Angeles: From Urban Restructuring to Regional Urbanization* (Berkeley: University of California Press, 2014); Allen J. Scott, *Technopolis: High-Technology Industry and Regional Development in Southern California* (Berkeley: University of California Press, 1993), 3–9; Mike Davis, "Ozzie and Harriet in Hell," *Harvard Design Magazine* 1 S/S (1997); Roger Waldinger and Mehdi Bozorgmehr, eds., *Ethnic Los Angeles* (New York: Russell Sage Foundation, 1996).

5. Soja, *Postmodern Geographies*, 201–203; Mike Davis, "The New Industrial Peonage," *Heritage newsletter* (Summer 1991) 7; Davis, "Ozzie and Harriet in Hell"; "Lockheed," Industrial Los Angeles, accessed March, 2, 2023, https://industrial-los-angeles.com/lockheed/; Scott, *Technopolis*, 15; Layne Karafantis and Stuart W. Leslie, "'Suburban Warriors': The Blue-Collar and Blue-Sky Communities of Southern California's Aerospace Industry," *Journal of Planning History* 18, 1 (2019), 3–26.

6. Soja, *Postmodern Geographies*, 207; Scott, *Technopolis*, 10–11; "Bold Fashion Statement Amid Aerospace Decline," *LAT*, March 12, 1995; Ruth Milkman, *L.A. Story: Immigrant Workers and the Future of the U.S. Labor Movement* (New York: Russell Sage Foundation, 2006), 87–92; "Slavery's Long Gone? Don't Bet on It," *LAT*, August 4, 1995; "INS Got Tip on Sweatshop 3 Years Ago," *LAT*, August 4, 1995; "Of Neighbors and Fences: 'Slave' Shop Generated Few Suspicions," *LAT*, August 5, 1995; Alex Sayf Cummings, "Dreams of Escape and Belonging," in *East of East: The Making of Greater El Monte*, edited by Romeo Guzmán, Carribean Fragoza, Alex Sayf Cummings, and Ryan Reft (Rutgers: Rutgers University Press, 2020), 135–145.

7. "An Overcrowded Housing Crisis," *LAT*, October 24, 2022. LA was the leader in overcrowding, among all large counties in the United States.

8. Dick Degnon, "Suburbs Now Blocks of Neighborly Neighbors," *LAT*, May 25, 1958. Section title refers to *Get Out*, directed by Jordan Peele (Universal Pictures, 2017), 104 min.

9. Eric Avila, *Popular Culture in the Age of White Flight* (Berkeley: University of California Press, 2004).

10. See Table A2.1 (Whites in suburbs of LA, 1950–2010)

11. Wendy Plotkin, "Restrictive Covenants," in *Encyclopedia of American Urban History*, vol. 2, edited by David Goldfield (Thousand Oaks: Sage, 2007), 679–681; Douglas Flamming, *Bound for Freedom: Black Los Angeles in Jim Crow America* (Berkeley: University of California Press, 2005), 69, 156, 223; Laura Redford, "The Intertwined History of Class and Race Segregation in Los Angeles," *Journal of Planning History* 16, 4 (2017), 308; George Sánchez, "The History of Segregation in Los Angeles: A Report on Racial Discrimination and Its Legacy" (Scheff & Washington, PC, in legal case *American Civil Rights Foundation v. Los Angeles Unified School District*, 2007); Richard Rothstein, *The Color of Law: A Forgotten History of How Our Government Segregated America* (New York: Liveright Publishing Corp, 2017), 81.

12. Lawrence B. de Graaf, Kevin Mulroy, and Quintard Taylor, eds., *Seeking El Dorado: African Americans in California* (Seattle: University of Washington Press, 2001), 25.

13. Lawrence B. de Graaf, "The City of Black Angels: Emergence of the Los Angeles Ghetto, 1890–1930," *Pacific Historical Review* 39 (1970), quote at 337; Flamming, *Bound for Freedom*, 69, 221; Arnold R. Hirsch, "With or Without Jim Crow: Black Residential Segregation in the United States," in *Urban Policy in Twentieth Century America*, edited by Arnold R. Hirsch and Raymond A. Mohl (New Brunswick: Rutgers University Press, 1993), 75; Scott Kurashige, *The Shifting Grounds of Race: Black and Japanese Americans in the Making of Multiethnic Los Angeles* (Princeton: Princeton University Press, 2008), 22–23.

14. Kurashige, *The Shifting Grounds of Race*, 31–33.

15. Becky Nicolaides, *My Blue Heaven: Life and Politics in the Working-Class Suburbs of Los Angeles, 1920–1965* (Chicago: University of Chicago Press, 2002), 19; "Race Restrictions in South Gate," File 1018 "South Gate", Box 160, Works Progress Administration Collection 306, UCLA Special Collections.

16. "Editorial," *Crescenta Valley Ledger*, April 10, 1941; "La Canada Race Restrictions Program Assured; Underwriting Fund Sought," *Crescenta Valley Ledger*, May 8, 1941; "Race Restriction Drive Underway," *Crescenta Valley Ledger*, November 6, 1941, "Editorial," *Crescenta Valley Ledger*, November 13, 1941, Lanterman Family Collection, Lanterman House Archives.

17. Windsor Hills Summary of Building Restrictions, Series 3, Box 2ov Folder 1, Fritz Burns Papers, CSLA-2, Department of Archives and Special Collections, William H. Hannon Library, Loyola Marymount University.

18. Kurashige, *The Shifting Grounds of Race*, 28.

19. Kurashige, *The Shifting Grounds of Race*, 22, 25; and see Redford, "The Intertwined History of Class and Race," 308–312.

20. Flamming, *Bound for Freedom*, 69; Josh Sides, *L.A. City Limits: African American Los Angeles from the Great Depression to the Present* (Berkeley: University of California Press, 2003), 107. A notable exception was Lewis Homes in the Pomona Valley, committed to racial integration. See the excellent discussion in Genevieve Carpio, *Collision at the Crossroads: How Place and Mobility Make Race* (Oakland: University of California Press, 2019), 189–195.

21. Sánchez, "History of Segregation," 8; Sides, *L.A. City Limits*, 101–106; Andrea Gibbons, *City of Segregation: One Hundred Years of Struggle for Housing in Los Angeles* (New York: Verso Books, 2018), 30–31; Lonnie G. Bunch, "A Past Not Necessarily Prologue: The Afro-American in Los Angeles," in *20th Century Los Angeles: Power, Promotion and Social Conflict*, edited by Norman Klein and Martin Schiesl (Claremont: Regina Books, 1990), 106; Nicolaides, *My Blue Heaven*, 165; Gary Keyes and Mike Lawler, *Crescenta Valley's Dirty Laundry* (Mount Pleasant, SC: Arcadia Books, 2021), 11–12, 17, 66. On the KKK in Pasadena, see Chapter 4, and in Lakewood, see Chapter 7; on El Monte, see Dan Cady, "Rise, Fall, Repeat: El Monte's White Supremacy Movements," in *East of East: The Making of Greater El Monte*, edited by Romeo Guzmán, Carribean Fragoza, Alex Sayf Cummings, and Ryan Reft (New Brunswick: Rutgers University Press, 2020), 59–67.

22. Sánchez, "History of Segregation," 4; Flamming, *Bound for Freedom*, 220–221.

23. Quotes from Hirsch, "With or Without Jim Crow," 75.

24. Sides, *L.A. City Limits*, 106; Flamming, *Bound for Freedom*, 219–221; Gibbons, *City of Segregation*, 25–27; Gene Slater, *Freedom to Discriminate: How Realtors Conspired to Segregate Housing and Divide America* (Berkeley: Heyday, 2021).

25. Sánchez, "History of Segregation," 8; Jerry González, *In Search of the Mexican Beverly Hills: Latino Suburbanization in Postwar Los Angeles* (Rutgers University Press, 2018), 64; Sides, *L.A. City Limits*, 106.

26. Area D-50, City Survey File for Los Angeles, Record Group 195, Records of the Federal Home Loan Bank Board, National Archives, Washington, DC.

27. A, B, C, D worksheets, City Survey File for Los Angeles, Record Group 195, Records of the Federal Home Loan Bank Board, National Archives, Washington, DC.

    My analysis of the Los Angeles HOLC appraisals found that no Blacks were present in A-green and B-blue rated areas; they were present in just 3 out of 166 C-yellow rated neighborhoods, where they comprised just 1% of the population. By contrast, 45 of the C-yellow areas contained Mexicans, Japanese, Jews, and other non-Caucasian groups. Of 71 D-red areas in Los Angeles, 69 had racial minorities in them, 35 included African Americans.

28. Kenneth T. Jackson, *Crabgrass Frontier* (New York: Oxford University Press, 1985), 208.

29. Rothstein, *Color of Law*, 70; Sides, *L.A. City Limits*, 107–108; Flamming, *Bound for Freedom*, 352–353; Nicolaides, *My Blue Heaven*, 179.

30. Avila, *Popular Culture*, chapter 2; Rothstein, *Color of Law*.

31. Jackson, *Crabgrass Frontier*, 213–217; Rothstein, *Color of Law*, 88–91.

32. Daniel Martinez HoSang, *Racial Propositions: Ballot Initiatives and the Making of Postwar California* (Berkeley: University of California Press, 2010), 64, 73.

33. For example, see Keeanga-Yamahtta Taylor, *Race for Profit: How Banks and the Real Estate Industry Undermined Black Homeownership* (Chapel Hill: University of North Carolina Press, 2019).

34. Mike Davis, *City of Quartz: Excavating the Future in Los Angeles* (New York: Vintage, 1992), 159.

35. Davis, *City of Quartz*, chapter 3; James Zarsadiaz, *Resisting Change in Suburbia: Asian Immigrants and Frontier Nostalgia in L.A.* (Oakland: University of California Press, 2022), chapter 5; Andrew Whittemore, "Zoning Los Angeles: A Brief History of Four Regimes," *Planning Perspectives* 27, 3 (2012), 399–404; Greg Morrow, "The Homeowner Revolution: Democracy, Land Use, and the Los Angeles Slow-Growth Movement, 1965–1992," (PhD dissertation, University of California Los Angeles, 2013); "An Overcrowded Housing Crisis."

36. For example, see Nicolaides, *My Blue Heaven*, chapter 7; Jack Schneider, "Escape from Los Angeles: White Flight from Los Angeles and Its Schools, 1960-1980," *Journal of Urban History* 34, 6 (September 2008), 995-1012; HoSang, *Racial Propositions.*

37. Sánchez, "History of Segregation," 11–12, citing Camille Zubrinsky Charles, *Won't You Be My Neighbor?: Race, Class, and Residence in Los Angeles* (New York: Russell Sage Foundation, 2006), 120; Carolyn B. Aldama and Gary A. Dymski, "Urban Sprawl, Racial Separation, and Federal Housing Policy," in *Up Against the Sprawl: Public Policy and the Making of Southern California*, edited by Jennifer Wolch, Manuel Pastor, and Peter Dreier (Minneapolis: University of Minnesota Press, 2004), 113.

38. Clayton Howard, "Building a 'Family-Friendly' Metropolis: Sexuality, the State, and Postwar Housing Policy," *Journal of Urban History* 39, 5 (2013), 934, 937–938; Clayton Howard, *The Closet and the Cul-de-Sac: The Politics of Sexual Privacy in Northern California* (Philadelphia: University of Pennsylvania Press, 2019); Cohen, *A Consumers' Republic*, 141, 147; Hayden, *Building Suburbia*, 147.

    On the preponderance of young, straight, white nuclear families in postwar suburbs, see Otis Dudley Duncan and Albert J Reiss, Jr., "Suburbs and Urban Fringe," in *The Suburban Community*, edited by William M. Dobriner (New York: G. P. Putnam's Sons, 1958), 48–61; Ernest Mowrer, "The Family in Suburbia," in *The Suburban Community*, edited by William M. Dobriner (New York: G. P. Putnam Sons, 1958), 158; Hugh A. Wilson, "The Family in Suburbia: From Tradition to Pluralism," in *Suburbia Re-examined*, edited by Barbara M. Kelly (New York: Greenwood Press, 1989), 85–86; Gwendolyn Wright, *Building the Dream: A Social History of Housing in America* (Cambridge, MA: MIT Press, 1988), 256.

39. Degnon, "Suburbs Now Blocks of Neighborly Neighbors"; Keyes and Lawler, *Crescenta Valley's Dirty Laundry*, 11.

40. This section relies on US Census dataset on sources and methodology, see Note 1.

    On these broad patterns in LA, important works include Lawrence Bobo, et al., *Prismatic Metropolis: Inequality in Los Angeles* (New York: Russell Sage Foundation, 2000); Waldinger and Bozorgmehr, eds., *Ethnic Los Angeles*; Allen and Turner, *The Ethnic Quilt*; Wendy Cheng, *The Changs Next Door to the Díazes: Remapping Race in Suburban California* (Minneapolis: University of Minnesota Press, 2013).

41. Laura Pulido, *Black, Brown, Yellow, and Left: Radical Activism in Los Angeles* (Berkeley: University of California Press, 2006), 53.

42. Sides, *L.A. City Limits*, 126–127.

43. González, *In Search of the Mexican Beverly Hills*, 64–65.

44. On this meaning of suburban life for Black Americans, see the remarkable story of Ted Wheeler who lived in the suburbs of Chicago. He articulated the notion of integrated neighborhoods as a "training ground for competition in a multiracial society," in Andrew Wiese, *Places of Their Own: African American Suburbanization in the 20th Century* (Chicago: University of Chicago Press, 2004), 232–243.

45. These data are drawn from the book's dataset, US Census 1950–2010. The suburban number (or, non-city number) is arrived at by subtracting the LA City population from the LA County population, a method used by a number of geographers to arrive at "suburban" data. In turn, this approach skirts a lot of nuance; i.e., it does not account for the San Fernando Valley, which lies within LA City. But even the Valley diversified quite rapidly, keeping pace with (if not surpassing) broader County trends.

46. Waldinger and Bozorgmehr assert that Los Angeles led the nation in immigration by 1990. Waldinger and Bozorgmehr, eds., *Ethnic Los Angeles* 14.

Demographer William Frey classified Los Angeles as the second highest metro area receiving international migration, from 1990 to 1999, behind New York. William H. Frey, "The Fading of City/Suburb and Metro/Nonmetro distinctions in the United States," in *New Forms of Urbanization: Beyond the Urban-Rural Dichotomy*, edited by Tony Champion and Graeme Hugo (London: Routledge, 2004), 69–71.

47. Eileen O'Brien, *The Racial Middle: Latinos and Asian Americans Living Beyond the Racial Divide* (New York: New York University Press, 2008); Lisa Lowe, *Immigrant Acts: On Asian American Cultural Politics* (Durham: Duke University Press, 1996); González, *In Search of the Mexican Beverly Hills*, 9, 46–49; Max Felker-Kantor, "Fighting the Segregation Amendment," in *Black and Brown in Los Angeles*, edited by Josh Kun and Laura Pulido (Berkeley: University of California Press, 2014), 146.

48. Charlotte Brooks, *Alien Neighbors, Foreign Friends: Asian Americans, Housing, and the Transformation of Urban California* (Chicago: University of Chicago Press, 2009), especially chapters 7–9.

49. Claire Jean Kim, "The Racial Triangulation of Asian Americans," *Politics & Society* 27, 1 (March 1999), 105–138; Cindy I-Fen Cheng, "Out of Chinatown and into the Suburbs: Chinese Americans and the Politics of Cultural Citizenship in Early Cold War America," *American Quarterly* 58, 4 (December 2006), 1067–1090; Brooks, *Alien Neighbors*, chapters 7–8; Xiaojian Zhao, *Remaking Chinese America: Immigration, Family, and Community, 1940-1965* (New Brunswick: Rutgers University Press, 2002); Hillary Jenks, "Seasoned Long Enough in Concentration: Suburbanization and Transnational Citizenship in Southern California's South Bay," *Journal of Urban History* 40, 1 (2014), 6–30. Also see Becky Nicolaides, "Introduction: Asian American Suburban History," *Journal of American Ethnic History* 34, 2 (Winter 2015), 5–17.

50. Bill Ong Hing, *Making and Remaking Asian America Through Immigration Policy, 1850-1990* (Stanford: Stanford University Press, 1993), 79–86; Mae M. Ngai, *Impossible Subjects: Illegal Aliens and the Making of Modern America* (Princeton: Princeton

University Press, 2004), 258–263; Waldinger and Bozorgmehr, eds., *Ethnic Los Angeles*, 9–10. Also see Michael B. Katz, Mathew J. Creighton, Daniel Amsterdam, and Merlin Chowkwanyun, "Immigration and the New Metropolitan Geography," *Journal of Urban Affairs* 32, 5 (2010), 523–547; Lucie Cheng and Philip Q. Yang, "Asians: The 'Model Minority' Deconstructed," in *Ethnic Los Angeles*, edited by Roger Waldinger and Mehdi Bozorgmehr (New York: Russell Sage Foundation, 1996), 305–344.

51. Cheng, *Changs Next Door*; Merlin Chowkwanyun and Jordan Segall, "The Rise of Majority Asian Suburbs," *Bloomburg CityLab*, August 24, 2012; Zarsadiaz, *Resisting Change in Suburbia*; Cheng and Yang, "Asians," 334–336; Elisabeth Orr, "Living Along the Fault Line: Community, Suburbia, and Multiethnicity in Garden Grove and Westminster, California, 1900–1995" (PhD dissertation, Indiana University, 1999); Becky M. Nicolaides and James Zarsadiaz, "Design Assimilation in Suburbia: Asian Americans, Built Landscapes, and Suburban Advantage in Los Angeles' San Gabriel Valley since 1970," *Journal of Urban History* 43, 2 (2017), 332–371.

52. See Table A2.2 (Asians in suburbs)

53. González, *In Search of the Mexican Beverly Hills*, 65–66.

54. See Table A2.3 (Latinos in suburbs)

55. Matt Garcia, *A World of Its Own: Race, Labor and the Making of Greater Los Angeles, 1900–1970* (Chapel Hill: University of North Carolina Press, 2001); González, *In Search of the Mexican Beverly Hills*, chapters 1–2; George Sánchez, *Boyle Heights: How a Los Angeles Neighborhood Became the Future of American Democracy* (Oakland: University of California Press, 2021); Cheng, *Changs Next Door*.

56. Rudolfo F. Acuña, *Occupied America: A History of Chicanos*, 8th edition (New York: Pearson Longman, 2014), 297–298; Allen and Turner, *Ethnic Quilt*, 108; Pierrette Hondagneu-Sotelo and Manuel Pastor, *South Central Dreams: Finding Home and Building Community in South L.A.* (New York: New York University Press, 2021); Manuel Pastor, Pierrette Hondagneu-Sotelo, Alejandro Sanchez-Lopez, Pamela Stephens, Vanessa Carter, and Walter Thompson-Hernandez, "Roots/Raíces: Latino Engagement, Place Identities, and Shared Futures in South Los Angeles" (USC Center for the Study of Immigrant Integration, November 2016), 34; Manuel Pastor, "Maywood, not Mayberry: Latinos and Suburbia in Los Angeles County," in *Social Justice in Diverse Suburbs*, edited by Christopher Niedt (Philadelphia: Temple University Press, 2013), 129–154; Laura Pulido and Manuel Pastor, "Where in the World Is Juan—and What Color Is He? The Geography of Latina/o Racial Identity in Southern California," *American Quarterly* 65, 2 (2013), 309–341; Raymond Rocco, "Latino Los Angeles: Reframing Boundaries/Borders," in *The City: Los Angeles and Urban Theory at the End of the Twentieth Century*, edited by Allen J. Scott and Edward W. Soja (Berkeley: University of California Press, 1996), 365–389.

57. Sides, *L.A. City Limits*, 129; see Table A2.4 (Black Americans in suburbs).

58. Michele Zack, *Altadena: Between Wilderness and City* (Altadena: Altadena Historical Society, 2004), 182–187; Harold Zellman and Roger Friedland, "Broadacre in Brentwood? The Politics of Architectural Aesthetics," in *Looking for Los Angeles*, edited by Charles G. Salas and Michael Roth (Los Angeles: Getty Research Institute, 2001), 188–190.

59. James P. Allen and Eugene Turner, *Changing Faces, Changing Places: Mapping Southern California* (Northridge: Cal State Northridge Center for Geographical Studies, 2002), 16–18; Edward W. Soja, "Los Angeles, 1965–1992," in *The City: Los Angeles and Urban Theory at the End of the Twentieth Century*, edited by Allen J. Scott and Edward W. Soja (Berkeley: University of California Press, 1996), 440; David Grant, Melvin Oliver, and Angela James, "African Americans: Social and Economic Bifurcation," in *Ethnic Los Angeles*, edited by Waldinger and Bozorgmehr, 400–402; Lawrence B. deGraaf, "African American Suburbanization in California, 1960 through 1990," in *Seeking El Dorado: African Americans in California*, edited by Lawrence B. de Graaf, Kevin Mulroy, and Quintard Taylor (Seattle: University of Washington Press, 2001), 405–449. On national trends, see Wiese, *Places of Their Own*.

By 2000, Moreno Valley was 19% African American, 38% Latino, 32% white, and "solidly middle class," a suburban space of stable diversity "in an environment that is becoming increasingly safe and prosperous," as a 2004 report put it (Jon C. Teaford, *The American Suburb: The Basics* (New York: Routledge, 2008), 63–64). Also see "Lancaster Is a Successful Portrait in Black and White," *LAT*, December 19, 2011.

60. Lou et al., "Racially Balanced Cities in Southern California, 1990–2010," 6.

61. Allen and Turner, *Changing Faces*, 12; Philip J. Ethington, "The Spatial and Demographic Growth of Los Angeles," in *The Development of Los Angeles City Government: An Institutional History, 1850–2000*, edited by Hynda Rudd et al. (Los Angeles: Los Angeles City Historical Society, 2007), 666–667. While whites in nearly all five Southern California counties declined, LA County saw the biggest drop.

62. Waldinger and Bozorgmehr, eds., *Ethnic Los Angeles*, 12–29, quote at 29; Allen and Turner, *Ethnic Quilt*; Allen and Turner, *Changing Faces*; Frey, "Fading," 71.

63. See Table A2.5 (Foreign-born in suburbs).

64. Deborah Dash Moore, *To the Golden Cities: Pursuing the American Jewish Dream in Miami and L.A.* (Cambridge, MA: Harvard University Press, 1994) 23, 43; Sánchez, *Boyle Heights*.

65. On Southeast LA, see sources in Note 56; on the San Gabriel Valley: Cheng, *Changs Next Door*; Wei Li, *Ethnoburb: The New Ethnic Community in Urban America* (Honolulu: University of Hawai'i Press, 2009); Leland Saito, *Race and Politics: Asian Americans, Latinos and Whites in a Los Angeles Suburb* (Urbana: University of Illinois Press, 1998); Garcia, *A World of Its Own*; Timothy Fong, *The First Suburban Chinatown: The Remaking of Monterey Park, California* (Philadelphia: Temple University Press, 2001); John Horton, *The Politics of Diversity: Immigration, Resistance, and Change in Monterey Park, California* (Philadelphia: Temple University Press, 1995); Mary Pardo, *Mexican American Women Activists: Identity and Resistance in Two Los Angeles Communities* (Philadelphia: Temple University Press, 1998).

66. Tanachai Mark Padoongpatt, "'A Landmark for Sun Valley': Wat Thai of Los Angeles and Thai American Suburban Culture in 1980s San Fernando Valley," *Journal of American Ethnic History* 34, 2 (Winter 2015), 87–90; Allen and Turner, *Ethnic Quilt*; Waldinger and Bozorgmehr, eds., *Ethnic Los Angeles*.

67. Moving from the municipal to the neighborhood level, studies are in some disagreement about whether LA's suburbs were integrating or segregating. (These studies used Census tract data to reflect a finer-grained view of neighborhood patterns.) One study found that, by 2010, LA was among the more integrated large cities in the United States, showing a dramatic reversal of trends since 1970 (Edward Glaeser and Jacob Vigdor, "The End of the Segregated Century: Racial Separation in America's Neighborhoods, 1890–2010," Manhattan Institute, January 2012, 4–6). Another study by two of LA's leading geographers concurred, contending that LA had become "more open and fluid" since 1970, so much so that they abandoned the term "segregation" because it was too harsh a descriptor for what they observed, preferring the less coercive word "separation." Yet still they documented some persistence of racial separation, a holdover of historic patterns and social attitudes (Turner and Allen, *Changing Faces*, quote at 46). By contrast, a USC study found that LA went from severe segregation before 1965, to a general resegregation of the county's ethnoracial groups. Majority white areas seeped to the periphery of the county, while Latinos and Asians moved toward increased ethnic isolation. Blacks remained the most isolated racial group, and, when they did integrate, it tended to be with Latinos. For all the progress at the municipal level, whites were still the most likely to live among whites, while other groups were less likely to have white neighbors than any other group (Philip J. Ethington, William H. Frey, and Dowell Myers, "The Racial Re-segregation of Los Angeles County, 1940–2000," Public Research Report 2001-04, Race Contours 2000 Study, USC and University of Michigan, May 12, 2001, 1–22).

    The findings of these studies can still coexist with municipal-level patterns. They suggest that while entire suburbs may have diversified, blocks and neighborhoods tended toward ethnoracial clustering or segregation. So, in larger edge cities like Pasadena and Santa Monica, for example, groups tended to live amongst themselves in their own pockets.

    Some scholars see signals that LA is headed toward greater resegregation. Even so, they acknowledge that, of all metro areas, "durable integration" seems most promising in the suburbs, a conclusion revealing how radically the suburbs had changed. ("L.A. Is Resegregating—and Whites Are a Major Reason Why," *LAT*, April 1, 2016; Michael Bader and Siri Warkentien, "The Fragmented Evolution of Racial Integration since the Civil Rights Movement," *Sociological Science*, March 2, 2016, https://www. sociologicalscience.com/articles-v3-8-135.)

68. On rising income inequality in LA, see Bobo et al., *Prismatic Metropolis*, chapter 2; Becky M. Nicolaides and Andrew Wiese, "Suburban Disequilibrium," *NYT*, April 6, 2013. On metro inequality nationally, see Todd Swanstrom, Colleen Casey, Robert Flack, and Peter Dreier, "Pulling Apart: Economic Segregation among Suburbs and Central Cities in Major Metropolitan Areas" (Living Cities Census Series, Brookings Institution, October 2004); Richard Fry and Paul Taylor, "The Rise of Residential Segregation by Income" (Social and Demographic Trends, Pew Research Center, 2012); Anacker, ed., *The New American Suburb*; Hanlon, et al., *Cities and Suburbs*; Maginn and Anacker, eds., *Suburbia in the 21st Century*. One national study offered these stunning numbers: from 1970 to 2009, the proportion of American families living in poor or rich neighborhoods

doubled from 15% to 33% while those living in middle-class neighborhoods declined from 65% to 42% (Kendra Bischoff and Sean F. Reardon, "Residential Segregation by Income, 1970–2009," in *Diversity and Disparities: America Enters a New Century*, edited by John Logan (New York: Russell Sage Foundation, 2014).

On broader national trends, also see Bennett Harrison and Barry Bluestone, *The Great U-Turn: Corporate Restructuring and the Polarizing of America* (New York: Basic Books, 1988); Melvin Oliver and Thomas Shapiro, *Black Wealth/White Wealth: A New Perspective on Racial Inequality* (New York: Routledge, 1995).

69. For example, see Nicolaides, *My Blue Heaven*.

70. See Table A2.6 (Suburbs divided by class group)

71. Table A2.7 (Suburbs ranked by median family income), Table A2.8 (Suburbs ranked by median home value), Table A2.9 (Indices of relative town wealth over time). On the power of wealthy towns to hold their advantages over time, see John R. Logan and Harvey L. Molotch, *Urban Fortunes: The Political Economy of Place* (Berkeley: University of California Press, 1987); James S. Duncan and Nancy G. Duncan, *Landscapes of Privilege: The Politics of the Aesthetic in an American Suburb* (New York: Routledge, 2004).

72. Elsa Devienne, *Sand Rush: The Beach in Twentieth-Century Los Angeles* (New York: Oxford University Press, 2024); Elsa Devienne, "Urban Renewal by the Sea: Reinventing the Beach for the Suburban Age in Postwar Los Angeles," *Journal of Urban History* 45, 1 (2019), 99–125; Alex Jacoby, "Bringing the Beach to Los Angeles: The Politics and Environment of the Southern California Coast, 1880–1970" (PhD dissertation, UC Irvine, 2017), chapter 4; Andrew A. Kahrl, *The Land Was Ours: African American Beaches from Jim Crow to the Sunbelt South* (Cambridge, MA: Harvard University Press, 2012), 4.

73. US Census dataset; also see Myron Orfield and Thomas Luce, "California Metropatterns: A Regional Agenda for Community Stability in California" (Metropolitan Area Research Corporation, April 2002), 9, 15; Myron Orfield, "Los Angeles Metropatterns: Social Separation and Sprawl in the Los Angeles Region" (University of Minnesota, Metropolitan Area Research Corporation, May 2000).

74. See Table A2.10 (Families in poverty by suburb); Bernadette Hanlon, *Once the American Dream: Inner-Ring Suburbs of the Metropolitan United States* (Philadelphia: Temple University Press, 2010); Davis, "Ozzie and Harriet in Hell"; Orfield, *American Metropolitics*.

75. On domestic service suburbia, see Wiese, *Places of Their Own*.

76. Alan Ehrenhalt, *The Great Inversion and the Future of the American City* (New York: Vintage, 2012); Leigh Gallagher, *The End of the Suburbs: Where the American Dream is Moving* (New York: Portfolio, 2013).

77. Hope VI was criticized for reducing the overall number of public housing units, as in the Pico-Aliso public housing development in Boyle House, slated to lose half its units in a Hope VI redo—a move resisted by local tenants. See Jacqueline Leavitt, "More Than Design: Injustice and Hope VI," AIA California, February 21, 2018, https://aiacalifornia.org/design-injustice-hope-vi/; Jacqueline Leavitt, "A Public-Housing Policy That Says Fewer Units Is More," *LAT*, October 25, 1998.

78. Edward G. Goetz, "Housing Dispersal Programs," *Journal of Planning Literature* 18, 1 (August 2003), 3–16.

79. Elizabeth Kneebone and Alan Berube, *Confronting Suburban Poverty in America* (Washington, DC: Brookings Institution Press, 2013), 9, 17–18. Their data were drawn from the 100 most populous metropolitan areas in the United States.

80. Elizabeth Kneebone, "The Growth and Spread of Concentrated Poverty, 2000 to 2008–2012" (Brookings Metropolitan Opportunity Series, July 31, 2014), https://www.brookings.edu/interactives/the-growth-and-spread-of-concentrated-poverty-2000-to-2008-2012/. For the most part, the poorest suburbs stayed poor over the years, a pattern more salient in LA compared to a place like Chicago; see Elizabeth Delmelle, "Mapping the DNA of Urban Neighborhoods," *Annals of the American Association of Geographers* 106, 1 (2016), 36–56. Delmelle mapped socioeconomic change across census tracts in both cities, 1970–2010.

81. Jacob Wegmann, "'We Just Built It': Code Enforcement, Local Politics, and the Informal Housing Market in Southeast Los Angeles County" (PhD dissertation, UC Berkeley, 2014); "An Overcrowded Housing Crisis"; see Table A2.11 (Data on rich and poor suburbs).

82. See Table A2.9 (Indices of relative town wealth over time), on the differing economic fortunes of middle-class suburbs.

83. Analysis based on proportion of married adults in suburban municipalities, US Census dataset. Reference to Jan and Dean, "The Little Old Lady (from Pasadena)," March 21, 1964, Liberty, 1964, single record.

84. Michael Gutowski and Tracey Feild, *The Graying of Suburbia* (Washington, DC: The Urban Institute, May 1979), xi, 23.

85. On generational conflicts in the Fairfax district, see "Vying for Space in the New L.A.," *LAT*, October 31, 1990.

86. Tanvi Misra, "We're at Peak Multigenerational," *Bloomberg CityLab*, August 11, 2016.

87. Ian Baldwin, "Family, Housing, and the Political Geography of Gay Liberation in Los Angeles County, 1960–1986" (PhD dissertation, University of Nevada Las Vegas, 2016), 132, quote at 136. Baldwin suggested that this federal policy shift likely facilitated gay suburban access (conversation with author, November 2015).

88. Baldwin, "Family, Housing," 184–185. Baldwin emphasizes the limits of this accomplishment, however, seeing it as a geographic constriction of gay activism—from county-wide to a much narrower spatial scope.

89. Lillian Faderman and Stuart Timmons, *Gay L.A.: A History of Sexual Outlaws, Power Politics, and Lipstick Lesbians* (New York: Basic Books, 2006), quote at 247. Also see Daniel Hurewitz, *Bohemian Los Angeles and the Making of Modern Politics* (Berkeley: University of California Press, 2007); Craig Loftin, *Masked Voices: Gay Men and Lesbians in Cold War America* (Albany: State University of New York Press, 2012); Stacy I. Macías, "A Gay Bar, Some Familia, and Latina Butch-Femme: Rounding Out the Eastside Circle in El Monte's Sugar Shack," in *East of East: The Making of Greater El Monte*, edited by Romeo Guzmán, Carribean Fragoza, Alex Sayf Cummings, and Ryan Reft (New Brunswick: Rutgers University Press, 2020), 250–260.

On broader trends and experiences of LGBTQ suburbanization, see Gary J. Gates, "Geographic Trends Among Same-Sex Couples in the U.S. Census and the American Community Survey," Williams Institute, UCLA School of Law, November 2007; Katrin B. Anacker, "Queering the Suburbs: Analyzing Property Values in Male and Female Same-Sex Suburbs in the United States," in *Queering Planning: Challenging Heteronormative Assumptions and Reframing Planning Practice*, edited by Petra L. Doan (Farnham, UK: Ashgate, 2011), 107–125.

90. Karen Tongson, *Relocations: Queer Suburban Imaginaries* (New York: NYU Press, 2011) 162–166.

91. Suzanne Kahn, "Divorce and the Politics of the American Social Welfare Regime, 1969–2001" (PhD dissertation, Columbia University, 2015), 125; Martha L. Garrison, "Credit-Ability for Women," *The Family Coordinator* 25, 3 (1976), 245.

92. Leo Grebler and Frank G. Mittelbach, *The Inflation of House Prices: Its Extent, Causes, and Consequences* (Lexington, MA: Lexington Books, 1979), 5, 55, 100–101; Louis Hyman, *Debtor Nation: A History of America in Red Ink* (Princeton: Princeton University Press, 2011), 171, 218.

93. Some groups had historically higher levels of working women, including women over 40, low-income households, childless married women, and African Americans. Stephanie Coontz, *The Way We Never Were* (New York: Basic Books, 1992), 162. See Table A2.12 (Working married women in suburbs).

94. Paul M. Ong and J. Eugene Grigsby III, "Race and Life-Cycle Effects on Homeownership in Los Angeles 1970 to 1980," *Urban Affairs Quarterly* 23, 4 (June 1988), 608; Sides, *L.A. City Limits*, 122.

95. Becky Nicolaides, "Map Room: Stay-at-Home Moms in Los Angeles County, 1950–2000," *California History* 93, 3 (Fall 2016), 2–8. See Table A2.13 (Stay-at-home wives in suburbs).

96. In 2000, suburbs with between 50% and 90% single-family homes ranged from rich to middling and working class such as Lakewood (81.4%), Palmdale (76.3%), Diamond Bar (70.2%), Malibu (63%), Rolling Hills (99%), Pico Rivera (75.2%), Compton (67%), Carson (70%), Lynwood (54.6%), and South Gate (50.9%).

97. Mike Davis dubbed these stucco apartments "six-pack stucco tenements" in "The New Industrial Peonage," 10. LA did have high-rise buildings in the periphery, especially in edge city areas like Century City, and along the freeways in Glendale and Pasadena. But low-slung, condos and townhomes were more prevalent.

98. Matthew Lasner, *High Life: Condo Living in the Suburban Century* (New Haven: Yale University Press, 2012), 4, 6, 7–17, 206–230. Lasner details how LA was at the vanguard of advancements in the postwar condo. He also makes the striking point that, nationally, the share of households living in owner-occupied single-family homes was roughly the same in 1960 and 2007 (49%), although homeownership rates as a whole rose from 62% to 68%, suggesting the growth occurred in multifamily-owned housing.

99. Tracy M. Gordon, "Planned Developments in California: Private Communities and Public Life" (San Francisco: Public Policy Institute of California, 2004), 3, 11, 13–14, 21–22, 28, 35.

100. National Public Radio, "L.A. Gated Communities" (broadcast August 11, 1992) in *Rights and the Common Good: The Communitarian Perspective*, edited by Amitai Etzioni (New York: St. Martin's Press, 1995), 243–250; Thomas W. Sanchez, Robert E. Lang, and Dawn M. Dhavale, "Security Versus Status? A First Look at the Census' Gated Community Data," *Journal of Planning Education and Research* 24 (2005), 281–291. On elite gated communities in Los Angeles, see Blanca Barragan, "An Introduction to L.A.'s Private and Gated Communities," Curbed L.A., May 1, 2014, https://la.curbed.com/maps/an-introduction-to-las-private-and-gated-neighb orhoods.

101. See Table A2.14 (Rate of growth in LA suburbs).

102. Roger W. Lotchin, "Population Concentration in Los Angeles, 1940–2000," *Pacific Historical Review* 77, 1 (2008), 90; "Despite the Sprawl, L.A. Is America's Most Overcrowded Place," *LAT*, October 23, 2022; "An Overcrowded Housing Crisis." In 2000, density rates in LA and New York were 7,068 and 5,309 persons/square mile, respectively.

103. Lotchin, "Population Concentration," 97–99.

104. As a pair of urban land experts from UCLA wrote in 1979, "As a general, time-honored rule of thumb, the house price should not exceed 2 to 2-1/2 times the annual income," a ratio accepted by both mortgage lenders and the buying public in the 1970s. Grebler and Mittelbach, *The Inflation of House Prices*, 39.

105. Analysts have identified a host of factors that drove up housing prices in LA, starting with the region's first housing bubble in the 1970s. They included demographic changes (i.e., the coming of age of baby boomers); psychological impacts of inflation, income of more working mothers; slow growth movements that choked off the housing supply; rising land costs; rising building costs; California's surging economy; Proposition 13, which diminished incentives to promote home building in municipalities; the impacts of global finance structures; and a phenomenon that economist Robert Schiller calls "irrational exuberance." See Dowell Myers, *Immigrants and Boomers: Forging a New Social Contract for the Future of America* (New York: Russell Sage Foundation, 2007), 232; Grebler and Mittelbach, *Inflation of House Prices*, 5, 55, 79, 100–101; Hyman, *Debtor Nation*, 171, 218; Katrin B. Anacker, "Introduction: Housing Affordability and Affordable Housing," *International Journal of Housing Policy* 19, 1 (March 2019, online); Mac Taylor, "California's High Housing Costs: Causes and Consequences" (California Legislative Analyst's Office, 2015), 3–20; Myers, *Immigrants and Boomers*, 232; Fulton, *Reluctant Metropolis*, 260–261; Conor Dougherty, *Golden Gates: The Housing Crisis and a Reckoning for the American Dream* (New York: Penguin Press, 2020); Davis, *City of Quartz*, chapter 3; Andrew Wiese, "'The Giddy Rise of the Environmentalists': Corporate Real Estate Development and Environmental Politics in San Diego, California, 1968–73," *Environmental History* 19 (January 2014), 28–54; Whittemore, "Zoning Los Angeles," 399–404; Robert J. Shiller, *Irrational Exuberance*, 3rd edition (Princeton: Princeton University Press, 2015), chapter 3.

106. Myers, *Immigrants and Boomers*, 228. From 1950 to 2010 in LA County as a whole, homeowners fell from bare majority to minority—50.9% to 44.8%.

107. See Table A2.15 (Homeownership rates in suburbs).

108. Sides, *L.A. City Limits*, 129.

109. See Table A2.16 (Nonwhite homeownership in suburbs); Matt Reynolds, "Banks' Reverse Redlining Cost It $1 Billion, Los Angeles Claims," *Courthouse News Service*, December 9, 2013.

110. See Table A2.17 (Housing tenure by race 1990); Ong and Grigsby, "Race and Life-Cycle Effects," 609–611; Camille Zubrinsky Charles, "Residential Segregation in Los Angeles," in *Prismatic Metropolis: Inequality in Los Angeles*, edited by Bobo, et al., 172–174; Clark, *Immigrants and the American Dream*, 150.

111. George Sánchez, *Becoming Mexican American: Ethnicity, Culture and Identity in Chicano Los Angeles, 1900–1945* (New York: Oxford University Press, 1993), 199–200; Carpio, *Collision at the Crossroads*, chapter 5.

112. Taylor, *Race for Profit*; for LA examples, see "Woman Evicted Near End of 30-Year Loan," *LAT*, November 1, 1999; "Watts 'Home of Hope' Built in Only 96 Hours," *LAT*, November 13, 1968; "South Central's 'Pride' Housing Hopes Shattered," *LAT*, June 22, 1970. Taylor's book raises many important questions that merit future research, such as to what extent predatory inclusion operated in LA, among not just Blacks but also Latinos and Asians, and how did it manifest in suburbia?

113. B. Marchand, *The Emergence of Los Angeles: Population and Housing in the City of Dreams* (London: Pion, 1986), 143–145.

114. Hondagneu-Sotelo and Pastor, *South Central Dreams*, 10, 32.

115. Sánchez, *Becoming Mexican American*, 197–201; Myers, *Immigrants and Boomers*, 225.

116. Myers, *Immigrants and Boomers*, 229; Clark, *Immigrants and the American Dream*, 127, 150; Zubrinsky Charles, "Residential Segregation," 172–174.

117. For example, among Latino immigrants in the United States for less than 10 years, 16.4% of households owned homes; for those in the United States for more than 30 years, the rate jumped to 64.6% of households. Myers, *Immigrants and Boomers*, 109–111, 116–117, 228–232.

118. Jana Kasperkevic, "The American Dream: How Undocumented Immigrants Buy Homes in the U.S.," Marketplace, Minnesota Public Radio, September 11, 2017, https://www.marketplace.org/2017/09/11/american-dream-how-undocumented-immigrants-buy-homes-us/; Reema Khrais, "What Happens to Your House when You Get Deported?" Marketplace, Minnesota Public Radio, August 10, 2017, https://www.marketplace.org/2017/08/10/little-noticed-effect-deportations-foreclosures/; "Illegal Immigrants Good Mortgage Risk," NPR Morning Edition, December 25, 2007, https://www.npr.org/templates/story/story.php?storyId=17597739.

119. Clark, *Immigrants and the American Dream*, 126. As demographer William Clark noted, "it is ownership which increases the affiliations that unify people at local scales and bind them—however loosely—to the host society."

120. Myers, *Immigrants and Boomers*, 231–232.

121. Alisa Belinkoff Katz et al., "'People Are Simply Unable To Pay The Rent': What History Tells Us About Rent Control in Los Angeles" (UCLA Luskin Center for History and Public Policy, October 2018).

Chapter 3

1. This follows the approaches taken in two works that contrast suburban responses to immigrant issues: Laura Barraclough, "Contested Cowboys: Ethnic Mexican Charros and the Struggle for Suburban Space in 1970s Los Angeles," *Aztlán* 37, 2 (Fall 2012), 95–124; Genevieve Carpio, Clara Irazábal, and Laura Pulido, "Right to the Suburb? Rethinking Lefebvre and Immigrant Activism," *Journal of Urban Affairs* 33, 2 (2011), 185–208.

   Also see the excellent essays in Audrey Singer, Susan W. Hardwick, Caroline B. Brettell, eds., *Twentieth First Century Gateways: Immigrant Incorporation in Suburban America* (Washington, DC: Brookings Institution Press, 2008) and Katrin B. Anacker, ed., *The New American Suburb: Poverty, Race, and the Economic Crisis* (New York: Routledge, 2016).

2. On contested articulations of the suburban ideal, see Mary Corbin Sies, "North American Suburbs, 1880–1950: Cultural and Social Reconsiderations," *Journal of Urban History* 27, 3 (March 2001), 313–346; Andrew Wiese, "Stubborn Diversity: A Commentary on Middle-Class Influence in Working-Class Suburbs," *Journal of Urban History* 27, 3 (March 2001), 347–354. Key works in the vast scholarship on defensive homeowner politics in the postwar years include Matthew Lassiter, *Silent Majority: Suburban Politics in the Sunbelt South* (Princeton: Princeton University Press, 2006); Thomas Sugrue, *Origins of the Urban Crisis: Race and Inequality in Postwar Detroit* (Princeton: Princeton University Press, 1996); Thomas Sugrue, *Sweet Land of Liberty: The Forgotten Struggle for Civil Rights in the North* (New York: Random House, 2009); Kevin Kruse, *White Flight: Atlanta and the Making of Modern Conservatism* (Princeton: Princeton University Press, 2005); Becky Nicolaides, *My Blue Heaven: Life and Politics in the Working-Class Suburbs of Los Angeles, 1920–1965* (Chicago: University of Chicago Press, 2002); Lily Geismer, *Don't Blame Us: Suburban Liberals and the Transformation of the Democratic Party* (Princeton: Princeton University Press, 2014); Kyle Riismandel, *Neighborhood of Fear: The Suburban Crisis in American Culture, 1975–2001* (Baltimore: Johns Hopkins University Press, 2020).

3. For an articulation of this multicultural suburban ideal, see Tom Hogen-Esch and Martin Saiz, "An Anatomy of Defeat: Why San Fernando Valley Failed to Secede from Los Angeles," *California Policy Issues* (November 2001), 58. Two notable studies of progressivism in suburbia include Sylvie Murray, *The Progressive Housewife: Community Activism in Suburban Queens, 1945–1965* (Philadelphia: University of Pennsylvania Press, 2003) and Amanda Kolson Hurley, *Radical Suburbs: Experimental Living on the Fringes of the American City* (Cleveland: Belt Publishing, 2019).

4. Lassiter, *Silent Majority*; Riismandel, *Neighborhood of Fear*; Geismer, *Don't Blame Us*.

5. Manual Pastor, *State of Resistance: What California's Dizzying Descent and Remarkable Resurgence Mean for America's Future* (New York: The New Press, 2018); Daniel HoSang, *Racial Propositions: Ballot Initiatives and the Making of Postwar California* (Berkeley: University of California Press, 2010).

6. For voter registration data in LA suburbs, see Table A3.1 (Partisan leanings in LA County suburbs) and Table A3.2 (Voter registration in LA County suburbs). For

a map series of dominant voter registration in LA suburbs from 1962 to 2000, see Figure A3.1 (Map of voters in suburbs). Works that emphasize suburban conservatism in Southern California include Lisa McGirr, *Suburban Warriors* (Princeton: Princeton University Press, 2001); Michelle Nickerson, *Mothers of Conservatism: Women and the Postwar Right* (Princeton: Princeton University Press, 2012); Nicolaides, *My Blue Heaven*.

7. The category of DTS was also tied to California's somewhat complex primary system. See "California's Unaffiliated Voters Are Sometimes Unreachable," *NYT*, January 29, 2008.

8. Raphael Sonenshein email to author, May 26, 2021.

9. Lassiter, *Silent Majority*; McGirr, *Suburban Warriors*; Geismer, *Don't Blame Us*; Kenneth T. Jackson, *Crabgrass Frontier: The Suburbanization of the United States* (New York: Oxford University Press, 1985); Sugrue, *Origins of the Urban Crisis*; Sugrue, *Sweet Land of Liberty*; David M. P. Freund, *Colored Property: State Policy and White Racial Politics in Suburban America* (Chicago: University of Chicago Press, 2007); Kruse, *White Flight*; Nicolaides, *My Blue Heaven*.

10. In addition to works cited in Notes 2 and 9, other examples of this extensive literature include Arnold Hirsch, *Making the Second Ghetto: Race and Housing in Chicago, 1940–1960* (Cambridge: Cambridge University Press, 1983); Robert Self, *American Babylon: Race and the Struggle for Postwar Oakland* (Princeton: Princeton University Press, 2003); Kenneth D. Durr, *Behind the Backlash: White Working-Class Politics in Baltimore, 1940–1980* (Chapel Hill: University of North Carolina Press, 2007); Murray, *The Progressive Housewife*, chapter 3; Thomas J. Sugrue, "Jim Crow's Last Stand: The Struggle to Integrate Levittown," in *Second Suburb: Levittown, Pennsylvania*, edited by Dianne Harris (Pittsburgh: University of Pittsburgh Press, 2010), 175–199; Andrew Wiese, *Places of Their Own: African American Suburbanization in the Twentieth Century* (Chicago: University of Chicago Press, 2004); Riismandel, *Neighborhood of Fear*; Becky Nicolaides and Andrew Wiese, eds., *The Suburb Reader*, 2nd edition (New York: Routledge, 2016).

11. Josh Sides, *L.A. City Limits* (Berkeley: University of California Press, 2003); Andrea Gibbons, *City of Segregation: 100 Years of Struggle for Housing in Los Angeles* (London: Verso, 2018); HoSang, *Racial Propositions*, chapter 4; Scott Kurashige, *The Shifting Grounds of Race: Black and Japanese Americans in the Making of Multiethnic Los Angeles* (Princeton: Princeton University Press, 2008); Darnell Hunt and Ana-Christina Ramon, eds., *Black Los Angeles: American Dreams and Racial Realities* (New York: New York University Press, 2010); Nicolaides, *My Blue Heaven*, chapter 7; on slow growth, see Mike Davis, *City of Quartz* (New York: Vintage, 1992), chapters 3 and 4; William Fulton, *The Reluctant Metropolis: The Politics of Urban Growth in Los Angeles* (Point Arena, CA: Solano Press Books, 1997); Andrew Whittemore, "Zoning Los Angeles: A Brief History of Four Regimes," *Planning Perspectives* 27, 3 (2012), 393–415; Greg Morrow, "The Homeowner Revolution: Democracy, Land Use, and the Los Angeles Slow-Growth Movement, 1965–1992" (PhD dissertation, University of California Los Angeles, 2013); James Zarsadiaz, *Resisting Change in Suburbia: Asian Immigrants and Frontier Nostalgia in L.A.* (Oakland: University of California Press, 2022), chapter 5; "An Overcrowded Housing Crisis," *LAT*, October 24, 2022.

12. Davis, *City of Quartz*, 213; Laura Barraclough, *Making the San Fernando Valley: Rural Landscapes, Urban Development, and White Privilege* (Athens: University of Georgia Press, 2011); Zarsadiaz, *Resisting Change in Suburbia*; Michael Storper, Thomas Kemeny, Naji Philip Makarem, and Taner Osman, *The Rise and Fall of Urban Economies* (Stanford: Stanford University Press, 2015), 159.

13. Michael Danielson, *Politics of Exclusion* (New York: Columbia University Press, 1976), 99–100, quote at 151; on South Gate, see Chapter 6. The US Supreme Court in *James v. Valtierra* (1971) upheld the rights of Californians to hold local votes on whether or not residents wanted public housing in their communities. See Danielson, *Politics of Exclusion*, 180–181; Lassiter, *The Silent Majority*, 307; Aaron Cavin, "A Right to Housing in the Suburbs: *James v. Valtierra* and the Campaign Against Economic Discrimination," *Journal of Urban History* 45, 3 (2019), 427–451.

14. Jon C. Teaford, *The American Suburb: The Basics* (New York: Routledge, 2008), 182–183; William C. Baer, "California's Housing Element," *The Town Planning Review* 59, 3 (July 1988), 263–274.

15. Barraclough, "Contested Cowboys," 98–100; Carpio et al., "Right to the Suburb?"

16. John Mollenkopf and Manuel Pastor, eds., *Unsettled Americans: Metropolitan Context and Civic Leadership for Immigrant Integration* (Ithaca: Cornell University Press, 2016), 2–4.

17. The concept was first developed by Wei Li, *Ethnoburb: The New Ethnic Community in Urban America* (Honolulu: University of Hawai'i Press, 2009).

18. Leland Saito makes the important point that discrimination was a critical catalyst in the formation of the Chinese ethnic economy. As many highly trained Chinese immigrants hit the glass ceiling working in fields like engineering, they left those American companies to start their own businesses. Leland T. Saito, *Race and Politics: Asian Americans, Latinos and Whites in a Los Angeles Suburb* (Urbana: University of Illinois Press, 1998), 62.

19. Li, *Ethnoburb*; Merlin Chowkwanyun and Jordan Segall, "The Rise of Majority Asian Suburbs," *Bloomburg CityLab*, August 24, 2012.

20. Li, Zhou, and others contested this linear model, arguing that Asian (especially Chinese) suburban settlement defies this simplistic process, especially in the ethnoburbs. Moreover, the class diversity of these suburbs complicates the older spatial assimilation model, which posits that movement into suburbia meant automatic upward mobility and assimilation. See Li, *Ethnoburb*; Min Zhou, Yen-Fen Tseng, and Rebecca Y. Kim, "Rethinking Residential Assimilation: The Case of a Chinese Ethnoburb in the San Gabriel Valley, California," *Amerasia Journal* 34, 3 (2008), 55–83; Emily Skop and Wei Li, "Asians in America's Suburbs: Patterns and Consequences of Settlement," *The Geographical Review* 95, 2 (April 2005), 173–174. For an excellent discussion of theories around immigrant identity and assimilation, see Pierrette Hondagneu- Sotelo and Manuel Pastor, *South Central Dreams: Finding Home and Building Community in South L.A.* (New York: New York University Press, 2021), 13–19.

21. George Sánchez, *Boyle Heights: How a Los Angeles Neighborhood Became the Future of American Democracy* (Oakland: University of California Press, 2021); Kurashige, *Shifting Grounds of Race*, 249–258.

22. Timothy Fong, *First Suburban Chinatown: The Remaking of Monterey Park, Ca.* (Philadelphia: Temple University Press, 1994); Saito, *Race and Politics*; "Stronger Rules on English in Signs Pushed by Council," *LAT*, December 5, 1985; "Monterey Park, America's First Suburban Chinatown," *LAT*, April 6, 1987.

23. Becky M. Nicolaides and James Zarsadiaz, "Design Assimilation in Suburbia: Asian Americans, Built Landscapes, and Suburban Advantage in Los Angeles' San Gabriel Valley since 1970," *Journal of Urban History* 43, 2 (2017), 332–371.

24. Nicolaides and Zarsadiaz, "Design Assimilation in Suburbia"; Zarsadiaz, *Resisting Change in Suburbia*; Jan Lin and Melody Chiong, "How Chinese Entrepreneurs Transformed the San Gabriel Valley," KCET website, May 20, 2016, https://www.kcet.org/shows/departures/how-chinese-entrepreneurs-transformed-the-san-gabriel-valley.

25. James Rojas, "The Enacted Environment of East Los Angeles," *Places* 8, 3 (Spring 1993), 42–53; James Rojas, "The Cultural Landscape of a Latino Community," in *Landscape and Race in the United States*, edited by Richard H. Schein (New York: Routledge, 2006), 185. A. K. Sandoval-Strausz describes similar patterns of Latino urbanism on a broader scale in *Barrio America: How Latino Immigrants Saved the American City* (New York: Basic Books, 2019).

26. See Chapter 6; Becky M. Nicolaides, "Are Latinx Suburbs Ethnoburbs? And Why It Matters," in *MetropoLatinx: The Significance of Latinidad in Urban History*, edited by A. Sandoval-Strausz (Chicago: University of Chicago Press, forthcoming); Enrique Ochoa and Gilda Ochoa, eds., *Latino LA: Transformations, Communities, and Activism* (Tucson: University of Arizona Press, 2005), 306; Mark Villianatos, "A More Delicious City: How to Legalize Street Food," in *The Informal American City*, edited by Vinit Mukhija and Anastasia Loukaitou-Sideris (Cambridge, MA: MIT Press, 2014), 215–217.

27. Nicolaides and Zarsadiaz, "Design Assimilation in Suburbia"; Emily Skop and Wei Li, "From the Ghetto to the Invisiburb: Shifting Patterns of Immigrant Settlement in Contemporary America," in *Multicultural Geographies: Persistence and Change in U.S. Racial/Ethnic Patterns*, edited by John W. Frazier and Florence Margai (Albany: State University of New York Press, 2010), 113–124. For an excellent study that probes the ways Japanese Americans in rural Washington concealed the ethnic appearance of their settlements as a way of avoiding racism, see Gail Dubrow, "Deru Kugi Wa Utareru or The Nail That Sticks Up Gets Hit: The Architecture of Japanese American Identity, 1885–1942," *Journal of Architectural and Planning Research* 19, 4 (Winter 2002), 319–333.

28. See Chapter 5, and Figure A3.2 (Design-assimilated suburbs); Nicolaides and Zarsadiaz, "Design Assimilation in Suburbia"; Denise Lawrence-Zúñiga, "Residential Design Guidelines, Aesthetic Governmentality, and Contested Notions of Southern California Suburban Places," *Economic Anthropology* 2, 1 (2015), 121.

   On landscape aesthetics as they reflect cultural and racial power, especially in suburban contexts, see James S. Duncan and Nancy G. Duncan, *Landscapes of Privilege: The Politics of the Aesthetic in an American Suburb* (New York: Routledge, 2004); Willow Lung-Amam, "That 'Monster House' Is My Home: The Social and Cultural Politics of Design Reviews and Regulations," *Journal of Urban Design*, 18, 2 (2013),

220–241; Lawrence-Zuñiga, "Residential Design Guidelines"; Brian K. Ray, Greg Halseth, and Benjamin Johnson, "The Changing 'Face' of the Suburbs: Issues of Ethnicity and Residential Change in Suburban Vancouver," *International Journal of Urban & Regional Research* 21, 1 (March 1997), 75–99; Richard Schein, ed., *Landscape and Race in the United States* (New York: Routledge, 2006); Sies, "North American Suburbs, 1880–1950"; Zarsadiaz, *Resisting Change in Suburbia.*

29. HoSang, *Racial Propositions*, chapter 5.

30. On San Marino and South Gate, see Chapters 5 and 6; "Post Signs in English, New City Law Says," *LAT*, December 20, 1982; "Rights Groups Hail Ruling Against Pomona Sign Law," *LAT*, July 28, 1989; "Sign Law to Ease English Requirements," *LAT*, July 12, 1990.

31. "Rival to English Initiative Proposed," *LAT*, November 10, 1985; "A City Is Divided by Its Languages," *LAT*, April 10, 1987.

32. "Rival to English Initiative Proposed"; "Proposed English-Only Plan Invalidated," *LAT*, November 20, 1985; "Language Issue Spreads to Alhambra," *LAT*, November 21, 1985; "Official-English Proposals Rejected; Dialogue Urged," *LAT*, November 28, 1985; "Further Split Feared over Suit to Force English Vote," *LAT*, December 8, 1985; Saito, *Race and Politics*, 64; Wendy Cheng, *The Changs Next Door to the Díazes: Remapping Race in Suburban California* (Minneapolis: University of Minnesota Press, 2013). Chu went on to serve in the US Congress.

33. The case was presided over by Judge Robert Takasugo, a Japanese American who was incarcerated in detention facilities during World War II.

34. "Lawsuit Filed Over Pomona Sign Law," *LAT*, February 16, 1989; "Rights Groups Hail Ruling Against Pomona Sign Law"; "Temple City Strives for Sign Law That's Acceptable to All," *LAT*, October 19, 1989; "Rosemead Amends Sign Law to Ease English Requirements"; "Temple City: Sign Ordinance Softened," *LAT*, November 8, 1990; Haley Chung, "Coercive Assimilation: The Constitutionality of Enforcing English Signage," *Columbia Undergraduate Law Review* (October 2, 2020).

35. HoSang, *Racial Propositions*, 132, 159.

36. "Growing Diversity Fuels a War of Words," *LAT*, March 19, 2006.

37. Nicolaides and Zarsadiaz, "Design Assimilation in Suburbia."

38. See Chapter 6.

39. Max Felker-Kantor, *Policing Los Angeles: Race, Resistance, and the Rise of the LAPD* (Chapel Hill: University of North Carolina Press, 2018), 183.

40. Jumping forward to 2012, one study found that LA County public health enforcers filled a 20,000-square foot warehouse with confiscated food carts and equipment every 45 days—most of which was sold off for scrap metal since the vendors were reluctant to appear in court to try to reclaim their carts. Villianatos, "A More Delicious City," 214.

41. "Street Vendors Finding It Harder to Ply Their Wares," *LAT*, September 23, 1990; "Local Laws '94," *LAT*, December 30, 1994.

42. Margaret Crawford, "The Garage Sale as Informal Economy and Transformative Urbanism," in *The Informal American City*, edited by Vinit Mukhija and Anastasia Loukaitou-Sideris (Cambridge, MA: MIT Press, 2014), 33.

43. "San Gabriel Valley Notebook: Azusa," *LAT*, December 10, 1981; "San Gabriel Valley Digest: Azusa," *LAT*, April 21, 1983; "Garage Sale Cop Cuts City in on Profits," *LAT*, May 10, 1990; "Garage Sale Savvy," *LAT*, May 23, 1990; "Not All Favor Restrictions on Garage Sales," *LAT*, December 3, 1993; "Proposed Rules Would Slam Door on Garage Sales as a Way of Life," *LAT*, December 26, 1993; "Council Moves to Put Curbs on Yard Sales," *LAT*, September 25, 1996; "Local Laws '98," *LAT*, December 29, 1998; "New Rules for Illegal Daily Yard Sales Approved by L.A. County Supervisors," *Los Angeles Daily News*, May 28, 2015; L.A. County Ordinance No. 94-0082, 1994; L.A. County Ordinance No. 2021-0013.

44. "Suburbia's Simmering Class Struggle," *LAT*, September 28, 1998.

45. Li, *Ethnoburb*, 100.

46. Lin and Chiong, "How Chinese Entrepreneurs"; "From Healing Hands to Haute Handbags," *LAT*, March 31, 2005.

47. Li, *Ethnoburb*, 108–110, 173.

48. Nicolaides and Zarsadiaz, "Design Assimilation in Suburbia."

49. Nicolaides, "Are Latinx Suburbs Ethnoburbs?"; G. Aron Ramirez, "Business as Usual: Ethnic Commerce and the Making of a Mexican American Middle Class in Southeast Los Angeles, 1981–1995," *Journal of Urban History* (2022), 1–22.

50. See Chapter 6.

51. Monica Varsanyi, "City Ordinances as 'Immigration Policing by Proxy': Local Governments and the Regulation of Undocumented Day Laborers," in *Taking Local Control: Immigration Policy Activism in U.S. Cities and States*, edited by Monica W. Varsanyi (Stanford: Stanford University Press, 2010), 135–136.

52. Jennifer Ridgley, "Cities of Refuge: Immigration Enforcement, Police, and the Insurgent Genealogies of Citizenship in U.S. Sanctuary Cities," *Urban Geography* 29, 1 (2008), 54; Carpio et al., "Right to the Suburb"; Bernadette Hanlon and Thomas J. Vicino, "Local Immigration Legislation in Two Suburbs: An Examination of Immigration Policies in Farmers Branch, Texas, and Carpentersville, Illinois," in *The New American Suburb: Poverty, Race, and the Economic Crisis*, edited by Katrin B. Anacker (New York: Routledge, 2016), 113–130.

   One national study suggested that suburban places most likely to support harsh anti-immigrant measures were exurbs and places with relatively higher rates of home-ownership (Kyle E. Walker and Helga Leitner, "The Variegated Landscape of Local Immigration Policies in the United States," *Urban Geography* 32, 2 (2011), 156–178). LA suburbs supporting anti-immigrant measures seemed to show greater variation.

53. Adam Goodman, *The Deportation Machine: America's Long History of Expelling Immigrants* (Princeton: Princeton University Press, 2020), 34. For data from 2012, see https://trac.syr.edu/immigration/reports/350/; on post 9/11 crackdowns on South Asian Americans, see Erika Lee, *The Making of Asian America: A History* (New York: Simon & Schuster, 2016).

54. Ridgley, "Cities of Refuge," 55. Another team estimated that nearly 100 cities and counties in the United States had proposed or passed sanctuary ordinances by 2011 (Walker and Leitner, "The Variegated Landscape," 157).

55. For the earlier period, equally important was LAPD Special Order 40, a measure passed in 1979 that forbade officers from inquiring about a person's immigration status during routine encounters or arrests. Yet the LAPD circumvented the spirit of this measure in numerous ways, as detailed in Felker-Kantor, *Policing Los Angeles*, 174–189.

56. Sean T. Dempsey, *City of Dignity: Christianity, Liberalism, and the Making of Global Los Angeles* (Chicago: University of Chicago Press, 2023); "Trump's Crackdown on Illegal Immigration Leaves a Lot Unanswered for Sanctuary Cities Like L.A.," *LAT*, November 15, 2016; "Anxiety for Immigrants Living in 'Sanctuary Cities,'" *LAT*, January 27, 2017; "Being a Sanctuary City: What It Means, What Cities Can Do, and What They Can't," *Orange County Register*, December 16, 2016; "Maywood, la ciudad santuario," *LO*, May 15 2006; "Cuestionan designación de ciudad santuario," *LO*, November 16, 2006; "L.A. County's Latest 'Sanctuary City' Stands Its Ground Against Trump," *L.A. Weekly*, January 12, 2017; "Map: Here's Where the 'Sanctuary Cities' and 'Safe Haven' Schools Are in the San Gabriel Valley," *San Gabriel Valley Tribune*, February 16, 2017; "'Sanctuary' Cities Los Angeles County," Los Angeles Almanac © 1998–2019 Given Place Media, publishing as Los Angeles Almanac, November 2, 2022, https://www.laalmanac.com/immigration/im04c.php.
   Sanctuary suburbs centered in Latino, not Asian, areas.

57. "Cae propuesta contra santuarios," *LO*, April 10, 2008; "Lancaster se suma a la Ley Arizona," *LO*, July 14, 2010; "Councilman's 'Proud Racist' Comment Splits Santa Clarita," *LAT*, January 28, 2021; "Santa Clarita Opposes California's 'Sanctuary' Law, the First City in L.A. County To Do So," *LAT*, May 9, 2018; "Jim Gilchrist's Minutemen Project," Library of Congress, accessed March 3, 2023 at https://www.loc.gov/item/lcwaN0002871/.

58. Richard Harris, *Building a Market: The Rise of the Home Improvement Industry, 1914–1960* (Chicago: University of Chicago Press, 2012); Kristen Hill Maher, "Border and Social Distinction in the Global Suburb," *American Quarterly* 56, 3 (2004), 781–806.

59. "City Opens Center to Help Day Laborers," *PSN*, February 25, 2001.

60. Abel Valenzuela Jr., "Regulating Day Labor: Worker Centers and Organizing in the Informal Economy," in *The Informal American City*, edited by Vinit Mukhija and Anastasia Loukaitou-Sideris (Cambridge, MA: MIT Press, 2014), 261–265; Abel Valenzuela, Jr., Nik Theodore, Edwin Meléndez, and Ana Luz González, *On the Corner: Day Labor in the United States* (Los Angeles: UCLA Center for the Study of Urban Poverty, 2006).

61. Varsanyi, "City Ordinances," 137.

62. Duncan and Duncan, *Landscapes of Privilege*, 184, 186.

63. This continued a long, historic pattern in Southern California of working-class Mexicans being relegated to a lower position on the racial hierarchy than other groups. See Tomás Almaguer, *Racial Fault Lines: The Historical Origins of White Supremacy in California* (Berkeley: University of California Press, 1994), 72; Douglas Monroy, *Thrown Among Strangers: The Making of Mexican Culture in Frontier California* (Berkeley: University of California Press, 1990); Juan Gomez-Quiñones,

Mexican American Labor, 1790–1990 (Albuquerque: University of New Mexico Press, 1994).

64. "Merchants Say Day Laborers are Driving Business Away," *LAT*, September 22, 1985.

65. "INS Gets Tough on Steady Use of Day Laborers," *LAT*, July 29, 1988; "Illegals in Glendale Rounded Up," *LAT*, August 11, 1988; "Council Studies Ban on Street-Corner Job Solicitation," *LAT*, January 26, 1989; "Patrols to Control Day Laborers Are Being Stepped Up in Santa Clarita," *LAT*, March 30, 1990.

66. "Agoura Hills Council Votes to Ban Job-Seeking by Day Laborers," *LAT*, July 13, 1990; "Outcry Against Immigrants Is Loud in Valley," *LAT*, August 1, 1993; Varsanyi, "City Ordinances," 139–142; "Day Laborers Win Supreme Court Free-Speech Case," *SFGate*, February 22, 2012.

67. "La Mirada: Ordinance Bans Day Labor Solicitations on Sidewalks," *LAT*, May 21, 1992; "City Council Moves to Evict Day Laborers," *LAT*, August 27, 1992; "City Ready to Adopt Day Labor Rules," *LAT*, February 21, 1993.

68. "A Case of Overkill to Curb Day Laborers," *LAT*, January 25, 1994; "Proposed Limits on Laborers Protested," *LAT*, January 30, 1994; "Day Laborers Face Opposition from Merchants," *LAT*, March 6, 1994; "Community Clashes with Day Workers," *LAT*, March 14, 1994. For another example of African American opposition to day laborers, see Carol Lynn McKibben, *Racial Beachhead: Diversity and Democracy in a Military Town* (Stanford: Stanford University Press, 2011), 264–265.

69. *Xiloj-Itzep v. City of Agoura Hills*, 24 Cal. App. 4th 620, 29 Cal. Rptr. 2nd 879 (1994).

70. "County Limits, But Does Not Ban, Day Laborers," *LAT*, March 16, 1994; "More Limits Sought on Day Laborers," *LAT*, March 27, 1994; "Appeals Court Upholds Day Laborer Guidelines," *LAT*, April 29, 1994; "Antonovich Seeks Curbside Ban on Job-Seekers in County Areas," *LAT*, May 19, 1994; "Supervisors Ban Curbside Job Solicitation," *LAT*, May 25, 1994.

71. "Supervisor Defends Vote to Restrict Day Laborers," *LAT*, May 26, 1994; "Backers Praise Ban on Day Laborers," *LAT*, May 29, 1994.

72. "Calabasas: Proposal Would Target Day Laborers," *LAT*, July 8, 1995; "2-Pronged Plan for Street-Side Job Seekers," *LAT*, September 13, 1996; "Local Laws '96," *LAT*, January 1, 1997; "Many Expect Little from Law Aimed at Day Laborers (Santa Clarita)," *LAT*, March 10, 1997; "Home Depot Project to Regulate Hiring of Laborers at New Site," *LAT*, December 11, 1997; "Local Laws '97," *LAT*, January 1, 1998; "Local Laws '98," *LAT*, December 29, 1998; "Officials Reworking Rules on Day Labor," *LAT*, August 25, 2001; "Cities Work on Day-Laborer Policies," *PSN*, March 21, 2004.

    The proportions of non-Hispanic whites in these towns, in 2000, were Pasadena (38.8%), Glendale (54.1%), Alhambra (13.8%), Monrovia (46.2%), Duarte (31.9%), Azusa (23.4%), Santa Clarita (69.2%), Malibu (88.8%), and Lawndale (22.1%).

73. *Xiloj-Itzep v. City of Agoura Hills*, 24 Cal. App. 4th 620, 29 Cal. Rptr. 2nd 879 (1994); Varsanyi, "City Ordinances," 142; "Law on Laborers Too Vague, Judge Says," *LAT*, August 22, 2000; "Federal Judge Voids Ban on Soliciting by Day Laborers," *LAT*, September 15, 2000.

74. "Curbside Laborers Still in Business Despite Ordinance," *LAT*, August 22, 1994; "Agoura Hills: City to Continue Job Placement Services," *LAT*, February 1, 1996;

"The Guys Police Themselves, Nobody Drinks, Nobody Gambles," *LAT*, September 7, 1996; "*Jornaleros* Deserve Dignity," *LAT*, July 27, 2001; "Officials Reworking Rules on Day Labor."

75. "No Citations Issued as Enforcement of Day-Laborer Law Begins (Santa Clarita)," *LAT*, May 15, 1997; "Judge Blocks Crackdown on Redondo Beach's Day Laborers," *LAT*, December 14, 2004; "Pasadena Cracks Down on Laborers," *LAT*, March 27, 2003; "Law Prohibits Hiring Workers in the Street," *LAT*, June 11, 2003; "Laborer Center Clears Hurdle," *PSN*, January 17, 2000; "Laborer Center in Need of Cash," *PSN*, March 10, 2001; "Laborers Protest Crackdown," *PSN*, January 11, 2003; "Council OKs Ban on Hires from Car," *PSN*, June 10, 2003; "Day Laborers Say They're Staying Despite New Law," *PSN*, July 22, 2003; "Crowd Control," *Pasadena Weekly*, April 17, 2003, 13; "Handouts Slapped," *PSN*, March 27, 2004; "Pasadena Hoping to Curb Laborers," *PSN*, April 27, 2004; "Life on the Margins," *Pasadena Weekly*, February 18, 2010; "Day Laborer Tries to Survive While Helping Kin in Mexico," *PSN*, March 21, 2004.

76. "Day Laborers Win Supreme Court Free-Speech Case"; "Day Laborers Win in High Court," *LAT*, February 22, 2012; "Rebuffing Redondo," *LAT*, February 26, 2012; "Striking Down a Bad Law, Piece by Piece," *NYT*, March 7, 2012; *Comite De Jornaleros De Redondo Beach v. City of Redondo Beach*, 657 F.3d 936 (9th Cir. 2011); "The Legal Fight to Protect the First Amendment Rights of Day Laborers," MALDEF in History, December 13, 2021, https://www.maldef.org/2021/12/the-legal-fight-to-protect-the-first-amendment-right-of-day-laborers/. Also see Gabriela Garcia Kornzweig, "Note: Commercial Speech in the Street: Regulation of Day Labor Solicitation," *Southern California Interdisciplinary Law Journal* 9 (Spring 2000), 499–519.

77. In recent years, a notable exception to this was Pasadena, where local groups like Pasadenans Organizing for Progress advocated for the rights of day laborers.

78. Mollenkopf and Pastor, eds., *Unsettled Americans*, 3.

79. In LA County, many of the strongest progressive efforts centered in regional-level groups, especially after 1980. LA, in fact, was a national leader in creating an infrastructure for immigrant rights and social services. Key groups included the Coalition for Humane Immigrant Rights (CHIRLA, formed in 1986), Los Angeles Alliance for a New Economy (LAANE, founded in 1993), Strategic Actions for a Just Economy (SAJE, founded in 1996), and the National Day Laborer Organizing Network (NDLON, formed in 2001). All had strong ties to labor unions, another bastion of regional social activism by the 1990s, when Los Angeles led the nation in a resurgence of organized labor. This labor activism was invigorated by the energies of Latino immigrants who brought strong pro-labor traditions with them from home countries. See Hondagneu-Sotelo and Pastor, *South Central Dreams*, 18; Storper et al., *Rise and Fall*, 159–160; Manuel Pastor, "Contemporary Voice: Contradictions, Coalitions, and Common Ground," in *A Companion to Los Angeles*, edited by William Deverell and Greg Hise (Chichester, UK: Wiley-Blackwell, 2010), 250–266; Edward W. Soja, *Seeking Spatial Justice* (Minneapolis: University of Minnesota Press, 2010); Ruth Milkman, *L.A. Story: Immigrant Workers and the Future of the U.S. Labor Movement* (New York: Russell Sage Foundation, 2006); John Laslett, *Sunshine Was Never Enough: Los Angeles Workers, 1880–2010* (Berkeley: University of California Press, 2012), chapter 12.

80. See sources in Note 3. The presence of suburban progressivism also adds to the reframing of LA political culture from conservatism to something more contested, in works such as Mike Davis and Jon Weiner, *Set the Night on Fire: L.A. In the Sixties* (London: Verso, 2021); Danny Widener, *Black Arts West: Culture and Struggle in Postwar Los Angeles* (Durham, NC: Duke University Press, 2010); Laura Pulido, *Black, Brown, Yellow & Left: Radical Activism in Los Angeles* (Berkeley: University of California Press, 2006); Josh Kun and Laura Pulido, eds., *Black and Brown in Los Angeles: Beyond Conflict and Coalition* (Berkeley: University of California Press, 2014); and, for the recent era, Manuel Pastor, *State of Resistance: What California's Dizzying Descent and Remarkable Resurgence Mean for America's Future* (New York: The New Press, 2018).

81. Jean-Paul deGuzman, "'And Make the San Fernando Valley My Home': Contested Spaces, Identities, and Activism on the Edge of Los Angeles" (Ph.D. dissertation, UCLA, 2014), 143–167.

82. Tanachai Mark Padoongpatt, "'A Landmark for Sun Valley': Wat Thai of Los Angeles and Thai American Suburban Culture in 1980s San Fernando Valley," *Journal of American Ethnic History* 34, 2 (Winter 2015), 83–114.

83. Dempsey, *City of Dignity*; the conservative story is detailed in Darren Dochuk, *From Bible Belt to Sunbelt: Plain-Folk Religion, Grassroots Politics, and the Rise of Evangelical Conservatism* (New York: W.W. Norton, 2010); McGirr, *Suburban Warriors*.

84. Pasadena, in fact, had a coterie of liberal/progressive groups, from Democratic clubs to the Coalition Against Police Abuse; see Chapter 4.

85. See Chapter 6.

86. See Chapter 6; Carpio et al., "Right to the Suburb," 198; Laura Pulido, "Rethinking Environmental Racism: White Privilege and Urban Development in Southern California," *Annals of the Association of American Geographers* 90 (2000), 12–40; Karen Brodkin, *Power Politics: Environmental Activism in South Los Angeles* (New Brunswick: Rutgers University Press, 2009).

87. "In 'People's Republic of Santa Monica,' Voters Turn to the Right," *NYT*, April 17, 1983. This sensibility was eventually diluted in the face of gentrification in the area.

88. Kurashige, *Shifting Grounds of Race*, 256–258.

89. Cheng, *Changs Next Door*, chapter 1, quote at 59.

90. Hondagneu-Sotelo and Pastor, *South Central Dreams*, 9.

91. Romeo Guzmán, Carribean Fragoza, Alex Sayf Cummings, and Ryan Reft, eds., *East of East: The Making of Greater El Monte* (New Brunswick: Rutgers University Press, 2020), 9.

92. Genevieve Carpio, *Collision at the Crossroads: How Place and Mobility Make Race* (Oakland: University of California Press, 2019), 189–195, quote at 189.

93. Barraclough, "Contested Cowboys," 104–118.

94. Jerry González, *In Search of the Mexican Beverly Hills: Latino Suburbanization in Postwar Los Angeles* (New Brunswick: Rutgers University Press, 2018), 131–135; "Cruisers Win Boulevard, but Montebello Finds Peace," *LAT*, July 20, 1980. On the Eastside music scene which helped spawn this cruising culture, see Matt Garcia, *A World of Its Own* (Chapel Hill: University of North Carolina Press, 2002), 199–201.

95. González, *In Search of the Mexican Beverly Hills*, chapter 4.

96. Gilda L. Ochoa, *Becoming Neighbors in a Mexican American Community: Power, Conflict, and Solidarity* (Austin: University of Texas Press, 2004).

97. For example, see James S. Lai, *Asian American Political Action: Suburban Transformations* (Boulder, CO: Lynne Rienner Publishers, 2011); Benjamin Francis-Fallon, *Rise of the Latino Vote* (Cambridge, MA: Harvard University Press, 2019); Geraldo L. Cadava, *The Hispanic Republican: The Shaping of an American Political Identity, from Nixon to Trump* (New York: Ecco/Harper Collins, 2020).

98. This conclusion contradicts one national study, which found that municipal anti-immigrant policies were most prevalent in Republican areas. Karthick Ramakrishnan and Tom Wong, "Partisanship, Not Spanish: Explaining Municipal Ordinances Affecting Undocumented Immigrants," in *Taking Local Control: Immigration Policy Activism in U.S. Cities and States*, edited by Monica W. Varsanyi (Stanford: Stanford University Press, 2010), 73–92.

99. Fully 13 of 16 suburbs passing strict restrictions on yard sales were predominantly Democratic. Similarly, six of nine suburbs passing day laborer laws had more registered Democrats than Republicans in 1990, seven in 2000.

100. Voter registration from California Secretary of State, *Report of Registration*, October 1980, October 1990 and September 2000.

101. A sample of the 15 suburbs with the highest proportion of nonwhite homeowners in 2000, along with the book's four case study suburbs, was used for this analysis. Also see Table A2.16 (nonwhite homeownership in suburbs).

102. Pastor, *State of Resistance*, especially chapters 4 and 5.

103. HoSang, *Racial Propositions*, chapter 6; Philip Martin, "Proposition 187 in California," *International Migration Review* 29, 1 (1995), 255–263; "Groups Organize to Fight Prop. 187," *LAT*, October 9, 1994; "Crime, Immigration Issues Helped Wilson, Poll Finds," *LAT*, November 9, 1994. Two different statewide exit polls showed opposite voting patterns by Asian Americans and Black Americans: the poll cited in Martin, "Proposition 187," showed they voted "yes" on the measure; the poll cited in "Crime, Immigration Issues," *LAT*, November 9, 1994, showed they voted "no." This contradiction suggests the evidence may still be inconclusive on where these groups stood, statewide, on the measure.

104. Pastor, *State of Resistance*, 79–81; on Lakewood, see Chapter 7.

Chapter 4

1. Andrew Wiese, *Places of Their Own: African American Suburbanization in the Twentieth Century* (Chicago: University of Chicago Press, 2004), 35; George Regas oral history conducted by Becky Nicolaides, October 27, 2010, Pasadena, CA; Michael E. James, *The Conspiracy of the Good: Civil Rights and the Struggle for Community in Two American Cities, 1875–2000* (New York: Peter Lang, 2005), ix; Peter Dreier, "Separate and Unequal," *PW*, September 13, 2007.

2. Julia Child, *My Life in France* (New York: Anchor Books, 2007), 23; *Thurston's Residence and Business Directory of Pasadena, 1921-22* (Los Angeles: Los Angeles Directory Company, 1922).

3. Jackie Robinson, *I Never Had It Made* (Hopewell, NJ: Ecco Press, 1995), 5-6. Willa Mae was the sister of Jackie Robinson.

4. Bruce Schulman, *From Cotton Belt to Sunbelt* (New York: Oxford University Press, 1991); Matthew D. Lassiter, *Silent Majority: Suburban Politics in the Sunbelt South* (Princeton: Princeton University Press, 2006); Kevin Kruse, *White Flight: Atlanta and the Making of Modern Conservatism* (Princeton: Princeton University Press, 2005). Atlanta was the city "too busy to hate," Charlotte underscored its racial moderation.

5. Wiese, *Places of Their Own*, 25.

6. Lynn M. Hudson, *West of Jim Crow: The Fight Against California's Color Line* (Urbana: University of Illinois Press, 2020), chapter 6; James, *Conspiracy of the Good*.

7. Hudson, *West of Jim Crow*, chapter 6.

8. On the limits of this federal commitment, see Lassiter, *Silent Majority*; Robert O. Self, *American Babylon: Race and the Struggle for Postwar Oakland* (Princeton: Princeton University Press, 2003).

9. William H. Frey, "Metro Magnets for Minorities and Whites: Melting Pots, the New Sunbelt, and the Heartland," Population Studies Center Research Report No. 02-496, February 2002.

10. An excellent discussion of this trend of civic withdrawal is in Kruse, *White Flight*.

11. I base this on my analysis of local media coverage on race relations in Pasadena in the twentieth century. Also see Hudson, *West of Jim Crow*, chapter 6.

12. Laura Voisin George, "Cultivating an Ideal: The Agrarian Aspirations of Pasadena, California, 1873-1895" (MA thesis, University of Virginia, 2010), quote at 40, 46, see 31 for the local use of A. J. Downing designs; Yvette Saavedra, *Pasadena Before the Roses: Race Identity, and Land Use in Southern California, 1771-1890* (Tucson: University of Arizona Press, 2018).

13. George, "Cultivating an Ideal," 56-79; Ann Scheid, *Pasadena: Crown of the Valley* (Northridge, CA: Windsor Publications, 1986).

14. Scheid, *Pasadena*, 25, 27, 120-123.

15. Scheid, *Pasadena*, 59-61, 81.

16. See Table A4.1 (Race/ethnicity in Pasadena, 1900-2010).

17. James, *Conspiracy of the Good*; Robin D. G. Kelley, "Black History Project," notes, PMH; Earl F. Cartland, "A Study of the Negroes Living in Pasadena" (master's thesis, Whittier College, 1948); James E. Crimi, "The Social Status of the Negro in Pasadena, California" (master's thesis, University of Southern California, 1941); Manuel Pineda and F. Caswell Perry, *Pasadena Area History* (Pasadena: James W. Anderson, 1972); Carson Anderson, "Ethnic History Research Project, Pasadena, California" (report of survey findings prepared for the City of Pasadena, March 1995); Roberta H. Martínez, *Latinos in Pasadena* (Charleston, SC: Arcadia Books, 2009); Christine Lofstedt, "The Mexican Population of Pasadena, California," *Journal of Applied Sociology* 7 (May-June 1923), 262-263. On the early zoning measure, see Ordinance 1433, March 30,

1914, and Ordinance 1982, March 31, 1922 (which includes a map), City Clerk's Office, City of Pasadena.

18. Beverly Wayte, *At the Arroyo's Edge: A History of Linda Vista* (Los Angeles: Historical Society of Southern California and Linda Vista/Annandale Association, 1993), 55–66.

19. City of Pasadena Architectural and Historical Inventory, "Survey Area Twenty-Eight North Raymond-Summit Neighborhood" (City of Pasadena, Urban Conservation Program, October 1985), 24; Robert Winter and Alexander Vertikoff, *Craftsman Style* (New York: Harry N. Abrams, Inc., 2004), 165–166.

20. Franklin D. Howell, "A Study of the History and Development of Hastings Ranch Into a Single Family Tract House" (paper for Urban and Regional Planning Pl. 612), 6–9, CRPPL.

21. James, *Conspiracy of the Good*, 29–30.

22. Crimi, "Social Status," 72–75. The Pasadena Improvement Association's directors included bankers, real estate men, attorneys, and one member of the city council.

23. See Chapter 2 on racial covenant campaigns in La Cañada, Flintridge, Glendale, Alhambra, and South Pasadena in the 1940s. Charlotta Bass describes a 1939 campaign by realtors to shut Blacks out of Arcadia, Monrovia, and Sierra Madre, although it was not completely successful. Charlotta Bass, *Forty Years: Memoirs from the Pages of a Newspaper* (Los Angeles: C. A. Bass, 1960), 101–102.

24. "Glendale Method Cited as Neighbors Hold Meet to Keep Altadena White," *Crown City Press*, December 6, 1956. The segregated racial geography of Pasadena is visible in Figure A4.1 (Pasadena's racial geography, 1950), and Figure A4.2 (HOLC map of Pasadena, 1939).

25. Scheid, *Pasadena*, 96–99; Cartland, "Study of the Negroes," chapter 5; Crimi, "Social Status"; Kelley, "Black History Project" notes; Anderson, "Ethnic History," 21–23, 27, 44–55; Hudson, *West of Jim Crow*, chapter 6; "A Brief History of St. Barnabas Church," St. Barnabas Church, Pasadena, CA; Bill Lane Doulos, *Hearts on Fire: The Evolution of an Urban Church* (Pasadena, CA: All Saints Church, 1995), 13; "The Saint Barnabas Church Family 100 Year Story," https://stbarnabaspasadena.org/who-we-are/our-story, accessed March 24, 2023.

26. Scheid, *Pasadena*, 132, and chapter 5.

27. Edward L. Thorndike, *Your City* (New York: Harcourt, Brace & Co., 1939), 33.

28. Pineda and Perry, *Pasadena Area History*, 60, 61, 70–75; Scheid, *Pasadena*, chapters 6 and 7; Patrick Conyers, Cedar Phillips, and the Pasadena Museum of History, *Pasadena, 1940–2008* (Charleston, SC: Arcadia Books, 2009); "Cities, Schools Seek to Solve Twin Problems," *LAT*, January 4, 1970. On suburban shopping centers, see Lizabeth Cohen, *A Consumers' Republic: The Politics of Mass Consumption in Postwar America* (New York: Vintage, 2004), chapter 6.

29. "Pasadena Wants It Both Ways," *Business Week* (June 1, 1957), 37–38; Scheid, *Pasadena*, 172–174; US Department of Commerce, Bureau of the Census, *1980 Census of Population, Characteristics of the Population, General Social and Economic Characteristics, California* (Washington, DC: GPO, 1982), 6–223. On postwar urban "magic lands" and "cities of knowledge," see John Findlay, *Magic Lands: Western*

Cityscapes and American Culture After 1940 (Berkeley: University of California Press, 1993); Margaret Pugh O'Mara, *Cities of Knowledge: Cold War Science and the Search for the Next Silicon Valley* (Princeton: Princeton University Press, 2004).

30. Scheid, *Pasadena*, 173–174, 181–184; Ann Scheid Lund, *Historic Pasadena: An Illustrated History* (San Antonio: Historical Publishing Network, 1999), 93.

31. Joel Garreau, *Edge City: Life on the New Frontier* (New York: Doubleday, 1991), 329.

32. See Table A4.2 (Demographic data for Pasadena, 1950–2010).

33. In Pasadena, their numbers were significantly higher than the LA County average. This lent some demographic truth to the stereotype of the "little old lady from Pasadena," from the 1964 Jan and Dean song.

34. See Table A4.2 (Demographic data for Pasadena, 1950–2010).

35. James, *Conspiracy of the Good*; vertical files of a number of individual organizations, CRPPL. See Table A4.3, for detailed numbers on Pasadena associations and Figure A4.3 (Per capita club data). Sources used to reconstruct the history of associations include *Thurston's Pasadena City Directory, 1947* (Los Angeles: Los Angeles Directory Co., 1947); *Sixteenth Annual Register of the Organizations of Pasadena and Vicinity, 1950*, Bertha K. Shaw compiler (Pasadena: Turner and Stevens Co., 1950); *Thurston's Pasadena City Directory, 1951* (Los Angeles: Los Angeles Directory Co., 1951); *Twenty-First Annual Register of the Organizations of Pasadena and Vicinity, 1955*, Bertha K. Shaw compiler (Pasadena: Turner and Stevens Co., 1955); *Polk's Pasadena City Directory, 1961* (Los Angeles: R. L. Polk & Co., 1961); *Thirty-Second Annual Register of the Organizations of Pasadena and Vicinity, 1966*, Mrs. Stanley H. Stevens, compiler (Pasadena: Bank of Pasadena, 1966); *Polk's Pasadena City Directory, 1971* (Monterey Park, Ca.: R. L. Polk & Co., 1971); *Pasadena Community Organizations Directory, 1979–1980*, edited by Frederick Olsen (Pasadena: Pasadena Public Library, 1979); *Pacific Telephone, Bell System Yellow Pages, Pasadena, 1980* (Pacific Telephone, 1980); Pasadena Chamber of Commerce and Civic Association, *1991 Business Directory and Community Guide* (San Diego: Marcoa Publishing, 1991); *Pacific Bell Smart Yellow Pages, Pasadena, 1989–90* (Pacific Bell, 1990); for 2011, Pasadena Public Library Community Directory (online in 2011).

36. Vance Packard, *The Status Seekers* (Philadelphia: David McKay, 1959). Packard offered a useful class profile of popular postwar groups, nationally.

37. "Rose Bowl Rites Induct 1200 Nobles," *LAT*, June 18, 1950; "2000 Masons Will Picnic in Pasadena," *LAT*, July 18, 1954; "Public Schools Week Programs Readied for Observance in Valley," *LAT*, April 16, 1965; "Eastern Star 108 Now 75 years old," *PSN*, May 12, 1965; "Pooh-Bah . . . " *PW*, September 17, 1998; *Pasadena Scottish Rite Bulletin*, vol. 72, no. 2, February 2009, Pasadena Scottish Rite vertical file, CRPPL; "Elks Divided by Dilemma over Property," *PSN*, December 11, 1988.

38. In 1948, it honored Mae Reese Johnson, an African American woman who was director of the Scattergood Association. Woman Civic League Vertical File, for miscellaneous clippings from 1945–1973, CRPPL; "Woman's Civic League to Mark 30th Anniversary," *PSN*, October 1, 1941; "Certificates of Merit Awarded by Woman's Civic League," *PSN*, May 6, 1946.

39. Lizabeth Cohen documented the importance of these groups in the interwar years, assuming their demise by the 1930s and 1940s with the arrival of state-based welfare

and unionization. Lizabeth Cohen, *Making a New Deal* (Cambridge: Cambridge University Press, 1991), 218–238.

40. Some scholars have assumed the assimilation capacity of suburbia for whites ethnic Americans, reflecting a desire among suburbanites to shed old ethnic identities upon their move into these new "American dream" communities. See Karen Brodkin, *How Jews Became White Folks and What That Says About Race in America* (New Brunswick: Rutgers University Press, 1998); David Roediger, *Working Toward Whiteness: How America's Immigrants Became White: The Strange Journey from Ellis Island to the Suburbs* (New York: Basic Books, 2006); George Lipsitz, *The Possessive Investment in Whiteness: How White People Profit from Identity Politics* (Philadelphia: Temple University Press, 1998). Others have noted the persistence and transformation of white ethnic identities in suburbs, including Lila Corwin Berman, *Metropolitan Jews: Politics, Race, and Religion in Postwar Detroit* (Chicago: University of Chicago Press, 2015); Deborah Dash Moore, *To the Golden Cities: Pursuing the American Jewish Dream in Miami and L.A.* (New York: The Free Press, 1994).

41. Rates of membership from Elbie Hickabottom oral history, in *Advocates for Change: Oral History Interviews on the Desegregation of the Pasadena Unified School District* (Pasadena: Pasadena Heritage, 2007), 190, and *Crown City Press*, November 22, 1956, cited in Kelley, "Black History Notes" and "The Church," Kelley notes, PMH; church information from *Thurston's Pasadena City Directory 1951*; Saundra Knox oral history, in *Advocates for Change*, 74–75.

42. This type of event was not uncommon in this period, when progressive activism was occurring in Los Angeles around the issue of race. See Shana Bernstein, *Bridge of Reform: Interracial Civil Rights Activism in Twentieth Century Los Angeles* (New York: Oxford University Press, 2011); Sean Dempsey, *City of Dignity: Christianity, Liberalism, and the Making of Global Los Angeles* (Chicago: University of Chicago Press, 2023).

43. "The Pasadena Interracial Women's Club: A Plus Quality, Organized December 9, 1946," pamphlet, 1978, Interracial Women's Club vertical file, CRPPL; "Mrs. Owen Troy Heads Pasadena Interracial Club," *LAS*, September 26, 1957; "Interracial Club Begins 11th Year," *LAS*, October 17, 1957.

44. Quotes from Georgina Hickey, "Social Seasons and Settlement Houses: Privileged Women and the Development of Cities," *Journal of Urban History* 29 (May 2003), 464. Though referencing a different time and place, Hickey's descriptions of elite women applied well to elites in postwar Pasadena.

45. Many of the early members hailed from large cities of the East Coast and Midwest—including Jared Torrance, a wealthy real estate developer, president of 23 California corporations, and CFO of Union Oil; Dr. Francis Rowland; and other "old money" transplants. Ann Scheid, *The Valley Hunt Club, One Hundred Years, 1888–1988* (Pasadena: Valley Hunt Club, 1988), 21–22, 41.

46. In contrast to these other clubs, the Valley Hunt Club welcomed women from the outset. They joined the hunting excursions in carriages, wearing long dresses and fancy hats, carrying lunches for the gentlemen hunters. Scheid, *Valley Hunt Club*, 15–17.

47. Scheid, *Valley Hunt Club*, 14–65, especially 14, 15, 33.

48. Scheid, *Valley Hunt Club*, 41, 111–112, 125, 164.

49. The Club's rise in membership in the 1950s—to 550 by 1960—reflected both a spike in local population and the recent closure of two other clubs in the area, the Midwick Country Club in Alhambra and the Flintridge Golf Club in nearby La Cañada, which both went under during the Depression. Scheid, *Valley Hunt Club*, 98, 128.

50. Scheid, *Valley Hunt Club*, 126–150; "Clubs: Can Everyone Join in the Hunt?" *PW*, January 2, 1986. In 1959, a local judge observed the inequity when it came to policing—gambling was tacitly allowed at five elite private clubs in Pasadena, while the police targeted Black Americans at gaming parties, including in private homes. Moreover, five private clubs in Pasadena excluded Jews, according to a 1967 report conducted by the Anti-Defamation League of B'nai B'rith. See "Clubs Allow Gambling, Judge Says," *LAT*, March 13, 1959; "Anti-Semitism Found Waning in Private Clubs," *LAT*, February 21, 1967.

51. The *Los Angeles Times* regularly covered debutante activities in Pasadena starting in the 1910s, accelerating after 1930. A small sampling includes "Los Angeles County— Its Cities and Towns," *LAT*, December 31, 1908; "New Year's First Debutante Bows in Pasadena," *LAT*, January 10, 1937; "Valley Hunt Club Will Host Debutante Ball," *LAT*, October 18, 1949; "Yuletide Décor Set for Hunt Club Debs," *LAT*, December 20, 1955; "Debutantes Blossom in Summer," *LAT*, June 25, 1962.

    In 1971, the Valley Hunt Club debs were notable for their lack of service activities and emphasis on leisure travel and self-enrichment. Debs who came out through other organizations—such as the Las Madrinas—were more apt to spend time volunteering at a hospital or other social service institution. "Debs Seeing and Doing Their Duty," *LAT*, July 11, 1971.

    On debutante culture as a means of enacting class privilege, see Karal Ann Marling, *Debutante: Rites and Regalia of American Debdom* (Lawrence: University Press of Kansas, 2004).

52. Scheid, *Pasadena*, 133; quote from "Fetes City Birthday Historical Society," *PSN*, January 30, 1963; "Queen Presented at Traditional Breakfast," *PSN*, December 19, 1947; "Historic Shakespeare Club Active Civic Group," *PSN*, April 11, 1948; "Shakespeare Club Philanthropy Day," *PSN*, May 6, 1984; "Gently to Hear, Kindly to Judge," *PW*, March 15, 2001; "Shakespeare Century," *LAT*, November 24, 1988.

53. Examples of extensive press coverage include "Junior League Takes Voyage," *LAT*, December 9, 1926; "Junior League Has Frolic," *LAT*, December 11, 1928; "Pasadena Junior League Plans Series of Affairs," *LAT*, November 27, 1932.

54. Barbara Slattery, "Our League: Post War Years," 1952[?], 27–29, Junior League vertical file, CRPPL.

55. Slattery, "Our League," 28.

56. Slattery, "Our League"; Pasadena Junior League, "Annual Report of the President, 1960–1961," November 28, 1961, Junior League vertical file, CRPPL; "Pasadena League Will Set Program," *LAT*, September 14, 1947; "Juniors Hail New Members," *LAT*, April 27, 1960; "Pasadena Junior League Meeting to Observe 40th Year," *LAT*, April 21, 1966; newspaper clippings from Junior League vertical file, CRPPL. An excellent historical analysis of the Junior League is Elise Chenier, "Class, Gender, and

the Social Standard: The Montreal Junior League, 1912–1939," *Canadian Historical Review*, 90, 4 (December 2009), 671–710.

57. See Table A4.4 (Percentage of private school children in LA suburbs).

58. US Census, *Census of Population and Housing: 1960. Census Tracts: Los Angeles-Long Beach, Calif. SMSA* (Washington, DC: GPO, 1963), 101–103; the number of private schools from *Thurston's Pasadena City Directory, 1951* (Los Angeles: Los Angeles Directory Co., 1951); *Polk's Pasadena City Directory, 1961* (Los Angeles: R. L. Polk & Co., 1961); racial statistics from an analysis of yearbooks of LaSalle, Mayfield Senior, Polytechnic, and Westridge, conducted by Jennifer Vanore, 2011.

59. "Graduation Waited by Subdeb," *LAT*, June 8, 1947; "Colorful Commencement Rites Arranged by Schools for Girls," *LAT*, June 5, 1949.

60. Ave Maria DeVanon Bortz, *Mayfield: The Early Years, 1931–1950* (Pasadena: Mayfield Senior School, 2000).

61. "Crown City Citizen's Corner," *LAS*, April 2, 1953; "Debutante Assembly at Pasadena Civic," *LAS*, May 7, 1953; "Six Crown City Lovelies Presented," *LAS*, March 1, 1956.

62. "Pasadena Delts Fete Debutantes at Luncheon," *LAS*, October 18, 1962; "Mothers Beam as Daughters Bow at Delta Ball," *LAS*, May 8, 1969.

63. The importance of the "local" as a site of civic activism is well described in Michelle M. Nickerson, *Mothers of Conservatism: Women and the Postwar Right* (Princeton: Princeton University Press, 2011).

64. An excellent treatment of these educational conflicts is in Nickerson, *Mothers of Conservatism*; also see James, *Conspiracy of the Good*; David Hulburd, *This Happened in Pasadena* (New York: Macmillan, 1951).

65. Ironically, Jürgen Habermas, who posited a distinction between "deliberative democracy" and "plebiscitary democracy," largely dismissed the legitimacy of suburban civic engagement, a conclusion belied by the vibrancy of suburban political activism across the nation. See Robyn Muncy, "Cooperative Motherhood and Democratic Civic Culture in Postwar Suburbia, 1940–1965," *Journal of Social History* (winter 2004), 285; Robyn Muncy, "Disconnecting: Social and Civic Life in America Since 1965," *Reviews in American History* 29 (2001), 141–149.

66. See sources in note 35; *Sixteenth Annual Register of the Organizations of Pasadena and Vicinity, 1950*, Bertha K. Shaw compiler (Pasadena: Turner and Stevens Co., 1950). These figures include both men's groups and women's auxiliaries.

67. Nickerson, *Mothers of Conservatism*, 40–45.

68. Hulburd, *This Happened*, "mansion" quote at 59; Nickerson, *Mothers of Conservatism*, 71–85; Pasadena City Directories of 1949. Examples of national media coverage include "Man Out of a Job," *Life*, December 11, 1950; "Education: Pasadena Revisited," *Time*, May 7, 1951; "Educators Should be Warned by the Pasadena Revolt," *Saturday Evening Post*, July 14, 1951, 10.

69. Nickerson, *Mothers of Conservatism*, 84–85.

70. Marvin Schachter oral history, conducted by Becky Nicolaides, December 28, 2010, Pasadena, CA; Esther and Marvin Schachter oral history, conducted by Becky Nicolaides, April 7, 2011, Pasadena. CA; Francis Carney, "The Palsy of the CDC," *Nation* (May 4, 1970), 526–530; Jonathan Bell, "Social Democracy and the Rise of

the Democratic Party in California, 1950–1964," *The Historical Journal*, 49, 2 (2006), 497–524; Carlotta Mellon, "The Rise and Fall of Grassroots Politics: the California Democratic Council, 1953–1966" (PhD dissertation, Claremont Graduate University, 1973), chapter 6 on Joe Wyatt. On the Democratic Club movement, also see Francis Carney, *The Rise of the Democratic Clubs in California* (New York: Holt, 1958). Many thanks to David Levitus for alerting me to these sources.

71. Marvin Schachter oral history; Esther and Marvin Schachter oral history.

72. Vertical files on these associations, CRPPL; "Boys of Blue Hold Banquet," *LAT*, May 17, 1926; "Lauds Heroes of Civil Strife," *LAT*, May 18, 1926; sources in note 35; on pro-Union sentiment in Pasadena, see Scheid, *Pasadena*, 48. Pro-Union figures included the sons of abolitionist martyr John Brown, who settled in Altadena in the 1880s.

73. Lassiter, *Silent Majority*, 305.

74. Hudson, *West of Jim Crow*, chapter 6; Kelley, "Black History Project" notes, sections on civil rights and labor, PMH; James, *Conspiracy of the Good*, 246–247. After the protest over unfair hiring practices at Pasadena City Hall, the NAACP received a letter that revealed the depth of racial animosity among some Pasadenans. It read: "Hi Nigger: I read your dirty rag with nothing but contempt for all you black rats. The whole situation is this: The sooner you niggers learn that we WHITES will NEVER accept you niggers the sooner you will be happier. Pasadena (is) being polluted with negroes we WHITES have lost fortunes in DEVALUED PROPERTY VALUES. I will curse the day my White race introduced you black bastards to our White hemisphere." *Crown City Press*, October 11, 1956, cited in Kelley, "Black History Notes," on "Civil Rights," PMH.

75. One key principle established in this case was Judge Roger Traynor's assertion that enforcing restrictive covenants conflicted with the public interest, in particular the congestion which was "a consequence of residential segregation of the colored population" caused not by municipal racial zoning ordinances (which were deemed unconstitutional in *Buchanan v. Worley*), but "by agreements between private persons." Traynor cited social scientific evidence in his opinion, setting a precedent that the NAACP would use as it built its case against restrictive covenants, leading to the Supreme Court case *Shelley v. Kraemer*. Many thanks to Greg Hise for pointing out the *Fairchild* case and its significance to me.

76. Wiese, *Places of their Own*, 220–221; Loren Miller, "A Right Secured," *The Nation*, May 29, 1948, 600; the *Fairchild v. Raines* case is at http://www.lawlink.com/research/CaseLevel3/2419.; Josh Sides, *L.A. City Limits: African American Los Angeles from the Great Depression to the Present* (Berkeley: University of California Press, 2003), 101–108; on incidents of racial violence, see Kelley "Black History Project" notes on "Race Relations," "Civil Rights," and "Housing, Settlement, Population," PMH.

77. Wiese, *Places of Their Own*, 129–133, quote at 133.

78. In 1970, Hastings had 15 Blacks out of 6,200 residents, Sierra Madre 12 Blacks out of 12,100. US Bureau of Census, *Census of Population and Housing: 1970. Census Tracts, Los Angeles-Long Beach, Calif., SMSA*. Part 1 (Washington, DC: GPO, 1972), P89–91.

79. Ralph Schloming, "Road Blocks to Effective and Integrated Schools in Pasadena," Pasadena Chapter CORE, February 1966, CRPPL, 20. As the Pasadena CORE report pointed out, Blacks were shut out more tightly in these towns from 1950 to 1960, when their miniscule Black populations declined even further. Also see Figure A4.4 (Racial geography of Pasadena, 1950-1970).

80. "Pasadenans March for 4 Bomb Victims," *PSN*, September 23, 1963; "NAACP Parley May Set Rose Tourney Protest," *LAT*, November 15, 1963; "NAACP OKs Picketing of Rose Parade," *LAT*, December 5, 1963; "NAACP Withdraws Plan to Picket Parade," *LAT*, December 29, 1963; "Rights March During Rose Parade Considered," *LAT*, December 29, 1963; "Patience Yielding Big Payoff in Pasadena," *Washington Post*, January 21, 1986; "Tournament of Roses: Diversity Remains a Work in Progress," *PSN*, December 4, 2010; Kelley, "Black History Project," Rose Parade notes, PMH; City of Pasadena Independent Financial and Legal Audit (with Carolyn H. Carlburg), *Executive Summary of the Report on the Contractual and Financial Relationships between the City of Pasadena and the Tournament of Roses Association* (Pasadena, 1993).

81. "1,000 Picket Segregationists," *LAS*, July 2, 1964; "White Council Meeting Runs Into Trouble Here," *LAT*, June 25, 1964; "Citizens Group Still Plans to Hold Meeting," *LAT*, June 26, 1964; "Civil Rights Forces Find Joint Issue," *LAT*, July 5, 1964; "Board Reluctantly Oks Auditorium Use for Alabaman's Talk," *LAT*, November 10, 1965; "Pasadena Hecklers Halt Alabama Sheriff's Talk," *LAT*, November 16, 1965; "Free Speech and Sheriff Jim Clark," *LAT*, November 17, 1965; "Incident in Pasadena," *Frontier*, 17, December 1965, 11-12, cited in Kelley, "Black History Project" notes, and Kelley, general notes, "Civil Rights," PMH.

82. Marge Wyatt oral history, in *Advocates for Change*, 156-159; Marge Wyatt telephone interview with author, April 5, 2011.

83. "An Unreconstructed Radical Still Takes His Case to the Streets," *LAT*, July 28, 1986; on CAPA, see Max Felker-Kantor, *Policing Los Angeles* (Chapel Hill: University of North Carolina Press, 2018), 121-125.

84. The literature on this topic is large. Key works include John Logan and Harvey Molotch, *Urban Fortunes: The Political Economy of Place* (Berkeley: University of California Press, 1987); Jon C. Teaford, *The Rough Road to Renaissance* (Baltimore: Johns Hopkins University Press, 1990); June Manning Thomas, *Redevelopment and Race: Planning a Finer City in Detroit* (Baltimore: Johns Hopkins University Press, 1997); Lawrence Vale, *Purging the Poorest: Public Housing and the Design Politics of Twice-Cleared Communities* (Chicago: University of Chicago Press, 2013).

85. Self, *American Babylon*, 143; Logan and Molotch, *Urban Fortunes*.

86. See, for example, Andrew Highsmith, *Demolition Means Progress: Flint, Michigan, and the Fate of the American Metropolis* (Chicago: University of Chicago Press, 2015), chapter 4.

87. "Pasadena's Rehabilitation Program," *American City* 69 (July 1954), 116-117.

88. The best treatment of the Pepper Project is in Michele Zack, *Altadena: Between Wilderness and City* (Altadena: Altadena Historical Society, 2004), 173-175.

89. Zack, *Altadena*, 174-175; on the Black suburban ideal, see Wiese, *Places of Their Own*, chapter 3.

90. Zack, *Altadena*, 175; *Pasadena Eagle*, May 10, 17, June 1, 8, 15, 1969, cited in Kelley, "Black History Project" notes on "Housing Settlement, Population," PMH; Pasadena Community Services Commission, *Poverty in the City of Roses: A Statistical Analysis* (October 1973), 18–19.

91. "Pasadena Sees Freeway as Business Bonanza," *LAT*, May 30, 1971.

92. "Pasadena Stands Fast on Freeway Position," *LAT*, September 2, 1964; "Angriest Freeway Revolt Brews Over New Routes," *LAT*, November 20, 1964; also see Anastasia Loukaitou-Sideris, et al., "The Implications of Freeway Siting in California: Four Case Studies on the Effects of Freeways on Neighborhoods of Color" Pacific Southwest Region University Transportation Center/UCLA, March 2023, viii-x, 83-131.

93. "La Cañada Loses Fight on Freeway," *LAT*, June 15, 1966; Zack, *Altadena*, 173; "State Relents, Pasadena Families Facing Eviction Get Brief Reprieve," *LAT*, March 19, 1970; "Marchers at Pasadena City Hall Demand Homes for Poor," *LAT*, March 26, 1970; "Pasadena Blacks Say Little Done to End Their Plight," *LAT*, May 28, 1972. On the displacement of nonwhite communities by freeways, see Raymond Mohl, "Stop the Road: Freeway Revolts in American Cities," *Journal of Urban History* 30 (July 2004), 674–706; Eric Avila, *The Folklore of the Freeway: Race and Revolt in the Modernist City* (Minneapolis: University of Minnesota Press, 2014); Ryan Reft, Amanda K. Phillips de Lucas, and Rebecca C. Retzlaff, eds., *Justice and the Interstates: The Racist Truth about Urban Highways* (Washington DC: Island Press, 2023).

94. Joel Sheldon oral history, in *Advocates for Change*, 136.

95. Art Seidenbaum, "The Neighborly Thing to Do," *LAT*, January 7, 1976.

96. Lassiter, *Silent Majority*; Ellen Goldring, Lora Cohen-Vogel, Claire Smrekar, and Cynthia Taylor, "Schooling Closer to Home: Desegregation Policy and Neighborhood Contexts," *American Journal of Education* 112, 3 (2006), 335–363; Ansley Erickson, *Making the Unequal Metropolis: School Desegregation and Its Limits* (Chicago: University of Chicago Press, 2016).

97. "Schools in Pasadena Confronted by Classic Segregation Crisis," *NYT*, April 7, 1969.

98. "Pasadena Nears Crossroads on Integration of Schools," *LAT*, June 18, 1967; "Schools in Pasadena Confronted by Classic Segregation Crisis"; Sides, *L.A. City Limits*, 160. On La Cañada's formation of its own district, see "La Canadans OK Unified School Plan," *LAT*, October 20, 1960; "School Unity Debated," scrapbook, La Cañada Unified School District collection, Lanterman House Archive, La Cañada.

99. This one-way busing formula was known as the "Geographic and Controlled Open District" plan, which was implemented in 1965. It actually achieved modest success in desegregating the high school—by 1969, PHS had 9.7% Blacks, Blair had 21.6%, while Muir had 37%. None reflected the racial composition of the actual population, but it showed modest progress. "Integration Plan Called Success by Pasadenans," *LAT*, January 12, 1969; League of Women Voters of Pasadena, "A Summary of Facts Compiled as Part of a Study and Evaluation of Long-Range Planning and Equality of Educational Opportunity in the Pasadena Unified School District" (December 1968), 9, CRPPL.

"Recall Election Viewed as Crucial to Pasadena School Integration," *LAT*, October 11, 1970; this article dates the "open district plan" as starting in 1964.

100. "Schools in Pasadena Confronted by Classic Segregation Crisis"; "The Problems of Pasadena High Schools," *PSN*, July 28, 1968.

   At this point, PHS was bursting at the seams, with 3,400 students and a classroom shortage; Muir had 2,100 and classrooms to spare. "Busing: 30 Years After Landmark Decision," *PSN*, January 23, 2000.

101. The two white fathers were James Spangler, a stockbroker, and Skip Rostker, an insurance broker; the African American father was Wilton Clarke, a furniture manufacturer. "Schools in Pasadena Confronted by Classic Segregation Crisis"; Zack, *Altadena*, 185.

102. James Spangler oral history, in *Advocates for Change*, 1–5; "Schools in Pasadena Confronted by Classic Segregation Crisis"; "Recall Election Viewed as Crucial."

103. "Schools in Pasadena Confronted by Classic Segregation Crisis"; "U.S.Presses a Landmark Case in Pasadena," *NYT*, January 11, 1970. The "black leader" was not identified in the *New York Times* article of January 11, however it was likely former Pasadena NAACP chair George Jones, who was quoted later in the article.

104. "Uniform School Rulings Asked," *NYT*, January 24, 1970; "Southerners Act in Pasadena Case," *NYT*, February 14, 1970; "Pasadena Integration Approved," *NYT*, March 5, 1970; Lassiter, *Silent Majority*, 247–248; "Busing: 30 Years After Landmark Decision." Judge Manuel Real ultimately rejected the Southerners' petition to intervene.

105. "U.S. Presses a Landmark Case in Pasadena"; "Pasadena Schools Told to Integrate," *NYT*, January 21, 1970; "Southerners Act in Pasadena Case."

106. "Recall Election Viewed as Crucial."

107. James Spangler oral history, in *Advocates for Change*, 8.

108. Lassiter and others have explored how regional solutions to school inequality have never gained traction, lacking sufficient political backing at all levels of governance. See Lassiter, *Silent Majority*.

109. "Anti-Poverty Program Delay Asked," *LAT*, December 10, 1964; "School Bonds 'Strike' Urged in Pasadena," *LAT*, March 28, 1968; "New Threat Faces Pasadena Trustees," *LAT*, March 4, 1970.

110. "School Cluster. Tool for Forced Integration," flyer of the Greater LA Citizens' Council, Marvin Schachter personal files.

111. "Pasadenans Will Battle School Integration Edict," *LAT*, February 12, 1970; "Board Will Confer on Integration Plans," *LAT*, February 17, 1970; "Integration Foes Raise Funds," *LAT*, March 3, 1970; "Pasadenans Seek Appeal on Schools," *LAT*, March 4, 1970; "Antibussing Group Wins Court Round," *LAT*, March 20, 1970.

112. "Group Forms to Oppose Bus Plan," *LAT*, September 9, 1970; "Pasadena and Inglewood Begin Integration by Bus Smoothly," *LAT*, September 15, 1970.

113. "Black Community Split Over Integration Order," *LAT*, January 22, 1970; "Psychology of Bussing Black Youth Criticized," *LAT*, April 14, 1970; "Black Culture Center Urged for Pasadena Community," *PSN*, February 1, 1970; Kelley, "Pasadena Black History Project-Report I," 3, PMH.

114. "Pasadenans Pave Way for Integration Quietly," *LAT*, June 14, 1970; Lassiter, *Silent Majority*, 58–64; Louise M. Young, *In the Public Interest: The League of Women Voters, 1920–1970* (New York: Greenwood Press, 1989).

115. "Group Forms to Help Solve School Issue," *LAT*, May 2, 1963; "PACE Attacks School Staffing in Pasadena," *LAT*, November 7, 1963; "Board to Act on Integration Plan," *LAT*, May 11, 1964; Marge Wyatt oral history, in *Advocates for Change*, 161.

116. "Pasadenans Pave Way."

117. "Pasadenans Pave Way."

118. Joel V. Sheldon III oral history, in *Advocates for Change*, 136.

119. "250 in Pasadena Integration Rally," *LAT*, December 15, 1974; "Schools Act to Prevent Nazi Demonstration," *LAT*, April 24, 1975. The photo shown in Figure 4.11 lacked clear identifying information; it was taken by a *Pasadena Star News* photographer, but no story accompanied the photo. The Pasadena location of the demonstration was determined by consulting Pasadena city directories from 1975 to 1985, to identify buildings shown in the photo located along Colorado Boulevard. Many thanks to Young Phong, of the Pasadena Public Library, for helping identify the place and time of this photograph.

120. The best treatment of the 1970s controversy between the fundamentalists and liberal progressives is Julie Salley Gray, "To Fight the Good Fight: The Battle Over Control of the Pasadena City Schools, 1969–1979," *Essays in History*, 37 (1995), published by Corcoran Department of History, University of Virginia.

121. Joel Sheldon oral history, in *Advocates for Change*, 132–140; on their court fight and boycotts of Audubon during the pro-fundamental regime, see "Picketing, Boycott Hit School Plan," *LAT*, June 19, 1975; "Audubon Pupils Pawns in Battle," *LAT*, December 18, 1975; "Court Stays Audubon Order," *LAT*, August 8, 1976.

122. Joel Sheldon oral history, in *Advocates for Change*, 130–131; George Van Alstine oral history, conducted by Becky Nicolaides, April 12, 2011, Altadena, CA.

123. California Secretary of State, *Report of Registration: State of California*, 1962, November 3, 1970, October 1980, October 9, 1990, September 8, 2000, October 18, 2010.

124. "Patience Yielding Payoff in Pasadena," *Washington Post*, January 21, 1986; "Political Power in Pasadena: Loretta Thompson Glickman is Mayor of the City of Roses," *Ebony* (August 1982), 113–115; "Pasadena Mom Is on Fast Track," *PSN*, October 25, 1991.

  Thompson Glickman was the nation's first Black woman to serve as mayor of a city with a population over 100,000. She was elected to the Pasadena Board of Directors in 1977.

125. Nicolaides and Wiese, eds., *Suburb Reader*, chapters 15 and 16; Alex Schafran, *Road to Resegregation: Northern California and the Failure of Politics* (Oakland: University of California Press, 2018).

126. US Department of Commerce, Bureau of the Census, *Census of Population and Housing 1980: Census Tracts, Los Angeles-Long Beach Calif.*, Sections 1–3 (Washington, DC: GPO, 1983); US Census tract data 2000. For details, see Table A4.5 (Race by neighborhood in Pasadena, 1980, 2000), and Figure A4.5 (Racial geography of Pasadena, 1980–2000).

127. Dreier, "Separate and Unequal."

128. Dreier, "Separate and Unequal." In January 2011, Dreier noted that the recent Pasadena General Plan was overly focused on service for the affluent, with scant mention about the needs of low-income and poor residents. Dreier public lecture at All Saints Church, Pasadena, January 6, 2011.

129. US Census tract data 1980; US Census data set 1950–2000; Bill Trimble telephone interview with author, April 25, 2011.

130. Robert D. Putnam, *Bowling Alone: The Collapse and Revival of American Community* (New York: Simon & Schuster, 2000).

131. J. Eric Oliver, *The Paradoxes of Integration: Race, Neighborhood, and Civic Life in Multiethnic America* (Chicago: University of Chicago Press, 2010); Robert D. Putnam and Lewis M. Feldstein, *Better Together: Restoring American Community* (New York: Simon & Schuster, 2003).

132. Latino groups in Pasadena included El Centro de Accion, the Latino Heritage Association, and El Teatro de los Niños, among others.

133. "Shakespeare Century"; "Scholarships Awarded," *PSN*, June 25, 2004; "Gently to Hear, Kindly to Judge." As of 2004, the group was still awarding scholarships to local public high school students.

134. Nickerson, *Mothers of Conservatism*; Lisa McGirr, *Suburban Warriors: The Origins of the New American Right* (Princeton: Princeton University Press, 2002), 199, 207, 262–273; Jo Freeman, *A Room at a Time: How Women Entered Party Politics* (New York: Rowman & Littlefield, 2000), 160–166; Marvin Schachter oral history; Esther Schachter and Marvin Schachter oral history; Carney, "The Palsy of the CDC," 526–530; meeting minutes, 1966 to 1980, San Gabriel Valley Democratic Women's Club collection, Huntington Library, San Marino, CA.

135. Basil Entwistle, *Making Cities Work: How a Community Mobilized to Meet Its Needs* (Pasadena: Hope Publishing House, 1990); Doulos, *Hearts on Fire*, chapter 13; "A Chronology of Inclusion, 2010," All Saints Church records.

136. Lian Dolan, *Helen of Pasadena* (Altadena, CA: Prospect Park Books, 2010), 43; on recent coverage of Pasadena galas and fundraisers, see issues of *Pasadena Outlook*, since 2007, and *LAT* coverage since the 1980s; Lian Dolan interview with author, August 24, 2012, Pasadena CA.

137. Scheid, *The Valley Hunt Club*, 162.

138. "Clubs: Can Everyone Join in the Hunt?"; "Don't Even Think About Joining This Club," *LAT*, September 18, 2004.

139. On Pasadena-Altadena chapter of LINKS, see https://pasadenaaltadenalinksinc.org/membership-login/chapter-notes/, accessed November 1, 2020; on Women in Action, see https://womennaction.tripod.com/, accessed November 1, 2020; "And the Dance Goes on," *LAT*, February 27, 2000; on the Deltas, see regular coverage in the *LA Sentinel*, including "Pasadena Deltas Celebrate Elegant Energy in Motion," *LAS*, May 1, 2003.

140. "Changing Junior League Image," *PSN*, February 28, 1987.

141. The national Junior League had adopted "multiculturalism" as a goal at its annual convention the previous year.

142. Scott reflected upper-class African American life in Pasadena. She married a doctor and became a stay-at-home mother to her three children who attended private schools. She made her connection to the League through the mothers of children at her kids' private schools. "Junior League Aims for Diversity," *LAT*, June 9, 1991. See Table A4.6 (Junior League membership rates, 1960–2010).

143. "Junior League Aid-Involved," *PSN*, August 9, 1970; "Junior League, Women in Action Team up to Help Local Schools," *PSN*, January 20, 1984; "Changing Junior League"; "Junior League Donates $5,500 to PUSD Program," *PSN*, November 9, 1988; "Pasadena Mom on Fast Track," *PSN*, October 25, 1991; "Pasadena's Junior League Grants Total Almost $14,000," *PSN*, January 29, 1992; "Junior League Will Fix Depot," *PSN*, February 6, 1992; "League Tells Our Politicians What's Up," *PSN*, May 9, 1992; "No Stereotyping These Junior Leaguers," *PSN*, March 13, 1993; "It Was a Spring Thing for the Junior League," *PSN*, April 15, 2004; "Junior League Aims for Diversity"; Nicole Weaver-Goller telephone interview with author, December 17, 2010.

144. "Empower to the People," *LAT*, June 2, 1994; "Sleeves rolled up: It's the fashion here," *LAT*, June 20, 2004; Bill Trimble oral history, conducted by Becky Nicolaides, November 19, 2010, Pasadena CA; Brian Biery interview with author, June 28, 2023, via Zoom; Brian Biery, "A Brief and Partial History of Neighborhood Organizing in Pasadena," City Council District 5, April 29, 2021; Garfield Heights Neighborhood Association, https://www.garfieldheights.org/; Bungalow Heaven Neighborhood Association, https://www.bungalowheaven.org/our-history/orig ins/; City of Pasadena Landmark District Designation, https://www.cityofpasadena. net/planning/planning-division/design-and-historic-preservation/historic-prese rvation/historic-preservation-incentives/#landmark-district; Survey of Pasadena Neighborhood Associations conducted by Becky Nicolaides, November 2010.

   NC was dismantled in 2017 by the city council, and the number of active neigh-borhood associations has declined to approximately 30 to 35.

145. Kruse, *White Flight*; Lily Geismer, *Left Behind: The Democrats' Failed Attempt to Solve Inequality* (New York: Public Affairs, 2022).

146. Gary Orfield, *The Growth of Segregation in American Schools: Changing Patterns of Separations and Poverty Since 1968* (Washington, DC: National School Boards Association, 1993); Gary Orfield and Susan Eaton, *Dismantling Desegregation: The Quiet Reversal of Brown v. Board of Education* (New York: New Press, 1997); Erickson, *Making the Unequal Metropolis*; Lassiter, *Silent Majority*; Matthew Delmont, *Why Busing Failed: Race, Media, and the National Resistance to School Desegregation* (Oakland: University of California Press, 2016); Daniel Amsterdam, "Toward the Resegregation of Southern Schools: African American Suburbanization and Historical Erasure in *Freeman v. Pitts*," *History of Education Quarterly* 57, 4 (November 2017), 451–479.

147. Amy Stuart Wells et al., *Both Sides Now: The Story of School Desegregation's Graduates* (Berkeley: University of California Press, 2009), 214–217, and espe-cially chapter 6; "Rock 'n' Roll 101 in Pasadena," *LAT*, October 19, 2020. On the benefits of the busing experience, see *Advocates for Change*; *Can We All Get Along? The Segregation of John Muir High School* (49 min., Arroyo Seco Films, dir. Pablo Miralles, 2019).

148. Richard D. Kahlenberg, "One Pasadena: Tapping the Community's Resources to Strengthen the Public Schools," A Report to the Pasadena Educational Foundation, May 24, 2006, 14. The court's release of Pasadena from the busing mandate reflected a political and judicial retreat from busing nationally. In Pasadena, from 1980 to

2006, the number of bused students fell from 12,000 to fewer than 2,000, after it became a voluntary program.

149. Wells et al., *Both Sides Now*, 274; school data 2000–2020, from Data Reporting Office, California Department of Education, accessed on January 15, 2022, at https://dq.cde.ca.gov/dataquest/dataquest.asp. Also see Tables A4.7 (PUSD demographics) and A4.8 (Private school pupil demographics).

150. "Nine Injured in Militant Clash at Pasadena High," *LAT*, May 10, 1969; "Students Resentful at Expulsion from School," *LAT*, May 12, 1969; "10,000 Back Action by Trustees in Riot," *LAT*, May 14, 1969; "Students Raise $435 to Help Fix Damage at Muir," *LAT*, September 25, 1969; "60 Suspended in First Week of Integration," *LAT*, September 23, 1970; "Adult Aid Will Ride School Bus," *LAT*, October 20, 1970; "Integration as Seen by Pupils and Teachers," *LAT*, November 26, 1970; Mary Carter oral history, in *Advocates for Change*, 99; John Kennedy oral history, in *Advocates for Change*, 94.

151. Wells et al., *Both Sides Now*, 107–111.

152. Wells et al., *Both Sides Now*, 271–275. Notably, by the 2000s, roughly two-thirds of students in PUSD qualified for free or reduced-price lunch.

153. Harold Kurtz, "The Educational and Demographic Consequences of Four Years of School Desegregation in the Pasadena Unified School District," Pasadena Unified School District, 1975; Stephen Mulherin and Monique N. Hernandez, "Pasadena Unified School District: The Abandonment of a Public Institution," *California Politics and Policy* (June 2006), 93, 99, 107–108; Kahlenberg, "One Pasadena," 12; Wells et al., *Both Sides Now*, 111.

154. Mulherin and Hernandez, "Pasadena Unified School District," 93, 99.

155. Harriet McGinley Webster oral history, conducted by Becky Nicolaides, November 19, 2010, Pasadena, CA; Ann Hight oral history, in *Advocates for Change*, 114; "Busing" letter to the editor, *Pasadena Eagle*, March 9, 1972; "PTA Reappraises Role in Wake of Integration Rule," *LAT*, March 1, 1970.

156. Bill Trimble oral history.

157. "PTA Shaken by Puzzling Membership Decline," *LAT*, April 24, 1966; "PTA Retains Traditions, Broadens Role," *LAT*, March 16, 1975; Susan Crawford and Peggy Levitt, "Social Change and Civic Engagement: The Case of the PTA," in *Civic Engagement in American Democracy*, edited by Theda Skocpol and Morris P. Fiorina (Washington, DC: Brookings Institution Press, 1999), 249–296.

158. "PTA Reappraises Role"; "Pasadena School Busing Hit, Defended at Hearing," *LAT*, April 15, 1976; "Group Approves Integration," *PSN*, February 10, 1970; "PTA Battle" (letter to editor, signed "Disgusted Mother"), *PSN*, March 30, 1974; "Wanted: More Parents," *PSN*, March 15, 1998. The PTA Council of Pasadena consistently took a stand in favor of busing and integration. For example, see "Pasadenans Pave Way"; "Pasadena Trustees Slam Door in Face of Opposition," *LAT*, November 30, 1975.

159. "PTA Reappraises Role"; "Wanted: More Parents"; Anne Pursel oral history, in *Advocates for Change*, 209; Marge Wyatt oral history, in *Advocates for Change*, 165; Mulherin and Hernandez, "Pasadena Unified School District," 104, 106. On similar challenges in other suburbs of the region, see "Use of Dues, Stiff Formality Chip at

PTA Membership," *LAT*, March 20, 1977; "Educators Stress Need for Involvement," *LAT*, February 10, 1986; "Beyond the Bake Sale: Building a New PTA," *LAT*, June 22, 1996.

On the historical tradition of fundraising by PTA units, see Christine Woyshner, *The National PTA, Race, and Civic Engagement, 1897–1970* (Columbus: Ohio State University Press, 2009), 108–118. Woyshner points out that PTA fundraising was particularly important in poorer, Black schools.

160. On Black parent leadership and involvement in PTAs in northwest Pasadena, see "Pasadena Jottings," *LAS*, March 11, 1954 (on Hilda Grant at Washington School PTA), "Crown City Citizen's Corner" (on Esther Hutcherson and Eugenia Peters at Washington Junior High PTA), "PTA Series at Lincoln," *LAS*, February 9, 1956 (on Shirley Price as president of the Lincoln Elementary PTA); "Lilian Mims, Pasadena Civic Leader," *LAS*, July 5, 1956 (on Lillian Mims as treasurer of the Pasadena PTA Council); "Henry Clark Appointed to Board of Ed.," *LAS*, February 19, 1970 (on Mrs. Henry Clark as president of the Loma Alta Elementary PTA; her husband was a conservative African American appointed to the school board in 1970).

Segregated PTAs had a long history in the United States; Southern Blacks had their own PTA organizations since the 1920s, which gave them some measure of autonomy. See Woyshner, *The National PTA*, and 102 on California.

161. "A PTA Convention Minus the Funny Hats," *LAT*, June 20, 1985; Woyshner, *The National PTA*, 152–153, 246n2.

162. Woyshner, *The National PTA*, 102; "The PTA: Educational Organization," *LAS*, June 3, 1971; "Forced Busing a 'Hot Potato' for the PTA," *LAT*, October 17, 1977; Joe C. Hopkins, "PTA: The Life You Save May Be Your Little Jelly Bean," *Pasadena Journal*, September 12, 2002. Also see "Flexibility Within a Framework at PTA Convention," *LAT*, April 11, 1972.

There is passing mention that in some desegregated districts, white parents tended to take over leadership roles in the PTAs, in Wells, et al., *Both Sides Now*, 98.

163. "Wanted: More Parents," *PSN*, March 15, 1998; see Figure A4.6 (PTA membership).

164. *Polk's Pasadena City Directory* 1971; PUSD Consolidated Funding Office, "ECIA Chapter 2, 1991–1992, Private Non-Profit Schools," Private School vertical file, CRPPL; "Public, Private School Chasm Grows Wider," *PSN*, January 23, 2000; see Table A4.4 (Percentage of private school children in LA suburbs). One 1990 article referenced an LA County Department of Education figure that counted 69 private schools in the PUSD area, however other sources showed a lower figure ("Private Schools' 'Public' Problems," *PSN*, March 18, 1990).

165. As Table A4.8 indicates, Black families showed a slight uptick in the proportion of kids in private schools from 1970 to 2000. Given their overall declining population numbers, this seemed to have less of an impact on the overall race/ethnic pattern in private schools, than did the Latino presence.

166. The following schools were included in this survey: La Salle High (Catholic), Mayfield Senior School (Catholic), St. Elizabeth's (Catholic), St. Mark's Elementary (Catholic), Polytechnic, Waverly, and Westridge Girls School. Racial data were

gleaned from yearbooks from La Salle, Mayfield Senior, Polytechnic, and Westridge. Many thanks to Jen Vanore for her assistance with this research.

The largest race/ethnic groups broke down as follows: the Catholic schools tended to have large numbers of Latinos, followed by Asians; at Westridge, African Americans were the largest nonwhite group, and at Polytechnic, it was Asians.

167. "Private Schools Seeking Better Racial Balance," *LAT*, December 2, 1984; Heidi Johnson interview with author, November 15, 2010, Pasadena, CA. On "A Better Chance," see http://www.abetterchance.org/, accessed April 6, 2023; "A Better Chance for Children of Minorities," *NYT*, November 9, 1980; "The ABCs of Getting Ahead," *NYT*, September 20, 1998; "Tapping the Potential of Gifted Minority Students," *LAT*, December 27, 1979.

168. Survey of Pasadena area private schools, see note 166.

169. *Oak Tree Times*, Polytechnic School, February 1991, 9; "Parent Support Group for Black Children," *The Oak Tree Times*, Polytechnic School, March 1992, 4, Polytechnic vertical file, CRPPL.

170. Heidi Johnson interview; Survey of parents at the Waverly School, conducted by Becky Nicolaides, Winter 2010 (survey yielded 22 responses out of 300 queried).

171. Rande Sotomayor oral history, conducted by Becky Nicolaides, April 3, 2011, Altadena, CA.

172. Wells et al., *Both Sides Now*; Orfield and Eaton, *Dismantling Desegregation*.

173. Wells et al., *Both Sides Now*, 236–263, 275. The film *Can We All Get Along?* emphasizes the families embracing diversity in the post-busing era.

174. "Fond Memories" (letter to editor), *PW*, May 10, 2007.

175. Wells et al., *Both Sides Now*, 207–213.

176. Dempsey, *City of Dignity*; Mark Wild, *Renewal: Liberal Protestants and the American City after World War II* (Chicago: University of Chicago Press, 2019).

177. For broader context, see Lily Geismer, "More Than Megachurches: Liberal Religion and Politics in the Suburbs," in *Faithful Republic: Religion and Politics in Modern America*, edited by Andrew Preston, Bruce J. Schulman and Julian E. Zelizer (Philadelphia: University of Pennsylvania Press, 2015), 117-130.

178. "Negro Artists Will Exhibit Their Work," *LAT*, August 16, 1968; "Church Will Have Showing of Negro Art," *LAT*, September 8, 1969; "Episcopalians to Consider Aid for Blacks," *LAT*, September 27, 1969; "Church Will Present Minority Group Series," *LAT*, April 19, 1970.

179. "4 Seminarians Tackle White Racism Problem in Suburbs," *LAT*, December 21, 1969; "More Funds Awarded to Fight Prejudice," *LAT*, May 28, 1970; "$434,000 Fight to Start on Racism in Churches," *LAT*, June 24, 1972; Joseph C. Hough, Jr. and Dan D. Rhoades, "Project Understanding: Report and Evaluation," School of Theology at Claremont, August 1971, 30. Also see Philip A. Amerson and Jackson W. Carroll, "The Suburban Church and Racism: Is Change Possible?" *Review of Religious Research*, 20, 3 (Summer 1979), 335–349; Joseph C. Hough telephone interview with author, October 25, 2010.

180. In 1989, whites comprised 89% and Black Americans 4% of the congregation, when Pasadena as a whole was 47% white and 18% Black. By 1998, the racial profile had changed only slightly: 85% white, 4% Black, 3% Asian, and 3% Latino (the latter two

groups were imperceptible in 1989). Barry Jay Seltser, "Demographics and Decisions: A Parish Survey of All Saints Church, Pasadena," Social Issues Research, San Gabriel, CA, February 1989; Program Review Committee, "Parish Survey Report to Congregation; Report Summary, Areas of Strength/Areas for Growth, Comparison of 1988 and 1998 Survey Results," March 21, 1999, All Saints Church records. The 1989 survey only included financially contributing members. The surveys revealed significant diversification by other measures in 1998—a notable increase in gay/lesbians, singles, and cohabiting couples, as well as an increase in wealth.

181. George Regas oral history. In a separate oral history, Regas reiterated this assessment, conceding that the segregation of All Saints was "a stressful phenomenon." George Regas oral history, conducted by Elizabeth McBroom, California Social Work Archives, USC School of Social Work, September 19, 1990. Regas acknowledged that the church struggled with racial inclusion on various occasions; see, e.g., "They've Dared to be Different at All Saints," *LAT*, December 12, 1971. On the robust social activism of All Saints, see copious coverage in *LAT*, 1967 to 2000s; Doulos, *Hearts on Fire*; Entwistle, *Making Cities Work*; George Regas, *Kiss Yourself and Hug the World* (Waco, TX: Word Books, 1987).

182. George Van Alstine oral history; "Pasadena New School Board Head," *LAT*, May 9, 1993.

183. Alice Blackwood interview with author, April 12, 2011, Altadena, CA.

184. Alice Blackwood interview; George Van Alstine oral history.

185. Media coverage of All Saints and Altadena Baptist was a study in contrasts—the *Los Angeles Times* had more than 1,500 articles on All Saints in the post-1967 period; Altadena Baptist was covered in a few dozen articles, mostly about weddings and Easter services.

186. For a similar milieu in the suburbs of Boston, see Lily Geismer, *Don't Blame Us: Suburban Liberals and the Transformation of the Democratic Party* (Princeton: Princeton University Press, 2014).

187. On All Saints Church, see Doulos, *Hearts on Fire*; Pasadenas Organizing for Progress has become a center of progressive activism, see https://www.poppasadena.org/, accessed on April 6, 2023. From 2018 to 2023, whites comprised 17% of all school pupils in the PUSD. Data from https://www.pusd.us/site/handlers/filedownload.ashx?moduleinstanceid=12689&dataid=35339&FileName=2022-23%20District-wide%20Norm%20Day%20Enrollment%20by%20Ethnicity%20Trend.pdf, accessed April 6, 2023.

188. Mulhern and Hernandez, "Pasadena Unified School District," 99.

189. Quote from "Pasadena's History of Racism Trickles into Present," *PSN*, August 24, 2013; school statistics from Kahlenberg, "One Pasadena," 10–11.

Chapter 5

1. On communities bound by NIMBYism, see James S. Duncan and Nancy G. Duncan, *Landscapes of Privilege: The Politics of the Aesthetic in an American Suburb* (New York: Routledge, 2004), 5.

2. "Housing Bust Didn't Touch San Marino," *LAT*, January 31, 2011.

3. Lisa Sun-Hee Park, *Consuming Citizenship: Children of Asian Immigrant Entrepreneurs* (Stanford: Stanford University Press, 2005), 4–16; also see James Zarsadiaz, *Resisting Change in Suburbia: Asian Immigrants and Frontier Nostalgia in L.A.* (Oakland: University of California Press, 2022).

4. Duncan and Duncan, *Landscapes of Privilege*, quote at 26. Also see Kristen Hill Maher, "Borders and Social Distinction in the Global Suburb," *American Quarterly* 56, 3 (2004), 781–806.

5. Michael B. Katz, Mathew J. Creighton, Daniel Amsterdam, and Merlin Chowkwanyun, "Immigration and the New Metropolitan Geography," *Journal of Urban Affairs* 32, 5 (2010), 523–547; Willow Lung-Amam, *Trespassers? Asian Americans and the Battle for Suburbia* (Oakland: University of California Press, 2017); David Ley, *Millionaire Migrants: Trans-Pacific Life Lines* (Chichester, UK: Wiley-Blackwell, 2010); Noriko Matsumoto, *Beyond the City and the Bridge: East Asian Immigration in a New Jersey Suburb* (New Brunswick: Rutgers University Press, 2018).

6. On internal class dynamics within Asian America, see Xiaojian Zhao, *The New Chinese America: Class, Economy, and Social Hierarchy* (New Brunswick: Rutgers University Press, 2010); Wei Li, *Ethnoburb: The New Ethnic Community in Urban America* (Honolulu: University of Hawai'i Press, 2009), 134–143, and chapter 7; Aihwa Ong, "Cultural Citizenship as Subject-Making," *Current Anthropology* 37, 5 (December 1996), 737–762; "Transitions on a Personal Scale Mirror Region's Transformation," *LAT*, April 16, 1987.

7. Stoneman went on to serve as governor of California in the 1880s. Elizabeth Pomeroy, *San Marino: A Centennial History* (San Marino: San Marino Historical Society, 2012), 29–31.

8. Patton Sr. was also father of the storied World War II general. Pomeroy, *San Marino*, 54–64.

9. Pomeroy, *San Marino*, 2, 8, 15, 29–31, 53–54, 59, 83–84.

10. Pomeroy, *San Marino*, 70. The emphasis on local social inequality is mine, not Pomeroy's.

11. Pomeroy, *San Marino*, 59, 65–67, 83–89. With proceeds from his transit and real estate empire, Huntington went on a buying spree of epic proportions, purchasing precious European art and entire collections of rare books (that included Shakespeare quartos and folios and a Gutenberg Bible), all within a span of less than 20 years.

12. Pomeroy, *San Marino*, 76–77; William Friedricks, *Henry Huntington and Creation of Southern California* (Columbus: Ohio State University Press, 1992), 125; William Friedricks, "Henry E. Huntington and Real Estate Development in Southern California, 1898–1917," *Southern California Quarterly* 71, 4 (Winter 1989), 327–340; Robert M. Fogelson, *The Fragmented Metropolis: Los Angeles, 1850–1930* (Berkeley: University of California Press, 1993). While Huntington never served in local office, his landscape man William Hertrich served on the city council from 1922–1945. Patton served as mayor (1913–1924), and on the city council (1922–1927) (Pomeroy, *San Marino*, 228).

13. William Friedricks notes that an earlier tract named Oak Knoll in west San Marino was subdivided in the 1890s and began selling in 1906. Oak Knoll Marino was in this same area ("Henry E. Huntington and Real Estate Development," 332–334).

14. "Oak Knoll Marino – To Complete an Ideal," sales brochure, the Frank Meline Co., representing the Huntington Land and Improvement Company, [192–?], RB 194420, Huntington Library, San Marino, CA; "Community Development: Oak Knoll Marino," *LAT*, September 7, 1924. An earlier iteration of Oak Knoll also had tight race restrictions. See Friedricks, "Henry E. Huntington and Real Estate Development," 333. On country club districts, see Becky Nicolaides and Andrew Wiese, eds., *The Suburb Reader*, 2nd ed. (New York: Routledge, 2016), 225–227, 230–234; Kenneth T. Jackson, *Crabgrass Frontier* (New York: Oxford University Press, 1985), 177–178.

15. "Huntington Hill" display ad, *LAT*, April 27, 1927.

16. "Gainsborough Heath" display ads, *LAT*, January 29 and March 4, 1928; O. Nicholas Gabriel, "The Story of Gainsborough Heath and the Old Adobe," 1928, RB 268804, Huntington Library, San Marino, CA; Pomeroy, *San Marino*, 96–97; "San Marino Tract to Go on Market," *LAT*, December 18, 1927.

17. Pomeroy, *San Marino*, 93–97, 202–203.

18. "Large Subdivision Prepared at San Marino Opens Today," *LAT*, June 13, 1937; "San Marino Building Increase Expected to be Large in 1938," *LAT*, March 6, 1938; "Development Plans Prepared for New San Marino Tract," *LAT*, January 22, 1939; "New Subdivision Opens Today," *LAT*, October 8, 1939.

19. US Department of Commerce, Bureau of the Census, *Sixteenth Census of the United States: 1940. Housing. Vol. I. Data for Small Areas. Part 1* (Washington, DC: GPO, 1943), 160; US Department of Commerce, Bureau of the Census, *Eighteenth Census of the United States: 1960. Census of Housing. Vol. I. Part 2* (Washington, DC: GPO, 1963), 6–109; "sub-Marino" from Judith Carter oral history, conducted by Becky Nicolaides, July 3, 2012, San Marino, CA.

20. Pomeroy, *San Marino*, 78–79 (on early ordinances); Gabriel, "The Story," 11, 17. The earliest zoning ordinances were San Marino City Ordinances No. 93 (April 22, 1925) and No. 174 (March 16, 1928), which established three zones: commercial, multifamily residential, and single-family residential. (San Marino Zoning ordinances, City Clerk's Office, SMCH.)

    On Palos Verdes, see Margaret Marsh, *Suburban Lives* (New Brunswick: Rutgers University Press, 1990), 168–173.

21. "San Marino Board Will Check New Home Plans," *LAT*, May 15, 1952.

22. "San Marino Forms New City Planning Board," *LAT*, May 3, 1953.

23. City Survey Files for Los Angeles, Record Group 195, Records of the Federal Home Loan Bank Board, National Archives, Washington, DC, worksheets A-14 and A-16.

24. Charlotte Brooks, *Alien Neighbors, Foreign Friends: Asian Americans, Housing, and the Transformation of Urban California* (Chicago: University of Chicago Press, 2009), 167.

25. Pomeroy, *San Marino*, 83–84.

26. "Oak Knoll Marino – To Complete an Ideal" sales brochure.

27. Merlin Chowkwanyun and Jordan Segall, "How an Exclusive Los Angeles Suburb Lost Its Whiteness," *Bloomburg CityLab*, August 27, 2012; Wendy Cheng, *The Changs*

Next Door to the Díazes: Remapping Race in Suburban California (Minneapolis: University of Minnesota Press, 2013), 36–37; Allan Yung oral history, conducted by Becky Nicolaides, May 30, 2012, and June 29, 2012, San Marino, CA.

28. "Chinese Scions Take Root," *LAT*, January 21, 2006; Pomeroy, *San Marino*, 132; Mamie Chandler Breitkreutz, "Reminisces of Early San Marino," transcript, Oral History Project by Friends of the San Marino Public Library, 1976, SMHS, 9; Richard Sun oral history, conducted by Becky Nicolaides, July 25, 2012, San Marino, CA. Breitkreutz recalled a number of Mexican workers laboring in the local orange groves of the early twentieth century, "but most of them didn't live here" (9). On the anti-Asian rhetoric of Patton's son, who became famous as the bombastic, controversial World War II general, see Charles M. Province, *The Unknown Patton* (New York: Bonanza Books, 1983), 99–100.

   In a survey of city ordinances from 1913–1929, there were no explicit references to race. San Marino City Council Minutes and Ordinances, 1913–1929, SMCH.

29. Joe Austin and Michael Nevin Willard, eds., *Generations of Youth: Youth Cultures and History in Twentieth-Century America* (New York: NYU Press, 1998); William Graebner, "The 'Containment' of Juvenile Delinquency: Social Engineering and American Youth Culture in the Postwar Era," *American Studies* 27, 1 (spring 1986), 81–97; James Gilbert, *A Cycle of Outrage: America's Reaction to the Juvenile Delinquent in the 1950s* (New York: Oxford University Press, 1988); Elaine Tyler May, *Homeward Bound: American Families in the Cold War Era* (New York: Basic Books, 2017). More and more suburban schools in LA adopted the Grad Night tradition—from South Gate to La Puente to Santa Monica—over the next several years. See coverage in the *LAT*.

30. "San Marino to Rock 'n' Roll at Grad Party," *LAT*, June 10, 1956.

31. "San Marino Grads Plan Big Time," *LAT*, June 13, 1965.

32. "Not Knowing Better, One Could Think He's a Worker," *SMT*, March 31, 1982; "Former Grad Night Chairmen Discuss 'Old Times' at Reunion," *SMT*, May 27, 1982; Judith Carter oral history; Tom Santley and Perta Santley oral history, conducted by Becky Nicolaides, July 8, 2012, San Marino, CA; "Grad Night" vertical file, SMHS.

33. Matthew Lassiter, *The Suburban Crisis: White America and the War on Drugs* (Princeton: Princeton University Press, 2023); Matthew Lassiter, "Pushers, Victims, and the Lost Innocence of White Suburbia: California's War on Narcotics during the 1950s," *Journal of Urban History*, 41, 5 (2015), 787–807; Kyle Riismandel, *Neighborhood of Fear: The Suburban Crisis in American Culture, 1975–2001* (Baltimore: Johns Hopkins University Press, 2020); Matthew Lassiter, *Silent Majority: Suburban Politics in the Sunbelt South* (Princeton: Princeton University Press, 2006); Lily Geismer, *Don't Blame Us: Suburban Liberals and the Transformation of the Democratic Party* (Princeton: Princeton University Press, 2014); Charles M. Haar, ed., *The End of Innocence: A Suburban Reader* (Glenview, Ill: Scott, Foresman & Co., 1972); Charles M. Haar, ed., *The President's Task Force on Suburban Problems: Final Report* (Cambridge, MA: Ballinger Publishing Company, 1974).

34. See Tables A2.7 and A2.8.

35. Tribid Banerjee and William C. Baer, *Beyond the Neighborhood Unit* (New York: Plenum Press, 1984), 47.

36. "Serene Enclave: San Marino, U.S.," *NYT*, August 16, 1964.

37. See Table A2.13 (Stay-at-home wives in suburbs, 1950–2010). Also see Table A5.1 (Full San Marino demographic data).

38. Paul Crowley oral history, conducted by Ave Maria Bortz, April 23, 2007, San Marino, CA, SMHS (audio interview); Pomeroy, *San Marino*, 170.

39. "Neighborly Advice: The Well-Tended Garden That Is San Marino," *LAT*, January 5, 2003; Tom Santley and Perta Santley oral history; Judith Carter oral history.

40. In the *New York Times*, "society" coverage peaked in the 1930s and 1940s, dropped somewhat in the 1950s, then picked up again in the 1960s, lasting well through the 1990s. The *Los Angeles Times* also carried frequent "society" news about San Marino residents.

41. See *New York Times* coverage of San Marino, 1950s and 1960s.

42. "Junior Leagues Elect Head," *NYT*, May 9, 1964.

43. Judith Carter oral history; "snobbish" quote from Hal Harrigian and Julie O'Reilly oral history, conducted by Becky Nicolaides, June 25, 2012, San Marino, CA. Harrigian also came from working-class roots.

44. *San Marino City Directory 1971* (San Marino: California Directory Publishing Co., 1971). The City Club began as the San Marino Civic Improvement Association and changed its name to the City Club in 1927. See Table A5.2 (Clubs per capita in San Marino, 1950–2011), and Figure A4.3 (Clubs in San Marino and Pasadena over time).

45. Pomeroy, *San Marino*, 110; Mildred Seidell, "Once Upon a Time," typed manuscript, April 1983, San Marino Woman's Club vertical file, SMHS; Arlene Kelly, "San Marino Woman's Club: Keeping Up with Changing Times for 71 Years," *The Quarterly Magazine* (Fall 2007), 52–53; *San Marino City Directory 1973* (San Marino: California Directory Publishing Co., 1973), 9–16; "A Guide for Residents of San Marino" (City of San Marino, 1980), SMHS; Terry Golden telephone interview with author, November 26, 2012; on NCL, see https://www.nationalcharityleague.org/chapter/sanmarinoarea/, accessed April 6, 2023.

46. California Secretary of State, *Report of Registration: State of California* (November 1962), 29–30; Secretary of State, *Report of Registration: State of California* (November 1970), 48–50. Also see Table A3.2.

47. Michelle Nickerson, *Mothers of Conservatism: Women and the Postwar Right* (Princeton: Princeton University Press, 2012), 27–30, 138–143; California Legislature, *Twelfth Report of the Senate Factfinding Subcommittee on Un-American Activities* (Sacramento, 1963), 58–59 (thanks to Michelle Nickerson for sharing this report); "New Birch Office is Opened in West," *NYT*, March 16, 1963; "Serene Enclave: San Marino, U.S.," *NYT*, August 16, 1964; "Regrouping in the Cold War," *LAT*, March 16, 1989; "Obituary, John Rousselot," *LAT*, May 12, 2003. The UN was a favored target of the Birchers, as Nickerson ably demonstrates.

48. Other affluent suburbs in LA with volunteer city councils, as of 2021, included Arcadia, Bradbury, Hidden Hills, La Habra Heights, Palos Verdes Estates, Rolling Hills, and Rolling Hills Estates. Source: http://publicpay.ca.gov/Reports/Cities/Cities.aspx, accessed June 1, 2021.

49. Richard Sun oral history; "She's Gained Respect 'Just for Being Me,'" *LAT*, November 28, 1993; "Message from Mayor Dr. Allan Yung," *San Marino City Directory 2011–12*, 7th ed. (San Marino: Association of Directory Publishers, 2011); Matt Ballantyne oral history, conducted by Becky Nicolaides, July 19, 2012, San Marino, CA; Hal Harrigian and Julie O'Reilly oral history.

50. Judith Carter oral history; Hal Harrigian and Julie O'Reilly oral history.

51. Pomeroy, *San Marino*, 110, 194; *San Marino City Directory 1978* (San Marino: California Directory Publishing Co., 1978), 14–26; "Community Groups Vital to Grad Night Success," *SMT*, June 1, 1978. One particularly tragic event that centered on a San Marino youngster drew the national spotlight, as detailed in William Deverell, *Kathy Fiscus: A Tragedy That Transfixed the Nation* (Los Angeles: Angel City Press, 2021).

52. Pomeroy, *San Marino*, 197; Hal Harrigian and Julie O'Reilly oral history; Tom Santley and Perta Santley oral history. The *San Marino Tribune* described "A wonderfully crazy, mad, ingenious world of Father's Night, a San Marino institution" (quoted in Pomeroy, *San Marino*, 197). On the USC culture in San Marino, also see "Well Regulated Lifestyle Suits Them Just Fine," *LAT*, December 22, 1991.

53. "Serene Enclave: San Marino, U.S.," *NYT*, August 16, 1964.

54. Governor's Commission on the Los Angeles Riots, *Violence in the City – An End or a Beginning? A Report* (Los Angeles: Governor's Commission on the Los Angeles Riots, 1965); Robert M. Fogelson, "White on Black: A Critique of the McCone Commission Report on the Los Angeles Riots," *Political Science Quarterly*, 82, 3 (September 1967), 337–367.

55. In scant coverage in the *Los Angeles Sentinel*, the middle-class oriented African American newspaper, San Marino had something of a Janus face—reviled for its racism, yet fawned over for its lovely homes and clubhouses by the African American "society" set. For example, see "Wash's Wash," *LAS*, September 10, 1959; "The Inside Story," *LAS*, March 31, 1966; "Pyramids Make Bow to Greek Society," *LAS*, November 15, 1962.

56. "Nearby Cities Seen as Pasadena Ghetto Relief," *LAT*, October 13, 1968; "No Community a Racial Island, San Marino Told," *LAT*, March 4, 1970; "Good Neighbors Come in All Colors," display ad, *LAT*, April 9, 1970; "San Marino Relations Group Hears Mexican-American Equality Plan," *LAT*, May 3, 1970; "More Ethnic Contact Asked for San Marino," *LAT*, May 5, 1970.

57. "Serene Enclave: San Marino, U.S."

58. John R. Logan and Harvey L. Molotch, *Urban Fortunes: The Political Economy of Place* (Berkeley: University of California Press, 1987); Myron Orfield, *Metropolitics* (Washington, DC: Brookings Institution Press, 1997); Nicolaides and Wiese, eds., *Suburb Reader*, chapters 4, 15.

59. William A. Fischel, "How Serrano Caused Proposition 13," *Journal of Law and Politics* (Fall 1996), 607–636; Peter Schrag, *Paradise Lost: California's Experience, America's Future* (New York: New Press, 1998), 149. Schrag questions whether the *Serrano* decisions actually caused the passage of Proposition 13, as Fischel claimed, though he acknowledges that it "certainly undermined one powerful reason to vote against it" (149).

Although the US Supreme Court invalidated the premise of the Serrano decision in the case *San Antonio v. Rodriguez* (1973), the California legislature pressed for compliance with Serrano in 1977 and beyond. Matthew Lassiter argues that without federal muscle behind the mandate for school equalization, it languished in most regions of the country as state legislatures refused to follow through in any effective way. Lassiter, *Silent Majority*, 318.

60. Also see Scott Vandehey, "Suburban Citizenship" (PhD dissertation, UC San Diego, 2009), chapter 8, which develops the idea that the privatization of public services in suburbia acted as a spur to parental participation.

61. "Covenant Case Continued by Court in L.A.," *Pacific Citizen*, November 15, 1947. This article describes a suit filed against a mixed-race couple (Chinese and white), seeking to enforce the race-restrictive covenant on the property. Thanks to Jean-Paul deGuzman for locating this article. On civil rights housing breakthroughs by Asians, see Brooks, *Alien Neighbors*; Scott Kurashige, *The Shifting Grounds of Race: Blacks and Japanese Americans in the Making of Multiethnic Los Angeles* (Princeton: Princeton University Press, 2008), 241–249; Lung-Amam, *Trespassers?*; Cheng, *The Changs Next Door*; Hillary Jenks, "Seasoned Long Enough in Concentration: Suburbanization and Transnational Citizenship in Southern California's South Bay," *Journal of Urban History* 40, 1 (2014), 6–30.

62. Chowkwanyun and Segall, "How an Exclusive Los Angeles Suburb." The authors also suggest the possibility of price discrimination by white sellers, who hiked up prices to meet high Asian demand.

63. Becky M. Nicolaides and James Zarsadiaz, "Design Assimilation in Suburbia: Asian Americans, Built Landscapes, and Suburban Advantage in Los Angeles' San Gabriel Valley since 1970," *Journal of Urban History* 43, 2 (2017), 335.

64. On the nuanced impacts on property values when Asians moved to white suburbs, see Lung-Amam, *Trespassers?*; Cheng, *Changs Next Door*.

65. Madeline Y. Hsu and Sucheng Chan, eds., *Chinese Americans and the Politics of Race and Culture* (Philadelphia: Temple University Press, 2008), chapters 3–5, especially 174.

66. "Lily Wong Remembers Hard Times," *LAT*, August 14, 1988; http://www.campaignmo ney.com/political/contributions/lily-wong.asp?cycle=08, accessed April 6, 2023.

67. Rosa Zee oral history, conducted by Becky Nicolaides, June 4 and 18, July 6, 2012, San Marino, CA.

68. Allan Yung oral history, May 30, June 29, 2012. Also see the story of immigrant Henry Hwang, a San Marino resident who rose from laundryman to president/CEO of Far East National Bank, in Li, *Ethnoburb*, 161–167.

69. David Freund, *Colored Property: State Policy and White Racial Politics in Suburban America* (Chicago: University of Chicago Press, 2007); Lassiter, *Silent Majority*.

A recent study spotlights Taiwanese immigrant students who mobilized politically against their own experiences of injustice and for self-determination. See Wendy Cheng, *Island X: Taiwanese Student Migrants, Campus Spies, and Cold War Activism* (Seattle: University of Washington Press, 2023).

70. On this broader concept, see Chan and Hsu, eds., *Chinese Americans*, x.

71. "San Marino Schools, City Struggle to Make Ends Meet," *LAT*, November 29, 1979.

72. Jean Wang, "A Reflection of the Birth of CCSM – Trudging Through a Rugged Path," [San Marino, n.d.], Jean Wang personal files; Jean Wang oral history, conducted by Becky Nicolaides, September 29, 2012, San Marino, CA.

73. Wang, "A Reflection of the Birth of CCSM," 1.

74. Wang, "A Reflection of the Birth of CCSM"; Jean Wang oral history.

75. Wang, "A Reflection of the Birth of CCSM," 2.

76. As Zhou and Li note, the three pillars of the Chinese diasporic community (Chinese schools, ethnic media, and family/clan associations) were more inward focused, and not inclined toward acculturation. Min Zhou and Xiyuan Li, "Ethnic Language Schools and the Development of Supplementary Education in the Immigrant Chinese Community in the U.S.," *New Directions for Youth Development* (Winter 2003), 57–73; Min Zhou, *Contemporary Chinese America* (Philadelphia: Temple University Press, 2009); "Asian Parents Find Schools an Education," *LAT*, September 18, 1986.

77. Rosa Zee oral history. Chinese unfamiliarity with school-based voluntarism was also observed in nearby suburbs like Monterey Park and Rosemead. Assistant principal Elena Wong explained, "When you ask an Asian parent to come to a meeting after school and ask how they think their child's education could be improved, they think, 'Why are you asking me? You're supposed to know.' That kind of participation is not part of Asian culture. So we are asking our parents to change completely." From "Ethnic Diversity Puts School District to Test," *LAT*, April 9, 1987.

78. "Asian Parents Find Schools an Education."

79. Jean Wang oral history.

80. Scholars have noted that public schools often represented the first suburban institution to deal with newly arrived immigrants, since they were mandated by law to provide education to children. Mary E. Odem, "Unsettled in the Suburbs: Latino Immigration and Ethnic Diversity in Metro Atlanta," in *Twenty-First Century Gateways: Immigrant Incorporation in Suburban America*, edited by Audrey Singer, Susan W. Hardwick, and Caroline B. Brettell (Washington DC: Brookings Institution Press, 2008), 123.

81. "Schools Divided? Racial Tension Surfaces in San Marino," *PSN*, March [n.d.] 1984; Jean Wang oral history; "Summary Report on San Marino Community Conflict" (June 20, 1984), San Marino Human Relations Committee, Jean Wang personal files.

82. "Summary Report on San Marino Community Conflict" (June 20, 1984); Jean Wang oral history; "Human Relations Plans Announced," *SMT*, June 7, 1984; "Panel Tackles Racial Problems in San Marino," *PSN*, June 13, 1984.

83. "County Asks Communities to Resolve Ethnic Tensions," *LAT*, July 6, 1980.

84. "Human Relations Issues" list, n.d., San Marino Human Relations Committee, Jean Wang personal files (emphasis in original).

85. "Human Relations Issues" list, n.d.

86. "Human Relations Get High Grades," *SMT*, October 18, 1984.

87. Leland T. Saito, *Race and Politics: Asian Americans, Latinos and Whites in a Los Angeles Suburb* (Urbana: University of Illinois Press, 1998), chapters 3 and 4; Timothy Fong, *First Suburban Chinatown: The Remaking of Monterey Park, Ca.* (Philadelphia: Temple University Press, 1994), chapters 4–7; John Horton, *The Politics of Diversity:*

Immigration, Resistance, and Change in Monterey Park, California (Philadelphia: Temple University Press, 1995); Li, *Ethnoburb*.

88. Nicolaides and Zarsadiaz, "Design Assimilation."

89. The *Los Angeles Times* conducted a survey of 13 municipalities on the matter and found San Marino's law to be the "most stringent" among them. "Arcadia Delays Decision on Home Sizes," *LAT*, December 21, 1989; "San Marino New Building Curbs Aim to Limit Density," *LAT*, October 8, 1987.

90. Willow Lung-Amam, "That 'Monster House' Is My Home: The Social and Cultural Politics of Design Reviews and Regulations," *Journal of Urban Design* 18, 2 (2013), 220–241; Jan Lin and Melody Chiong, "How Chinese Entrepreneurs Transformed the San Gabriel Valley," KCET website, May 20, 2016, accessed at: https://www.kcet.org/shows/departures/how-chinese-entrepreneurs-transformed-the-san-gabriel-valley; Judith Carter oral history; Willow S. Lung-Amam, "A New Generation of Single-Family Homes: Multigenerational Homebuilding in the Suburbs of Phoenix, Arizona," in *The Routledge Handbook of Housing Policy and Planning*, edited by Katrin B. Anacker, Mai Thi Nguyen, and David P. Varady (New York: Routledge, 2019), 357–370.

91. "Owner Cramped in Mansion San Marino Calls Plenty Big," *LAT*, October 28, 1990; "San Marino Estate District Offers Peace and Quiet at a Price," *LAT*, November 27, 1991.

92. Paul Crowley explained, "The Design Review Commission started in the 1990s. I precipitated it because I realized that the Planning Commission told me there were a lot of things that don't look good that are legal. And they don't have to go to the Planning Commission to be approved. . . . it doesn't look right, but it meets all the code. The Design Review we formed to give a subjective view on things." Paul Crowley oral history.

93. Paul Crowley oral history; "Monterey Park, Nation's First Suburban Chinatown," *LAT*, April 6, 1987; "San Gabriel Valley Asian Influx Alters Life in Suburbia," *LAT*, April 5, 1987; "Asian Newcomers Create Consternation in Arcadia," *LAT*, September 19, 1985; "Design Review Committee Members," roster of members, City Clerk's office, SMCH; "25.15.01 Design Review Committee Established," city zoning ordinances, SMCH.

94. "City of San Marino," a booklet for San Marino Residents (San Marino: San Marino City Hall, 1959–60); "City of San Marino," a booklet for San Marino Residents (San Marino: San Marino City Hall, 1967–68); "City of San Marino," a booklet for San Marino Residents (San Marino: San Marino City Hall, 1972); "City of San Marino," a booklet for San Marino Residents (San Marino: San Marino City Hall, 1980); "An Information Guide for Residents of San Marino" (San Marino: San Marino City Club, 1989), all from "Guides for Residents" vertical file, SMHS.

95. "City of San Marino: Residential Design Guidelines" (final revision: December 15, 1999), 53, City of San Marino; on the idea of historical continuity and design, see Duncan and Duncan, *Landscapes of Privilege*.

96. Paul Crowley oral history.

97. Alan Yung oral history; Robert Lay oral history, conducted by Becky Nicolaides, March 3 and April 20, 2015, San Marino, CA; Mark Chen oral history, conducted by Becky Nicolaides, March 5, 2015, San Marino, CA; Jean Wang oral history; Rosa Zee oral history; "Design Review Committee Members," roster of members.

98. Richard Sun oral history; "1990s: The Gold Decade, San Marino," *LAT*, January 15, 1990. On extended families in Chinese households, also see Lung-Amam, "That Monster House," 231–232.

99. Duncan and Duncan, *Landscapes of Privilege*, 221. The Duncans offer an excellent discussion of the powerful symbolism of old trees (219–223).

100. "Council Approves 45-Day Moratorium on Tree Removal," *SMT*, October 15, 1987; Paul Crowley oral history; Judith Carter oral history; Jean Wang oral history; Robert Lay oral history. While local press coverage did not associate Chinese residents with tree removal, several oral history informants made that connection explicit.

101. "1990s: The Gold Decade, San Marino," *LAT*, January 15, 1990; "SM Moves Closer to Tree USA Status," *SMT*, May 1, 1997; "City of San Marino Proclamation for Arbor Day," March 12, 1992, from Mark Chen personal files; Mark Chen oral history; Robert Lay oral history. Robert Lay noted that trees peaked as a contentious issue in the 1980s, but died down by the 1990s when a kind of interethnic consensus was reached.

102. Fong, *First Suburban Chinatown*, 63, 69, 105–106, 110–113, 145–146; "Stronger Rules on English in Signs Pushed by Council," *LAT*, December 5, 1985; "Monterey Park, America's First Suburban Chinatown," *LAT*, April 6, 1987.

103. Daniel HoSang, *Racial Propositions: Ballot Initiatives and the Making of Postwar California* (Berkeley: University of California Press, 2010), chapter 5; "Youth to Make San Marino 4th City to Weigh English Issue," *LAT*, March 9, 1986; "San Marino Youth Vows to Take English Issue to Voters," *LAT*, March 16, 1986; "In Praise of Freedom of Speech," *LAT*, March 27, 1986; "'Shocking' Coverage," *LAT*, April 3, 1986; "Council Hopefuls Against Proposal," *SMT*, March 20, 1986; "San Marino Language Petition Dropped," *LAT*, June 5, 1986.

   Forbes tried to revive the issue by circulating a petition to get the measure on the June ballot, but collected only 500 signatures, which fell short of the required 900. By contrast, the statewide "Official English" movement succeeded in California, with the passage of Proposition 63 in 1986. An excellent description of this movement is in HoSang, *Racial Propositions*, chapter 5.

104. "City Council Answers to Upset Citizens," *SMT*, October 22, 1987. San Marino's muted press coverage contrasted starkly with coverage of signage politics in Monterey Park, which dominated local media for years.

   The San Marino City Council minutes noted the following: "The Planning Commission conducted a public hearing on the proposed ordinance (No. 931) and unanimously recommended its adoption." The minutes of that Planning Commission hearing—presumably held on September 23, 1987—were missing from city records. San Marino City Council minutes, October 14, 1987; San Marino Planning Commission minutes, file for 1987/88, SMCH.

105. "City Council Answers to Upset Citizens," *SMT*, October 22, 1987; San Marino City Council minutes, July 8, August 12, October 14, 1987, SMCH; "1990s: The Gold Decade, San Marino," *LAT*, January 15, 1990; "Man Fights Thefts of Chinese Sign," *LAT*, January 14, 1989; Jean Wang oral history.

None of my oral history subjects—Chinese and Anglo alike—recalled the passage of the signage ordinance, suggesting a lack of public awareness of the issue or a reluctance to discuss it.

106. "Chinese Characters on Business Sign Bring Deep Resentments to the Surface," *SMT*, November 24, 1988; "In Any Language Vandalism Means Breaking the Law," *SMT*, November 24, 1988; "Man Fights Thefts of Chinese Sign," *LAT*, January 14, 1989; "Asian Broker Says 8 Teens Didn't Steal Chinese Signs," *LAT*, March 5, 1989.

When the vandals were caught and turned out to be local high school students, the realty office owner Caesar Wu asked the DA's office to drop the charges, noting: "Having this mark against them will affect them for the rest of their lives. It is too much for them to pay."

107. Mark Chen oral history; Robert Lay oral history; Rosa Zee oral history.

In nearby Arcadia, a similar interethnic consensus against Chinese-language signage existed. See "Challenge to Arcadia Sign Law Rebuffed: Discrimination," *LAT*, January 27, 1991.

108. "Through Thick and Thin," *PW*, March 31, 2011. This article mentions owners Frank and Linda Chen, who took over the restaurant in 2003.

109. San Marino maintained its position among the top wealthiest municipalities in LA County from 1950 to 2010; see Tables A2.7 and A2.8.

110. Allan Yung oral history; Robert Lay oral history. Jean Wang expressed similar sentiments.

111. Robert Lay oral history.

112. Mark Chen oral history; Robert Lay oral history; Becky Lei Ung oral history, conducted by Becky Nicolaides, via Skype (Taiwan to Los Angeles), March 8, 2015.

113. Janice Lee-McMahon oral history, conducted by Becky Nicolaides, August 16, 2012, San Marino, CA.

114. Matt Ballantyne oral history, conducted by Becky Nicolaides, July 19, 2012, San Marino, CA.

115. Denise Lawrence-Zuñiga, "Residential Design Guidelines, Aesthetic Governmentality, and Contested Notions of Southern California Suburban Places," *Economic Anthropology* 2, 1 (2015), 124, emphasizes the role of the state in shaping "a dominant aesthetic order."

116. Lung-Amam, "That 'Monster House.'" She makes the key point that archival silences around such issues might be plausibly explained by these factors.

117. Allan Yung oral history.

118. "She's Gained Respect 'Just for Being Me.'"

119. Rosa Zee oral history.

120. Allan Yung oral history.

121. Jean Wang oral history; Richard Sun oral history.

122. Jean Wang oral history; Allan Yung oral history; Rosa Zee oral history; Janice Lee-McMahon oral history; Richard Sun oral history.

123. Janice Lee-McMahon oral history.

124. Allan Yung oral history.

125. Rosa Zee oral history.

126. See Table A2.7 and Table A2.8.

127. See Table A2.13 (Stay-at-home wives in suburbs, 1950–2010); Nicolaides, "Map Room: Stay-at-Home Moms in Los Angeles County, 1950–2000," 2–8.

128. Pomeroy, *San Marino*, 216; "Alleged Drug Kingpin Seized in San Marino," *LAT*, December 14, 1990; "Drug Suspect Stood out in Posh Enclave," *LAT*, December 15, 1990; "Obituary: Jean Webb Vaughan Smith," *LAT*, January 27, 2012.

129. For example, see regular columns by Mary Lou Loper in the 1980s; an example of Rose Court is "Musical Whiz, Scholar Named '88 Rose Queen," *LAT*, October 28, 1987; that year, three San Marino students were princesses on the court; Pomeroy, *San Marino*, 229.

130. "Human Relations Get High Grades"; "1990s: The Gold Decade, San Marino," *LAT*, January 15, 1990.

131. Rosa Zee oral history.

132. "Meet Rosa Zee" campaign flyer, Rosa Zee personal files; "Q and A: School Board Candidates Give their Views," *SMT*, October 14, 1993; "She's Gained Respect." By her count, Zee put in thousands of hours of volunteer work, counseling students and parents and serving in various capacities in San Marino. When she ran for School Board, Zee was owner of a flower shop in Arcadia.

133. "Human Relations Get High Grades"; "Asian Parents Find Schools an Education."

134. "San Marino's Schools: Pockets of Poverty in a Community of Wealth," *LAT*, September 18, 1986.

135. "San Gabriel Valley Elections: San Marino," *LAT*, March 30, 1986; "Local Elections: Polished Rivals Face Lone School Tax Foe," *LAT*, May 29, 1986; "Special Tax for Schools Rejected in San Marino," *LAT*, June 6, 1986; "San Marino to Vote on Tax," *LAT*, October 27, 1994; "As States Cut Funding, More Districts Turn to Voters," *LAT*, June 15, 2009.

136. "San Marino's Schools," *LAT*, September 18, 1986; Johann Diel phone interview with author, August 1, 2012; San Marino Schools Foundation website at www.smsf. org; 1991 San Marino City Directory. The Schools Foundation did not track ethnic data on its donors.

137. Rosa Zee oral history; "San Marino's Schools," *LAT*, September 18, 1986. While Schrag, *Paradise Lost*, argues that Prop 13 killed civic spirits, that did not apply to a wealthy suburb like San Marino.

138. The groups that existed from 1950 onward included the American Legion, City Club, Daughters of the American Revolution, Garden Club, Lions Club, Rotary Club, Toastmasters Club, Woman's Club, and Republican (Women's) Club. (The last was listed as the Republican Women's Club in 1950, then opened its membership to men by 2000.) The groups that existed from 1960 onward included the National Charity League, Newcomers Club, Chamber of Commerce, and San Marino Guild of Huntington Hospital. See Figure A4.3 (Clubs in Pasadena and San Marino over time).

139. In contrast to nearby Pasadena, San Marino had only one "white lineage" organization—the Daughters of the American Revolution, which existed through 2010. Besides the Chinese Club, this was the only overtly ethnic group in the suburb.

140. The fate of the PEO—an ultra-secret women's organization—was more difficult to determine. One of my respondents claimed that the local PEO existed in 2012, however they had dropped out of listings in local city directories by the mid-1970s.

141. The Rotary Club first established a chapter in mainland China in 1919.

142. Robert Lay oral history; "San Marino Lion's Club, California, 1988–1989, Membership Roster," Robert Lay personal files.

143. For Lions, information accessed on May 15, 2015, at http://www.lionsclubs.org/EN/index.php. For Rotary, information accessed at https://my.rotary.org/en/club-search. For Kiwanis, information accessed at https://www.kiwanis.org/clubs. See Table A5.3 (International fraternal groups).

144. "San Marino: 2 Factions, 4 Candidates," LAT, March 30, 1986; "New Members List," San Marino City Club, February 20, 1990 and February 16, 1993, City Club vertical file, SMHS; Allan Yung oral history.

145. "San Marino Mayor Quits Club That Bars Women," LAT, February 3, 1996; "Lungren Visits Mens-Only Club, Draws Criticism," LAT, January 23, 1998; "An Uneasy Time at the Club," LAT, January 24, 1998; "San Marino City Club Opens Membership to Women," LAT, October 22, 1999; Janice Lee-McMahon oral history; Janice Lee-McMahon email to author, January 20 and 23, 2013; Tom and Perta Santley oral history. While the Santleys observed the City Club as on a decline, their standards were very high—Tom had been vigorously involved in numerous civic groups for decades.

146. Patricia Mar oral history, conducted by Becky Nicolaides, January 27, 2013, via telephone; https://sanmarinoarea.nationalcharityleague.org/our-chapter-history/, accessed January 15, 2013. After joining the NCL in 1997, Mar served as the first Chinese American president of the San Marino NCL Juniors (the adult chapter) in 2003.

   While some debutante groups slipped into cultural irrelevance or derision in the 1970s, this did not happen to the NCL in San Marino where its social status remained strong.

147. Pomeroy, San Marino, 194; Terry Golden telephone interview with author, November 26, 2012.

148. Shirley Donovan telephone interview with author, November 28, 2012; Newcomers Club, vertical file, SMHS.

149. Zhou and Li, "Ethnic Language Schools"; Zhou, Contemporary Chinese America; Becky Lei Ung oral history; Mark Chen oral history; Robert Lay oral history; Rosa Zee oral history; Allan Yung oral history.

150. Allan Yung oral history.

151. Rosa Zee oral history.

152. The Chinese Club underwrote the cost of the trip.

153. Rosa Zee oral history.

154. Tom and Perta Santley oral history.

155. Allan Yung oral history.

156. Around Chicago in the 1990s, "diversity dinners" were held in Park Forest, Illinois, and other nearby suburbs undergoing racial change. They were organized by the South Metropolitan Regional Leadership Council at Governors State University. "Diversity Dinners Foster Racial Understanding," *Park Forest Star*, April 29, 1999; "Diversity dinners reach 4th year," *The Star*, April 29, 2001 (from Local History Files, Park Forest Public Library).

157. Allan Yung oral history; "1990s: The Gold Decade, San Marino," *LAT*, January 15, 1990. Similar recollections of "Dinner for Eight" in Richard Sun oral history, Janice Lee-McMahon oral history.

158. "Manhattan Magic" San Marino High School Grad Night 1988 program, Grad Night vertical file, SMHS; "Grad Night: Parents Pass Tradition on to Children," *SMT*, June 2, 1988.

159. Allan Yung oral history.

160. Robert Lay oral history.

161. "Pirates of the Caribbean" San Marino High School Grad Night booklet, 1990, Grad Night vertical file, SMHS; Becky Lei Ung oral history; "Social Circuits," *LAT*, July 11, 2000.

162. "1990s: The Gold Decade, San Marino," *LAT*, January 15, 1990, parentheses in original; "San Marino's Schools: Pockets of Poverty," *LAT*, September 18, 1986; Rosa Zee oral history; Allan Yung oral history.

163. "School Parties for Grads," *LAT*, June 6, 1985; "Mira Costa High Revamps Grad Night," *LAT*, June 17, 1990; "Sobering Thoughts About Grad Nights," *LAT*, May 7, 1995.

164. Louisa Lim, *The People's Republic of Amnesia: Tiananmen Revisited* (New York: Oxford University Press, 2014); Jonathan D. Spence, *The Gate of Heavenly Peace: The Chinese and Their Revolution, 1895–1980* (New York: Penguin Books, 1981), 17–18.

165. Lim, *People's Republic*, 206–207.

166. Li Zhang, *In Search of Paradise: Middle Class Living in a Chinese Metropolis* (Ithaca: Cornell University Press, 2010), 1–9, chapter 3; Shenglin Chang, *The Global Silicon Valley Home: Lives and Landscapes Within Taiwanese American Trans-Pacific Culture* (Stanford: Stanford University Press, 2006); Park, *Consuming Citizenship*.

167. By the late 1990s, East West Bank was the region's fourth largest commercial bank. "California Becoming a Favorite Chinese Investment," *LAT*, June 29, 1997.

168. Peter J. Rimmer and Howard Dick, *The City in Southeast Asia: Patterns, Processes and Policy* (Honolulu: University of Hawaii Press, 2009), 28–42; Zhang, *In Search of Paradise*.

169. Class, more than ethnic identity, seemed to influence party preference, evident in more mixed voter registration in middle-class Asian suburbs. See Table A5.4 (Political profile Asian suburbs).

170. In San Marino, the proportion of registered voters was 97% of adults (18 and older) in 1980 and 85% in 2000, well above the state average (73%). On broader trends of voter engagement among Asian Americans, see Janelle S. Wong, *Democracy's*

Promise: Immigrants and American Civic Institutions (Ann Arbor: University of Michigan Press, 2006); James S. Lai, *Asian American Political Actions: Suburban Transformations* (Boulder, CO: Lynne Rienner Publishers, 2011).

171. "Regrouping in the Cold War"; "Cold War Still Has Bitter Chill for San Marino Bookstore Volunteers," *LAT*, June 9, 1989; "Inside the New (Old) Right," *PSN*, May 8, 1994; "Voice Regained; Birchers Resurge as Communism Fades," *LAT*, June 26, 1990. The JBS was even skeptical of the pro-democracy movement quelled in Tiananmen Square.

172. "Hong Kong, One Country, Two Systems, but Will It Be Free?" *LAT*, June 15, 1997; "Community Softens Line on Taiwan, China," *LAT*, November 2, 1997.

173. "She's Gained Respect"; Rosa Tao Zee campaign folder, Rosa Tao Zee personal files.

174. "Newcomers Add Lots of Cash to Race," *LAT*, April 5, 1992; "1992 Elections San Marino City Council," *LAT*, April 5, 1992; "Minorities Poised for Gains at Ballot Box," *LAT*, April 14, 1992; "Asian Americans Flex Growing Political Muscle," *LAT*, September 12, 2001; Allan Yung oral history; "City Council Members of San Marino, 1913–present," accessed at https://www.cityofsanmarino.org/government/mayor__ _city_council_/state_federal_local_resources.php. Yung's strategy of downplaying his ethnic heritage was typical of Asian Americans running for local office in the San Gabriel Valley in the 1990s.

175. Josie Huang, "In San Marino Election, Mansionization Is Top Worry," 89.3 KPCC, November 2, 2015, at https://www.scpr.org/news/2015/11/02/55374/in-san-mar ino-election-mansionization-is-leading-c/; "Quota Creativity: Wealthy Cities Plan to Call Servants' Quarters Low-Income Housing," *LAT*, April 23, 1993; "In the Neighborhood: San Marino, the Affluent Grapple with Low-Income Housing," *LAT*, June 14, 1993; Richard Sun oral history. Sun, who served on the city council from 2009 to 2017, suggested that accessory dwelling units (ADUs) were "probably one way we can meet that requirement, even without R-2 and R-3" zoning. Because of its small size, San Marino was required to provide a mere 13 units of affordable housing to fulfill its regional fair share.

176. Pomeroy, *San Marino*, 102–105; "San Marino's Lacy Park," *LAT*, March 26, 1987.

177. "Dogs, Lovers: Outsiders Flocking to San Marino Park," *LAT*, December 16, 1973; "Commission Views Letters on Future of SM's Lacy Park," *SMT*, April 4, 1974.

178. "Commission Views Letters on Future of SM's Lacy Park," *SMT*, April 4, 1974; "Commissioners to Study Lacy Park Question More," *SMT*, June 6, 1974.

179. "San Marino's Lacy Park," *LAT*, March 26, 1987.

180. "Prop. 13 Cited in Closure of Lacy Park on Weekends," *LAT*, July 13, 1978; "Postscript: San Marino Still Locks Park," *LAT*, August 11, 1980; "San Marino's Lacy Park," *LAT*, March 26, 1987.

181. "San Marino Oks Plan for Saturday Park Use," *LAT*, January 17, 1988; "San Marino Lacy Park Opens Saturdays," *LAT*, June 30, 1988.

182. "'Elitism' Seen in Park Policy," *LAT*, January 28, 1988.

183. "San Marino 170 People Use Park on Saturday," *LAT*, September 8, 1988; "San Marino Lacy Park open Sundays," *LAT*, May 12, 1991.

184. Steve Lopez, "You Pay to Play in Posh San Marino," *LAT*, December 12, 2007.

Chapter 6

1. James Botting, *Bullets, Bombs and Fast Talk: Twenty-Five Years of FBI War Stories* (Washington, DC: Potomac Books, Inc., 2008), 210; Sandra Martinez oral history, conducted by Becky Nicolaides (translated by Crystal Yanez), April 1, 2017, South Gate, CA. This bifurcated subjectivity around suburban life is also explored in Paul Maginn and Katrin Anacker, eds., *Suburbia in the 21st Century: From Dreamscape to Nightmare?* (New York: Routledge, 2023).

2. Becky Nicolaides, *My Blue Heaven: Life and Politics in the Working-Class Suburbs of Los Angeles, 1920–1965* (Chicago: University of Chicago Press, 2002), chapter 1; Juan de Lara, *Inland Shift: Race, Space, and Capital in Southern California* (Berkeley: University of California Press, 2018); Jacob Wegmann, "'We Just Built It': Code Enforcement, Local Politics, and the Informal Housing Market in Southeast Los Angeles County" (PhD dissertation, UC Berkeley, 2014); Raymond A. Rocco, "Latino Los Angeles: Reframing Boundaries/Borders," in *The City: Los Angeles and Urban Theory at the End of the Twentieth Century*, edited by Allen J. Scott and Edward W. Soja (Berkeley: University of California Press, 1996), 365–389; Manuel Pastor, "Maywood Not Mayberry: Latinos and Suburbia in Los Angeles County," in *Social Justice in Diverse Suburbs*, edited by Christopher Niedt (Philadelphia: Temple University Press, 2013), 129–154. On the class continuity of this area, see James R. Curtis, "Barrio Space and Place in Southeast Los Angeles, California," in *Hispanic Spaces, Latino Places: Community and Cultural Diversity in Contemporary America*, edited by Daniel D. Arreola (Austin: University of Texas Press, 2004), 137.

3. William Hudnut, *Halfway to Everywhere: A Portrait of America's First-Tier Suburbs* (Washington, DC: Urban Land Institute, 2003); Bernadette Hanlon, *Once the American Dream: Inner-Ring Suburbs of the Metropolitan United States* (Philadelphia: Temple University Press, 2010); Katrin Anacker, ed., *The New American Suburb: Poverty, Race and the Economic Crisis* (New York: Routledge, 2016); Bernadette Hanlon, John Rennie Short, and Thomas J. Vicino, *Cities and Suburbs: New Metropolitan Realities* (New York: Routledge, 2010), 132–133 on gateway suburbs.

4. Manuel Pastor, "Looking for Regionalism in All the Wrong Places: Demography, Geography, and Community in Los Angeles County," *Urban Affairs Review* 36 (July 2001), 727–782. One existing entity is the Gateway Cities Council of Governments, but it is mostly an advisory body.

5. On the whiteness of the American working class in this era, see Jefferson Cowie, *Stayin' Alive: The 1970s and the Last Days of the Working Class* (New York: New Press, 2010), 236.

6. Cowie, *Stayin' Alive*, 362; John Laslett, *Sunshine Was Never Enough: Los Angeles Workers, 1880–2010* (Berkeley: University of California Press, 2012).

7. A. K. Sandoval-Strausz, *Barrio America: How Latino Immigrants Saved the American City* (New York: Basic Books, 2019); A. K. Sandoval-Strausz, "Latino Landscapes: Postwar Cities and the Transnational Origins of a New Urban America," *Journal of American History* 101, 3 (December 2014), 804–831; Llana Barber, *Latino City:*

Immigration and Urban Crisis in Lawrence, Massachusetts (Chapel Hill: University of North Carolina Press, 2017); Mike Davis, *Magical Urbanism: Latinos Reinvent the U.S. Big City* (London: Verso, 2000).

8. David Harvey, *A Brief History of Neoliberalism* (New York: Oxford University Press, 2005); Douglas Massey, Jorge Durand, and Nolan Malone, *Beyond Smoke and Mirrors: Mexican Immigration in an Era of Economic Integration* (New York: Russell Sage Foundation, 2002).

9. Scholars have emphasized intraethnic conflict, solidarity, and everything in between. See, for example, David Gutiérrez, *Walls and Mirrors: Mexican American, Mexican Immigrants, and the Politics of Ethnicity* (Berkeley: University of California Press, 1995); Gilda Ochoa, *Becoming Neighbors in a Mexican American Community: Power, Conflict and Solidarity* (Austin: University of Texas Press, 2004), Lisa García Bedolla, *Fluid Borders: Latino Power, Identity, and Politics in Los Angeles* (Berkeley: University of California Press, 2005); Genevieve Carpio, Clara Irazábal, and Laura Pulido, "Right to the Suburb? Rethinking Lefebvre and Immigrant Activism," *Journal of Urban Affairs* 32, 2 (2011), 197–198; Matt Garcia, *A World of Its Own: Race, Labor and the Making of Greater Los Angeles, 1900–1970* (Chapel Hill: University of North Carolina Press, 2001); Jerry González, *In Search of the Mexican Beverly Hills* (New Brunswick: Rutgers University Press, 2017).

10. Nicolaides, *My Blue Heaven*, chapter 1.

11. González, *In Search of the Mexican Beverly Hills*, chapter 2.

12. For 1930, I estimate that 36 people in South Gate were part of this Mexican Mormon diaspora (based on sources cited in Note 14). On Mormon colonies in Mexico around this time, see John B. Wright, "Mormon Colonias of Chihuahua," *Geographical Review* 91, 3 (July 2001), 586–596; Thomas Romney, *The Mormon Colonies in Mexico* (Salt Lake City: University of Utah Press, 1938, reprinted 2005).

13. South Gate's median home value was $4,200.

14. Nicolaides, *My Blue Heaven*, 42. Information on South Gate's early Mexican residents reconstructed from US Bureau of the Census, *Fifteenth Census of the United States, 1930* (Washington, DC: GPO, 1930), Census Place: *South Gate, Los Angeles, California; Roll:* 171, *Page:* 15A, Enumeration District: *1353;* FHL microfilm: 2339906 (accessed at Ancestry.com). I cross-checked with additional 1940s records on Ancrestry.com, including US Census, Naturalization records, and city directories.

On repatriation policies in Los Angeles, see George Sánchez, *Becoming Mexican American: Ethnicity, Culture and Identity in Chicano Los Angeles, 1900–1945* (New York: Oxford University Press, 1993), 211–221; Gutiérrez, *Walls and Mirrors*, 72; Zaragosa Vargas, *Crucible of Struggle* (New York: Oxford University Press, 2011), 220.

15. Nicolaides, *My Blue Heaven*, chapters 1–4. While George Sánchez describes how homeownership represented permanence for Mexican Americans—a symbolic retort against an image as a perpetually mobile, unrooted people—in South Gate, with many immigrants, some undocumented, this was less true. Sánchez, *Becoming Mexican American*, 200.

16. Nicolaides, *My Blue Heaven*, 24–26, 76–77, 138.

17. Home movies are from the Prelinger Archives, accessed at https://archive.org/details/ HMScenesinPhoenix97239; https://archive.org/details/97246_hm_fishing_at_monmouth_lake_and_klamath_falls_home_at_south_gate_calif; https://archive.org/ details/97240_hm_scenes_around_phoenix_arizona_and_south_gate_california. I deduced the likely address and owner of the home using Google Earth and *South Gate City Directory* 1951.

18. Nicolaides, *My Blue Heaven*, 199, 226–230.

19. LA County Regional Planning Commission (LARPC), *The East Central Area, A Portion of Los Angeles County* (July 1, 1963), 20–22.

20. LARPC, *The East Central Area*, 21–22, 39; Gordon Whitnall and Associates, "Report on Proposed Comprehensive General Plan for South Gate, California," 1959, 16, SGHWL.

21. Nicolaides, *My Blue Heaven*, 199, 226–230; South Gate Chamber of Commerce, "Standard Industrial Survey Report," October 1970, SGHWL; 1973 figures from "S. Gate's 606 Industries Provide Jobs for 25,000," *HPDS*, January 19, 1973.

22. *South Gate "Blue Book" Criss Cross City Directory, 1961* (Anaheim: Luskey Brothers & Co., 1961); Bicentennial Heritage Committee, *South Gate 1776–1976* (South Gate: South Gate Press, 1976), 32–33; "Postwar Building Program for City of South Gate," *Architect and Engineer* (May 1944), 33–36; "South Gate Park Heart of City," *HPDS*, January 19, 1973. County and WPA funds also helped finance these facilities.

23. See Table A2.7 (Median family income).

24. US Census data set; Nicolaides, *My Blue Heaven*, chapter 6.

25. Nicolaides, *My Blue Heaven*, 194; US Census data set 1950–2000. From 1930 to 1960, the Census did not enumerate Latinos as a distinct group, but instead lumped them in with "whites"; the Census did conduct separate counts of "Spanish Surname" people in 1950 and 1960, used here.

26. On the racial position of Latinos, see Tomás Almaguer, *Racial Fault Lines: The Historical Origins of White Supremacy in California* (Berkeley: University of California Press, 2008); Eileen O'Brien, *The Racial Middle: Latinos and Asian Americans Living Beyond the Racial Divide* (New York: New York University Press, 2008); González, *In Search of the Mexican Beverly Hills*, 9.

27. Nicolaides, *My Blue Heaven*, 210–212, chapter 7; Matthew Lassiter, *The Silent Majority: Suburban Politics in the Sunbelt South* (Princeton: Princeton University Press, 2006) on the vulnerability of working-class neighborhoods to the burdens of school desegregation mandates.

28. On federal defense housing programs locally, see Nicolaides, *My Blue Heaven*, 190; Greg Hise, *Magnetic Los Angeles: Planning the Twentieth Century Metropolis* (Baltimore: Johns Hopkins University Press, 1997), 115, 120–121; on the national situation, see Sarah Jo Peterson, *Planning the Home Front* (Chicago: University of Chicago Press, 2013).

29. US Census data set; Nicolaides, *My Blue Heaven*, 220; "Veterans Demand Action on South Gate Housing," *LAT*, August 14, 1946.

30. "Local Housing Situation Serious," *SGP*, January 1, 1944; "Veteran and His Family Move into Trailer Home," *LAT*, November 11, 1945; "VFW Takes up Drive for

Vet Housing," *SGP*, January 17, 1946; "Veteran Ousts Parents Amid Mother's Protests," *LAT*, July 24, 1946; "Suspect in Killing Found at Hide-out," *LAT*, April 8, 1952; "Illegal Income Units May Prove Expensive," *LAT*, March 16, 1961; Kenneth Jackson, *Crabgrass Frontier* (New York: Oxford, 1985), 232; Becky Nicolaides, "From Resourceful to Illegal: The Racialized History of Garage Housing in Los Angeles," Boom California, January 31, 2019, https://boomcalifornia.org/2019/01/31/from-resourceful-to-illegal/; Wegmann, "We Just Built It," 18–23.

31. "Converting an Orchard Garage," *LAT*, April 14, 1946; "Tom Thumb Living," *LAT*, September 15, 1946; "A Garage Goes Formal," *LAT*, September 2, 1945; "The Cart Before the Horse," *LAT*, August 17, 1947; "Apartment in the Country," *LAT*, August 8, 1948; "Garage Transformation," *LAT*, May 15, 1949; Nicolaides, "From Resourceful."

32. US Bureau of Census, *1970 Census of Housing*, vol. 1 Housing Characteristics for States, Cities, and Counties, part 6 California (Washington, DC: GPO, 1972), 247.

33. James A. Jacobs, *Detached America: Building Houses in Postwar Suburbia* (Charlottesville: University of Virginia Press, 2015), 20–21.

34. "New Subdivision," *SGP*, February 21, 1946; "SG Commission to Act on New Subdivision," *SGP*, February 28, 1946; "Meadow Park" ad, *SGP*, May 8, 1947; Nicolaides, *My Blue Heaven*, 206–209.

35. South Gate density calculated using 7.5 square miles and population total of 53,831 in 1960, from Table A6.1 and *South Gate "Blue Book" Criss Cross City Directory*, 1961.

36. US Bureau of Census, *1970 Census of Housing*, vol. 1 Housing Characteristics for States, Cities, and Counties, part 6 California (Washington, DC: GPO, 1972), 247.

37. See Table A6.1 (Full South Gate data) and Table A6.2 (Housing tenure).

38. South Gate City Council minutes, 1950–1965, provide numerous examples of these complaints, as well as the council's incessant approval of new and used car lots in the 1950s (City Clerk's Office, SGCH). Also, Nicolaides, *My Blue Heaven*, 264–267.

South Gate also lacked a unifying master plan for growth, resulting in a fairly haphazard development process. See Whitnall "Report on Proposed Comprehensive General Plan," 9–14.

39. Ralph Guzman, "The Hand of Esau: Words Change, Practices Remain in Racial Covenants," *Frontier* 7 (June 1956), 13, 16; González, *In Search of the Mexican Beverly Hills*, 66–67; Gutiérrez, *Walls and Mirrors*. As with Asians, Latinos occupied a position in the "racial middle" between whites and Black Americans, making them more acceptable to white suburbanites. See González, *Mexican Beverly Hills*, 9; Josh Sides, *L.A. City Limits: African American Los Angeles from the Great Depression to the Present* (Berkeley: University of California Press, 2006); Max Felker-Kantor, "Fighting the Segregation Amendment," in *Black and Brown in Los Angeles*, edited by Josh Kun and Laura Pulido (Berkeley: University of California Press, 2014), 146; Charlotte Brooks, *Alien Neighbors, Foreign Friends* (Chicago: University of Chicago Press, 2009), 227.

40. Henry Gonzalez oral history, conducted by Becky Nicolaides, February 16, 2017, South Gate, CA.

41. Theresa Gonzalez oral history, conducted by Becky Nicolaides, April 24, 2017, South Gate, CA.

42. Theresa Gonzalez oral history; Henry Gonzalez oral history.

43. Theresa Gonzalez oral history; Henry Gonzalez oral history.
44. On Huntington Park, see "Cultures Follow Separate Paths in Huntington Park," *LAT*, April 7, 1990. This article mentions that the few Latinos who lived in Huntington Park in the early 1960s were "middle-class professionals who participated in civic activities."
45. US Census dataset; Nicolaides, *My Blue Heaven*, 194.
46. Mercedes González-Ontañon, "The Remaking of Los Angeles: Latino Suburbs, the Case of South Gate, 1966–2014" (unpublished seminar paper, Claremont Graduate University, December 2014), 2, 8–9.
47. Nicolaides, *My Blue Heaven*, chapter 7.
48. Guzman, "The Hand of Esau," 13, 16.
49. Guzman, "The Hand of Esau"; Davis McEntire, *Residence and Race: Final and Comprehensive Report to the Commission on Race and Housing* (Berkeley: University of California Press, 1960), 241–242; Rose Helper, *Racial Policies and Practices of Real Estate Brokers* (Minneapolis: University of Minnesota Press, 1969), 234–235; Milton L. McGhee and Ann Fagan Ginger, "House I Live In: A Study of Housing for Minorities," *Cornell Law Review* 45, 2 (Winter 1961), 249; "California Suits Against Housing Discrimination May Have Effect Here," *Honolulu Record* 9, 2 (August 9, 1956), 7. The two suits were *Wing v. Southeast Realty Board* and *Beddoe v. Southeast Realty Board*, Los Angeles County Superior Court, Department A, SG C-1125 and SG C-1050 (1956).
50. On Latino entry into suburbia, see González, *In Search of the Mexican Beverly Hills*, 46–69; Genevieve Carpio, *Collision at the Crossroads* (Oakland: University of California Press, 2019), chapter 5.
51. On Black Americans, see Emily E. Straus, *Death of a Suburban Dream: Race and Schools in Compton, California* (Philadelphia: University of Pennsylvania Press, 2014); Sides, *L.A. City Limits*.
52. Herbert Gans, *The Levittowners* (New York: Columbia University Press, 1967), 26–27.
53. Persistence rates in South Gate were fairly average. See Table A6.3 (Persistence rates).
54. Henry Gonzalez oral history; "Club Calendar," *SGP*, January 3, 1960; Dorothea Lombardo Letter to the Editor, *SGP*, April 24, 1982.
55. Bicentennial, *South Gate 1776–1976*, 47–57; Henry Gonzalez oral history; Nicolaides, *My Blue Heaven*, 261–262.
56. The clubs were from Compton, Crenshaw-Los Angeles, El Monte, Downey, Huntington Park, Montebello, Norwalk, South Gate-Lynwood, and Whittier. "Soroptimists Build Village for Seniors," *LAT*, June 30, 1963.
57. The federal Housing and Home Finance Agency (1947–1965) was a precursor to HUD. The Soroptimist's housing project was aided by Section 207 of the Federal Housing Act (1934), which helped finance multifamily housing projects, including for the elderly.
58. "Women: Soroptimist Clubs Give Unselfishly," *LAT*, January 21, 1951; "Low-Cost Rental Village for Aged is Aim of Drive," *LAT*, September 3, 1957; "Area Soroptimist Clubs Seek Housing for the Elderly," *LAT*, December 2, 1957; "New FHA Plan Houses Aging," *LAT*, April 9, 1958; "Soroptimists Build Village for Seniors"; "Dream Project

Became Model in Housing for Senior Citizens," *LAT*, January 9, 1972; "Norwalk 'Village' Marks 25th Year of Low Rents," *LAT*, July 1, 1988.

59. Nicolaides, *My Blue Heaven*, 232, 260–262; Henry Gonzalez oral history.

60. "Azalea Festival 1969, 4th Annual" (South Gate City and Chamber of Commerce, March 1969); "South Gate's 6th Annual Azalea Festival" (South Gate City and Chamber of Commerce, March 1971); "Azalea Festival 1980" (South Gate City and Chamber of Commerce, March 1980), all at SGHWL; "Service Award Honors Woman in South Gate," *LAT*, February 16, 1975; "Parent-Teacher Group Lauds Woman's Record," *SGP*, April 1, 1981.

61. Theresa Gonzalez oral history; South Gate Coordinating Council, Directory 1965–1966, Box 3, File 18, SGHWL.

62. Nicolaides, *My Blue Heaven*, 249–255, 280–281; Myrna Cherkoss Donahoe, "Workers' Response to Plant Closures: The Case of Steel and Auto in Southeast Los Angeles, 1936–1986" (PhD dissertation, UC Irvine, 1987), 242–243; "Mexican wedding," from City Council Minutes, August 22, 1960, SGCH, September 12, 1960. The word "Mexican" was redacted from the minutes with a taped-on strip of paper.

63. Kathy Seal, *American Daughter* (unpublished manuscript), 59–60; Kathy Seal oral history, conducted by Becky Nicolaides, May 6, 2017, via Skype; Virgil Collins oral history, conducted by Becky Nicolaides, August 20, 1991, Artesia, CA. On the October League, see Robert J. Alexander, *Maoism in the Developed World* (Westport, CT: Prager 2001), 31–32.

64. Nicolaides, *My Blue Heaven*, 257–258; "Top Amateurs Clash Tonight," *LAT*, January 17, 1950; "Tiscareno and Jimenez Top Card at South Gate," *LAT*, December 14, 1953.

65. "L.A. Women's Bowling Meet," *LAS*, March 8, 1956; "Bowling," *LAS*, May 23 and June 6, 1963; "LAWBA Opens Meeting," *LAS*, March 23, 1967; "Bowling Around L.A.," *LAS*, April 6 and November 9, 1967.

66. These activities were similar to other cultural practices in Los Angeles—like music, custom cars, and even foodways—that were transgressing ethnoracial boundaries and shifting the meaning of suburban culture. See Daniel Widener, *Black Arts West: Culture and Struggle in Postwar Los Angeles* (Durham: Duke University Press, 2010); González, *In Search of the Mexican Beverly Hills*, 131–135; Garcia, *A World of Its Own*; Mark Padoongpatt, "A Landmark for Sun Valley: Wat Thai of Los Angeles and Thai American Suburban Culture in 1980s San Fernando Valley," *Journal of American Ethnic History* 34, 2 (Winter 2015), 83–114.

67. "Floats and Choral Groups Expected to Attract Thousands," *SGP*, December 18, 1947; "'Beauty and Beast' Takes First Place in Colorful Christmas Parade," *SGP*, December 25, 1947; "100,000 Line Street to See Huge SG Parade," *SGP*, December 14, 1950; "Santa Greets Thousands in Tweedy Blvd. Parade," *SGP*, December 20, 1951; "Boulevard Parade is Success," *SGP*, December 9, 1954; "60,000 to Watch Parade," *SGP*, December 1, 1957; "Casimir Sparked Growth," *SGP*, June 20, 1963; "Top Local Events of '79," *SGP*, January 2, 1980; "'Tis the Season to Spread Happiness Along the Tinsel Parade Routes," *LAT*, November 28, 1985; "All the World's a Parade for South Gate Couple," *LAT*, March 31, 1991.

68. "'Apartment House' Population Increase Worries Co-Council," *SGP*, November 3, 1955; "South Gate Expansion is Over, Leaders Leaving," *SGP*, December 8, 1955; "City Delinquency Survey Suggests Many Projects," *SGP* April 5, 1956. While this negative view of renters reflected widespread attitudes, it contradicted William Whyte's study of Park Forest, Illinois, which found that transiency and renting could spark high levels of community engagement among suburbanites. See Constance Perin, *Everything in Its Place: Social Order and Land Use in America* (Princeton: Princeton University Press, 1977); William H. Whyte, *The Organization Man* (New York: Simon and Schuster, 1956), 287.

69. Whitnall, "Report on Comprehensive General Plan for South Gate," 3, 6.

70. Ordinance No. 647 (May 1, 1954), Ordinance No. 824 (February 8, 1960), Ordinance 863 (January 22, 1962), City Clerk's Office, SGCH. The 1961 zoning map for South Gate showed a majority of lots zoned as R-3 (multifamily dwellings), even though many of those properties were built with single-family homes. 1961 map printed in *SGP*, August 3, 1961.

71. "Evaluation and Summary of Planning Study: City of South Gate" (unpublished paper, Planning Studio Class 1964–65, USC Graduate Program in City and Regional Planning, May 1965), SGHWL; South Gate City Council minutes, June 2, 1965, SGCH.

72. Nicolaides, *My Blue Heaven*, chapter 7, quotes at 295, 303.

73. "Skip" Marilyn Echols, "Lynwood/South Gate, California" (unpublished manuscript, December 1990), 5–6, quote at 6, SGHWL; Bicentennial, *South Gate 1776–1976*, 38; "South Gate Azalea Festival to Begin 10-Day Run Friday," *LAT*, March 11, 1976; "Azalea Festival" file, SGHWL; "History of Azalea Festival," files of Ruth Lampmann, in author's possession.

74. "Inquests on 30 Riot Dead to Begin Tuesday," *LAT*, September 12, 1965; Nicolaides, *My Blue Heaven*, 323.

75. Charles M. Haar, ed., *The End of Innocence: A Suburban Reader* (Glenview, IL: Scott, Foresman & Co., 1972), 16–18; Charles M. Haar, ed., *The President's Task Force on Suburban Problems: Final Report* (Cambridge, MA: Ballinger Publishing Co, 1974), 28–29. Works that explore different angles of the suburban crisis include Matt Lassiter, *The Suburban Crisis: White America and the War on Drugs* (Princeton: Princeton University Press, 2023); Kyle Riismandel, *Neighborhood of Fear: The Suburban Crisis in American Culture, 1975–2001* (Baltimore: Johns Hopkins University Press, 2020).

76. "Firestone a Force for Good in City" and "GM Makes 4 Millionth Car," *SGP*, May 1977, Box 3, file 36, SGHWL; "GM Adds $92 Million to Economy," *SGP*, January 2, 1980; "Firestone Tire Pumps $34.6 Million into Area," *SGP*, February 6, 1980.

77. "UAW Leader Tries but Fails to Ease Anger over Layoffs," *LAT*, January 14, 1974.

78. "Expected Happens: Firestone Shutdown to Idle 990 Workers," *SGP*, March 22, 1980; "City Politics, Plant Closures Make Top Stories," *SGP*, January 3, 1981.

79. "GM Layoffs Take Personal Toll," *SGP*, November 21, 1981.

80. "GM: 'Sleeping Giant' to Reawaken," *SGP*, January 3; 1981; "GM Enthusiastic About Future," *SGP*, February 14, 1981; "Meeting to Focus on Plant Closures," *SGP*, April 18, 1981; "Coalition to Hear Economist, Author," *SGP*, April 22,1981; "Plant

Closures Are a National Problem," *SGP*, May 2, 1981; Donahoe, "Workers' Response to Plant Closures," 297–311. Also see *SGP* coverage on October 24, November 11, 21, 1981.

81. "Festival Events Continue Despite Weather," *SGP*, March 17, 1982; "Saturday UAW Rally Draws 200 to Union Hall," *SGP*, March 20, 1982. As though in a state of existential denial, the *South Gate Press* ran more coverage of the Azalea Festival than the GM plant closure at this time.

82. GM's Guaranteed Income Stream, the name of its severance benefit, was offered only to workers with at least 10 years seniority at GM.

83. Seal, *American Daughter*, 151–162. Seal raised the idea that the union should draw up a list of volunteers to go to Oklahoma as a way of pushing back against GM.

84. Ed Soja, *Postmodern Geographies: The Reassertion of Space in Critical Social Theory* (London: Verso, 1989), chapter 8; Curtis, "Barrio Space and Place," 133–136; Saskia Sassen, *The Mobility of Labor and Capital: A Study in International Investment and Labor Flow* (Cambridge: Cambridge University Press, 1988).

85. David R. Dias, *Barrio Urbanism: Chicanos, Planning and American Cities* (New York: Routledge, 2005), 103–105; Gregory Squires, "Capital Mobility Versus Upward Mobility: The Racially Discriminatory Consequences of Plant Closings and Corporate Relocations," in *Sunbelt/Snowbelt*, edited by Larry Sawers and William K. Tabb (New York: Oxford University Press, 1984), 152-162; John R. Logan and Harvey L. Molotch, *Urban Fortunes: The Political Economy of Place* (Berkeley: University of California Press, 1987), 282–283.

86. Rocco, "Latino Los Angeles," 374–375; Curtis, "Barrio Space and Place," 138; "Recall Election, Gas Panic," *SGP*, January 2, 1980.

87. "Chamber Expresses Concern," *SGP*, April 7, 1982; "Reopening of GM Plant Considered a Possibility," *SGP*, April 17, 1982; "Local Groups Band Together," *SGP*, June 30, 1982; "Volunteers Work to Bring Holiday Cheer to Needy," *LAT*, December 8, 1983. Huntington Park and South Gate were leading an effort with the California Employment Development Department to designate the southeast suburbs a "high unemployment region"—including South Gate, Bell, Bell Gardens, Cudahy, Huntington Park, Lynwood, and Maywood ("EDD Effort Could Lead to More Jobs," *SGP*, September 22, 1982).

88. Pierrette Hondagneu-Sotelo and Manuel Pastor, *South Central Dreams: Finding Home and Building Community in South L.A.* (New York: New York University Press, 2021), 6; Josh Sides, "Straight into Compton: American Dreams, Urban Nightmares, and the Metamorphosis of a Black Suburb," *American Quarterly*, 56 (September 2004), 585–605; Josh Sides, ed., *Post Ghetto: Reimagining South Los Angeles* (Berkeley: University of California Press and Huntington Library, 2012); Susan Phillips, *Operation Fly Trap: LA Gangs, Drugs, and the Law* (Chicago: University of Chicago Press, 2012).

89. Sandoval-Strausz, *Barrio America*; Vargas, *Crucible of Struggle*, 344–346.

90. See Table A6.4 ("Hispanics" in gateway suburbs).

91. Rudolfo F. Acuña, *Occupied America: A History of Chicanos* (New York: Pearson Longman, 2007), 297–298; Allen and Turner, *Ethnic Quilt*, 108; Hondagneu-Sotelo and Pastor, *South Central Dreams*.

92. In 1990, the median age of Latinos was 24, compared to 51 for whites. US Census dataset 1970, 1990. Also see Jorge Leal, "Ephemeral Forums, Enduring Communities: Latina/o Community Building and Belonging in 1990s South East Los Angeles" (PhD dissertation, UC San Diego, 2018).

93. See Table A6.5 (Occupations of Latinos in South Gate). South Gate also had a relatively high proportion of stay-at-home-wives. See Table A2.13 (Stay-at-home wives in suburbs).

94. Table A6.1 (Full South Gate data); Nicolaides, *My Blue Heaven*, 194; US Census of Housing, 1960–2010; González, *In Search of the Mexican Beverly Hills*, 10–11; "Living the Dream," *LAT*, September 24, 1995. South Gate's homeownership rates were on the high end compared to other gateway suburbs. (Wegmann, "We Just Built It," 76). On Latino homeownership in South LA, see Hondagneu-Sotelo and Pastor, *South Central Dreams*, 67–70.

95. Karen Brodkin, *Power Politics: Environmental Activism in South Los Angeles* (New Brunswick: Rutgers University Press, 2009), 33–34.

96. "Inland Communities Get Rich Ethnic Mix," *LAT*, December 5, 1982; "Prices Lure Buyers; Friendliness Keeps Them," *LAT*, September 22, 1991; "Anderson Says Busing Could Improve Education Quality," *SGP*, May 9, 1984; Sandra Martinez oral history; Celene Leyva oral history, conducted by Becky Nicolaides (Crystal Yanez translator), May 23, 2017, South Gate, CA.

97. Graham McNeill, "Deindustrialization and the Evolution of the Working-Class Suburban Dream in Southeast Los Angeles (1965–1990)" (unpublished seminar paper, Claremont Graduate University, 2014), 5, 9; González-Ontañon, "The Remaking of Los Angeles," 9–10; "Two Anti-Blockbusting Laws Win Approval in South Gate," *LAT*, November 30, 1972; "Fear, Mistrust Develop in Wake of 2-City Realty Boom," *LAT*, December 24, 1972; "Efforts to Resolve South Gate Realty Sign Issue Stalemated," *LAT*, March 1, 1973; "South Gate Attempts to Rectify Improper Vote," *LAT*, March 18,1973; "South Gate Realty Sign Ban Proposal Fails," *LAT*, April 12, 1973.

98. Virgil Collins oral history, conducted by Becky Nicolaides, August 25, 1991, Laguna Hills, CA.

99. Brodkin, *Power Politics*, 21; Jose Valenzuela oral history, conducted by Becky Nicolaides, May 21, 2020, via Zoom.

100. Letters quotes from *SGP*, July 9, 16, August 2, 9, 1980; ads in *SGP* in 1980, 1981. More letters to the editor appeared in *SGP*, August 9, September 9, 24, 1980, July 11, 1981.

101. McNeill, "Deindustrialization," 9–10.

102. Sides, *L.A. City Limits*; González, *In Search of the Mexican Beverly Hills*; Felker-Kantor, "Fighting the Segregation Amendment," 146.

103. Veronica Lopez oral history, conducted by Becky Nicolaides, March 6, 2017, South Gate, CA.

104. On informal housing practices more broadly, see Vinit Mukhija, "Outlaw In-Laws: Informal Second Units and the Stealth Reinvention of Single-Family Housing," in *The Informal American City*, edited by Vinit Mukhija and Anastasia Loukaitou-Sideris (Cambridge, MA: MIT Press, 2014), 39–45; Diana R. Gordon, *Village of Immigrants: Latinos in an Emerging America* (New Brunswick: Rutgers University Press, 2015); Tim Keogh, *In Levittown's Shadow: Poverty in America's Wealthiest*

Postwar Suburb (Chicago: University of Chicago Press, 2023); Katrin Anacker and Christopher Niedt, "Classifying Regulatory Approaches of Jurisdictions for Accessory Dwelling Units: The Case of Long Island," *Journal of Planning Education and Research* (2019), 1–21.

105. McNeill, "Deindustrialization," 11–21.

106. "Watching a Dream Become a Nightmare," *LAT*, October 1, 1989.

107. Both cases were dismissed on a procedural technicality. "Communities Fight Misuse of Funds," *El Chicano*, March 10, 1977, 10, SGHWL; CDBG Training Advisory Committee, "An Advocacy Guide to the Community Development Block Grant Program," 12 *Clearinghouse Review* 601 (1979, January Supplement), 667.

108. "South Gate Housing Element Rejected by HUD," *SGP*, April 24, 1982; "City Revises Housing Element," *SGP*, September 29, 1982; "Apartment Construction Ban Wins Approval," *SGP*, April 18, 1984; "City Council Moves on Ban of New Multi-Unit Housing," *SGP*, May 16, 1984; Wegmann, "We Just Built It," 166, 219–220.

109. Mike Davis, "The New Industrial Peonage," *Heritage* (newsletter of the Southern California Library for Social Studies and Research), Summer 1991, 10–11.

110. "Watching a Dream Become a Nightmare."

111. Jake Wegmann, "Research Notes: The Hidden Cityscapes of Informal Housing in Suburban Los Angeles and the Paradox of Horizontal Density," *Buildings and Landscapes* 22, 2 (Fall 2015), 89–110; Jake Wegmann and Sarah Mawhorter, "Measuring Informal Housing Production in California Cities," *Journal of the American Planning Association* 83, 2 (Spring 2017), 119–130.

112. "Illegal Garage and Shed Habitations Becoming Rife Throughout Southeast," *SGP*, April 29, 1981; "Garage Conversions Are Problem for Cities," *SGP*, June 20, 1984; "Southeast Cities Launch Crackdown on Eyesores," *LAT*, September 8, 1983; "Garages: Immigrants In, Cars Out," *LAT*, May 24, 1987. Mukhija, "Outlaw In-Laws," shows the ubiquity of these informal units across LA City, not just in poor neighborhoods. By 1997, LA City reported between 50,000 and 100,000 illegal garage conversions within the city limits (*LAT*, May 28, 1997). On informal housing nationally, see Noah J. Durst and Jake Wegmann, "Informal Housing in the United States," *International Journal of Urban and Regional Research* 41, 2 (March 2017), 282–297.

113. "South Gate Proposal Would Crack Down on Illegal Housing," *LAT*, March 14, 1985.

114. Figures come from "South Gate Race Focuses on City Code Crackdown," *LAT*, February 9, 1986; "Garages: Immigrants In, Cars Out"; "Illegal Garage and Shed Habitations"; US Census, *General Population Characteristics, California*, 1990, 1097. Also see other coverage in *LAT*, September 8, 1983, March 14, 1985.

   I arrived at this estimate using the following reported data: one report suggested that converted dwellings housed an average of five people. The US Census counted 4.52 persons per Hispanic family in South Gate in 1990. From 1984 to 1987, in South Gate, 1,000 families had been evicted from garage dwellings and about 4,000 occupied garages remained. Taking these data, I calculated the following:

   1,000 evicted families (4.52 persons/family) = 4,520 people
   4,000 remaining garage units (5 people/unit) = 20,000 people
   Total: 24,520 living in the units over the years 1984–1987. This is an approximation.

115. "Tough Stance on Garage Conversions," *LAT*, December 21, 1996.

116. "Garages: Immigrants In, Cars Out"; "Garage Conversions Are Problem for Cities" (on cost estimates); Veronica Lopez oral history.

117. "Fire Started by 6-Year-Old Kills 3," *LAT*, September 15, 1994; "Tough Stance on Garage Conversions." Unfortunately, the *SGP* after 1984 was unavailable at area libraries.

118. Veronica Lopez oral history; "Illegal Garage and Shed Habitations"; "Garages: Immigrants In, Cars Out"; Wegmann, "We Just Built It," 140–148. Such practices resembled the *encarcado* system flourishing at this time in suburban Long Island among Salvadoran immigrants; see Sarah J. Mahler, *American Dreaming: Immigrant Life on the Margins* (Princeton: Princeton University Press, 1995), chapter 8. On other informal housing arrangements among Latinos in Long Island, see Keogh, *In Levittown's Shadow*; Gordon, *Village of Immigrants*, chapter 7.

119. Wegmann, "We Just Built It," 146. Wegmann's excellent study of the period 2011–2014 reveals the dynamics of the system, which we might cautiously assume applied to the 1980–2000 period as well.

120. Jose Valenzuela oral history; Veronica Lopez oral history; "Illegal Garage and Shed Habitations."

121. Wegmann, "We Just Built It," 144–146; Veronica Lopez oral history; "Garages: Immigrants In, Cars Out"; John Sheehy oral history, conducted by Becky Nicolaides, June 19, 1990, South Gate, CA.

　　In late 1998, a landlord named Ted Ross—based in South Gate—owned a property in Watts used as an immigrant "drop house." That year, 36 smuggled immigrants were held at the property in a converted garage in squalid conditions until payment could be made to smugglers to release them. (*LAT*, June 17, 1998).

122. "Housing Strained at Seams," *LAT*, December 19, 1999; I calculated South Gate's density level based on its 2000 population of 96,418, and its area of 7.5 square miles. Since the census likely undercounted, the density level was probably higher. For more details on density, see Wegmann, "We Just Built It," 65, 120–130; Nicolaides, "From Resourceful to Illegal."

123. James Rojas, "The Enacted Environment of East Los Angeles," *Places* 8, 3 (Spring 1993), 42–53.

124. Wegmann, "We Just Built It," 112–113; "Hue and Cry over Colors of Homes," *LAT*, September 22, 1998; Veronica Lopez oral history.

125. Wegmann, "We Just Built It," 90.

126. City of South Gate, "Housing Element," in South Gate General Plan 2035, January 2014, p 24, accessed at http://www.southgatecc.org/community/planning-division/. In 2011, South Gate had 199 unhoused individuals, comprising 0.21% of the total population. The LA County rate was 0.46% of the total population.

127. Historian Zaragosa Vargas described this nativism as "the racist blowback of economic globalization"; in California, it materialized as Propositions 187 and 209, which denied immigrants access to public services and abolished affirmative action. Vargas, *Crucible of Struggle*, 344–347, 356–359.

128. David Gutiérrez, "Migration, Emergent Ethnicity, and the 'Third Space': The Shifting Politics of Nationalism in Greater Mexico," *Journal of American History*

(September 1999), 481–517; Brodkin, *Power Politics*, 34; Sam Quinones, *Antonio's Gun and Delfino's Dream: True Tales of Mexican Migration* (Albuquerque: University of New Mexico Press, 2007), 72.

129. Adam Goodman, *The Deportation Machine: America's Long History of Expelling Immigrants* (Princeton: Princeton University Press, 2020).

130. For an excellent discussion of local authority over immigration enforcement, see Monica Varsanyi, "City Ordinances as 'Immigration Policing by Proxy': Local Governments and the Regulation of Undocumented Day Laborers," in *Taking Local Control: Immigration Policy Activism in U.S. Cities and States*, edited by Monica W. Varsanyi (Stanford: Stanford University Press, 2010), 135-154. My thanks to Genevieve Carpio for highlighting the theme of "insecurity" among Latinos in suburbs in this era.

131. Goodman, *Deportation Machine*, 107–126. Goodman shows how the US expelled 13 million immigrants from 1965 to 1985, most of them Mexicans including many long-term residents.

132. "400 Illegal Aliens Seized as Coast Roundup Goes On," *NYT*, June 10, 1973; "Latinos Join to Condemn Raids," *LAT*, May 9, 1982.

133. Goodman, *Deportation Machine*, 131; "South Gate Woman's Story: Threats, Abuses Claimed in Raid," *LAT*, May 9, 1982; "Deportation Didn't Last Long," *LAT*, October 28, 1979.

134. Goodman, *Deportation Machine*, 124.

135. Goodman, *Deportation Machine*, 121–130; Jose Valenzuela oral history.

136. "Neighborhood Raids for Illegal Aliens Resumed," *LAT*, October 10, 1979; "Deportation Didn't Last Long"; "The Raids Are Wrong," *LAT*, October 30, 1979; Goodman, *Deportation Machine*, 130; Max Felker-Kantor, *Policing Los Angeles: Race, Resistance, and the Rise of the LAPD* (Chapel Hill: University of North Carolina Press, 2018), chapter 7.

137. Leal, "Ephemeral Forums," 7, 14–15; "Huntington Park Department Leads Southeast in Police Brutality Claims," *LAT*, July 6, 1986; Carpio, et al., "Right to the Suburb?" 197–198.

138. "Illegal Aliens Said to Take Most New Jobs," *SGP*, June 20, 1984; though this article navigated between the positions of the RAND report, organized labor, and employers, the headline conveyed a critical view of undocumented workers.

139. For examples of the extensive press coverage of school overcrowding in this period, see *SGP*, April 16; June 7, 14; September 13; October 8; August 16, 1980; January 3, 1981; *LAT*, October 9, 1978, February 9, 1986.

140. "Southeast Cities Launch Crackdown on Eyesores."

141. "Enforcement Change for City Building Code," *SGP*, January 17, 1981; "Southeast Cities Launch Crackdown on Eyesores"; South Gate Ordinance No. 1562, April 11, 1983, City Clerk's Office, SGCH.

142. "Southeast Cities Launch Crackdown on Eyesores"; "South Gate Escalates Fight Against Blight," *LAT*, September 6, 1984; "South Gate Race Focuses on City Code Crackdown." South Gate budgeted $265,000 in 1984, and $335,000 in 1986 for the enforcement of municipal building codes.

498 NOTES TO PAGES 315–319

143. South Gate Ordinance No. 1651-A, April 3, 1985, City Clerk's Office, SGCH "South Gate Proposal Would Crack Down on Illegal Housing."

144. Veronica Lopez oral history; Wegmann, "We Just Built It," 150–152. Also see Mukhija, "Outlaw In-Laws."

145. South Gate City Council minutes, January 27, 1986, 7, February 10, 1986, 5, SGCH.

146. "'City of Hollydale' Considered," SGP, September 25, 1986 (Box 6, file 14, SGHWL); South Gate City Council minutes, May 27, 1986, SGCH. Swisher was part of a citizen movement to overturn South Gate's laws against garage conversions.

147. South Gate City Council minutes, January 27, 1986, February 10, 1986, SGCH.

148. "Tough Stance on Garage Conversions." One councilman, for example, reported on complaints from a resident that "illegal aliens" were living in a garage on their street (South Gate City Council minutes, May 27, 1986).

149. "Watching a Dream Become a Nightmare."

150. Veronica Lopez oral history; Wegmann, "We Just Built It," 216.

151. South Gate City Council minutes, May 27, 1986, 8, SGCH; "Park Traffic Problems Get Council Attention," SGP, November 12, 1980; "Hollydale Park's Soccer Fields Will Be Relocated," SGP, March 18, 1981.

152. "Vendors Finding It Harder to Ply Wares," LAT, September 23, 1990.

153. South Gate Ordinance 1952 (June 22, 1993); South Gate Ordinance 1951 (June 22, 1993) and Ordinance 2301 (December 11, 2012); South Gate Ordinance 1948 (May 25, 1993), and associated city council minutes, SGCH; also see http://www.codepub lishing.com/CA/SouthGate/#!/SouthGate07/SouthGate0742.html#7.42.   Other sources claim South Gate passed measures outlawing piñata parties at the park and overnight street parking; see Quinones, Antonio's Gun, 70; Brodkin, Power Politics, 98.

154. "Sign Law Would Require English in South Gate," LAT, October 20, 1985; "Letter to Editor: English Sign Law Example of Bias," LAT, November 3, 1985; "More Study Urged on Proposed Sign Ordinance," LAT, November 10, 1985; "English-Only Sign Bill Sidetracked," LAT, November 17, 1985; South Gate City Council minutes, December 18, 1985, 5, January 13, 1986, 4; South Gate Ordinance 1718 (1986), SGCH. Nearby Bellflower launched a similar effort in 1987, which also met with Latino resistance (LAT, February 15, 1987).

155. "Hue and Cry over Color of Homes"; "South Gate Council Postpones Vote," LAT, September 24, 1998; Nita Lelyveld, "Infusion of Fuchsia Rattles a California City's Staid Beige," Philadelphia Inquirer, October 5, 1998; Carol Morello, "California Town May Tone Down Loud House Hues," USA Today, November 6, 1998; South Gate Community Development "Agenda Bill" for city council, Item #7, August 31, 1998, City Clerk's office, SGCH.

156. See Figure A6.1.

157. Many suburbs embraced the same "retail" emphasis to recover from Proposition 13 cuts to municipal revenue. See William Fulton, The Reluctant Metropolis: The Politics of Urban Growth in Los Angeles (Point Arena, CA: Solano Press Books, 1997), 261.

158. "South Gate City Is Tops in Area for Entrepreneurs," LAT, October 23, 1994; Brent Keltner, et al., "Sustaining Innovation in South Gate: A Framework for Restructuring City Government," RAND Corporation report, 1996, 18.

159. "Successful Latinos Team Up to Help Others Make It," *LAT*, July 24, 1983; South Gate Chamber of Commerce files, SGHWL; Jorge Leal conversation with author, May 4, 2018; on Downey, see G. Aron Ramirez, "Business as Usual: Ethnic Commerce and the Making of a Mexican American Middle Class in Southeast Los Angeles, 1981–1995," *Journal of Urban History*, online first, December 8, 2022.

160. A vivid exception was the Latino-owned coffee chain Tierra Mia, which originated in South Gate, predating the local Starbucks. The huge success of Tierra Mia, in fact, attracted Starbucks to the community. Thanks to Jorge Leal for pointing this out.

161. "L.A. Fails to Be a Refuge for Some," *LAT*, May 9, 1992; "Latino Yes, but with New Tastes," *LAT*, May 28, 2008; "A New Latino Clout, South Gate Shopping Center Goes Mainstream," *LAT*, September 24, 2015; *South Gate Progress*, Spring 1999, Box 6/File 37, SGHWL; Jorge Leal, "Las Plazas of South Los Angeles," in *Post-Ghetto: Reimagining South Los Angeles*, edited by Josh Sides (Berkeley: University of California Press, 2012), 11–32; Clara Irázabal and Macarena Gómez-Barris, "Bounded Tourism: Immigrant Politics, Consumption and Traditions at Plaza Mexico," *Journal of Tourism and Cultural Change* 5, 3 (2007), 191; Anastasia Loukaitou-Sideris, "Regeneration of Urban Commercial Strips: Ethnicity and Space in Three Los Angeles Neighborhoods," *Journal of Architectural and Planning Research* 19, 4 (Winter 2002), 338–340; Bob Rodino, "Capturing the Latino Market: Repositioning for Fun and Profit," *California Centers* (Spring 1994), 44–46; Bob Rodino telephone interview with author, January 29, 2018.

    Also see Becky Nicolaides, "Are Latino Suburbs Ethnoburbs? And Why it Matters," in *MetropoLatinx: The Significance of Latinidad in Urban History*, edited by A. Sandoval-Strausz (Chicago: University of Chicago Press, forthcoming).

162. Gutiérrez, *Walls and Mirrors*, explores the history of this fractured experience.

163. "Illegal Garage and Shed Habitations"; "South Gate Escalates Fight," *LAT*, September 6, 1984; on similar recalcitrance among first-generation Latino settlers in South LA, see Hondagneu-Sotelo and Pastor, *South Central Dreams*.

164. Latino population figures for 1980 to 2000, see Table A6.1; "Human Relations Agency Enlists Help of Community Groups to Ease Tensions," *LAT*, July 6, 1980.

165. Henry Gonzalez oral history.

166. Henry Gonzalez oral history; Kenneth C. Burt, *The Search for a Civic Voice: California Latino Politics* (Claremont, CA: Regina Books, 2007), 265.

167. Henry Gonzalez oral history; "South Gate Rotary Honors Its Presidents," *SGP*, March 12, 1980; Burt, *Search for a Civic Voice*, 289.

168. By 1977, Latinas had risen to hold the office of PTA president at three elementary schools; by 1990, Latina/os held leadership positions at four schools, including the large junior high. As late as 1990, reps from other groups were uniformly Anglo. South Gate Coordinating Council Directory 1977–1978; South Gate Coordinating Council Directory 1990–91, SGHWL.

169. Theresa Gonzalez oral history.

170. "Noticias en Espanol," *SGP*, January 2, 5, April 2, 1980; "Schools Will Celebrate Cinco de Mayo Holiday," *SGP*, May 2, 1980; "Chicano: It's Time to Get Rid of That Label," *SGP*, September 19, 1981; "South Gate," *LAT*, May 5, 1983. In the 1990s,

councilman Albert Robles tried to replace the Azalea Festival with a Cinco de Mayo festival. Opposition to Robles's proposal came from both whites and Latinos, the latter sensitive to South Gate's pan-Latino diversity.

171. "Recall Election, Gas Panic"; "Laura Ramirez Named Miss South Gate 1981," *SGP*, November 26, 1980; "5,000 to March in Sunday Parade," *SGP*, December 13, 1980; "Record Turnout Views Christmas Parade," *SGP*, December 17, 1980.

172. "Celebration Continues," *SGP*, March 18, 1981; Azalea Festival clip file, Box 3/ Folder 31, SGHWL; Quinones, *Antonio's Gun*, 71. See Figure A6.2.

173. Nicolaides, *My Blue Heaven*, 103; Theresa Gonzalez oral history; South Gate Women's Club membership list, 2013, files of Theresa Gonzalez; Maria Davila oral history, conducted by Becky Nicolaides, June 29 and July 31, 2017, South Gate, CA.

174. "Couple Toil to Make a Political Impact," *LAT*, January 26, 1984. Belmontez was in a job retraining program for a $6/hour job, compared to the $11/hour he earned at GM. Another local group was the Latin Association of South Gate, founded by city councilman John Sheehy. That group helped residents become citizens ("Candidates Tell Platforms," *SGP*, April 2, 1980).

175. "Successful Latinos Team Up"; "Friends, Colleagues Mourn Raul Perez," *LAT*, October 29, 1996.

176. "South Gate Chamber of Commerce," supplement to *SGP*, June 6, 1984; Chamber of Commerce file, Box 3/file 36, SGHWL.

177. By 1994, Latino majorities were elected to city councils in Maywood, Cudahy, Huntington Park, and Bell Gardens.

178. "South Gate Councilmen Say Harmony," *LAT*, April 15, 1990; "Latinos Emerge as Southeast Political Force," *LAT*, April 17, 1994. See Figure A6.3.

179. Alvaro Huerta, "South Gate, California: The Latinization of a Formerly White, Blue Collar Suburb and a Case Study of Environmental Racism" (UCLA paper, June 9, 2004), SGHWL, 12; "De Witt Seeks Re-Election to South Gate City Council," South Gate-Lynwood Patch, December 21, 2012, accessed at https://patch.com/califor nia/southgate-lynwood/incumbent-seeks-re-election-for-south-gate-city-council; "South Gate City Council Members 1923 to present," City Clerk's Office, SGCH.

180. Sam Quinones, "How Mexicans Became Americans," *NYT*, January 17, 2015; Gutiérrez, "Migration, Emergent Ethnicity and the 'Third Space'"; Leal, "Ephemeral Forums." Leal contends many residents in the gateway suburbs came from cities in Mexico.

181. Hondagneu-Sotelo and Pastor, *South Central Dreams*, 86.

182. Social scientists offer differing interpretations of the patterns and implications of remittances on civic capacity and rootedness (indicated by measures like homeown- ership) in the United States. For example, one study of immigrants in 1990 found that homeowners tended not to remit; a study of immigrants in 2000 suggested the opposite; a third study complicated the framework of "transnationality" altogether. See Cecelia Menjívar, Julie DaVanso, Lisa Greenwell, and R. B. Baldez, "Remittance Behavior Among Salvadoran and Filipino Immigrants in Los Angeles," *International Migration Review* 32, 1 (1998), 97–126; Enrico Marcelli and B. Lindsay Lowell, "Transnational Twist: Pecuniary Remittances and the Socioeconomic Integration of Authorized and Unauthorized Mexican Immigrants in Los Angeles County," *International Migration Review* 39, 1 (Spring 2005), 69–102; Roger Waldinger,

"Between 'Here' and 'There': Immigrant Cross-Border Activities and Loyalties," *International Migration Review* 42, 1 (Spring 2008), 3–29.

183. In 1990, 400,000 residents of Los Angeles were from Jalisco.

184. "Jalisco Native Helping Other Immigrants," *LAT*, December 27, 1990; "L.A. to Send Disaster Experts to Guadalajara," *LAT*, April 25, 1992; "Southland Opens Its Heart to Aid Victims," *LAT*, May 21, 1992; "Immigrants Tapped to Fund Jobs in Mexico," *LAT*, August 6, 1999; "Mexican 'Hometown Clubs' Turn Activist," *LAT*, June 8, 2000; "The Go-Between for Mexico, U.S. Harmony," *LAT*, February 25, 2001; Carol Zabin and Luis Escala Rabadan, "Mexican Hometown Associations and Mexican Immigrant Political Empowerment in Los Angeles," Aspen Institute Working Paper (Winter 1998), 17–18; http://fedjalisco.org/, accessed May 16, 2018; Enrique C. Ochoa and Gilda L. Ochoa, *Latino LA: Transformations, Communities and Activism* (Tucson: University of Arizona Press, 1995), 130.

185. As early as 1994, the year it passed, federal court rulings barred Prop 187 from taking effect. The 1997 ruling nullified Prop 187, except for provisions relating to higher education and false documents. In 1999, newly elected Governor Gray Davis withdrew the state's appeal of the case, which effectively killed Prop 187. "U.S. Judge Bars Most Sections of Prop. 187," *LAT*, December 15, 1994; "Prop. 187 Found Unconstitutional by Federal Judge," *LAT*, November 15, 1997.

186. The same thing happened in Bell Gardens, Huntington Park, and Maywood, where registration increases were even higher. The increase in voter registration from 1990 to 2000 in those towns was Bell Gardens (67%), Huntington Park (57%), and Maywood (64%). In nearby Lakewood, by contrast, the increase was 6%. (*Reports of Registration*, State of California.)

187. Quinones, *Antonio's Gun*, 71.

188. "They're Speaking Language of Cooperation at South Gate PTA," *LAT*, October 21, 1990; Brodkin, *Power Politics*, 117.

189. "They're Speaking Language of Cooperation"; "South Gate: Newcomer Center Offer to Help Latino Immigrants," *LAT*, November 22, 1990. The LAUSD had launched a Newcomer Center program in 1989, which referred to separate schools for non-English speaking new immigrants. This program ran into trouble in 1991, in Bellflower, accused of promoting segregation of immigrants. It is unclear whether the South Gate program was part of this broader LAUSD initiative (see *LAT*, August 12, 1989, February 24, 1991, March 21, 1991).

190. The Bracero Program was enacted by the US Congress in 1942, as Public Law 45. It was an agreement between the United States and Mexico that brought Mexican workers to the United States as emergency contract labor to fulfill labor needs during World War II. Vargas, *Crucible of Struggle*, 263.

191. Celene Leyva oral history; Maria Davila oral history; Sandra Martinez oral history.

192. "'Las comadres' los quieren uniformados," *LO*, August 25, 1996.

193. Maria Davila oral history; Quinones, *Antonio's Gun*, 102; Brodkin, *Power Politics*, 117; "New Schools a Mixed Blessing for South Gate," *LAT*, March 2, 2005. Some South Gate city councilmen and small business owners did not support the school construction, fearing it would displace potential sales tax revenue.

194. Maria Davila oral history.

195. Celene Leyva oral history.

196. On Latino opposition to busing, see Celene Leyva oral history; "Jordan High as alternative," *SGP*, August 8, 1981; "Anderson says busing could improve education quality," *SGP*, May 9, 1984; on the lawsuit, see "Black Teachers: Racism Rampant at S. Gate School," *LAS*, September 11, 1997; "Discrimination Alleged at School in South Gate," *LAT*, September 4, 1997; "Is There Discrimination at South Gate?" *LAT*, September 27, 1997; "3 Black Teachers Win $242,000 in Bias Case," *LAT*, March 16, 1999; "District Settles Bias Suit by 3 Black Teachers," *LAT*, January 5, 2002. Jerry González found similar anti-Black sentiment among upwardly mobile Latino suburbanites, in *In Search of the Mexican Beverly Hills*, 67-69. School board member Victoria Castro claimed the South Gate situation would not have gotten so bad had there been a human relations commission within the district. See "L.A. Schools to Replace Panels on Minorities," *LAT*, April 14, 1998.

197. As of 2017, 15 Latino gangs were active in South Gate. http://www.streetgangs. com/hispanic/southgate, accessed June 1, 2017. On the plight of aging inner-ring suburbs, see Hanlon, *Once the American Dream*; Hudnut, *Halfway to Everywhere*; Bernadette Hanlon and Thomas Vicino, eds., *Routledge Companion to the Suburbs* (New York: Routledge, 2019).

198. Quinones, *Antonio's Gun*, 100–103; Celene Leyva oral history; Community in Action flyers and meeting records, from Celene Leyva personal files; "South Gate Citizens March Against Violence," *Southside News*, November 1998; "Vecinos en Accion," *LO*, September 27, 2000 (from personal files of Celene Leyva). Leyva added that this moment of unity between residents and police was ultimately short-lived.

199. Quinones, *Antonio's Gun*, 102–105, quote at 104.

200. These were churches with Spanish-language names and/or Latino ministers. Some of these churches included Iglesia Bautista Libro Church, Iglesia Bautista Fundamental Hispana, and Iglesia Evangelic de Naverine. Coordinating Council directories, 1977 and 1990, Box 3, File 19, SGHWL.

201. "South Gate Wins All-America City Honors," *LAT*, June 14, 1990; "Prices Lure Buyers"; Sandra Martinez oral history.

202. "Worshippers Flock to Huntington Park Church," *LAT*, December 16, 1984; "Cultures Follow Separate Paths in Huntington Park"; "South Gate Wins All-America City Honors"; "Prices Lure Buyers."

203. Leal, "Ephemeral Forums."

204. Quinones, *Antonio's Gun*, chapter 3; Brodkin, *Power Politics*; Raphael J. Sonenshein, *The City at Stake* (Princeton: Princeton University Press, 2004), 264–265; Alvaro Huerta, "Report from Los Angeles: South Gate, Ca., Environmental Racism Defeated in a Blue-Collar Latino Suburb," *Critical Planning* (Summer 2005), 93–102. On racial self-identification in the southeast suburbs, which were drastically re-segregated spaces, see Laura Pulido and Manuel Pastor, "Where in the World Is Juan – and What Color Is He? The Geography of Latina/o Racial Identity in Southern California," *American Quarterly* 65, 2 (2013), 309–341. While I take issue with Pulido and Pastor's definition of "suburb," they offer excellent insights on racial self-identification across metropolitan space; they find a greater tendency to

identify as "some other race" (rather than white) in the southeast suburbs, which had resegregated.

205. Sandoval-Strausz, *Barrio America*.

206. "South Gate Wins All-America City Honors"; "South Gate: 3 Officials to Accept Award," *LAT*, August 2, 1990; "South Gate Is All-American," *SGP*, June 14, 1990; "City Finally Gets Deserved Attention," *SGP*, July [n.d.], 1990; "Next Stop, the White House," *SGP*, July 12, 1990 (from Box 17, files 24, 30, 33, SGHWL).

207. A detailed account of the Robles scandal is in Quinones, *Antonio's Gun*. By the late 1990s, South Gate's local newspapers had all folded, compounding the sense of community disconnection.

208. Wegmann, "We Just Built It," 219–220; Transportation & Land Use Collaborative of Southern California, memo to South Gate Regional Advisory Group, August 12, 2004, 4. I was a member of that advisory group. This study queried 30 residents, city, and business leaders in South Gate.

209. Manuel Pastor, South Gate Regional Advisory Group Interview, February 18, 2005, 2 (Transportation & Land Use Collaborative of Southern California, 2005).

210. Wegmann, "We Just Built It," 154; Veronica Lopez oral history.

211. In the absence of political activism around this issue—suppressed by the enduring suburban ideal in these communities—South Gate officials never fully explored options that would legalize converted dwellings or accommodate them in ways that would promote safer conditions. On what such alternative policies might look like, see Wegmann, "We Just Built It," 220–223.

212. Carpio et al., "Right to the Suburb?"; James Holston and Arjun Appadurai, "Cities and Citizenship," *Public Culture* 8 (1996), 187–204.

213. Steve Costley telephone interview with author, March 7, 2018. Costley was deputy director of the South Gate Parks and Recreation Department.

214. Maria Davila oral history, August 30, 2017.

215. Ana Medina, South Gate Parks and Recreation Department, telephone interview with author, November 14, 2022; City of South Gate, "Azalea Festival," https://www.cityofsouthgate.org/Government/Departments/Parks-and-Recreation/Search-Programs-Activities/Azalea-Festival#section-3.

Chapter 7

1. I am indebted to Allison Baker, who generously shared her dissertation research materials with me, a gesture that took on greater significance when COVID-19 closed public libraries and archives just as I began work on this chapter. Allison's dissertation on Lakewood, particularly its insights on local recreation and public safety culture, were crucial to my understanding of the community's history. See Allison Baker, "The Lakewood Story: Defending the Recreational Good Life in Postwar Southern California Suburbia, 1950–1999" (PhD dissertation, University of Pennsylvania, 1999).

2. William A. Garnett photographs of Lakewood, CA, J. Paul Getty Museum, Los Angeles; "A New Mayor, a New Councilwoman . . . and 400 New Angels Every Day," *Life* 35, 2 (July 13, 1953), 23+; Harry Henderson, "The Mass-Produced Suburbs. I. How People Live in America's Newest Towns," *Harper's Magazine*, November 1953, 25–32; Dolores Hayden, *Building Suburbia: Green Fields and Urban Growth, 1820–2000* (New York: Pantheon, 2003), chapter 7; Barbara Lane Miller, *Houses for a New World: Builders and Buyers in American Suburbs, 1945–1965* (Princeton: Princeton University Press, 2015); D. J. Waldie, *Holy Land: A Suburban Memoir* (New York: St. Martin's Press, 1996).

3. Lewis Mumford, *The City in History: Its Origin, Its Transformation, and Its Prospects* (New York: Harcourt, Brace, 1961), 486.

4. Waldie, *Holy Land*, 5; D. J. Waldie, "Beautiful and Terrible: Aeriality and the Image of Suburbia," *Places* (February 2013).

5. "A New Mayor, a New Councilwoman," 24–25; Robert Beuka, *SuburbiaNation: Reading Suburban Landscapes in Twentieth-Century American Fiction and Film* (New York: Palgrave, 2004); Catherine Jurca, *White Diaspora: The Suburbs and the Twentieth-Century American Novel* (Princeton: Princeton University Press, 2001); Becky Nicolaides and Andrew Wiese, eds., *The Suburb Reader*, 2nd ed. (New York: Routledge, 2016), chapter 10.

6. Dianne Harris, ed., *Second Suburb: Levittown, Pennsylvania* (Pittsburgh: University of Pennsylvania Press, 2010); Ellen-Dunham Jones and June Williamson, *Retrofitting Suburbia, Updated Edition: Urban Design Solutions for Redesigning Suburbs* (Hoboken: Wiley, 2011).

7. Max Felker-Kantor, *Policing Los Angeles: Race, Resistance, and the Rise of the LAPD* (Chapel Hill: University of North Carolina Press, 2018); Mike Davis, *City of Quartz* (New York: Vintage, 1992); Matthew D. Lassiter, *The Suburban Crisis: White America and the War on Drugs* (Princeton: Princeton University Press, 2023); Matthew D. Lassiter, "Pushers, Victims, and the Lost Innocence of White Suburbia: California's War on Narcotics during the 1950s," *Journal of Urban History* 41, 5 (2015), 787–807; Matthew D. Lassiter, *The Silent Majority: Suburban Politics in the Sunbelt South* (Princeton: Princeton University Press, 2006); Kevin Kruse: *White Flight: Atlanta and the Making of Modern Conservatism* (Princeton: Princeton University Press, 2005); Lily Geismer, *Don't Blame Us: Suburban Liberals and the Transformation of the Democratic Party* (Princeton: Princeton University Press, 2015); Paul Renfro, *Stranger Danger: Family Values, Childhood, and the American Carceral State* (New York: Oxford University Press, 2020); Kyle Riismandel, *Neighborhood of Fear: The Suburban Crisis in American Culture, 1975–2001* (Baltimore: Johns Hopkins University Press, 2020).

8. On the racially discriminatory application of policing, see Lassiter, *Suburban Crisis*. On the rise of "law and order" in nearby Compton, see Emily E. Straus, *Death of a Suburban Dream: Race and Schools in Compton, California* (Philadelphia: University of Pennsylvania Press, 2014).

9. Andrea S. Boyles, *Race, Place, and Suburban Policing: Too Close for Comfort* (Oakland: University of California Press, 2015), 6–7.

10. Linda Lou, Hyojung Lee, Anthony Guardado, and Dowell Myers, "Racially Balanced Cities in Southern California, 1990–2010" (USC Sol Price School of Public Policy, February 2012), Exhibit 3. Of the 10 towns that qualified as having a balanced four-way mix, six were in the Southeast: Bellflower, Carson, Gardena, Lakewood, Long Beach, and Signal Hill.

11. "Lakewood: Instant City 20 Years Later," *LBIPT*, December 31, 1972.

12. "Diversity Spoken in 39 Languages," *LAT*, June 16, 2004; "A Melting Pot That's Brimming with Alphabet Soup," *LAT*, July 1, 2004.

13. "Staying for Good," *LBPT*, August 12, 1997.

14. Joan Didion, "Trouble in Lakewood," *New Yorker*, July 26, 1993, 46–48. "Era of limits" coined by California governor Jerry Brown, as cited in Danielle Wiggins, "'Our Worst Crisis Since Slavery': The Crisis of the Black Family and the Politics of Familial Responsibility" (paper presented at the LA History and Metro Studies Group, February 23, 2021).

15. This is a key theme of Baker, "The Lakewood Story." Don Waldie, who worked as Director of Public Information in Lakewood from 1977 to 2010, was always aware of Lakewood's racially checkered past and wrote about it in many places. Still, the official Lakewood narrative for years mostly excluded the experience and voices of people of color. See Waldie, *Holy Land*; D. J. Waldie, "What L.A.'s Suburbs Can Teach Us," *LAT*, December 22, 2004; https://www.lakewoodcity.org/about/history/history/default.asp, accessed February 1, 2020. On the power of historical mythmaking and its capacity to shape the prospects for social justice in LA, see William Deverell, *Whitewashed Adobe: The Rise of Los Angeles and the Remaking of Its Mexican Past* (Berkeley: University of California Press, 2004); Romeo Guzmán, Carribean Fragoza, Alex Sayf Cummings, Ryan Reft, eds., *East of East: The Making of Greater El Monte* (New Brunswick: Rutgers University Press, 2020), 1–14.

16. Alida Brill wrote powerfully about this narrative in "Lakewood, California: 'Tomorrowland' at 40," in *Rethinking Los Angeles*, edited by Michael J. Dear, H. Eric Schockman, and Greg Hise (Thousand Oaks: Sage Publications, 1996), 97–112.

17. D. J. Waldie makes this point in Brill, "Tomorrowland," 108.

18. "Diversity Spoken in 39 Languages." Also see the excellent study on communities just west of Lakewood, Pierrette Hondagneu-Sotelo and Manuel Pastor, *South Central Dreams: Finding Home and Building Community in South L.A.* (New York: NYU Press, 2021).

19. City of Lakewood, "The Lakewood Story," chapter 1, https://www.lakewoodcity.org/About/Our-History/The-Lakewood-Story/01-The-Story-Begins; Harry Klissner, "How Agencies of Communications Can Convert a Gigantic Real Estate Operation (Lakewood) into a Socially Cohesive Community" (MS thesis, UCLA, 1954), 36, 132.

20. Fred Viehe, "Black Gold Suburbs: The Influence of the Extractive Industry on the Suburbanization of Los Angeles, 1890–1930," *Journal of Urban History* 8 (1981), 3–26; Nancy Quam-Wickham, "Another World: Work, Home, and Autonomy in Blue-Collar Suburbs," in *Metropolis in the Making: Los Angeles in the 1920s*, edited by Tom Sitton and William Deverell (Berkeley: University of California Press, 2001), 123–141; on Petroleum Gardens, "Tiny Lots Legacy of Oil Boom," *LAT*, July 3, 1977; "Large

Petroleum Gardens Tract To Be Put on Market," *LBP*, December 10, 1922; "Come to Petroleum Gardens - Ad" *LBP*, January 20, 1923 (thanks to Don Waldie for finding the latter two articles).

21. City of Lakewood, "The Lakewood Story," chapter 1; Waldie, *Holy Land*, 28; on the imagined but unrealized plan of an industrial and residential complex centered on aircraft in Lakewood, see "Janss Will Take Over Huge Tract," *LAT*, January 27, 1929.

22. City of Lakewood, "The Lakewood Story," chapter 1; "Huge New Tract Launched," *LAT*, August 28, 1932; on suburbia's inherent class diversity, see Lizabeth Cohen, *A Consumers' Republic: The Politics of Mass Consumption in Postwar America* (New York: Vintage, 2003), chapter 5.

23. City of Lakewood, "The Lakewood Story," chapter 1; "Famous Rancho's Land Scheduled for Market," *LAT*, September 23, 1934; "New Village Sales Ready," *LAT*, September 30, 1934; "Successful Sales Start for Tract," *LAT*, October 7, 1934; City Survey Files for Los Angeles, U.S. Home Owners Loan Corporation, RG 195, National Archives (hereafter HOLC City Survey Files) A-56 (Lakewood Village); on nearby working-class suburbs, see Becky Nicolaides, *My Blue Heaven: Life and Politics in the Working-Class Suburbs of Los Angeles, 1920–1965* (Chicago: University of Chicago Press, 2002), chapter 1.

24. Nicolaides, *My Blue Heaven*, 187–193; Greg Hise, *Magnetic Los Angeles: Planning the Twentieth Century Metropolis* (Baltimore: Johns Hopkins University Press, 1997); Arthur Verge, *Paradise Transformed: Los Angeles During the Second World War* (Dubuque: Kendall/Hunt Publishing, 1993).

25. City of Lakewood, "The Lakewood Story," chapter 1.

26. City of Lakewood, "The Lakewood Story," chapter 1; "Death Takes C. J. Bonner," *LAT*, January 14, 1947.

27. City of Lakewood, "The Lakewood Story," chapter 2, https://www.lakewoodcity. org/About/Our-History/The-Lakewood-Story/02-City-of-Tomorrow; Waldie, *Holy Land*, 165–170; Hayden, *Building Suburbia*, 132. The LPC owners manipulated the federal home financing system in ways that landed them in a US Senate inquiry in 1954 but were technically legal.

28. City of Lakewood, "The Lakewood Story," chapters 2 and 3, https://www.lakew oodcity.org/About/Our-History/The-Lakewood-Story/02-City-of-Tomorrow, and https://www.lakewoodcity.org/About/Our-History/The-Lakewood-Story/03-Subur ban-Pioneers; Waldie, *Holy Land*, 7–12, 33. Narrative accounts claim the population exceeded 70,000 by the late 1950s; the US Census reported 67,000 in 1960.

29. James A. Jacobs, *Detached America: Building Houses in Postwar America* (Charlottesville: University of Virginia Press, 2015), 124; Baker, "Lakewood Story," 68–71; Miller, *Houses for a New World*, 16; "Lakewood, Built on Youth, Shows Its Age," *LBPT*, February 28, 1982.

30. Baker, "Lakewood Story," 67, 401; also see Waldie, *Holy Land*, 1. Lakewood resident Janet MacHale described residents as "middle-class wage earners" (Thomas and Janet MacHale oral history, conducted by Allison Baker, September 24, 1996, Lakewood, CA). Allison Baker called Lakewood a "not quite middle-class suburb" (401).

31. Miller, *Houses for a New World*, 14; Hise, *Magnetic Los Angeles*.

32. Klissner, "How Agencies of Communications," 8; Richard Longstreth, *From City Center to Regional Mall: Architecture, the Automobile, and Retailing in Los Angeles, 1920–1950* (Cambridge, MA.: MIT Press, 1997), 334–343; City of Lakewood, "The Lakewood Story," chapter 2. On postwar malls nationally and their myriad social dimensions, see Cohen, *Consumers' Republic*, chapter 6 and Lizabeth Cohen, "From Town Center to Shopping Center: The Reconfiguration of Community Marketplaces in Postwar America," *American Historical Review* 10, 4 (October 1996), 1050–1081.

33. Waldie, *Holy Land*, 12–13, 102; Baker, "Lakewood Story," 112–119, 175–180; Christopher C. Seller, *Crabgrass Crucible: Suburban Nature and the Rise of Environmentalism in Twentieth-Century America* (Chapel Hill: University of North Carolina Press, 2012), 185–188; City of Lakewood, "The Lakewood Story," chapter 2.

34. Hayden, *Building Suburbia*, 128, 139–140.

35. HOLC City Survey File, A-56 (Lakewood Village).

36. Baker, "Lakewood Story," 93.

37. Allen and Turner, *Ethnic Quilt*, 109; Waldie, *Holy Land*, 103.

38. "County Purchase Scored," *LAS*, October 19, 1950; "First Class Blunder," *LAS*, October 19, 1950; and see Scott Kurashige, *The Shifting Grounds of Race* (Princeton: Princeton University Press, 2008), 239–240.

39. Baker, "Lakewood Story," 98–99; HOLC City Survey Files, C-137 (Norwalk), C-138 (Bellflower, Clearwater & Hynes), D-59 (Artesia); Waldie, *Holy Land*, 73.

40. "Lakewood: Instant City 20 Years Later"; Waldie, *Holy Land*, 37. In this way, Lakewood was similar to Park Forest and Levittown; see Gregory Randall, *America's Original G.I. Town: Park Forest, Illinois* (Baltimore: Johns Hopkins University Press, 2000); Barbara Kelley, *Expanding the American Dream: Building and Rebuilding Levittown* (Albany: State University of New York Press, 1993).

41. "Lakewood: Instant City 20 Years Later"; Waldie, *Holy Land*, 37, 89–90; Bobbe Frankenberg oral history, conducted by Allison Baker, May 29, 1996, Beverly Hills, CA; "A New Mayor, a New Councilwoman," 23+.

42. On the "kitchen debates," see Karal Ann Marling, *As Seen on TV: The Visual Culture of Everyday Life in the 1950s* (Cambridge, MA: Harvard University Press, 1994), chapter 7.

43. Michan Connor, "'Public Benefits from Public Choice': Producing Decentralization in Metropolitan Los Angeles, 1954–1973," *Journal of Urban History* 39, 1 (2013), 85.

44. Klissner, "How Agencies of Communications," 106–109. The group also studied the Nassau Plan in New York, whereby Nassau County supplied services to the area.

45. City of Lakewood, "The Lakewood Story," chapter 4, https://www.lakewoodcity.org/About/Our-History/The-Lakewood-Story/04-Birth-of-a-City; Klissner, "How Agencies of Communications," 4, 95–131; Baker, "Lakewood Story," 53–57; "Lakewood Women Fight Honor Farm," *LAT*, February 11, 1953. Both Klissner and Baker referred to pro-incorporation materials as "propaganda."

46. Upon incorporation, Lakewood affiliated with two school districts—Bellflower Elementary and Long Beach Unified. In subsequent years, it joined the ABC and Paramount School Districts. Klissner, "How Agencies of Communications," 19; "Lakewood: Education Panel Rejects Proposed School District," *LAT*, August 28, 1998.

47. Connor, "Public Benefits," 81; City of Lakewood, "The Lakewood Story," chapter 5, https://www.lakewoodcity.org/About/Our-History/The-Lakewood-Story/05-The-Lakewood-Plan; Davis, *City of Quartz*, 165–169; Gary J. Miller, *Cities by Contract: The Politics of Municipal Incorporation* (Cambridge, MA: MIT Press, 1981). In the 1950s and 1960s, 31 new towns incorporated in LA County and there were 28 contract cities by 1970.

48. "Lakewood: Tomorrow's City Turns 40," *LBPT*, March 6, 1994; US Census dataset 1960 on homes; Klissner, "How Agencies of Communications," 9, 25, 32; material on eastern Lakewood from Don Waldie email to author, November 9, 2020; Ari Pe oral history, conducted by Becky Nicolaides, November 10, 2020, via Zoom; City of Lakewood, "The Lakewood Story," chapter 2; "Tiny Lots Legacy of Oil Boom."

49. Klissner, "How Agencies of Communications," 17, 21; US Census dataset 1960.

50. On the importance of life cycle stage and children in forging suburban affiliations in Dublin, Ireland, see Mary P. Corcoran, Jane Gray, and Michel Peillon, *Suburban Affiliations: Social Relations in the Greater Dublin Area* (Syracuse: Syracuse University Press, 2010).

51. Waldie, *Holy Land*, 162.

52. US Bureau of Census, *U.S. Census of Population: 1960*, Vol. I, *Characteristics of the Population. Part 6, California. General Population Characteristics* (Washington, DC: GPO, 1963), 6–135.

53. Bill Baca oral history, conducted by Becky Nicolaides, November 30, 2020, via Zoom.

54. For full demographic, social, and housing data on Lakewood, see Table A7.1.

55. US Bureau of Census, *U.S. Census of Population: 1960*, vol. I, *Characteristics of the Population. Part 6, California. General Population Characteristics* (Washington, DC: GPO, 1963), 6–135, 6–196, 6–274.

56. Baker, "Lakewood Story," 196–197; California Secretary of State, *Report of Registration: State of California*, 1962, November 3, 1970.

57. See Table A2.7 (Median family income).

58. US Bureau of Census, *U.S. Census of Population: 1960*, Vol. I, *Characteristics of the Population. Part 6, California. General Social and Economic Characteristics: California, 1960*, 6–314, 6–334, 6–354; on aerospace, see Baker, "Lakewood Story," 80; John Rae oral history, conducted by Allison Baker, March 13, 1997, Lakewood, CA; on the Douglas plant, "Historic American Engineering Record (HAER): Douglas Aircraft Company Long Beach Plant" (HAER CA-315), National Park Service, San Francisco, CA, May 2006, 2. On national trends, Joanne Meyerowitz, ed., *Not June Cleaver: Women and Gender in Postwar America, 1945–1960* (Philadelphia: Temple University Press, 1994); Nancy Rubin, *The New Suburban Woman: Beyond Myth and Motherhood* (New York: Coward, McCann & Geoghegan, 1982), chapter 3.

59. Henderson, "The Mass-Produced Suburbs," 31. Harry Henderson's profile of postwar mass-produced suburbia was based on his first-hand observations in six suburbs from 1950–1953, of which he only identified Levittown and Park Forest by name. While he did not identify the other four suburbs, we can surmise that one was Lakewood since he mentioned it in the opening of his article. I draw on this article as a useful point of

reference to other sitcom suburbs; Henderson made many astute observations about everyday life in these instant communities, some of which were reiterated by William Whyte in his reporting on Park Forest, IL. See William Whyte, *Organization Man* (New York: Simon and Schuster, 1956).

60. Waldie, *Holy Land*, 38; Baker, "Lakewood Story," 75–80.

61. They comprised about 70% of all married women in 1960.

62. Baker, "Lakewood Story," 79–80, 127–137; Janet MacHale oral history.

63. "An Oral History with Lois Smith," conducted by Denise Spooner, September 10, 1988, Lakewood, CA, courtesy of Lawrence de Graaf Center for Oral and Public History, California State University Fullerton.

64. Becky Nicolaides, "How Hell Moved from the City to the Suburbs: Urban Scholars and Changing Perceptions of Authentic Community," in *The New Suburban History*, edited by Kevin M. Kruse and Thomas J. Sugrue (Chicago: University of Chicago Press, 2006), 80–98.

65. Waldie quotes from Baker, "Lakewood Story, 136–138, 157.

66. Anne Pechin Emigh oral history, conducted by Allison Baker, June 11, 1997, Long Beach, CA; Sandra Jenkins Janich oral history, conducted by Allison Baker, September 18, 1996, Long Beach, CA; also Margie Lehner Armstrong oral history, conducted by Allison Baker, June 25, 1997, Huntington Beach, CA.

67. Margie Lehner Armstrong oral history; Linda Kay Gahan oral history, conducted by Allison Baker, January 27, 1996, Lakewood, CA; Henderson, "The Mass-Produced Suburbs," 32. On the culture of mutual aid and DIY in postwar suburbia, see Whyte, *Organization Man*; Richard Harris, *Building a Market: The Rise of the Home Improvement Industry, 1914–1960* (Chicago: University of Chicago Press, 2012); Rosalyn Baxandall and Elizabeth Ewen, *Picture Windows: How the Suburbs Happened* (New York: Basic Books, 2000), 153–54; Robyn Muncy, "Cooperative Motherhood and Democratic Civic Culture in Postwar Suburbia, 1940–1965," *Journal of Social History* (Winter 2004), 285–310.

68. Shirley William oral history, conducted by Allison Baker, October 21, 1996, Westminster, CA.

69. Baker, "Lakewood Story," 126–131, 138–139. On similar maternal politics in suburban and urban settings, see Sylvie Murray, *The Progressive Housewife: Community Activism in Queens, New York, 1945–1960* (Philadelphia: University of Pennsylvania Press, 2003); Michelle Nickerson, *Mothers of Conservatism: Women and the Postwar Right* (Princeton: Princeton University Press, 2012); Marta Gutman, *A City for Children: Women, Architecture, and the Charitable Landscapes of Oakland, 1850–1950* (Chicago: University of Chicago Press, 2014).

70. Journalist Harry Henderson observed in 1953, "Children love living in these towns, the first large communities in American which have literally been built for them." Harry Henderson, "Rugged American Collectivism: The Mass Produced-Suburbs, Part II," *Harper's*, December 1953, 83.

71. Baker, "Lakewood Story," chapter 3.

72. Baker, "Lakewood Story," 112–119, 176. Baker emphasizes recreation as central to Lakewood's community identity and social history.

73. Baker, "Lakewood Story," 148–156. In the case of Jackie Rynerson, this service was a springboard to the Lakewood city council. On the "tot lots" see "Investing in Young Lakewood" (film, produced by Lakewood Water and Power Co., 1955).

74. Bill Grady, Lakewood Public Information Officer, email to author, April 12, 2020.

75. Mike Rae oral history, conducted by Allison Baker, January 28, 1997, Long Beach, CA; John Rae oral history. Mike Rae went on to become a player in the NFL.

76. Keith Sharon oral history, conducted by Allison Baker, March 22, 1997, Lakewood, CA.

77. Henderson, "Rugged American Collectivism," 83.

78. Baker, "Lakewood Story," 188–189, 234–237, quote at 234.

79. Rebecca Jo Plant, *Mom: The Transformation of Motherhood in Modern America* (Chicago: University of Chicago Press, 2010).

80. On this point, also see Harry Henderson, "Rugged American Collectivism," 83–84.

81. Klissner, "How Agencies of Communications," 27–31; Waldie, *Holy Land*, 16; John Rae oral history; Baker, "Lakewood Story," 150–152; "Golf Fans Swarm to Public, Private Links," *LAT*, February 1, 1959; Henderson, "Rugged American Collectivism," 86.

82. Longstreth, *City Center to Regional Mall*, 311; Cohen, *Consumers' Republic*, 270.

83. Baker, "Lakewood Story," 94.

84. "L.A. Confidential," *LAS*, October 31, 1957.

85. Baker, "Lakewood Story," 99; Connor, "Public Benefits," 85.

86. "CORE to Propose Strike," *LAT*, September 4, 1963; Brill, "Tomorrowland," 105; on the broader racial climate in sitcom suburbia, see Henderson, "Rugged American Collectivism," 85. The enormous literature on postwar white suburban resistance is referenced in Chapter 2.

87. Larry Aubry, "Census Figures Out: The Redistricting Process Is Critical," *LAS*, April 12, 2001. Also see Darnell Hunt and Ana-Christina Ramon, eds., *Black Los Angeles: American Dreams and Racial Realities* (New York: New York University Press, 2010).

88. "Local Suburbs More Diverse," *LAT*, December 12, 2008; "Human Relations Agency Enlists Help of Community Groups to Ease Tensions," *LAT*, July 6, 1980.

89. Ari Pe oral history, conducted by Becky Nicolaides, November 10, 2020 and November 13, 2020, via Zoom.

90. Cassandra Chase oral history, conducted by Becky Nicolaides, November 17, 2020, December 3, 2020, and March 4, 2021, via Zoom; Louis Chase oral history, conducted by Becky Nicolaides, April 29, 2022 and May 2, 2022, via Zoom.

91. Pamela Williams and Derrick Williams oral history, conducted by Becky Nicolaides, November 20, 2020 and December 6, 2020, via Zoom.

92. Lassiter, *Silent Majority*; Matthew Delmont, *Why Busing Failed: Race, Media, and the National Resistance to School Desegregation* (Oakland: University of California Press, 2016); and the classic, J. Anthony Lukas, *Common Ground: A Turbulent Decade in the Lives of Three American Families* (New York: Vintage, 1986).

93. It was the Rampart Division; on Rampart, see Felker-Kantor, *Policing Los Angeles*, 240–242.

94. Bill Baca oral history; Joseph Esquivel oral history, conducted by Becky Nicolaides, December 8, 2020, via Zoom; Cassandra Chase oral history; Vicki Stuckey oral history, conducted by Becky Nicolaides, November 11 and November 19, 2020, via Zoom.

95. "Minorities Still Face Obstacles to Housing, Report Finds," *LAT*, September 6, 1996.

96. "Tilting the Balance of Black Bank," *LAT*, July 3, 1998.

97. This influx reflected immigration flows in the wake of the 1965 Hart-Celler Act and the end of the Vietnam War.

98. Ari Pe oral history; Beverlee Nye Perez oral history, conducted by Allison Baker, October 31, 1996, Lakewood, CA; Birdie and Meyer Levy oral history; Sandra Jenkins Janich oral history; James P. Allen and Eugene Turner, *Ethnic Quilt: Population Diversity in Southern California* (Northridge: Center for Geographical Studies, Cal State Northridge, 1979), 244.

99. See Figure A7.1 (Maps of Lakewood by race/ethnic groups, 1950–2020).

100. "Human Relations Agency Enlists Help of Community Groups to Ease Tensions," *LAT*, July 6, 1980. The LA County Human Relations Commission faced budget challenges through the 1980s, resorting to private fundraising by 1990. See "Awareness a Weapon in Fighting Hate Crimes," *LAT*, January 2, 1990; "L.A. County Agency's Mailers Ask for Money," *LAT*, February 10, 1990.

    The placement of human relations work in the Lakewood Recreation and Community Services Commission, and the recollection of retired staff, is from Bill Grady email to author, March 16, 2023.

101. Bill Baca oral history.

102. "Tireless Crusader is Making Inroads," *LAT*, December 8, 1993.

103. "Lakewood Matron Vows Rights Fight Despite Bomb Scare," *LAS*, September 10, 1964; "I'm Not Going to Back Down," *LAS*, September 10, 1964.

104. Cassandra Chase oral history.

105. By 1978, the number of Blacks rose to 270, while whites had dropped to 78% of students.

106. "Teachers Split on Racial Tension, Confrontations at Lakewood High," *LBPT*, September 13, 1979; Baker, "Lakewood Story," 426.

107. "Lakewood Mayor Replies to Slur," *LBPT*, September 19, 1979.

108. Brill, "Tomorrowland," 108–110; Baker, "Lakewood Story," 428–439.

109. Elaine Lewinnek, Gustavo Arellano, and Thuy Vo Dang, *A People's Guide to Orange County* (Berkeley: University of California Press, 2022); examples of media coverage include "Skinhead Suspects Admit to Bombings, Court Is Told," *LAT*, September 8, 1993; "Leader of Skinheads Pleads Guilty to Violence, Plot," *LAT*, October 21, 1993; a recent example is "Easter Surprise: Huntington [Beach] Residents Find Fliers by KKK," *LAT*, April 6, 2021.

110. Alex Alonso, "Out of the Void: Street Gangs in Black Los Angeles," in *Black Los Angeles: American Dreams and Racial Realities*, edited by Darnell Hunt and Ana-Christina Ramón (New York: New York University Press, 2010), 141.

111. "Family's Dream Turns to Nightmare in Cerritos," *LAS*, August 10, 1972; "Harassment Reported in Cerritos," *LAS*, July 26, 1973; the women were nurses.

112. "NAACP Decries Racial Terror," *LAS*, May 20, 1976.

113. "Five-Minute Rule Permits Klansman to Have His Say," *LAT*, March 4, 1981; "Klan Appears in Paramount," *LAT*, March 5, 1981. Soon after the KKK's appearance, the Paramount City Council adopted a resolution condemning racist and violent

organizations and thwarted another appearance by the Klavern by failing to convene a quorum. "Paramount Resolution Blasts Racists," *LAT*, June 6, 1981; "Klan Gets Media but No Hearing," *LAT*, July 9, 1981.

114. "Vandals Paint Swastika on Synagogue," *LBPT*, May 15, 1991.

115. Ari Pe oral history.

116. Louis Chase oral history.

117. "East Lakewood Area Survey Data Weighed," *LAT*, November 10, 1974; "Independent-Minded East Lakewood," *LAT*, July 27, 1975; Memo on "Comments received in Lakewood questionnaire," from F. Juarez to City Planning Commission Members, City of Lakewood, April 25, 1969, LHCIL, 8, 10; "Tiny Lots Legacy of Oil Boom."

118. "Bias Hits Home for Families," *LBPT*, April 4, 1997; "Black Families Win $1.5 Mil in Bias Suit," *LAS*, April 24, 1997.

119. Fifty other tenants eventually joined the lawsuit.

120. Baker, "Lakewood Story," 399; "Housing Bias Suit Is Settled for $1.7 Million," *LAT*, April 3, 1997; "Families in Housing Suit Recall Pain of Bias," *LAT*, April 4, 1997; *Nelson Walker, et al. v. Lakewood Condominium Owners Association*, et. al., CV 93-4531-KM; "Introduction of Motion for approval of attorney fees," submitted by Bert Voorhees; Bert Voorhees email to author, November 4, 2020. The apartment complex was located at 12350 E. Del Amo Boulevard, in Lakewood. The lengthy discovery battle in the case resulted in over 25,000 pages of documents, mostly tenant files.

121. *Nelson Walker and Fair Housing Foundation of Long Beach v. City of Lakewood*, U.S. Court of Appeals for the Ninth Circuit, D.C. No. CV-93-04531-DT (2001). Also see "Discrimination Cases Might Not Be Over," *LBPT*, April 4, 1997. This article claims the FHF suit against Lakewood and LA County included charges that the LA Sheriffs "conspired to make warrantless detentions and otherwise unlawfully harassed African-American tenants and non-tenants in the vicinity of Park Apartments."

122. Brill, "Tomorrowland," 108-110; Baker, "Lakewood Story," 428-439.

123. Rubin, *The New Suburban Woman*, 78. As of 1975 nationally, there were more working women in suburbia than cities and rural areas. See Table A2.12 (Working women in suburbs) and Table A2.13 (Stay-at-home wives in suburbs).

124. "Staying Put," *LAT*, May 12, 1996; see Table A7.1 (Full Lakewood data).

125. See Table A7.1.

126. Information on the senior housing complex, from Bill Grady email to author, April 12, 2021.

127. See Table A7.2 (Median income by race group in Lakewood, 1989). US Bureau of Census, *1990 Census of Population, Social and Economic Characteristics: California* (Washington, DC: GPO, 1993), 1126, 1165, 1282, 1321, 1740.

128. "The Storied History of Douglas Park," *Long Beach Business Journal*, May 7, 2018; "Long Beach: A History of Hard Workers Making Big Important Things," *LBPT*, January 12, 2014.

129. "Aircraft Company to Cut 17,000 Jobs," *NYT*, July 17, 1990; "Battling the Lethargy at Douglas," *NYT*, July 22, 1990; "McDonnell Is Criticized in U.S. Study," *NYT*,

September 27, 1990; "Douglas Aircraft Cutting 1,200 Jobs," *NYT*, October 17, 1990; "Many Workers Fear the Worst Is Yet to Come," *LAT*, July 17, 1990; "These Trying Times, The Stormy Economy Shatters Lives and Scatters Dreams Series," *LAT*, May 19, 1991; Didion, "Trouble in Lakewood," 48, 60–65.

130. Andrew Wiese, *Places of Their Own: African American Suburbanization in the Twentieth Century* (Chicago: University of Chicago Press, 2004), 125; Rubin, *New Suburban Woman*, 245.

131. I gleaned that African American women were welcomed since the event was publicized in the Black newspaper, *LA Sentinel*. "Free Expertise at Sewing Fair," *LAS*, September 14, 1972.

132. "NCNW Luncheon Set for Beah Richards Tribute," *LAS*, November 6, 1977; "'Try It on for Size' Brings Mirth," *LAS*, November 15, 1979. Bullocks Lakewood also supplied fashions for other Black women's groups held in other venues, such as the Alpha Chi Pi Omega's annual lunch and fashion show at the Beverly Hilton and the Alpha Wives (auxiliary of the Black fraternity Alpha Phi Alpha) at the Bonaventure Hotel downtown. For example, see "Coordinating Council Celebrates Its Founding with Luncheon Show," *LAS*, November 10, 1977; "Alpha Wives Schedule Fashion Extravaganza," *LAS*, April 28, 1977.

133. "Eta Phi Beta Sorority: Kappa Chapter Celebrates in Spirit of National Motto," *LAS*, January 20, 1994; "NCNW Compton Section Holds Awards Luncheon," *LAS*, June 12, 2003. I identified 38 articles in the *LA Sentinel* reporting on these social events held in Lakewood between 1976 and 2005.

134. Wiggins, "'Our Worst Crisis Since Slavery,'" 9–10.

135. "Cosmopolitan Golf Club Auxiliary Elects Officers," *LAS*, May 6, 1954; "Pop Warner Loop Hosts Grid Clinic," *LAS*, July 28, 1966; "Wanda on National TV," *LAS*, December 14, 1972; "L.A. 600 Club News," *LAS*, August 10, 1978; "Divot Diggings," *LAS*, October 12, 1978; "Bowling: Triple Tee Results," *LAS*, September 8, 1988; "Bowling: L.A. 600 Dates," *LAS*, October 4, 1990.

136. Bill Baca oral history.

137. Joe Esquivel oral history. Esquivel was president of Steelworkers Union Local 5031 for 17 years at the American Can Company, where he had worked for years.

138. Cassandra Chase oral history.

139. Pamela and Derrick Williams oral history.

140. Pamela and Derrick Williams oral history.

141. Cassandra Chase oral history; "The Pulpit's Plight on Abortion," *LAT*, October 11, 1989; "Letter to Editor," *LAT*, April 8, 1991; "On Fear and Violence," *LAT*, April 5, 1993; "We Must Never Substitute Charity for Justice," *LAT*, January 31, 1994. On religious social justice activism in LA at this time, see Sean Dempsey, *City of Dignity: Religion and the Making of Global Los Angeles* (Chicago: University of Chicago Press, 2022).

142. Ari Pe oral history.

143. "Lakewood: Back to the Future," *LBPT*, May 14, 1995.

144. The excellent recent scholarship on the suburban crisis begins with Lassiter, *Suburban Crisis*; Lassiter, "Pushers, Victims, and the Lost Innocence"; Riismandel,

Neighborhood of Fear; Renfro, *Stranger Danger*. Also see Gillian Frank, "Save Our Children: The Sexual Politics of Child Protection in the United States, 1965–1990" (PhD dissertation, Brown University, 2009).

145. "Marauders from Inner City Prey on L.A.'s Suburbs," *LAT*, July 12, 1981; "Our Reckoning with Racism," *LAT*, September 27, 2020, in which the newspaper apologized for its own "failures on race," featured the "Marauders" story prominently.

146. Lassiter, *Suburban Crisis*; Renfro, *Stranger Danger*; and see Riismandel, *Neighborhood of Fear*, chapter 3, on the rise of suburban fears about crime. On a broader level, the policies arising from this sense of suburban victimhood drove the expansion of the carceral state.

147. Daniel T. Rogers, *Age of Fracture* (Cambridge, MA: Belknap Press of Harvard University Press, 2012); Renfro, *Stranger Danger*, 15–17; Robert Self, *All in the Family: The Realignment of American Democracy Since the 1960s* (New York: Hill and Wang, 2012), 10; and see Natasha Zaretsky, *No Direction Home: The American Family the Fear of National Decline* (Chapel Hill: University of North Carolina Press, 2007).

148. "Six More Beaten Up by Hoodlum Gangs," *LAT*, April 24, 1950; "Eight Seized as Police Press Marijuana Drive," *LAT*, August 11, 1950; "Housewife Roughed up by Prowler," *LAT*, August 21, 1958; "Mother's Plea Saves Money from Bandits," *LAT*, December 25, 1961.

149. Davis, *City of Quartz*, chapter 5; Alonso, "Out of the Void," 157–161; Felker-Kantor, *Policing Los Angeles*, chapter 8.

150. "Rise of Suburban Asian Gangs Strikes a Paradox," *LAT*, January 28, 1996; "The Rise of a Small Street Gang, Armenian Power, Is Causing a Tragic Cycle of Fear and Death," *LAT*, August 17, 1997; "Call of the Wild In the Upscale Suburbs," *LAT*, June 25, 1989. On migration of gangs to the exurbs, see "Class Struggle Unfolds in Antelope Valley Tracts," *LAT*, June 24, 1996.

151. Lassiter, *Suburban Crisis*.

152. "Youth Gang Rivalry Spawns Crime, Violence," *LAT*, August 27, 1972.

153. "Sheriff's Project Puts Heat on 'Hype'-Related Crimes," *LAT*, December 9, 1976; "Cities OK Funds to Fight Burglars," *LAT*, February 20, 1977.

154. "Color Them Trouble: Lakewood Detects First Signs of Gangs on Its Sleepy Streets," *LAT*, June 5, 1988; also "Sweeps Indicate Average Age of Gang Members Is Falling," *LAT*, September 8, 1988.

155. Didion, "Trouble in Lakewood," 52.

156. Didion, "Trouble in Lakewood," 46-56, quotes at 52; "8 High School Students Held in Rape, Assault Case," *LAT*, March 19, 1993; "A Stain Spreads in Suburbia," *LAT*, April 6, 1993. The Spur Posse arrests attracted national media attention. A few examples include Didion, "Trouble in Lakewood"; "A Town's Divided Loyalties," *Newsweek*, April 12, 1993; Jane Gross, "Where 'Boys Will Be Boys' and Adults Are Befuddled," *NYT*, March 29, 1993; Jill Smolowe, "Sex with a Scorecard," *Time*, April 5, 1993; Jennifer Allen, "Hanging with the Spur Posse," *Rolling Stone*, July 8-22, 1993.

Among the Spur Posse members, by 1996, founder Dana Belman was serving a 10-year prison sentence, Chris Albert was killed in a Huntington Beach fight, two others were arrested in a near-fatal stabbing in Seal Beach, another was stabbed in a fight after he was released from jail. "An American Tragedy: Some Never Got Back on Track," *LAT*, March 22, 1996.

157. "The Young Victims: Age, Innocence Magnify Tragedy," *LAT*, September 7, 1978.

158. "Idle Threats?" *LAS*, March 16, 1989; "4 Arrested on Drug Charges in H. Gardens," *LAT*, March 28, 1974; "Boy Kidnapped, Drugged, Held in Suitcase," *LAT*, July 3, 1979; "Drug Sales Still Plague L.B.'s El Dorado Park," *LAT*, January 24, 1982; "Surviving Victims of Murder Unite to Ease Nightmares," *LAT*, May 6, 1984.

159. "Drug Agents Finish Smuggling Probe with 156 Arrests," *LAT*, May 3, 1996; "3 Injured as Gunfire Erupts Inside Theater," *LAT*, November 8, 1996.

    Even the high-profile death of Tupac Shakur in Las Vegas had connections to Lakewood. Some of the conflict between rival Crip and Blood gangs that resulted in Shakur's death began in a fight at the Lakewood Mall, and at least one gang member from Lakewood was caught up in the gang sweeps connected to this case. "Police Raids Target Violence Provoked by Tupac Shakur's Death," *LAT*, October 3, 1996; "Ex-Suspect in Shakur's Death Sues Estate," *LAT*, September 10, 1997.

160. Baker, "Lakewood Story," 384.

161. Baker, "Lakewood Story," 383.

162. "Letters to the Editor: Crime in Lakewood," *LBPT*, April 6, 1992.

163. Brill, "Tomorrowland," 104–110; https://patch.com/california/cerritos/lakewood-councilman-larry-van-nostran-dies-of-lung-dib65da016af.

164. Baker, "Lakewood Story," 385–387, quote at 386.

165. Interviews from Baker, "Lakewood Story," 383.

166. Lakewood crime statistics for 1973–1980: County of Los Angeles Department of Sheriff, "Fiscal Year 1973–74 Statistical Summary (Prepared by Management Staff Services); County of Los Angeles Department of Sheriff, "Fiscal Year 1975–76 Statistical Summary (Prepared by Management Staff Services); County of Los Angeles Department of Sheriff, "Fiscal Year 1980–81 Statistical Summary (Records & Statistics Bureau); for 1985–2020: "Reported Crimes & Crime Rates by Jurisdiction Los Angeles County, 2021," for years 1985–2020, Los Angeles Almanac. © 1998–2022 Given Place Media, publishing as Los Angeles Almanac. https://www.laalmanac.com/crime/cr03.php.

167. See Table A7.3 (Crime rates in LA suburbs).

168. Baker, "Lakewood Story," 377. Baker uses the phrase "police state," noting that it came from a quote of the League of California Cities in their opposition to the Lakewood plan, "arguing it would result in 'the creation of a police state.'" Lakewood's suburban story aligns with the "fortress" mentality described in Davis, *City of Quartz*, chapter 4.

169. On Black support of law enforcement in urban areas, see James Forman, Jr., *Locking Up Our Own: Crime and Punishment in Black America* (New York: Farrar, Straus and Giroux, 2017).

170. Felker-Kantor, *Policing Los Angeles*; Davis, *City of Quartz*; Lassiter, *Suburban Crisis*; Edward Escobar, *Race, Police, and the Making of a Political Identity: Mexican Americans and the Los Angeles Police Department, 1900–1945* (Berkeley: University

of California Press, 1999); Kelly Lytle Hernandez, *City of Inmates: Conquest, Rebellion, and the Rise of Human Caging in Los Angeles, 1771–1965* (Chapel Hill: University of North Carolina Press, 2017); Susan A. Phillips, *Operation Fly Trap: L. A. Gangs, Drugs, and the Law* (Chicago: University of Chicago Press, 2012).

171. City of Lakewood, "The Lakewood Story," chapter 9, https://www.lakewoodcity.org/About/Our-History/The-Lakewood-Story/09-Safe-City.

172. Felker-Kantor, *Policing Los Angeles*, 41, 50–57.

173. Felker-Kantor, *Policing Los Angeles*, 55; on the Douglas F3D-2, see Waldie, *Holy Land*, 14.

174. Lauren Wasserman, "Lakewood's Airborne Police Augment Ground Patrol," *Western City* 43, 2 (February 1967), 21–22, 33; Harold Becker, "Do Police Helicopters Justify Their Cost?" *American City* 84, 11 (November 1969), 70. The Becker story notes that New York City first pioneered the use of helicopters in law enforcement in the late 1940s (71).

175. "Project Sky Knight," *American City* 82, 8 (August 1967), 33.

176. Linda Kay Gahan oral history.

177. Bill Baca oral history.

178. Felker-Kantor, *Policing Los Angeles*, 55; "Sky Knight a Local Hero," *LBPT*, November 4, 1996.

179. "Lakewood to Place Greater Stress on Law Enforcement," *LAT*, September 10, 1972; "Annual Budget Document Fiscal Period 1972–73," Lakewood City Council, LHCIL.

180. "4 Lakewood Councilmen Targets of Recall Campaign," *LAT*, October 16, 1975; "Recall Effort in Lakewood Fails," *LAT*, December 18, 1975; "Divided Council Erases Post of Safety Director," *LAT*, May 13, 1976; "Lakewood Recall Attempt," *LBPT*, October 15, 1975.

181. "Cities OK Funds to Fight Burglars," *LAT*, February 20, 1977; "2 Cities Join Sheriff's Task Force on Crime," *LAT*, September 28, 1986; "6 Cities Pitching in Funds to Keep Anti-Drug Task Force in Business," *LAT*, November 2, 1986; "Sheriff's Matching Fund Grows," *LAT*, October 15, 1987; "Funds for Anti-Drug Class," *LAT*, November 24, 1988; "Lakewood Votes Rewards for Turning in Graffiti Vandals," *LAT*, March 18, 1990.

Lakewood city budgets from 1960 to 2012 showed a steady rise in spending on law enforcement by two measures: per capita spending and percentage of total city budget allocated to law enforcement. The increases persisted even as crime rates began dropping after 1980. Lakewood annual budgets, 1962–1963, 1972–1973, 1981–1982, 1990–1992, 2002–2003, 2012, LHCIL.

182. Renfro, *Stranger Danger*, 183; "Lakewood," *LAT*, May 5, 1983; "Lakewood Uses Decals to Scare Off Car Thieves," *LAT*, November 12, 1989.

For the car decal program, residents placed a yellow and green decal on their car which essentially authorized the sheriffs to pull the car over if it was spotted anywhere on the roads between 1 and 5 A.M. Operation L.A.W. (Lakewood Auto Watch) was the first of its kind in LA County, modeled on similar programs in New York City and San Diego.

183. Barry Wulwick oral history, conducted by Allison Baker, May 3, 1996, Lakewood, CA; Baker, "Lakewood Story," 384; "Special Deputies Work 'Hot Spots' in Lakewood Area," *LBPT*, August 9, 1992.

184. "Getting Soft(ware) on Crime," *LAT*, December 8, 1997; Barry Wulwick oral history; Baker, "Lakewood Story," 398.

185. Baker, "Lakewood Story," 396–397. Charles Ebner, Lakewood's director of community development, noted that eastern Lakewood was a particularly problematic area in terms of dilapidated housing. The area was hard hit by the closure of the Long Beach Naval Hospital and aerospace layoffs, and residents were generally of lower socioeconomic status there.

186. Brill, "Tomorrowland," 106; Baker, "Lakewood Story," 411.

187. Baker, "Lakewood Story," 413.

188. Brill, "Tomorrowland," 107; Baker, "Lakewood Story," 409–414. For a similar community dynamic around local parks in Seaside, California, see Carol McKibben, *Racial Beachhead: Diversity and Democracy in a Military Town* (Stanford: Stanford University Press, 2011).

189. "Campus Clamps Down on Conflict," *LBPT*, September 30, 1994; Baker, "Lakewood Story," 427; also "Blacks, Latinos Fight at Lakewood High," *LBPT*, December 9, 1993. Policing in the Long Beach district had tragic consequences in 2021; see "School Safety Officers Don't Make Students Feel Safe," *LAT*, October 5, 2021.

On the differential policing and disciplining of students by race, in broader context, see Davison M. Douglas, *Reading, Writing, and Race: The Desegregation of the Charlotte Schools* (Chapel Hill: University of North Carolina Press, 1995), 226; Straus, *Death of a Suburban Dream*; Lassiter, *Suburban Crisis*; Robert F. Kennedy Memorial Fund and Southern Regional Council, *The Student Pushout: Victim of Continued Resistance to Desegregation* (Atlanta: Southern Regional Council; Washington DC: Robert F. Kennedy Memorial Fund, 1973).

190. Riismandel, *Neighborhood of Fear*, chapter 3.

191. Luis Gascón and Aaron Roussell, *The Limits of Community Policing: Civilian Power and Police Accountability in Black and Brown Los Angeles* (New York: NYU Press, 2019). Gascón and Roussell take a critical view of urban community policing, arguing that it amplified rather than alleviated racial tensions.

192. "Lakewood to Place Greater Stress on Law Enforcement," *LAT*, September 10, 1972; "We TIP: Crime Information Plan Has its Rewards," *LAT*, January 22, 1978; "Color Them Trouble"; "Crime Fighting Expo Saturday June 10," *Lakewood Community News*, June 1995, 1.

193. "Neighborhood Watch Plan Cuts Crime," *LAT*, March 25, 1979; also see, "Neighbors Unite in Fight Against Crime," *LAT*, August 31, 1979. Parker's checkered record on race and policing made him a controversial leader.

194. "Don't Gamble with Your Safety, Join Lakewood Neighborhood Watch," undated pamphlet, Allison Baker personal archive.

195. "Crime Prevention Program," *LAT*, August 4, 1977; City of Lakewood, "The Lakewood Story," chapter 9; "Neighborhood Watch Instructs Residents How to Cut Crime," *LAT*, January 24, 1982; "Tips from . . . Neighborhood Watch: Senior Power," *LAT*, February

14, 1982; "Neighborhood Watch: Rape Information," *LAT*, February 28, 1982; "Neighborhood Watch: An Education on Child Abuse," *LAT*, March 21, 1982.

196. "Neighborhood Watch: Meeting the Police," *LAT*, March 28, 1982.

197. "Crime Watch Block Captains to Hold Picnic," *LAT*, July 8, 1990; Baker, "Lakewood Story," 377; Barry Wulwick oral history; "Volunteer Patrol Expands Lakewood Law Enforcement," *Lakewood Community News*, June 1995, 1. Percentage calculated from US Census dataset 2000.

198. *Lakewood Neighborhood Watch News*, August 1994 to October 1999, Allison Baker personal archive; Baker, "Lakewood Story," 380.

199. Barry Wulwick oral history.

200. Baker, "Lakewood Story," 380.

201. Pamela and Derrick Williams oral history; Eric Morgan email to author, January 3, 2021; Mrs. J (pseudonym) telephone interview with author, March 17, 2021; Mrs. P (pseudonym) telephone interview with author, March 17, 2021.

202. Pamela and Derrick Williams oral history; Joe Esquivel oral history; Eric Morgan email to author, January 3, 2021; Mrs. J telephone interview; Mrs. P telephone interview.

In 2021, Lakewood Public Information officer Bill Grady explained that Lakewood did not collect ethnic-racial data on Neighborhood Watch block captains, but city staff sensed growing ethnic diversification of participation in the program. In recent years, the city had worked to recruit more block captains and to encourage participation by residents of diverse backgrounds. From 2016 to 2021, three of the six people selected as Neighborhood Watch Block Captain of the Year included two African Americans and one person of Middle Eastern descent. Bill Grady email to author, August 4, 2021.

203. Pamela and Derrick Williams oral history.

204. Mrs. J telephone interview.

205. "Volunteer Patrol Expands Lakewood Law Enforcement," *Lakewood Community News*, June 1995, 1.

206. Barry Wulwick oral history.

207. Bill Baca oral history; Bill Baca email to author, March 29, 2021; "Deputies Seek Residents for Patrol Program," *LAT*, January 5, 1995.

208. Baker, "Lakewood Story," 377–378; "Results of 1998 Community Survey," conducted by J. D. Franz Research.

209. "Cities Ponder Problems of Regional Enforcement," *LAT*, April 13, 1980.

210. Pamela and Derrick Williams oral history; Louis Chase oral history.

211. The latter deputy had formerly worked in the Lakewood Station but planted the drugs while on the LAPD. "2 Indicted by Federal Jury in Cocaine Case," *LAT*, February 24, 1983; "Ex-Deputy Convicted of Drug Sales," *LAT*, July 13, 1983; "6 Officers on L.A. Drug Task Force Are Indicted," *LAT*, January 11, 1991.

212. Two years later, video captured the Rodney King beating by the LAPD.

213. "Neighborhood Cries Foul Over Police Tactics Against Samoans," *LAT*, May 23, 1991; "No Deputies Disciplined Since Costly 1989 Brawl," *LAT*, May 12, 1998.

214. Felker-Kantor, *Policing Los Angeles*, 208–209; Davis, *City of Quartz*, chapter 5.

215. Cassandra Chase oral history; Louis Chase oral history.

216. Los Angeles County Sheriff's Department, "A Report by Special Counsel James G. Kolts & Staff," July 1992, 19–20.

217. "Town Hall #2 on Racial Equity," Lakewood CityTV, September 30, 2020, https://vimeo.com/466223575, accessed April 7, 2023.

218. Pamela and Derrick Williams oral history.

219. "Charges of Brutality Beset Deputies, Cost L.A. County," *LAT*, May 27, 1990.

220. "Two Stations Led by Baca Known for Personnel Problems," *LAT*, November 13, 1998.

221. "A Report by Special Counsel James G. Kolts," 176, 179, quotes at 351; "Lynwood Deputies Cited for Brutality in Kolts Report, Law Enforcement, Norwalk and Lakewood Stations Also Criticized," *LAT*, July 23, 1992.

　　Four shootings by LASD deputies triggered the Kolts inquiry. One of those deaths was 15-year-old David Angel Ortiz, in 1991, by Deputy Jose Belmares while he was assigned to the Lakewood Station. In 1995, Belmares was reinstated after an inquiry by the LA County Civil Service Commission, which leaned heavily on the testimony of Lakewood Sheriff captain John Anderson, who testified that the shooting was within departmental policy. "Panel Orders Sheriff's Deputy Who Killed Youth Reinstated," *LAT*, November 22, 1995.

222. "Panels Seek to Ease Relations Between Deputies, Residents," *LAT*, September 12, 1993.

223. "Citizen Complaints Against Sheriff's Dept. on Rise, ACLU Says," *LAT*, September 11, 1997; "Area Sheriff's Stations Top in Complaints," *LBPT*, September 11, 1997. The original report is "Disturbing Trends: Examining Complaints Against the Los Angeles County Sheriff's Department, 1994–1996," ACLU Foundation of Southern California, September 1997.

224. At the same time, some believed the sheriffs did not show racial bias on the job. Ari Pe, for example, did not recall any racial bias by the Lakewood Sheriffs toward him or his Black, Mexican, Cambodian, and white friends when he was a teen and into his early 20s. Ari Pe oral history.

Conclusion

1. For an excellent discussion and debate around this suburban ideal, albeit referring to an earlier historical period, see Mary Corbin Sies, "North American Suburbs, 1880-1950: Cultural and Social Reconsiderations," *Journal of Urban History* 27, 3 (March 2001), 313–346; Andrew Wiese, "Stubborn Diversity: A Commentary on Middle-Class Influence in Working-Class Suburbs," *Journal of Urban History* 27, 3 (March 2001), 347–54.

2. "Racist Remarks in Leaked Audio of Politicians Spark Outrage," *LAT*, October 10, 2022; "Calls Mount for Politicians to Step Down," *LAT*, October 11, 2022, and extensive coverage in subsequent days. Particularly insightful commentaries included Jean Guerrero, "Our City Needs a New Generation of Latino Leaders," *LAT*, October 13, 2022; "Frank Shyong, "Racial Coalitions Define Life in Los Angeles," *LAT*, October 18, 2022; Sandy Banks, "Let's Drop the 'People of Color' Label," *LAT*, November 21, 2022.

3. Nicholas De Genova, eds., *Racial Transformations: Latinos and Asians Remaking the United States* (Durham: Duke University Press, 2006), 17.

4. "Women in Suburbia Are Not Too Worried About Its Ruin, Polls Say," *NYT*, September 21, 2020. These polls were taken in the wake of Donald Trump's campaign assertion that he would "save the suburbs" from decline by putting the brakes on integration; that appeal ultimately failed to resonate with suburban voters.

5. "C.A.R. Issues Formal Apology for Past Discriminatory Policies," October 14, 2022, https://www.car.org/aboutus/mediacenter/newsreleases/2022releases/apology.

6. Conor Dougherty, "After Years of Failure, California Lawmakers Pave the Way for More Housing," *NYT*, August 26, 2021; "Editorial: Shame on SoCal Leaders for Backing a Ballot Measure to Roll Back Housing Fixes," *LAT*, January 18, 2022; also see, Conor Dougherty, "Where the Suburbs End," *NYT*, October 28, 2021; Conor Dougherty, *Golden Gates: The Housing Crisis and a Reckoning for the American Dream* (New York: Penguin, 2020).

7. Mitch Lehman, "Students Host Passionate, Peaceful BLM Protest," *San Marino Tribune*, June 11, 2020; Amy Powell, "Deputies Fire Tear Gas at Crowd During Protest in Lakewood After Declaring Unlawful Assembly," ABC 7 Eyewitness News, June 7, 2020, https://abc7.com/deputies-fire-tear-gas-at-crowd-during-protest-in-lakewood/6235358/; for video on the protesters' confrontation with the Lakewood Sheriffs, see https://twitter.com/greg_doucette/status/126909059779 4701312?lang=en.

8. Veronica Hernandez and Amanda Tapia interview with author via Zoom, August 6, 2020.

9. "Glendale Confronts Its Racist Past, Apologizing for 'Sundown' Laws," *LAT*, October 15, 2020; South Pasadena Sundown Town resolution 7750, February 2, 2022, https://www.southpasadenaca.gov/home/showpublisheddocument/28302/637805957085730000; "When South Pasadena Was a Sundown Town," coloradoboulevard.net, April 17, 2022; "A Century After Its Seizure, a Vote to Return Bruce's Beach," *LAT*, June 29, 2022; "Church Hosts Talks on City's Race-Based Housing," *La Canada Flintridge Outlook Valley Sun*, October 17, 2022, https://outlookvalleysun.outlooknewspapers.com/2022/10/17/church-hosts-talks-on-citys-race-based-housing/.

10. Powell, "Deputies Fire Tear Gas," https://abc7.com/deputies-fire-tear-gas-at-crowd-during-protest-in-lakewood/6235358/; for video on the protesters' confrontation with the Lakewood Sheriffs, see https://twitter.com/greg_doucette/status/12690905 97794701312?lang=en.

11. "Town Hall #1 on Racial Equity," Lakewood CityTV, September 26, 2020, https://vimeo.com/466222625; "Town Hall #2 on Racial Equity," Lakewood CityTV, September 30, 2020, https://vimeo.com/466223575.

12. Lakewood City Council Agenda Item, "Community Dialogue Action Plan," January 26, 2021; https://www.lakewoodcity.org/Things-to-Do/Community-Events/Fest-Of-All; "Lakewood's Race, Equity, Diversity and Inclusion Plan Gets Top Honors," Lakewood Connect e-Magazine, September 28, 2022.

13. Joe Esquivel oral history.

14. The fact that Lakewood's city council racially integrated while also evincing strong support for law enforcement reflected broader political trends in LA suburbia. In 2000, for example, a race for the 29th state senate district—encompassing the east San Gabriel Valley and some southeast suburbs—revealed a rising block of suburban swing voters, mostly Latino and Asian, who were liberal on social programs and tough on crime. "New Diversity of Voters Sparks Battle in Suburbs," *LAT*, November 1, 2000.

15. Cassandra Chase oral history; "Lakewood election results," July 5, 2022, City of Lakewood.

16. Paragraph is drawn from Pamela and Derrick Williams oral history.

Index

For the benefit of digital users, indexed terms that span two pages (e.g., 52–53) may, on occasion, appear on only one of those pages.